D0939054

THE FRENCH RENAISSANCE COURT

THE FRENCH
RENAISSANCE COURT
1483–1589

ROBERT J. KNECHT

YALE UNIVERSITY PRESS
NEW HAVEN AND LONDON

Published with assistance from the foundation established in memory of Oliver Baty Cunningham of the Class of 1917, Yale College.

For information about this and other Yale University Press publications please contact:

U.S. Office: sales.press@yale.edu   yalebooks.com
Europe Office: sales@yaleup.co.uk   www.yalebooks.co.uk

Set in Caslon by J&L Composition Ltd, Filey, North Yorkshire
Printed in Great Britain by Biddles Ltd, King's Lynn

Library of Congress Cataloging-in-Publication Data

Knecht, R. J. (Robert Jean)
    The French Renaissance Court, 1483–1589 / Robert J. Knecht.
        p. cm.
    Includes bibliographical references and index.
    ISBN 978–0–300–11851–3 (alk. paper)
    1. France—History—Charles VIII, 1483–1498. 2. France—History—16th century.
3. France—Court and courtiers—History—16th century. 4. France—Social life and customs—16th century. I. Title
    DC107.K64 2008
    994′.027—dc22
                                                              2007026101

A catalogue record for this book is available from the British Library

10 9 8 7 6 5 4 3 2 1

To Maureen

Contents

Illustrations and Maps

Figures

Colour plates

Maps

Abbreviations

AN   Archives Nationales, Paris
AS   Archivio di Stato
BNF   Bibliothèque nationale de France, Paris
CAF   *Catalogue des actes de François Ier*, 19 vols (Paris, 1887–1910)
CSP Span.   *Calendar of State Papers, Spanish*, ed. G.A. Bergenroth, P. de Gayangos and M.A.S. Hume, 12 vols (London, 1862–95)
CSP Ven.   *Calendar of State Papers, Venetian*, ed. R. Brown, C. Bentinck and H. Brown, 9 vols (London, 1864–98)
EHR   *English Historical Review*
EQR   *European Quarterly Review*
GBA   *Gazette des Beaux-Arts*
JWCI   *Journal of the Warburg and Courtauld Institutes*
LP   *Letters and Papers, Foreign and Domestic, of the Reign of Henry VIII*, ed. J.S. Brewer, J. Gairdner and R.H. Brodie, 21 vols (London, 1862–1910)
RH   *Revue historique*
RHMC   *Revue d'histoire moderne et contemporaine*
RQH   *Revue des questions historiques*
St P   *State Papers of Henry VIII*, 11 vols (London, 1830–52)

Note on Coinage

Sums of money mentioned in this book reflect the division between the two kinds of money that co-existed in sixteenth-century France: money of account and actual coin. The most common money of account was the *livre tournois* (abridged as *l.*), which was subdivided into *sous* (or *sols*) and *deniers* (abridged as *s.* and *d.*). The *livre* was worth about 2 English shillings. Actual coin was of gold, silver and billon. The gold *écu au soleil* was worth 45 *sous* in 1533. The silver *teston* issued from 1514 was the first coin to carry the king's portrait. It was worth 10 *s.* 8 *d.* in 1533. It remained the principal silver coin till Henry III introduced the *franc* in 1576. Billon was a mixture of silver with a high proportion of copper. Billon coinage included the *douzain*, *dizain* and *sizain*. In addition to royal coins, provincial and foreign coins circulated in France. In March 1541 Francis I authorised the circulation of thirty-three kinds of foreign coin.

Note on Names

French names and titles, such as *duc*, *comte* and *vicomte*, are given in French, but the names of kings are anglicized. Thus François duc d'Angoulême becomes Francis I following his accession in 1515, and Henri duc d'Anjou becomes Henry III in 1574.

Preface

Courts have long interested a certain reading public: the love affairs of kings, queens and royal mistresses – what the French aptly sum up as *histoire d'alcôve* – have been the stuff of popular historiography for centuries. That is not, however, what this book is about; at least I have tried to avoid it as far as possible in order to concentrate on the court as an institution. This has received comparatively less attention, though recently it has captured the interest of a number of historians. In 1977 A.G. Dickens edited a volume entitled *The Courts of Europe: Politics, Patronage and Royalty, 1400–1800*. This has been followed by other works on the same theme. Some have focused on individual courts, such as those of David Starkey and David Loades on the Tudor court. The court of Spain has been the object of fine studies, including *A Palace for a King: The Buen Retiro and the Court of Philip IV* by Jonathan Brown and J.H. Elliott. *The Princely Courts of Europe, 1500–1750*, edited by John Adamson, was published in 1999, and two years later Malcolm Vale carried the subject back in time in *The Princely Courts: Medieval Courts and Culture in North-Western Europe*. So the subject is now well established. It has even prompted the creation in Britain of a Society for Court Studies with its own scholarly journal.

The court of France has not been neglected, but much of the attention has focused on Louis XIV and Versailles. This provided the evidence for Norbert Elias's influential, albeit controversial study *Court Society*; but, as I hope to demonstrate, the court of Renaissance France was very different for it was still evolving. For much of the sixteenth century it remained nomadic, as it had been since its beginnings: it only developed an etiquette once it had become more or less fixed under Henry III. Jean-François Solnon's *La Cour de France* is a valuable overview, but its treatment of the sixteenth century is rather skimpy. So much research has been done recently by historians and art historians that the court needs a more in-depth treatment. Among recent French works two stand out as pre-eminent: Monique Chatenet's *La cour de France au XVIe siècle: vie sociale et architecture* (2002) and Nicolas Le Roux's *La faveur du roi: mignons et courtisans au temps des derniers Valois (vers 1547–vers 1589)* (2000). My indebtedness to both is immense.

Writing a synthesis of recent work on a subject as vast and multifaceted as the court of France between 1483 and 1589 is fraught with difficulties of presentation: above all, how to cover so much ground within a limited number of words. The court was significant politically, socially and culturally. Politically it was the centre of decision-making; socially, it attracted all those people looking for advancement for themselves and their relatives by capturing some morsel of royal largesse; and culturally, it promoted innovation and excellence, notably in the visual arts, often as a means of projecting the king's image to the world at large. The political aspect has presented me with a special problem: how to consider the court without describing the political background – the Italian Wars or the Wars of Religion – which have been exhaustively covered by historians. I have tried to give just the right amount of background for the institution to be intelligible. Another difficulty has been the familiar one of blending themes and chronology. Broadly, my book is divided into two parts, the division falling in 1559 when Henry II was accidentally killed, plunging the kingdom into a crisis that nearly destroyed it. Some themes receive more attention in the first half than in the second, and vice versa. Nor could I ignore the personalities that made the court, for as the contemporary soldier and writer François de La Noue put it: 'The court is in the image of the prince.'

My own interest in the French Renaissance court stems partly from my work on the reign of Francis I and partly from an interest in the art and architecture of the period which led me in my youth to cycle round the châteaux of the Loire. I also had a personal reason for my interest: my maternal ancestors came from Macé, a village outside Blois, within striking distance of the great château of Chambord. My research has also uncovered a certain Étienne Dinocheau, almost certainly an ancestor, who was one of Francis I's hard-pressed quartermasters or *fourriers*. I also remember standing as a small child at an open dormer window of the château of Écouen, once the home of the constable Anne de Montmorency, now the Musée National de la Renaissance, looking across a plain that had seen so much history. I was there when the château was a school for the daughters of French officers; my mother was of their number and later became a teacher there. In recent years my interest in the architecture has been enlarged and stimulated thanks to a close association with Jean Guillaume and his circle of international art historians, who have kindly invited me to join them in their conferences and study tours.

I have been greatly helped over the years by a large number of scholars, many of them friends. In addition to all that I have learnt from the book cited above, I am most grateful to Monique Chatenet for kindly letting me share the fruits of her research in the Italian archives; to Raffaele Tamalio, who first drew my attention to the correspondence of Federico Gonzaga; to Hervé Oursel for his warm hospitality at Écouen; to Vincent Droguet for generously taking me through every nook and cranny of the château of Fontainebleau; to Thierry Crépin-Leblond for doing likewise at Blois, Écouen and Villers-Cotterêts. I am also grateful to Mary Clark for kindly letting me share her transcript of Claude Chappuys's *Discours de la Cour;* and to Mark Greengrass for drawing my attention to a fascinating drawing at the Folger Library and for some constructive suggestions following a reading of my text. Others who have assisted me with advice and in other ways include Sydney Anglo, Joseph Bergin, Denis Crouzet, Philippe Hamon, Maurice Howard, Eric Ives, Nicolas Le Roux, Cédric Michon, François Nawrocki, David Potter, Hamish Scott, Pauline Smith, Lynn Tamalio, Denise Turrel and Laurent Vissière. I am grateful to my editor, Heather McCallum, for her encouragement and guidance, to Rachael Lonsdale for her kind help in gathering illustrations and to Candida Brazil for her tactful efficiency as senior editor. As always, my greatest debt is to my wife, Maureen, who has helped me overcome moments of despondency, listened stoically to some of my drafts and often supplied me with the *mot juste.*

Birmingham, 2007

Introduction

'We were following the court with the weariest trouble and fatigue; the reason of this was that the train of the King drags itself along with never less than 12,000 horse behind it; this calculation is the very lowest; for when the court is complete in times of peace, there are some 18,000, which makes 12,000 less than the average.'[1] Thus wrote Benvenuto Cellini, the Florentine goldsmith and sculptor, in his *Autobiography*, recalling his second visit to the court of the French king, Francis I, in September 1540. The number of horses provides an indication of the size of the French court, for there may have been twice as many horses as people. Its size, however, varied according to circumstances. In wartime when the king and his courtiers were with the armies, the court was smaller than in peacetime, and even then its population fluctuated as visitors came and went, some of them noblemen with large suites of their own. At its largest the court could attain the size of an average French town, containing somewhere between eight and ten thousand people. Moving such a mass of people over long distances when communications remained primitive was a taxing operation, particularly as the court carried its own furniture from place to place. Today English visitors, used to their own well-filled country houses, are often surprised and disappointed by the emptiness of some French châteaux. Guides tell them that the contents were stripped at the Revolution. Maybe so in certain instances, but many royal châteaux were never furnished in the first place. No purpose could have been served by furnishing a residence that might only be visited once in a blue moon.

The slowness of the court's progress was not Cellini's only complaint. 'Consequently,' he continued, 'we had to journey after it through places where sometimes there were scarcely two houses to be found; and then we set up canvas tents like gipsies, and suffered at times very great discomfort.' Finding accommodation for the court was a major headache for its *fourriers* or quartermasters. Though the population of France in the early sixteenth century was among the largest in Europe, it was only about sixteen million. France's surface area was smaller than it is today, for certain provinces, such as Alsace-Lorraine, had not yet been absorbed into it. Even so, much of the countryside was unoccupied. Not even the king could be sure of finding a roof for the night. He could use his own châteaux in the Loire Valley and the Paris region; elsewhere he might rely on the hospitality of courtiers whose châteaux were often as palatial as his own. The Constable of Montmorency, to name but one, was immensely wealthy and often entertained the king at Chantilly or Écouen. Elsewhere Francis might put up at a religious house or an inn, but he was not fussy: if necessary, he was prepared to sleep in the humblest dwelling. The rest of the court had to be equally adaptable: wherever it stopped for a night, there was a mad scramble for shelter, often extending over several square miles.

Why, we may ask, was the court prepared to put up with so much discomfort? Hunting was one reason. The king loved to discover new hunting grounds; but tradition also played its part. The court had always picked up its food at the point of production rather than have it brought from afar. By the sixteenth century the habit had become ingrained, but there were also political reasons for the nomadic lifestyle. In an age without media the king had to affirm his authority by making his presence known; otherwise his subjects might know him only from his portrait on the coinage. He was surprisingly approachable: he and his subjects liked to meet each other. The latter might use the opportunity to ask for some favour such as the confirmation of a privilege. A town would offer him a formal reception or 'joyous entry' when he visited it for the first time. This would be an occasion for the inhabitants to rejoice, demonstrate their loyalty and point to their expectations. The street decorations which they devised for the occasion reflected a town's prosperity: there might be triumphal arches made of wood and brightly painted canvas. Symbolism would run riot in the form of inscriptions, plaster statues and roadside theatricals evoking some biblical or mythological tale. Francis I visited many towns in the course of his long reign, yet he preferred the countryside: he liked nothing better than to hunt deer with his 'fair band' of ladies and male friends. A hunt was a jolly social occasion offering opportunities of feasting and dalliance, the kind of bucolic activity one sees depicted in many contemporary tapestries.

The king's sylvan escapades, which could last as long as a week, were enormously frustrating to foreign ambassadors who had serious business to conduct. The bishop of Saluzzo expressed his annoyance in a letter to Cosimo de' Medici. 'This court', he wrote, 'is like no other. Here we are completely cut off from business, and if by chance there is any, no hour, day or month is set aside for certain to deal with it. Here one thinks of nothing but hunting, women, banquets and moving house.'[2] Politics, however, could not be entirely avoided. The court's itinerary was seldom haphazard: some places may have been visited on an impulse, but the overall strategy was preordained. It usually had a political objective, such as meeting a foreign ruler. The king also needed sometimes to inspect the kingdom's border fortifications or to join his army for a military campaign. Nor could he ignore Paris, where parts of his administration were permanently based. France had in effect two capitals: the court, where the king and his council took all major political decisions, and Paris – the largest town in the kingdom – where parts of the medieval *curia regis* had settled during the Middle Ages after going 'out of court'. The most important was the Parlement of Paris, the highest court of law under the king. Its work was mainly judicial, but it also had political responsibilities: legislation emanating from the king and his council could only be applied once it had been registered by the Parlement. This was no mere formality, for the Parlement had to ensure that the king had not broken the so-called 'fundamental laws'. One was the Salic law debarring women from the throne; another forbade the disposal of any part of the royal domain. The king never broke the Salic law, but was often tempted to sell off parts of his domain in order to enlarge his income. If the Parlement objected to a legislative proposal submitted by him and his council, it could remonstrate verbally or in writing; the king might agree to amend the proposal or he might insist on its being registered. In extreme cases this might result in a ceremony called a *lit de justice*, when the king would attend the Parlement in person and impose his will. There were other causes that might bring him to Paris. It was the traditional venue for state occasions, such as marriages, funerals, visits by foreign princes and services of thanksgiving. The king also came to buy jewellery or other luxury goods.

One fascinating aspect of the French court is the way it reflected the personality of the monarch. Not every king was as keen on travel as Francis I. If Cellini had come to France during the reign of Charles VIII or Louis XII, he might have had less cause to complain, for both kings liked urban living. Francis was the most peripatetic of the later Valois kings. Yet even he was not always on the road. In winter the court usually stayed put in one or other of the royal residences near Paris. Those within the capital had been built at times of domestic unrest or civil war; none was suitable for a Renaissance court which rated comfort and magnificence more highly than defence. The old palace of the Tournelles, where Louis XII had died, was a rambling complex of buildings in desperate need of repair; the Louvre was a grim fortress with a massive keep instead of a spacious courtyard; the Palais on the Île-de-la-Cité was occupied by the Parlement; the Bastille was another fortress, as was the château of Vincennes to the east of the city. Francis I began to modernize the Louvre, but the task was unfinished at his death. In the meantime he built a ring of châteaux around Paris, his favourite being Fontainebleau.

Returning to Cellini, we may wonder why he was so keen to come to France when so much might have detained him in his own native Italy. His purpose in coming to France was to capture the patronage of Francis I, who had acquired an international reputation for his interest in art and wide-ranging munificence. Cellini was not the first Italian – or the last – to be drawn to his court. Contacts, political and cultural, between France and Italy had already flourished in the Middle Ages, but the Italian Wars, begun by King Charles VIII in 1494, had intensified them. Successive military campaigns brought the French kings and their nobles into direct contact with the classical culture of the Italian Renaissance. Charles VIII had returned from Naples with sculptors and gardeners, Louis XII may have employed Leonardo da Vinci, while Francis I actually invited the old man to France and gave him a desirable residence outside Amboise. Other artists followed, including Andrea del Sarto, Rosso and Primaticcio. They were honoured as few were elsewhere in Europe. Rosso, it was said, lived like a prince. Cellini was keen to join this happy band. A first visit had failed to produce a commission, but another sponsored by Cardinal Ippolito d'Este, a close friend of the king, resulted in a commission to make a set of giant candelabra. Leonardo had been too old and infirm to produce anything other than drawings during his last years spent in France, but Cellini was young enough to turn the Petit Nesle, a building in Paris given to him by the king, into a thriving studio where he and his apprentices beat sheets of silver into shape under the admiring gaze of Francis and his court.

In addition to being a political and cultural centre, the court was a microcosm of French society. All social classes, except the peasantry, were represented there. In addition, the sixteenth century was marked by a notable expansion of the role given to women. 'A court without women', Francis allegedly said, 'is like a garden without flowers.' The court also acted as a magnet for people anxious to better themselves socially. They might secure an *office*, which was a uniquely French institution: a post in the royal administration that could, in some cases, automatically confer nobility. By acquiring one by gift or purchase a man could move from the third estate into the second. The first estate, the clergy, was also well represented at court, for the king was by virtue of his *sacre* or coronation a semi-priestly figure supposedly endowed with the miraculous power of healing the sick. Proud holder of the papal title of 'The Most Christian King', he had sworn at his coronation to protect the church and to drive heretics out of his kingdom. He dispensed not only offices, but also ecclesiastical benefices: consequently, ambitious churchmen had as much cause to come to court as ambitious bourgeois. A lucrative bishopric or abbey might be had for the asking. As for the so-called old nobility – families of ancient lineage – its members came to court as the king's right hand. However absolute the king may have been in his own estimation, he would have achieved little without the support of the nobility. Handling it required tact and skill. Francis I had both, except when he alienated the duc de Bourbon. Nor was there much faction at his court before his declining years. It was only following the accidental death of King Henry II in 1559 and the rise of the House of Guise that the court's unity began to crumble. A powerful solvent was the rise of Protestantism, which began in the 1520s but only became a serious threat in the 1560s after many nobles had converted to it. For more than half a century France had been blessed with domestic peace, 'golden years', but in 1562 aristocratic unrest and religious dissent combined to ignite the first of a series of bloody civil wars – the so-called Wars of Religion – which inevitably affected the court. For some time its presiding genius was no longer a man, but a woman and an Italian: the queen mother, Catherine de' Medici. She tried to reconcile the factions and to restore religious unity, but in the end she failed. A woman, however able, could not command the same authority in sixteenth-century France as a man.

Ballets and other entertainments continued to be held at court, but they now took place against a background of mounting violence. Not even Catherine and her son Charles IX were safe. In 1568 they narrowly escaped being kidnapped by Protestant nobles before being besieged in Paris. In August 1572 a royal marriage in Paris was followed by the Massacre of St Bartholomew's Day, which bloodied not only the streets of the capital, but also the courtyard of the Louvre and the monarchy's reputation. Thereafter the climate at court altered completely, reflecting yet again a change in the monarch's personality. Though highly intelligent and well-meaning, Henry III committed every sin in the manual of good political conduct. No one could have been further removed from Francis I than his grandson. Whereas the former had been accessible, gregarious and pleasure-loving, albeit author-itarian, the latter was a recluse who tried to enhance his authority by distancing himself physically from his subjects and by creating a rigid court etiquette. At the same time he alienated many courtiers by favouring just a few: the famous *mignons*. Nor was Henry keen on travel. He fixed his court in Paris, leaving it only for short breaks in private at a château in the vicinity. Despite an empty purse which prevented him from dealing effectively with the Protestant threat to his authority, he promoted lavish festivities at court which contrasted with high food prices and hunger outside. The king was accused of profligacy and also of hypocrisy as he fervently embraced peniten-tial exercises ranging from retreats in religious houses to hooded processions through the streets of the capital. In 1589 Henry III was assassinated by a Jacobin friar. The court, however, survived, for it was the person of the king, not the institution of monarchy, that had been challenged.

CHAPTER 1

The Golden Years, 1483–1559

The history of France in the sixteenth century may be divided into two periods of roughly equal length. The first, which lasted from 1483 until 1559, was one of domestic peace, whereas the second, which continued till the end of the century, was disfigured by prolonged and bloody civil wars. The accession of Charles VIII in 1483 coincided with a process of reconstruction, both economic and political, which rescued France from the horrors and divisions of the Hundred Years War. As peace returned, agriculture and trade prospered, and urban life boomed. Peace at home encouraged the kings of France to seek an extension of their dominion across the Alps, bringing them into direct contact with the art and culture of the Italian Renaissance. The French court reflected these changes. After lagging far behind the court of the dukes of Burgundy in magnificence, it soon became renowned as the most splendid in Christendom. All over France noblemen built new outward-looking homes, with windows rather than arrow-slits, designed for comfort and pleasure instead of defence. This was the great period of château-building when a new classical style of decoration became fashionable.

When Louis XI died on 30 August 1483, his son, Charles VIII, was only thirteen years old, ten months short of the age of majority for a king of France. Among possible regents, two seemed best qualified: his sister Anne and her husband, Pierre de Beaujeu. They already had custody of the young king and the support of the royal civil service, but they could not rely completely on that of the nobility. Their main rival was the king's cousin Louis duc d'Orléans. He plotted to abduct Charles after his coronation on 30 May, but was foiled by the Beaujeus who carried the king off to Montargis. Supporters of Louis were dismissed from court while he retired to his *gouvernement* (governorship) of the Île-de-France.

The minority of Charles VIII was bedevilled by the so-called 'Mad War', a series of aristocratic revolts against the Beaujeus.[1] A major source of trouble for the French crown was Brittany, as yet an independent duchy, which offered a safe haven to French rebels and often sought English assistance. The problem was eventually solved by military action which ended in 1488 with a royal victory. Charles VIII, now a full-fledged monarch, married the defeated duchess, Anne of Brittany, on 6 December 1491.[2] Her duchy effectively became part of the French kingdom, though in theory it remained independent, and Anne was determined to keep it so.

Once rid of the Breton question, Charles VIII turned his attention to Italy. Keen to emulate his distant forebear, the Emperor Charlemagne, who in the ninth century had fought the Saracens, he planned to lead a crusade against the Turks and liberate Constantinople and the Holy Places from their domination; as a first step, however, he needed to realise a claim to the kingdom of Naples inherited from his Angevin forebears. A majority of his councillors opposed his Italian designs, but a few, including his favourites, Guillaume Briçonnet and Étienne de Vesc, encouraged him, if only for the opportunities of self-enrichment which they could see in Italy. In August 1494 Charles invaded the peninsula, thereby inaugurating a series of French military campaigns known as the Italian Wars. They lasted on and off till 1559. The king's march south turned into a triumphal progress: wherever he passed crowds flocked to see him. Some may have been disappointed by his appearance. 'The king of France', a Venetian wrote,

> is twenty-two years old. Small and ill-shaped, facially ugly, his eyes are large and pale and inclined to see badly rather than well; likewise, his aquiline nose is larger and fatter than is fitting; his lips are thick and he keeps them continually open. His hand is convulsed by spasms which are very ugly to see. He speaks slowly. In my opinion, which may well be wrong, I believe that in body and mind he is of little worth.[3]

Yet Charles was welcomed by the people of Florence as their liberator from Medici rule. The historian Guicciardini thought his achievement surpassed that of Caesar, for he had conquered even before seeing. Marsilio Ficino, the Florentine humanist, said that Charles 'had shaken the world with a nod'. Ultimately, however, his conquest of Naples proved short-lived: a coalition of Italian states drove the French out of Italy. Charles himself narrowly avoided defeat at the Battle of Fornovo, and lost much of the booty he had taken from Naples. He hoped to avenge this humiliation, but was prevented by the death of his infant son, Charles-Orland, and also by a lack of money. On 7 April 1498 Charles himself died, aged twenty-seven, after hitting his head against the lintel of a door at the château of Amboise.

As Charles VIII's only son had predeceased him, the throne passed to his erstwhile troublesome cousin, Louis d'Orléans, who now became King

Louis XII. Thirty-six years old, he was physically unattractive and subject to frequent bouts of ill health. His first aim as king was to get rid of his wife, Jeanne de France, whom he had been forced to marry by her father, Louis XI. This had been a cynical ploy on the part of the old king, who had rightly assumed that his ill-favoured daughter would be barren. He wanted to ensure

1. *King Louis XII of France.* Painting attributed to Jean Pérréal, a French painter, illuminator of manuscripts and designer of funerary monuments. Having entered the royal court by 1494, Pérréal became its chief artist.

the early termination of the Orléans branch of the royal family and the absorption of its lands into the king's domain. For a long time Louis d'Orléans refused to live with Jeanne, preferring a life of debauchery, but eventually he agreed to see her from time to time and even slept with her despite the physical revulsion she inspired in him. He did not try to repudiate Jeanne during her father's lifetime or that of her brother, Charles VIII, but on reaching the throne, he sought an annulment from Pope Alexander VI, who willingly obliged as a means of advancing his own political and family interests. Louis expressed his appreciation by making the pope's bastard, Cesare Borgia, duc de Valentinois. A papal tribunal was set up in France, and Jeanne underwent a humiliating public examination. Her marriage was then annulled. She received the duchy of Berry by way of compensation and devoted the rest of her life to pious works. She died in 1505 and was canonised in 1950.[4]

Louis XII was now free to marry his predecessor's widow, Anne of Brittany, who attracted him for two reasons: first, at twenty-two she was capable of child-bearing; secondly, by marrying her he would retain control of Brittany. Anne accepted Louis on strict conditions aimed at preserving her duchy's independence. The marriage took place at Nantes on 8 January 1499. Though praised for her beauty, Anne had one leg shorter than the other, an infirmity she concealed by wearing a high heel. Her first child by Louis was a daughter, Claude, born on 13 October 1499. For eleven years she was the only child in the royal nursery and the pivot of Louis's matrimonial diplomacy. Though plain, she was desirable on account of her rich dowry, which included the Orléans patrimony, the duchy of Brittany and the French claims to Asti, Milan, Genoa and Naples.

From the start of his reign Louis XII sought popularity and he succeeded to the extent of being acclaimed in 1506 as 'father of his people'.[5] Believing that a king should live 'of his own' (i.e., on the income from his domain), he avoided excessive expenditure on his court. He reduced the annual amount spent on gifts and pensions, much to the annoyance of courtiers, who nicknamed him *le roi roturier* (the commoner king). His parsimony was also derided in satirical plays staged by a company of Parisian actors called the Basoche, but Louis did not care. 'I much prefer', he said, 'to make fops laugh at my miserliness than to make the people weep over my generosity.' While curbing expenditure, he trebled the revenue from his domain by more efficient accounting. In the last two years of his reign he ran into difficulties, yet his efforts to keep taxes low, to dispense justice and to give his subjects security were not forgotten: throughout the sixteenth century people looked back nostalgically to the 'good old days of King Louis'.[6] In the XVIIIth century Louis XII was held up by writers, such as Fénelon and Voltaire, as an example of 'enlightened monarchy'.[7]

He continued the policy of armed intervention in Italy begun by his predecessor. He conquered Naples in 1501, but soon lost it to Ferdinand of Aragon after foolishly dividing the kingdom with him. Thereafter he set his sights on the duchy of Milan, to which he had a claim inherited from his grandmother Valentina Visconti. This brought him into conflict with a coalition of mainly Italian states called the 'Holy League' and led by the warlike Pope Julius II. A French victory at Ravenna in April 1512 was followed paradoxically by the French army's headlong retreat across the Lombard plain. In September 1513 the Swiss, who were part of the League, invaded France and laid siege to Dijon. The local commander, La Trémoille, bought them off by signing a treaty that Louis then refused to ratify.[8] The Swiss were infuriated and harboured a grudge against France for several years.

In the absence of a son, Louis XII's nearest male heir was a second cousin, François d'Angoulême, who was six years old in 1500. Born in Cognac, he and his sister, Marguerite, were brought up at Amboise by their mother, Louise of Savoy. She was the daughter of Philippe de Bresse, duke of Savoy, and Marguerite de Bourbon. In 1488, at the age of fourteen, she had married Charles comte d'Angoulême, who died in 1496, leaving her with two young children to bring up.[9] Louis XII forced her to share their guardianship with him and placed them in the care of Pierre de Rohan, seigneur de Gié, a Breton strongly committed to Brittany's union with France. This ran counter to the wishes of the queen, Anne of Brittany. Louise deeply resented Gié's tutelage and protested vehemently when one of his subordinates intruded on her privacy. Louise, however, was allowed a free hand in educating her children. She commissioned books for them and employed François Demoulins, a distinguished humanist, as her son's tutor. Passionately committed to his advancement, Louise consulted the saintly hermit Francis of Paola, who prophesied that he would become king one day.[10]

Gié wanted François to marry the king's daughter, but her mother, Anne of Brittany, had other ideas linked to the determination to preserve her duchy's independence at all costs. She wanted Claude to marry Charles of Habsburg, the grandson of Emperor Maximilian, even if this meant dismembering France. Caught in the crossfire between Gié and Anne, Louis XII made a secret declaration nullifying in advance any marriage between Claude and anyone other than François. Anne, meanwhile, arranged Claude's betrothal to Charles, whose parents, Philip the Fair and Juana of Castile, came to France to see their prospective daughter-in-law. In April 1505, however, the king made a will in which he ordered Claude's marriage to François when she was old enough to wed. He forbade her to leave the kingdom in the meantime, and appointed a council of regency capable of standing up to the queen.[11] The queen, for her part, retired to Brittany where she remained for five months.

2. Louise of Savoy, countess of Angoulême. Miniature from an anonymous manuscript entitled *Le Compas du daulphin* (Bibliothèque nationale de France, ms. fr. 2285, fo. 5). The large compass is a symbol of Louise's role in guiding her son (who stands beside her), along the paths of virtue.

Her absence enabled her husband to pursue his own agenda: he summoned an Assembly of Notables, which met at Tours in May 1506.[12] They begged him to marry his daughter to François, whom they commended to him as being a true Frenchman ('tout français'), a request that Louis graciously conceded.[13]

In August 1508 François left his mother to settle at court. At fourteen he was old enough to be king, but this depended on Louis XII having no son. In

Ce price romaine come reatet leure
historiographie et oratenre solonit dne
qne en regardant lee ymages honorablee
et arez detriniplze de leure predecessenre aunit.

3. The Assembly of Notables held at Tours in 1506 and the betrothal of François d'Angoulême (the future Francis I) and Louis XII's daughter, Claude de France. Miniature (Bibliothèque nationale de France, ms. fr. 5083, fo. 1 verso). Claude's mother, Anne of Brittany, stands, crowned, next to her daughter, and Louise of Savoy next to her son.

1512 Queen Anne gave birth to a boy, but he died almost at once, much to the relief of Louise of Savoy. 'Anne, queen of France', she wrote in her diary, 'gave birth to a son on 21 January, the feast of St Agnes, but he failed to prevent the exaltation of my Caesar for he was stillborn.'[14] Now known as the dauphin, François was admitted to the king's council and given a military command in Navarre. In 1514, following the queen's death, he and Claude were married. Eyewitnesses, noting Louis XII's sickly appearance, did not give him long to live. In October, however, he surprised everyone by marrying Mary, the sister of the English king, Henry VIII.[15] Public opinion was shocked by this match between the gout-ridden monarch, aged fifty-three, and an eighteen-year-old princess, noted for her looks, but Mary herself seemed resigned. Louis's days were doubtless numbered and Henry VIII had promised her a free choice of second husband. Meanwhile, she would become queen of France.[16] Mary and Louis were married at Abbeville on 9 October 1514. Within a short time, however, he began to show signs of wear and tear, much to the amusement of the clerks of the Basoche, who put on a play showing the king being carried off to heaven or to hell by an English filly.[17] On 1 January 1515 Louis died in Paris and François d'Angoulême succeeded him as King Francis I.[18]

Francis I was not bound to retain his predecessor's ministers, although it was not unusual for a monarch to do so in return for appropriate fees. Among the survivors in 1515 was Florimond Robertet, now remembered as 'the father of the secretaries of state'.[19] Continuity, however, was not everything: the new administration badly needed fresh blood and Francis's childhood companions, and the men who had attached themselves to his rising star, expected their reward. Among them was Antoine Duprat, who now became Chancellor of France. Another vacant office in 1515 was the Constableship of France, to which Charles III, duc de Bourbon, was appointed. This made him in effect commander-in-chief of the king's army. He also became governor of Languedoc and *Grand chambrier de France*. In January 1515 Francis created two marshals of France – Odet de Foix, seigneur de Lautrec, and Jacques Chabannes, seigneur de Lapalisse – in addition to the two already in post, namely Stuart d'Aubigny and Gian-Giacomo Trivulzio. Lautrec ceded his office of *Grand Maître* to Artus Gouffier, seigneur de Boisy, who became one of Francis I's most trusted councillors but died in May 1519. His younger brother, Guillaume seigneur de Bonnivet, one of Francis's childhood companions, became Admiral of France in 1517. This, however, did not entail any command at sea: rather, it conferred supreme jurisdiction over all maritime affairs and commanded a sizeable income from wrecks and prizes.

We owe the best description of Francis I at the age of twenty-six to Ellis Griffith, a Welsh soldier who observed him at the Field of Cloth of Gold in 1520. The king, observed Griffith, was six feet tall with a head rightly proportioned for his height. The nape of his neck was unusually broad, his hair brown, smooth and neatly combed, his beard of three months' growth darker in colour, his nose long, his eyes hazel and bloodshot, and his complexion the colour of watery milk. He had muscular buttocks and thighs, but his legs below the knees were thin and bandy, while his feet were long, slender and completely flat. He had a pleasing voice and in conversation a lively manner marred only by the unkingly habit of continually rolling his eyes upwards.[20]

Women played a significant part in Francis I's life. Two in particular were important: his mother, Louise of Savoy, and his sister, Marguerite d'Angoulême. Louise was forty in 1515 and had another sixteen years to look forward to. An Italian visitor, Antonio de Beatis, described her in 1517 as 'an unusually tall woman, still finely complexioned, very rubicund and lively and seems to me to be about forty years old but more than good, one could say, for at least another ten. She always accompanies her son and the Queen and plays the governess without restraint.'[21] Louise never remarried and was therefore able to devote herself completely to her son's service. She sat in his council and was twice regent during his reign: first, when he invaded Italy in 1515, and, secondly, in 1525–6 when he was a prisoner in Spain. Louise became an expert in foreign affairs. Cardinal Wolsey, Henry VIII's chief minister, described her as 'mother and nourisher of peace', but she was seen by many contemporaries as excessively grasping and ambitious. A formidable lady, she exercised a powerful influence on the court. The king's sister, Marguerite, was not beautiful, but was intelligent and vivacious and, like her brother whom she worshipped, had a well-developed sense of humour. She married twice: first, Charles duc d'Alençon, in December 1509, and secondly, Henri d'Albret, king of Navarre, in 1527. Despite these princely attachments, she spent most of her time before 1534 at the French court. Like her mother, she often acted as government mouthpiece and talked to foreign ambassadors with a candour that surprised them. Sometimes, one suspects, her behaviour was not always free from calculation. The duke of Norfolk described Marguerite as 'one of the wisest frank women, and best setter forth of her purpose' he had ever spoken to.[22] But it is as an author and champion of religious reform that Marguerite is best remembered. In addition to the *Heptaméron*, a series of stories modelled on those of Boccaccio's *Decameron*, she wrote several religious poems.[23] Marguerite never became a Lutheran, but was strongly attracted to evangelical faith and offered her protection to preachers and scholars whose views were sometimes more extreme than her own.

Queen Claude, Francis I's first wife, counted for little politically. 'The Queen is young,' wrote de Beatis in 1517, 'and though small in stature, plain and badly lame in both hips, is said to be very cultivated, generous and pious.' Surprisingly enough, given Francis's well-founded reputation as a libertine, he seems to have been genuinely fond of her. 'It is a matter of common report', wrote de Beatis, 'that he holds his wife the Queen in such honour and respect that when in France and with her he has never failed to sleep with her each night.'[24] Claude bore Francis three sons and four daughters in nine years. Such intensive child-bearing inevitably precluded her from any prominent share in public life. She died at Blois on 26 July 1524.

Louise, Francis I's first child, was born at Amboise on 19 August 1515 while the king was in Italy. She was followed a year later, on 23 October, by another daughter, Charlotte, named after the king of Castile whose ambassador held her over the font at her christening. In November 1517 Francis went on pilgrimage to the abbey of St Martin of Tours to pray for a son. He was granted his wish when the Dauphin, François, was born at Amboise on 28 February 1518. A second son was born at Saint-Germain-en-Laye on 31 March 1519. He was called Henry after his godfather, King Henry VIII of England. That is why his name is spelt Henry, not Henri, in contemporary documents. On 10 August 1520 Claude gave birth to a third daughter, Madeleine, who eventually became the wife of James V of Scotland. The king's third son, Charles, was born at Saint-Germain-en-Laye on 22 January 1522 and his fourth daughter, Marguerite, on 5 June 1523. She eventually became duchess of Savoy. She and Henry were the only two children to outlive their father.[25]

A royal marriage in the sixteenth century was seldom a sentimental union; more often than not it was a political arrangement between parties of different nationalities. This being so, it was almost inevitable that a king would take a mistress. Francis had several in the course of his reign, but only two were *maîtresses en titre*, or official mistresses. They were official in the sense that no attempt was made to conceal their existence: known to everyone, they were given an honourable place at court. The first was Françoise de Foix, who in 1509 had married Jean de Laval, sieur de Châteaubriant. We do not know where or when the king first met her, but she was present at court in June 1516 as one of the queen's twelve ladies-in-waiting. Noted for her elegance, she may also have used her influence with the king to assist the careers of her three brothers, Odet, Thomas and André, who all obtained high military commands. She died in 1537 after being superseded in the king's affections in about 1526 by Anne de Pisseleu, who eventually became the duchesse d'Étampes. Her career will be discussed later.

Francis continued the policy of military intervention south of the Alps. In August 1515 he crossed them and conquered Milan after crushing the Swiss, who had been defending the duchy, at Marignano. This, however, was to be his only great victory; he hoped to repeat it some day but never did. In 1519 Charles of Habsburg, who ruled Spain and the Netherlands, was elected Holy Roman Emperor. France thus became almost encircled by a hostile power. In 1521 a war broke out between Francis and Charles which continued on and off until 1559. They became lifelong enemies but for an interlude of about ten years between 1530 and 1540.

Francis on the whole got on well with his nobility; his court was largely free of faction. The only serious discord was the treason of Charles III de Bourbon, the Constable of France. In 1521, during a military campaign in northern France, the king gave command of his army's vanguard to his own brother-in-law, Alençon, instead of the Constable, who was entitled to it. Charles bottled up his resentment, but relations with the king broke down following the death of his wife, Suzanne, in April 1521. A will she had made in her husband's favour was challenged by the king and his mother, Louise of Savoy. The rival claims were submitted to the Parlement, but before a verdict could be given, Louise did homage to her son for part of Suzanne's inheritance. This, however, was not the constable's only grievance. As a childless widower, he needed to remarry in order to perpetuate his line. He soon came under pressure from two directions: while imperial agents offered him the hand of Charles V's sister, the French crown urged him to marry a French princess. Like Anne of Brittany before him, Bourbon, who was the last of the great feudal lords, was anxious to maintain his ducal independence. Early in 1523, as he was dining with Queen Claude, Francis entered the room and accused him of becoming secretly engaged, whereupon Bourbon left the court in high dudgeon, followed, it was alleged, by many nobles.[26] In May he confessed to a friend that he no longer trusted the king, and in July he signed a secret treaty with Charles V in which he agreed to rebel in return for the hand of the emperor's sister. News of the plot, however, soon leaked out. Francis called on Bourbon at his château of Moulins as he was travelling south to join his army at Lyon on the eve of another invasion of Italy. The king tried to persuade the duke to follow him and Charles agreed to do so, but as soon as Francis's back was turned he reneged on his promise and came to a secret understanding with an English agent. Realising that he had been duped, Francis took steps to nip the conspiracy in the bud. Bourbon managed to evade arrest and fled to imperial territory beyond the Saône, where he took up a new career as one of Charles V's commanders. This was to end ignominiously in 1527 with his death in the Sack of Rome. Serious as it had been, Bourbon's treason had failed to ignite a major aristocratic revolt in France.[27]

In the autumn of 1524 Francis invaded Italy, hoping to repeat his triumph at Marignano and reconquer Milan, which had slipped from his grasp in 1522. Only this time he was fighting not the Swiss but the imperial army commanded by Charles de Lannoy, viceroy of Naples. Refusing to believe that any town could hold out against a king of France, Francis made the fatal mistake of besieging Pavia in midwinter, thus sentencing his army to cold and hunger in the open. On 24 February 1525 he was decisively defeated outside the town and taken prisoner. The dead included many of his closest friends, including the seigneur de Bonnivet. Marshal Lescun and the king's uncle, René of Savoy, died of their wounds. The only prominent Frenchman to escape defeat or capture was Francis's brother-in-law, Charles d'Alençon, but he died on 15 April soon after returning to France, some said of shame. Two years later, his widow, the king's sister, Marguerite, married Henri d'Albret, king of Navarre.

Francis expected to have to pay a ransom for his freedom, but the Emperor Charles V demanded nothing less than the return of the duchy of Burgundy which, he claimed, had been wrongfully taken from his ancestors by Louis XI in 1477. As Francis would not comply with this demand, Charles kept him in prison, first in Italy, then in Spain. For more than a year France had no king.[28] Francis's mother, Louise of Savoy, ruled as regent, ably seconded by the chancellor, Duprat. Their task was arduous, as France was still at war with England and the Holy Roman Empire. The remnants of its defeated army were trickling back across the Alps, demoralised, bedraggled and unpaid. Louise settled at the monastery of Saint-Just, near Lyon, leaving the Parlement to oversee the defence of northern France. She warded off the threat of English invasion by detaching Henry VIII from his alliance with Charles V and laid the foundations of an international coalition, called the League of Cognac, aimed at forcing the emperor to release her son on the best possible terms.[29]

Francis was in Spain when the traitor Bourbon came there to claim the hand of the emperor's sister, Eleanor, whose first husband, King Manuel I of Portugal, had died in 1521. Her hand had been promised to the duke, but Francis put in a counterbid of his own. He may have calculated that such a move would facilitate his liberation on favourable terms. Charles was left with no choice: the hand of a king of France, albeit a prisoner, was far worthier of his sister's rank than that of a dispossessed French duke; so the matter was decided in Francis's favour and the betrothal, which was celebrated by proxy on 20 January 1526, sealed the Treaty of Madrid, signed six days earlier, in which Francis promised to cede Burgundy to the emperor. In February, following his release from prison, the king and Charles went to Illescas, where Francis was introduced to his future wife. Eleanor was the eldest child of Philip the Fair, archduke of Austria, and Juana 'the Mad', queen of Castile. Born in Louvain on 15 November 1498, she was only four years younger than Francis. She had been brought up in Flanders by her aunt, Margaret of Austria, who had given her an excellent all-round education. She was an accomplished musician. Though not beautiful (she had the heavy jaw characteristic of the Habsburgs), she was praised for her grace and elegance. By temperament she was gentle and submissive. In 1517 she had been married off to the old king of Portugal, Manuel I 'the Fortunate', and had given him two children: Charles, who died in infancy, and Maria, who never married and lived until 1577. When Manuel died in 1521, Eleanor joined her brother Charles V in Spain. She would have liked to take her daughter with her, but was prevented by the Portuguese authorities.[30]

In March 1526 Francis returned home in order to fulfil the Treaty of Madrid. By way of security he had to hand over to the emperor his eldest sons, François and Henri. They were exchanged for their father at the Pyrenean border. Eleanor, too, had to remain in Spain for the time being. Having regained his freedom, however, Francis refused to ratify the treaty. His homecoming was followed by an almost complete renewal of his administration. Bourbon's treason and the mass slaughter of French noblemen at Pavia had left numerous vacancies at court. Foremost among the new appointees were Anne de Montmorency and Philippe Chabot, who became Grand Master and Admiral of France respectively.[31]

Francis I's failure to honour the Treaty of Madrid led inevitably to a new war with the emperor, which lasted till August 1529 when the so-called 'Peace of the Ladies', was signed at Cambrai. By this Francis gave up all his claims in Italy, but retained Burgundy and recovered his sons in return for an enormous cash ransom. Montmorency was responsible for collecting the money, transporting it to Bayonne and handing it over to imperial commissioners. The peace also enabled Eleanor of Austria to join her fiancé at last. She and the king's two sons crossed the River Bidassoa on 1 July 1530 and six days later she and Francis were married quietly in the chapel of the monastery of Saint-Laurent-de-Beyries, near Mont-de-Marsan. Eleanor's coronation at Saint-Denis followed on 5 March 1531. Montmorency, who supervised preparations for the ceremony, admired her greatly. Frenchmen, he thought, should thank God for giving them 'so beautiful and virtuous a lady'.[32] Her husband, however, was less enthusiastic. He had by now acquired a new mistress in the person of Anne d'Heilly, the eighteen-year-old daughter of Guillaume de Pisseleu, a Picard nobleman. She was lady-in-waiting to Marie de Luxembourg, duchesse de Vendôme. The king made no secret of his new passion, even displaying it publicly at Eleanor's entry into Paris on 16 March. 'He . . . took Hely and set her before him in an open window and there stood devising with her two long hours in the sight and face of all the people, which was not a little marvelled at of the beholders.' Anne's position at court soon grew in importance. She became governess to the king's daughters, Madeleine and Marguerite. In 1534 Francis married her off to Jean de Brosse, seigneur de Penthièvre, and on 23 June he gave them the *comté* of Étampes, raising it two years later to ducal status. Thus did Anne become duchesse d'Étampes, the title by which she is now best known. She continued to live at court and exerted a powerful influence on the king and his entourage till the end of his reign.[33]

It soon became clear to everyone that the king's marriage was a sham. Sir Francis Bryan reported to Henry VIII:

> For the first, being both in one house they lie not together once in four nights; another he [Francis] speaks very seldom unto her openly; another, he is never out of my lady's [Louise of Savoy's] chamber, and all for Hely's sake, his old lover; another is, there has been no feast or banquet yet, since the beginning of the triumph, but, the table furnished, he has come and sat in the midst of the board, where Hely has sat, and the Cardinal of Lorraine and the Admiral likewise with their lovers. He has also divers times ridden six or seven miles from the Queen and lain out four or five days together, as it is said, at the houses of his old lovers.[34]

Two years later Marguerite de Navarre told the duke of Norfolk that no man could be less satisfied with his wife than her brother. For the past seven months 'he neither lay with her, not yet meddled with her'. Norfolk asked for the reason. 'Parce quil ne le trouve plesaunt a son apetyde,' she replied, 'nor when he doth lie with her, he cannot sleep; and when he lieth from her no man sleepeth better.' Pressed for an explanation, Marguerite burst out laughing and said: 'She is very hot in bed and desireth to be too much embraced.'[35]

Eleanor has been largely ignored by historians, yet the impact of her presence at the French court ought not to be underestimated, for she had a number of Spanish ladies-in-waiting and imported a concern for etiquette hitherto unknown there.[36] The queen adhered to Spanish timekeeping, taking her evening meal much later than the rest of the court.[37] Apart from trying to mend fences between her husband and her brother, she lived in semi-retirement, listening to music and devoting herself to good works. Eleanor did not get on well with her mother-in-law, but she did not have to put up with her for long. Louise died of plague at Grez-sur-Loing on 22 September 1531. Marguerite was at her bedside, but not her beloved son, who was at Chantilly with Montmorency. He made up for his absence by giving Louise, who had never been queen, a regal funeral modelled on that of his first wife, Claude. Louise's legacy was even larger than her legendary greed had led people to expect.

In 1533 an alliance between Francis and Pope Clement VII was sealed by the marriage in Marseille of the king's second son, Henry (the future Henry II), with the pope's niece, Catherine. Clement was a member of the Florentine family of Medici and Francis hoped that the match would advance his interests in Italy. Catherine de' Medici soon adapted to her new environment. She came to admire her father-in-law and he became quite fond of her, if only because she was an excellent horsewoman and joined his hunting parties with gusto. In September 1533, however, Clement VII died and was succeeded by Paul III, who was a Farnese, not a Medici. Catherine's marriage was accordingly robbed of its *raison d'être*. Her position became even more precarious following the sudden death of her brother-in-law, the Dauphin François, on 10 August 1536, which caused her husband, Henry, to become the new heir to the throne. Catherine's situation would not have been so bad had she given birth to a son, thereby ensuring the future of the dynasty, but so far her marriage had proved barren. According to the late sixteenth-century writer, Brantôme, 'Many people advised the king and the dauphin to repudiate her, since it was necessary to continue the line of France.'[38] Francis ruled out a divorce after Catherine had moved him deeply by offering to cede her place to another and retire to a convent. Fortunately for her, ten years after her wedding, on 20 January 1544, she produced a son, an event loudly acclaimed by court poets. Francis shed tears of joy.

Catherine adored her husband, but she had to share him with his mistress, Diane de Poitiers, the widow of Louis de Brézé, Grand Sénéchal of Normandy, whom she had met in 1538 when she was thirty-eight and he only nineteen. According to the Venetian ambassador Marino Cavalli, Henry's love for Diane was purely platonic, but the idea that he was uninterested in sex is belied by his numerous love affairs and by his fathering of at least two bastards.[39] Cavalli may have been taken in by Diane's clever propaganda. During Francis I's reign her morals were frequently called into question by friends of the duchesse d'Étampes. In 1551 the Venetian ambassador, Lorenzo Contarini, cited popular gossip alleging that Diane had been the mistress of Francis I and of many other men before she had become Henry's. Her true personality is not easily disentangled from the myth she created about herself. By encouraging her identification with Diana, the chaste goddess of hunting, she raised herself above the level of a mere royal mistress, disguising the true nature of her relations with Henry.[40]

In June 1535 Charles V launched an attack on the Turks in North Africa. Montmorency promised that Francis would not take advantage of the situation to attack him. In November 1535, however, the death of Francesco Sforza, duke of Milan, reopened the thorny question of the succession to the duchy. Francis still wanted it, if not for himself then at least for one of his sons. In February 1536 a French army, commanded by Admiral Chabot, invaded Savoy, whose duke, Carlo III, was the emperor's ally. The move was aimed at providing Francis with a bargaining counter in talks over Milan's future, but Charles V denounced it as an act of aggression against himself and, in July, invaded Provence. Montmorency, who was put in charge of defending the province, forced the emperor to withdraw by adopting a scorched-earth strategy. His success earned him promotion to the exalted office of Constable of France, which had been vacant since Bourbon's treason.

Montmorency now set about reconciling Francis and Charles V, a policy which had the wholehearted support of the latter's sister, Eleanor. It represented a complete volte-face in French foreign policy and did not meet with universal approval at the French court. Montmorency, however, could count on the backing of Pope Paul III, who viewed the peace of Christendom as the essential precondition for a future crusade against the Turks. A meeting in Nice in May and June 1538, at which the king and the emperor negotiated with him separately, resulted in a ten-year truce (see plate 9). Eleanor seized the opportunity to call on her brother at Villefranche. She and her ladies went there by sea. As they disembarked a wooden pier collapsed, pitching them into the sea, but the water was shallow at this point so that no one suffered more than a soaking. A separate meeting in Aigues-Mortes between Francis and Charles V in July marked the start of a rapprochement which Montmorency intended as a first step towards the peaceful recovery of Milan by Francis. In October Mary of Hungary, the governess of the Low Countries, visited Compiègne. The triumph of Montmorency's policy sealed the fate of his rival, Chabot, who, after being excluded from the meetings at Nice and Aigues-Mortes, retired to his Burgundian home. Montmorency meanwhile tightened his grip on the court.[41]

In 1539 Charles V needed to travel from Spain to the Netherlands by the fastest possible route to quell a serious tax revolt in Ghent. With some hesitation he accepted an invitation from Francis to cross his kingdom. He was received with the utmost courtesy.[42] All talk of business was avoided during his visit, but it did not yield the result that Montmorency had hoped for. Charles, instead of inviting him to Brussels for talks, submitted wholly unacceptable proposals and followed them up by conferring the investiture of Milan on his own son, Philip. This destroyed Montmorency's credit at the French court and played into the hands of the so-called war party led by Chabot and the duchesse d'Étampes. Montmorency fell from power and was replaced as the king's chief adviser by Chabot, but on 1 June 1543 the latter died. This opened the way for two younger councillors – Claude d'Annebault and Cardinal François de Tournon – to rise to prominence. Annebault became Admiral of France in February 1544.

In June 1543 England and the Empire declared war on France and in December they agreed to invade France jointly. While the imperial army overran Luxemburg, capturing Saint-Dizier, Henry VIII seized Boulogne. Francis promised to live and die with the Parisians as Charles V's army advanced on the capital, but the emperor suddenly sued for peace: he was short of money and needed urgently to attend to the political situation in Germany. In September 1544 he signed the Peace of Crépy, which provided for the marriage of Francis's third son, Charles duc d'Orléans, with either the emperor's sister, Maria, or his niece, Anna. Either way, the duke was to receive a handsome dowry in the form of the Netherlands and Franche-Comté or Milan. Francis promised him four French duchies as *apanages* and gave up his rights in Italy. Charles V, for his part, finally abandoned his claim to Burgundy. The treaty aroused mixed feelings in France. Queen Eleanor was, of course, delighted. She joined her sister, Mary of Hungary, in Brussels, where they celebrated the peace together. Charles d'Orléans also attended the celebrations, as did, more surprisingly, Madame d'Étampes, who, frightened by an illness that Francis had suffered in 1538, had drawn closer to the queen and duc d'Orléans. Francis's son, Henry, on the other hand, was furious, as the treaty stripped him of his rights in Italy and threatened to dismember the kingdom he hoped would one day be his. He need not have worried, however, for his brother Charles died on 9 September 1545 before the agreement could be implemented. Heartbroken, Francis drew nearer to Henry. He admitted him to his council, but the new dauphin preferred to wait in the wings until the stage could be his alone. During the last five years of his life, Francis's health gave cause for concern. Everyone knew that his days were numbered and that his death would be followed by a palace revolution. He died at Rambouillet on 31 March 1547 at the age of fifty-two.

Henry II has often been portrayed as a gloomy monarch, but he shed the melancholia that had marked his unhappy youth once he became king. A Venetian described him as 'joyful, rubicund and with an excellent colour'.[43] Tall and muscular, he shared his father's love of outdoor exercise, especially tennis, riding and jousting. Though less gifted intellectually, he was interested in architecture and used art to project his authority. His private life was only marginally more respectable than his father's had been. Henry's faults and qualities were evenly balanced: kind to his offspring and loyal to his friends, he could also be vindictive and stubborn.[44]

Henry's accession was followed by the expected palace revolution. The main victim was the duchesse d'Étampes, who had upset many people by her arrogance and nepotism. Saint-Mauris, the imperial envoy, believed that she would have been stoned if she had dared to appear in public. She lost her apartment at Saint-Germain-en-Laye, had to disgorge the jewels given to her by Francis I, and lost part of her lands.[45] These were now given to Diane de Poitiers, who also received the château of Chenonceau and the title of duchesse de Valentinois. As for Queen Eleanor, she was badly treated by Henry. She was not allowed to bid him farewell when she returned to the Netherlands in November 1548; nor was she even given an escort. She travelled with a handful of companions and had to suffer the indignity of having her baggage searched. In 1551 her dowry, worth 60,000 *l.* per annum, was confiscated by Henry and given to Orazio Farnese. Eleonor only got it back in 1556, when she and her sister, Mary of Hungary, returned to Spain with their brother, Charles V, after his abdication. She had long wished to see the daughter whom she had been obliged to leave in Portugal in 1521. A meeting was arranged at Badajoz, but Maria refused to join her mother in Spain. Eleanor died of asthma at Talavera la Real in February 1558.[46]

With the accession of Henry II, his close friend Montmorency re-emerged from retirement, becoming president of the king's council, took his oath as Constable of France and was confirmed as Grand Master. His arrears were settled and he recovered the governorship of Languedoc. In July 1551 he became a duke and a peer, an unprecedented elevation for a mere baron, placing him on a par with the highest noblemen in the land.[47] Among newcomers to the council were François de Guise, comte d'Aumale, and his younger brother, Charles, archbishop of Reims. The former was a soldier and brilliant tactician, and the latter a highly intelligent man and a fine public speaker. Within a few months of Henry II's accession, François became the second duc de Guise and Charles cardinal of Lorraine.[48]

Henry II was anxious to recover Boulogne, which had been lost to the English in 1544, but it was in Scotland that he struck his first blow against them. He had two good reasons for so doing: one was the 'Auld Alliance', which had enabled France to distract the English from the continent by stirring up trouble for them in the north; the second was Guise influence in Scotland. Henry saw political advantage to be gained from a marriage between the Guises' cousin, Mary, queen of Scots, who had a claim to the English throne, and his son, François. Such a union, he thought, would promote French ascendancy over Scotland and perhaps over England as well. Early in August 1543 a French fleet picked Mary up at Dumbarton and carried her to France, where her arrival was acclaimed by Henry as a triumph. 'France and Scotland', Henry declared, 'are now one country.'[49] Only then did he besiege Boulogne. In March 1550, it was handed back to France for 400,000 crowns.

Henry also had Italy in his sights. He controlled much of Piedmont, but Milan belonged to Charles V. As always, French fortunes in the peninsula depended on the Holy See's support. Fortunately for Henry, Pope Paul III wanted to draw closer to France, having fallen out with the emperor. A link existed in the person of his grandson, Orazio Farnese, who had been brought up at the court of Francis I. On 30 June 1547 Orazio married Henry's natural daughter, Diane de France. In 1548 the king mounted a show of force south of the Alps. He set off in April with a large escort of nobles. Among the Italian princes who met him at Turin was Ercole d'Este, duke of Ferrara, who used the opportunity to arrange a marriage between his daughter, Anne, and François de Guise. This brought the Guise family into even closer union with the royal family, as Anne d'Este was Louis XII's granddaughter.[50]

The queen, Catherine de' Medici, was not allowed much political influence during Henry II's reign, though she did serve him twice as regent. By contrast, it seems that Henry listened to Diane de Poitiers. He allegedly spent one-third of each day in her company and gave her daily reports of his activities. Then, sitting on Diane's lap, he would play the cittern while fondling her breasts, and invite Montmorency or the duc d'Aumale to admire her charms. Though deeply saddened by Henry's love for Diane, Catherine concealed her true feelings. In 1584, however, she told the minister Pomponne de Bellièvre: 'If I was polite to Madame de Valentinois, it was for the king's sake, yet I always told him that I was doing so against my will, for no wife who loses her husband has ever loved his whore. The word is ugly, but such a woman deserves no other name.'[51] Diane, for her part, was intelligent enough to realize her proper place at court. She nursed Catherine when she was ill or was in labour, sang her praises to the king and even encouraged him to sleep with his wife.[52] In spite of his infidelity, Catherine adored her husband. She lived in fear of losing him and went into mourning whenever he was absent.[53] She begged Montmorency to keep her regularly informed about his health. Meanwhile she continued to produce children. After the two – François and Elizabeth – born in Francis I's reign, she produced eight more during the twelve years of Henry II's reign. They were Claude, born on 12 November 1547; Louis, born on 3 February 1549 (he died on 24 October 1550); Charles-Maximilien – the future Charles IX – on 27 June 1550; Édouard-Alexandre – the future Henry III – on 19 September 1551; Marguerite – the future 'reine Margot' – on 14 May 1553; Hercule – the future François duc d'Alençon – on 18 March 1555; and, lastly, twin daughters – Jeanne and Victoire – on 24 June 1556. This double birth, it seems, nearly killed Catherine: Victoire was stillborn and Jeanne lived only for a month and a half.[54]

By 1547 the French monarchy seemed resolutely committed to defending the Catholic faith against the rising tide of Protestantism. This had begun under Francis I, not long after Martin Luther had launched the Protestant Reformation in Germany by putting up his ninety-five theses on the church door at Wittemberg. His ideas had soon spread to France and had been well received in certain quarters, including the court. Francis I had had to cope with mounting religious dissent, culminating in the Affair of the Placards of October 1534, when posters attacking the mass had appeared in the streets of Paris. After vacillating for a time, he had thrown in his lot with the party of Catholic orthodoxy mainly represented by the Faculty of Theology of the University of Paris and the Parlement of Paris. It was under Henry II that the religious situation in France became fraught as many noblemen converted to the new faith. Henry himself was staunchly orthodox. In October 1547 he set up a special court in the Parlement of Paris to deal with cases of heresy, and in June 1551 issued an edict strengthening the heresy laws.[55] His action helped to swell the ranks of religious dissenters fleeing to Geneva where John Calvin was seeking to set up a city ruled by God.[56]

In February 1551 Henry II, after declaring war on the emperor, announced that he would lead his army to the borders of Champagne and, if necessary, beyond. French forces occupied Metz and Toul in April, and soon afterwards the king visited Nancy, capital of Lorraine. Violating the duchy's independence, he marched on the Rhine but, after meeting stiff resistance, withdrew. His 'German Voyage', however, secured for him three strategic bases in northeast France – Metz, Toul and Verdun – and a permanent foothold in Lorraine. Although riddled with gout and ageing rapidly, Charles V mounted a counteroffensive. He laid siege to Metz only to be beaten off by Guise, who added to his laurels in January 1558 by capturing Calais from the English. His reward was the marriage of his niece, Mary Stuart, to the Dauphin François.[57]

In the summer of 1557 King Philip II of Spain launched an invasion of northern France under the command of Emmanuel-Philibert of Savoy. Montmorency and a huge army engaged the enemy outside Saint-Quentin on 10 August only to be crushed. The constable was taken prisoner, leaving the way clear for the rise to power of the Guises.[58] By the autumn of 1558 Henry was too poor to continue the war and wanted to focus his energies on fighting heresy at home. Charles V was equally keen to end the conflict. In October 1558 peace talks began after Montmorency had been released on parole. The outcome was the famous Peace of Cateau-Cambrésis (3–4 April 1559), which effectively ended the Italian Wars. Two marriages sealed the treaty: one between Emmanuel-Philibert and Henry II's sister, Marguerite; the other, between Philip II and Henry's eldest daughter, Elizabeth. The peace was denounced as shameful by many Frenchmen, particularly by veterans of the Italian Wars, yet it was not wholly bad for their nation: outside Italy, France retained all of its territories, including Calais and the three towns in Lorraine.[59]

On 18 June 1559 the peace was sworn at Notre-Dame de Paris. Four days later the marriage of Philip II of Spain and Elizabeth de Valois was celebrated, the groom being represented by the duke of Alba. The duke of Savoy came to Paris for his marriage to Marguerite. To honour the two marriages, Henry II staged a magnificent tournament in the rue Saint-Antoine, taking part in it himself. On the third day, however, he was fatally wounded.[60] His death, on 10 July, plunged the kingdom into one of the worst crises of its history. Henry left a widow and four young sons. Catherine de' Medici was inconsolable. French queens traditionally wore white on being widowed, but she wore black as she took leave of her husband's corpse and continued to do so for the rest of her life. A broken lance, instead of a rainbow, became her emblem. As for Diane de Poitiers, she suffered the fate of every royal mistress: having left the court before Henry's death, she never returned. She had to surrender the jewels given to her by the late king, and to exchange the pretty château of Chenonceau for the less attractive one of Chaumont-sur-Loire. Diane returned to Anet, where she died in April 1566.

CHAPTER 2

One Kingdom, Two Capitals

France in the early sixteenth century was neither as large nor as unified as it is today: it lacked well-defined frontiers, a common language and a single legal system. The eastern border from the North Sea to the Mediterranean more or less followed the rivers Scheldt, Meuse, Saône and Rhône: people living west of this line were vassals of the French king; those to the east owed allegiance to the Holy Roman Emperor. Lorraine and Alsace lay outside the kingdom. In the south, Dauphiné and Provence were not yet fully integrated: the king was obeyed as 'dauphin' in the one, as 'count' in the other. The southwest border roughly followed the Pyrenees, avoiding Roussillon, ruled by the House of Aragon, and the small kingdom of Navarre, ruled by the House of Albret. Within France there were three foreign enclaves: Calais belonged to England, the Comtat-Venaissin to the Holy See and the principality of Orange to the House of Chalon. Some great fiefs, notably the duchies of Brittany and Bourbon, were virtually independent.[1]

The surface area of France was 459,000 square kilometres as against 550,986 today. Communications were primitive: country roads were unpaved and turned readily into quagmires under heavy rain; the rivers were often flooded or frozen in the winter and traffic along them was frequently obstructed by tolls. Travelling times were consequently slow. Normally it took two days to travel on horseback from Paris to Amiens, eight to ten to Lyon, sixteen to twenty to Marseille.[2] Faster speeds were possible if one travelled by post horse: this allowed one to cover the 90 kilometres between Lyon and Roanne in one day. Couriers bearing letters or packages could move faster still: on Italian roads they could cover 150 or 200 kilometres in a single day.[3]

In the absence of any contemporary census figures, no precise number for the population of France can be given, but the evidence of parish registers and fiscal returns indicates that it had recovered some of the losses it had sustained in the fourteenth century. It is unlikely, however, to have exceeded eighteen million by the mid-sixteenth century. Two million lived in towns.

England, by contrast, had a population of around three million. The demographic rise in France was due mainly to a fall in the incidence of plague and to the fact that the kingdom, except for a few border areas, was now largely peaceful. The absence of any serious grain famine between 1440 and 1520 was also helpful. The need to feed more mouths stimulated agriculture, which was achieved mainly by reclaiming land rather than by improved farming techniques. Reclamation varied from region to region: it began sooner in the Paris region and the south-west than in the Midi.[4]

The population increase was reflected in urban growth. A fiscal document of 1538 enables us to rank the towns according to size. Paris with a population of around 200,000 was by far the largest. Below it were Rouen, Lyon, Toulouse and Orléans with between 40,000 and 70,000 each. After a score of towns of between 10,000 and 30,000, another forty or so had between 5,000 and 10,000 inhabitants. Many smaller towns had fewer than 5,000. The distinction between a town and a large village is not easily drawn: a town was usually enclosed by a wall; it also enjoyed certain privileges and contained more occupations and social types than a village. Walled towns were commonly referred to as 'good towns' (*bonnes villes*) to distinguish them from large villages. Many town walls, which had fallen into disrepair by the thirteenth century, were now being repaired at the towns' own expense. Although the threat of civil conflict had largely receded, companies of disbanded soldiers and brigands continued to terrorize the countryside from time to time and towns needed to keep them out. Trade was important to all of them, but some were also administrative, intellectual or ecclesiastical centres. Seven had a *parlement*, ninety were capitals of *bailliages* or *sénéchaussées*, fifteen had a university and about 110 were ecclesiastical sees.[5]

In 1500 France was in the midst of an economic boom which had begun in the 1460s and lasted till the 1520s. It was largely self-sufficient in respect of basic necessities, producing enough grain for its own needs and exporting any surplus. Wine consumption increased as more vineyards were established in the Bordeaux region and around Paris, Lyon and some other cities. As trade developed, no fewer than 344 markets and fairs were set up between 1483 and 1500, the most famous being the four annual fairs of Lyon which drew many foreigners, especially Italians, Germans and Swiss. Though banks had existed in France since the thirteenth century, they only became important as agencies of credit and exchange in the fifteenth. Many Italian bankers settled in Lyon on account of the large amount of business transacted there.[6] The expansion of trade was linked to industrial growth. Cloth-making, centred in the north of the country, was France's main industry. The cloth was mainly of ordinary quality, suitable for daily use by the lower classes of society. The silk industry that had been set up at Tours, then at Lyon, could not satisfy the needs of the court and nobility. The finest textiles were imported from the Netherlands and Germany; velvet, damask, satin and cloth of gold from Italy. A rapidly growing industry was printing. Whereas in 1480 only nine French towns had printing presses, by 1500 the number had risen to forty. Paris alone had seventy-five. [7]

Society

French society around 1500 consisted mainly of peasants, who lived in the kingdom's thirty thousand villages, each with its own hierarchy. At the top was the *seigneur*, who was not necessarily a nobleman, for a *seigneurie* or lordship could be purchased. It consisted usually of the lord's demesne, which he cultivated himself, and the *censives* or *tenures* that he left the peasants to cultivate in return for obligations known as *redevances*, the main one being the *cens*, or annual rent, paid on a fixed day and often quite light. The *seigneur* usually retained the mill, wine-press and oven, and expected to be paid for their use. He also had judicial powers: his court judged cases among the *censitaires*. The closing years of the Middle Ages witnessed a reduction in the wealth and authority of the *seigneur* and the rise of a village aristocracy consisting of *fermiers* owning more than 30 hectares each. [8]

Urban society was more complex than rural society. Contemporaries tended to divide it into two groups: the *aisés* or well-to-do, and the *menu peuple* or proletariat. In reality, however, it was more complex. The well-to-do were divided into merchants and office-holders. In some towns they were fairly well balanced, but in others, like Lyon, merchants were pre-eminent. The core of urban society consisted of artisans and small-to-middling merchants. Artisans were of two kinds: those who employed large numbers of workmen and those who employed no one outside their own families. The lower stratum of French society – the *menu peuple* – consisted of manual workers. [9]

Sixteenth-century Frenchmen classified everyone, great and small, rich or poor, into three estates: clergy, nobility and the third estate (see plate 3). In theory, these were regarded as divinely ordained and permanently fixed; in practice, however, it was possible for an individual to pass from one to another, each having its distinctive function, lifestyle and privileges. Clergy had to be ordained or at least to have taken minor orders. The secular clergy may have numbered 100,000, made up of about 100 bishops, many suffragan bishops and canons, about 30,000 parish priests and a huge crowd of unbeneficed clergy. The second estate, the nobility, may have numbered as many as 200,000, of whom only a small proportion would have attended the court with any frequency. To be accepted as a nobleman, a man needed an ancient family line, called *race*, and a style of living that conformed to a social ideal.[10] To be truly ancient, the family line needed to stretch back beyond the memory of the oldest living witness; in practice, three generations. A nobleman had to be seen to be living 'nobly'. He could not dabble in a trade or craft that might soil his hands. If he broke this rule, he risked losing his noble status under the law of *dérogeance*. Nobility was equated with military virtue by sixteenth-century writers: that is, a combination of courage, physical endurance, strong nerves, mental alertness and the desire to gain renown. The creation of the *compagnies d'ordonnance* in the fifteenth century had given nobles opportunities of military service, and the Italian Wars enabled many of them to demonstrate their virtue.

Nobility was not a closed caste. Had it been so, it would soon have become extinct; it needed to replenish its ranks by recruiting new members from lower down the social scale. A commoner could become a nobleman in various ways. One was to buy an *office*. This was a uniquely French institution: in addition to being a post in the royal administration commanding wages, it could, if important enough, confer nobility on the holder. Offices were not merely given, but sold. Their sale – known as venality – was used by the crown to raise money at a time when the cost of war was fast escalating. As the practice grew, two kinds of nobility developed: *noblesse de race* and *noblesse de robe*.[11] The most popular way for a commoner to enter the nobility was by assimilation or *agrégation*: a commoner would act as if he were a nobleman. He might, for example, acquire a *seigneurie*. The poet, Agrippa d'Aubigné, passed himself off as a nobleman although his grandfather had been a cobbler. Nobles were exempt from direct taxation, the theory being that they gave their blood to the crown rather than their money; but the exemption did not apply to areas of *taille réelle*, in which tax was assessed according to the value of land rather than personal status. Historians used to believe that the nobility of sixteenth-century France experienced a serious economic decline, but it was not a single economic unit capable of only one response to economic pressure. Variations in wealth were considerable: some nobles were enormously rich; others exceedingly poor.[12]

The bulk of France's population belonged to the third estate, made up of people of widely different fortunes and occupations. Seyssel in his *La monarchie de France* (1519) distinguished between middling people (*peuple moyen*) and lesser folk (*peuple menu*). The former, he explained, were merchants and officers of finance and justice. The *peuple menu* were people mainly engaged in 'the cultivation of the land, the mechanical arts and other inferior crafts'. Such people, he believed, should not be 'in too great liberty or immeasurably rich and especially not generally trained in the use of arms'.[13]

Government

Any account, however brief, of the government of sixteenth-century France must begin with the king, for he was the ultimate authority. A recent, and largely otiose, debate has focused on the nature of that power: was it truly absolute, as the king himself claimed, or was it limited?[14] Absolute it certainly was, as the king had no superior save God, whose lieutenant on earth he was deemed to be. His coronation, or *sacre*, was the ceremonial manifestation of that relationship: it conferred on him a semi-priestly character. It did not empower him to say mass, but unlike the laity he could take communion in both kinds. The *sacre* also conferred on him the miraculous power of healing the sick. That said, however, his power was not absolute. The king was expected to abide by the so-called 'fundamental laws' which prevented him from altering the order of succession to the throne or disposing at will of any part of his domain.[15] Expediency also demanded that he should treat with consideration and respect the many customs and privileges that had been traditionally built into the nation's fabric. And whatever the theory may have been, the king could not possibly rule alone: he needed advice and support. A machinery of government, both central and local, capable of adapting to circumstances, was required to execute his wishes, and the effectiveness of that machinery depended in turn on adequate funding. By the sixteenth century, the king could no longer 'live of his own': that is, on the revenue from his domain.

The fiscal administration was built around two forms of royal revenue, called 'ordinary' and 'extraordinary'. The first was revenue from the royal domain, while the second was from taxation. The only direct tax, the *taille*, was levied annually, the amount being decided by the king's council. It was of two kinds: *taille réelle* and *taille personnelle*. The former, found only in the south of France, was a land tax payable by all regardless of rank; the latter fell mainly on property owned by commoners. The nobility and clergy were exempt, as were many professional groups and even certain towns, including Paris. Indirect taxation included the *gabelle* or tax on salt that was levied in different ways. In some areas the salt was taken to royal warehouses, called *greniers à sel*, where it was weighed and allowed to dry for two years before being weighed a second time. Only then was it sold to merchants for public distribution. The *aides* were duties levied on commodities, such as wine, that were sold regularly and in large quantities. The most lucrative tax was the *taille* which, in 1515, amounted to 2.4 million *l.* out of a total revenue of 4.9 million *l.* It was followed by the *aides*, which brought in about a third of that amount. The *gabelle* yielded 284,000 *l.*[16] The fiscal administration around 1500 comprised two organisations corresponding to the two kinds of revenue. Four *trésoriers de France* supervised the collection and disbursement of the ordinary revenue, while four *généraux des finances* were responsible for the 'extraordinary' revenues. They had virtually the same powers as the *trésoriers*, each being in charge of an area, called *généralité*. The two administrations were not entirely separate, for the *trésoriers* and *généraux* (known collectively as *gens des finances*) were expected to reside at court when they were not on tours of inspection. They formed a financial committee meeting independently of the king's council and drew up an annual budget based on accounts sent by each financial district.[17] Rapid changes in military technology (the development of firearms, for instance) made particularly heavy demands on the royal purse. Taxation could not always meet them, forcing the king to borrow from bankers or to resort to various expedients, such as the sale of offices.

Among the various organs of central government in the early sixteenth century four were particularly important: the king's council, the chancery, the *Grand Conseil* and the Parlement of Paris. Originally they had all been part of the court or *Curia Regis,* but during the Middle Ages they had parted company. While the Parlement and other so-called 'sovereign courts' had 'gone out of court' and settled permanently in Paris, the king's council, chancery and *Grand Conseil* had remained attached to the court, following it on its travels. Thus France at the time may be said to have had two capitals: Paris and the court. The Parlement of Paris occupied the old royal palace (known simply as the Palais) on the Île-de-la-Cité. Unlike its English name-sake, it was not a representative body, but the highest court of justice under the king, staffed by magistrates, called councillors. They compared themselves to the senators of ancient Rome, an analogy resented by the king. Relations were often strained, for the Parlement's view of royal authority differed from his own. While admitting that supreme authority lay with him, the Parlement distinguished between the ideal sovereign and the human being sitting on the throne; it saw its role as protecting the former from the latter. In practice this meant ensuring that the king observed the 'fundamental laws'. Originally the Parlement's *ressort*, or area of jurisdiction, had covered the whole kingdom, but in time other parlements were established at Toulouse, Grenoble, Bordeaux, Dijon, Rouen and Aix-en-Provence. Even so, the *ressort* of the Parlement of Paris covered two-thirds of the kingdom. Excluding Normandy, it reached as far south as the Lyonnais and Upper Auvergne. Within this area it judged a wide variety of cases. But it was not just a lawcourt: it regulated matters such as public hygiene, the upkeep of roads, bridges and quays, and the quality and price of bread. It fixed wages and hours of work, punished shoddy workmanship and intervened in academic matters. More importantly, it ratified royal legislation. If a proposed law was acceptable, it was registered at once; if not, the Parlement could submit one or more remonstrances to the king. He might amend the law accordingly or send a *lettre de jussion* ordering its registration regardless. If the Parlement continued to object, he might hold a *lit de justice*: he would come to the Parlement in person and force through the registration. Each parlement was sovereign within its *ressort*; thus a law registered in Paris could not be applied in Languedoc unless it had been registered in Toulouse.[18]

While the Parlement and other 'sovereign courts' were fixed in Paris, the other organs of central government – the king's council, chancery and *Grand Conseil* – remained attached to the court, sharing its nomadic existence.[19] This can be explained on several grounds. In an age devoid of media it was necessary for the king to show himself to his subjects; it was a way of affirming his authority. Hunting was also a major reason; for most kings and their courtiers it was the principal open-air activity in peacetime. They liked to look for game in many different forests. And urban life was not especially agreeable: it was often cramped and unhygienic. So the court was nomadic and, as the kingdom became more peaceful internally, it travelled more extensively than before, never more so than under Francis I. Yet it was not always on the road: in winter, when communications were hampered by bad weather, it tended to stay put in one or other of the royal châteaux in or near Paris.

The king's council, where important policy decisions were taken, consisted of a group of individuals meeting under the king's chairmanship who exercised his authority collectively across all matters of state. The council's name sometimes changed according to the business in hand. If this was finance, specialists, collectively known as *messieurs des finances*, would be admitted and the council would be described temporarily as the *conseil des finances*. The council might also sit as a lawcourt. If some matter of exceptional importance and urgency turned up, the king would summon a handful of advisers and their meeting would be known as the *Conseil étroit*. The council's development between 1483 and 1526 is not easily traced as no complete set of minutes exists. Acts and ordinances were usually signed only by the king and a secretary, rarely by councillors. It seems that, between August 1484 and January 1485, there were as many as 120 councillors, of whom only a few attended meetings regularly; a core of working councillors presumably existed within the larger body. The council might also split up on occasion. There were many routes to council membership – birth, skill in the law, diplomacy or administration, regional importance, ecclesiastical dignity and influential patrons or relatives – but membership was by royal invitation only. Councillors were appointed at the king's pleasure, not for life. Their role was purely consultative; only the king could decide and sometimes he chose to act as he thought best. Charles VIII, for example, invaded Italy in 1494 against the advice of the majority of his councillors. We can assume, however, that the king was normally content to endorse a majority decision. This would then be described as having been taken by 'the king in his council'.[20]

Only in respect of justice did the council throw out a specialised offshoot that achieved autonomy: this was the *Grand Conseil*. It originated under Charles VII, but was only formally established by two edicts in 1497 and 1498. Its members were given the same powers as members of the parlements. Though independent, they continued to follow the court until the reign of Henry III and dealt with a variety of lawsuits. These were mostly disputes over ecclesiastical benefices, but there were also cases (*évocations*) removed by the king from the courts which would have tried them normally. He tended to intervene when he had reason to believe that the judges might reach a verdict unacceptable to himself. As the *Grand Conseil* followed him about the kingdom, he was well placed to influence its judgment.[21]

The body responsible for turning conciliar decisions into laws was the chancery, headed by the Chancellor of France. He was always an eminent jurist who had served his apprenticeship in a parlement; sometimes he was also a churchman. His powers and duties ranged widely: he was a sort of prime minister without the title. He kept the Great Seal and other seals of state and supervised the sealing of all documents emanating from the king's council. He had to ensure that they were correctly drafted and could refuse to seal any that were not. As head of the judiciary, he could preside over any sovereign court, including the Parlement of Paris. He appointed judges and received their oaths of office. Deemed to represent the monarchy itself, the chancellor did not go into mourning when the king died; nor did he attend the funeral. The chancellor was appointed for life; he could not be dismissed, but his duties could, if necessary, be performed by a keeper of the seals. Closely associated with him were the *maîtres des requêtes de l'hôtel*.[22] There were eight of these about 1500, but their number increased rapidly thereafter. The chancery was the nearest equivalent to a modern ministry. In 1500 it had a staff of 120, which grew during the rest of the century. The *clercs du secret*, who drafted documents that came directly from the king, eventually became known as secretaries.[23]

Paris

The monarchy had neglected Paris since the fourteenth century when Charles VII had been driven to Bourges by political adversity. Although he eventually returned to the capital, neither he nor his immediate successors showed much affection for it, preferring the valley of the Loire. Charles VIII spent only a total of 169 days in Paris. He went there each year, usually in February and March, but his visits were brief.[24] This pattern changed after he invaded Italy.

4. *Map of Paris in the Sixteenth-century.* From Georg Braun and Franz Hogenberg, *Civitates Orbis Terrarum* (1572). The map shows the division of the city into three parts: Ville, Cité, and Université; also the walls of Philip-Augustus and Charles V and the axial rue Saint-Jacques cutting through the city from north to south.

He pointedly avoided Paris in March 1496, travelling from Amboise to Saint-Denis, then returning to Lyon by way of Sens and Moulins. He thereby expressed his displeasure with the Parisians, who had denied him financial aid.[25] Louis XII scored 264 days. He spent longer in the capital in 1513 and especially 1514 following his peace treaty with England and his marriage to Mary Tudor; and he died in Paris.[26] It was under Francis I that Paris recovered its role as the capital of France. For all his love of the countryside, Francis could not ignore the capital.[27] He visited it more often than any other town: at least once each year, except in 1525 (when he was a prisoner in Spain), 1526, 1541 and 1547. He spent more than a month there in each of seventeen years and less than ten days in only four years. Altogether, he spent 1,291 days in Paris.[28] Admittedly he was rarely there in summer, but he could not

stay away for long for political and economic reasons. The king also came to
Paris to shop: his accounts are full of payments to Parisian jewellers. Indeed,
the growth of luxury industries in the capital, including the creation of the
Gobelin tapestry works in the fifteenth century, has been seen as a response
to the court's demands (see plate 3).[29]

Important state occasions were traditionally held in Paris. Every king in the
sixteenth century, except Francis II and Henry III, was given a formal entry,
or *entrée joyeuse*, after his coronation at Reims.[30] Queens, too, were given
entries. Foreign ambassadors were similarly honoured. In January 1517 the
court came to Paris to receive Adrien de Croy, the imperial ambassador.
The following year an English embassy was given a memorable banquet in
the Bastille.[31] Parisians doubtless had mixed feelings about the court's
visits. The presence of so many extra mouths caused food prices to rise and
the behaviour of courtiers was resented. In May 1517, for example, Francis
I and his courtiers, disguised and masked, frequented houses of ill-repute.
Two years later some distinguished English visitors were invited to join
them: they 'rode daily disguysed through Parys, throwyng Egges, stones
and other foolishe trifles at the people, which light demeanoure of a kyng
was muche discommended and gested at'.[32]

Francis I looked to Paris for financial support. The fact that it was a *ville
franche*, exempt from the *taille*, did not deter him from appealing directly to
the generosity of the citizens. In 1522 he asked them to subsidize five
hundred infantry. As the Parisians debated the matter, he went to Rouen and
persuaded its citizens to pay for twice that number. Returning to the capital,
he shamed it into doubling its contribution.[33] Francis was not always popular
in Paris. His absence in 1523, when an English invasion threatened the
capital, was resented. The treason of the duc de Bourbon gave Parisians a
chance to vent their feelings; they showed sympathy for him in popular songs,
and rejoiced when his chief accomplice was reprieved. They were not even
moved by the king's defeat at Pavia in 1525. Some tried to unseat his mother
as regent, and the success of her foreign policy was imperilled by the capital's
refusal to provide the financial guarantees demanded by the English in a
peace treaty. The Parlement also took advantage of Francis's captivity in 1525
to challenge some of his policies. No wonder the king kept away from Paris
for more than a year after his release! His reappearance in April 1527 was
heralded by the arrest of eight leading burgesses and followed by a *lit de justice*
in which Francis put the Parlement firmly in its place.[34] He was seldom
vindictive, however. On 15 March 1528 he ended almost a century of royal
absence. 'Dearest and well-beloved,' he wrote to the town council, 'it is our
intention henceforth to stay most of the time in our good city of Paris and its
neighbourhood and, knowing that our castle of the Louvre is most suitable

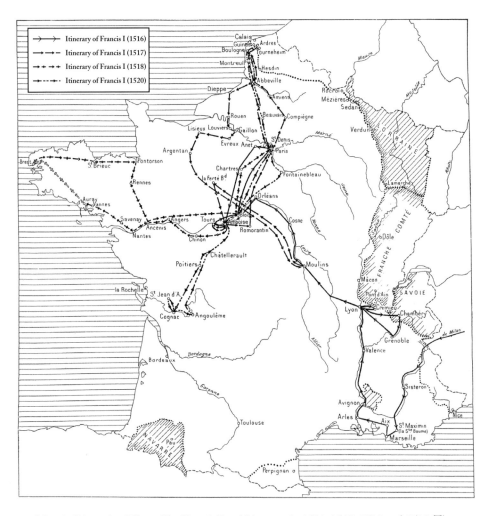

Map 1. Itineraries followed by Francis I and his court in 1516, 1517, 1518 and 1519. The court remained largely nomadic until the reign of Henry III (1574–89) when it tended to remain fixed in Paris.

and appropriate to our purpose, we have decided to repair and refurbish it.'[35] The king began converting the Louvre into a Renaissance palace, work that continued till the end of his reign. In the meantime Francis stayed at Saint-Germain-en-Laye or Fontainebleau.

Despite his stated intention, Francis I continued to travel widely in his kingdom. His successor, Henry II, spent most of his time in or near Paris, as did his queen, Catherine de' Medici. So by degrees the space that had divided France's two capitals narrowed. Eventually, under Henry III, as we shall see, they virtually coalesced as the court settled in Paris.[36]

CHAPTER 3

The Court

The word 'court', as applied to the French monarchy, commonly conjures up a picture of the court of Louis XIV at Versailles – a huge gathering of nobles and ladies revolving around the royal person, and controlled by a rigid code of etiquette. This image does not help us to understand the French court during the Renaissance, say between 1483 and 1589. This was a motley crowd of people, who sometimes resided in one place, but were more often moving across the kingdom unaware of any etiquette. The king was surprisingly accessible to his subjects. An edict of 1530 showed how easy it was for anyone to enter his lodging:

> Because of the great flow of people who each day come into our lodging when we are there, several thefts have taken place of ornaments from our chapel, of silver plate and of clothes belonging to us and to others by people who by virtue of being decently dressed are allowed to enter everywhere without being observed, and likewise by others who, by claiming acquaintance with some members of our suite, penetrate everywhere.

Such thefts were to be punished in future by death regardless of the value of the objects stolen.[1]

A historian has recently written: 'In the Middle Ages, the kings of France had no court.'[2] This cannot be so. Although many relevant archives were lost when the *Chambre des comptes* burnt down in the eighteenth century, there is evidence in plenty of a flourishing court in medieval France. At its heart was the *hôtel du roi*, or king's household, which consisted essentially of his domestic servants. Household ordinances dating back to 1261 list the officials responsible for different services. They were distributed among a number of departments, called *métiers*. The court also included the households of the queen and of the king's sons, if they were old enough to have them.[3] Household officials were almost certainly appointed by the king. Each department had several heads, as it would have been impractical to entrust the king's daily requirements to a single individual. The ordinances list those officials who were entitled to eat at the king's expense, the amount of fodder each was allowed for his horse, the number of candles and logs he might use for lighting and heating, his wine ration and how many gowns he might be allowed each year; for the officials were clothed and fed by the king. In time, payments in kind were replaced by cash.

The size of the medieval household is hard to estimate. The ordinances indicate the relative strengths of the various departments. In 1291, for example, the household's population was 165; under Philip V it numbered 500, to which must be added another 200 for the households of the queen and royal children. The staff were not always present as they served in rotation. Only 164 were officially entitled to eat at court, but the actual number who did was certainly larger. An ordinance of 1291 laid down that ushers should clear the dining hall of 'all manner of strangers'.[4] The household was also expensive. Already high under Louis IX, its cost escalated under Charles VI and his successors. After depending for three centuries on revenues from the royal domain, it eventually drew its income from indirect taxes, or *aides*. As it grew larger, the *Chambre aux deniers,* the department responsible for its financial management, also became a storehouse for the king's furniture and jewels. By 1315 a new department – the *argenterie* – had developed. This supplied furniture and clothes for the royal family and organised court festivals.

The court did not just cater for the king's bodily needs: it was also a 'theatre of magnificence' for which Charles V laid down certain rules. He enlarged the royal apartment at the Louvre. His chamber was readily accessible to noblemen. Among them were chamberlains, who slept in his chamber and attended his *lever* and *coucher*. Some were 'favourites' whose political influence was much criticised by contemporary writers. In 1387 the number of chamberlains fell from forty-five to twenty. The king's bodily needs were catered for by *valets de chambre*, numbering fifty-two in 1378.

Early in the fifteenth century, civil war between the Armagnacs and Burgundians forced the court to leave Paris and settle first at Bourges, then at Montilz-lez-Tours.[5] It failed to compete with the court of the dukes of Burgundy, which in the late Middle Ages became a byword for magnificence. By the end of the century, however, a revival was under way at the French court. A fragmentary series of payrolls points to a notable increase in its size from the late fifteenth century onwards. There were 366 household officials in 1495, four times as many as in 1465.[6]

In 1523, under Francis I, the household comprised 540 officials, more than twice as many as in 1480. These included a confessor, almoners, chaplains, physicians, surgeons, an apothecary, barbers, stewards, gentlemen of the chamber, valets, ushers, bread-carriers, cupbearers, carvers, squires, grooms, pages, secretaries, a librarian, quartermasters, porters, musicians, sumpters, coopers, spit-turners, saucemakers, pastry cooks, tapestry makers and laundresses. The staff were distributed across several departments, the principal ones being the *Hôtel*, the *Chambre* and the *Chapelle*. The *hôtel*, which fed the king and his entourage, was subdivided into three departments: the *paneterie*, *échansonnerie* and *fruiterie*, providing respectively bread, wine and fruit. The *cuisine de bouche* fed the king, and the *cuisine du commun* the officials claiming board and lodging at court, known as *domestiques et commensaux du roi*. The *fourrière* was responsible for moving the court. Its staff of *maréchaux des logis* and *fourriers* transported the furniture, allocated lodgings and issued lodging permits. The *argenterie* purchased clothes, furniture and other necessities, and the *écurie* looked after the king's horses. It also had a large staff of messengers (*chevaucheurs*) and a riding school for pages, sons of noblemen trained at the king's expense for a military career.[7] The *vénerie* and *fauconnerie* shared the organisation of the royal hunts.[8]

The *Chambre*, under the *Grand chambellan*, was concerned with the day-to-day activities of the royal bedchamber, including the king's *lever* and *coucher*. This was also where the privy council met. Francis I created the *gentilshommes de la chambre* (gentlemen of the chamber), who performed essentially the same duties as the *chambellans* had done previously. The new title enabled the king to honour artists and scholars with the title of *valet de chambre*, which no longer implied domestic duties. The gentlemen of the chamber were the king's constant companions, enjoying free access to his presence, but they were not all present simultaneously. They were often sent abroad as ambassadors and could be absent for long periods. The seigneur de Castillon, for example, was paid in September 1533 for 120 days' service as ambassador in England.[9] Guillaume du Bellay, seigneur de Langey, served as diplomat, soldier and administrator. Such activities conferred on the chamber a special cultural significance, as the gentlemen brought back impressions gathered abroad. One way of demonstrating friendship and trust to a foreign ruler was for the king to admit his ambassador to his chamber. Sir Thomas Cheney was accorded this privilege in 1526. 'He [Francis I] commanded me', he informed his master, Henry VIII, 'to use myself in his chamber at all hours, as Your Grace has appointed me in yours.' When the ambassador accepted the honour, the Grand Master asked him to present the king's towel at his *lever*, saying that 'Henry had used him so at his being in England'.[10] The normal wage for a gentleman of the chamber was fairly modest: 1,200 *l*. per annum, but the perks were considerable. The chamber staff also included the *maître de la garderobe* and a number of valets who looked after the king's clothes as well as artisans, such as tailors, *savetiers*, *pelletiers*, painters and carpenters.

5. *Charles de Maigny, Captain of the Guard of the King's Chamber.* Statue by Pierre Bontemps (Musée du Louvre, Paris). Maigny is portrayed sleeping but the monument is meant to show that he has died on duty.

There were also physicians, a surgeon and apothecaries. A barber attended to the king's toilette, and notaries and secretaries to '*affaires*' or conciliar business.

Under Francis I the chamber was administered by the *Premier gentilhomme de la chambre*, who was entitled to sleep there and could thus see the king before he rose from bed in the morning. The office was held for much of the reign by Jean de La Barre, comte d'Étampes, whose duties included looking after the crown jewels, holding the king's privy purse and signing contracts for work on royal châteaux. He coupled his office with that of *Maître de la garderobe*. La Barre was rewarded for his services with gifts of land, offices and money.

The *Chapelle* attended to the king's spiritual needs by providing masses, sermons and confessions. It was completely reorganised by Francis I and Henry II. The former changed the title of *Grand aumônier du roi*, created by Charles VIII, to *Grand aumônier de France*. Its holder was, in effect, the court's bishop, ruling over a diocese whose limits were defined by the king's movements. Following its reorganisation, the chapel had three subdivisions: the *aumônerie*, under the first almoner, which was responsible for charitable works and certain hospitals; the *chapelle de musique*, under the *maître de la chapelle*, made up of choristers, which organised high masses; and the *oratoire*, under the *maître de l'oratoire*, for low ones. In 1544 each office was held by a different cardinal. The chapel staff also included the king's confessor as well as a number of preachers and, after 1530, the royal lecturers (*lecteurs royaux*).[11]

By 1535 the number of household officials at Francis I's court had risen from 540 to 622, and the amount spent on wages from 65,915 *l.* in 1517 to 214,918 *l.*[12] But the court's expansion was variable: while some sections grew, others dwindled in size or vanished altogether. The number of almoners, for example, grew from 14 in 1515 to 56 in 1546, of gentlemen of the chamber from 20 in 1515 to 68 in 1545. But the *enfants d'honneur* dropped from 47 in 1515 to 17 in 1536: they then vanished from the payroll. This may have resulted from an ordinance of July 1534 which forbade the admission to the household of any *enfant d'honneur* who had not served for at least four years in the *compagnies d'ordonnance*, or heavy cavalry.[13] Some household departments appear to have reached their maximum size about 1523, when the government ran into financial difficulties and had to economize. Political events inevitably made an impact on the court, none more so than the king's defeat and capture at Pavia in February 1525. For more than a year the kingdom was administered by his mother from the monastery of Saint-Just, near Lyon. The accounts of the *Chambre* for this period show that many of the staff were put on half-pay or sent home, while almoners, chaplains and other clerics were renumerated with benefices instead of wages.[14]

In January 1542 the papal nuncio Capodiferro stated that Francis I was grossly extravagant.[15] Yet, according to recent research, his reign marked 'a phase of level-pegging between the substantial rises during the reigns of Charles VIII, Louis XII and Henri II'. Between 1516 and 1546 expenditure on the court rose from 622,899 *l.* to 811,236 *l.*, an increase of only 30 per cent over thirty years. Certain departments of the household were more expensive than others. The cost of the *vénerie* and *fauconnerie* increased by 71 per cent, from 33,773 *l.* per annum in 1516–20 to 57,988 *l.* per annum in 1542–6.[16]

The court also had a military establishment made up of units created at different times, the oldest being the *garde écossaise*, founded by Charles VII, which was the king's personal bodyguard. The *archers de la garde* consisted of three companies of one hundred archers each, the last being Francis I's own creation. The *Cent suisses* had been set up by Charles VIII. Lastly, there were the *Deux cents gentilshommes de l'hôtel*, divided into two companies. All the troops were mounted, except the Swiss, who escorted the king in public ceremonies. In 1539 they carried him in a litter when he was too infirm to ride.[17]

Law and order at court were maintained by the *Prévôt de l'hôtel* who punished crimes committed in a royal residence or within five miles of the king's person. He was assisted by three lieutenants and thirty archers. When the court was travelling, the *Prévôt* had to ensure adequate supplies at a reasonable cost. The annual budget of the *Chambre aux deniers* was subject to the approval of the *Chambre des comptes*, but the king's privy purse, called *menus plaisirs*, escaped this scrutiny.

The queen's household, though smaller than the king's, was still sizeable. It had more or less the same number of departments, but the chamber staff were entirely female, including various *dames, femmes* and *filles de la reine*. The *chevalier d'honneur* performed the same duties as the *Grand Maître* in the king's household.[18] Francis I's mother, Louise of Savoy, and his children also had households. In 1523 the latter had a staff of 240, including five chamberlains, nine stewards and some twenty pages.

Many people who were not household staff had to attend the court on business. They included councillors, *maîtres des requêtes*, notaries and secretaries, as well as guests, such as princes of the blood, foreign princes, prelates and ambassadors. Finally, there were numerous hangers-on, including merchants and artisans, who were exempt from tolls and guild regulations as long as they served only the crown. Under Louis XII they numbered about a hundred; in March 1544 Francis raised it to 160. Among the hangers-on were the camp followers, or *filles de joie suivant la cour*. They received a New Year's gift of 20 *écus* from the king, and in May they gave him a bouquet of flowers for which he paid them another 20 *écus*.

Overall control of the court was vested in the *Grand Maître*, who was one of the *grands officiers de la couronne*. He drew up the roll of the household staff each year, supervised appointments, controlled expenditure, kept the keys of the king's residence and ensured the security of his person. Such an office could only be given to someone who enjoyed the king's trust. It was held first by Artus Gouffier, seigneur de Boisy, then by the king's uncle, René of Savoy, but the most famous holder of the office was Anne de Montmorency, who held it for more than thirty years. He also became Constable of France and virtually ran the government from 1528 until 1541. He necessarily had to delegate his household duties to the *Premier maître d'hôtel*, but whenever possible Montmorency himself introduced foreign ambassadors to the king.[19]

Although it was customary for the royal household to be dissolved on the king's death, Francis I reappointed many of Louis XII's officials; those who were too old were pensioned off. The procession for Francis I's entry into Paris in 1515 included members of Louis's household wearing his emblem of a porcupine while Francis's archers wore the salamander. By the end of the reign the household had become so large that it would have been difficult to rebuild. Henry II therefore decided that in future the household would outlive the king.

Size

The size of the French court in the sixteenth century varied according to time and place. Historians differ in their estimates: some favour a figure as high as ten thousand; others as low as eight thousand. The court has been compared to 'a nebula with evanescent edges'.[20] Contemporaries spoke of it as being 'large' or 'small'. On 25 May 1518 the Mantuan secretary, Stazio Gadio, wrote to Federico Gonzaga from Chinon:

> There are very few people at the court here: the queen has not yet arrived and Duke Lorenzo has gone in post to see his wife at Amboise. We expect the queen to arrive any day, and it is said that next Monday we shall leave for Angers in order to resume our journey.[21]

The whole court tended to unite for major occasions. Writing from Villeneuve on 8 June 1538, Marcantonio Bendidio, a Mantuan envoy, reported:

> His Majesty arrived here at Villeneuve on the penultimate day of last month with the court which is truly larger and more magnificent than it has been for many years, especially on account of the pomp brought by the ladies who have left no ornament behind in order to present themselves most honourably as much by their clothes as by jewellery and gold.[22]

At its largest, the court may have contained as many as ten thousand people: only twenty-five towns in France had larger populations. It was bigger in times of peace than of war, when the king and his able-bodied courtiers would absent themselves, leaving behind a rump of women, elderly men and clerics.

Young noblemen were in the habit of rushing off to fight as soon as a war seemed imminent. Even in peacetime, however, the court's population varied: as it travelled across the kingdom, noblemen from one region would tag along for a few days or weeks, then go home, leaving their places to be filled by others from another region. Such visitors seldom stayed for long as life at court was expensive; nor was it always rewarding. Few noblemen chose to reside there permanently; even the greatest liked to return to their châteaux periodically to attend to their own affairs. Household accounts list the staff of the various departments, but imponderables remain, as many served on a quarterly basis; nor did they necessarily live at court once their spell of duty had passed. 'The court was not an administrative body in which a fixed number of officials would be found at their desks in working hours and leave once their duties were over.'[23] The number of wives who accompanied their husbands is also unknown.

Archives provide only glimpses of the suites that accompanied important visitors. Writing from Lyon on 9 April 1516, Federico Gonzaga informed his father, the marquis of Mantua, that he had been forced to cut down his suite to forty-one horses and fifty mouths.[24] That seems modest enough; other suites were much larger. In 1540 the marquis of Saluzzo spent two days shopping in Lyon in order to impress the court. Such was the volume of stuff which he and the maréchale de Montéjean acquired that six large boats were needed to carry it down the Loire.[25]

Mobility

The court of France in the sixteenth century was wherever the king happened to be. As the kingdom grew larger and more peaceful, the court travelled more extensively, but its mobility varied. Some kings preferred to live in towns rather than the countryside; others were differently inclined; each had his own itinerary. Charles VIII preferred living in a town rather than in the countryside: he spent a total of 528 days in Lyon, doubtless because it was the doorway to Italy. Lyon was followed by Plessis-lès-Tours (402), Amboise (279) and Moulins (225).[26] It was commonly believed that one's 'native air' was essential to good health: hence the need felt by Charles VIII to reside at his birthplace, Amboise. He also loved gardens. Wherever he stayed, he employed a carpenter to build him a staircase leading out of his chamber. Louis XII spent on average four months each year in his native Blois. Over seventeen years he spent 2,273 days there and 721 at Lyon. His decision to make Blois his capital caused its population to rise within a few years to almost eighteen thousand, roughly twice the medieval figure. It was exempted of all taxes, and local speculators, particularly the religious houses, cashed in

6. *The Court of France Leaving the château of Anet.* Drawing by Antoine Caron (Musée du Louvre, Paris). The purpose of the court's progress here may be a hunt. A bear and birdcatcher are in the foreground. Anet was the home of Diane de Poitiers, Henry II's mistress.

on the land market.[27] Louis travelled mainly between the Loire and the Rhône, and thence to Lombardy, which he visited four times. He also visited Nantes twice, made one brief stay in Normandy, two in Burgundy and another on the frontier of Picardy.[28]

Francis I was a compulsive traveller. Hunting loomed large in his thinking: whereas his predecessors had only hunted deer in summer, he did so all the year round.[29] Writing in 1535, a Venetian complained that during his embassy, which had lasted forty-five months, he had travelled almost incessantly. 'Soon after my arrival in Paris,' he wrote,

the king left for Marseille; in excessively hot weather, we crossed the Bourbonnais, the Lyonnais, Auvergne and Languedoc, and came to Provence. The meeting with the pope was so long delayed that it only took place in November when everyone had assumed that it would be in the summer. Ambassadors who had brought only summer clothing had to acquire clothes for the winter. We were overcharged by fifty per cent for furs. I lost a horse and a mule during this voyage. From Marseille we travelled across Provence, the Dauphiné, the Lyonnais, Burgundy and Champagne as far as Lorraine where the king had talks with the landgrave of Hesse and we returned from thence to Paris . . . In the course of my embassy the court never stayed in the same place for a fortnight: it transported itself first to Lorraine, to Poitou; then to different places in Belgium; then to Normandy, the Île-de-France and again to Normandy, to Picardy, to Champagne, to Burgundy. The cost of these journeys was excessive, not only for me, who am but a poor gentleman as everyone knows; even the wealthiest lords will have felt the pinch.[30]

Francis's progresses were not haphazard. He tried to visit different provinces each year: Provence in 1516, Picardy in 1517, Anjou and Brittany in 1518, Poitou and Angoumois in 1519, Picardy again in 1520 and Burgundy in 1521. After 1521, when he went to war with the emperor, Francis's movements had to take account of military needs. As soon as the fighting ended, however, he resumed his progresses as before.

Francis I's most extensive progress lasted from November 1531 until October 1532. Setting off from Compiègne, he visited Amiens, Abbeville, Boulogne, Dieppe, Rouen, Argentan, Caen, Rennes, Châteaubriant, Vannes and Nantes, before returning along the Loire to Fontainebleau and Paris. In 1533 he went south after making a détour to Reims. He stopped at Fontainebleau, then visited Gien, Bourges, Moulins and Lyon. Moving westwards, he went to Clermont, Issoire, Le Puy, Rodez and Toulouse before turning east to Carcassonne, Montpellier, Avignon and Arles. After meeting the pope at Marseille, he travelled to Lyon *via* Romans and Crémieu. In 1534 Francis visited Dijon and Bar in Lorraine before returning to Fontainebleau and Paris. He then set off again on a progress which took him to Chambord, Blois, Amboise and Châtellerault. After spending the winter at Saint-Germain-en-Laye and Paris, he departed in March on another journey, this time to Normandy and Picardy, then across to Lorraine and south to Dijon and Pagny. Even in poor health Francis continued to travel. He was still hunting in February 1547, a month before his death.

Italian visitors, used to a more sedentary lifestyle within their relatively small city-states, were bewildered by the French king's ceaseless peregrinations. In 1541 the envoy Gambara complained to the duchess of Mantua about Francis I's restlessness. 'His Majesty', he wrote,

did not stay here longer than a day, but departed suddenly with his usual company and explores the strangest places in the country while chasing the poor deer. It is said that His Majesty will be here for the feast of All Saints. Opinions, however, differ: some say he will go directly to Fontainebleau; others that he will go to Picardy to inspect its frontiers; for my part, I believe that His said Majesty does not know which path to follow, as is his custom.

Francis I's pattern of travel was seasonal. In winter he tended to stay put. In 1516, for example, he remained at Amboise (except for a brief sojourn at Blois) from 25 October until mid-January 1517. He then moved to Paris, remaining there until 19 May, when he set off for Picardy. On 10 December he was back at Amboise, where he remained until 2 June.[31] The court travelled mainly in the spring, summer and early autumn, not always at the same pace. Sometimes the king liked to stay put for more than a few days. In 1528 he announced that he would spend more time in and around Paris, but he did not abandon the Loire Valley completely. He spent more time at Fontainebleau after 1528 than anywhere save Paris: it figures 624 times in his itinerary, as compared with Saint-Germain-en-Laye (405), Blois (107), Villers-Cotterêts (81) and Amboise (77). Paris is mentioned 712 times.

Travel in sixteenth-century France was not easy. The roads were unsurfaced, often narrow, winding and poorly maintained; in heavy rain they became quagmires. Rivers, much used for transporting merchandise, often burst their banks or froze in the winter; ice flows sometimes carried away bridges. When this happened, the court had to throw a pontoon or find an alternative route. An epidemic of plague affecting a particular locality might also force a diversion. For all of these reasons travel was painfully slow for all except royal messengers, who used post horses. A guidebook published by Charles Estienne in 1553 indicates that 15–16 leagues could be covered in a day when the terrain was flat, 14 when it rose gently and only 11–13 where it rose steeply.[32] Only the king, members of his family and chief courtiers travelled by boat; the rest of the court travelled overland. In May 1534 a payment was made to men who had dragged 'the king's great boat and that of his kitchens from Paris to Melun'.[33] In the fifteenth century portolan maps intended to assist sailors were only interested in France's coastlines, and maps based on Ptolemy's *Geography* were of no practical use. In 1525, however, a more scientific map was produced by Oronce Finé. This was large enough for use as a wall map; it also gave an idea of the size and general shape of France, but no information on the road system.[34] When planning a progress, the king and his officials had to rely on past experience or local knowledge. Towns sometimes placed a local guide at their disposal.

Moving the court was like moving an army. The baggage train was enormous, including furniture, gold and silver plate, and tapestries. Only royal châteaux where the court resided for relatively lengthy periods were kept furnished; the rest remained empty from one royal visit to the next. Amboise, Blois, Fontainebleau, Saint-Germain-en-Laye and the Louvre had special rooms where furniture and tapestries were stored during the court's absences.[35] In 1533, when Francis I met the pope at Marseille, the sum of 4,623 *l*. was spent on moving the court's furniture, plate and tapestries.

Guillaume Monnier, the king's *tapissier*, was ordered to assemble 'several items of furniture, gold and silver plate, tapestries and other things that we have asked to be taken from our châteaux of the Louvre, Blois and Amboise'. The tapestries, *objets d'art*, gold cloth, etc. were packed in chests and, early in May, were transported overland to Orléans in two separate convoys. They were then carried up the Loire to Roanne in two large boats. From here waggons pulled by oxen transported the cargo to Lyon, where it remained awaiting the king's pleasure until 12 August. It was then taken down the Rhône to Arles and put on a ship for the final leg of the journey to Marseille. This had lasted from early May to 26 August. The return proved even more arduous as the River Yonne was frozen. The cargo did not return to Paris until 3 February 1534.[36]

The court did not travel in a long, disciplined, single file: it split up into parallel columns which moved across the countryside in isolated bands. Without necessarily keeping to the roads, they would take short cuts, trampling over cultivated fields if need be. The bulk might meet up at some agreed point along the route; stragglers, moving at their own pace, would turn up later. Riders, forming the vanguard, were always well ahead of the menials who had to walk. A man of quality was expected to ride a horse. Montaigne, writing at the end of the century, had no time for any other mode of transport: 'Now I cannot put up for long with coach, litter or boat (and could do so less still in my youth). I loathe all means of conveyance but the horse, both for town and country.'[37] A litter was favoured by anyone too tired, ill or old to ride a horse. Francis I hunted from a litter at the end of his life, and Montmorency used one at the age of seventy-two. Litters were carried by men or mules. Carts pulled by horses were used to carry merchandise. Coaches only made their appearance at court around 1540 when Francis was given one by the duke of Mantua. Accompanied by Madame d'Étampes and Madame de Massy, he drove it at speed around the park of the Tournelles and was so thrilled by the experience that he took the vehicle on a longer ride to Vincennes. He commissioned a carpenter to make an awning to shield him from the sun. Queen Eleanor liked the vehicle so much that she spoke of nothing else for two days and wanted it for herself, but the king ignored her wish. 'This coach', wrote the Mantuan envoy Gambara, 'is highly favoured. His Majesty wants to use it for stag hunting. He also wants to take some mares out of his stud farm in order to train them for this exercise, and wants other chariots to be made here in Paris.'[38] Passenger coaches only reached France from Italy around the mid-century. There were three in Paris in 1550 owned respectively by Catherine de' Medici, Henry II's illegimate daughter, Diane, and a nobleman no longer able to ride. The fashion soon spread. In

1562 a coach was made for Charles IX and a few years later several *chariots branlants* (jolting waggons) were to be found in the royal stables.

Finding accommodation for the court was the responsibility of the *prévôté de l'hôtel* and its staff of *fourriers*. Machiavelli, who visited France between 1501 and 1511, was impressed by their efficiency. 'The court's *fourriers*', he wrote,

> are the people responsible for accommodating the court when it is on the move. There are thirty-two of them who are paid wages of 300 francs per annum and given a livery in the king's colour. Above them are four *maréchaux des logis* who are paid 600 francs. The order they keep is as follows: they are divided into three bands: the first, under the command of a *maréchal des logis* or his lieutenant, remains at a place which the court has left in order to settle up and pay the people with whom it has lodged; the second goes with the king; and the third goes ahead to where the court is due to arrive or the king is due to sleep next day so as to arrange the lodgings. Their order is admirable, for as soon as each one arrives, even the most insignificant member of the court finds his lodging ready.[39]

An ordinance of 1560 provides more information. The *fourriers* drew up a register of available lodgings and, on the eve of the court's arrival in a given place, the *fourriers* of princes, ambassadors and others were given tickets signed by a *maréchal des logis* authorising their masters to claim a lodging. This, at least, was the theory; in practice things may have gone less smoothly. The bishop of Saluzzo complained that an isolated house containing only a few rooms would be found for Francis I and his ladies, while the rest of the court had to fend for itself three, four or six miles away.[40] 'I believe', wrote an Italian envoy, 'that he [Francis] does it to inconvenience the whole court rather than for any other reason.'[41] Writing from Loches in December 1539, Gambara complained of extreme confusion on the eve of the emperor's visit. Only the great nobles were catered for; the rest, particularly foreign ambassadors, left to fend for themselves, were grossly exploited by the natives. 'The English ambassador', wrote Gambara,

> has had to pay 15 *écus* for a lodging, as I have learnt from one of his secretaries. As for other expenditure, Your Eminence may be sure that it is intolerable. I myself cannot manage on less than three *écus* per day and only by making the most of them, especially when looking for oats, hay and straw which are hard to find, especially oats. They are excessively dear: salt, wine, bread and other foodstuffs are cheaper. I have never seen more extortionate

people than these Frenchmen. They are never satisfied and do not care about piercing the hearts of all Italians.[42]

'We ambassadors', wrote the papal nuncio from Bar-le-Duc in April 1564, 'are put up as well as possible, and those who are new to the game are more disgruntled than I whose bones have become accustomed to discomfort.'[43] The situation was no better later in the century. In 1577 the Venetian ambassador Lippomano reported:

> to find lodgings a prince must be three or four leagues distant from the next; not even towns can accommodate the entire court which makes do with the surrounding villages. Even if there is enough room for the court, there is not enough for the large number of horses and other beasts of burden.[44]

Wherever possible, Francis I stayed in one of his own châteaux or accepted the hospitality of a courtier: he stayed with his Bourbon-Vendôme cousins at La Fère, Admiral Chabot at Pagny, Florimond Robertet at Bury, Duprat at Nantouillet, Cardinal du Bellay at Saint-Maur, Louis de Brézé at Mauny and Philibert Babou at La Bourdaisière. He also stayed with ladies at Châteaubriant and Challuau. Where no château existed, the king would put up at an abbey or inn and his followers would seek lodgings in the vicinity. Francis often chose a remote spot, usually in a forest, where no building existed capable of housing the court. A modest dwelling would be adapted to serve his minimum requirements. In March 1540 he put up at a stable at Novion. Wooden partitions were run up to form a hall (*salle*) and a chapel. The king said he was better housed than the pope, but the Mantuan ambassador begged to differ: 'There is no worse place to be seen', he wrote. 'The queen has only a very small room, as have Madame Marguerite, Madame la Dauphine and the others.' The rest of the court stayed in Abbeville, where everything was exorbitant.[45]

Feeding the court could be difficult too. Its presence, even in a town as large and prosperous as Lyon, was likely to strain local resources and provoke a sharp rise in food prices.[46] In May 1533 the Venetian ambassador reported:

> This town [Lyon] cannot accommodate so many men and horses, and this has caused a great scarcity of all things; most especially of lodgings, bread, corn, stabling; and the quantity of bread sold for one French *sou*, equal to rather more than three *marchetti*, is so small that I never remember to have got less for three *marchetti* in Venice, however great the scarcity may have been there. The people eat very coarse and bad bread, corn has trebled in

price: and should the court remain here some days longer, the cost will become unbearable.[47]

In August 1540 France was hit by drought, and the imperial ambassador described the court's plight as it travelled to Le Havre: no fodder for the horses, no wine or cider for the men. All the wells were dry so that courtiers had to drink polluted water, with predictable consequences. Monsieur de Lautrec and the son of the duc de Guise fell gravely ill, and the duc d'Orléans had a 'bloody flux'. The king, too, suffered stomach pains, but they were not regarded as serious; they were blamed on his love of hunting: for three weeks he had done nothing else.[48]

Plague could seriously hinder the court's movements. The disease still broke out from time to time, although there were no more pandemics of the kind that had swept across France between 1348 and 1440. Epidemics were now limited to one or two provinces at most, and destructive ones were less frequent. They occurred on average once in eleven years before 1536 and once in fifteen thereafter. The most effective antidote was flight. In 1521 'the people of Moulins absented themselves on account of the danger of plague'. Fugitives were, of course, only the better off who could afford to move.[49] The court on its travels had to watch for pockets of contagion and avoid them as far as possible. On several occasions it had to leave precipitately in response to a warning of plague: hence Francis I's hasty departure from Bordeaux in July 1531. The epidemic was evidently widespread. In September his mother, who had been unwell for some time, left Fontainebleau which was threatened by plague. She set off for Romorantin 'for a change of air', but died on the way of the disease she had been trying to avoid.[50]

CHAPTER 4

The Courtier

The court of France in the early sixteenth century was a microcosm of French society as well as an instrument of royal power. Both sexes and all social groups with the exception of the peasantry were represented among its members; but the nobility and the upper clergy occupied a privileged position. They were the courtiers who attended the king's *lever* and *coucher*, who stood beside him as he took his meals, who shared in his pastimes and entertainments, and who benefited most from his largesse. For the king was the fount of patronage to whom nobles looked for gifts and favours for themselves and their clients. The wealthiest courtiers, however, were not just recipients of royal largesse; they gave their obedience in return and, being themselves patrons commanding a vast network of clients and *fidèles* in parts of the kingdom where their estates were situated, they could ensure that the king's authority was widely obeyed.[1] Churchmen, too, had much to gain from going to court as the king had many benefices in his gift.

An important reason for attendance at court was to acquire an office from the king. In 1522 Francis I systematised the sale of offices by setting up a special department – the *recettes des parties casuelles* – to receive the revenues from it. Once bought, an office could be exchanged or sold with royal permission in return for a fee, the only restriction being that the seller should outlive the official permit by forty days; if he died in the meantime the office reverted to the king. This was greatly to his advantage as the fee for a *résignation* was less than could be obtained from a sale. Such was the success of venality that the king also created offices in order to sell them. Over the century their number increased dramatically.[2]

The king was also responsible for most appointments to major church benefices. Although royal control of the church hierarchy reached back to the Middle Ages, it was the Concordat of Bologna of 1516 between Francis I and Pope Leo X that enabled the king to appoint to most major benefices with papal approval.[3] Some important sees and abbeys retained the right of electing their superiors; they lost this privilege in 1531 as a result of another agreement with the Holy See. The pope kept the right to set aside any royal appointment in breach of the canonical rules regarding age or worthiness, but in practice he seldom interfered. The king thus disposed of an extensive ecclesiastical patronage. Most of the bishops he appointed were drawn from the nobility. In 1516, out of 102 bishops sixty were from the 'old' nobility and fourteen from recently ennobled families. Four others were commoners and sixteen were foreigners, mostly Italians.[4] The commoners owed their sees to their reputation as humanists. The most lucrative benefices were given to members of the king's entourage. Pluralism and absenteeism were rampant among them. Under Francis I fifty sees passed through the hands of only eight prelates. The wealthiest pluralist was Jean de Lorraine, who had nine sees and six abbeys. He was closely followed by Louis and Charles de Bourbon, who held seven sees and numerous abbeys. The most blatant pluralists were Italians. Ippolito d'Este, for instance, was archbishop of Lyon, Arles and Narbonne, and bishop of Autun and Tréguier. He also held the sees of Milan and Ferrara. Service to the crown, notably as diplomats, was the main criterion for nomination. Consequently, many bishops were almost permanently at court or abroad. Others were expected to represent the king's interests in the provinces where their sees were located. After taking possession of them, they leased the revenues to the highest bidder. They would appoint a vicar-general, invariably a lawyer, to run the diocese, while a suffragan, often a regular qualified in theology, was entrusted with the pontifical duties.

Apart from the royal family, the king's friends and the great officers of state, all kinds of noblemen frequented the court, but they formed only a small part of the nobility as a whole; for attendance at court was a costly business which many nobles could ill afford. Nor did it always achieve the hoped-for results. In 1556, for example, the seigneur de Gouberville left his manor in Normandy for the first time in fourteen years. He travelled to the court at Blois, hoping to obtain an office for which he was ready to pay 1,300 *écus*. He remained there for a month and a half, only to return empty-handed, having spent 65 *l.* on food and lodging; his annual expenditure was normally between 150 and 200 *l.*[5]

Contemporary writers identified nobility with military virtue: in other words, courage, endurance, strong nerves, mental alertness and the desire to achieve fame. The Italian Wars gave French noblemen many opportunities of displaying their virtue; for more than fifty years Italy was a *champ d'honneur* where they might seek fame at the point of a sword.[6] By going to court, a young nobleman, keen on achieving fame, would stand a better chance of serving in the king's army than if he stayed in some remote château. Even as children, nobles played more or less violent games which, by the time they had grown up, assumed the appearance of real combats. Mock battles, jousts and tournaments were part of the stock-in-trade of court entertainments. Honour played an important part in war. In 1552, at the siege of Metz, young noblemen could not wait to take part in a dangerous sortie. They rejoiced, we are told, at the prospect of laying down their lives on the *lit d'honneur*.[7] If they survived, they could show their frontal wounds as evidence of their virtue. Several noblemen achieved fame on this account: François and Henri de Guise shared the nickname of *le balafré* (scarface), Monluc wore a nose of leather after being wounded at the siege of Rabastens, and La Noue became known as *bras de fer* (arm of iron).[8] Many courtiers were captains of the *compagnies d'ordonnance*, units of heavy cavalry that were the core and pride of the royal army.

Though the king liked to think that his authority was God-given and therefore absolute, he could not have ruled his kingdom without the support of the nobility and they looked to him for gifts and favours. The dependence was mutual and it was sealed at court. The steady rise in the number of courtiers during the sixteenth century reflected the expansion of royal patronage. Only by attending the court could nobles hope to acquire the most lucrative honours. It was there that they shared the king's authority by serving on his council or by drawing his officials into their own clienteles. It was also there that pressure groups or factions, consisting of friends, clients or allies, were formed, often around the royal mistresses. Finally, the court was the stage on which courtiers could proclaim their prestige by the magnificence of their dress, the size of their suites and their proximity to the monarch.

Going to court was not necessarily a one-way process. In the course of his progresses the king often stayed with his subjects. The duration of his visit could be taken as a measure of the favour enjoyed by the host. Receiving the court could be rewarding, but it was also expensive as the host had to entertain not only the king, but also his retinue. Monsieur de Vieilleville, who received Henry II at Durtal in 1550, in addition to providing the courtiers with food in abundance, placed his two wine cellars at their disposal. Each was given two bottles of wine, red and white, and even the meanest servant was able to drink as much as he liked. Some courtiers were particularly skilful at acquiring properties strategically situated along the roads most often used by the court, a favourite target being the one used by Henry II to call on his mistress, Diane de Poitiers, at Anet. From his châteaux at Meudon and Dampierre, the cardinal of Lorraine commanded the road to the south, while the Constable of Montmorency, who ruled the area north of Paris, was able to receive Henry II thirty-seven times in thirteen years. Courtiers, who could not compete with the constable as landowners, could at least try to lure the king to their homes by commissioning a building specially for his use.

Marshal Saint-André set the example at Vallery and was soon copied by Cosme Clausse at Fleury-en-Bière. Sometimes a château had a room set aside specially for the king's use. In the absence of such a room it was customary for the host to give up his own room to the king, a gesture that was not only an honour, but also a demonstration of allegiance. In 1510 Cardinal Georges d'Amboise moved out of his magnificent room at Gaillon for the benefit of Louis XII, who was not used to such luxury in his own châteaux.[9] Montmorency created an apartment specifically for the king's use at Écouen.[10]

The king did not have a sufficiently large civil service or standing army to impose his will alone; he needed the support of the great nobles, whose power and prestige could be measured by the number of kinsmen, friends or clients they could mobilise. Great nobles surrounded themselves with cohorts of dependants and clients. In 1560 Louis prince de Condé travelled with a retinue of five hundred noblemen; Anne de Montmorency turned up at Fontainebleau with eight hundred. It was to such men that the king looked to control the provinces. The provincial governor was a sort of viceroy. In 1500 there were eleven governorships (*gouvernements*), corresponding roughly to the kingdom's border provinces. Governors were normally princes of the blood or high-ranking nobles whose powers were laid down in a commission. Thus in 1560 Antoine de Bourbon was governor of Guyenne, Anne de Montmorency governor of Languedoc, François de Guise governor of Champagne and Jacques d'Albon governor of the Lyonnais. Without the local knowledge and influence of such men, the king would have had difficulty raising the *compagnies d'ordonnance*. When a provincial governor was away at court or in the army, his local duties were performed by a *lieutenant*, who was usually a lesser nobleman or a prelate, but even from afar a governor could assist his province by defending its interests in the king's council. His large private household provided employment for local noblemen and education for their children.[11] Clientage was 'a complex, multifaceted social institution, and far more varied than vassalage'. Clients came from all levels of society and their relationship to a great lord varied in strength, permanence and the nature of the goods and services exchanged. The patron's protection took various forms, such as gifts of employment or money, intercession with the king to obtain public offices, honours or pensions, judicial assistance or acting as godparent to the client's children. Many clients came to court, not on their own account, but in the wake of their masters.[12]

Courtiers who were particularly favoured by the king became known as *favoris* or *mignons*. The word *favori* reached France from Italy around 1500, when *mignon* was already in use. A favourite was a courtier who was intimate with the king without being a member of his family. Such a man was the young Jacques d'Albon de Saint-André, who, it was said, was the only courtier allowed to enter Henry II's chamber in the morning before he was dressed. The relationship between king and favourite depended to a large extent on the latter being continually present at court; if he absented himself for any length of time, the relationship was likely to cool, particularly as there was always a courtier at hand ready to take his place. A favourite also needed to be a yes man. Charles VIII's favourites supported his invasion of Italy and helped to organise it. There were favourites throughout the sixteenth century. Under Charles VIII they included Guillaume Briçonnet and Étienne de Vesc. Briçonnet became *général des finances* for Languedoc in 1483, and the next year a royal councillor. On becoming a widower, he entered the church and was appointed bishop of Saint-Malo. In return for supporting Charles VIII's invasion of Italy, he was given a cardinal's hat. Several more benefices followed, including Reims, the abbey of Saint-Germain-des-Prés and two sees near Rome. Like other successful commoners, Guillaume used his position at court to advance his kinsmen. His brother, Pierre, who succeeded him as *général des finances* for Languedoc, married his eight daughters to future financial officials of the crown. The cardinal did likewise for his own daughters. Thomas Bohier, paymaster of the royal armies in Italy and owner of Chenonceau, became Briçonnet's son-in-law. Another brother, Robert, became successively a president in the Parlement of Paris, archbishop of Reims, president of the *Chambre des comptes* and Chancellor of France.[13] De Vesc, a nobleman from Dauphiné, had served Louis XI as chamberlain and *bailli* of Meaux. In 1489 he became president of the *Chambre des comptes* and in 1491 *sénéchal* of Beaucaire. His contacts with shipowners in Marseille and in Italy helped the king prepare his Italian campaign.

Georges d'Amboise, cardinal-archbishop of Rouen, was until his death in 1510 Louis XII's constant companion and adviser. 'The king', wrote a contemporary, 'knowing him to be an excellent man endowed with common sense, experience, loyalty and good principles, kept him close to his person. Whether he was dealing with serious matters or seeking mental relaxation, he was always either alone with him in his chamber or his perpetual travel companion.' Being on equally good terms with the queen, Amboise frequently acted as go-between in disputes between the royal couple. He failed in his bid to become pope following the death of Alexander VI in 1503, but was eventually appointed papal legate for life in France, thereby greatly enhancing his authority.

Among Francis I's many favourites were Guillaume Gouffier de Bonnivet, Anne de Montmorency, Philippe Chabot, Jean de La Barre and Claude d'Annebault. Two others were high-ranking churchmen: Jean de Lorraine and Ippolito d'Este. The former, a member of the House of Guise, became the king's close companion: although a bishop from an early age (he was said

7. *Guillaume Gouffier, seigneur de Bonnivet.* Drawing by Jean Clouet (Musée Condé, Chantilly). One of Francis I's childhood companions, Guillaume Gouffier (*c.* 1482–1525) also became the king's favourite. Admiral of France in 1517, he was killed at the Battle of Pavia in 1525.

to have been a bishop in his mother's womb), and a cardinal from 1518, he hunted and played tennis, appeared dressed as a satyr and in other disguises in court masques, and shared the king's sexual adventures. Though both a councillor and a diplomat, he was never as influential politically as Anne de Montmorency.[14] Ippolito d'Este was the son of Lucrezia Borgia and Alfonso I, duke of Ferrara. It was following the marriage of his brother Ercole to the

French king's sister-in-law, Renée, that Ippolito became involved with France, but he did not go to the court until 1536. He, too, took an active part in its festive, not to say dissipated, life. He became a cardinal in December 1538 at the request of Francis I. Known as the 'cardinal of Ferrara', he acquired several lucrative benefices in France in addition to those he already held in Italy. The large income he drew from them enabled him to live ostentatiously. He has been described as 'one of the most prestigious and powerful men at court'. A leading art patron, Ippolito encouraged Benvenuto Cellini, and in 1546 commissioned Sebastiano Serlio to build the 'Grand Ferrare', a small but luxurious residence at Fontainebleau. When Francis I came to see how the work was progressing in 1546, the cardinal laid on a superb banquet to which all the most beautiful ladies of the court were invited. The dauphin and his friends rounded off the proceedings by riding up a flight of steps 'with so much bravery and applause from the spectators that it was the greatest fun in the world'.[15]

Not all courtiers were noblemen; a fair number were commoners who possessed the experience and skills required for certain ministerial functions. This was especially true of the chancery and the fiscal administration. Such men had often been trained as lawyers or had first-hand commercial experience. Among them were Guillaume Briçonnet II, Florimond Robertet, Antoine Duprat and Jacques de Beaune. Briçonnet belonged to a bourgeois family from Touraine that had served the crown in various capacities since the late fourteenth century. The youngest of six boys, he began his career in the *boutique de l'argenterie* that supplied the court of Louis XI with luxury textiles and goldsmith's work. In 1480, after marrying Raoulette de Beaune, he became *secrétaire des finances*. Antoine Duprat belonged to a merchant family from Upper Auvergne. His ancestors had traded in cloth and wine before turning to moneylending and banking. After studying civil and canon law, Duprat became *avocat du roi* in the Parlement of Toulouse, and in 1503 was appointed *maître des requêtes*, an office that entitled him to sit in the Parlement of Paris. In 1508 he became its First President. After serving Anne of Brittany, Duprat turned to Louise of Savoy and in 1515, following her son's accession to the throne, he was appointed Chancellor of France. As such, Duprat needed to be constantly with the king. During Francis's captivity in 1525–6, Duprat virtually ran the kingdom alongside the regent. By then, he was a widower and ordained. He became archbishop of Sens and abbot of Saint-Benoît-sur-Loire. Promoted to cardinal in 1527, he was appointed papal legate *a latere* two years later. Duprat used his power to advance his relatives: his brother and his son succeeded each other as bishop of Clermont. Duprat died in 1535, leaving a vast fortune which the crown promptly borrowed.[16]

8. *Cardinal Antoine Duprat.* Bust in terracotta. (Musée du Louvre, Paris). Duprat (*c.* 1463–1535), who became Chancellor of France in 1515 and a cardinal in 1527, was a powerful figure at the court of Francis I. He was noted for his avarice.

Among commoners who rose to prominence at court during the early sixteenth century two – Florimond Robertet and Jacques de Beaune – deserve to be singled out. The former belonged to a family from Forez that had served the House of Bourbon, and became a royal notary and secretary by 1490. Thereafter he acquired several financial offices, but soon specialised in foreign affairs where his knowledge of foreign languages (including English allegedly) stood him in good stead. Under Louis XII he became a close confidant of Georges d'Amboise. His presence at court is attested by his counter-signature on numerous treaties. A Florentine envoy described him as 'the linchpin of the court; his advice always prevails, for one can be sure that in all things he remains the ear and tongue of the king'. Robertet used his influence to advance his kinsmen. His uncle Gabriel secured a benefice 'to reward the said *Maître* Florimond Robertet for his good and great services to the king'. In addition to drawing substantial wages from the crown, Robertet received valuable gifts from visiting diplomats. He acquired many properties and collected works of art, including a bronze *David* by Michelangelo and a painting of the Virgin by Leonardo da Vinci.[17]

Jacques de Beaune is best remembered under his baronial name of Semblançay. He belonged to a family from Touraine which had risen from the cloth trade. His ancestor Jean had been a prime mover in Louis XI's *boutique de l'argenterie*. He had then started a moneylending business and became *argentier* to the dauphin in 1470. A striking feature of the families of financiers from Touraine was the amount of intermarriage. Jacques married Jeanne Ruzé, the daughter of a royal financier. After serving Anne of Brittany, he entered the service of Louise of Savoy, whose son, Francis I, appointed him *général des finances*, an office which he subsequently resigned to his son. Jacques lent money to the king and was given overall control of the royal revenues, but, accused of peculation, he was tried and executed in 1527. His family and friends were dragged down in a mass prosecution by the crown of its financial officers.[18]

Competition for the king's favour or the need to direct his policy in a particular direction divided the courtiers into factions or groups with a common interest to pursue. There could be many such groups within the court, but more often there were just two operating as rivals. Their objective might be to secure a lucrative office, but also to effect a change in royal policy. Faction was largely absent from the court of Francis I before 1526. The rebellion of the Constable of Bourbon failed to prompt an aristocratic revolt on a scale that might have divided the court. It was only after 1526 that faction appeared in the form of a rivalry between two of the king's favourites: Anne de Montmorency and Philippe Chabot de Brion. Montmorency was thirty-three and a member of one of the oldest and wealthiest houses in France (see plates 12 and 13).[19] Brought up with the king, he had taken part in many military campaigns. He had become a marshal of France, Grand Master of the household and governor of Languedoc. In 1527 he married Madeleine, the daughter of the king's uncle, René of Savoy.[20] The career of Philippe Chabot, who became Admiral of France in 1527, was similar to that of Montmorency. Of roughly the same age, he too had been one of the king's childhood companions. In addition to the admiralship, he became governor of Burgundy, and in January 1527 he also joined the royal family by marrying Françoise de Longwy, the daughter of the king's natural sister. In 1536 Montmorency enhanced his reputation by successfully defending Provence against Charles V. Following his promotion to Constable of France, he instigated a radical change in French foreign policy aimed at recovering the duchy of Milan by peaceful means instead of war. In 1538 he secured the appointment of Guillaume Poyet as Chancellor. Among the constable's friends at court were the Dauphin Henri, his mistress Diane de Poitiers, the cardinal of Lorraine and other members of the Guise family. In the meantime, Chabot fell victim to rumour-mongers. An enquiry revealed malpractices by his subordinates and in 1540 his own conduct came under scrutiny. Accused of corruption, he was tried by a special commission under Poyet's chairmanship. In February 1541 Chabot was stripped of his offices, heavily fined, banished from court and imprisoned at Vincennes, but not for long. Montmorency's policy was soon found wanting and denounced by the duchesse d'Étampes. 'He is a great scoundrel,' she exclaimed, 'for he has deceived the king by saying that the Emperor would give him Milan at once when he knew that the opposite was true.' Francis did not ditch the constable immediately, but deprived him of any say in foreign affairs. In March 1541 Chabot was reinstated: he recovered his offices and a year later was cleared of *lèse-majesté*. His rehabilitation led inevitably to Poyet's fall and imprisonment in the Bastille.

Although Francis I's authority remained unchallenged, his court began to fracture in the 1540s. As Nicholas Wotton reported, 'The Court everywhere is the Court, that is to say, a place where is used good shouldering and lifting at each other.'[21] Following the death of the Dauphin François, in 1536, factions formed around his brothers, Henri and Charles. While Montmorency's friends gathered round Henri, his enemies, led by the duchesse d'Étampes, supported Charles. Their rivalry was exacerbated by the contrasting fortunes of the two princes in the war of 1542. While Charles conquered Luxemburg, Henri was defeated at Perpignan. In October the English envoy Paget identified two rival camps at the French court: on the one hand, Marguerite de Navarre, Charles d'Orléans, the duchesse d'Étampes and Philippe Chabot; on the other, Queen Eleanor, the Dauphin Henri, Montmorency and most of the cardinals.[22] Then, in June 1543, Chabot died suddenly, clearing the way for the rise of two younger men: Claude d'Annebault and François de Tournon. Annebault succeeded Chabot as admiral in February 1544, and in May an Englishman noted 'the admiral is the king's factor to whom he commands all things'. In December a Florentine reported: 'The admiral rules everything; without him one cannot speak to the king or obtain anything.'[23] In September 1544 Francis I signed the Peace of Crépy which provided for the marriage of his son Charles to the emperor's sister or niece. This angered his brother, Henri, as it seriously threatened his inheritance. Charles, however, died in September 1545 and the treaty lapsed. Henri succeeded to the throne in March 1547 and one of his first acts was to invite his friend Montmorency to return to court and to banish Madame d'Étampes and her friends.

Women at Court

The court's population was predominantly male, but women were present in significant numbers. Except among servants, however, the sexes lived apart much of the time. Queens, princesses and mistresses had their own households comprising mainly female attendants and servants. At the highest level, of course, the sexes would meet to socialise at banquets or balls. Francis I's *petite bande*, which accompanied him on his hunting expeditions, included a number of young women, but the day-to-day life of the king's household was mainly controlled by men.

The attention given to the education of women by Erasmus, Vives and other humanists and Castiglione's description of the cultured lives of women at the court of Urbino have given the impression that the status of women was raised by the Renaissance. This impression is reinforced by statements regarding the role of women at the court of France, yet the Renaissance was not a period of emancipation for Frenchwomen generally: a wide gulf existed between the ladies of the court and the majority of their sex. Women's rights declined during the sixteenth century. If in certain provinces their rights were to a degree protected by customary law, in France as a whole the increased use of marriage contracts during the century strengthened a husband's control over family property. At the same time, the spread of Roman law stressed his authority.[24] At court, however, things were different: women began to figure more prominently than before.

Francis I regarded women as an essential adornment of his court and wanted them to be fashionable. Isabella d'Este, the marchioness of Mantua, who was internationally reputed for her taste in clothes, set the tone. On 19 November 1515 her son, Federico, wrote to her from the French court:

> My Lord de Morette has told me that the king would like you to send him a doll dressed in the fashion you wear: the chemise, sleeves, undergarment and overgarment; that is, everything including the headdress and hairstyle that you wear. However, by sending various styles of headdress Your Ladyship will satisfy the king all the more as he intends to have some of this clothing made as gifts for ladies in France. May it please you to send them as speedily as possible.[25]

Italian fashions soon conquered the French court. On 11 July 1516 Stazio Gadio wrote from L'Arbresle to Isabella d'Este:

That Sunday, after the departure of Bartholomew the courier, the king held a banquet and reception at which fourteen ladies-in-waiting wore dresses in the Italian style which he had brought back from Italy. Twelve were the queen's ladies and two were Madame de Bourbon's. Among the former was Mademoiselle de Châteaubriant, the sister of Monsieur de Lautrec, wearing a dress of dark crimson velvet embroidered all over with gold chains among which were cunningly placed tablets of silver with 'SPONTE' written on them. One lady, called Este, a lady attached to the king's mother, was the fifteenth dressed in the Italian style: she wore a long, ample dress of black velvet embroidered with broken feathers. Another had one made in quarters of cloth of gold and crimson velvet: spent torches were embroidered on the cloth of gold and obelisks cleverly on the velvet. Mademoiselle d'Estrac wore a dress of green velvet covered in knots and hammers in golden embroidery. Still others wore various dresses, some of crimson satin, others of velvet with flames of cloth of gold, but the richest and best were those I have described above. On their heads they wore golden caps with velvet berets on top, but these were not worn properly; if Messer Rozone had not assisted them to dress they would have looked even worse, yet, compared to those dressed in the French style who all sat on a dais, they looked like goddesses; nor can I be accused of Italian partisanship for the same opinion was expressed by the king and many other judicious Frenchmen.[26]

According to Brantôme, Francis I was accused of causing

several evils at court and in France, not only during his reign but also during those of his successors. The first was the introduction at court of large numbers of ladies as visitors or residents: one has to admit that before his time they neither stayed at court nor frequented it often, and, if they did, they were few in number. It is true that Queen Anne [of Brittany] enlarged her circle of ladies more than earlier queens had done, and, but for her, the king would not have troubled to do so. On his accession, however, Francis considered that the court's adornment consisted entirely of ladies and wished to have more than had been the custom. True it is that a court without ladies is like a garden without beautiful flowers.[27]

This statement is backed up by statistics. Under Charles VII and Louis XI the queen's household was relatively small. That of Charlotte of Savoy, Louis XI's queen, comprised between 74 and 113 people, including about 20 women. The situation changed dramatically under Charles VIII. Anne of Brittany's household grew from 244 people in 1492 to 325 in 1496, and the number of women from 47 to 53 (see plate 1). Thus it seems that Brantôme was correct in describing Anne as 'the first who set up the large court of ladies which we have seen since her day until now; for she had a very large suite of ladies and girls and never refused any; she would question noblemen at court if they had daughters, who they were and ask for them'.[28] Yet the household of Francis's first queen, Claude, was relatively small: only 12 women out of a total complement of 209.[29] By contrast, his mother, Louise of Savoy, had 31 women in her household of 295 in 1531. Among them were members of Francis's *petite bande*: Anne de Pisseleu, Marie de Canaples and Diane de Poitiers. His second queen, Eleanor, had an even larger household: in 1531 it comprised 348 people, including 50 women. By 1547 the number had risen to 391, including 98 women, many of them Spanish.[30]

The Courtier under Fire

The courtier has never been popular. Throughout the Middle Ages and the Renaissance, the court was portrayed as a hell. It was described as such by Aeneas Sylvius Piccolomini in the fifteenth century. Courtiers fared no better than the court. From antiquity onwards the courtier has been denounced as a flatterer, hypocrite, deceiver, spendthrift and debauchee. In 1405, in a sermon preached before the queen of France, Jacques Le Grand condemned debauchery and effeminacy at court. For the medieval critic, the life of the courtier could not be otherwise than degenerate, for corruption was the essential prerequisite of success at court. Medieval anti-courtier literature is best exemplified by Alain Chartier's *De Vita Curiali*, better known as *Le Curial*. On a pretext of dissuading his brother from pursuing a career at court, Chartier attacks its moral corruption and material discomforts, and eulogizes the simple life. *Le Jouvencel*, written by Jean de Bueil in 1466, offers an interesting variation on the theme of court versus country by comparing the soldier and the courtier. He underscores the contempt of the *noblesse d'épée* for the new *noblesse de robe* that is increasingly discharging various functions at court. Of all medieval writers the bitterest critic of courtiers was Eustache Deschamps. He pitches into the soft-living, pleasure-seeking, irresponsible younger courtiers and regrets the passing of chivalrous values and manners. Deschamps also inveighs against the new male fashions at court: the absurdly short cloak, the shoes that do not conform to the natural shape of the foot. All this Deschamps sees as evidence of moral laxity. In the *Champion des Dames* (1442), Martin Le Franc criticises breeches designed to protect masculine vanity from public appraisal. The frivolity of ephemeral court fashions, in his view, betrays the degeneration of the inner man.

The early sixteenth century in France witnessed an increase in the number of works tilting at courtiers. These reflected a popular perception of social change rather than what was actually happening. The Italian Wars were allegedly accompanied by a great influx at court of adventurers, including Italians whose only purpose was gain. The latter, it was claimed, were usurping lucrative and influential positions and importing a way of life that departed from traditional French values. More serious, perhaps, was the charge that the courtier was becoming more professional and, therefore, more remote from the rest of society. Whereas in the past courtiers had been vassals often more powerful than the king who came to court for a limited period to discharge a function or duty, courtiers now looked upon the court as a source of livelihood. Another butt of satirists was the court's lavishness which, it was believed, had been built on the backs of the poor.

Critics of the court in sixteenth-century France could turn to the works of ancient authors such as Terence, Homer, Plutarch and Lucian for inspiration. Horace, in addition to satirising fortune-hunters, praised the quiet country life in contrast to the dangers, irritations and complexities of the Roman forum. Plutarch offered an inexhaustible supply of vivid portraits of the flatterer in his many guises. Lucian's attacks on flattery in the Athens of his day could be readily applied to the French court. His pamphlet *Rhetorum Praeceptor* was the prototype for Renaissance satires offering ironic advice, a device quickly seized upon by Erasmus who, in his *Praise of Folly*, attacked the typical courtier as a man content to wear the trappings of office without shouldering any of its responsibilities.

Not all the court literature of the early sixteenth century was hostile. A notable exception is Baldassare Castiglione's *Il Cortegiano* (*The Book of the Courtier*), first published in Italy in 1528 and soon translated. The first French edition appeared in Paris in 1537, and several more followed in quick succession. While condemning all the timeworn courtly vices, Castiglione ignores earlier anti-court writing. He is concerned with behaviour. He was influenced both by chivalric tradition and by Italian courts, such as Urbino and Ferrara, where, apart from war, there was little to do but practise refinement and the art of elegant conversation. *Il Cortegiano* takes the form of a dialogue spread over four nights and covering a number of seemingly unrelated topics. Castiglione discusses love and the role of women at court, but his chief concern is to define the perfect courtier and how he should develop his talents in order to be successful. His ideal courtier has to be a warrior, but also learned, a conjunction achievable through a classical education and rigorous physical training. Castiglione stresses appearance. The courtier must have *grazia*, or grace, and *sprezzatura*, a studied nonchalance. He must steal his grace from others 'as a bee chooses flowers in a meadow'. He should tackle difficult matters with a deceptive ease, but his nonchalance should never become obvious: its purpose is to make everything seem natural. It has the effect of enhancing achievement as it impresses on the minds of observers 'that who so can so slightly do well hath a great deal more knowledge than indeed he hath'. In athletics and other accomplishments such as music, the courtier must avoid all sign of effort; whatever his expertise may be, he must give the impression that he devotes little time to such pursuits. He must consider his reputation, ensuring that 'there goes first a good opinion of him before he comes in person'. In conversation, he should prepare himself before-hand while pretending 'the whole to be done extempore'. When dealing with unfamiliar matters, he should give the impression that he 'hath a great deal more cunning therein than he uttereth'. He needs to fashion himself like a work of art. He must ingratiate himself with 'great men, gentlemen and the ladies'. *Il Cortegiano* was 'without doubt the most significant book in the history of courtly literature'. Castiglione's courtier became a model for all to follow.[31] Yet paradoxically in France his work served to fuel anti-courtier satire, for many of its prescriptions, notably *sprezzatura*, were deemed incompatible with the robust candour (*franchise gauloise*) Frenchmen liked to think part of their national character.[32]

Even more influential in France than *Il Cortegiano* was the *Menosprecio de Corte*, an outright condemnation of court life by the Spaniard Antonio de Guevara. A French translation published in Lyon in 1542 was rapidly followed by no fewer than twenty-six French editions. Guevara uses religious terminology to pour scorn on the tenets of the courtier's profession: just as the monk gives his life to God, so the courtier sacrifices his freedom and integrity for an uncertain, indeed improbable, advancement. Guevara's satire is based on contrast and antithesis: rural life is held up as the yardstick by which the court's degradation can be measured.[33]

One of the most interesting French responses to Castiglione's *Il Cortegiano* is the *Philosophe de Court* by Philibert de Vienne (1547), a work clearly influenced by Lucian's attempt to define the art of the Parasite. He attacks *Il Cortegiano* at its weakest points. Firstly, he calls into question Castiglione's tacit acceptance of the court as the highest arbiter in respect of virtue and good reputation; secondly, Philibert attacks Castiglione's goal for the perfect courtier by insisting on the interested aim of court philosophy; his account of the reception that awaits the unwary visitor to court exposes all that is contrived and deliberate in the projection of a 'good appearance'. He shows that Castiglione has substituted the carefully cultivated appearance of virtue for virtue itself and also that the aim of his courtly virtue is merely success and high esteem.[34] Philibert despises the 'rude youths and minions of the court' who 'simper it in outward show, making pretty mouths and marching with a stalking pace like cranes'. They have curled hair, dress foppishly and sprinkle their conversation with a few words of French, Italian and Spanish, yet they are counterfeit courtiers whose pretensions are all too obvious. Philibert also shows that courtly justice differs from the law or morality. The courtly philosopher holds it 'tolerable to beguile, filch and cog, and do the worst we can, so that neither law, judge nor justice may touch or catch hold of us for it'. Humility is extolled by our sages, writes Philibert, but courtly virtue lies elsewhere: the best way to achieve worldly honour is to be liberal, especially with other men's goods. All deeds, however, should seem to conform to reason, for 'such as we seem, such are we judged here'. Castiglione's art of pleasing is thus reduced to absurdity. The courtier must give advice according to his master's desires, not according to the truth. Openness and simplicity are only suitable for 'beasts and idiots'. The courtier, Philibert argues, must be pliant: he must do whatever is expected of him, even if he is otherwise inclined. His dissimulation, however, must be prudent; it must seem natural. Such satire in France fell on ground manured by Italophobia. Every aspect of court life was ridiculed and abused. Courtiers were even accused of mispronouncing words in imitation of ladies unwilling to open their mouths wide.[35] But satire could not alter the realities of court life, however contemptible these might be. In the words of Sydney Anglo: 'The fundamental difficulty facing satirical critics of courtly ethics was that, as they themselves frequently acknowledged, the necessary qualities for prospering at court were precisely those they felt obliged to mock. . . . Temporal success is usually obtained by sedulously cultivating the good opinion of those who already enjoy it.'[36]

CHAPTER 5

The Daily Round

In the absence of household ordinances for the early sixteenth century, the historian of the French court has to rely on information contained in the reports of foreign ambassadors, contemporary memoirs or biographies. One document in particular has been much used as a guide to the day-to-day life of the court. This is a letter, probably written in 1574, by Catherine de' Medici to her son, Henry III, in which she urges him to follow the routine that had been observed by his father and grandfather.[1] Helpful as the letter is, it needs to be read with care, for a routine that could be followed in the stable environment of a royal château could not have been so easily observed when the court was on progress and having to adapt to conditions that were sometimes primitive.

The king's day, as described by Catherine, began with his *lever* in the presence of his main courtiers and distinguished guests. This took place in the *chambre*, one of four rooms into which the king's lodging was divided. The courtiers and guests entered the chamber before the king had risen from bed. Cardinal Jean du Bellay once boasted that he had spoken to the king for an hour as he lay in bed.[2] The courtiers watched the king as he got up, prayed, washed and dressed. He was handed his shirt by the most distinguished person present. The king spoke to his entourage as he took a morning drink (*collation du matin*). The company then dispersed, except for councillors and secretaries, with whom the king now retired to his *cabinet* to deal with state papers; alternatively, he might hold a small council meeting. In 1561 this was described as follows by a Venetian:

The *conseil des affaires* consists of very few people who are the king's intimates. Sometimes it consists of only one, such as the constable in the days of King Henry or the cardinal of Lorraine in the time of Francis I. This council was created by Francis I, who disliked having too many councillors; he was the first to take upon himself important decisions on matters of state. It is called *conseil des affaires* because the king held it with his most intimate courtiers at the hour of his *lever* and even as he satisfied his bodily needs, known in French as *les affaires* (his business). It has kept this name although its form has changed considerably. Today, it is a kind of ordinary council to which are admitted the principal courtiers and those most trusted by the king.[3]

About 10 a.m. the king left his chamber escorted by princes and lords to attend mass. This was normally celebrated in a chapel situated at some distance from the king's lodging so that he had an opportunity to show himself to many people. Federico Gonzaga, who was not among the privileged few who attended the *lever*, seized this chance of ingratiating himself with Francis I. As his secretary, Stazio Gadio, explained to the marquis of Mantua: 'He rises early in the morning and walks to mass outside Paris in one church or another by way of exercise; he then goes to court and accompanies the king to church and remains for the sermon. Once this is finished, he dines and immediately afterwards attends the king's dinner.'[4] Attendance at mass was for the king a duty that could not be avoided. Not even ill health could stand in the way. On 6 December 1538 Edmund Bonner wrote to Thomas Cromwell from the French court:

> The French King came out of his chamber by his secret stair into the chapel, wearing a gown of taffeta with sables, his buskin furred, and under his bonnet a velvet night cap, and looking very pale. At the mass, which was not long, he kneeled near the altar and had to be helped up by the Cardinal of Lorraine on one side and by the count of Saint Pol on the other. He turned to where the dauphiness was with Madame de Etampes, with whom he talked a good while and then went up his privy stairs again.[5]

The return from mass was the moment when traditionally members of the public could bring petitions to the king, who would read them before passing them on to the chancery for action.

The king's dinner, which followed mass at about 11 a.m., was another public ceremony intended to demonstrate the love binding him to his people. At Saint-Germain, he sat either alone or with guests at a table set up at the far end of the *salle* in front of a fireplace. He had his back to it in order to be seen by the public. The table, a board resting on trestles, could be folded away to make way for the audience that followed the meal. The table was divided into two parts: the *haut bout* on the king's right hand, and the *bas bout* on his left. The *haut bout* was reserved for honoured guests; the *bas bout* was for others. The queen seems not to have shared the king's table. Whether he sat alone or had guests, he was surrounded by great lords, who stood beside him along with his confessor, doctors and various household officials. His viands were brought to him from the *cuisine de bouche* by archers, stewards and pages walking in procession. Following ancient tradition, he was served by the *panetier*, *échanson* and the *écuyer tranchant*. The nef or saltcellar, an elaborate piece of goldsmith's work in the form of a ship, stood on the table. Lesser courtiers, meanwhile, were kept at a distance by stewards and archers. Music often accompanied the meal. An account of one served to Charles VIII in Rome indicates the importance that was attached to his personal safety. A morsel from each dish was tasted by the official who served it; any leftovers were placed in the nef. A group of doctors sat at the table ready to advise the monarch on his food and drink. Whether such precautions were taken in France is unclear.

Francis I used the time immediately after dinner to show off his learning. He would hold forth on almost any subject to an entourage that often included scholars and artists. His table acquired the reputation of being a centre of learned discourse. Hubert Thomas, a humanist from Liège, who witnessed the scene at the end of Francis's reign, was much impressed. He had observed other princely tables, but none, in his judgment, surpassed this one. 'The readings that took place,' he wrote, 'the subjects that were discussed, the conversations that were held were so instructive that even the most learned men could still learn something.' He had some difficulty, however, understanding Francis, whose speech had become impeded following the excision of his uvula.[6] Cellini, in his *Autobiography*, offers a vivid glimpse of the royal table. As he waited impatiently for some commission from the king, the cardinal of Ferrara advised him to attend his dinner. 'This I did,' writes Cellini, 'and one morning at his dinner, the King called me. He began to talk to me in Italian, saying he had it in mind to execute several great works, and that he would soon give orders where I was to labour, and provide me with all necessaries.'[7]

The king would often call on the queen in the afternoon before retiring to the privacy of his *cabinet*. Afterwards he would take part in some 'honest exercise' such as a walk, a horse ride or a game of tennis. This was when the men and women, who had spent the morning apart, got together to socialise. The evening at court began with supper, which was also *en public* but, being less formal than dinner, has left comparatively few traces in the records. Later in the century, under Henry III, rules were laid down whereby the king was to sup with the queen from Sunday to Thursday, and alone on Friday and Saturday, but this may not have applied to earlier reigns. Supper was immediately followed by a ball several times a week. According to Catherine de' Medici, Francis I used to say that he needed to give a ball at least twice a week to live at peace with his subjects, who liked to be kept merry and engaged in some honest exercise, yet it is not known how often he called upon his courtiers to dance. A masque held as part of the celebrations for the wedding of the duc de Nevers and Mademoiselle de Vendôme was described by a Mantuan observer as 'very honourable and fine'. Among a group of courtiers dressed as satyrs was the cardinal of Lorraine. The popularity of dancing at the French court was already established by the reign of Louis XII, who was a keen dancer. In June 1507 he and Ferdinand of Aragon danced together during their meeting at Savona. A few days later in Milan, cardinals danced for the king. Robert Dallington, who visited France later in the century, was particularly struck by the popularity of dancing; he even suggested that it might have impeded the progress of the Protestant Reformation across the Channel, for Huguenots disapproved of dancing. Until around 1530 the *basse-danse*, characterised by a relatively slow tempo, was most commonly performed. Then, from the second quarter of the century, other kinds of dance, both rapid (*saltarello*, *gaillarde*) and slow (*pavane* or *passa-mezzo*), became very popular.[8]

The king's day ended with the *coucher*, which, like the *lever*, was witnessed by the principal courtiers. The king did not sleep alone: one of the duties of the first gentleman of the chamber was to sleep in the same room. The *valets de chambre* and some royal favourites did likewise. The king shared his bed on occasion. Henry II invited Montmorency to do so more than once. The king's *coucher* was the signal for the doors of the royal residence to be locked and to remain so until the next *lever*.[9]

Francis I's life cannot have been as tightly regulated as Catherine's letter suggests, given the fact that he was constantly on the move, sometimes detaching himself from the main body of the court for days on end and putting up in some very inhospitable places. Yet the accounts given by Brantôme and foreign diplomats do not substantially depart from Catherine's account. The Venetian ambassador, Giovanni Capello, for example, describes Henry II's day in 1554 as follows: in summer, he rises at daybreak and in winter uses a light. He starts the day with a prayer, then attends a meeting of his privy council at which matters of peace and war are discussed. Mass follows, then dinner and another council meeting, which the king seldom attends, preferring instead to read 'for he knows that letters can bring more honour to princes than anything else'. Henry then goes riding to relax mentally and to exercise his body. He enjoys hunting, especially the stag. 'All his amusements are honest,' writes Capello, 'unless he is particularly clever at concealing his illicit pleasures.'[10]

The king of France was proud of his accessibility. An ordinance of 1523 states that 'a greater conglutination, bond and conjunction of true love, pure devotion, cordial harmony and intimate affection has always existed between the kings of France and their subjects than in any other monarchy or Christian nation'.[11] Except in time of plague, as in October 1520, when Francis I was confined to his room, the king was easily approached. In 1562 the Venetian ambassador Michele Soriano commented on Charles IX's accessibility:

> The king of France is so familiar with his subjects that he treats them all as his companions and no one is ever excluded from his presence so that even lackeys of the lowest sort are bold enough to wish to enter his privy chamber in order to see all that is going on there and to hear all that is being said. Anyone who needs to deal with a matter of importance must have the patience to do so in such a crowd and to speak as quietly as possible in order not to be overheard. This familiarity, if it makes the nation insolent and arrogant, nevertheless inspires love, devotion and loyalty to its prince.[12]

Access to the court was open to anyone who was decently dressed or could claim acquaintance with a member of the royal entourage.

The chaotic scenes that resulted from this climate of familiarity sometimes called for extreme police measures. In 1515 the Mantuan envoy, Giovan Francesco Grossi, congratulated himself on emerging unscathed from San Petronio in Bologna: as he left the church, Francis I's servants cleared his way through a crowd by hitting out with sticks. They inflicted serious blows on many Italian noblemen. Not even the pope's servants were spared. In 1539, as Francis I was having a meal with ladies by the roadside, he ordered some of his Gascon soldiers to stop horses and litters that were passing by. This they did by administering a *gran bastonate*. In 1559 there were chaotic scenes during the marriage of the duke of Savoy: people were thrown to the ground and smothered as the constable fell upon them with 'a devil's bastinade'.[13] Italian ambassadors were shocked by the absence of decorum at the French court. Their difficulty in understanding it was well expressed by Castiglione in his *Il Cortegiano*: 'Thus if you will consider the Court of France, which today is among the noblest of all Christendom, you will find that all those who there enjoy universal favour tend to be arrogant, not only among themselves but even towards the King.' 'Do not say so', replies Federico.

> On the contrary, the gentlemen of France are very courteous and modest. It is true that they allow themselves a certain liberty as well as an uncere-monious familiarity which is peculiar and natural to them and should not,

therefore, be called presumption. For in the way they conduct themselves, whereas they laugh at and mock the arrogant, they greatly esteem those they believe to be worthy and modest.[14]

Italian ambassadors were continually comparing the rigidity of court etiquette at the Spanish court with the laxity of the French court; in their view Italy stood in the middle.[15]

Each day, after dinner, Francis I would give audience. If foreign ambassadors were involved, it would have been a formal occasion with the king seated and wearing a hat, and the ambassadors standing bareheaded. They would kiss the king's hand (later in the century, his knee) and submit their letters of credence. Francis, however, did not care for such formalities, as Venetian ambassadors found to their dismay in 1531. They were quite overwhelmed by the warmth of their reception. Francis was standing in his chamber surrounded by courtiers when the ambassadors entered. As they approached, he doffed his hat, saying repeatedly: 'You are most welcome!' He then embraced them in a manner calculated to prevent them kissing his hand and received their credentials standing up.[16] The following year Francis curtly refused to allow Marino Giustiniani, the new Venetian ambassador, to make the customary speech after presenting his credentials. 'I do not want the new ambassador to make a speech', he said. Thoroughly disconcerted, Giustiniani complied with 'the brevity which His Majesty seems to want for his affairs, or rather for his pleasures'. The king was unpredictable, however; sometimes he chose to be formal. The papal nuncio Acciaiuoli was taken aback in 1526 when he was welcomed at the French court in a manner that he viewed as excessively respectful.[17]

Ambassadors who managed to get an audience with Francis I were usually treated informally. When, in 1541, the imperial representative tried to pass in front of the Venetian envoy Matteo Dandolo, the king settled the matter by beckoning Dandolo with his hand and even pulling at his gown. Once the audience was over the king sent him away and humiliated his rival by slamming a door in his face. When Dandolo visited the French court for a second time in the reign of Henry II, he noticed a greater formality. He was escorted into the royal presence by archers, but instructed by the king to keep his hat on. Much importance was attached to this item of clothing. It was an honour for an ambassador to be invited to remain covered. When, in 1461, a Florentine envoy refused such a request from Louis XI, the king took off his own hat. In 1549 Louis de Gonzague, duc de Nevers, also refused an invitation from Catherine de' Medici to keep his hat on and to sit down.[18]

Italians frequently commented on the fact that the king of France seemed to be continually surrounded by a large crowd of courtiers, so that it was extremely difficult for them to conduct any business, especially if this called for secrecy. Often this could only be achieved by talking to the king in a window recess. French ambassadors, for their part, were astonished at the disciplined manner with which foreign rulers conducted their audiences. When Bellièvre called on Don John of Austria in the Low Countries in 1578, he was surprised when the gentlemen in the room withdrew to let him pass.[19] An audience with Francis I was often chaotic. Ambassadors, who sometimes had difficulty passing through the scrum of courtiers surrounding him, would seek the assistance of the constable. In 1540, for example, Francis left the room before the Mantuan envoy was able to make his presence known to him whereupon the envoy tugged at Montmorency's cloak (*vesta*), and Montmorency then pulled at the king's.[20] Francis, however, could also be deliberately elusive. In 1520 Stazio Gadio complained:

> M. Suardino and I have been at court all day in order to speak to the king and to Madame [Louise of Savoy] but our fate has decided otherwise: I have now been at court ten days and have not yet succeeded in getting an audience because each day the king goes hunting early in the morning and does not want anyone to follow him; when he returns in the evening, he puts on a mask (*si veste maschara*) and dines privately . . . Today, however, after deciding to accost the king before he goes hunting, we went early to the door of his *garde-robe* in the house of Villeroy where he is staying with all the ladies and we waited there till he came out.[21]

The Queen's Day

Though debarred by the Salic law from exercising royal authority, the queen of France was accorded regal dignity. She was crowned at Saint-Denis and had an impressive household, but her day-to-day life is less well documented than her husband's.[22] The historian has to rely on occasional glimpses provided by foreign ambassadors in their dispatches or on semi-contemporary biographies, such as those of Brantôme or Hilarion de Coste, which are subject to caution. Pierre de Bourdeille, seigneur de Brantôme, wrote his biographies of famous ladies (*Dames galantes*) after an accident in 1584 which obliged him to give up the adventurous life that he had followed hitherto. He relied not only on his own memories of court life (he had been a gentleman of Charles IX's chamber) but also on a good deal of hearsay.[23]

Judging from a report written in 1570 by the secretary of Cardinal Alessandrini, the daily routine followed by Catherine de' Medici was similar to that of the king. Her day began, like his, with the *lever*, ended with the *coucher*, and her meals were taken 'in public', but her *lever* differed from the king's in one important respect: whereas only men attended his *lever*, both sexes were represented at the queen's.[24] This was followed by mass. Both Anne of Brittany and her daughter, Claude, were noted for their piety and seem to have spent an inordinate amount of time making altarcloths. Catherine de' Medici was fond of musical services. According to Brantôme, she never failed to attend mass and vespers, and enlivened them with music; she recruited to her chapel the finest choristers available.[25] No information exists for the period before 1585, yet it seems that for most of the century the queen did not accompany the king at daily mass and that her church services were more private than his. However, on feast days in 1516 and 1517, Francis I and Queen Claude are known to have attended services together.

Mass was followed by dinner. Marguerite de Navarre was served by her ladies, who ate in the same room but not at the same table. According to a report dating from 1550, Catherine de' Medici regularly shared her table with Henry II's illegitimate daughter, Diane, who was eleven, and also with the sister of the duc de Nemours and Mademoiselle de Rohan, but these sat at the end of the table furthest from the queen. Once she had dined, the queen received visitors. These were often foreign ambassadors, who paid their respects after saluting the king.[26] In February 1517, for example, Francis I invited five ambassadors to dine with him after mass. They then called on the queen, the king's mother and his sister, who had gathered in the queen's presence chamber. The ladies kissed one of the ambassadors, Monsieur de Rens, as a special honour, while indicating to the others simply a desire to kiss them.[27]

During the afternoon the ladies of the court would either watch the men at sport, betting on their respective champions and distributing prizes to the victors, or they might take part in sports of their own: pall-mall (an early form of croquet), riding or archery. As a young woman, Catherine de' Medici was an excellent rider. She is even credited with introducing into France the side-saddle, which enabled women to ride as fast as men. Previously they had used a saddle called a *sambue*, a kind of armchair in which they sat sideways with their feet resting on a board. Queen Eleanor, too, was a keen huntress. The ladies' afternoon might also be filled with less energetic pursuits, such as polite conversation with the queen in her antechamber or needlework. A little music-making might also take place. In December 1544 Bernardo de' Medici, the Tuscan ambassador, sent the following report to Cosimo I: 'The prince of Salerno is still here and every evening these ladies invite him to sing two Neapolitan songs, and there are so many guitars here that each lady has her own.' The afternoon ended with a public supper, which was invariably followed by a concert or a ball.[28]

The Banquet at the Bastille, 22 December 1518

The daily round of the court was frequently broken by celebrations of various kinds. Sometimes a distinguished guest would be entertained or the court might celebrate a religious feast day, such as Epiphany. In December 1518 a distinguished English embassy arrived in Paris to ratify the Treaty of London.[29] They were received by Francis I at the Palais on the Île-de-la-Cité, then went to Notre-Dame for the official ratification. Various celebrations followed, culminating on the evening of 22 December with a banquet at the Bastille, which may have been chosen on account of its proximity to the rue Saint-Antoine where a tournament preceded the banquet. The central courtyard of the fortress was turned into a makeshift hall for the occasion. This was an innovation in France, but such halls had been used in Italy, notably in 1507 when Gian-Giacomo Trivulzio had set one up in Milan for the reception of Louis XII. Among several contemporary descriptions of the Bastille banquet the most interesting is by Bernardino Rincio, a Milanese doctor attached to the household of Chancellor Duprat.[30] The banquet, he explains, had been 'elaborated to perfection on the orders of the Most Christian King by the illustrious Count Galeazzo Visconti', who had fought against him at Marignano. He had since been pardoned by the king and had settled in France with his family.[31]

Entry to the Bastille in the early sixteenth century was through a gateway on the rue Saint-Antoine. A path running alongside the moat led to a fore-court, then across a bridge and through two portcullises to an inner courtyard. For the ambassadors' visit the gateway had been adorned with pillars and pilasters. A Latin inscription above the gateway read in translation: 'Praise the Lord, all the nations.' Beyond lay a gallery, 90 metres long and 7.20 metres wide, consisting of a trellis of box supported by sixty wooden columns, painted silver, and supporting busts (*effigies*) of famous men. Springing from the columns, hoops of wood entwined with ivy formed a vault from which hung wreaths displaying the arms of England and France. The columns and pilasters, flanking the entrance to the bridge, supported, on the right, the two lions of England and, on the left, a dolphin. Above the gateway were the arms of France framed by the collar of the Order of St Michael. The entrance to the fortress also had columns bearing trophies and a Latin inscription: 'The Temple of Peace comes into view.'

The Bastille courtyard had been made to look more symmetrical and given a wooden floor. Some 16 metres above the floor, ropes, stretched across the courtyard, supported large sheets of canvas arranged to form a pitched roof. Beneath this, a ceiling of blue cloth supported by ropes, crisscrossed and tightly stretched, was adorned with stars and signs of the Zodiac. Hanging from it were thirty large chandeliers, each with twelve cornucopias and wax torches. The illumination they provided was reflected by mirrors attached to the ceiling and augmented by two hundred torches bracketed to the walls of the hall. Measuring 60 metres by 24, this was divided into three parts: the *theatrum*, *orchestra* and *tribuna*. The *theatrum* consisted of two superimposed porticos and three tiers of galleries running along three sides of the hall. The *orchestra* was the central area where tables were set up for 'ordinary guests'. The *tribuna*, at the upper end of the hall facing the entrance, was a raised platform reserved for the king, his sister and principal guests. A space on the right was kept for Queen Claude, Louise of Savoy and Antonia, the wife of Galeazzo Visconti. Sixty pillars supported the *theatrum*, each adorned with torchbearing cornucopias, and the balustrades of the galleries carried the arms of the kings, queens and dauphin inside wreaths of box trailing gold and silver ribbons. Behind the *tribuna* was a large canopy made of cloth of gold, and in front five columns decorated with trophies. The *tribuna* had a fretwork ceiling decorated with box and ivy, red and white roses and various kinds of fruit. A variety of evergreen trees were distributed about the platform. Also in the hall were four large sideboards (*buffets*) on which gold and silver plate were displayed.[32] Inscriptions and images on the *theatrum* and *tribuna* celebrated the peace. Above the king's throne a bright sun carried the words: 'Here is the true serene day under the brilliant light of God.' A panel showing Aeolus asleep in the house of Morpheus bore the inscription: 'This sleep will do me no harm.' Other images – a riderless horse and a philosopher – pointed to the royal virtues of physical endurance and wisdom which had made the peace possible. Francis I's personal responsibility was emphasised by the floor covering in his own colours of white, tawny and black. Other inscriptions on the *tribuna* claimed that the kings of France and England had made peace of their own free will without prompting by the goddess Fortune. A quote from the *Bucolics* acclaimed it as a return to the Age of Gold; another from Scripture implied that the peace was providential. As for the stars and signs of the Zodiac, they celebrated a conjunction of the planets pointing to present and future happiness. A huge fire-breathing salamander, occupying the place normally given to the bear, served to remind guests of Francis I's recent victory over the Swiss at Marignano. A viper, emblem of the Visconti, wound itself around the salamander's tail.[33]

At 4 p.m. Francis I entered the brightly lit hall accompanied by the English ambassadors, the papal legate, Cardinal Bibbiena, his escort of bishops, and French princes. Queen Claude, Louise of Savoy, the duchess of Alençon and some thirty of the queen's ladies awaited them on the *tribuna*. Musicians performed a pavane, and the king danced with several ladies. At 7 p.m. tables were set up on the *tribuna* and in the *orchestra*. The guests at the high tables,

numbering about thirty, sat with their backs to the wall in order to be served
from the front, as was the custom at court and in noble households. In the
orchestra, 250 guests sat on either side of long tables. Men and women sat
alongside each other. This was an innovation for the French court, where
traditionally they sat at separate tables.

The next stage of the banquet was the procession of royal viands: twenty-
five pages preceded by trumpeters, archers, heralds and officials of the household led by the Grand Master carried them on large gold platters. They
marched solemnly along the full length of the hall to the *tribuna*. While the
king and his guests were served, two hundred archers and twenty provosts
served the guests in the *orchestra* off silver platters. Fifty *échansons* were also
in attendance. Up to nine courses were served. At 9 p.m. the tables were
removed and dancing began. Groups of masquers, wearing bizarre costumes,
succeeded each other on the floor while spectators assembled in the galleries.
The dancers included the king, who wore a long gown of white satin embroidered with astrological symbols. As the musicians, playing wooden or copper
flutes, struck up a pavane, the masquers were joined by ladies so as to form
forty couples. The female dancers wore Milanese dresses that were very décol-
leté made by ladies of the court under the direction of Visconti's two daughters.[34] The dancing itself was new and Italianate. The king and his male
courtiers had long been known to dance in disguise, but never before had they
invited ladies from among the spectators to dance with them.[35] Dancing
continued late into the night, after which young ladies dispensed sweetmeats
(*zucheri*) and preserves, as Ethiopian perfumes wafted across the hall.

The example set by the Bastille banquet was soon followed elsewhere. In
April and May 1518 the courtyard of the château of Amboise was transformed to celebrate the dauphin's baptism and the marriage of Lorenzo de'
Medici to Madeleine de La Tour d'Auvergne. The courtyard was covered
with sheets of cloth strewn with fleurs-de-lys and supported by ropes attached
to three tall masts. Tapestries, depicting scenes from antiquity, covered the
walls. A month later, on 18 June, Francis offered a banquet and a ball at the
manor of Clos-Lucé, near Amboise, where Leonardo da Vinci was living.
The impresario was once again Galeazzo Visconti. Around the courtyard
were columns on two levels entwined with ivy; the wooden floor was covered
with sheets bearing the king's device; and the roof consisted of blue sheets
adorned with golden stars, planets and signs of the Zodiac. A dais beyond the
courtyard was reserved for the ladies. Lighting was provided by four hundred
torches. Each male guest at the banquet sat between two ladies.[36]

The Feast of the Bean

The feast of Epiphany, or Twelfth Night as it was called in England, prompted much jollification at the French court. Part of this consisted in electing a King and a Queen of the Bean. This was done by concealing a bean in a cake; whoever found the bean was the 'king', who, like his English equivalent, the Lord of Misrule, was supposed to reign for the duration of the fun and games – originally twelve days. The choice of a king seems to have caused less stir than that of the queen which elicited much competition among the court's beauties. Writing in 1550, the Venetian ambassador, Giovanni Soranzo, tells us how Henry II came into the queen's chamber at Blois and picked out of a hat the name of the Queen of the Bean. Chance, it seems, played no part in his choice, for he discarded several names before alighting on that of a 'young, really beautiful and most charming' lady, who belonged to the circle of his sister Marguerite. His choice was greeted with the cry 'La reine est faite!' from the assembled company, and the lady concerned, after touching Henry's hand, retired to dress 'honourably'. The rest of the ceremony is described by the Mantuan envoy Bendidio in a report dating back to 1539. On the evening of the Queen of the Bean's election, Francis I ordered new and beautiful clothes to be brought to her and to eighteen ladies who were to attend upon her. The style of the clothes was Flemish: the undergarment was of crimson velvet with slashed sleeves held together by gold clasps, and the top garment was of grey satin fringed with velvet and lined with mink fur. The headdress, a long golden or silver snood, was adorned with precious stones or pearls and worn under a plumed bonnet. Belts, necklaces and bracelets completed the attire. When it was time for supper, the Queen of the Bean rose from her seat on the right of Queen Eleanor, and, taking the king's hand, led her band of ladies and the rest of the court to a hall where two tables, one very long, the other less so, were laid. The procession was accompanied by instrumental music. The Queen of the Bean sat above Queen Eleanor, the dauphin's wife, Catherine de' Medici, and the king's sister, Marguerite, at the shorter table, while Francis joined the ladies at the other table. During the meal the Queen of the Bean was served with a ceremony usually reserved for the real queen, who had to do without during the twenty-four hours of her rival's reign.[37]

In 1550 a different seating plan was observed at the banquet. Henry II sat in the middle of the shorter table, flanked on his right by the Queen of the Bean, and on his left by Diane de Poitiers, the cardinal of Lorraine, the duchesse de Guise and the Constable of Montmorency. The real queen (Catherine de' Medici), Mary Stuart and the king's sister, Madame Marguerite, sat next to the Queen of the Bean. All the other ladies sat at a longer table running off at a right angle from the king's table. The banquet was followed by a ball which lasted far into the night. Next day being the feast of Epiphany, the king walked to the chapel of the château escorted by the Queen of the Bean, who walked in front of the real queen. Following behind were Mary Stuart, the king's sister, Marguerite, more ladies and all the courtiers. After mass everyone dined in the same order as on the previous evening before retiring, then took up positions at windows overlooking the palace courtyard to watch a joust. This lasted two hours and was followed by another banquet and ball.[38]

The King's Lodging

The king's lodging at Saint-Germain-en-Laye, dating from the end of Francis I's reign, may serve to exemplify the distribution of rooms in a royal palace.[39] It was situated on the far side of the courtyard and on the second floor of the left wing. The lodging occupied a surprisingly small space, given the overall size of the court. It consisted of only four rooms: the *salle*, the *chambre*, the *garde-robe* and the *cabinet*. The royal chapel was situated some distance away. The king reached it by descending the main staircase and crossing the courtyard. His lodging was also far from the château's entrance and from the ballroom. However, it did communicate directly with the queen's *salle* by means of a small external passage, and a concealed staircase led from it to the château's *chemin de ronde* and to a bridge across the moat leading to the garden. Near this bridge, another small staircase led down into the dry moat where the tennis court and lists were situated.

The king's *salle*, a vast room of about 165 square metres, was a public room accessible to virtually anyone. Order was maintained by the archers of the guard who were expected to remain there all day. The *salle* was reached directly from the courtyard by means of a dog-legged staircase. In other châteaux the *salle* varied in size: 100 square metres at Fontainebleau and Blois, and 250 square metres at Chambord and Villers-Cotterêts. At Saint-Germain-en-Laye it was lit from four window bays and heated by two fireplaces. It was where the king dined. While he sat on a chair, guests had to be content with stools. The only major piece of furniture in the *salle* was the sideboard or *buffet* on which the royal plate was displayed. Apart from meals and audiences, the *salle* was a favourite meeting place for courtiers. If they felt tired, they could sit on one of the benches that ran along the walls. The entrances to the *salle* at Saint-Germain were not aligned, so that the king had to walk diagonally from one to the other. More courtiers were thus able to see him and the archers' task of fraying a passage for him was facilitated.[40]

The *chambre* at Saint-Germain was also vast, measuring nearly 100 square metres. It was lit on both sides by five large windows which overlooked the garden, the park and the River Seine. The king's bed stood next to the fireplace, flanked on one side by the *chaire* or close-stool and enclosed by a balustrade. The chamber was lavishly decorated. At Fontainebleau, it was adorned with paintings and stuccowork above the wainscoting, as Sir John Wallop was able to see for himself in 1540. 'And within a while,' he wrote,

> the said Cunstable cam to the chamber dore, agayn saying, 'Le Roy vous demaunde, Monsr l'Ambassadour', and so we went into his bedde chambre, whiche I do assure your Majestie is very syngulier, aswell with antycall borders, as costly seeling, and a chemeney right wel made. And for bycause in suche my communication had with Hym before, I did not gretely prease the mattyer and stuff that the said borders was made of, geving no good luster, the said Frenche King required me to go uppon a benche to feele the said matier and stuff; unto whom I saied, 'Sir, the benche is to highe, and shal hardly gett upp', and began tassaye. He, like a good gratiouse Prince did help me forward with hande, orelle, to be playne with Your Majestie, I shud hardly have gotton upp; and likewise at my cummyng downe stayed me agayn.

At the new Louvre the chamber had splendid woodcarvings by Scibec de Carpi after designs by Pierre Lescot. Furniture included hangings and tapestries. Carpets were laid on the rush matting that covered the floor. A bench ran along the wall, but courtiers were normally expected to stand in the chamber. There was also a buffet from which the king was served his early morning drink.[41]

The *garde-robe* at Saint-Germain was a rectangular room sandwiched between the *salle* and the *chambre*. It measured only 28 square metres yet could accommodate a bunk where the valets slept. It was also here that the king's clothes were stored in large chests. Under Francis I and Henry II the morning session of the king's council was sometimes held in the *garde-robe*, which for much of the century was virtually the only part of the king's lodging offering privacy.

The *cabinet* was a circular room measuring only 12 square metres. It was lit from three windows and heated by a small fireplace. In 1556 the walls were covered by tall wainscoting. Too small to accommodate the *conseil des affaires*, the room was used by the king as a study where he would work with his secretaries. It was also where he kept his valuables. In 1505, for example, Anne of Brittany's gold plate was kept in Louis XII's *cabinet* at Blois. Writing in 1567, Philibert de l'Orme said: 'It is necessary and more than reasonable for the chambers of kings, great princes and lords to be accompanied by a *cabinet* so that they may withdraw in privacy either to write or talk business in secret or otherwise.'[42] Though the pattern of four rooms – *salle, chambre, garde-robe* and *cabinet* – was repeated in all the royal palaces, the size and location of each were variable.[43] At Chambord there was no king's lodging in the strict sense. It was one of thirty-two identical lodgings, though its decoration was slightly more elaborate than the rest. Cruciform *salles*, one on each of three floors, were common to eight lodgings. The arrangement became typical in all Francis I's hunting lodges. At the château of Madrid instead of a single *salle* there was one on each floor, and at Villers-Cotterêts, instead of being a suite of rooms, the king's lodging was more like a cluster around the chamber. At Fontainebleau the king had two successive lodgings. The first was a modest affair, but in 1531 he took over his mother's lodging after her death. This enabled him to incorporate the long gallery that bears his name so that it became an extension of his chamber.[44] Below it was a suite of rooms: some were baths, others were used to display part of his art collection. Staircases were of different kinds. The gigantic double-spiral staircase at Chambord, providing access to all three floors and also to the terraced roof, was unique, as was the short-lived monumental staircase that Francis I set up in the Cour Ovale at Fontainebleau.

Under Henry II the king's lodging acquired an additional room in the form of the *antichambre*, a relatively small room sandwiched between the *salle* and the *chambre*. The idea was not new, but there were no antechambers in royal châteaux until 1547. Thereafter they caught on rapidly: we find them in five royal châteaux (the Louvre, Fontainebleau, Saint-Léger, Amboise and the Château-Neuf at Saint-Germain-en-Laye) and in three owned by royal favourites (Anet, Beynes and Vallery). The earliest court regulation in which the antechamber's function is defined dates from the reign of Henry III. It was the room where courtiers waited to see the king and where he normally dined. The reason for this development is easily guessed. Under Francis I the *salle* was accessible to everyone, save lackeys and the Swiss guard. Noblemen had to rub shoulders with social inferiors. The antechamber served as a filter: an usher effected a selection at the door. Courtiers were thus able to wait among their own kind before being invited to meet the king in his chamber or until he emerged on his way to mass. Henry III also chose to eat in the antechamber. As Richard Cook wrote in 1585:

> The place where He dynneth is allwaies for the most his antechamber . . ..
> The King beinge sett at his table & whilest he is at dynner it is permitted
> & lawfull for all men to enter into the antechamber, to see him dyne & to
> heare him talk & devise amongst his nobylitie.[45]

The appearance of the antechamber in French royal châteaux marked the beginning of an architectural revolution with serious implications for the life of the court: by increasing the distance between the king and his courtiers, it ran counter to the age-old tradition of 'familiarity' that had characterised the French court, and brought it into closer alignment with English and Spanish usage; secondly, it created a hierarchy among the nobles between those who could enter the chamber directly, those who had to wait in the antechamber before entering it, and those sentenced to remain in the *salle*. These developments only came into their own in the second half of the century.[46]

CHAPTER 6

Outdoor Pursuits

Hunting

When Antonio de Beatis visited the château of Blois in 1517, he reached the garden through a passage that he describes as

> adorned on every side with real stag's antlers set on miniature stags carved from wood and coloured quite realistically. However, they are built into the wall at a height of about ten spans, one opposite the other, with only the neck, breast and forelegs showing. There are also many wooden dogs – hounds and greyhounds – set in facing pairs on projecting stones, which are lifelike not only in size and form but also in their coats, and some falcons set in similar fashion on hands which are also built into the wall, dogs and falcons having been favourites of King Louis. There is also an imitation reindeer with real antlers which extend their branches each over a hand wide, the rest of the animal has all the features of a stag, except that it is longer and has a great beard under its muzzle. In the garden, to the left of the entrance, is an imitation of a hind with a great pair of horns that came from a real hind, which according to the inscription was killed by the Marquis de Bau and given by him to the Duke of Lorraine, who in turn presented them to King Louis.[1]

Hunting loomed large in the day-to-day life of the French court in the sixteenth century. Much of its socialising was built up around the sport. Sir Anthony Browne, who witnessed a royal hunt near Amiens in August 1527, wrote:

> The king's bed is always carried with him, when he hunts, and anon, after that the deer is killed, he repairs to some house near at hand, where the same is set up, and there reposes himself three or four hours, and against

his return there is provided for him a supper by some nobleman, as by Monsr. de Vendôme, Monsr. de Guise or other; whereupon a great number of ladies and gentlewomen used to be in his company be sent for, and there he passes his time until ten or eleven o'clock.[2]

Italian ambassadors were astonished by Francis I's willingness to subordinate politics to hunting and to allow it to dictate his court's movements.

Hunting was seen as the perfect antidote to idleness. Man's senses were kept in tune by studying the ways of wild animals and outwitting them; it enabled him to maintain a range of mental and physical skills that he might soon require in war.[3] Hunting was mainly of two kinds: with hounds (*vénerie*) or with birds of prey (*fauconnerie*), both being represented in the court's organisation. Each monarch had his preference: Guillaume Tardif wrote a treatise on falconry for Charles VIII, who spent more than 20,000 *l.* on the sport. Louis XII favoured it, but also rode to hounds. In August 1500 Machiavelli was unable to deliver his credentials to the king because the latter had injured his shoulder after being thrown by his horse.[4] Francis I was addicted to riding to hounds. A contemporary miniature shows him chasing a stag, surrounded by his pack of hounds and accompanied by his favourite huntsman, Perrot (plate 5).[5] The king continued to hunt even in old age: when he could no longer ride, he hunted from a litter and thought of using a chariot given to him by the duke of Mantua. He told a Venetian ambassador that he hoped to continue hunting from his coffin.

Traditionally, the hunting season was divided into two parts: one for *fauconnerie*, the other for *vénerie*. According to Florange,

> The *veneurs* and *fauconniers* treated each other oddly. When May arrived and the birds are cooped up, the *veneurs*, wearing green and carrying their horns and green staves (*gaules*), drove the *fauconniers* from the court, for it was the stag-hunting season; but at the start of winter, the *Grand fauconnier* came to court and expelled the *veneurs*, who had to put their dogs into kennels, as the stags were no longer worth hunting.[6]

Francis I changed all that: he hunted stag all the year round and, for this reason, was given the title of *père des veneurs* ('father of huntsmen') by Jacques du Fouilloux in a treatise published in 1561. As a result, the stag population was soon so depleted that younger deer had to be hunted.

Whereas Louis XII had had about fifty hunting dogs cared for by six valets, Francis greatly increased their number. He allegedly knew every dog by its coat and name (*de poil et de nom*). Many, of various breeds, had been given to him. Some were bred at an abbey in the Ardennes dedicated to

St Hubert, who was said to cure victims of rabies.[7] Kennels built by Francis at Fontainebleau contained between ten and twelve pens, each with a small lodge for a *valet des chiens*. The other royal châteaux did not have such buildings; here the dogs were presumably given temporary quarters. The *vénerie* was under the control of the *Grand veneur*, one of the great officers of the crown. When Louis de Vendôme died in 1526, his office passed to Claude de Lorraine, first duc de Guise, who was paid 12,000 *l.* in wages in addition to sums for feeding the dogs and for the upkeep of the valets. The *Grand veneur* handed to the king the *estortoire*, a stick used by a mounted huntsman to part low-hanging branches, and a *houssine* (switch) for restraining dogs during the quarry. Hunts were organised by the *lieutenant de la vénerie*, an office held by Perrot de Ruthie, whose staff wore a special tunic with pleated skirts reaching down to the knees: green for stag-hunting, grey for boar-hunting. The king wore a felt garment.[8] The English ambassador Sir William Fitwilliam often talked of hunting with him. In 1521 Fitzwilliam reported to Henry VIII: 'I assure Your Grace they know their deer right well, as well by his view, feeding and feumyshing, as also by such other tokens as a woodman should have.' Francis promised to send Henry some wild boar each year. He advised him to empark them in the thickest ground he could find and leave them there to breed.[9] Francis spent lavishly on acquiring and enclosing new hunting grounds, opening up bridlepaths, and on all the gamekeepers, foresters and other staff who supervised the royal hunts. Many of the châteaux he built were hunting pavilions, some specifically designed as belvederes from which to view the sport. La Muette, for example, was built near a marsh, 'where the red deer (*les bestes rousses*) retire exhausted from the labours of the chase . . . in order [that I might] have the pleasure of seeing their end (*leur fin*)'.[10]

Since the fourteenth century the crown had tried to restrict the number of people entitled to hunt; by the early sixteenth century the privilege was restricted to the king and nobility. Francis I went a stage further by conceding the right only to fiefholders. In Languedoc he tried to revoke a custom allowing the province's commoners to hunt. 'We forbid', he declared, 'all persons of whatever estate, quality or condition to hunt in our forests, bushes and warrens or to capture red and black animals, hares, rabbits, herons, pheasants, partridges and other game by means of dogs, crossbows, bows, nets, ropes, collars, tunnels and nooses.' Severe penalties were laid down for poaching on royal land, recidivists being threatened with death. Steps were also taken to extend the royal hunting grounds at the expense of neighbouring properties. Francis set up the first *capitaineries*, areas where he alone could hunt. Each was placed under a captain, who judged offenders against the hunting laws and ensured the king a sufficient supply of game.[11]

The royal library contained several hunting books, the most famous being the *Livre des chasses*, written by Gaston Phébus in the fourteenth century.[12] Francis I carried a copy even on the battlefield at Pavia. Phébus divided the animal world into two kinds of beasts: 'ignoble' and 'noble'. 'Ignoble animals', such as the wolf or wild boar – the so-called *bêtes noires* – were traditionally linked to Satan, whereas 'noble animals', like red deer (*bêtes rousses*), were associated with Christ. The former could be taken by ruse, whereas the latter had to be treated with 'nobility and kindness'. The end result for both kinds of animal was much the same, however. A contemporary miniature shows Francis standing sword in hand in front of a stag at bay (*forcé à courre*). 'He [Francis] is very fond of the chase,' wrote de Beatis, 'especially of hunting stag with a spear.'[13] Used as a royal emblem from Charles VI to Louis XII, the stag was highly regarded on account of its supposed longevity, virility and handsome crown of antlers. The rut was seen as a kind of tournament. Certain forms of hunting, such as shooting animals from afar with crossbows or arquebuses, were regarded as below the dignity of French monarchs, yet they felt no compunction about driving wild animals into nets. Henri de Ferrière in his *Livre du roi Modus et de la reine Ratio*, written between 1354 and 1376, regarded this as the royal sport par excellence. It was undertaken by a special department called the *vénerie des toiles*, under a captain (*capitaine des toiles*). The office, created by Louis XII, was held under Francis I by Jean d'Annebault. His staff of one hundred archers set up the nets and to this end disposed of some fifty waggons, each pulled by six horses. They also had about fifty dogs that were given protective coats or *jacques*. The *vénerie des toiles* cost 18,000 *l.* per annum. The wild boar was the principal victim of hunting with nets. Hugues Salel, a *valet de chambre ordinaire* of Francis I, wrote an allegorical poem in 1539 called *Discord*, in which Charles V and Francis I, armed with spears, kill a boar. Budé, in his book on hunting, addressed Francis I as follows: 'I have sometimes seen you on horseback assailing a foaming boar and killing it with your sword while I watched from a place of safety.'[14] In April 1520 Sir Richard Wingfield, writing to Henry VIII, described a boar hunt at the French court:

> Soon after three o'clock in the afternoon, he [Francis] went to hunt for the wild boar, and caused me to go with him, which boar was killed after such manner as here follows. When he came to the place in which the boar lay, there was cast off one hound only to him, the which incontinently had him at the bay, and then immediately was thrown off upon a twenty couple of hounds, with three or four brace of mastiffs let slip, all of which drew to the bay, and there plucked down the poor boar, and the king, with divers

others, being afoot, with their boar spears had dispatched him shortly, and then the king himself, after their fashion, cut off the right foot of the said boar.[15]

Most royal residences had parks attached to them where wild animals were kept. Enclosed by walls or fences, they varied in size. Some were large enough to permit hunting, but most were not. Sometimes the larger animals – deer and boar – were kept separate from the smaller game: hares, rabbits, pheasants and partridges. Francis I created new parks, in addition to those he had inherited. At Saint-Germain-en-Laye he enclosed 416 acres of forest into which he introduced deer and wild boar imported from Fontainebleau. Similar reservations existed at Madrid and Chambord. In 1528 the king had the enclosure of the Petit Parc at Villers-Cotterêts restored. This had a pool and its walls were shaped so as to allow hunting within a narrow space (*chasses rapprochées*).[16]

Not all forms of hunting brought man and beast into direct confrontation. In hawking (*la volerie*) a bird acted as intermediary. For this reason Francis I did not enjoy the sport as much as hunting deer or boar. Wingfield, writing to Henry VIII in April 1520, describes how the king, after a boar hunt,

> mounted on horseback, and passed through the forest to have seen a flight to the heron, at the request of M. de Lautrec, unto which disport I assure Your Grace he has no more affection than Your Highness has. Notwithstanding, the said Seigneur de Lautrec, with divers others, do what they can possible to fashion one appetite to be in him, which shall be hard for them to bring about, after my conceit.[17]

The appetite, it seems, was fashioned by 1539, when the bishop of Saluzzo reported from the French court:

> Here one thinks only of hunting. When one comes across one of these lodgings one stays as long as there are herons and kites in the area. Numerous as they are, they do not last long as the king and the great courtiers have more than five hundred falcons between them.[18]

Budé, in his book on hunting, put the following words into Francis's mouth:

> I look upon the flight of birds simply as recreation. *Vénerie* has given me more pleasure hitherto because it exercises the body, yet I have followed and practised falconry with diligence, and now by way of recreation I willingly watch birds of prey as they fly over fields and marshes.[19]

Birds of prey were expensive, as they had to be imported from distant lands. Francis paid 112 *l.* – an exceptional sum – for a 'bastard sakeret of strange and handsome plumage'. A saker normally cost 33.75 *l.*, a falcon 23 *l.* and a sakeret 17 *l.* Birds were also often sent as diplomatic gifts. The royal accounts show that nearly 6,000 *l.* were spent on feeding the birds in 1538 and 8,000 *l.* in the following year. They also had to be trained and fitted with hoods and small bells. Isabella d'Este sent three dozen such bells and hoods bearing the royal arms to Louis XII. His aviary was administered by the *Grand fauconnier*, who was paid 12,000 *l.* per annum and had the right to hawk wherever he wished. In 1521 the office was held by René de Cossé, in whose family it remained for the rest of the century. He had a staff of fifty noblemen and as many assistants, who between them had about three hundred birds. Their main victim was the heron, whose breeding was encouraged by the establishment of heronries – nesting places situated alongside streams and pools – in the parks of châteaux. There were some at Chambord and Fontainebleau. Hunting the heron provided a spectacle animated by the bird's size and pugnacity; it did not benefit the king's table, however, for heron meat is not palatable.[20]

The leopard, another hunting auxiliary, seems to have been imported from Italy, where several princely courts had used it to hunt hares, wolves and roe deer since the fifteenth century. Louis XII returned from Milan with leopards given to him by Ludovico Sforza. He used them at Amboise, but their employment was not risk-free, as a leopard is never completely tamed. The royal library at Blois contained at least one book of advice on the subject, called the *Livre de la chasse des Lyons*.[21] Francis I kept various large cats, called 'onces' or 'lions'. One was a lynx, which evidently posed problems. In August 1527 it was left at an inn in the faubourg Saint-Honoré. The innkeeper's wife was paid 67 *l.* by the king for feeding the animal – and to care for her husband who had suffered a nasty leg bite.[22]

In 1551 Henry II staged a hunt at Fontainebleau for the benefit of German guests. The sieur de Marconnet, *lieutenant de la vénerie*, released a stag across their path as they were about to leave the forest. The stag fled for cover across a clearing, only to find its way barred by a brace of hounds which soon brought it down. About a hundred *picqueurs* (huntsmen) announced the stag's death by blowing their horns. This form of hunting, the ambassadors said, was unknown in their country; they were accustomed to arquebuses and crossbows being used in addition to dogs.[23] Denis Lambin, the cardinal of Tournon's secretary, described Henry II following a hunt in the forest of Écouen. In a gallery leading to the king's chamber, Tournon met the Constable of Montmorency, as he walked behind a huntsman carrying a huge pair of antlers. 'See', he exclaimed, 'how the king treats my forests and how superbly I entertain him. This is the third stag he has killed today.'[24]

Charles IX, too, was a keen huntsman. 'He was so mad about this painful exercise,' wrote Papyre Masson, 'that he forgot to drink, eat and even sleep.' Fouilloux dedicated his treatise on hunting (1561) to the young king, as did Clamorgan, author of *La chasse au loup*. Charles IX himself wrote a book on hunting and commissioned a French translation of Budé's treatise on the subject.[25]

Ball Games

The seigneur de Florange, who spent part of his youth with Francis I at Amboise, described some of their games in his memoirs. One, called *l'escaigne*, involved hitting a large inflated ball with a bat shaped like a stool with legs filled with lead; another consisted of hitting a ball 'as large as a barrel and filled with air' with a piece of tin, lined with felt and strapped to the forearm. The *jeu de paume* – the ancestor of modern tennis – was very popular in sixteenth-century France. The ball, called an *esteuf*, was about twice the size of a modern tennis ball and much harder, being made of leather filled with dogs' hair. It was originally hit with the hand or with a padded glove, but

9. Game of jeu de paume or tennis and a game of chess. Fifteenth-century French minia-ture from Valerius Maximus, *Faits et dits mémorables* (British Library, 4375, fo. 151 verso).

rackets had come into use by the sixteenth century. Games were played in an open space or a specially equipped court. This, in a château, was usually a rectangular hall surrounded on three sides by a spectators' gallery with a sloping roof. At the far end of the hall was a high wall, painted black. The court was normally covered, daylight entering through large open windows situated directly under the roof. The floor was covered with stone slabs, each one foot square.

Every royal château had at least one tennis court; the Louvre had two. On 23 October 1529 Sir Nicholas Carew and Dr Richard Sampson stopped in Paris on their way to Italy. After giving them dinner at the Louvre, Francis I went on his mule to a tennis court in the rue du Temple, where he, the cardinal de Lorraine and the Grand Master played against the king of Navarre and two other gentlemen.[26] Henry II was also a keen tennis player. On 12 November 1551 a Venetian watched him play. 'After dinner,' he wrote,

> the king returned to the Louvre, and to his game of ball and racket. He began to play with My Lord of Guise and other noblemen. He was dressed all in white, had white shoes and wore a straw hat but of the finest kind. He played in his doublet. He is tall, perhaps a trifle stout, but on the whole well proportioned. When one sees him thus at play one would never imagine that he is the king, for he cares neither for ceremony nor etiquette, except that the rope is lifted up for him to pass underneath and that only one ball is used per racket; otherwise no one would know that the king is playing. Even errors are discussed, and I have seen him being faulted several times. Anyone wishing to watch him may do so. That day, I do not know how, a ball missed by Monsieur de Guise struck him in the face, splitting his lip. The said Monsieur de Guise hastily withdrew to his chambers and His Majesty stopped the match. The blow was not at all serious.

The king never played at *paume* from the first line; always from the second or third, which, according to Brantôme, were 'the two most difficult and dangerous places'. Henry bet on the result of a game, as did his courtiers. If he won, he gave his winnings to his team; if he lost, he paid his bet and those of all his team. Bets could be as high as 200 or 300 *écus*.[27]

Mock Battles and Tournaments

Even allowing for split lips, tennis was among the court's less violent sports. Mock sieges were very different. At Amboise in April 1518 six hundred men, led by the king and the duc d'Alençon, defended a model town, complete with moat and gun battery, against an equal number of men, led by the dukes of Bourbon and Vendôme. 'It was the finest battle ever seen,' wrote Florange, 'and the nearest to real warfare, but the entertainment did not please everyone, for some were killed and others scared.'[28] At Marseille, in January 1516 Francis took part in a battle of oranges laid on for his benefit. A local chronicler wrote: 'This prince, who had so much ardour for real combats, wanted also to be a party to this one; having seized a large shield, he began to shoot and scored many fine hits, having received a few himself to his head and body.'[29]

On the feast of Epiphany in 1521 Francis I was almost killed during a mock siege at Romorantin. About 3 p.m. the sénéchal of Normandy, who had just been elected King of the Bean, led a party, including Francis and gentlemen of his chamber, to attack the lodging of the comte de Saint-Pol. Apprised of their approach, the count and his servants fastened the doors and took up defensive positions at upstairs windows. Both sides then bombarded each other with oranges, eggs, stones and whatever else was at hand. As the defenders ran out of ammunition, one of them seized a burning log and threw it out of a window. It fell on a buckler the king was holding up, but bounced off, hitting his head. Francis suffered a gash 'almost four fingers long', and skin had to be removed from his scalp to minimise the risk of infection. It took him more than two months to recover.[30] His head had to be shaved, and this upset his vanity. Afraid of looking ridiculous, he ordered all the men at his court to be shaved likewise, much to the alarm of the Mantuan ambassador:

> *Mignons*, gentlemen of the chamber, princes and officials were taken to him [Francis] by force and only set free once they had been shaven. It is said that ambassadors are also to be shaved, so much so that I would like my embassy to end in order to be spared the fate of other ambassadors.[31]

Tournaments were staged to entertain distinguished visitors or to celebrate an event such as a royal marriage. An elaborate one took place at the Field of Cloth of Gold in 1520 and another for Emperor Charles V's visit to Paris in 1540.[32] Henry II often practised jousting with one of his courtiers. He would wear only a half-suit of armour, leaving his lower limbs unprotected; the central barrier or tilt kept the horses apart. In addition to jousting at the barrier, other forms of combat were practised, such as tilting at the ring or at the quintain, which involved detaching rings or toppling emblems or figures disposed around the tournament field. Valets stood in the counter-lists ready to assist a jouster in difficulties or to round up a riderless horse. Spectators watched from a safe distance, sitting in tribunes or standing at the windows of an adjacent château. Tournaments tried to re-create some episode from a tale of chivalry such as the arrival at court of strange knights intent on redressing an alleged offence, usually the slighting of a lady. As proof of her surpassing beauty and virtue, they offered to fight as a group or individually.

Tournaments were held in June 1549 to celebrate Henry II's accession and entry into Paris, in February 1554 for the wedding of René de Lorraine, marquis d'Elbeuf, with Louise de Rieux, and in February 1559 for the double wedding of Philibert de Marcilly, seigneur de Cypierre, with Louise de Piennes, and of M. de Barbazan with Charlotte d'Humières. A fortnight before this event a notice announced that a group of knights would fight with pike or sword anyone who so wished, in or out of the lists. The challenge, written in verse by the poet Mellin de Saint-Gelais, bore the signatures of

10. A tilt and counter-lists (Bibliothèque nationale de France, ms. fr. 20,360, fo. 138).

knights in Ariosto's *Orlando furioso*. On the day, devices, emblems and banners in the colours of the defendants adorned the lists. The four marshals of the field, acting as judges, took up their places in the counter-lists along with valets and pages. Gorgeously attired ladies filled the tribunes that were hung with rich tapestries. Trumpets sounded, then heralds proclaimed the rules of combat, whereupon the rival champions entered the lists, each wearing a richly embossed suit of armour and a plumed helmet. The caparisons of the horses and the pennons of the lances bore their respective colours. They fought each other using several weapons in turn: a lance, a heavy rebated sword, a battle-axe and a pike. A camp master stood by ready to separate them if they became violent; but a joust was meant to be ruled by courtesy.

Animals were often cruelly abused to entertain courtiers. Francis I was proud of his physical strength and from an early age liked to take on a savage beast single-handed. When he was about ten years old and staying at Plessis-lès-Tours, Louis XII ordered animals 'to be caught in the forest of Chinon and elsewhere and brought to the park to entertain (*desennuy*) his young nephew'.[33] Francis once pitted his strength against a boar. The marriage of Antoine duc de Lorraine to Renée of Bourbon on 28 June 1515 drew a crowd of lords and ladies to Amboise. For their amusement Francis ordered his huntsmen to capture a wild boar in the neighbouring forest. After trapping the animal, they put it inside a strong chest and placed it behind branches and leaves in the courtyard of the château. Francis wanted to pit his strength against the boar in single combat, but was dissuaded by his queen and mother. So the boar was left to fight dummies hanging from ropes stretched across the courtyard. Spectators gathered in a gallery that was reached from the courtyard by four separate spiral staircases, the entrances having been blocked by heavy chests and other objects. There were loud cheers as the boar charged the dummies, tossed them into the air and tore them to pieces, but the cheers turned to screams of panic as the victorious animal then forced its way up one of the staircases. Some of the spectators climbed on to a balustrade, others thought of jumping into the courtyard, but Francis, bold as ever, faced the boar sword in hand. As it charged, he stepped aside as nimbly as a skilled matador, transfixing the animal with his sword. Fatally wounded, the boar crashed down a staircase to expire in the courtyard.[34]

Later in the century the court became a venue for sadistic spectacles in which different species of animals were made to fight each other. François de Scépeaux, the future Marshal de Vieilleville, during a visit to England, witnessed a fight between mastiffs and bulls. He had never seen the like and was so impressed that he introduced this new type of combat to France after acquiring a large number of mastiffs and a battle-hardened bull.[35] Henry II became an enthusiast, as did his courtiers, who took to collecting mastiffs.

Bulls were brought to court from Provence. In June 1550 Costanze Preti, writing to the duke of Mantua from Saint-Germain-en-Laye, described a fight between two lions, four bears and two leopards laid on for the king of Navarre. 'It was', he wrote, 'the finest entertainment in the world.' Charles IX also enjoyed animal fights. He arranged for the royal menagerie at Vincennes to be provided with an arena surrounded by galleries so that courtiers might watch them.[36] Animal fights flourished at court until the 1560s, when the civil wars appear to have dampened enthusiasm for such bloodshed.

Duels

Tournaments and duels were condemned by the church. Their purposes, however, were different: a tournament was essentially a game whereas a duel had a serious judicial function. The Italian jurist Alciati, writing in 1550, described the latter as 'a combat in which God is the judge'. If a tournament was a show of bravery, a duel was an affirmation of honour. There were few duels at the French court in the early sixteenth century, but two were sensational. On 17 February 1538 the sieur de Sarzay and the sieur de Véniers fought one at Moulins. The former had accused the sieur de La Tour Landry of cowardice at the Battle of Pavia. On being asked for his source of information, Sarzay named Véniers, who hotly denied the charge. To accuse a man of lying was to impugn his honour. Montaigne called it 'the ultimate verbal insult'.[37] The offence could only be expunged by single combat. The injured party, or *défendeur*, was legally entitled to issue a challenge, but instead of throwing down a gauntlet as in the past, he now did so verbally or in a written document, called a *cartel*. A duel could only be fought with the king's permission; if granted, he also fixed the time and place of the duel and appointed the witnesses.

The duel between Sarzay and Véniers was allowed by Francis I, who also chose Moulins as the venue. The combatants, however, were left to choose their own weapons and equipment. Véniers decided to wear a corselet with sleeves of mail and gauntlets; he also chose to fight the first round of the duel with a sword in each hand, and the second with a sword in one hand and a dagger in the other. Duels were sometimes fought on foot, but more often on horseback. The entry of the champions into the duelling ground was one of several preliminary steps. The king did nothing except preside, but the constable and marshal of the field supervised preparations.[38] At Moulins, the Constable of Montmorency was flanked by the comte de Nevers, the comte de Saint-Pol and Marshal d'Annebault, each holding a halberd and wearing a suit of velvet trimmed with gold or silver. Around the château's courtyard were tribunes for spectators. Four heralds cried, 'Venez au champ faire votre devoir' (come to the field and do your duty). The first to respond was Sarzay who stepped forward accompanied by the king's drummers and fifers, his second or *parrain* and a large group of noble kinsmen. Véniers followed, likewise escorted. After declaring their names, the duellists retired to their tents at opposite ends of the courtyard. All demonstrations by spectators were banned. Anyone caught signalling with feet or hands, or speaking, coughing, blowing his nose or spitting, was liable to have a fist cut off. After the combatants had been searched for hidden weapons, relics, charms or talismans, the heralds shouted: 'Laissez aller les vaillants combattans' (let the bold combatants go forward)!' After first wielding their swords, Sarzay and Véniers cast them aside and grappled with each other. As one drew a dagger, Francis I stopped the fight by throwing down a baton. He declared himself satisfied with both combatants and gave them each 500 *écus*. He then testified that La Tour Landry had not been a coward at Pavia. Véniers, however, was bleeding profusely and died soon afterwards.[39]

The second duel – the most famous in French history – was fought in the presence of Henry II and his court on 10 July 1547 at Saint-Germain-en-Laye between two young noblemen: François de Vivonne, seigneur de La Châtaigneraye, and Guy Chabot, seigneur de Montlieu, eldest son of Charles baron de Jarnac.[40] Their quarrel had begun during the reign of Francis I. Both had powerful connexions at court. La Châtaigneraye was a close friend of the Dauphin Henri, and Diane de Poitiers; Jarnac (the name by which Chabot is remembered) was the brother-in-law of the duchesse d'Étampes. La Châtaigneraye was ten years older and a distinguished soldier, having fought valiantly at Ceresole. Their quarrel sprang from a rumour emanating from the dauphin's circle concerning Jarnac's extravagant lifestyle. It was said that he was receiving money from Madame d'Étampes and there was talk of incest. Jarnac felt bound to defend his honour, but could not easily challenge the heir to the throne. His dilemma was solved when La Châtaigneraye volunteered to take on the challenge. Francis I, however, would not allow the duel.

One of Henry II's first acts on gaining the throne was to reverse his father's decision. He assumed that La Châtaigneraye would win and may have seen the duel as a kind of ritual purging of the old order. His court began to take sides: while the Guises supported La Châtaigneraye, Montmorency and the Bourbons backed Jarnac. A huge crowd of nobles and commoners flocked to Saint-Germain to watch the fight. The odds favoured La Châtaigneraye, who was the more experienced fighter, and his confidence was such that he planned a victory banquet. Jarnac, for his part, tried to delay the duel while he took fencing lessons. When asked to choose his weapons, he chose some that were expensive and difficult to find. The outcome of the duel, therefore, came as a complete surprise. Jarnac struck a fatal blow with his sword at the back of his opponent's leg (hence the French phrase *le coup de Jarnac* meaning an unexpected mishap). Unable to believe his eyes, Jarnac appealed to the king to stop the fight, but Henry did nothing, leaving La Châtaigneraye to bleed to death. It was already too late when Henry threw down his baton. He was much criticised for this. 'The king', wrote Monluc in his *Commentaires*, 'should stop the mouths of ladies who tittle-tattle at court . . . a chatterbox caused the death of M. de La Châtaigneraye . . . the king should order them to mind their own business.'[41] More serious was the charge that Henry had not been impartial. He had certainly miscalculated by leaving the final decision to God, instead of asserting his own authority. The historian Jules Michelet described the *coup de Jarnac* as a 'defeat for the monarchy'.[42] Having begun his reign with a bloody duel, Henry ended it with a tournament in which he himself fell.[43]

The court, then, was by no means the victim of routine. Despite the somewhat rigid timetable prescribed by Catherine de' Medici in her famous letter to Henry III, the king and his courtiers in the first half of the century found plenty of time for exercise in the open air. Hunting dominated much of their lives, providing them with an excitement akin to war. It tested their mettle, while mock battles and tournaments enabled them to identify with the knights of medieval romance. Nor was this all; the court was frequently called upon to display its authority through magnificence in a frequent round of festivals.

CHAPTER 7

Ceremonies

Two kinds of festival took place at the French court in the sixteenth century: ceremonies and spectacles. Ceremonies created power structures. The coronation, for example, created the monarch, who gained his authority through anointing, taking of the oath, and investiture with the insignia of royalty: the orb and sceptre. The solemn entry of a monarch into a town was another ceremony that embodied a legal contract between him and his subjects. He was formally greeted outside the entrance to the town and presented with its keys, which he then returned. The ruler and the town thus entered into a relationship of mutual obligation. Royal baptisms, marriages and funerals were also ceremonies as they ensured the dynastic succession in different ways. Ceremonies needed to be witnessed by the people in order to be legally binding. They had a theatrical dimension, but were also constitutionally significant. Spectacles were different: they could be banquets, balls, ballets, tournaments or jousts in which courtiers were actors and audience. Some of these have been described above. Here we are only concerned with ceremonies.[1]

The Coronation or *Sacre*

By the sixteenth century the coronation, or *sacre*, at Reims was no longer considered essential to the exercise of kingship: the king succeeded to the throne from the instant his predecessor died. The *sacre*, however, remained important as the symbol of divine election and of the close alliance between church and state. An essential feature of the French mythology of kingship was the Holy Ampulla. According to Hincmar, a ninth-century archbishop of Reims, a dove brought down from heaven a vessel or ampulla containing a sacred chrism just as Saint Remi was about to baptise the Frankish king Clovis in 496. The chrism, whereby God demonstrated his special regard for France, continued to be used until the end of the monarchy. Between coronations the

Holy Ampulla was kept at the abbey of Saint-Remi in Reims, where, allegedly, it was miraculously replenished in preparation for its next use.

Henry II's coronation on 26 July 1547 may serve as an example of the sixteenth-century ceremony, which was governed by regulations laid down in the *Ordo* of King Charles V of 1365.[2] The king and his court arrived at Reims on 25 July and entered the city accompanied by all the customary pageantry. The temporary monuments included a huge pyramid outside the archbishop's palace, topped by a golden sphere and a silver crescent. The pyramid was encircled by a scroll bearing the archbishop's motto, *Crescam et testante, virebo* ('I will grow and in the eyes of all cover myself with foliage'). That afternoon, Henry was greeted at the west door of the cathedral by the archbishop, Charles de Lorraine, and other prelates. Before entering, Henry, flanked by the bishops of Langres and Beauvais, knelt in prayer on a red carpet. At the high altar he made the traditional offering: a magnificent gilt reliquary of the Resurrection. Henry then retired to the archbishop's palace to rest and sup. He returned to the cathedral later to pray and make his confession.

The *sacre* took place the following day. The choir of the cathedral was adorned with tapestries and its floor covered with a red carpet. Two thrones – one for the king, the other for the archbishop – faced each other in the

11. *The Oath and Anointing at the King's Coronation.* Drawing (Musée du Louvre, Paris).

choir, both covered in cloth of gold. The ritual began when the grand prior of Saint-Remi brought the Holy Ampulla to the cathedral and received an assurance of its safe return in the form of hostages. Twelve peers, six ecclesiastical and six lay, now took their places in the choir. Two bishops then went to the archbishop's palace to fetch the king whom they found lying on a bed – this seems to have been a relic of the medieval ceremony of initiation into knighthood. Charles VIII underwent a night vigil before his coronation in 1484. After hearing vespers, he returned to church to pray before returning to the archbishop's palace. Here he rested overnight until he was fetched by two bishops. They found him 'seated or leaning on one elbow, and half-lying on a daybed'. In 1561 Charles IX was fetched, not just by two bishops, but by all twelve peers. As they came to his chamber door, they called out: 'Where is our king, whom God has given us to rule and govern us?' 'He is within,' replied the acting Great chamberlain. 'What is he doing?' asked the peers. 'He is resting', came the response. 'Awaken him,' replied the peers, 'in order that we may salute him and do reverence to him.' The door was then opened and the king found to be awake.

When Henry II was fetched by the bishops of Langres and Beauvais in 1547, he was wearing a linen shirt slit in two places to allow his chest and back to be anointed. After receiving a silk surplice with similar splits, he was escorted to the cathedral, where the nobility had gathered. The king advanced up the nave, then sat on his throne, flanked by the peers, whereupon the archbishop received the Holy Ampulla at the cathedral porch. The next step was the king's oath. This fell into two parts: the ecclesiastical oath and the oath of the kingdom. In the first, Henry promised to uphold the privileges of the church and to defend it; in the second, he promised to promote the peace of Christendom, to protect Christians against injury and injustice, to dispense justice fairly and mercifully, and to extirpate heresy from his kingdom. This was followed by the anointing. The archbishop extracted the sacred balm from the Holy Ampulla with a gold needle and mixed it with a chrism. Then, thrusting his hand through the specially contrived openings in the king's tunic and shirt, he touched his body nine times with the sacred mixture, thereby conferring on him a semi-priestly character. Although the king was not allowed to celebrate mass, he could henceforth take communion in both kinds.

Henry then put on the royal mantle, or *soccus*, which according to a medieval treatise signified the king's rejection of the 'worldly estate' in favour of the 'royal religion'. The archbishop also slipped a ring on a finger of the king's right hand, and handed him the royal insignia: the sword, sceptre and hand of justice. Henry placed the sword, symbolising military authority, on the high altar before handing it to the constable, who held it upright for the rest of the ceremony. The scene was now set for the coronation proper. This began with the king praying in silence. The peers then gathered round him and helped the archbishop place the heavy 'crown of Charlemagne' upon his head. They did so by stretching out their hands as if to hold up the crown. The peers then escorted Henry to a throne on a platform elevated above the screen. The archbishop removed his mitre, made a low bow, embraced the king and cried out three times: 'Vivat rex in aeternum!', an acclamation taken up by the peers. A fanfare on silver trumpets sounded and the entire congregation shouted: 'Vive le roi!' Heralds threw a shower of gold and silver medals among the congregation. This was followed by the singing of the *Te Deum* and by high mass during which Orazio Farnese offered wine in a large gold vase and the duc d'Étampes presented a large silver loaf. The king's crown was now replaced by a smaller one and his robes were removed. He then returned in procession to the archbishop's palace for a banquet.[3]

Although women were debarred from the French throne by the Salic law, the queen was also crowned, but always after the king's coronation and at the abbey of Saint-Denis instead of in Reims. Her coronation was thus clearly differentiated from her husband's. The two ceremonies also differed in other respects. The queen did not take the oath, nor did she receive the insignia of chivalry or wear the three vestments symbolising membership of the church hierarchy. Her anointing was done with a sacred oil, not the chrism from the Holy Ampulla, and she was anointed only twice, on the head and breast, instead of nine times. Claude de France, for some reason, was anointed three times. The queen, like her husband, received a ring, sceptre (smaller than his and differently shaped) and hand of justice. Her crown was not with the so-called 'crown of Charlemagne' but the 'crown of Jeanne d'Évreux', and her crowning was assisted by barons and princes, not the peers of France. Anne of Brittany was given the 'crown of St Louis'. The mass was similar to the king's: the queen made an offering, received the kiss of peace and took communion in both kinds (see plate 2).

Kings were crowned as soon as possible after their accession; not so the queen, who often had to wait a long time. Some queens were never crowned at all: neither Mary Stuart nor Louise de Lorraine was crowned. Whereas the king's coronation followed a set pattern with only minor variations, the queen's was subject to greater improvisation. The officiating prelate varied: Claude de France was crowned by the cardinal of Le Mans, Eleanor of Austria by the cardinal de Bourbon, and Elizabeth of Austria by the cardinal of Lorraine.

Whereas the king owed the crown to his accession, the queen owed hers to her marriage. She was doubly subservient: to her husband by her marriage, and to the state by her coronation. The size and shape of her sceptre were not accidental. Whereas the king's sceptre symbolised his exercise of divine authority, the queen's lacked that authority. Yet her *sacre* did elevate her to a position halfway between the king and his subjects. The fact that she took communion in both kinds demonstrated that she alone shared in the sacredness of monarchy, though not in its authority. It was precisely because her position was unique that its limitations needed definition. The *sacre* effectively ritualised the Salic law.[4]

The King's Touch

From Reims the king went to the shrine of Saint-Marcoul at the priory of Corbeny in the Aisne Valley. This pilgrimage was connected with his thaumaturgical power: that is to say, his miraculous power of healing the sick (see plate 14). It was in the early Middle Ages that the king of France was first credited with this power; the only other Christian monarch who claimed it was the king of England. In time it became restricted to curing scrofula, a disease more disgusting than serious and subject to periods of remission. Originally it was assumed that the king owed his power to his anointing, but in about the twelfth century an obscure Norman saint called Saint Marcoul acquired a posthumous reputation for curing scrofula. By the late Middle Ages it had become customary for the king to visit the saint's shrine after his coronation as if to boost his own thaumaturgical power. This soon led to the idea that he owed his power to Saint Marcoul, not to his anointing. The queen could not heal the sick, for she had not been anointed with the sacred chrism.

The pilgrimage to Corbeny was carefully regulated. The monks went in procession to meet the king, who received the saint's skull from the prior and carried it to the church. After praying before the shrine, he retired to a lodging at the priory. The next day a number of sick people were formed into groups and examined by the court's doctor, presumably to ensure that they were not infectious. Before touching them, the king took communion in both kinds, as though to underline further the sacredness of his monarchy. He then approached the crowd followed by his almoner. Passing his bare hand over the sores or tumours of the afflicted, he made the sign of the cross over each one, saying, 'The king touches you and God cures you.' Each recipient was given two small silver coins. A sixteenth-century miniature shows Henry II performing the ceremony in full royal regalia, but normally the king was simply dressed.

A careful record was kept of the money distributed on these occasions. They tell us how many people were touched by each king. Louis XII touched 528 between 1 October 1507 and 30 September 1508; Francis I at least 1,326 in 1528, more than 988 in 1529, and no fewer than 1,731 in 1530. Charles IX holds the record: he touched 2,092 in 1569. The ceremony varied in frequency. Louis XI touched every week; Charles VIII less often. Francis I would touch on his travels. Normally a feast day was chosen for the ceremony, though Francis sometimes acted on the spur of the moment. In January 1530 he touched a few people at each stop on his way through Champagne; he was even moved to heal a poor old man standing alone by the roadside. Francis also touched people at Roquefort on 8 July 1530, possibly to impress his new queen, Eleanor. The venue could also vary. On 8 September 1528 it took place at Notre-Dame in Paris where 205 people had gathered in the nave. In August 1527 Cardinal Wolsey watched Francis heal some two hundred sick people in the episcopal palace at Amiens.[5] People flocked from far and near to be cured by the king of France; they included foreigners, who received money to help pay for their homeward journey. Spaniards were not deterred by Franco-Spanish hostility: whenever peace was declared caravans of sick people, led by so-called 'captains', entered France. Kings of France even exercised their miraculous power outside France. On 20 January 1495 Charles VIII touched about five hundred people in Rome. In December 1515 Francis I touched the sick in the papal chapel at Bologna. Even during his Spanish captivity, large crowds in Barcelona and Valencia sought his healing touch.[6]

Royal Entries

Whenever the king visited a town for the first time, he was given a 'joyous entry' (*entrée joyeuse*). Neither royal proclamations nor official tracts could move the hearts of the people as much as a ceremony in which the king appeared in person amid a décor carefully designed to project his idealised personality and the nature of his rule. A coronation was witnessed by relatively few people whereas an entry allowed the monarch to be seen by many people in different places. As it was organised by the townspeople themselves, it also served to identify them with the mystery of kingship. The ceremony was as old as the monarchy itself. From a relatively simple affair in which the townspeople offered the king victuals and sometimes fodder, by the end of the fifteenth century the entry had become a colourful spectacle.[7]

Although it underwent changes over time, the entry's original purpose was never forgotten: it was to honour the king in return for his protection. He was met outside the town by the clergy, town officials and citizens wearing colourful liveries, and escorted in to the sound of public cheering, church bells, trumpeters, drummers and other musicians.[8] The presentation of a gift by the town, in the form of either money or an *objet d'art*, was preceded by an exchange of oaths: the king promised to maintain the town's privileges and the citizens swore to obey him. After receiving the town's keys, the king rode through the streets in procession under a rich canopy, almost certainly a transference to him of the ritual used to honour the Blessed Sacrament on the feast of Corpus Christi.

Over time, it became customary for descriptions of an entry in verse or prose to be printed and published. A large number of such *livrets* or 'festival books' survive. At first they were only interested in the processions, but gradually they gave more attention to the street *apparati* or decorations. The earliest French *livret* dates from the reign of Charles VIII. Early in the sixteenth century illustrations appeared: the earliest illustrated *livret* was a manuscript offered to Mary Tudor, the wife of Louis XII, for her entry into Paris on 6 November 1514.[9] A few months later a similar manuscript was produced for Francis I's entry into Lyon. Printed festival books enabled many people who had not witnessed an event to visualise it, and for that reason they need to be read circumspectly: they may exaggerate the splendour of the occasions. Although a festival book might claim to be a factual record, one should remember that it was commissioned with the purpose of glorifying the monarch or prince for whom the event was being staged.[10] The author may not even have witnessed the entry, and if he did, he may not have been sufficiently well placed to observe all that was happening: etiquette might have prevented this. Maurice Scève, the author of a description of Henry II's entry into Lyon in 1548, changed some of its inscriptions and suppressed other material.[11] This is clear from a comparison of his work with ambassadors' reports of the same event. Some festival books were even printed in advance for distribution at the event being described. Unfortunately, the festival books cannot make us hear the music that accompanied an entry, but we know that it was of many kinds, ranging from the pealing of church bells to polyphony specially composed for the occasion. When Louis XI left Reims for Paris in 1461 he was accompanied by fifty-four trumpeters and, at one point along the route, was entertained by three girls who sang 'little motets and *bergerettes*' (pastoral ditties).[12]

Entertainments for a royal entry took weeks to prepare. Some *tableaux vivants* were religious, others historical. The religious tableaux depicted scenes from the life of Christ. The Passion was performed in Paris in 1494, and the Crucifixion for Louis XII's entry in 1498.[13] At the cemetery of the Innocents, a tableau depicted Herod and the Archangel Gabriel baptising the massacred children in their own blood. For Anne of Brittany's entry in 1504, members of the Confraternity of the Passion performed the mystery of the Transfiguration; the *fripiers* performed the Adoration of the Magi. David and Solomon were chosen as monarchs who could stand comparison with the king of France. At Rouen in 1485 David appeared as an old man surrounded by people symbolising the virtues of the late king, Louis XI. A deputation of ladies and esquires, led by Bathsheba, begged him to crown Solomon, who was given the features of the reigning monarch. The prophet Nathan and the high priest Padoch, holding a picture of the Holy Ampulla, backed the queen's request. Solomon was then shown being crowned by David, as girls representing various French provinces sang joyful ditties.[14]

Secular history also supplied themes exalting the king or the town he was entering. The wolf giving suck to Romulus and Remus was staged at Reims for Charles VIII's coronation in 1484. That same day the baptism and coronation of Clovis were performed at one street corner, and the king healing the sick at another. Other tableaux showed the coronations of Pharamond, legendary founder of the French monarchy, and of Charlemagne. At Rouen in 1485 the victory of the Emperor Constantine over Maxentius was performed to symbolise the king's Christian faith and his hope of victory over the Infidel.[15]

Organisers of entries also found inspiration in contemporary art. They made frequent use of the Tree of Jesse, substituting Charles V or St Louis for Jesse. Portraits of the monarch's ancestors were placed inside the flowers of a giant lily. In Paris in 1498 a lily with seven flowers sprang from the head of King Charles V.[16] Stained glass seems to have inspired an elaborate tableau presented by the citizens of Rouen in 1485. About fifty people took part and a wooden machine enabled the tableau to operate on three levels. At the top God the Father, surrounded by angels, cherubim and seraphim, sat at the centre of a multicoloured circle, his feet resting on a rainbow. The four animals symbolising the Evangelists occupied the corners. Below them was the Lamb of God, emblem of Rouen. Thanks to a clever device, this saluted the king, then climbed up to God, who handed it the book with seven seals. After opening it, the lamb resumed its original place. Around it lamps symbolised the seven gifts of the Spirit and the seven Norman bishoprics. On a second level twenty-four old men played lutes, harps and other instruments, and beneath them were St John and an angel holding the inscription: 'Ascende hunc et ostendam tibi quae oportet fieri cito.'[17]

In the early sixteenth century much of the medieval imagery disappeared from royal entries, but allegory survived. Animals were much used as royal symbols: the porcupine for Louis XII; the ermine for Anne of Brittany; the salamander for Francis I. At Rouen in 1508 a dragon with three heads, representing Milan, Genoa and Rome, emerged from a rock symbolising Italy, only to be slain by the porcupine, which came out of a wood representing France.[18] The porcupine that greeted Louis XII at his first entry into Paris had rolling eyes and moving quills. The king also encountered a winged stag 25 feet tall, also with moving parts.[19] The virtues deemed essential to good government were also represented. At Rouen in 1485 the king, holding the sceptre and crown, was portrayed flanked by Justice and Peace on one side, and Prudence and Temperance on the other, while Peace crouched at his feet. In 1498 Louis XII, flanked by Good Counsel and Justice, was shown trampling Injustice under foot while other figures, representing the Church, the People, Lordship, Power, Unity and Peace, sang his praise. If the king was commonly represented by a lily, the kingdom was often portrayed as a garden or *verger.*

The medieval and ancient worlds combined to shape two legends commonly illustrated in royal entries. The first was the legend of the Nine Heroes, or *preux.* These were chosen from three different periods: Hector, Alexander and Caesar from the classical world; David, Joshua and Judas Maccabeus from the biblical past; and Arthur, Charlemagne and Godefroy de Bouillon from medieval chivalry. The *preux* remained popular in the sixteenth century. In 1532 Francis I was met outside Caen by the nine *preux* followed by Mars in his chariot. The first three *preux* were dressed as Hebrews: Joshua rode an elephant, David a camel and Judas Maccabeus a stag. The three ancient heroes wore Turkish clothes and rode a unicorn (Hector), a griffin (Alexander) and a dromedary (Caesar). The last three Christian paladins, riding horses, wore French clothes. Mars informed Francis that a divine consistory had elected him as the tenth *preu.*[20] Another legend was that of France's Trojan origin. Just as Aeneas was thought to have landed in Italy and founded Alba from which Rome had sprung, so it was claimed that Francus, son of Hector, had fled to the west after the fall of Troy and become the first king of the French. The legend appeared in royal entries. When the Dauphin François entered Caen in 1532, he was acclaimed as

Noble dauphin, Royal géniture
Vray sang troyen plein de perfection.[21]

Ancient mythology influenced theatrical displays as early as 1494. Venus and Cupid figured in a spectacle offered to Charles VIII at Reims. Another tableau recalled the city's legendary foundation by Remus. Hercules figured prominently in many entries. Following Charles VIII's invasion of Italy in 1494, a new element characterised the royal entry in France. This was the 'Roman triumph', a dominant element of Italian entries for some time. Ever since Petrarch had revealed the pomp of ancient Roman ceremonial in his epic poem *Africa,* Italians had been fascinated by the triumph: a procession in which the victor seated in a chariot is escorted by prisoners and the bearers of trophies. Drawing inspiration from the writings of Suetonius, Appian and Plutarch, and from the bas-reliefs on Trajan's Column and other ancient monuments, Italian princes sought to enhance their own authority and renown by reviving the triumphs of antiquity.[22] The Italian Wars introduced the kings of France to the ancient Roman triumph.

On 12 July 1515 Francis joined his army in Lyon. A detailed account of his entry into the city is contained in a manuscript now at Wolfenbüttel.[23] The king and his suite were met outside the town by officials led by the archbishop. After the usual exchange of formalities, the royal party was led to the city. Along the way Francis was invited to watch a nautical display on the River Saône. A large seagoing vessel pulled by a white winged stag was seen approaching. Around the stag's neck was the Bourbon emblem, the 'belt of hope' (*ceinture d'espérance*). A man wearing the duc de Bourbon's colours stood on the stag, holding a flaming sword in one hand and an antler in the other. In the ship's forecastle a tall man, wearing armour but no helmet and holding a battle-axe, impersonated the king. Two ladies, representing Queen Claude and her sister Renée, stood amidships. A second man at the rear controlled the rudder. He wore the colours (yellow and green) of Marshal Gian-Giacomo Trivulzio, leader of the francophile party in Lombardy and governor of Lyon. A cherub in the crow's-nest, using bellows, puffed wind into the ship's sail. From the mast flew a banner showing the arms of France and a large salamander. The display evidently symbolised the king's forthcoming Italian expedition, the cherub promising a fair wind. The prominence given to the Constable of Bourbon is easily explained: he commanded the vanguard and was Lyon's most powerful neighbour. As for Claude and Renée, they provided the chivalrous justification for the forthcoming campaign. Had they not asked Francis to take up their just quarrel with the Moor (Lodovico il Moro), who had usurped the garden of Milan? The stag pulling the ship recalled the legend of King Clovis, to whom a stag had indicated a ford by which he might invade Germany.[24]

Francis I entered Lyon through a temporary triumphal arch erected in front of an old fortified gate. The new structure, made of brightly coloured wood, included a platform supported by pillars. An inscription acclaimed Lyon as a town that had never been ruled by a tyrant. On the platform was an elaborate *tableau vivant*. Two ladies, one representing Lyon, the other Loyalty, stood on each side. Between them, rising out of a grassy mound on which lay a salamander, was a tall lily with three open flowers and two buds. Each flower on the lowest branch contained a lady: Divine Grace and France. The buds stood for hope of a dauphin. Standing in the topmost flower was Francis, crowned and holding a sceptre. Above him, two angels sitting on clouds held a large golden crown. The lily grew in an enclosure – the garden of France – guarded by two armed men, one holding a flaming sword, the other leaning on a halberd.[25]

Within the city, eight tall pillars stood one hundred paces apart. Standing on each one beneath a floral wreath was a pretty girl, richly dressed and covered in jewels. In one hand, she held one letter of the king's name and, in the other, the symbol of one of the virtues making up his name (François): Faith, Reason, Temperance (*Atrampance*), Nobility, Charity, Obedience, Justice and Wisdom (*Sapience*). As Francis passed by, each girl made a speech praising him and the virtue she represented.[26] Outside an inn another tableau was performed on two superimposed platforms. Above sat God the Father on his heavenly throne surrounded by cherubim and seraphim, while angels climbed up and down the platforms. Below was enacted the baptism of Clovis, shown standing in a font half-naked between Saint-Remi and Saint-Vaast. Above Clovis were three toads, the coat of arms traditionally attributed to the pagan kings of France. As Francis arrived, God declared himself satisfied with Clovis and sent down angels bearing gifts: the Holy Ampulla, the *oriflamme*, a banner with three fleurs-de-lys against a blue background and the power to heal scrofula. Clovis was popularly regarded as a saint in whom the Christian virtues and chivalrous heroism were combined. The Lyonnais looked to Francis to follow his example.[27]

It was customary for the king of France to make his entry into Paris as soon as possible after his coronation. The inhabitants, who would gather along the processional route in huge numbers, were not necessarily disciplined. In 1498 the Parlement of Paris was afraid that its deputation would not be able to go from La Chapelle to Paris in good order on account of the crowds. It relieved the pressure by allowing windows along the route to be rented for 10 *l.* Whereas the coronation was a ceremony fixed by tradition, an entry was less rigid: a fair degree of freedom was allowed to the devisers of *tableaux vivants* staged at various points along the route. These were meant to convey not only the joy of the inhabitants, but also their hopes. On his first entry into Paris on 2 July 1498, Louis XII was presented with seven tableaux articulated around three topics: religious (crusade), political (unity, justice and good government) and military (the Italian Wars). While his right to the throne by virtue of his ancestry was recognised, Louis was nevertheless reminded of the virtues that would enhance his right to wear the crown, which were represented at the top of a tall lily springing from the recumbent figure of King Charles V.[28]

Francis I's entry on 15 February 1515 consisted, as usual, of two elements: first a procession of the various corporations, civil and religious, from the city, followed the king and his court; secondly, various *apparati*, such as theatrical sideshows, fountains flowing with wine, or street decorations. No festival book was published for the entry; the only detailed description appeared three years later in a book entitled *La Mer des hystoires*. This deals only with the procession, omitting all mention of the *apparati*, yet payments are known to have been made for a 'mystery' outside the porte Saint-Denis. Was this the only one? Possibly so, for the Parisians may not have been able to stage another entry so soon after Mary Tudor's, yet the chronicle of the *Bourgeois de Paris* describes it as 'the most beautiful entry that was ever seen' and the register of the Bureau de la Ville also praises its magnificence. The processional route had been carefully prepared: its surface covered with sand or rushes, and tapestries hung over the façades of houses lining the route. Ladies wearing gorgeous dresses sat at open windows. On 15 February the mayor (*prévôt des marchands*), aldermen (*échevins*), representatives of the seventeen trade guilds, and members of the Parlement and 'sovereign courts' met the king at La Chapelle Saint-Denis and escorted him back into the capital. First to enter were the *gens de ville*; then came the *gens du roi*, some wearing the late king's badge of the crowned porcupine, others Francis's salamander. They were followed by the four marshals of France and the Grand Master, all in suits of cloth of gold and silver, and by gentlemen pensioners and others wearing the king's colours. Chancellor Duprat then appeared, preceded by his staff and a riderless horse carrying a blue velvet coffer containing the Great Seal. A flurry of pages, musicians and heralds came next, then four gentlemen carrying the king's hat, cloak, sword and helmet. Behind rode members of his household. The canopy over the king was carried in turns by the aldermen and representatives of the various guilds.

Only then did Francis appear, in a dazzling suit of silver cloth and wearing a white hat flashing with jewels. Bounding forward on his horse, he threw fistfuls of coins into the crowd lining the route. Behind him rode the princes of the blood and other nobles, also superbly dressed. The rear of the procession was brought up by the *Cent gentilshommes de l'hôtel* and four hundred archers. To reach Notre-Dame, the king needed to cross the River Seine. Traditionally, the Pont au Change was used, but Francis chose the Pont Notre-Dame instead. Recently rebuilt by the Veronese architect Fra Giocondo, it had six arches, sixty-eight identical houses and four turrets. By choosing it instead of the old bridge, Francis may have intended to demonstrate his love of novelty. A service of thanksgiving at Notre-Dame was followed by a splendid banquet, dancing and an entertainment by the Basoche. Thereafter jousts and tournaments took place for several days in the rue Saint-Antoine. On 11 March the Bureau de la Ville gave Francis a statue in solid gold of his patron saint.[29]

In the early sixteenth century, the queen was also given an entry into Paris, but only after the king's. She was received in the same way and handed the keys to the city, while the king effaced himself completely. In 1514, when Louis XII met Mary Tudor outside Abbeville, he did not enter the city with

12. Tableau-vivant staged at the Porte du Palais in Paris, devised by Pierre Gringore for the entry of Queen Claude on 12 May 1517. Miniature (Bibliothèque nationale de France, ms. fr. 5750, fo. 49 verso). On the upper level: Saint Louis flanked by his mother, Blanche of Castile, and Justice; below: Labour, a wretched beggar and a soldier or *aventurier*.

her; instead he 'went along the walls'. Francis I watched the Parisian entry of Queen Eleanor from an open window. The show was hers alone and its symbolism was modified to focus on her marriage, maternal duties, desire for peace and intercessionary role. She was seen as the person best able to influence the king. Her attributes identified her more closely with the lives of ordinary French people than did those of the king.

Henry II's entry into Paris prompted the publication of an official account with engravings of the monuments erected for the occasion.[30] The entry, which took place on 16 June 1549, nearly two years after his coronation, involved the participation of several thousand men. Women had to watch from open windows. The entry fell into two parts, as usual: first, the procession out of the city by its principal citizens; secondly, that into the city by the king and his court. The first procession began early in the morning and was watched by the king from a tribune specially erected near the priory of Saint-Lazare outside the city's walls. The procession of citizens, in strict pecking order from the least to the most important, lasted several hours. As each group passed in front of the king, a representative detached himself from the rest to mount the tribune and deliver a welcoming address to Henry, who sat on a chair flanked by the constable and chancellor. The latter responded to each speech on the king's behalf. The most important speech was, of course, that of the *prévôt des marchands*, who also handed the keys of the city to the king in return for confirmation of its liberties and privileges. Once the procession had filed past, it turned around and led Henry and his court into Paris.

At various points along the route to Notre-Dame were monuments specially erected for the occasion. It was under Henry II that the essential prerequisites for the reconstruction of a Roman triumph in art and poetry were met in France. These were a determination to link policy and image-making, adequate resources, properly trained artists, and models from which to work. By the mid-1540s these conditions had all been met.[31] The Paris entry of 1549 had been organised by Jean Martin, a distinguished humanist, with the assistance of the sculptor Jean Goujon and the poet Thomas Sébillet. The first of several themes developed in the entry was that of Force and Authority, as symbolised by Hercules, who was given the features of the late king, Francis. Hercules had a special appeal for French humanists: while the Gallic Hercules stood for the god's civilising role, the Libyan Hercules symbolised military prowess. The theme of triumph was expressed in motifs concerning the Argosy and the Golden Fleece. The Argo was identifiable with the ship of state successfully piloted by the king, and also with Paris whose emblem was a ship. The citizens would see themselves as the Argonauts following the king on his journey to success. A third major theme was Fortune. This appeared on the Fontaine du Ponceau, with Jupiter at the apex denoting divine authority, and the three Fortunes representing justice, the nobles and the Third Estate.[32]

The monuments included several triumphal arches displaying different classical Orders. One of them had two pairs of Corinthian pilasters and a statue of Gaul crowned by three towers. On top, two angels held aloft the

13. An arch erected at the Porte Saint-Denis for the entry of King Henry II into Paris on 16 June 1549. Engraving from the festival book published by Jean Dallier. The traditional theme of Force and Authority is developed by the classical myth of Hercules, shown on the top of the arch as the Gallic Hercules linked to representatives of the estates by gold and silver chains implying his use of persuasion rather than force.

imperial crown and beneath it the shield of France framed by the collar of the Order of St Michael. Paintings beneath the vault represented the rivers Seine and Marne. The message here was that fertile Gaul nourishes her subjects. Just as Zephyr causes Flora to produce fruit and flowers, so the king promises to give happiness to France. Further on, an obelisk, 70 feet tall, stood on the back of a rhinoceros beneath which could be seen a heap of animal corpses. Cartouches enjoined the king to use force and vigilance in defence of his kingdom. One monument was intended to last. This was the Fontaine des Innocents, with bas-reliefs of smiling nymphs by Jean Goujon. Water flowed from spouts shaped as masks around the base, while an open loggia above provided a vantage point for distinguished spectators.[33] At the Châtelet, a long portico of painted plaster had eight Ionic columns behind which an urban panorama unfolded. At the centre sat the New Pandora, her left arm

14. The Fontaine des Innocents in Paris, the only monument to survive from Henry II's entry into Paris on 16 June 1549. Originally in the rue Saint-Denis, it was demolished and rebuilt on the present site (the place Joachim Du Bellay) in 1786, when it was also given two additional façades. The upper level was used in 1549 as a platform from which to observe the entry procession. The elegant bas-reliefs around two sides of the fountain, from which water used to flow, are by Jean Goujon.

raised in salute and her right holding a vase filled with divine gifts. Two more triumphal arches, this time celebrating Typhis and the Argonauts, stood at each end of the Pont Notre-Dame.

The entry of Queen Catherine de' Medici into Paris on 18 June 1549 was closely modelled on the king's except for the inclusion of women in the procession. Some of the participants also changed their clothes for her. The *prévôt des marchands*, for example, who had worn crimson-brown velvet for the king's entry, now put on 'bright colours'. The change was meant to show that the prévôt, having effaced himself in the monarch's presence, could now display an authority given to him by the king which the queen could not confer.[34] The *prévôt de Paris*, who had been armed for the king's entry, now appeared in a gown of gold cloth. Similar changes were made by the *enfants de la ville*, the *échevins* and members of the trade guilds. Catherine made her entry preceded by six foreign ambassadors, each accompanied by a bishop, and by riders carrying her coronation accoutrements. Her servants wore her white and green livery. Borne in an open litter draped in cloth of silver, the queen wore a surcoat of ermine under the royal mantle and a crown encrusted with pearls and precious stones. Facing her in the litter was the king's sister, Marguerite. They were escorted by four cardinals and the Constable of Montmorency. Over the queen porters carried a magnificent canopy of cloth of gold fringed with red silk. Princesses riding white palfreys followed. Like her husband, Catherine prayed at Notre-Dame before going to the Palais for a supper served by the constable and princes of the blood.[35]

Following his coronation, Henry II spent five years touring his kingdom. His many entries were more lavish, expensive and classical than those of his father. The civic parades were huge. At Rouen in 1550 the entry fell into two parts: first, a procession of triumphal cars with hundreds of followers; secondly, the king's journey through the city (see plate 15). Four triumphal arches stood along the processional route, two at each end of the bridge crossing the Seine. One showed Orpheus, the Muses and Hercules destroying the Hydra; the other presented a vision of the Golden Age above Henry's device of a crescent moon. Outside the cathedral a statue of Hector in full armour stood on a platform supported by four caryatids, while the Fontaine de la Crosse was adorned with an image of the late king, Francis I. The triumphal cars evoked a Roman triumph. The first, depicting Fame, was drawn by four winged horses and decorated with battle scenes, spoils of war and representations of death; the second, symbolising religion, was adorned with statues and Vesta enthroned; the third displayed an effigy of Henry himself, holding the insignia of state and receiving the imperial crown from the goddess Good Fortune. Each car was preceded by soldiers, cavalry, musicians and standard-bearers wearing Roman armour. The musical instruments imitated the long tubular horns and trumpets of the Romans and, as in Caesar's triumphs, elephants carried the booty. Prisoners of war in chains walked dejectedly behind. Then came priests with sacrificial lambs, while Flora and her nymphs scattered flowers of welcome. Wave after wave of citizens dressed *à la romaine* marched past the king, who sat in a specially constructed gallery.[36]

In Lyon in 1548 seven thousand men marched past Henry II. They wore black and white for the king; green and white for the queen. The costumes were made of velvet, satin, taffeta, silk, and cloth of silver and gold depending on social status. Pages and musicians played fifes, tabors and trumpets.[37] When Henry returned to Lyon after a successful military campaign in Piedmont, he was greeted by the *enfants de la ville* wearing imitation Roman uniforms and armour. They also carried twin-headed lances. The merchants from Lucca wore cloth of silver shaded to look like armour. A re-enactment of a Roman gladiatorial combat so delighted the king that he asked for a repeat performance. Similar displays were put on by other towns. At Carpentras the citizens staged a Roman wrestling match lasting three hours. At Beaune Henry watched a mock siege in which two thousand soldiers, equipped with guns and siege engines, succeeded in capturing a fort after engagements that generated much noise and smoke and several casualties. At Rouen a famous battle was fought by two supposedly Brazilian tribes.

Water spectacles, or *naumachia*, became popular under Henry II. At Lyon two confraternities organised a battle on the river between a flotilla of ships and two galleys manned by crews wearing Roman attire. One of the galleys exploded during the engagement, giving rise to a spectacular fireworks display. The king and queen watched from the deck of a Venetian galley. A dining room below deck had a floor that opened up to allow a table, laden with food and wine, to rise up. During another *naumachia*, at Rouen, Henry was surrounded by sea monsters as he crossed a bridge and was offered dominion of the seas by Neptune.[38]

The taste for antiquarian classicism was firmly established by the Lyon entry of September 1548.[39] As the king rode through the city, he encountered a sequence of temporary monuments. The first was an obelisk made of wood and canvas and painted to look like grey marble. It had grass-filled cracks to denote antiquity. Matching it were two victory columns, one Doric, the other Corinthian. Behind the cathedral, an existing tower was given a matching one of wood and canvas. Niches in an apse behind steps leading to the river contained statues of river gods. Near the cathedral another apse was dedicated to Fortune. A tall column, topped by a golden fleur-de-lys, rose out of an antique vase at the centre. Temporary monuments adorned Henry II's other entries. In Tours two obelisks topped by a crescent stood on an arch built at the city gate. Classical architecture was frequently combined with sculpture. In Rouen a huge statue of Hector spurted blood from a wound. On reaching a cloud above, the blood turned into Henry II's device of three crescents.[40] The classical motif dominating the entry ceremony in several towns was the triumphal arch, which could be single with double columns or with pairs of Corinthian columns separated by niches containing statues. Ornament consisted of Victories in the spandrels and painted reliefs. Arches were also built on bridges. One that was erected in Lyon was topped by a temple and had a balustraded musicians' gallery.[41]

Royal Weddings

Weddings at the French Renaissance court were less consistently ceremonial than other events: while some were magnificently staged, others passed almost unnoticed. Much depended on circumstance, for marriages were political rather than sentimental unions. The marriage of Charles VIII and Anne, duchess of Brittany at Langeais on 6 December 1491 marked the end of a long series of Breton wars. Its validity was open to question following earlier engagements by both parties: Anne had been married by proxy to Maximilian of Habsburg and Charles had been engaged to Margaret of Austria. The couple should have obtained a papal dispensation for their marriage but had not done so and there were serious misgivings about their union. Anne, who was only fifteen, was the first to arrive at Langeais. Leaving Tours before daybreak, Charles travelled by boat down the Loire with a few courtiers. On arrival, he ordered the gates of the château to be closed so that no uninvited guest should enter. The exchange of vows in the great hall was followed by mass. After a little token rejoicing, the newlyweds retired to bed to consummate their union in the presence of witnesses, among whom were six bourgeois of Rennes, who hastily informed their fellow citizens that their duchess had been 'dépucelée' by the king of France. No one would be able to question the marriage's validity in future. Brittany was now firmly attached to France while retaining its formal independence.[42]

Anne's second marriage, on 8 January 1499, to Louis XII was also low-key. It took place without fuss in the chapel of her ancestral château of Nantes. Both parties were old hands at marriage and aware of the ease with which the most solemn engagements could be broken: hence the written assurance sent by Louis next day to the *Chambre des comptes* that the union had been consummated. A few public celebrations followed, but Anne, conscious of the fact that her previous marriage had not been blessed with issue, was more concerned to win divine approval of her new status by showering gifts on churches and places of pilgrimage. Louis remained in Brittany for a month, hunting incessantly. In 1500 there were celebrations in Amboise for Anne's return.[43]

In the sixteenth century the marriages of royal children normally took place in Paris on the Île-de-la-Cité, where the cathedral of Notre-Dame, the Palais and the episcopal palace offered a setting prestigious and spacious enough to accommodate many guests. Marriages of high-ranking noblemen also took place at court, but not necessarily in Paris. Thus the duc de Nemours and Mademoiselle de Longueville were married at Saint-Germain-en-Laye in January 1529, and the duke of Cleves and Jeanne d'Albret at Châtellerault in June 1541.

A marriage in which one of the parties was a distinguished foreigner commanded particular ostentation. Such a person was the king of Scots, James V, who came to France in 1536 to marry Francis I's daughter Madeleine.[44] The ceremony took place in Paris at Notre-Dame on 1 January 1537. A wooden platform, linking the bishop's palace to the cathedral's west front, had been erected and on it a golden canopy supported by four pillars, arrangements doubtless intended to offer the crowd assembled outside the cathedral a better view of the proceedings. Along the platform walked Francis I with his daughter 'on his arm', followed by Queen Eleanor, the dauphine (Catherine de' Medici), the bride's sister, Louise, Madame de Vendôme, the queen of Navarre and many noblewomen. As the bride waited under the canopy for cardinal de Bourbon to appear, a herald cried out three times: 'Largesse de par Madame Madeleine, la fille du Roy!' At the same time he threw into the crowd a large quantity of gold and silver coins. The bride then attended the nuptial mass celebrated by the cardinal. This was followed by dinner, dancing and other entertainments at the bishop's palace. Later that day a banquet was thrown in the great hall of the Palais, which was adorned as usual with rich tapestries and 'other precious and beautiful things'. Francis I sat at the marble table (*table de marbre*) with his new son-in-law, the bride, Queen Eleanor and other ladies. Close by were two sideboards laden with gold and silver plate, and further off two platforms on which musicians played. After the meal there was more dancing. The next day Francis, James and 'all the nobility' supped at the Louvre 'in great triumph', and on the morrow a fortnight's jousting began in the palace courtyard.

Foreign diplomats sent accounts of royal weddings to their masters in which they recorded the order of precedence, the colours of the liveries and the dimensions of the trains, but they paid most attention to the festivities that followed the religious service. The banquets, balls, masquerades and jousts often lasted a week or more. For the wedding of the duc de Nevers to Mademoiselle de Vendôme in January 1539 the *grande salle* of the Louvre was used first as a chapel, then as a ballroom. The bride wore a mantle fit for a queen, but its adornment of pearls and precious stones was so heavy that after the banquet she substituted a lighter crown with the assistance of a nobleman. The supper was followed by dancing. After the first dance, the queen partnered the bride, and a young girl in male attire performed a galliard. The men in the meantime withdrew to put on masks, before returning one by one. Each then took a lady by the hand and began dancing. Soon the hall was filled with couples. Last to appear was Francis I, preceded by an 'honourable company'. A Mantuan eyewitness was particularly impressed by the magnificence and grace of a masque in which five satyrs danced with as many nymphs, each a Syrinx turning into a reed. The satyrs wore suits of gold and silver cloth, garlands encrusted with pearls and precious stones on their heads and masks of crimson velvet. The nymphs wore ample round dresses that stopped above their ankles and barely covered their necks and breasts. They too had masks, except for Madame d'Étampes and Madame de Givry, who were deemed too beautiful for such dissimulation. The nymphs danced as the satyrs entered the hall blowing on their pipes. As for Francis, he appeared as Mars in a costume 'à l'antique' with rich embroidery, pearls and precious stones that beggared description. He was escorted by Cesare Fregoso. After a dance by the king, the ball ended. Masks were removed in an adjacent room and a collation served. Francis then retired, leaving the queen to lead the bride to the nuptial chamber. The groom was taken there by the dauphin, who recommended him to God before retiring to his lodging.[45]

The most spectacular royal wedding under Henry II was that of Mary Stuart and the Dauphin François, soon to become King Francis II. In the words of the Venetian ambassador:

> These nuptials were really considered the most regal and triumphant of any that have been witnessed in this kingdom for many years, whether from the concourse of the chief personages of the realm both temporal and spiritual thus assembled . . . or from the pomp and richness of the jewels and apparel both of the lords and ladies, as from the grandeur of the banquet and stately service of the table, or from the costly devices of the masquerades and similar revels.[46]

The marriage was a triumph not only for Henry II, but also for the House of Guise, for the bride was the niece of François duc de Guise who, acting as Grand Master in the absence of the Constable of Montmorency, had organised the wedding. As the husband of Anne d'Este, Louis XII's granddaughter, the duke was a member of the royal family and his niece's marriage to the dauphin reinforced that connexion. At the same time it was a triumph for Henry II, who had long resisted English attempts to control Scotland. The marriage seemed to unite France and Scotland indissolubly: by marrying Mary, a queen in her own right, the dauphin became king of Scots in his father's estimation: hence a proclamation made after the wedding to the effect that Mary would be styled 'queen-dauphiness' and François 'king-dauphin'.

The ceremony has been so often described that only a few details need be mentioned here.[47] The arrangements, such as the platform erected in front of Notre-Dame, evidently followed the model set by the marriage of James V and Madeleine de France. One change, however, was the bride's dress. Mary insisted on wearing white, which was traditionally the colour of mourning for French queens. 'Tall and elegant, she herself must have glittered like the goddess of a pageant, with diamonds round her neck, and on her head a golden crown garnished with pearls, rubies, sapphires and other precious stones, as well as one huge carbuncle worth over 500,000 crowns.'[48] As for James V's wedding, the nuptial mass was followed by a dinner at the bishop's palace and, later that day, by a banquet at the Palais. As the guests moved venue, huge crowds gathered to watch them pass, the men on horseback and the ladies in litters. The ball that followed the supper was spectacular. The dauphin's brothers and other young princes, mounted on twelve artificial horses, covered with gold and silver cloth, appeared pulling coaches in which bejewelled passengers sang melodiously. Six ships with silver sails were then drawn into the hall. A gentleman at each helm invited a lady to come aboard. Henry II predictably chose his new daughter-in-law, and the dauphin picked his mother. The Venetian observer believed the exceptional pomp to be due to the fact that no dauphin had married in Paris for two hundred years.[49] On this occasion, however, there were no jousts or tournaments. The reason, he explained, was cost: the nobles needed their money to equip themselves for war.

Royal Baptisms

An elaborate ritual surrounded royal births in sixteenth-century France. The queen gave birth in public and the horoscope of the newborn child was instantly determined by astrologers, as towns throughout the kingdom were invited to ring their bells and light bonfires. The festivities that accompanied the child's baptism usually coincided with the mother's churching. The ceremony was an opportunity to honour a foreign ally by making him the godfather. The baptism of Charles-Orland, the short-lived son of Charles VIII and Anne of Brittany, produced 'more blessings and acts of thanksgiving than were customary'.[50] The birth of Francis I's eldest son, François, at Amboise on 28 February 1518 was followed on 25 April by a spectacular baptism, which was delayed as the godfathers – Lorenzo de' Medici acting as proxy for his uncle, Pope Leo X, and Anthony, duke of Lorraine – had to come from afar. The godmother was Francis's sister, Marguerite.

The ceremony involved two buildings, the château of Amboise and the collegiate church of Saint-Florentin, linked by an elevated wooden walkway with a vaulted roof of trelliswork, covered with foliage and supported by golden pillars.[51] It crossed two courtyards of unequal size hung with rich tapestries depicting scenes from ancient history, such as the fall of Troy. Covering the larger courtyard was an awning of azure cloth powdered with fleurs-de-lys and supported by ropes attached to three ships' masts. Although

15. The baptism of the future king, Francis I (Bibliothèque nationale de France, ms. fr. 2275, fo. 4 verso). Dating from 1515, this miniature is taken from an anonymous manuscript that focuses on the significance of the king's name. The infant is already crowned. A female figure below the font points downwards to verses in praise of his name.

the baptism took place after dark, the scene was brightly lit by hundreds of candles, some attached to the walkway, others held by four hundred archers and Swiss troops. The baptism was preceded by a huge procession to the church along the walkway led by musicians beating drums and blowing trumpets and bugles.[52] Behind them walked, in strict order of precedence, heralds, stewards, gentlemen of the household, great lords, sons of noble families and knights of the Order of St Michael. At the centre, a group of nobles carried the sacred chrism, the basin and ewer, a candle of virgin wax, the salt and the cradle. Then came Lorenzo de' Medici, superbly attired and proudly wearing the collar of the Order of St Michael that the king had just conferred upon him. He was followed by Madame de Brissac, the dauphin's governess, who was to hold the babe's head at the christening. The infant himself was carried under a canopy of cloth of gold and silver by four princes who were followed by the king's mother, Louise of Savoy, the queen's sister, Renée, and the king's sister, Marguerite, each with a long train held up by one of their ladies. Two noblemen carried in their arms the dauphin's infant sisters, Louise and Charlotte. Waiting in the church were three cardinals and other prelates. Cardinal de Boisy, who officiated, had to climb six steps to reach the font, which was on a raised platform beneath a canopy supported by golden pillars. The knights of St Michael formed a circle around the font while the king and queen watched the christening from behind a grille. Once it was over, two heralds called out three times: 'Vive monseigneur le dauphin!', an acclamation taken up by choristers of the royal chapel in a work composed for the occasion by Jean Mouton.[53]

Royal baptisms at Fontainebleau in the 1540s aroused the admiration of Italian diplomats, who sent home detailed reports describing the rich hangings and tapestries that adorned every façade along the processional route as well as the resplendent costumes worn by the participants.[54] The preparation of the processional route for the baptism of the future Francis II in 1544 called for careful planning, as the upper chapel had not yet been built. The only way of reaching the lower one from Catherine de' Medici's chamber in the Porte Dorée was by means of a narrow spiral staircase. To avoid this inconvenience a temporary wooden staircase was built.

Another splendid baptism was that of Elisabeth, daughter of Dauphin Henri and Catherine de' Medici, whose birth at Fontainebleau on 2 April 1546 anticipated by only a few weeks the signing of a peace treaty with England. It thus became a double celebration. At Francis I's invitation Henry VIII agreed to be godfather. The child was carried to the chapel of the Holy Trinity by the English ambassador, Sir Thomas Cheyney, acting as proxy for his master, and was christened Elisabeth after Henry VIII's mother, Elisabeth of York. Queen Eleanor and Jeanne d'Albret, queen of Navarre, were the godmothers. Cardinal de Bourbon, who was a prince of the blood as well as archbishop of Sens, officiated. A fanfare of trumpets, bugles and hautbois and a discharge of firearms greeted the announcement of the child's name by French and English heralds.

The ceremony was accompanied by an exhibition of royal treasures assembled from all corners of the kingdom in the Cour du Donjon. An awning of blue silk with gold stars stretched across the courtyard was supported by a tall mast. At its base was a pyramid with nine shelves on which the king's gold plate was displayed along with other *objets d'art* and curiosities. Specially appointed guides told visitors about the provenance of each one: some, they explained, had been brought to France by Charlemagne; others were gifts from foreign potentates. After the baptism, Francis I offered a banquet, described as finer than any other in living memory, and a ball in which giants (*figures prodigieuses*) took part as well as ferocious beasts and birds of prey. The following day was given over to a tournament in which the dauphin and the comte de Laval each led a team of knights: the dauphin's dressed in white with crescent moons on their helms, and Laval's in bright red. The dauphin predictably won the prize for valour. The English ambassador, who had come with gifts from Henry VIII, including a goblet of jasper, a clock and a gold saltcellar, returned home well satisfied with his visit and laden with presents.[55]

Royal Funerals

Anne of Brittany and Claude de France were the only two queens of France during the sixteenth century to be given state funerals. The others – Mary Tudor, Eleanor of Portugal, Mary Stuart and Elizabeth of Austria – all died outside France. Catherine de' Medici died at Blois in 1589 in circumstances that precluded a state funeral, and Louise de Lorraine retired to a Capuchin convent following her husband's assassination, and was buried there without ceremony. Anne of Brittany, however, was given a spectacular funeral. She died at Blois on 9 January 1514, and for six days lay on her death bed surrounded by praying monks. Her body was then carried to the great hall of the château, splendidly adorned for the occasion, where it lay in state on a bed covered with cloth of gold. The queen was shown wearing her royal robes, crowned and holding a sceptre and hand of justice. She remained there for two more days surrounded by praying monks as an unbroken sequence of masses were sung. On 16 January, Anne's body was placed in a coffin and displayed in the same hall, now transformed into a *salle de deuil*. The walls were covered with black drapes, and the bier with a pall of black velvet divided in the middle by a white cross. The crown, sceptre and hand of justice lay on a cushion. This scenario lasted for a full month during which princes and princesses, in full mourning, filed past the coffin. On 3 February Anne's body was solemnly taken to the church of Saint-Sauveur for a funeral service. The bier was placed in a *chapelle ardente* and vigils for the dead were sung. The cardinal of Bayeux officiated that night and at three masses the next day. Afterwards a funeral sermon was delivered on the theme of thirty-seven virtues, one for each year of the queen's life. The body was then taken back to the château. On 5 April it left Blois for Paris, escorted by 450 torchbearers and a huge number of people marching in strict pecking order. The procession took eight days to reach the capital. At each halt on the way high mass was sung, and the queen was served two meals each day by her usual servants as if she were still alive.[56] It was only on 14 February, more than a month after her death, that the cortège made its entry into the capital. This was exceptionally sumptuous and, for the first time, the queen's effigy appeared. Placed on the coffin, it showed her in all the splendour of sovereignty, wearing her royal robes, crowned and holding the sceptre and hand of justice. The order of the cortège was carefully regulated and involved too many participants to be listed here. Suffice it to say that it was as triumphal as the finest king's entry. Following their arrival at Notre-Dame, the coffin and effigy were placed in a *chapelle ardente* illuminated by 3,800 candles and a service was celebrated by the cardinal of Le Mans. After mass on the following day, the cortège resumed its journey to Saint-Denis in the same order as before. On arrival, the coffin was placed in another *chapelle ardente* and mass celebrated. Another eulogy was preached, this time focusing on the late queen's genealogy. The coffin was then lowered into a vault and earth scattered upon it. Brittany herald shouted three times that the queen was dead. At his invitation three principal members of her household deposited her regalia in the tomb, and her stewards, after breaking their wands, threw the pieces into the tomb. Brittany herald removed his tabard. During the dinner that concluded the proceedings, he thanked the guests for having served the queen so well and broke his own wand to indicate that her household was dissolved. The queen's death was announced for the last time and her servants invited to provide for themselves.

The funeral of Anne of Brittany served as the model not only for that of her daughter, Claude de France, but also, more interestingly, for that of her mother-in-law, Louise of Savoy. On 23 September 1531 Francis I wrote to the Bureau de la Ville of Paris ordering a funeral for her on the model of that given to his first wife, Claude.[57] The king was in effect giving his mother posthumously the status of queen. After her body had been taken from Grès-sur-Loing to Saint-Maur-des-Fossés and embalmed, it was carried to the church of Saint-Martin-des-Champs outside Paris, where it lay in state until 17 October. On that day a huge procession of representatives from all walks of life accompanied the body and effigy to Notre-Dame for a funeral service.

The effigy, crowned and holding a sceptre in one hand, was borne under a canopy and the corners of the gold cloth on which it rested were held by the four presidents of the Parlement wearing their scarlet gowns. Everyone else was in deep mourning and the houses overlooking the cortège were draped in black. As was customary on such occasions, the king was not among the mourners.[58] Next morning the cortège made its way to Saint-Denis, where Louise's body was buried in the crypt alongside the remains of France's past kings and queens.

A king of France might die anywhere, but he was normally buried at the abbey of Saint-Denis outside Paris. An exception was Louis XI, who chose to be buried in the collegiate church of Notre-Dame-de-Cléry near Orléans. Burial at Saint-Denis was invariably preceded by a funeral entry into Paris and a service at the cathedral of Notre-Dame. This may be said to have paralleled the entry into Paris following the king's accession. If he died at some distance from Paris, a cortège had to be organised to transport his body with all the pomp due to his dignity. This could involve a large number of people. More than seven thousand accompanied Charles VIII on his last journey from Amboise to Paris. The cortège halted several times on the way, notably at Cléry where Charles had chosen to have his heart buried alongside his parents.[59] By contrast, Louis XII's funeral was simpler: as he had died in Paris, no preliminary procession or entry was required. His body was taken to Notre-Dame on 3 January 1515 and buried the next day. This may explain why Francis I spent only 13,000 *l.* on his predecessor's funeral whereas Louis XII, renowned for his parsimony, had spent 52,000 *l.* on that of Charles VIII.[60] A peculiar feature of any royal funeral was the king's effigy. This was made to look as lifelike as possible and was carried separately from the coffin in the Parisian entry in order to create the illusion that the king was still alive. All of these features and more figured in the funeral of Francis I.

Francis died at the château of Rambouillet, some 42 kilometres south-west of Paris, on 31 March 1547. He was not buried at Saint-Denis until 22 May. One reason for the delay was the need to transport the body to Paris; another was Henry II's decision to combine the king's funeral with those of his sons, François and Charles, who had predeceased him and whose bodies had remained where they had died. Charles's body only had to be brought from Beauvais, but François's had to come from Tournon, some 500 kilometres from Paris: it was not expected to reach the capital before 18 May. This allowed time for the preparation of a stupendous triple funeral. The artist François Clouet travelled from Paris to Rambouillet in order to make Francis I's death mask and to draw and take measurements for his effigy. This took a fortnight to make. On the night of 31 March mendicant friars prayed and stood vigil over the king's body and, on the following day, physicians and surgeons carried out a postmortem examination. Francis's heart and entrails were removed and placed in two caskets, while his body was embalmed and placed in a coffin. Next day, the coffin and caskets were carried in procession to the priory of Haute-Bruyère, a few miles from Rambouillet. For two days and nights the bells of the priory rang out ceaselessly as services were held. On 6 April the king's heart and entrails were buried in the priory; five days later his body was taken to Saint-Cloud, a palace belonging to the cardinal-bishop of Paris. This step was probably taken to have the body within striking distance of Paris by the time the dauphin's was due to arrive.[61]

On 28 April the focus of the ceremony shifted from the king's body to his effigy which lay, hands clasped, on a bed of state in the great hall at Saint-Cloud, which was decorated with hangings of blue velvet and cloth of gold. Never before had the effigy appeared before the entry into Paris. It wore the state robes, the collar of the Order of St Michael, and the closed, imperial crown. On either side, on pillows, lay the sceptre and hand of justice. There was a canopy over the bed and, at its foot, a crucifix and holy-water stoop. Two heralds kept watch day and night, and offered the aspergillum to anyone wishing to sprinkle the effigy with holy water. Four candles provided the only illumination. Along the walls were benches for nobles and clerics, who attended the religious services and meals served to the effigy. These were the strangest parts of the ceremonial. For eleven days the king's meals were served as if he were still alive. His table was laid and the courses brought in and tasted. The napkin, used to wipe his hands, was presented by the steward to the most eminent person in attendance, and wine was served twice during each meal. At the end, grace was said by a cardinal. The meal itself was not an innovation. At Charles VIII's funeral food had been served by stewards 'even as hitherto by the king in his lifetime', and a meal was also served during Anne of Brittany's funeral in 1514. The novelty at Saint-Cloud was not the meal, but the presence of the effigy. Its symbolic significance calls for comment. The idea of representing the deceased monarch by an effigy at his funeral was imported from England as part of the funeral of Charles VI in October 1422.[62] In England the effigy had no symbolic significance, it simply replaced the king's body; in France it was linked to the famous adage 'the king never dies' (*le roi ne meurt jamais*); in other words, the king's *dignitas* or authority outlived his bodily existence. As we have seen, the king succeeded to the throne on the death of his predecessor. He could exercise his monar-chical authority from that moment, but could not be seen to act as king until his predecessor had been buried. Only then could a herald cry out: 'Le roi est mort! Vive le roi!' The effigy was meant to create the illusion that the deceased monarch was still alive pending his burial, and the new king effaced himself in order not to destroy that illusion.[63]

On 4 May the last meal was served and the effigy removed. Overnight the *salle d'honneur* was turned into a *salle funèbre*. The blue and gold drapes were replaced by black ones, and the king's coffin, which had been in an adjacent room, was brought in and placed in the centre of the hall. On it were the crown, sceptre and hand of justice. On 18 May Henry II aspersed his father's body; this was his only public appearance between Francis's death and his own coronation. On 21 May the coffin was drawn on a waggon by six horses to Notre-Dame-des-Champs and placed in the choir alongside the coffins of his two sons. That evening a requiem mass was celebrated and all that night vigil was kept by Francis's officials and servants. Next morning, after another mass, the church was closed and the effigies of the king and his son were produced and attached to litters. Francis's effigy now had a different pair of hands: instead of being clasped in prayer, one held the sceptre and the other the hand of justice. Once everything was ready, members of the Parlement, who had come in solemn procession from Paris, were admitted to the church. They wore their red robes as an indication that justice never dies. About 2 p.m. the funeral cortège set off for Paris. The order was as follows: the parish clergy, five hundred poor carrying torches, the archers of the guard, the town criers and the watch. Marching on either side of the road were the mendicant orders, followed by students of the university and other clergy. Then came a group of royal officers, followed by trumpeters and the waggon bearing Francis's coffin. Immediately behind rode twelve pages and knights carrying his gauntlets, helmet, shield and coat of arms. Thirty-three prelates, including Cardinal Jean du Bellay, followed; then came the effigies of Francis's sons, each carried by gentlemen of their households, two knights carrying the king's spurs, his parade horse led by two grooms, and the Master of the Horse, Boisy, holding the sword of France; then a litter bearing the king's effigy. This was carried by the *hanouars* or salt-carriers of Paris, whose feet could be seen under the long gold drape covering the litter. Alongside marched eight gentlemen of the royal household attached to the litter by a kind of halter, and behind them rode Admiral Annebault with the banner of France, four princes in deep mourning and, finally, the papal legate, a group of cardinals and ambassadors, and troops of the guard.

After a brief service at Notre-Dame, the large company broke up, only to reassemble next day for the last rites. Each prince made an offering and Pierre du Chastel, bishop of Mâcon, delivered a eulogy of the deceased monarch.[64] After a lunch break the company set off in the same order as before for Saint-Denis. That evening vespers was celebrated and next morning the last rites were repeated. The effigies were removed and the coffins taken to a vault. The heralds deposited their tabards on a railing and the royal insignia were placed on the king's coffin, Boisy rested the point of the sword of France upon it,

Francis's stewards threw their wands into the grave, and the admiral, sitting near its edge, dipped the banner of France until its tip touched the coffin. 'Le Roy est mort!' cried Normandy herald three times, but the admiral was too distraught to respond with the cry 'Vive le Roy!' so the herald did so for him. Whereupon the sword and banner were raised and the various tabards retrieved. The company then retired to the abbey's refectory for supper. As it ended, Francis's chief steward, Mendoza, broke his wand to signify the dissolution of the late king's household. He told his fellow officials that they no longer had a master and should provide for themselves, but he held out the hope that the new king would treat them kindly.

CHAPTER 8

Summit Meetings

Writing in February 1517, the Dutch humanist, Erasmus, noted that the rulers of Christendom were reducing their armaments: he looked forward to a Golden Age in which moral virtues, Christian piety and true learning would come into their own.[1] He was soon to be disappointed. The peace of Christendom depended on three young rulers: Henry VIII of England, aged twenty-six; Francis I of France, aged twenty-three; and Charles I of Spain, aged seventeen. Only a blind optimist could have imagined any lasting peace between them; while paying lip service to Christian unity, none was willing to abandon any of his rights. Henry claimed the French crown, Francis the crowns of Milan and Naples, and Charles the duchy of Burgundy. Sooner or later they were bound to clash. For a time, however, they sank their differences. Francis and Charles signed a treaty in 1516; Henry and Francis did likewise in 1518. The Treaty of London (2 and 4 October 1518) was taken to mark the start of a Universal Peace.[2] It was celebrated on both sides of the Channel with pomp and ceremonial, and was followed two years later by a meeting of the two kings.[3]

The Field of Cloth of Gold, 1520

The idea of a meeting between the kings of England and France, mooted in 1518, was revived in 1519 after the election of Charles of Habsburg as Holy Roman Emperor had brought them together. Summit meetings, to be successful, need to be well prepared. In February 1520 a Frenchman warned against repeating the meeting between Philip Augustus and Henry II in 1189 from which no good had ensued.[4] Everyone hoped that the Field of Cloth of Gold would engender further meetings. The English Chancellor Wolsey stressed the need to avoid suspicion, jealousy or excessive expenditure. In the end, however, a vast amount of money was spent on both sides. The French crown may have spent 400,000 *l*.[5] In the words of du Bellay: 'many went there carrying their mills, forests and meadows on their shoulders.'[6]

One of the first matters to be decided was the venue. Henry VIII suggested Calais; Francis favoured a more open space. Eventually, a location halfway between the English town of Calais and the French town of Ardres was chosen. Francis generously agreed that it should be on English soil. Two commissioners – the earl of Worcester for England and Marshal Châtillon for France – picked a shallow valley, the Val Doré or Golden Valley, and made it more symmetrical by erecting two artificial mounds on either side.[7] A treaty, drawn up by Wolsey, banned the erection of tents and pavilions, but the English put one up for the convenience of the two kings: it was a pavilion of crimson and cloth of gold, furnished with two chairs, rich cushions and Turkish carpets.[8] Security was another problem. Even in the open, it was felt necessary to limit the number of participants. The kings accordingly drew up lists of their attendants, servants and horses.[9] The fair sex was expected to figure prominently. Francis hoped that Henry would not mind his bringing along suitable ladies.[10] Less indulgence, however, was shown to vagabonds; they were banished from the meeting place on pain of death. Everyone else had to hold a ticket.[11] Even so, an Anglo-French police force was set up. As

16. The meeting of the French and English kings, Francis I and Henry VIII, at the Field of Cloth of Gold, 7 June 1520. Bas-relief from the Hôtel Bourgtheroulde in Rouen. The French are on the right and the English (one of them carrying a longbow) on the left. The kings actually met on their own as their escorts looked on from a distance.

an additional precaution, all troops, except the garrisons of Boulogne and Calais, were forbidden to come within two days' march of the meeting site.[12]

Accommodation was probably the biggest headache for the organisers of the meeting. Ardres had been severely damaged in the war of 1512 and Guînes castle was a ruin, so Henry VIII erected a large temporary palace outside.[13] Some members of his entourage stayed there, but the English king preferred to sleep in the castle. Francis I, for his part, ordered a large number of tents and pavilions. They were made at Tours under the supervision of Galiot de Genouillac, *Grand maître de l'artillerie*. The tents of stout canvas were covered with rich materials, such as cloth of gold and silver, embroidered with various heraldic devices. Such enrichments were purchased far and wide: one official travelled seven times to Florence to buy fleurs-de-lys made of cloth of gold. Timber for the tent masts was taken from forests in Auvergne and Forez. Once made, the tents were transported to Ardres by 104 carters and 466 horses, and the ground was prepared by 200 pioneers. Eventually between 300 and 400 tents, emblazoned with the arms of their owners, were pitched in a meadow outside the town.[14] The finest was the French king's tent: it was 120 feet high and supported by two masts lashed together. The covering was of gold brocade with three broad stripes of blue velvet powdered with gold fleurs-de-lys. At the top was a life-size statue in walnut and painted blue and gold of St Michael, holding a dart in one hand and a shield in the other. The tent's ropes, striped in the king's colours, were thick enough to serve as cables for a ship of 300 tons or more. Near the great tent were three others, equally sumptuous, for the king's use as a chapel or secret chamber, wardrobe and council chamber respectively. Fifteen smaller pavilions stood nearby.[15] Francis started building a banqueting house: a rotunda on brick foundations with walls of board 30 inches high, painted to resemble brick. Almost certainly this was the 'hous of solas & sporte, of large and mightie compas' described by the chronicler, Edward Hall.[16] This, however, was not completed in time and thus never used.[17] The queen of France, the king's mother and great nobles had their own tents and pavilions which, according to one observer, surpassed in beauty the pyramids of Egypt and the angelic visages of the 'Heroydes princesses'. However, only four days after the start of the meeting the tents had to be taken down because of high winds and rain. The mast of the king's tent was shattered, but Francis was not entirely dependent on it as he had requisitioned four houses in Ardres and part of the abbey.[18]

Feeding everyone was another challenge for the organisers. Sir John Peachy reported from Calais on 18 April that the local butchers had beef and mutton only for three weeks and fuel only for one. The French, it seems, came to the rescue. Châtillon assured Worcester that there would be no shortage of supplies: he had ordered wine, meat and fodder to be provided at Merguyson and the English would be able to buy whatever they wanted there.[19] Food and drink, it seems, were plentiful at the Field of Cloth of Gold and reasonably priced.

Henry VIII arrived at Calais on 31 May. He should have been at Guînes on that day, but, as he explained to Francis, his ladies needed to recover from their Channel crossing. Without insisting on strict observance of Wolsey's rules, Francis reminded Henry to be at the meeting place on the appointed day. While the English court spent four days resting at Calais, Wolsey called on Francis. He was escorted by a hundred gentlemen clad in crimson velvet and wearing heavy gold chains or carrying maces. The cardinal was met along the way by high-ranking French courtiers and saluted by salvos fired by the guns of neighbouring castles. A treaty, signed on 6 June, bolstered the marriage alliance of 1518 and reaffirmed the French obligation of one million gold crowns.[20] Some last-minute hitches also had to be cleared up. Henry VIII threatened at one point to go home unless Francis removed troops that had been concealed near the meeting place.[21]

At 5 p.m. on 7 June, the feast of Corpus Christi, a signal was fired by a gun at Guînes to which another at Ardres replied. This was the cue for each king to mount his horse and for two enormous processions to begin moving towards the Val Doré from Guînes and Ardres respectively. The French were apparently more elegantly dressed than the English, but the heavy gold chains worn by the latter were much admired. The tall plumes worn by the Swiss troops in the French procession seemed to brush the sky. Eventually, the processions faced each other in silence on the mounds in the Val Doré. A fanfare of trumpets, sackbuts and clarions then gave the signal for the kings to detach themselves from their companies. They rode towards the centre of the valley, gathering speed as they did so. Spurring their horses as if to engage in combat, they suddenly pulled hard at their reins, drew alongside each other and embraced. They dismounted with agility and embraced again before retiring arm in arm to the tent that had been prepared for them. Here they were joined by Wolsey and Admiral Bonnivet while the marquis of Dorset and the duc de Bourbon, each holding a naked sword, guarded the entrance. About an hour later, the kings came into the open and introduced their courtiers to each other. As the afternoon was warm and everyone thirsty, wine in huge goblets and spice cakes were produced and avidly consumed. As darkness fell, the kings parted with a show of reluctance.[22]

The Field of Cloth of Gold lasted from 7 to 24 June. The meeting of the kings was followed on 9 June by the feat of arms. This, too, required careful preparation. First, it was proclaimed by English and French heralds in England, France and the Netherlands; secondly, a convenient site had to be found. Eventually, one was chosen on English soil. The field itself, about 900 feet by 320 feet, was surrounded by a ditch and bulwark. There were entries with triumphal arches at each end and, in line with them, ran the tilt about 240 feet in length. There were two stands for spectators and two arming chambers. An important feature was the Tree of Honour. This was an artificial tree, like an elm, around which were entwined a hawthorn for England and a raspberry bush for France. It was also adorned with over two thousand cherries of crimson satin and stood on a square mound with a railing on which were hung three shields representing the three successive parts of the challenge: tilt, tournament in the open field and armed combat at the barriers.[23] Preparations for the tournament and 'feat of arms' required a large number of horses as mounts and as gifts for exchange by the monarchs. Vast quantities of armour and weapons were also obtained, including hundreds of two-handed and heavy swords. Francis, who disliked such weapons, told Sir Richard Wingfield that the tourney on horseback would be better fought with a 'more nymble sworde'. Complicated regulations were drawn up to prevent participants from running too many courses and to limit accidents: sharp steel was banned, as was closing in on an adversary.

The kings came to the tournament field on 9 June with their retinues. Francis rode 'Dappled Duke', a magnificent horse from the Mantuan stud which Henry admired so much that Francis exchanged it for Henry's Neapolitan courser.[24] A problem of precedence posed by the Tree of Honour was neatly solved by placing the royal shields side by side and at the same height. The queens arrived on the field in litters covered with cloth of gold; their companions followed on palfreys or in waggons. The tilting was of variable quality. One eyewitness reported that both kings behaved valiantly, especially Francis, 'who shivered spears like reeds and never missed a stroke'; another wrote that few spears were shivered and no notable strokes given, except one that splintered Henry's spear. The kings did not compete with each other individually, but led rival teams, one English, the other French. The jousting was notable mainly for the lavish costumes and devices of the combatants. The French kept everyone guessing by means of a device in pictures and words, which ran as a serial intermittently throughout the first week of the tournament. The complete sentence read: 'Hart fastened in paine endles, when she delivereth me not of bondes.' The English contented themselves with shorter devices such as a heart on fire surmounted by a hand holding a watering can quenching the flames, inscribed: 'Pour réveiller'.[25]

The feat of arms was rounded off by a tournament on horseback using swords. The kings threw themselves into the fray, shattering plate armour and corselets, and striking sparks from their weapons. Francis had a plume sliced from his helm. This was followed by fighting at the barriers. A square stockade had been erected with a long bar about three feet high in the centre to which were attached two side bars which could be swung back and forth like a gate in order to force the combatants apart. The fighting, like the tourney on horseback, was between two men on each side: after fighting with rebated spears, they cudgelled each other with the stumps, and finally fought with swords. [26]

Feasting replaced combat on Sunday, 10 June: Henry VIII dined at Ardres with Queen Claude and Francis at Guînes with Catherine of Aragon. Their times of departure and return were announced by signal guns. Elaborate heraldic *entremets* were presented at Ardres, while a vast amount of food and drink was consumed at Guînes; both banquets were followed by music and dancing. At Guînes the ball was delayed while Francis kissed all the ladies, except four or five who were 'ould and not faire standing together'.[27] On 11 June the tournament was resumed, offering the ladies an opportunity to show off their finery. Foul weather, however, often interrupted play. To pass the time, the kings watched a wrestling match. This was followed by archery in which Henry demonstrated his skill. According to the memoirist Florange, he also tried to wrestle with Francis. Seizing the latter's arm, he exclaimed: 'Brother, let us wrestle!' Francis, however, reacting with lightning speed, crooked Henry's leg and laid him flat on his back. Henry got up flushed and angry, but a diplomatic incident was averted by an announcement that dinner was served.[28]

So far, a strict etiquette had regulated the events. Finding this tiresome, Francis paid a surprise visit to Henry at Guînes castle early on Sunday, 17 June. 'My brother,' he declared as he burst into his bedchamber, 'here am I your prisoner.' Such a gesture of trust greatly impressed the English. Not to be outdone, Henry turned up at Ardres two days later as Francis was getting out of bed.[29] The evening of 17 June was given over to feasting and dancing. Henry appeared in a Milanese outfit accompanied by six German drummers, eight 'Eastlanders' wearing red hats with yellow plumes, and ten people in long gowns of the kind worn by English doctors with mottoes embroidered on them.[30] The two nations doubtless learnt much about each other's manners at the Field of Cloth of Gold. 'From many most wanton creatures in the company of the French ladies,' wrote Polydore Vergil, 'the English ladies adopted a new garb which, on my oath, was singularly unfit for the chaste; even to-day there are some who dress in this style, abandoning for the most part the far more modest costume of their forbears.'[31]

On 23 June an altar was set up on the tournament field and Wolsey officiated at mass attended by mitred bishops with as much pomp as if he had been pope. Music was provided by the two royal chapels; they sang alternate parts of the mass, each accompanied by an organist.[32] During the service 'a great artificial salamander or dragon, four fathoms long and full of fire', appeared in the air from Ardres. Many onlookers were frightened, thinking it a comet or some monster as no attachment was visible. It flew over the chapel to Guînes 'as fast as a footman can go and as high as a bolt shot from a crossbow'. Was it a firework which pyrotechnicians had let off prematurely or a kite pulled by a wire? Historians are still debating the matter.[33] Once mass was over, the dean of St Paul's, Richard Pace, standing on a stage, proclaimed a plenary indulgence and conferred the pope's blessing on the two kings. An *al fresco* meal followed along with a display of foot combat with pikes and swords.

The final celebrations took place on Sunday, 24 June. Francis and some twenty couples rode to Guînes in masquing apparel. The ladies had horned headdresses and plumes. Francis himself was in murray (purple-red) brocade with a hood and hat in the German fashion decked with yellow and murray feathers. On arrival, he and his masquers dined before entering the apartment of Catherine of Aragon who pretended at first not to recognise them. They then unmasked and dancing began to the accompaniment of fifes. Francis then withdrew before returning dressed in an outfit that sparkled with emeralds under a black cape of satin and velvet slashed with gold. Once the dancing had ended, the English queen bestowed jewels, rings and collars on Frenchmen who had distinguished themselves in the joust. Francis received a diamond and ruby ring; he then left after kissing all the ladies present. In the meantime Henry and his sister went to Ardres with four companies of male and female masquers. Sad farewells followed. Louise of Savoy told the foreign ambassadors that the kings had parted with tears in their eyes, intending to build at their joint expense a palace in the Val Doré where they might meet each year, as well as a chapel dedicated to Our Lady of Friendship.[34] Neither was ever built. Francis and Henry remained on good terms for about a year before being pulled apart by the force of events. In May 1522 Henry declared war on Francis.

Henry VIII and Francis I's Second Meeting in Boulogne, 1532

By 1532 Francis I and Henry VIII had again sunk their differences. The widening rift between England and the papacy caused by Henry's repudiation of his wife, Catherine of Aragon, seriously concerned Francis, who needed to be on good terms with both pope and monarch. In April 1531 he sent Cardinal Gramont to Rome to help solve the problem of Henry's divorce and to propose a marriage between his own son Henri duc d'Orléans and the pope's niece Catherine de' Medici. Meanwhile, he and King Henry met for the second time. This encounter was less elaborate than the Field of Cloth

Gold: it lasted only eight days (21–29 October 1532), had far fewer participants and took place successively in Boulogne and Calais.[35] Women, except
for a few in Calais, were excluded as a direct consequence of Henry's determination to bring his mistress, Anne Boleyn. Finding a match for her on the
French side proved impossible. Francis's sister, Marguerite, initially agreed to
come, but backed out at the last minute. Even if Anne had been queen, her
presence at Boulogne would have posed problems since Queen Eleanor was
Catherine of Aragon's niece and consequently hostile to Henry's remarriage.
In the end Anne and her ladies remained in Calais; no French lady attended
the meeting.

The kings met on 21 October and went first to Boulogne, where they were
met by the dauphin and his brother. Henry VIII kissed them on the mouth
and they thanked him for his help in getting them released from their Spanish
prison. On 25 October the meeting moved to Calais, where Francis and his
suite were handsomely entertained. The French king, ever courteous, gave
Anne Boleyn a costly diamond. On Sunday, 27 October Henry offered his
French guests a lavish banquet followed by a dance in which Francis partnered Anne before having a long conversation with her in a window recess.[36]
A treaty was signed on 28 October, and next day Montmorency and Chabot
were made knights of the Garter.[37] Henry VIII also handed over to Francis
his illegitimate son, Henry Fitzroy, to be brought up at the French court.

The Meeting between Francis I and Pope Clement VII in Marseille, 1533

In January 1533 Pope Clement VII agreed to meet Francis I after accepting
his proposal for a marriage between his niece Catherine de' Medici and the
king's second son, Henri. The meeting, however, had to be postponed for
various reasons: the duke of Savoy's refusal to allow Nice to be the venue, the
activities of Turkish pirates off the Italian coast, bad weather in August and
enemy intrigues. Preparations resumed, however, once the venue had been
moved to Marseille. During the summer of 1533 a huge amount of furniture,
gold and silver plate and tapestries was taken out of three royal residences and
transported south.[38] In August the Constable of Montmorency arrived in
Marseille with the duke of Albany and a huge army which the town had difficulty accommodating. They also brought carts filled with gold and silver with
which to pay the troops. On 19 August a fleet of galleys under Albany's
command set off for Italy to fetch the pope, and on 28 August Montmorency
and a large crowd of nobles set off to meet Francis and his family at
Avignon.[39] 'I do believe', wrote the chronicler Honoré de Valbelle, 'that, in
addition to the blood royal, not a single nobleman remained in France who
had not accompanied the king.'[40] Meanwhile major building works were

undertaken in Marseille. A temporary palace was prepared for the pope next to the old palace of the counts of Provence where Francis was to stay. The two buildings were linked by a wooden bridge, and the street below was sealed off so as to form a large audience chamber and reception hall.

The cardinal of Bourbon, who arrived in Marseille on 22 September, was followed next day by Cardinal Duprat. Next to arrive were Montmorency's wife and the *grande maréchale* along with many young ladies; then Madame de Vendôme and more ladies. Ambassadors came from far and wide. Marseille became so crowded that stabling had to found in shops, houses and châteaux in the surrounding countryside. Francis, accompanied by his children, arrived at the 'king's garden' outside Marseille on 8 October. A barge that had just unloaded hay carried him on to Marseille, where he visited the pope's lodging before going to his own. Francis then took his children on a boat trip to the château d'If. Next day he met the queen at Aubagne.

Catherine de' Medici, who had set off on 6 September from La Spezia on one of Albany's galleys, landed at Villefranche, where she waited to be joined by her uncle, Pope Clement VII. He left Rome on 9 September with an escort that included thirteen cardinals among whom was Ippolito de' Medici, whose pages were dressed like Turks and armed with bows and scimitars. As the pope's galley entered the harbour at Marseille on 11 October, gun batteries fired a welcoming salvo. Clement was then taken to the 'king's garden' where many prelates and lords, both French and Italian, had gathered to welcome him. Musicians played as he dined.[41] That afternoon he went to the abbey of Saint-Victor, where he stayed overnight. On Sunday, 12 October Clement travelled to Marseille by barge accompanied by the dukes of Orléans and Angoulême. He landed near the Augustinian monastery and joined a large procession making its way to La Major, the principal church of Marseille. A white mare at the centre of the procession carried a casket containing the Blessed Sacrament. The pope, sitting under a golden canopy supported by leading noblemen, was preceded by a large number of noblemen, fourteen cardinals and some sixty prelates. The king's sons and many courtiers walked near Clement 'in good order and devoutly'.

Francis entered Marseille on 13 October accompanied by peers, knights of the Order of St Michael, local nobility, courtiers and cardinals. Flanked by two cardinals and accompanied by his sons, he went to the pope's residence where he knelt and kissed the pontiff's feet. He and Clement then retired to talk business. Next day Queen Eleanor entered Marseille. The local militia, municipal officials, courtiers and local nobles went in procession to welcome her. Eleanor sat with one of the king's daughters in a magnificent chariot flanked by the cardinals of Lorraine and Bourbon, while the dauphin trotted on a horse nearby. Behind came Montmorency and senior nobles. Then, in four waggons covered with cloth of gold, came Madame de Vendôme with another of the king's daughters and several ladies. Thirty elegantly dressed damsels followed on palfreys.

Catherine de' Medici, duchess of Urbino, arrived in Marseille on 23 October, and five days later she and Henri were married. The day began about noon when the dauphin and his brother, Henri, left the king's residence escorted by many courtiers to call on the pope. Francis followed them, leading the bride; both were covered with pearls and precious stones. Next came Queen Eleanor and the rest of the court. The marriage was celebrated in the chapel attached to the pope's residence. That night the newlyweds, both aged fourteen, were escorted by Eleanor and her ladies to a nuptial chamber where they allegedly consummated their union in the presence of Francis, who declared that 'each had shown valour in the joust'. An exchange of gifts rounded off the celebrations. Clement gave Francis a beautiful casket with panels of crystal engraved by Valerio Belli depicting scenes from the life of Christ; also a unicorn's horn (actually a narwhal's tusk). Traditionally the

17. Casket with incised rock crystal panels showing scenes from Christ's Passion. Made by Valerio Belli, the casket was presented by Pope Clement VII to Francis I at their meeting in Marseille in 1533. It returned to Italy with Christine of Lorraine, Catherine de Medici's granddaughter, who married Grand Duke Ferdinand I in 1589.

unicorn was thought capable of expelling poisonous creatures from fountains and of purifying their waters with its horn. The pope's gift, it was said, was intended 'to make him [Francis] understand that he should keep his kingdom safe from heresy'. In return Francis gave Clement a magnificent tapestry depicting the Last Supper.[42]

The Emperor Visits France, 1539–40

Francis I's foreign policy underwent a volte-face in 1538. After years of hostility towards the emperor, he suddenly became his friend. The architect of the new policy was Montmorency, whose aim was to recover Milan by peaceful means instead of force.[43] He was supported in this by Pope Paul III, who regarded a Christian peace as the essential precondition for a new crusade.[44] In December 1537 he persuaded Francis to meet him and the emperor in the summer. The meeting at Nice lasted from 15 May until 20 June (see plate 9). As the duke of Savoy would not place the local castle at the pope's disposal, Paul III had to put up at a monastery outside the town; Charles stayed on board one of his galleys off Villefranche; Francis resided in the town. There were four encounters between the pope and the emperor, and two between the pope and the king. Francis refused to meet Charles in the pope's presence or to promise assistance against the Turks unless Milan were first restored to him.[45] In the end a ten-year truce was signed instead of a peace.[46]

Although Francis and Charles did not meet in person at Nice, their courts were in frequent contact. On 11 June Eleanor and her ladies went to meet her brother at Villefranche. As they disembarked, a wooden pier collapsed, pitching them into the sea, but owing to its shallowness no one suffered more than a soaking. On 19 June Eleanor persuaded her brother to meet Francis after the pope's departure. Paul III left Nice on the following day, whereupon Charles V sailed to Aigues-Mortes in Languedoc for his meeting with the French king. The choice of venue was significant. Aigues-Mortes was strongly fortified and had been the port from which Louis IX of France had set off on crusade; a location with such associations might serve to counter the criticism that Francis had incurred by flirting with the Ottoman sultan. Great care was given to symmetry at the meeting: the arrivals of the two sovereigns were timed to coincide precisely. But Francis also threw protocol out of the window by going with a few companions in a small boat to greet the emperor aboard his galley. Forced to respond in kind, Charles stepped ashore next day. He then startled everyone by falling on his knees in front of the dauphin and his brother as if begging for pardon for the harsh treatment they had received as hostages in Spain.

Once inside Aigues-Mortes, the two sovereigns went arm in arm to the home of a local consul for a banquet. Charles again showed humility by using his own napkin rather than two offered by Francis's daughter and daughter-in-law. After watching a ballet, the sovereigns retired to their lodgings, which were linked by a bridge. Francis now sprang a surprise on his guest that recalled one sprung on Henry VIII in 1520: escorted by the cardinal of Lorraine, Montmorency and other lords, he entered the emperor's bedchamber while Charles was still in bed. 'How are you, my brother? Have you had a good rest?' said Francis as Charles leapt up. The emperor replied that he had slept well after so much feasting the previous evening. Expressing the wish that Charles should have as much authority in France as in his own dominions, Francis gave him a diamond ring worth 30,000 *écus*. Slipping it on his finger, Charles apologized for not being able to return the gift but, removing his collar of the Golden Fleece, he placed it around Francis's neck. This automatically turned the king into an imperial subject, but Francis had the last laugh: 'Since it pleases you that I should wear your order,' he said, 'may it please you to wear mine.' As he spoke, he placed his collar of St Michael around the emperor's neck. The two men then embraced and drank a toast. Observers rubbed their eyes in disbelief. 'It seems', wrote one, 'that what we are seeing is but a dream, considering all that we have seen in the past. God is letting us know that He governs the hearts of men as He pleases.'[47]

In October 1538 Francis met his sister-in-law, Mary of Hungary, regent of the Netherlands, at Compiègne. They spent most of the time hunting, feasting and dancing before signing a treaty: Francis promised not to assist the rebels in the Low Countries against the emperor and Mary undertook to satisfy French noblemen who had lost lands there during the recent war. On the eve of her departure Francis gave her a superb diamond.[48]

These demonstrations of Franco-imperial amity were followed in the winter of 1539–40 by an even more astonishing event: Charles V's visit to France. In April 1538 a serious tax revolt had broken out in Ghent, a city in Flanders under imperial rule. Charles V, who was in Spain at the time, needed to quell the unrest as soon as possible. Several routes for getting to the Low Countries lay open to him, but the quickest was across France. In August he received an invitation from Francis to cross his kingdom, but Charles's councillors feared a trap. Might not the king of France retaliate for his imprisonment in Spain after Pavia by detaining his old enemy? In September, however, Francis renewed his invitation as well as the assurances given at Aigues-Mortes.[49] Charles also received letters urging acceptance from the king's sons, Montmorency and other leading French courtiers. Plucking up courage, Charles accepted the offer on 22 October, much to the delight of his sister,

Queen Eleanor. Francis would have liked to meet him at the Franco-Spanish border but his health would not allow it; so the responsibility was delegated to the dauphin, the duc d'Orléans and Montmorency. As they travelled south they issued instructions to towns and local noblemen on how to receive the emperor.[50]

Charles V entered France on 27 November with an escort of some twenty noblemen and fifty horses. From the moment he set foot on French soil, he was empowered to appoint to offices and ecclesiastical benefices and to pardon all prisoners, with the exception of traitors. He was given entries in all the towns through which he passed.[51] Francis, meanwhile, was carried in a litter to Loches and greeted Charles there on 12 December. Sartorially the contrast between the two sovereigns could not have been sharper: whereas Francis wore a suit of purple satin and a bejewelled bonnet, Charles, who had just lost his wife, was dressed entirely in black, as was his entourage, and so they remained throughout their visit.[52] After their meeting, the two rulers fraternised, hunting together and visiting some of the finest Renaissance buildings. At Chenonceau Charles was able to admire the pretty château built by Thomas Bohier which the crown had confiscated.[53] The next port of call – Amboise – was the scene of an unfortunate accident. As the emperor and his suite rode up the ramp inside the Tour Hurtault, some tapestries caught fire. The tower filled with smoke, the horses panicked and the guests had to cover their mouths. Francis was understandably furious, particularly as the incident might have been given a sinister interpretation. He wanted to punish those responsible, but Charles dissuaded him from so doing; the fire, he said, had been an accident; no one was to blame.

From Amboise the royal party travelled to Blois and Chambord, where the emperor was able to admire the double-spiral staircase. At Orléans he was given an entry rich in symbols celebrating the new Franco-imperial friendship. The welcoming party included schoolboys disguised as Turks. Francis also put on a show of strength. Twenty thousand troops had been assembled, and Charles was greeted by volleys fired from 2,392 arquebuses. At Arthenay, eighteen miles away, he was shown a stretch of newly paved highway; but it was at Fontainebleau that the most spectacular welcome awaited him. According to Père Dan, the seventeenth-century historian, as the emperor entered the forest

he was greeted by a troop of people disguised as sylvan gods and goddesses, who at the sound of the hautboys had gathered and run forward. They performed a rustic dance, which was agreeable no less on account of the strange costumes they wore as of the order and movements they followed. After dancing thus for some time, they suddenly dispersed in the forest.[54]

Continuing his approach, Charles encountered a triumphal arch on which he and Francis were represented dressed in Roman attire accompanied by figures symbolising Peace and Concord.

Charles did not stay in the Pavillon des Poêles, as was once thought, but in Montmorency's apartment in the Porte Dorée. A Mantuan envoy wrote:

> I have seen Fontainebleau, but nothing finer than in Mantua. As one enters the great courtyard, there is on the left a tall column on the top of which stand the three Graces with imperial arms and above them a cauldron of copper into which pitch will be put so as to provide a torch which will burn for two or three days. Stones have been put below it so that the column should not burn. Around the courtyard there are statues: a man and a woman holding a torch. Above, where the waterspouts are, some garlands have been hung with the emperor's arms and around the courtyard there is a false tapestry which is a very ugly sight, and the same is true everywhere, including here in Paris.[55]

Several days of entertainment were laid on at Fontainebleau, including hunts, tournaments and other warlike games. Since it was Christmas, there were undoubtedly masques too. Some drawings by Primaticcio, now in Stockholm, of costumed people may be connected with the emperor's visit. A drawing by Rosso of an elaborately costumed Hercules holding an olive branch instead of a club may also be connected with it. On Christmas Day Francis touched for the king's evil in an alley near the pond.

From Fontainebleau, Francis and Charles travelled to Vincennes in the king's great barge, lavishly equipped with every comfort, including large fireplaces. Preparations for Charles V's entry into Paris had begun early in November 1539. The *échevins* or aldermen were given their instructions by the chancellor, Guillaume Poyet, and the Constable of Montmorency. They were ordered to prepare a magnificent entry and the richest gift possible. The streets were to be paved and the drains opened up so as to wash away the filth (*immondices*). The *échevins* were also ordered to find good painters and to take stock of the city's artillery, for Francis wanted Paris to be set 'on fire' for the emperor's entry. When the *échevins* complained that their resources were limited, Montmorency reminded them that the king had never refused them anything and that they should now obey him regardless of cost. On 17 November the captains of the militia were ordered to gather horses, harnesses, jerkins and staves, to muster their men and to ensure that there were enough of them for the entry.

On 30 November an *échevin*, named Jean Croquet, reported to the *prévôt des marchands* on his mission to Chancellor Poyet at Briare-sur-Loing.

Croquet had reminded the chancellor of a promise he had made to reimburse the cost of the entry. He had also objected to the king's request for the removal of paving in the rue Saint-Antoine in preparation for a tournament. Croquet had then called on Francis at Montargis and had shown him the design of a dresser (*buffet*) which Paris thought of giving to the emperor. Francis, however, rejected the proposal. The emperor, he explained, had once told him that he detested Flemish tapestries which seemed obsessed with gormandizing. The king suggested instead a gilded statue of Hercules with two pillars that might serve as candelabra and said that he wanted Rosso to design it. Croquet duly conveyed the king's wish to the artist at Fontainebleau and returned to Paris with his design. Francis also had views on the canopy to be carried over the emperor during his entry: he insisted that only Charles's arms should figure on it. As for the proposed street theatricals, he liked them well enough, but wanted the salamander to be replaced by the twin-headed eagle. When asked by Croquet about poetic eulogies, Francis said that he did not think Charles would stop to listen to their recital. He thought they should be displayed on hoardings and written down so that the emperor might read them at his leisure. Following Croquet's return to Paris, the rue Saint-Antoine was unpaved at great cost, only to be repaved when the king then changed his mind about the tournament; this was now to take place at the Louvre. At the same time, painters and goldsmiths were commissioned to prepare theatres and triumphs. Girolamo della Robbia, who was entrusted with providing two triumphal arches in the rue Saint-Antoine, employed three painters to decorate them while he himself provided backcloths and nails.[56]

Charles V's entry into Paris on 1 January 1540 differed from other royal entries into the capital in one important respect: instead of following the traditional route from the porte Saint-Denis in the north, he entered through the porte Saint-Antoine in the east. The change necessitated the construction of a temporary tribunal near the church of Saint-Antoine-des-Champs, about four miles outside the city, where the emperor might meet the Parisian corporations. The change of route may explain why paving was needed and why the emperor was offered only two theatrical displays compared with the six staged for his sister in 1531. The new route was narrower and more sinuous than the traditional one, and had fewer open spaces where stages might be set up. Otherwise, Charles V's entry followed the usual pattern. It began with a long procession of Parisians. Led by the clergy, this also comprised members of the university, the urban militia, the *enfants de la ville* (sons of rich bourgeois families), municipal officials and the masters of the six principal guilds. Then came a host of merchants and bourgeois, the magistrates of the Châtelet, 220 *sergents à verge* and, lastly, members of the Parlement. The procession lasted several hours. As each group marched past a tribunal specially built for the occasion, some of their leaders detached themselves from the procession and mounted it to make their obeisance to Charles. He received them sitting down, flanked by the French chancellor and constable. The *prévôt des marchands* made a speech of welcome and offered Charles the keys of the city. Other speeches were made by the rector of the university and First president of the Parlement.

The afternoon was taken up by a second procession in the opposite direction. This one entered Paris with the emperor. It consisted of officers of the king's household, great officers of state, princes of the blood, nobles and royal troops. As he approached the porte Saint-Antoine, Charles V was saluted with deafening salvos fired by guns at the Bastille and on the city's ramparts. Near the gate he was invited to stand under a superb canopy of cloth of gold adorned with imperial eagles and supported by four *échevins*. As the emperor made his way to the Palais on the Île-de-la-Cité, various dignitaries took turns at carrying the canopy. An enormous crowd of spectators had gathered at open windows and on roofs to watch the procession. At the Porte Baudoyer, Charles stopped to look at a tableau vivant depicting the garden of France. Filled with lilies, it had two gates representing War and Peace. The gate of War was closed, while that of Peace was open, and through it came a beautiful nymph called Alliance. A lamb – symbol of the Golden Fleece – in the middle of the garden faced a golden St Michael. Each carried a Latin inscription. The lamb's read: 'I shall walk in peace because you are with me'; St Michael's: 'I shall guard you in all your ways.' A second tableau, near the carrefour de la Vannerie, consisted of two eagles, one holding an asp and a basilisk in its talons, the other, a lion and a dragon. Above them, rising from a cloud, was a woman, Divine Will, with a scroll in each hand bearing appropriate inscriptions. Under one of the eagles, a figure, Accord, held a beehive, while under the other Armed Discord held fire and water. Between them Peace sat enthroned.[57]

The emperor next proceeded to the Île-de-la-Cité across the Pont Notre-Dame, much admired for its two rows of identical houses. Triumphal arches in the Roman style – the first to be seen in Paris – had been erected at each end of the bridge for Queen Eleanor's entry in 1531. An awning, from which hung wreaths (*chapeaux de triomphe*), covered the bridge's entire length, and tapestries adorned the house façades. Charles was received at Notre-Dame by the papal legate and by Jean du Bellay, cardinal-bishop of Paris. He prayed at the cathedral before going to the Palais where Francis I, the cardinal of Lorraine and several princes welcomed him at the foot of a staircase. Framed by a temporary porch with flanking columns of imitation marble, the staircase led to the Petite Salle, then to the Grande Salle. This was covered with an awning divided into squares containing heraldic devices. Magnificent tapestries depicting episodes from Homer's *Iliad* and the Acts of the Apostles covered the walls. Charles and Francis supped at 'the marble table' on a raised platform while other guests sat at tables set up along the length of the hall. Against one pillar was a dresser laden with gold and silver plate, while around other pillars were platters of meat and pastries. Lighting was provided by chandeliers, each with four flaming torches. Rush matting covered the floor. The emperor and the king were served by high-ranking nobles, Montmorency acting as *maître d'hôtel*, the comte d'Enghien as *écuyer tranchant*, the comte d'Aumale as *panetier* and the prince de la Roche-sur-Yon as *échanson*. After the banquet the queen and other ladies took their places on two tiers of seats around the hall to watch the princes and lords, richly attired and wearing masks, perform various dances. Charles then retired to a bedchamber specially decorated in his honour. The hangings were of crimson satin with gold embroideries, and the bedcover of cloth of gold was adorned with pearls and precious stones.

Despite a severe chill, on 2 January 1540 Charles visited the Sainte-Chapelle where he was shown the Crown of Thorns and other prestigious relics. He was then escorted to the Louvre by the constable, the Swiss guard and two hundred gentlemen pensioners. Next day his cold was worse and Francis sent some of his own doctors to treat him. On 4 January Charles had recovered sufficiently to receive officials of the city, who offered him their gift: a silver statue of Hercules, seven feet tall. Charles accepted it graciously, but Francis confided to Cellini that it was 'the ugliest work of art he had ever seen'. The trouble apparently lay with the Parisian goldsmiths. 'Not even the best masters', wrote Cellini in his *Trattato dell'Oreficeria*, 'were able to give to that statue either grace, beauty, or style; for the simple reason that they did not know how to solder properly, and so had to stick on the legs and the head and the arms by means of fastening them with silver wire.'[58]

The emperor spent five days at the Louvre, watching jousts, tournaments and combats by day, and attending banquets, dances and masques in the evening. Although the architect Pierre Lescot had not yet been commissioned to enlarge the palace, much had been done in preparation for the emperor's visit. A temporary gateway had been erected in the courtyard within which stood a gilded statue, fifteen feet high, of Vulcan, holding a torch that burned all night. In each corner of the courtyard a gilded hand held a flaming torch.[59] All doors and windows carried the arms of the emperor, the king and the queen. The lodgings of the two sovereigns faced each other across the courtyard. The walls of the great hall were covered with gold cloth and silk, and decorated with wreaths. Charles's bedchamber was hung with green velvet embroidered with hearts containing pastoral scenes taken from Virgil's *Bucolics*. The bed was again luxurious.

On 7 January Francis entertained Charles at the château of Madrid, which was still under construction.[60] Later that day the two monarchs went to the abbey of Saint-Denis, burial place of the kings and queens of France, which also had one of the richest treasuries in France. Charles was shown Solomon's gold cup, Virgil's mirror, Charlemagne's game of chess, Roland's ivory horn, Joan of Arc's sword and the longest unicorn's horn ever discovered. From 8 to 10 January he was entertained by Montmorency at Chantilly.[61] Charles took his leave of Francis at Saint-Quentin on 20 January 1540. He was escorted as far as Valenciennes by Dauphin François, his brother, Henri, and Montmorency. They returned four days later bearing gifts from the emperor. The constable hoped that the emperor's visit would soon be followed by talks on the future of Milan, but disappointment awaited him. The duchesse d'Étampes, who hated Montmorency, on the other hand was delighted. 'I hear from a good quarter', wrote the imperial envoy to his master, 'that the reason for her angry feelings is that when Your Majesty passed through the kingdom you did not make so much of her as she expected which has hardened her heart in such a way that it will be very difficult, nay, almost impossible to appease her.'[62] The emperor's refusal to respond to Francis's hospitality in the manner that Montmorency had expected prompted the minister's fall and the rise to power of his rival, Admiral Chabot, who favoured a more traditional, warlike policy.

Summit meetings were all very well. They offered grand opportunities for rulers to impress each other by their munificence, and offered courtiers opportunities to show off and enjoy themselves, but they seldom succeeded in altering political realities. The Field of Cloth of Gold, for all its extravagant demonstration of Franco-English cordiality, failed to bring about any lasting friendship between the two courts concerned. Likewise, Francis I's seemingly magnanimous invitation to the emperor to visit France in 1539 failed to generate a peaceful resolution of the Milanese question. Only the Marseille meeting of 1533 produced a tangible result in the form of a marriage compact between France and the Holy See, but even that foundered as a result of the premature death of Pope Clement VII.

CHAPTER 9

Royal Builders

The nomadic lifestyle and growth of the court encouraged the proliferation of residences across the royal domain as well as their modernisation. Until the mid-fifteenth century, defence rather than comfort had determined the design of châteaux. They had thick walls, few outside windows, massive angle towers, *chemins de ronde*, machicolations, portcullises and moats. Such features were no longer needed after the Hundred Years' War. A comparison of three châteaux – Langeais, Le Lude and Azay-le-Rideau – illustrates the transition.[1] Langeais, begun in 1465, was a grim fortress equipped with all the essential military features; it soon became obsolete and was never finished as originally intended. Military features, however, were not abandoned overnight. Force of habit connived at their survival, albeit with significant modifications: the *chemin de ronde*, towers and machicolations became status symbols pointing to aristocratic ownership at a time when wealthy bourgeois were acquiring landed estates. As Guy Coquille wrote in 1595:

> In France, where of old it was believed that the profession of arms was to be exercised only by a nobleman, if any commoner was employed to arms, he acquired nobility by his valour, and it is still the rule that a commoner employed in the cause of arms may call himself a nobleman.[2]

At Le Lude, which was rebuilt in the 1520s, military features were given a purely decorative role. At Azay-le-Rideau, a château built between 1518 and 1527, the *chemin de ronde* and machicolations became a frieze, while the angle towers were transformed into graceful *tourelles*.

The functional revolution of the early sixteenth century was accompanied by a stylistic change from Flamboyant Gothic to the classicism of the Italian High Renaissance. This process was largely a byproduct of the Italian Wars. Meillant, a château in central France partly built by Charles d'Amboise, bears no trace of Italianism. The Tour du Lion (*c.* 1510), with its delicately carved parapet, slender twisted columns and heraldic devices, including burning mounds (a pun on the owner's name), is a perfect example of Flamboyant Gothic. It is also a fine example of the tall, external spiral staircases that the nobility of this period liked to build. Nurtured on this style of building, the first generation of Frenchmen who fought in the Italian Wars were unmoved by the more austere classical architecture they encountered in Lombardy. Some buildings, however, did impress them, notably the Certosa at Pavia and the Colleoni mausoleum in Bergamo; they admired the exuberance of the decoration and before long applied classical decoration to the façades of their homes in France. At Fontaine-Henri, for example, which was built in the late fifteenth and early sixteenth centuries, classical ornamentation was added to the façade as it was being built.[3]

Among the châteaux of Renaissance France none illustrates better the twofold revolution than Chenonceau. This was originally a fortress owned by the aristocratic family of Marques. Finding themselves hard-pressed economically, they sold off their outlying estates, hoping to retain Chenonceau itself, but early in the sixteenth century they were expropriated by Thomas Bohier, one of Francis I's *gens de finance*. He knew Italy, having served as paymaster to the French army, and wanted a house near Amboise, where the court often resided. Chenonceau answered his need, but the building was too old-fashioned for his taste, so he pulled it down, retaining only the moat and one of the towers as status symbols. About 1513 he put up an elegant new château in the Renaissance style on the foundations of a water mill.[4]

Little remains of the château of Amboise as it was during the reign of Charles VIII: much of it was destroyed or insensitively restored during the nineteenth century. The king's architectural contribution should not be overlooked, however: he liked the château, which was his birthplace and had been his childhood home, and he set about embellishing it shortly before his invasion of Italy in 1494. He planned to enlarge it by bridging a moat and annexing a hill on which stood a church. At the same time, he ordered the construction of two large towers and two *corps de logis*, one for himself overlooking the River Loire, the other, called 'Des Sept Vertus', for his queen on the south side. In November 1492 he proudly showed a model of his new château to the Venetian envoy Gentile Becchi. Two years later, after seeing palaces in Italy, Charles became disenchanted with his French residences. 'At this hour,' wrote Bishop Briçonnet to the queen, 'he values neither Amboise nor any other place he has.' The king collected much artistic booty in Naples only to lose it at Fornovo, yet he did bring back twenty-two Italian artisans. Unfortunately their contribution at Amboise is unknown. Apart from a few minor details, the château remained essentially Flamboyant Gothic. Not even the wide ramps inside the towers, allowing horsemen to reach the terrace,

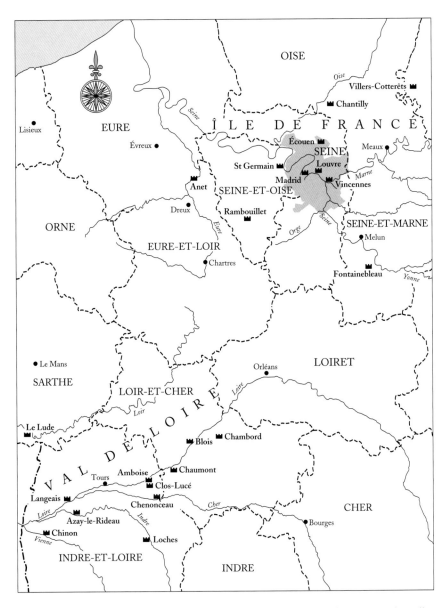

Map 2. The principal sixteenth-century châteaux. The court tended to stay in the valley of the Loire until 1528 when Francis I moved most of his building activities to the Île-de-France and Paris.

18. The château of Amboise. Situated on a spur overlooking the River Loire, this was the birthplace of Charles VIII (1483–98), who enlarged it. It was here, too, that he died after hitting his head against a lintel. Francis I spent much of his childhood here. In 1560 the château was the setting for the Tumult of Amboise. It houses the tomb of Leonardo da Vinci.

were an innovation: such a ramp already existed at Montreuil-Bellay. As Amboise was nearing completion, Charles VIII wanted a garden similar to those he had seen in Italy. After visiting Poggio Reale, he wrote: 'You cannot imagine the beautful gardens that I have seen . . . for by my faith it seems that they need only Adam and Eve to turn them into an earthly paradise.'[5] The Neapolitan gardener, Pacello da Mercogliano, whom the king invited to Amboise, designed borders and open arcades where the first orange trees introduced into France were displayed. Following Charles's death in April 1498, work at Amboise was continued by Louis XII, who settled there after his marriage to Anne of Brittany.[6]

Blois

Louis XII concentrated his attention on the château of Blois which had belonged to his family since 1397. It was also his birthplace and where he had been brought up. From December 1498 he started building a new wing.[7] The work was sufficiently advanced by 1501 for Archduke Philip of Austria to stay there, and was completed about 1503. The architecture of Louis XII's wing is remarkable for its balanced proportions, its abundance of ornamental detail and the lively contrast in the materials used – red brick overall with vertical mouldings of white stone. In a niche above the entrance gateway was the equestrian statue of the monarch by Guido Mazzoni. Destroyed in 1792, it was replaced in 1857 by a poor imitation. Such statues were common at the time over the entrances to aristocratic houses, a fashion doubtless inspired by Italian monuments glorifying *condottieri*. Louis XII's wing consists of two superimposed galleries. The lower one, which opens like a cloister on to the inner courtyard, is notable for the superb quality of the decoration. Italian motifs, such as candelabra, putti, dolphins and scrolls, are assimilated with more traditional ones, like leaves, human faces and angels. The columns are alternately round and square: the former are adorned with lozenges containing the lily of France or the ermine of Brittany, and the latter have flat pilasters with candelabra of Lombard design. In addition to his wing, Louis XII rebuilt the chapel of Saint-Calais of which only the choir remains.

Blois was especially famous for its garden designed by Pacello da Mercogliano. Situated on the far side of a ravine, it was on three levels. The lowest, called Jardin de la Bretonnerie, was connected to the château by a narrow viaduct spanning the ravine. The Jardin de la Reine, above, was a rectangle, 200 metres by 90, surrounded by latticework arbours and divided into perpendicular paths. At the central crossing was a fountain inside a wooden pavilion topped by a statue of St Michael. This is known as the Pavillon d'Anne de Bretagne; she was apparently very fond of gardens. Her Book of Hours containing three hundred paintings by Jean Bourdichon of flowers and fruit is a major source of information on the flora of Renaissance gardens. The Jardin du Roi, on the top level at Blois, was finished in 1505. The Italian architect, Fra Giocondo, was commissioned to bring water to the gardens by means of an aqueduct.[8] De Beatis has left us the following description of the gardens at Blois as they were in 1517:

> The great garden is completely surrounded by galleries, which are wide and long enough to ride horses down at full gallop. They have five pergolas resting on wooden trellises, but according to the Cardinal these would be somewhat low for the full manège and high jumping on powerful chargers. In the middle is a domed pavilion over a beautiful fountain which supplies water for those in the other gardens . . .. They contain almost all kinds of fruit to be found in Terra di Lavoro except figs, for although there are a few fig-trees they produce tiny fruit that hardly ever ripens. I saw many bitter-orange trees and other large citrus trees, which produce very decent fruit, but they are planted in wooden boxes full of earth and in winter are pulled in under a roomy loggia in the garden, safe from snow and harmful winds.

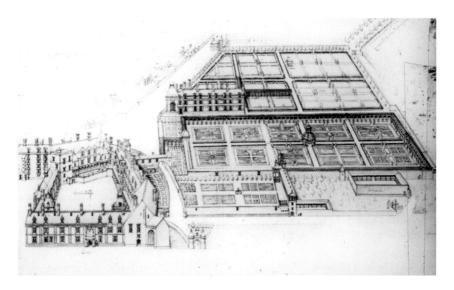

19. The château of Blois in the sixteenth century. Engraving from Jacques Androuet du Cerceau's *Les plus excellents bastiments de France* (1576–9). This was the birthplace and favourite residence of Louis XII (1498–1515), who built in the Flamboyant Gothic style the wing that bears his name. The west wing was destroyed and rebuilt in the seventeenth century. It was at Blois that Henri duc de Guise was assassinated by order of Henry III in 1588.

> Above this loggia are the quarters of the gardener-priest who has become very rich with benefices in comparison with his former situations. There are many plants and herbs for salads – endives and long-stalked cabbages as fine as in Rome.[9]

A large enamel plaque, now at the Louvre, depicts St Thomas, the patron saint of architects, with the features of Francis I (see plate 6). In the course of his reign he rebuilt or refurbished eleven châteaux, some of which survive. The Mantuan envoy, Fabrizzio Bobba, wrote from the French court on 23 July 1539:

> His Majesty is at present at one of his properties, called Becosso [Becoiseau] ten leagues from here . . .. The site is well suited to hunting, being situated in the midst of several fine forests. His Majesty has drawn with his own hand a large building which he wishes to have built. It so happens that wherever he goes, he draws plans, then nothing is done.[10]

Francis built two kinds of châteaux: some were 'standing houses', that is to say, palaces capable of accommodating the court over an extended period; others were smaller country houses, or *maisons de plaisance*, where the king liked to stay with a select group of friends. His earliest building activities were centred on the valley of the Loire at Blois, which belonged to his first wife.

In its present state, the château of Blois shows four distinct styles of construction reaching back to the Middle Ages. Francis began work there in June 1515. Stazio Gadio, the secretary of Federico Gonzaga, who spent two years at the French court, describes how the king led his young master by the hand at Blois. After showing him the gardens,

> his most gracious majesty, not content with such great proofs of affection as he had given him, wished to show him some parts of the château which has been very well arranged and embellished since he became king, on the side where the lodgings of King Louis once stood. Since demolishing these, he has rebuilt them and made a very beautiful façade of freestone decorated in the most excellent manner, with very beautiful galleries. It is actually being worked on now, both inside and out, while a beautiful façade all of stone is being erected on the courtyard side.[11]

20. The château of Blois: the façade of the Loggias. Around 1520 Francis I rebuilt one wing in the new classical style imported from Italy. Built by local masons not fully conversant with the rules of classical architecture, the façade is contemporary with loggias designed by Bramante for the Vatican and was probably influenced by them. In the sixteenth century it overlooked the château's gardens.

Francis I's wing was built on the site of an earlier medieval building, the outer wall of which was retained and used as a partition wall within the new structure. The work involved a realignment of the roof and the removal of some dormer windows. On the garden side Francis built the 'façade of the loggias', widening the original building by fifteen feet. This was the work of French master-masons, whose understanding of classical rules was evidently imperfect. There are two sets of loggias, one above the other, and above them a third floor of flat-headed openings separated by freestanding columns. The idea of an arcaded loggia on the outside of a château marked a radical break with tradition: French châteaux had hitherto been inward-looking structures. The loggias at Blois were meant to offer courtiers a view of the extensive garden and of the equestrian sports that took place there. On the courtyard side at Blois is a monumental staircase. Many external staircases were built in late medieval France, but that at Blois is more monumental, its decoration far removed from the light surface patterning of, earlier châteaux.[12]

Chambord

On 6 September 1519 Francis I announced that he had ordered the construction of 'a fine and sumptuous building' at Chambord, a village some twelve miles from Blois on the edge of a large forest where the medieval counts of Blois had hunted stags, wild boar and roe deer. [13] It had belonged to the House of Orléans since 1397 and had become part of the royal domain in 1498. A small château already existed at Chambord along with a priory where Francis I must have stayed before his new residence was built. It seems clear that, from the start, he intended it to be a *maison de plaisance*. When the Venetian ambassador, Giovanni Soranzo, in 1550, asked why Francis had chosen to reside in such a secluded and unhealthy spot, he was told:

> King Francis chose to build this great palace here for two reasons: first, because it was situated where none can live, which satisfied him as he did not like being followed by many people, for he wished to be left alone so as to rest quietly without disturbance and to devote much time to the ladies; then for the great commodity of the hunting which he much enjoyed.[14]

A Mantuan envoy reported in December 1519: 'It is said that the day after tomorrow or the next, the king and the ladies will come to Sanburgho [Chambord] four leagues from here, and that they will stay for three or four days. They will then set off for Cognac.'[15]

21. The château of Chambord. The first of many châteaux built by King Francis I (1515–47). Situated in a forest close to Blois, the huge building was essentially a hunting lodge, visited by the court only sixty-two times in thirty-two years.

The building of Chambord took from 1519 until about 1562, with an interruption of twenty-seven months following Francis I's departure to Italy in July 1524. The first floor of the keep was probably complete by then; dates inscribed on parts of the roof indicate that they were finished between 1533 and 1539; the rest of the château was built later. As work proceeded, the responsible team changed three times. Its members were all French, as were the master-masons. One of these, Jacques Sourdeau, who also served for a time as treasurer, could neither read nor write. He and his fellow workmen were doubtless experienced in building and technically competent, but their knowledge of the art of architecture must have been nil. Chambord cost a huge amount of money: 444,570 *l.* under Francis I and 91,008 *l.* under Henry II, but funding fluctuated as other calls were made on the royal finances.[16] It seems that Francis I, not for the last time, failed to consider the expense.

The plan of Chambord consists of a square keep flanked by four large round towers from which run lower buildings with towers at the corners. The château was originally surrounded by a moat filled with water. The keep is divided into four parts by a Greek cross, the centre being occupied by two intertwined spiral staircases within the same well. They are open on both sides, the newel being lit from above by a lantern. The arrangement leaves a

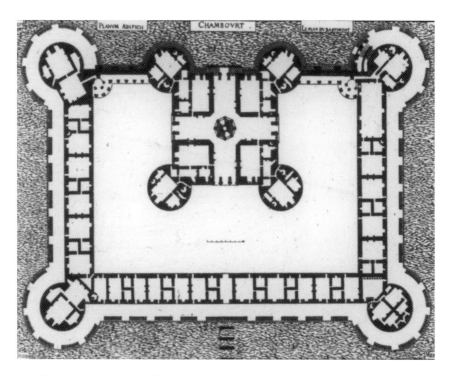

22. Plan of the château of Chambord. Engraving in Jacques Androuet du Cerceau, *Les plus excellents bastiments de France* (1576–9). The keep with its Greek cross and set of rooms in each angle recalls that of Poggio a Cajano, a villa built near Florence by Giuliano da Sangallo for Lorenzo de Medici in 1483–5. The double spiral staircase in the centre, however, is an innovation possibly inspired by Leonardo da Vinci.

square space in each angle, subdivided into a lodging of three rooms (*chambre, cabinet, garde-robe*). This ground-floor pattern is repeated on two floors providing altogether twelve lodgings of equal size. In addition there are twelve more lodgings in the towers and eight on the terraces bringing the total to thirty-two. The origin of the cruciform plan is Italian. Except for the staircase, it recalls the internal arrangement of Poggio a Cajano, a villa outside Florence built by Giuliano da Sangallo for Lorenzo de' Medici in the 1480s. The roof at Chambord is extraordinary: it consists of terraces commanding superb views of the surrounding forest, and is enlivened by a profusion of pinnacles, dormer windows and chimney stacks adorned with inlaid stones.

Who designed Chambord? Certainly not the superannuated officials and illiterate stonemasons listed in the building accounts. These make no mention of an architect, but only someone with genius could have produced such a design. Two names have been suggested: Domenico da Cortona and Leonardo da Vinci. Domenico, a pupil of Sangallo, was working in France early in Francis's reign. In 1532 he was paid a large sum for making wooden models over the past fifteen years of various buildings, including Chambord. Such a model could still be seen at Blois in the seventeenth century when it was drawn by the historian André Félibien. It looks like a model for the keep at Chambord, though it differs from the built work in several respects: a straight staircase occupies one of the arms of the cross instead of the double spiral at the centre, and the elevation presents semicircular bays regularly distributed across the entire structure. Can one deduce from this that Domenico designed Chambord? He was not just a model-maker. In 1532 he was commissioned to design a new town hall for Paris.

Leonardo had been employed as an architect in Milan by Galeazzo di San Severino and Charles d'Amboise, and his interest in architecture is manifest in the drawings made during his last years in France. True, he died in 1519 just as the first stone of Chambord was being laid. He can, therefore, be ruled out as the actual builder of Chambord, but his ideas could have been used.[17] Leonardo was still alive in June 1518 when Francis threw a banquet at the Clos-Lucé, and it seems inconceivable that he would not have consulted Leonardo, who was living there at the time, about his grand design. Two of Chambord's features point to Leonardo's authorship: the plan of the keep and the central spiral staircase. According to Jean Guillaume, the centralised plan had no precedent in civil architecture. It is to be found, however, among Leonardo's drawings. These also show a straight staircase occupying one arm of the cross dividing the keep, as in the wooden model. When Chambord was built, however, the straight staircase was abandoned in favour of the double spiral at the centre of the cross. Both staircases have precedents in Leonardo's drawings. The straight one is identical to one built by Leonardo for the villa of Charles d'Amboise in Milan. As for the spiral staircase, it recalls drawings of fortresses made by Leonardo some thirty years previously that reveal a fascination with multiple spirals enabling different kinds of troops to ascend and descend without obstructing each other. At Chambord, the purpose was similar: the staircase, which may originally have been conceived as quadruple, allowed courtiers to circulate freely in opposite directions without getting in each other's way. Although Leonardo died in 1519, it seems that his ideas lived on to be used and modified by Francis I between 1520 and 1540.[18]

Not everyone agrees with Guillaume. Monique Chatenet adheres to the view that the keep may have been inspired by Poggio a Cajano. She also points to similarities between the openwork spiral staircase at Blois and that at Chambord.[19] Henri Zerner finds Guillaume's suggestion appealing, but points to the existence of earlier French examples of spiral staircases with a double revolution. The Chambord staircase, he suggests, may be seen 'not as an invention of Leonardo da Vinci, but rather as a French motif introduced into an Italian layout'. Zerner also believes that 'the overall physiognomy of the château is at odds with the aesthetic that comes through so forcibly in Leonardo's drawings'. It is, on the other hand, perfectly in keeping with the spirit of other châteaux of the Loire – Bury, Chenonceau and Azay-le-Rideau – which may have served as models.[20] In the final analysis no one knows who designed Chambord: it may have been the king himself acting under the inspiration of Leonardo and others.

The Move to the Île-de-France

In March 1528 Francis wrote to the Parisian authorities announcing his intention 'henceforth to reside most of the time in our good town and city of Paris and its neighbourhood rather than elsewhere in the kingdom'.[21] In the event he continued to travel all over France, but he did shift the focus of his building activities from the Loire Valley to Paris and its surrounding neighbourhood. He began rebuilding the Louvre, erected the château of Madrid in the Bois de Boulogne, remodelled Saint-Germain-en-Laye, built Villers-Cotterêts to the north of the capital and embarked on the transformation of Fontainebleau. Various motives may have dictated this shift. Paris had been restless during his captivity in Spain and he may have felt the need to reassert his authority by making his presence felt. Strategic reasons may also have influenced him: the main zone of conflict with the Holy Roman Empire had moved from Italy to the northern and eastern borders of France, which were more easily reached from Paris than from the Loire. Another possible motive may have been the king's desire to be near his principal minister, Anne de Montmorency, whose châteaux – Chantilly, Écouen and Fère-en-Tardenois – stood near the capital. The minister frequently received Francis as his guest during this period.

In 1528 the Louvre remained a medieval fortress without a courtyard suitable for the kind of entertainments favoured by Renaissance princes. So the first step taken by Francis was to create one by demolishing the central keep. 'By command of the king,' writes the Bourgeois de Paris, 'work was begun on demolishing the great tower of the Louvre. This cost 200,000 *l.* to demolish and the king had this done to turn the Louvre into a *logis de plaisance* for his own residence.' The chronicler deplores the loss of the tower, which 'was very beautiful, tall and strong, and was a suitable prison for famous men. It was said to be eleven feet thick at the top and twenty-three at the base.'[22] The Louvre was also modernised in other ways: the moat was filled and access improved. Francis ordered a street on the east side to be made 'beautiful, wide and straight', and an embankment built 'giving passage to the horses pulling merchandise along the river'. Writing to Montmorency in August

1530, Nicolas de Neufville describes work newly commissioned by the king, including the construction of various offices and the refurbishment of a council chamber.[23] The royal lodging, in the Louvre's south wing, was smaller than that formerly occupied by Charles V, an adjustment possibly necessitated by the court's expansion in size since Charles's time.[24] The queen resided above the king, and her ladies occupied three rooms above hers.

Rebuilding the Louvre took a long time. For twenty years Francis was content merely to improve its convenience while giving it an occasional facelift. Many repairs were carried out for the emperor's visit in 1540.

All the weathercocks were regilded. The arms of France were in several places repainted and displayed . . .. Most of the casements were enlarged and the windows painted. The number of apartments was increased . . .. This château became so liveable that Charles V, the king, the queen, the dauphin, the dauphine, the king and queen of Navarre, the Children of France, Cardinal Tournon, the constable and even the duchesse d'Étampes, Francis I's mistress, each had apartments proportionate to their status. Such was the expenditure at that time that an entire register of the royal works is full of it and contains nothing else.[25]

23. The inner courtyard of the palace of the Louvre in Paris. In 1528 Francis I demolished the keep of the ancient fortress in order to create an open space suitable for tournaments and other activities. The courtyard, called the *Cour Carrée*, was begun by the architect, Pierre Lescot, and given its decoration of bas-reliefs by the sculptor, Jean Goujon.

It was only at the end of his reign that Francis ordered Pierre Lescot to demolish the west wing and replace it with the south-west wing of the present *Cour Carrée*. The work was continued after 1547 by Henry II.

In the 1540s the Italian architect Sebastiano Serlio submitted a project for the reconstruction of the Louvre which was never realised. This consisted of a huge rectangular building, 600 by 1,200 feet, laid out in a symmetrical manner along a central axis. Each of three large rectangles within the building contained a courtyard: one square, one octagonal and one circular. They were flanked by other rectangular courtyards and behind the residence lay a garden. Had Serlio's project been built, it would have given Francis I one of the most monumental princely residences of the time; but it departed radically from French tradition. In Italy it was usual for the elements of an architectural scheme to obey an overriding system; not so in France, where the predominant impulse was not unification but conglomeration: an architectural composition was conceived of as a piecing-together of disparate elements.[26] Serlio's design would also have entailed the clearance of a heavily built-up part of Paris and doubtless cost far more than Francis could afford.

Madrid

Nothing remains of the château of Madrid, which Francis built in the Bois de Boulogne, just outside Paris, though its plan and elevation are recorded in drawings, engravings and eyewitness accounts.[27] Work on the château began in 1528 and lasted for more than twenty years. Two-thirds of the roof had been completed by 1547. Why did Francis need a new residence only six kilometres from Paris? The answer is given in letters patent of 1 August 1528 in which he expresses the wish 'to find his pleasure and relaxation in hunting'.[28] Although much smaller than the other forests associated with royal houses, the Bois de Boulogne had the advantage of proximity to the capital. Earlier French kings had hunting parks, but so far none had built a palace inside one; Francis was the first to do so. When he appointed Duprat as the château's captain in May 1530, he described it as a *maison de plaisance* where the chancellor might escape the cares of state. It was close to Neuilly, where Francis normally crossed the Seine on his way to Saint-Germain-en-Laye.[29]

Madrid had neither courtyard nor moat and consisted of five blocks. The central block was occupied by a large vestibule or *salle* flanked by two open loggias. On either side was another block containing a small hall (*sallette*) on an *entresol* flanked by two *cabinets*. The *sallette* had a fireplace 'in the manner of Castile' with a tall overmantel and a hearth open on three sides.[30] At either end of the building there were large square pavilions, each containing four apartments consisting of two living rooms. This arrangement was repeated on

24. Elevation of the château of Madrid in the Bois de Boulogne, near Paris. Engraving from Jacques Androuet du Cerceau, *Les plus excellents bastiments de France* (1576–9). The actual building was smaller than is suggested here by the scale of the human figures. It was essentially a hunting lodge containing thirty-two apartments. Rectangular in plan, it was notable for its majolica decoration by Girolamo della Robbia.

three floors. The château thus had four large *salles*, each measuring 168 square metres. The *sallette* on the first floor opened on to a balustraded tribune overlooking the central hall. A fourth floor in each pavilion was divided into four large rooms lit by dormers. There was also an attic with four small, badly lit rooms. The various apartments were reached by spiral staircases housed in six towers, four square and two round, distributed around the building. Altogether there were thirty-two apartments, each with a fireplace and an alcove, an idea imported from Spain. The basement was occupied by kitchens and offices. The elevation comprised on the ground and first floors two horizontal tiers of open loggias running round the entire building between the square towers and linked by a corridor. The second floor had a terrace. High-pitched roofs covered the blocks and towers. Tall mullioned windows, spaced regularly, were flanked at the upper level by columns and pilasters. The dormers, instead of bearing complicated open-work designs, as at Blois or Chambord, were mostly covered by straight pediments.[31]

The most unusual feature at Madrid was the decoration of brightly coloured glazed terracotta. The columns and capitals of the loggias were covered with a grey or dark-brown glaze imitating marble, bronze or *pietra serena*. Medallions, containing busts of Roman emperors, occupied the spandrels above the columns, their white frames set against a bright blue background. The entablatures of the loggias were adorned with majolica, while the pilasters flanking the ground-floor windows had candelabra patterns containing dolphins, putti and satyrs. Two friezes on the second and third floors had white circles against a blue background. The dormers, too, had majolica adornments, as had the tall chimney stacks. The whole building must have been a riot of colour.[32]

Two men were responsible for Madrid's construction: Pierre Gadier, a master-mason from Touraine who had worked at Amboise and Tours, and Girolamo della Robbia, a member of the famous family of Florentine ceramicists. When Gadier died in 1531, he was replaced by Gatien François, a master-mason with a similar background. Born in 1488, the sculptor Girolamo was the youngest son of Andrea della Robbia and grand-nephew of the famous Luca. He first came to France early in the reign of Francis I, who appointed him *imagier et peintre du roi*. After a spell in Florence, he returned to France in 1527 and settled at Puteaux, where the king provided him with a workshop. Girolamo became quite prosperous: he built a house in Paris and, in about 1536, was appointed *valet de chambre du roi*. The king ordered from him a large wreath, or *chapeau de triomphe*, for Fontainebleau in about 1536 and two triumphal arches for Charles V's entry into Paris in December 1539.[33] In addition to such works, he was employed at Madrid from 1531 until 1552. In 1564 he carved the *gisant* of Catherine de' Medici for the tomb of Henry II. This, together with a few ceramic fragments at Sèvres Museum, are his only surviving works. Another thirty or so have been found recently, stored in the basement of the Musée Carnavalet in Paris. Although described as 'the king's architect' in 1566, Girolamo was never called this in any other document from the reign of Francis I. While conceding that he played a major part in the construction of Madrid and designed the arches for the loggias, Monique Chatenet does not believe that he designed the whole building. Its plan, in her view, is French in conception, as is much of the workmanship. In place of Girolamo, she plumps for an unidentified designer familiar with certain Italian architectural principles, but without any real understanding of building as practised in Italy.[34]

How did Madrid get its name? Officially it was called the château du Bois de Boulogne, but it became commonly known as Madrid. It may seem strange that the king should wish to be reminded of his most humiliating experience. The English diarist John Evelyn, who visited the château in 1644, wrote: 'We returned to Paris by Madrid, another villa of the king's built by Francis I, and called by that name to absolve him of his oath that he would not go from Madrid (where he was prisoner) in Spain, but whence he made his escape.'[35] Another explanation was given by Henri Sauval, historian of Paris, in 1724:

The château [has the name of Boulogne] and it allegedly owes that of Madrid to Francis I; for he enjoyed it and when he was there did not wish to be seen. It was as difficult to speak with him as when he was a prisoner in Madrid, so that his courtiers, speaking in jest, called the château Madrid instead of Boulogne and this became such a habit with them that the name stuck.[36]

These explanations, however, can all be set aside, as evidence has now come to light linking the château with the Casa de Campo, a country house built just outside Madrid between 1515 and 1519 by Francisco de Vargas, a royal treasurer and businessman. Though destroyed in the Spanish Civil War, the Casa's design is known from documents. It was a rectangular building with two storeys and an attic under sloping roofs. Two square pavilions, one at each end, were linked by a narrower central block. Each façade had arcaded galleries, open and superimposed. The arches rested on marble Corinthian columns imported from Italy with capitals adorned with escutcheons. The building was constructed of brick and faced with glazed tiles (*azulejos*). The square pavilions were subdivided internally by walls, while the central block consisted of a large vestibule. The Casa, however, was smaller than the French château. The similarity between the two buildings was noted in 1540 by a member of Charles V's entourage during his visit to Paris. He wrote that the emperor 'dined in a house called Boulogne modelled on that of the *licenciado* Vargas of Madrid although it is a little better'. Francis had presumably seen the Casa de Campo during his captivity and decided to build a larger version outside Paris for his lasting enjoyment.[37]

Saint-Germain-en-Laye, La Muette, Villers-Cotterêts

According to Jacques Androuet du Cerceau, Francis was so knowledgeable (*ententif*) about building that one could say that he alone was the architect of Saint-Germain-en-Laye. However, the king co-operated closely in the work with the Parisian master-mason Pierre Chambiges, who began rebuilding the château in September 1539. Keeping as much as he could of the medieval château, Chambiges added two storeys and completely renovated the inner façades. His chief innovation was the terraced roof constructed of large, superimposed stone slabs that were so heavy that the supporting edifice had to be strengthened with buttresses and held together by iron tie-bars. Though less exciting architecturally than Francis's other châteaux, he used it frequently. The château itself was only the principal component of a vast complex of buildings. On the west side there was an outer courtyard containing a well and a fountain and surrounded by outbuildings. On the north side lay the

25. The château of Saint-Germain-en-Laye: inner courtyard. Situated near Paris, this was a favourite residence of the French court in the early sixteenth century, particularly in winter. Unlike many other châteaux it was kept furnished. The buttresses were necessitated by the heavy paving of the flat roof from which hunts in the neighbouring forest could be observed.

gardens and, on the south and east, the park and forest. Three bridges linked the château to the park. Within the dry moat were a tennis court, the lists and a small arming chamber for the king. Near the future Château-Neuf stood the royal menagerie. Elsewhere in the park there was a quintain (*jeu de bague*) and a piece of equestrian equipment called a *chevalet de la jument*.[38] Finally, in the depths of the forest stood an ancillary residence, the château de La Muette, built from 1542 at a spot from which the king liked to watch deer retire after the chase. The Ferrarese ambassador, Giulio Alvarotti, reported on 17 January 1546 that Francis had gone from Saint-Germain to La Muette in order to hunt. With him were the dauphin, Madame d'Étampes, the admiral, the cardinal of Ferrara, Madame de Massy and all the *petite bande*. The queen, the dauphine and Madame Marguerite had stayed behind with the rest of the court, for the king was expected back in two or three days.[39]

La Muette resembled Saint-Germain in certain respects: it had a terraced roof and stone walls decorated with brick. But it was much smaller and the plan was different: it consisted of a square central block with four square pavilions, one at each corner. The chapel and a staircase were contained in two projecting wings, one on either side. There were superimposed galleries on two façades. Francis was fond of La Muette. As he lay dying, he asked his son to ensure that it was completed. Nothing remains of the château today.[40]

Another small château built by Francis in the Île-de-France was Challuau. It was demolished in 1803, but the plan and elevation are known from engravings by du Cerceau. It was another clever design with a central cube and four square angle pavilions. Superimposed galleries along the lateral façades provided independent access to the apartments. From the main

26. The château of Villers-Cotterêts. The staircase vault with coffers containing Francis I's emblem of a salamander and mythological scenes. The château was one of several built by the king in the Île-de-France after 1526. It was visited 135 times by Francis I, 247 times by Henry II and only forty-three times by Catherine de' Medici.

entrance a single-flight straight staircase led to the first floor. The walls were built of mortar and brick, and the flat roof was balustraded. It was built, possibly by Pierre Chambiges, between 1539 and 1545 and given by the king to Madame d'Étampes.[41] Yet Francis felt at home there. On 11 April 1546 Alvarotti informed his master, the duke of Ferrara, that the king would be staying at Challuau for five or six days 'because it is a fine place for hunting and hawking, and, as it only has this palace which cannot accommodate a large suite, he can be sure that no one will importune him with audiences and such like'.[42]

From 1532 onwards Francis was a frequent visitor at Villers-Cotterêts, 85 kilometres north-east of Paris. Work on this château began about 1533 and was largely completed in the king's lifetime. It was built around two rectangular courtyards, one serving as a tennis court. Today the main feature is the wing that divides the courtyards. This contains a chapel (now the Salle des États) and two straight staircases of which the larger has a coffered vault decorated with scenes from Colonna's *Il sogno di Polifilo*. Villers-Cotterêts is dreadfully neglected today, but even in 1539 it had been vandalised. A Mantuan envoy reported that servants had scrawled obscenities on the walls. 'What I find astonishing', he wrote, 'is not only that no remedy is forthcoming but that no officer or anyone else shows any concern for such bad behaviour, which I do not think would be the reaction of the most vulgar innkeeper, given the quality of the paintings in this palace.'[43]

Fontainebleau

A castle, roughly oval in shape, with a gatehouse, a square keep and flanking towers, had existed at Fontainebleau since the twelfth century. By the sixteenth century it could no longer serve the needs of a sizeable, sophisticated court. To enlarge it, a monastery, standing a short distance away to the west, needed to be removed. In 1528 Francis I accepted an estimate for the castle's reconstruction from Gilles Le Breton, a Parisian master-mason. As yet, however, the king had no grand design. Unlike Chambord and Madrid, which followed a set design, Fontainebleau developed in a piecemeal fashion. In 1528 the royal family consisted of the king, his mother and his three sons (his two daughters, for some unkown reason, were not brought up with the boys). Consequently, there were three lodgings within the old castle, each comprising a *chambre*, a *salle*, a *garde-robe* and a *cabinet*. The château was in a poor state of repair. The *donjon*, or keep, called the *grosse vieille tour*, was in reasonable shape, but the curtain walls and towers were crumbling. Francis set about repairing them at minimum cost. The keep was retained, as were the curtain walls up to a certain height, the angle towers and parts of the buildings in the courtyard. The gatehouse, however, was demolished and replaced by a monumental gateway – the Porte Dorée – with two superimposed loggias. Instead of the white stone used in the Loire Valley, Le Breton used *grès*, a hard local stone not easily carved.

The king planned to stay at the monastery while the château was under construction. A gallery linking it to the keep was accordingly built. Below the gallery, a footpath allowed public access to a pond situated to the south of the château. Except for the gallery, the château looked inwards and consisted of a sequence of independent lodgings, each accessible by means of a spiral staircase enclosed within an external round tower. Entrance to the courtyard (Cour du Donjon) was through the Porte Dorée. Francis I's lodging, in the north-west tower of the curtain wall, was sandwiched between his mother's, in the keep, and that of his sons. Francis and Louise each had a *salle* and a *cabinet*. A spiral staircase led from the *salle* to the courtyard and another from the *cabinet* to a garden. High-ranking courtiers were housed in the Porte Dorée, in one of two corps d'hôtel and in the *guet*. Even at this stage the gardens were extended and improved. Those at the foot of the curtain wall were retained, forming the Jardin du Roi on the north and west, and the Grand Jardin to the south. In 1530 a small garden was created for the king's sons. The château was thus entirely surrounded by gardens, except on the east side where there were meadows. In December 1529 Francis bought land immediately to the south of the gallery which became the Jardin des Pins.

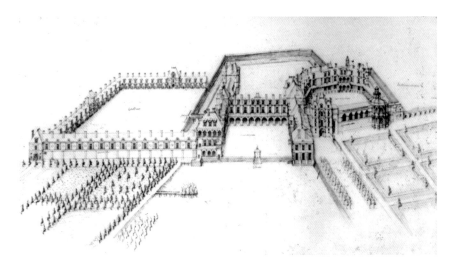

27. The château of Fontainebleau. Engraving from Jacques Androuet du Cerceau, *Les plus excellents bastiments de France* (1576–9). Built from 1528 on the site of an earlier royal castle, Fontainebleau became Francis I's favourite residence. He enlarged it considerably and collected his art treasures and books there.

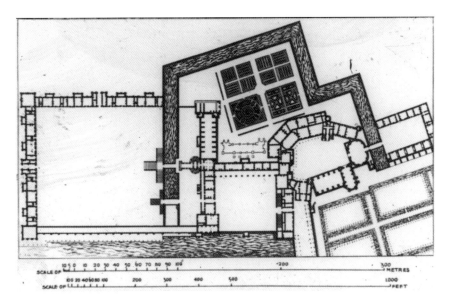

28. Plan of the château of Fontainebleau. Engraving from Jacques Androuet du Cerceau, *Les plus excellents bastiments de France* (1576–9). The chateau was at first an oval building with a central courtyard. Francis I then acquired a neighbouring monastery and linked it to the oval by a long gallery. He next built a new wing with pavilions on the monastic site and, beyond this, a large outer courtyard enclosed by more buildings. The moat was ordered by Catherine de' Medici in 1564 to protect the royal apartments from a surprise attack by Huguenots.

By 1531 the main work on the king's lodging was completed, but Francis no longer saw Fontainebleau simply as a hunting lodge, but as one of his principal residences. In August he decided to build a grand staircase in the courtyard leading to his lodging. This consisted of two converging straight flights leading to a central one and ending in a classical portico. The designer is unknown. The name of Rosso, who came to Fontainebleau in 1531, has been suggested.[44] Though he is remembered mainly as a painter, Vasari described him as an 'excellent architect' whose 'arches, colossi and such-like things were . . . the most stupendous ever made'.[45] Francis, however, never made use of his grand staircase, for after his mother's death in September 1531 he moved into her lodging in the keep, ceding his own to Queen Eleanor. His move may have been prompted by the desire to incorporate the gallery into his lodging, which he did by blocking one door and opening another between his chamber and the gallery.[46] The floor beneath was occupied by baths which may have been reached by means of a spiral staircase that no longer exists. The baths were heated and supplied with running water. They formed a suite of rooms which, from east to west, comprised a barber's shop (doubling as a *caldarium*), a *tepidarium*, the bath proper, two rest rooms (*salles de repos*), a *grande salle* and a vestibule. The bath measured 14 feet in length by 10 feet in width and 3 feet 6 inches in depth.[47] Francis did not keep his art collection in his baths, as was once thought. The paintings were almost certainly displayed in the two rooms furthest from the baths. In 1534 new kitchens were built backing on to the baths so that they could tap the same source of heat. A portico covered by a wide terrace was built on the south side of the gallery leading to the king's lodging. Major changes, meanwhile, took place in the Cour du Donjon. The external stair turrets were replaced by a raised walkway, or *coursière*, running on either side of the new monumental staircase to the Porte Dorée in one direction and to the princes' lodging in the other. It linked not only the various lodgings but also provided a viewing platform for festivals in the Oval courtyard.

The last ten years of Francis's reign were marked by the implementation of a 'Grand Design' for Fontainebleau: in 1535 the stonemasons shifted their attention from the Cour du Donjon to an enormous courtyard west of the Galerie François Ier. The new site, known as the Grande Basse Cour, was surrounded on three sides by long, low buildings made of red brick. The south wing consisted of a continuous portico, and the north and west wings of units of four rooms grouped around a staircase. They were probably intended to house court officials. The north and south wings were terminated at the east end by two identical pavilions, known as the Pavillon aux Armes and Pavillon des Poêles. These were intended as 'places of pleasure open on nature'. At the same time the adjacent gardens – the Jardin de la Fontaine and the Enclos de l'Étang – received much attention. Pines, willows, gooseberry bushes, roses and vines were planted and canals dug. In 1533–4 the Grand Jardin was enlarged, given canals, enclosed by walls and adorned with corner pavilions and towers.

The Pavillon aux Armes got its name after 1559 when it became a store for suits of armour. Built of stone and square in plan, it had three floors: the first two consisted of a chamber, cabinet, *garde-robe* and loggia; the third was a belvedere, a new idea imported from Italy. The pavilion, which could be entered independently from two sides, overlooked the king's garden and was given a very strange doorway flanked by Egyptian female herms. Above it are three groups of putti playing with a helmet and the royal 'F'. The design has been ascribed to Rosso or Serlio. Though the Pavillon des Poêles, like the Pavillon aux Armes, had three floors, a belvedere and two spiral staircases, its distribution was quite different. Each floor consisted of a single large room. The upper floor was open on three sides to provide views of the pond and gardens. The chamber on the first floor was a presence chamber heated by stoves and decorated with murals by Rosso.

Since 1531 Francis had used his mother's *cabinet*. It had a spiral staircase leading down to his garden, but was small, dark and commanded limited views, so about 1540 the king had a new one built as a projecting pavilion on the north side of the main building. This was no sooner completed than he commissioned another close to the pond. The main work was finished by February 1539 but the interior decoration was not completed in time for the emperor's visit in December, so he was given the king's lodging in the keep while Francis moved to Montmorency's in the Porte Dorée.

The south wing of the Grande Basse Cour was built in two stages. By 1539 a short wing had been constructed probably to enclose the Jardin des Pins; then, about 1541, it was extended and given an additional storey. A gallery, 115 metres long, on the first floor may been intended as a corridor linking the king's lodging with the Jardin des Pins. A magnificent portico covered by a terrace was erected in front of the wing's south façade. The only surviving part of the south wing is the Grotte des Pins with statues of giants emerging from a rocky background. The north wing of the Grande Basse Cour is more or less in its original state today, though it was shortened in 1565 to make way for a moat. In the 1540s a wing was added at the east end of the pond. This was a single-storey building covered by a long and wide terrace ending in a loggia that overlooked the pond. It was linked to the lodging of the duchesse d'Étampes, who could conveniently use the terrace to take the air, look down on the Grand Jardin and the pond, or, if she wished, take a boat. The pond became a focus of court life from the 1540s. A few years later Michelangelo's statue *Hercules* was erected at the water's edge.

Finally, the Cour du Donjon was radically transformed between 1541 and 1546. The monumental staircase, which obstructed the courtyard, was destroyed in 1541 and replaced by an internal one, the original portico being retained. At the same time, the lower of two superimposed chapels was completed. The future Francis II was baptised here in February 1544 and the ensuing festivities were held in an adjacent room, called the Salle du Roi. Francis planned to add a building with a first-floor loggia open on two sides. The walls were built by the end of 1546 and the ground floor served for the baptism of the king's granddaughter Elizabeth de Valois in July, but the loggia and terrace had to be abandoned in favour of an enclosed building better suited to the prevailing climate. By 1546 the Cour du Donjon was more or less complete.

Writing in 1535, the Venetian envoy Marino Giustiniani stated that Francis I had spent 25,000 *écus* (56,250 *l.*) on his private buildings and scarcely less on the public ones. He estimated the king's total revenue at 2,500,000 *écus* (5,625,000 *l.*).[48] Thus the private buildings – presumably the châteaux – accounted for one per cent of the royal budget. The official building accounts yield a slightly higher figure. In 1532–7 Francis spent 43,233 *l.* annually on his Parisian residences alone. The cost rose from 53,600 *l.* in 1528 to 85,000 *l.* in 1546; that is, about one per cent of the royal revenue, which rose from 5 million *l.* in 1523 to more than 9 million in 1546. The cost of the royal châteaux in the Paris region was monitored by an office of works set up in 1527. Three commissioners fixed the terms of contracts and controlled expenditure; the controller saw that work was carried out in accordance with the king's instructions; the treasurer paid the workforce and kept the accounts. There were three categories of royal works: large (costing more than 20,000 *l.* per annum); middling (between 10,000 and 15,000 *l.* per annum); and small (not more than 5,500 *l.* per annum). Chambord and Fontainebleau belonged to the first category; Saint-Germain-en-Laye, Villers-Cotterêts and Madrid to the second; and La Muette to the third.[49]

Henry II

Although less passionate about the arts than his father, Henry II still built a fair amount. He continued rebuilding the Louvre, erected the Château-Neuf at Saint-Germain-en-Laye, added a ballroom at Fontainebleau (see plate 16) and carried out improvements at Chambord and other royal châteaux. He also took a close interest in the château built by Diane de Poitiers at Anet. At the same time his friends vied with each other to build houses fit to receive him and the court. Montmorency carried out major works at Écouen, Chantilly and elsewhere. At Meudon the cardinal of Lorraine built a 'grotto' to house his many treasures. At Vallery, near Sens, Marshal Saint-André erected a château which Androuet du Cerceau compared to the Louvre.

Henry employed two outstanding architects: Pierre Lescot and Philibert de l'Orme. Lescot is now chiefly remembered for his work at the Louvre. He originally planned to build a *corps de logis*, two storeys high with a central projecting pavilion housing a staircase, on the site of the west wing of the old château. In the end, however, the staircase was moved to a pavilion at the north end, leaving a much larger space for a reception room (*salle*) on each floor; a projecting pavilion was added at the other end, and also a third storey. At the same time another building, the Pavillon du Roi, was added in the south-west corner, facing the river. The most striking feature of Lescot's façade, as decorated by the sculptor Jean Goujon, is its classicism, notably the correct treatment of the Orders.

The interior decoration of the Louvre is revolutionary. The *salle* on the ground floor has at the north end a gallery supported by four caryatids: 'the first time a passage from Vitruvius had been used to recreate an antique monument on the monumental scale and in a permanent form.'[50] At the south end is a tribunal separated from the main room by sixteen Doric columns in groups of four. As on the façade, the decorations are by Jean Goujon. Elsewhere in the Louvre, Lescot collaborated with the Italian woodcarver Scibec de Carpi, who made the remarkable ceiling in the king's *chambre de parade*. Previously French ceilings had beams running across them, usually with painted motifs; this one, by contrast, is coffered. The delicately carved friezes are more correctly Roman than anything yet seen in France.[51]

Philibert de l'Orme was 'the first French architect to have something of the universality of the great Italians'.[52] Born in Lyon about 1530, he was the son of a master-mason. About 1533 he visited Rome, where he attracted the attention of Cardinal du Bellay. After studying Roman antiquities for three years, de l'Orme returned to France and was commissioned by the cardinal to build the château of Saint-Maur-des-Fossés. Du Bellay also introduced him to the dauphin and Diane de Poitiers. She commissioned him in 1547 to build a château at Anet, which was completed about 1552. Although it has been largely destroyed, three major features survive: the frontispiece to the main block, the chapel and the entrance gateway. The frontispiece is remarkable for its monumentality and correct treatment of the Orders. The chapel is the first in France to invoke the Renaissance principle that the circle is the perfect figure, and therefore suitable for the house of God. The entrance gateway is unique. Except for the Doric columns flanking the door, it is almost free of classical elements. A sequence of rectangular blocks builds up to the central feature: a clock consisting of a bronze stag surrounded by hounds, which move at the striking of the hours. On either side are four sarcophagi, and open-work balustrades run round the structure.

Following Henry II's accession, de l'Orme was appointed as superintendent of royal buildings. He designed the tomb of Francis I at Saint-Denis, a chapel at Villers-Cotterêts and the Château-Neuf at Saint-Germain. The tomb is in general design a Roman triumphal arch with side arches set back. The Château-Neuf, begun in 1557, consisted of a central *corps de logis* to which were attached four pavilions, preceded by a courtyard enclosed by a wall and intended for festivities. Its unusual design may have been inspired by Hadrian's Villa at Tivoli which was being excavated at the time. When Henry II died, de l'Orme was dismissed as superintendent, only to be subsequently re-employed by Catherine de' Medici.

CHAPTER 10

Art Patronage

Art played a crucial role in the projection of monarchy in Renaissance France: it was a means by which the ruler demonstrated his power, good taste and munificence. The time was ripe for such display as royal residences were being built, inviting new forms of interior decoration. Contacts with Italian courts and their art became closer as a consequence of French involvement in the peninsula's affairs and Italian artists began to look upon the French court as a lucrative source of patronage. The kings of France were not content simply to employ artists; they also built up collections of works of art – paintings, statues, tapestries and *objets d'art*. Francis I was an outstanding collector; so much so that Vasari described his château at Fontainebleau as 'like a new Rome'.

Francis I's interest in art can be traced back to his childhood. On 12 June 1504 Niccolò Alamanni wrote from Blois to Francesco Gonzaga, marquis of Mantua:

> As I am the servant and familiar of our little prince of Angoulême, he has expressed the wish that I should obtain for him some pictures by those excellent Italian masters, as they give him so much pleasure. Since I know that M. Andrea Mantegna is among the best and also that he is liked by Your Lordship, I take the liberty of writing to beg you to cause M. Mantegna to suspend everything in order to make him something exceptional, as such a great prince deserves; the size and execution will be left to the painter's judgment. I know that no greater pleasure can be given to His Excellency. I have sent orders to Florence and elsewhere for others to be made'.[1]

Such artistic precocity on the part of a ten-year-old prince calls for an explanation. He did not appear regularly at the French court until 1508, nor did he go to Italy until 1515; so where did he pick up his taste for Italian art? The likeliest source was his mother, Louise of Savoy. In 1516 another Italian, Rozzoni, wrote to Isabella d'Este from Crémieu: 'An idea has occurred to me: it would not be a bad thing, indeed it would be a good one, if Your Ladyship were to offer her [Louise] some perfect picture of a saint, male or female, for she takes great pleasure in such things and is also knowledgeable.'[2] Art was among the topics that Federico Gonzaga discussed with Francis when he stayed at his court in 1516. The king listened with delight to the prince's description of the Mantuan collection and especially of Mantegna's *Triumphs of Caesar* (now at Hampton Court). As a child Federico had been in Rome when Michelangelo was painting the ceiling of the Sistine Chapel and Raphael the Stanze della Segnatura and *Galatea*. He may have communicated enthusiasm for these artists to the king.

Leonardo da Vinci and Andrea del Sarto

In 1818 Ingres painted his *Leonardo da Vinci Dying in the Arms of Francis I.*[3] He evidently drew his inspiration from Vasari's account of the artist's death at Amboise on 1 May 1519:

> Then, having confessed and shown his penitence with much lamentation, he [Leonardo] devoutly took the Sacrament out of his bed, supported by his friends and servants, as he could not stand. The king arriving, for he would often pay him friendly visits, he sat up in bed from respect, and related the circumstances of his sickness, showing how greatly he had offended God and man in not having worked in his art as he might. He was then seized with a paroxysm, the harbinger of death, so that the king rose and took his head to assist him and show him favour as well as to alleviate the pain. Leonardo's divine spirit, then recognising that he could not enjoy a greater honour, expired in the king's arms, at the age of seventy-five.[4]

This, unfortunately, is just another of many tall stories told about Francis I, for he was not at Amboise but at Saint-Germain-en-Laye when Leonardo died.

Leonardo's first contacts with France were with French intellectuals who visited Italy to study, such as Jean Pélerin Viator, a mathematician who promised to reveal to him the size of the sun. In 1499, when Louis XII regained the duchy of Milan, his courtiers were able to admire some of Leonardo's paintings and the giant clay model of a horse intended for an equestrian statue of Francesco Sforza. Someone discovered the *Last Supper* in the refectory of Santa Maria delle Grazie. Leonardo offered his services as a military

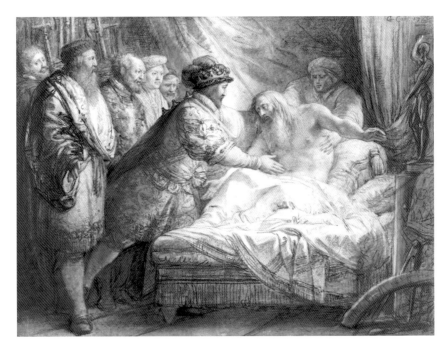

29. *Leonardo da Vinci Dying in the Arms of Francis I.* Pastel by Giuseppe Cades (1750–99) (Ashmolean Museum, Oxford). According to Giorgio Vasari's *Lives of the Most Excellent Italian Architects, Painters and Sculptors* (1550), Francis I was present when the artist died at Amboise in 1519, but the king is known to have been elsewhere at the time. Ingres is another artist who has illustrated the legend.

engineer to Ligny, the French commander; he also became acquainted with the Lyon painter Jean Perréal, the official artist of the campaign in 1500, who apparently gave him tips on how to use pastel.[5] Perréal, a shadowy figure in the history of French art, has been described as 'a jack of all trades'. In addition to devising programmes for royal entries, he painted portraits, including a *Charles VIII* and a *Pierre Sala*. He also designed tombs at Nantes and Brou.[6]

At the end of 1499 Leonardo left Milan for Venice before moving to Florence, where in April 1501 an agent of Isabella d'Este found him working on a painting for Florimond Robertet, Louis XII's treasurer and secretary. This was the *Madonna of the Yarn Winder*. An avid art collector, Robertet apparently also owned a bronze *David* by Michelangelo. Meanwhile, Louis XII probably acquired paintings that had belonged to Ludovico Sforza, including Leonardo's *La Belle Ferronière* and the *Virgin of the Rocks*. According to Vasari, the king also tried to take the *Last Supper* to France: 'He employed architects to frame it in wood and iron, so that it might be transported in safety, without any regard for the cost, so great was his desire. But the king was thwarted by its being done on the wall, and it remained with the Milanese.'[7]

In June 1506 Charles d'Amboise, comte de Chaumont, Louis XII's lieutenant-general in Lombardy, received Leonardo at his palace in Milan. Here the artist set to work on a tomb for Gian-Giacomo Trivulzio and on a second version of the *Virgin of the Rocks*. He also designed a large palace for Chaumont to be built in a suburb of Milan. The gardens and fountains were to include an artificial rock pierced by large arcades from which water was to pour into vases of granite, porphyry and serpentine. The possibility that Leonardo paid a brief visit to Louis XII's court at Blois in the company of Charles d'Amboise is hinted at in one of his notebooks, which also contains a mention of the architect and humanist Fra Giocondo, who had preceded him at the French court.

Charles d'Amboise defended Leonardo as he came under pressure from the Florentine *signoría* regarding a contract for the *Battle of Anghiari*. On 16 December 1506 Charles wrote a letter praising the artist: his greatness as a painter, he declared, could not surpass his excellence as an engineer and scientist. In January 1507 Louis XII asked the Florentine *signoría* to stop harassing Leonardo. Two days earlier he had told a Florentine envoy that he wanted Leonardo to paint for him 'some small pictures of Our Lady and others according to our pleasure; and I may also ask him to do my portrait'. In July Louis referred to him as 'our painter and engineer in ordinary'. A fortnight later Charles d'Amboise described Leonardo as 'painter to the Most Christian King'. In September 1507 the artist returned to Florence, where he remained until April 1508. Before returning to Milan, he informed Charles d'Amboise that he would bring two paintings of the Virgin on which he had been working in his spare time that were intended for 'the Most Christian King or whoever else you wish'. One may have been the new version of the *Virgin and St Anne* which Louis XII had ordered. Once back in Milan, Leonardo came into contact with the French treasurer-general, Étienne Grolier, and his son, Jean, the famous bibliophile.

In September 1513, following the death of Charles d'Amboise and the end of French rule in Lombardy, Leonardo secured the patronage in Rome of Giuliano de' Medici, duc de Nemours. Only after the latter's death on 17 March 1516 was Leonardo free to accept an invitation from Francis I to come to France. We do not know how or when the two men first met. The artist, who was attached to the household of Giuliano de' Medici in 1515, may have met the king at Bologna in December during his interview with Pope Leo X, Giuliano's brother. Leonardo was sixty-four and in poor health when he undertook the long journey to France. He spent some months preparing for it: his books and other effects had to be packed in cases and carts hired to transport them. Taking with him some of his most famous paintings, he left before the winter, accompanied by Francesco Melzi and his faithful servant, Batista de Vilanis.[8] Francis I gave him the manor of Cloux, now called the Clos-Lucé, near Amboise, and an annuity of 500 *l.* The artist also received letters of naturalisation which exempted him from the *droit d'aubaine* under which foreigners who died in France forfeited their property to the crown. Though not large, the Clos-Lucé suited Leonardo's needs as an artist. Vasari states that, although Francis wanted him to do 'the cartoon of St Anne in colours', the artist, 'as was his wont, gave him nothing but words for a long time'.[9] None of his paintings, not even the *St John* at the Louvre, can be dated to his time at Amboise.

On 10 October 1517 Leonardo was visited by Cardinal Luigi of Aragon, whose secretary, Antonio de Beatis, has left the following account:

> Our master went with the rest of us to one of the suburbs to see Messer Leonardo da Vinci of Florence, an old man of more than seventy, the most outstanding painter of our day. He showed the Cardinal three pictures, one of a certain Florentine woman portrayed from life at the request of the late Magnificent Giuliano de' Medici, another of St. John the Baptist as a young man, and one of the Madonna and Child set in the lap of St. Anne. All three works are quite perfect, though nothing good can now be expected from his brush as he suffers from paralysis in the right hand. He has successfully trained a Milanese pupil, who works extremely well. And although Messer Leonardo cannot colour with his former softness, yet he can still draw and teach. This gentleman has written on anatomy in a manner never yet attempted by anyone else: quite exhaustively, with painted illustrations not only of the limbs but of the muscles, tendons, veins, joints, intestines, and every other feature of the human body, both male and female. We saw this with our own eyes, and indeed he informed us that he has dissected more than thirty corpses, including males and females of all ages. He has also written (or so he said) innumerable volumes, all in the vernacular, on hydraulics, on various machines and on other subjects, which, if published, will be useful and most delightful books.

Some of Leonardo's drawings, which date from his last years in France, show an active interest in irrigation, town planning and architecture.[10]

Francis I seems to have appreciated Leonardo's versatility. Writing long afterwards, Benvenuto Cellini remembered a conversation with the king:

> And as he [Leonardo] was so abundantly endowed intellectually, having some knowledge of Latin and Greek, King Francis, who had so ardently

fallen for his great qualities, derived so much pleasure from listening to his discourse that he seldom parted from him; this was why he did not find time to give effect to the admirable studies he had conducted so rigorously. I must not forget to repeat the words which I heard the king speak about him and which he told me in the presence of the cardinal of Ferrara, the cardinal of Lorraine and the king of Navarre: he said that he did not think that any other man had come into this world with more knowledge than Leonardo, not only of painting, sculpture and architecture, but also of philosophy, for he was a very great philosopher.[11]

If he could no longer paint, the old man could still offer advice as an engineer and architect. Francis accordingly decided to entrust him with a project worthy of his genius: namely to transform Romorantin, a small town in the Sologne belonging to his mother, into a 'little Venice'.[12]

Leonardo died at the Clos-Lucé on 2 May 1519. His last note, written on 24 June, ends cryptically with the words 'for the soup is getting cold'. The main beneficiary of his will, dated 23 April 1519, was Francesco Melzi, who inherited his books, instruments and drawings. The absence of any mention of paintings suggests that these had already passed into the royal collection. Leonardo was buried in the church of Saint Florentin in Amboise. It was sacked during the Wars of Religion and demolished in 1808. In 1863 a certain Arsène Houssaye found the skeleton of a very tall man and three fragments of tombstone inscribed : LEO. . .INC/. . .EO. . .DUS VINC. . .[13]

Leonardo was not the only Italian artist employed by Francis I in the early part of his reign. Another was Andrea del Sarto, whom the king had invited to France after he had seen his *Christ Being Supported by Angels*. This had been sent by Giovanni Battista Puccini, an Italian merchant who served the king as artistic agent in Italy as early as 1516. Andrea was warmly received at court and given rich vestments and money. He painted a portrait of the infant dauphin as well the *Charity,* now in the Louvre. According to Vasari, Francis gave Andrea a large pension and did everything to retain his services. The artist also worked for the king's mother. One day, however, as he was working on a *St Jerome*, he received a letter from his wife urging him to come home. He requested the king's permission to do so, promising to return with his wife and valuable works of art. Francis allowed him to go and gave him money, but Andrea squandered it and failed to return. Francis swore that if ever he reappeared, he would give him more pain than pleasure regardless of his talent.[14]

Giovanni Battista Rosso

It was in 1531 that the Florentine artist Giovanni Battista Rosso came to France on a recommendation from Pietro Aretino, one of Francis's artistic agents in Italy. After working in Rome alongside Michelangelo and Raphael,

30. *Mars and Venus.* Drawing by Rosso Fiorentino (Musée du Louvre, Paris). This work was sent to Francis I by Pietro Aretino in around 1530 and may have served to introduce the artist to his future employer. The drawing is probably an allegory on the Peace of Cambrai (1529). Mars is being undressed by cherubs in order to make love, not war.

Rosso moved to Venice after the sack of 1527. Here, he did a drawing for
Aretino *Mars and Venus*, which has been interpreted as an allegory of the
Peace of Cambrai of 1529. Its presentation to Francis may have paved the way
for Rosso's invitation to France, though the king may already have possessed
a painting by him, *Moses and the Daughters of Jethro*.[15] Rosso made such a good
impression on the king that he was appointed First Painter and given a large
salary and a house in Paris. Antonio Mini informed Michelangelo in 1532
that Rosso was living like a lord: he had horses and servants and wore silk. In
May he was given letters of naturalisation, and in August he became a canon
of the Sainte-Chapelle.

In March 1532 Rosso was joined at Fontainebleau by Francesco
Primaticcio, a Bolognese artist who had spent six years assisting Giulio
Romano on the decoration of the Palazzo Tè in Mantua. Exactly how he
came to France is unclear. According to Vasari, Francis I, 'hearing of the
palace, wrote [to Federico Gonzaga] asking that a youth might be sent to him
who could paint and do stucco', but it seems that Primaticcio was sent to
France by his master, Giulio Romano.[16] The earliest reference to his being in
France is a document of 1532 recording a payment of 200 gold *écus* for a
journey he was about to make to Flanders.[17] His mission was to carry a
drawing by Giulio Romano of Scipio Africanus for a tapestry Francis was
having made in Brussels and to bring back the finished cartoon.[18] Four pieces
of the tapestry, already owned by the king, were used for his meeting with
Clement VII at Marseille in October 1533. He received the fifth and last in
April 1535. Francis, who had spent 23,448 gold *écus* on the tapestry, was
evidently anxious to recover the cartoon so that no one else should copy it.

Between them, Rosso and Primaticcio carried out much of the interior
decoration at the château of Fontainebleau. They worked separately, each
with a team of assistants, and between them created a new style of interior
decoration, combining painting with stucco, characteristic of the First School
of Fontainebleau. Which one introduced stucco to France is debatable. Vasari,
who met Primaticcio in Bologna in 1563, wrote:

> Although, as has been said, Rosso, the Florentine painter, had gone the
> previous year into the service of this same king and had executed quite a
> few pieces for him, . . . nevertheless, the first stuccos made in France and
> the first works in fresco of any consequence had, they say, their origin in
> Primaticcio.[19]

Archival documents confirm this. It seems that Primaticcio was given the task
of decorating the king's bedchamber at Fontainebleau even before Rosso set
to work on the Galerie François Ier. He may have brought with him a project

by Giulio Romano. The chamber no longer exists, but the project survives in the form of a drawing: two tableaux depicting the story of Psyche.[20]

Rosso, it seems, was responsible for the basic design of the Pavilion of Pomona, a small building in the Jardin des Pins that no longer exists. The decoration is known thanks to drawings and prints that survive. Two of the walls were open, and two were decorated with frescos – one by Rosso, the other by Primaticcio – surrounded by stuccos of satyr couples. In one fresco, Vertumnus, the Roman god of gardens, is seen disguised as an old woman about to seduce Pomona, goddess of fruit; in the other, Ceres is teaching humans how to cultivate the soil.[21]

The Galerie François Ier, the most important surviving vestige of Francis I's Fontainebleau, is a shadow of its original self (see plate 7). The frescos are 'little more than ruins' and the stucco work, though better preserved, has lost some of its original finish. Two oval paintings by Rosso were removed from the gallery when it was altered in the seventeenth and eighteenth centuries. Following restoration, a *Bacchus and Venus*, now in Luxemburg, has been identified as one of them; the other, a *Cupid and Bacchus*, remains lost.[22] The gallery's lighting was distorted as a result of a decision taken in 1786 to add a new wing on the gallery's north side, blotting out the windows. This also entailed the demolition of a projecting closet whose decoration formed an integral part of the whole. Under Louis-Philippe and Napoleon III, the ceiling was raised by 50 centimetres. It was subsequently lowered but not to the original height, so that it no longer rests on the caryatids and other horizontal decorations. The original floor, made of rich woods and patterned to match the ceiling, has also disappeared, yet the gallery continues to fascinate.

If the gallery originally served as a corridor, it had lost this role by the 1530s when an alternative passage from the château's keep to the Grande Basse Cour existed in the form of a terrace over the kitchens. The gallery was not really suitable for court gatherings on account of its length and narrowness. Its main purpose seems to have been as a private 'promenoir' which the king liked to show to distinguished guests.[23] The gallery's chief interest today resides in the decoration. The walls are divided into two roughly equal parts: the lower half contains carved wood panelling by Scibec de Carpi, and the upper a combination of stucco and painting. Each bay has a painted panel in the middle flanked by nudes, herms, putti, garlands of fruit and strap work, all in stucco. The meaning of the decoration has baffled generations of art historians. Some subjects, such as the *Death of Adonis*, are easily recognised; others have long puzzled the experts. Various theories were advanced about *Lost Youth* until it was found to refer to a legend popular in antiquity. Its source was Nicander of Colophon's poem *Theriaca*, a copy of which had just been acquired by Francis. Among the frescos that continue to mystify is *Venus*

Frustrated (*Vénus frustrée*). How is one to explain its mauve tritons or Venus standing in water? And who is the draped female standing behind Venus?[24] Another controversial fresco is *L'Ignorance chassée*. A Roman emperor, crowned with a laurel wreath, strides into a brightly lit temple; he carries a book under his left arm and holds a naked sword in his right hand. In the foreground, standing on clouds, a crowd of blindfolded people are groping, throwing up their arms or lying prostrate. The fresco has traditionally been taken to refer to Francis I's patronage of letters, but it has now been shown that Rosso was following a well-established topos in which the prince with a book and a sword combines endurance (*fortitudo*) with wisdom (*sapientia*).[25] As for the blindfolded figures, they represent Error and Misguidance, not the Vices, as was once suggested. The fresco, in short, shows the prince armed with two heroic virtues following the path to eternal glory, while the crowd below is untouched by wisdom or reason. An interesting parallel may be drawn between this fresco and another, *The Revenge of Nauplius*. This shows Nauplius's victims being dashed on rocks after a false signal has led them astray, while in the background a fleet is sailing peaceably towards a harbour under the sure guidance of a lighthouse.[26]

31. *L'Ignorance chassée*. Fresco by Rosso in the Galerie François Ier, Fontainebleau, showing Francis I in Roman attire striding through the open portal of a brightly lit temple. The king holds a sword in one hand and carries a book under his arm. Blindfolded figures are seen groping in the dark. Sometimes identified with the Vices, they are more probably the king's subjects whom he is leading from the darkness of ignorance into the light of truth.

Identifying the subjects of the frescos is not the only problem associated with the Galerie François Ier; another is understanding the programme that underlies it (see plate 8). It was once suggested that the murals formed 'a coherent and, on its own complex premises, consistent system' aiming at the king's glorification by referring mythologically to various moments in his life.[27] This interpretation assumed that a visitor to the gallery in Francis's day moved from west to east whereas the reverse was true; it also assumed that the gallery was decorated over a long period whereas Rosso and his team are now known to have finished their work in record time, presumably for the emperor's visit late in 1539. That said, the frescos are certainly related to the motifs surrounding them in each bay, and the distribution of subjects throughout the gallery rests on an underlying iconographical programme. For André Chastel, this was 'not narrative, but doctrinal': the twelve main panels display 'the principles of the French monarchy' while the oval panels follow a 'mythological programme'. For Pierre and Françoise Joukovsky, four themes permeate the gallery: peace, piety, immortality and empire.[28] Henri Zerner has suggested a possible link between the gallery's programme and the book of emblems, a genre created by Andrea Alciati that became very popular in early sixteenth-century France. Understanding an emblem as devised by Alciati depended on grasping the interplay of three components: image, text and *subscriptio*. In the Galerie François Ier, the images adjoining each fresco may function in the same way as the text of an emblem. In a few cases the connexion is fairly clear, but in many more it is not, and needs the assistance of someone 'in the know'. This may have been Francis I, to whom Rosso would have imparted the gallery's secret. The king held the key, not only to its door, but also to the enigma of its decoration. He may have liked to impress visitors by explaining what they could not figure out for themselves. This is suggested by a letter written to Francis by his sister. She looks forward to visiting Fontainebleau and is thankful that he will be there to show her around 'for to see your buildings without hearing your intention is like reading Hebrew'.[29]

Rosso's art at Fontainebleau was widely diffused under different forms. A number of engravings were executed there, somewhat clumsily, between 1542 and 1548 by artists such as Antonio Fantuzzi. Another studio, based in Paris and dominated by Pierre Milan and René Boyvin, produced engravings between 1545 and 1548, the best known being the *Nymph of Fontainebleau*. From the beginning of his stay in France, Rosso undertook various tasks: he designed costumes for spectacles, tableware, horse trappings and a tomb. He may also have been an architect. For the emperor's visit in 1539 he designed costumes, festival decorations and the statue of Hercules given to Charles V by the city of Paris. Rosso also worked for other patrons. In 1534 he designed a tapestry for the cardinal of Lorraine and in 1538 painted a *Pietà*, now in the Louvre, for Anne de Montmorency. Tragedy, however, awaited Rosso in 1540. Having wrongly accused a friend of theft, he committed suicide at Fontainebleau on 14 November. 'When the news was taken to the king,' writes Vasari, 'it caused him indescribable regret, since it was his opinion that in losing Rosso he had been deprived of the most excellent artist of his time.'[30]

Francesco Primaticcio

As a younger, less experienced artist, Primaticcio was paid less than Rosso and ranked second in importance. The backgrounds and characters of the two men were very different: whereas Primaticcio had been trained in the classical tradition associated with Raphael, Rosso was a typical Florentine: anti-classical, at least in his earlier years, and drawn to the bizarre and enigmatic. Primaticcio seems to have been a mild-mannered man, adaptable and concil-iatory. Under Rosso's influence, his art became more polished and sensual than that of Giulio Romano, and, following Rosso's death in 1540, it became even more distinctive. The last seven years of Francis I's reign were probably Primaticcio's most productive at Fontainebleau. He was mainly responsible

32. *Diana and Callisto*. Drawing by Francesco Primaticcio (Musée du Louvre, Paris). This was a sketch for one of the frescos painted by the artist in the château's baths, unfortunately destroyed in the eighteenth century. Callisto was loved by Zeus and bore him a son, Arcas. Here Diana is seen discovering Callisto's pregnancy.

for mural painting, but was content to design rather than execute, a task that he left mainly to assistants, among whom the most gifted was Niccolò dell'Abbate. In time Primaticcio also became an architect.

Primaticcio's art at Fontainebleau has suffered greatly from the destruction of public monuments in France between the time of Louis XV and Napoleon I. All that survives of his executed work before 1540 is the upper part of a fireplace in the Chambre de la Reine, but several of his drawings are still extant. At first he liked to draw with pen and wash, but later he preferred to use red chalk highlighted with white. In 1540 he was sent to Rome on an art-collecting mission by Francis and it seems that he made several trips to Italy in the next seven years. Primaticcio almost certainly returned to Mantua, where he would have seen the latest decorations by Giulio Romano. He may also have been to Parma and enlarged his understanding of Parmigianino's art. It was in Rome, however, that he familiarised himself with ancient

33. Stucco decoration by Francesco Primaticcio in the Chambre de la duchesse d'Étampes, château of Fountainebleau. The elongated female figures with small heads and regular profiles are typical of the Mannerist style imported by Primaticcio following his encounter around 1540 with the art of Parmigianino in Italy. The decoration projected a cultivated hedonism, 'at once sophisticated and playful' (Zerner).

remains.[31] The most important part of his mission was to secure plaster casts of famous statues mostly in the papal collection. These included the *Ariadne* (then called *Cleopatra*), *Laocoön*, *Apollo Belvedere*, *Cnidian Venus*, *Hercules Commodus*, *Tiber*, two sphinxes and two satyrs. Primaticcio also obtained moulds of reliefs from Trajan's Column and of Marcus Aurelius's horse on the

34. Fireplace mantel in the chamber of Queen Eleanor, château of Fountainebleau. The stucco decoration by Primaticcio is among the earliest examples of the genre at the château, dating from 1534–7. The central fresco showing *Venus and Adonis* is after a drawing by Giulio Romano.

Capitol. They were carefully packed in crates and sent to Fontainebleau to be turned into bronzes. This was done under the supervision of Vignola, the future architect, in a foundry set up within the château's precincts in 1541. The bronzes, once cast, had to undergo many repairs, hence a number of discrepancies between them and their ancient models. These repairs may have been necessitated by damage to the moulds while in transit from Rome or by faults in casting. Certain alterations may also represent a conscious attempt by Primaticcio to bring the originals into line with his own taste. Whatever their faults, the bronzes were much admired at the French court. The sight of the *Venus* prompted Francis to flatter his mistress, the duchesse d'Étampes: her body, he said, was as perfect as that of the goddess.[32]

Primaticcio's main work at Fontainebleau after 1540 was done in the Salle de Bal and Galerie d'Ulysse, but most of it dates from after Francis's reign. The gallery was destroyed in 1739 and none of its splendid murals was preserved. Scholars, however, have been able to reconstruct its iconographical programme from various documents. The story of Ulysses chosen by the artist for the vault and side walls reflected the vogue for Homeric poetry at Francis's court about 1540. The *Iliad* had been exploited for some time as a source for illustrations, but not the *Odyssey*. By choosing it, Primaticcio broke new ground as well as giving himself greater illustrative scope when painting the twenty-nine panels on each side of the gallery.

Jean and François Clouet

Francis I's artistic interests were not exclusively Italian. For portraiture, a genre that became extremely popular at the French court during his reign, he relied mainly on Jean Clouet, an artist who hailed almost certainly from the Low Countries. Clouet's date of birth and training are unknown, but he was evidently a full-fledged artist by the time he entered the king's service in 1516. He settled and married at Tours around 1520, before moving to Paris about 1532. After serving as *valet de garde-robe*, he joined the circle of royal painters and *gens de métier* in 1526. His annual salary rose from 180 to 240 *l.* in 1523. He was also paid for 'portraits and effigies from life', but was never granted letters of naturalisation. His son, François, who succeeded him as royal painter, was born in 1520. He continued to draw as his father had done and remained court portraitist under Henry II, Francis II and Charles IX.

The art of Jean and François Clouet is represented today by 360 drawings at Chantilly whose sitters straddle the period from 1516 to 1570.[33] They have not all been identified, but those who have belonged to the court. The intention may have been to turn some of the drawings into paintings, but most were finished products. Many contemporary copies of variable quality also exist. The drawings were put to different uses: they were sent to friends and relatives as photographs are today, or gathered into albums containing fifty or so drawings. Reading such portraits became a society game. An early collection, now at Aix-en-Provence, includes the names of the sitters and a few lines under their portraits. Removable cards allowed one to cover the name and inscription in order to guess the sitter's identity.[34]

Few paintings by Jean Clouet survive, the most famous being the large portrait of Francis I, aged about thirty, now in the Louvre (see plate 4). It is reminiscent of Jean Fouquet's portrait of Charles VII, which Clouet may have seen. It depicts the king half-length and three-quarter face against a back-cloth of red damask. Wearing a plumed cap, Francis is superbly attired in a garment of white silk with puffed-out sleeves, adorned with black stripes embroidered with gold. The collar of the Order of St Michael hangs around his neck. His left hand rests on the pommel of a sword. It has been suggested that this portrait was painted jointly by Jean and François Clouet, but a recent study has argued persuasively in favour of Jean's exclusive responsibility.[35] One of his earliest works was a series of six miniature portraits of the so-called 'Preux de Marignan', captains who fought alongside the king in 1516. They adorn the manuscript of the *Commentaire des guerres galliques* and are evidently related to larger drawings of the same sitters in the collection at Chantilly. Jean Clouet's works reveal a new conception of the portrait in which facial features are subordinated to physiognomy. By presenting the sitter three-quarter face, he gives the features mobility and is able to capture fleeting expressions.[36] While Clouet's practice of drawing in red and black chalk harks back to Fouquet, his graphic style – the modelling rendered through rhythmic parallel hatching – points to Italy and, more particularly, to Leonardo da Vinci, whose stay in France coincided exactly with Clouet's first appearance at court.

Benvenuto Cellini

Benvenuto Cellini, Florentine goldsmith and sculptor, occupies a special place among the Italian artists who worked for Francis I on account of the entertaining autobiography that he dictated, mostly between 1558 and 1562. Cellini was a dreadful man: greedy, hot-tempered, violent, promiscuous, jealous and boastful. Murders, fights and daring escapes filled his life. Not surprisingly, he acquired numerous enemies, including Francis I's mistress, the duchesse d'Étampes, who favoured Primaticcio. Many of the stories in Cellini's memoirs seem too good to be true, yet their substance has generally been confirmed by archival evidence. He seems not to have invented facts so much as coloured them.[37]

Cellini first came to France in 1537 in search of the ideal patron. Although well received, he did not get a royal commission and returned to Rome disappointed. In October 1538 he was imprisoned by Pope Paul III after being charged with murder and cheating the papal treasury. In December 1539, however, Ippolito d'Este, cardinal of Ferrara, acting on behalf of the king of France, secured his release. A letter from the papal nuncio, Filiberto Ferrerio, to Cardinal Farnese throws light on the king's role in the affair. Francis had told the nuncio of his wish to commission a number of silver statues to serve as candelabra in his gallery and wondered who might make them. Cardinal Gaddi suggested 'a certain Benvenuto, a very excellent goldsmith', who was being held prisoner by the pope. Francis said that he had written several times to the pope asking for Cellini's release, without success. He asked the nuncio to use his influence and explained that he wanted Cellini released as his servant.

Cellini was set free at Christmas 1539, but did not return to the French court immediately. Instead, Ippolito set him to work first in Rome, then in Ferrara, in order to ensure that he had lost none of his skill as a goldsmith, before sending him to France. Eventually Cellini received his marching orders. He arrived at the French court late in September 1540, carrying a ewer and basin which he had made in Italy. On seeing them, Francis allegedly exclaimed: 'Of a truth I hardly think the ancients can have seen a piece so beautiful as this. I well remember to have inspected all the best works, and by the greatest masters of all Italy, but I never set my eyes on anything which stirred me to such admiration.'[38] It was Ippolito d'Este, however, not Cellini, who presented the ewer and basin to the king at Blois on 16 March 1541. The occasion, witnessed by the Ferrarese ambassador, followed a banquet. The cardinal drank from the ewer to show that liquid flowed only from one of three spouts, and Madame d'Étampes followed suit. This was not Ippolito's first gift to the king: in December 1540 he had offered him a bronze copy of the *Spinario* at the Capitol.[39] The cardinal knew that his favour with the king depended largely on his reputation as an art connoisseur. It needed to be sustained by plying Francis with gifts of the highest quality.[40]

Cellini's second visit to France lasted five years. He began to follow the court on its travels, but needed a fixed abode in which to carry on his work. Ippolito d'Este advised him to appear as often as possible at the king's table. 'This I did then,' writes Cellini, 'and one morning at his dinner the King called me. He began to talk to me in Italian, saying that he had it in mind to execute several great works, and that he would soon give orders where I was to labour, and provide me with all necessaries.' He offered Cellini a salary of 300 *écus*, but the artist refused it and left the court, only to return soon afterwards under threat of imprisonment. He was now offered better terms, but Cellini's assertion that Francis promised him the same pension as had been paid to Leonardo is disproved by the archives. He received less than Leonardo − 1,460 *l.* instead of 2,000 *l.* − but nonetheless more than most Italian artists employed by Francis: Rosso was paid 1,200 *l.*, Primaticcio and Matteo del Nassaro 600 *l.*, Scibec de Carpi 400 *l.*, and Girolamo della Robbia 240 *l.* [41] For his accommodation Cellini was given the Petit Nesle, a medieval building on the left bank of the Seine opposite the Louvre. It contained a foundry where he cast two heads, one of Julius Caesar; the other of a beautiful girl whom he kept, as he said, for 'his pleasures'. Cellini never worked at Fontainebleau.

The first commission undertaken by Cellini for Francis I was for a life-size statue of Jupiter in silver, but being a goldsmith, not a sculptor, he lacked the experience required for work on a large scale. He accepted the task as a means of raising his status from artisan to artist. 'On the day following,' he writes,

> I went to thank the king [for his pension], who ordered me to make the models of twelve silver statues, which were to stand as candelabra round his table. He wanted them to represent six gods and six goddesses, and to have exactly the same height as his Majesty, which is a trifle under four cubits.

After receiving this commission in December 1540, Cellini made small wax models of Jupiter, Juno, Apollo and Vulcan, which he presented to the king at Blois about mid-March 1541. Francis liked them and ordered Cellini to proceed with the *Jupiter*, giving him the metal required. Cellini, however, decided to make the statue in bronze before venturing into silver. The casting failed miserably, and Cellini was reduced to adapting the simpler, albeit more arduous, method of hammering sheets of silver into shape on an anvil. He was thus engaged in December 1543 when the king, accompanied by Madame d'Étampes, the cardinal of Lorraine, the king and queen of Navarre, the dauphin and dauphine and other courtiers, called at the Petit Nesle. 'When the King arrived at the door of the castle, and heard our hammers going,' writes Cellini,

> he bade his company keep silence. Everybody in my house was busily employed, so that the unexpected entrance of his Majesty took me by surprise. The first thing he saw on coming into the great hall was myself with a huge plate of silver in my hand, which I was beating for the body of my Jupiter; one of my men was finishing the head, another the legs; and it is easy to imagine what a din we made between us . . .. He began to ask me what I was engaged upon, and told me to go on working; then he said that

35. *Juno*. Drawing by Benvenuto Cellini (Musée du Louvre, Paris). This drawing was a response to Francis I's request in 1540 for twelve life-size statues in silver of gods and goddesses to serve as candelabra around his table. Cellini made four small clay models, including one of Juno, but only completed the statue of Jupiter.

he would much rather have me not employ my strength on manual labour, but take as many men as I wanted, and make them do the rough work; he should like me to keep myself in health, in order that he might enjoy my services through many years to come. I replied to his Majesty that the moment I left off working I should fall ill; also that my art itself would suffer, and not attain the mark I aimed at for his Majesty.[42]

Apart from the *Jupiter*, Cellini began work on a statue of Juno, which is only known thanks to a drawing in the Louvre and a small bronze model.[43]

Another commission undertaken by Cellini for the king was a saltcellar. The project originated in Rome soon after his release from prison. He made a model for the cardinal of Ferrara, who decided that it was worthy of presentation to Francis. By a strange coincidence, the king subsequently asked Cellini in Paris to make him a saltcellar:

'On the following day,' he writes,

> he [Francis] sent for me at his dinner-hour. The Cardinal of Ferrara was there at meat with him. When I arrived, the King had reached his second course; he began at once to speak to me, saying, with a pleasant cheer, that having now so fine a basin and jug of my workmanship, he wanted an equally handsome salt-cellar to match them; and begged me to make a design, and to lose no time about it.[44]

Cellini fetched the model he had brought from Rome. 'When I appeared again before the King,' he writes, 'and uncovered my piece, he cried out in

36. Saltcellar by Benvenuto Cellini (Kunsthistorischesmuseum, Vienna). This famous piece of tableware was made between 1540 and 1543 for Francis I at the suggestion of Cardinal Ippolito d'Este, who was instrumental in bringing Cellini to the king's notice. The saltcellar, the only surviving work of art in gold by the artist, represents Sea and Land both seated, with their legs intertwined just as some branches of the sea run into the land.

astonishment: "This is a hundred times more divine a thing than I had ever dreamed of! What a miracle of a man! He ought never to stop working.'"[45] Ippolito warned the king that the saltcellar was a complex undertaking that might never be finished, but, heedless of the warning, Francis asked Cellini how much gold was needed for the task. 'A thousand *scudi*' was the reply, and the money was handed over forthwith. Cellini then set to work, dividing his time between the saltcellar and the *Jupiter*. The former was completed in 1543, and shown to the king in Paris. 'When I exhibited this piece to his Majesty,' writes Cellini,

> he uttered a loud outcry of astonishment, and could not satiate his eyes with gazing at it. Then he bade me take it back to my house, saying he would tell me at the proper time what I should have to do with it. So I carried it home, and sent at once to invite several of my best friends; we dined gaily together, placing the salt-cellar in the middle of the table, and thus we were the first to use it.[46]

In 1542 Cellini suggested two new projects to the king: one was a decorative scheme for the entrance gateway to the château of Fontainebleau; the other, a fountain topped by a colossal statue. Francis, who was about to go away, asked Cellini to make a model which he might judge on his return. On 18 February Cellini offered him two models: the first for the gateway, the other for the fountain. The gateway contained several elements: above the entrance a reclining female nude represented the spirit of Fontainebleau. She rested her left arm on a stag's neck and was surrounded with fawns, wild boars and various hunting dogs. Flanking the gateway were two satyrs, one holding a thick club, the other a lash with three balls attached to a chain. The whole composition was enclosed in an oblong, each angle containing a Victory holding a torch. It was the king, not Cellini, who had devised this programme. An unfinished relief, similar to one described by Cellini, could be seen above the entrance of the château after the king's death. The original design may have been Rosso's, but he died before it could be cast in bronze. Primaticcio was asked to take on the task, but for some unknown reason never did. The project stood thus in January 1542 when Cellini offered to rescue it. His enthusiasm, as usual, outstripped his ability to produce. Despite a contract, signed in June 1544, neither the satyrs nor the Victories were cast in bronze as long as Cellini remained in France. When he left in 1545, they remained unfinished in his workshop. Philibert de l'Orme eventually used them to decorate the château of Anet.[47]

The other model shown by Cellini to the king in February 1542 was of a fountain for Fontainebleau, square in shape and with steps all round. On a pedestal in the middle stood a nude male figure, holding a broken lance in his right hand and resting his left on a scimitar. His right foot rested on a richly decorated helmet. At each angle of the fountain sat a figure 'accompanied by many beautiful and appropriate emblems'. Though pleased by the design, Francis was baffled by its symbolism until Cellini explained that the central figure, intended to stand 54 feet above the ground, was the king himself in the guise of Mars, and the seated figures represented the arts and sciences which he so generously patronised.[48] Francis ordered his treasurers to disburse whatever money Cellini needed for the fountain even though he had not commissioned it. After making a model of the whole fountain, Cellini made two clay models of the central statue: one small, and the other 1.5 metres high. It was this larger one that he showed to the king at the Petit Nesle in June 1544. On 15 July Francis granted him the use of a small house, garden and tennis court adjoining the Petit Nesle, as his existing workshop was too small to accommodate the colossus and other incomplete works.[49] The colossus, however, was never completed.

Cellini's relations with the king deteriorated sharply around November 1544. The artist blamed the duchesse d'Étampes's malice, but Francis had reasons of his own to be exasperated. After four years he was still waiting for his silver candelabra. The time had come for a showdown, and Cellini cites the king's rebuke in all honesty:

'There is one important matter, Benvenuto, which men of your sort, though full of talent, ought always to bear in mind; it is that you cannot bring your great gifts to light by your own strength alone; you show your greatness only through the opportunities we give you. Now you ought to be a little more submissive, less arrogant and headstrong. I remember that I gave you express orders to make me twelve silver statues, and this was all I wanted. You have chosen to execute a saltcellar, and vases and busts and doors, and a heap of other things, which quite confound me, when I consider how you have neglected my wishes and worked for the fulfilment of your own. If you mean to go on in this way, I shall presently let you understand what is my own method of procedure when I choose to have things done in my own way. I tell you, therefore, plainly; do your utmost to obey my commands, for if you stick to your own fancies you will run your head against a wall.'[50]

Cellini offered various excuses: he recalled that Francis had ordered the gold needed for the saltcellar, that he had never received silver for the candelabra, save for the *Jupiter*, and that he could not have worked on the gateway without the consent of the king's treasurers. He admitted the colossal statue was his idea, but pointed out that the king had borne the cost. Adding that he was ready to return to Italy if he had lost the king's favour, he fell upon his knees. Francis, seemingly appeased, raised him up.

Cellini was jolted into two months of frenzied activity on the *Jupiter* which culminated in its presentation at Fontainebleau on 27 or 28 January 1545. The account in his autobiography is justly famous. The unveiling allegedly took place in the Galerie François Ier, where Primaticcio's bronzes were already on display. According to Cellini, the duchesse d'Étampes did her utmost to sabotage the event. She hoped that the bronzes would eclipse his work and delayed its presentation until nightfall when the gallery would be plunged into darkness. Cellini's ingenuity, however, overcame her malice. He had mounted his statue on a plinth with casters and, as the king entered the gallery, he inserted a lighted torch among the flames of Jupiter's thunderbolt. At the same instant Cellini's apprentice pushed the statue forward. The effect, he claims, was sensational, nullifying any possible competition from Primaticcio's bronzes. The duchess, however, was not defeated. As she set eyes on the *Jupiter*, she exclaimed: 'So this is what has cost ten thousand francs and has taken four years to make!' Pointing to a gauze veil hanging from the statue's shoulders, she suggested that it was there to conceal faults. Angered by her remark, Cellini tore off the veil, revealing the god's genitals to the amusement of everyone, save the duchess.[51] A letter from a Ferrarese eye-witness confirms the altercation. He puts the following words into Cellini's mouth: '"I gave it [the *Jupiter*] this shirt out of honesty, but since you do not want it, you won't have it" – and he tore the shirt off the back and said: "does he seem to you well endowed?" The king exploded with laughter.'[52]

The *Jupiter* was melted down in about 1570, but its appearance is known from a contemporary etching by Louis Davent. This shows the god holding a thunderbolt at waist height in his right hand and a globe in his left. No other statue of Jupiter, either ancient or modern, shows him thus equipped. He also wears elaborate sandals. The etching lends support to the duchesse d'Étampes's disparaging comments: the figure is gauche and static, the body thick and virtu-ally hipless, and its gestures are ill-balanced. Maybe Cellini realised its short-comings: this would explain the veil, which otherwise seems absurd. Prudery was hardly necessary at the court of Francis I, and there were better ways of concealing the god's private parts than draping a veil over his shoulders. As for the torch, Davent's etching shows the god's thunderbolt at waist height, thereby contradicting Cellini's statement that the statue was lit from above.

Even after this quarrel with Madame d'Étampes, Cellini continued to argue with her. 'I am accountable for my works to no one but his Majesty,' he said. She answered: 'What would you say if you were accountable to others as well?' 'If I were accountable to other people, I should not stay here,' he replied.

37. *Anne de Pisseleu, duchesse d'Étampes.* Painting attributed to Corneille de Lyon (Metropolitan Museum of Art, New York). Originally called Anne d'Heilly (1508–76), Anne became Francis I's mistress in 1526 and married Jean de Brosse, comte d'Étampes, in 1533. Promoted to the rank of duchess, she became powerful at court until 1547 when she was banished after the king's death.

Pressing the point, the duchess said: 'What would you say if you were accountable to me as well?' 'If I were accountable to you,' replied Cellini, 'I would not stay with his Majesty.' At this point, the king intervened: 'Enough, enough!' he said, bringing the conversation to an end.

Among the benefits Cellini received from Francis I were letters of natural-isation which committed him to spend the rest of his life in the king's service. In 1545, however, the artist returned to Italy. He gave various excuses, but the fact that he left his Italian apprentices at the Petit Nesle along with many unfinished works suggests that he intended to return. Why then did he leave? Almost certainly he feared for his life. In November 1544 the king had scolded the cardinal of Ferrara for not keeping a close watch on Cellini who, he considered, might abscond at any moment. He needed someone who would ensure that this did not happen. The comte de Saint-Pol promised to act in such a way that Cellini would never leave the kingdom.

'What is that?' asked the king. 'Madame sat by with an air of sullen irrita-tion, and Saint-Pol stood on his dignity, declining to answer the King's question. When the King repeated it, he said, to curry favour with Madame d'Étampes: 'I would hang that Benvenuto of yours by the neck, and thus you would keep him for ever in your kingdom.' She broke into a fit of laughter, protesting that I richly deserved it. The King, to keep them company, began to laugh, and said he had no objection to Saint-Pol hanging me, if he could first produce my equal in the arts; and although I had not earned such a fate, he gave him full liberty and licence.[53]

Cellini last met Francis I at Argentan in June 1545. He offered the king two vases and begged leave to go to Italy.

While I was uttering these words, the king kept gazing intently on the vases, and from time to time shot a terrible glance at me; nevertheless, I went on praying to the best of my ability that he would favour my petition. All of a sudden he rose angrily from his seat and said to me in Italian: 'Benvenuto, you are a great fool. Take these vases back to Paris for I want to have them gilt.' Without making any other answer, he then departed.

Ippolito d'Este advised Cellini to obey and wait in Paris for eight days; if no letter reached him in that time he would be free to depart. No letter came, so Cellini left after entrusting the Petit Nesle to his assistants, Ascanio and Paolo. Three silver vases that Cellini took with him later had to be returned after he was accused of stealing the king's silver.

It was a serious *faux pas* to leave Francis I's service without permission. Cellini offered various barely credible excuses: his real reason for going was almost certainly fear of what might happen to him following the king's death. Francis's days were numbered and Cellini was afraid of losing his protection. He probably intended to return to France eventually, but in the meantime he made a *Perseus* for Cosimo I, duke of Florence. Francis regretted his loss. 'Being the best man in the world, he often asked: "Why does not Benvenuto come back to us?"' Cellini's assistants in Paris replied that he was happy where he was and did not intend to return, whereupon the king exclaimed: 'Since he left us without any cause, I shall not recall him; let him e'en stay where he is.'[54] But he confided to the cardinal of Ferrara that it had been a great mistake to let Cellini go. To one of his treasurers Francis said: 'Send Benvenuto six thous- and *scudi* and tell him to come back and finish his great colossus, and I will make it up with him.' The king's death, however, dashed any hopes Cellini may have entertained of returning to France. 'Thus, was I deprived,' he writes, 'of the glory of my great work, the reward of all my labours, and of everything that I had left behind me.' In a poem written in 1556, he described himself as 'in part immortal, since the French king set me on the path of sculpture'.[55]

'Quasi un'altra Roma'

Some of the most important works in Francis I's art collection were diplo- matic gifts. In 1518 Pope Leo X sent four paintings by Raphael to the king. They were a *St Michael*, a *Holy Family*, a *St Margaret* and a portrait of Joanna of Aragon. All are now in the Louvre. The *St Michael* had been commissioned by the pope specifically as a gift for the king on the occasion of an alliance sealed by the visit to the French court of the pope's nephew, Lorenzo de' Medici. The painting was given to Francis at Nantes by the papal legate, Cardinal Bibbiena, after Lorenzo's departure. The gift was appropriate, as Francis was Grand Master of the Order of St Michael.[56] The *Holy Family* was intended for Queen Claude, possibly in celebration of the dauphin's birth. This at least is suggested by an original feature: the crowning of the Virgin by an angel with a wedding bouquet. The *St Margaret*, which shows its subject vanquishing a dragon, may have been a tribute to Francis's sister. As for the portrait of Joanna of Naples, who was renowned for her beauty, it may have been suggested by her cousin, Cardinal Luigi of Aragon, who was Bibbiena's friend and had recently visited the French court. Raphael's pupil Giulio Romano may have had a major share in this painting.[57]

Other diplomatic additions to Francis I's collection dating back to 1518 or soon after were a *Venus* by Lorenzo Costa, given by Francesco Gonzaga, and a *Visitation* by Sebastiano del Piombo, given by the Venetian republic. Federico de' Preti, who presented the Costa to the king, described his reaction as follows:

> He liked it very much and could not take his eyes off it. He asked me to give a thousand thanks to Your Lordship [Francesco Gonzaga]. He took it at once to the queen and his mother and showed it to them, who praised it

38. *St Michael Slaying the Demon.* Also known as *Le Grand Saint-Michel.* Painting by Raphael (Musée du Louvre, Paris). Given to Francis I at Nantes in 1518 by the papal nuncio, Cardinal Bibbiena, on the occasion of the marriage of Lorenzo de' Medici to Madeleine de la Tour d'Auvergne. It was later displayed in the chapel of the château of Fontainebleau. Francis I was Grand Master of the knightly Order of St Michael.

highly. His Majesty the king has asked me if it was the portrait *au naturel* of one of Madame's great ladies, but I stated that I did not know. The king shows her to all these lords and gentlemen.[58]

It may have been around the same time that Francis received a perfume burner, allegedly designed by Raphael and only known from an engraving.[59]

Among the more curious items in Francis's collection was a seven-headed beast with the skin of a crocodile brought back by Antonio Rincon from Constantinople in 1530 as a gift from the Ottoman sultan.[60] The marriage of Henri duc d'Orléans and Catherine de' Medici in 1533 produced gifts from her uncle, Pope Clement VII, including a unicorn's horn mounted in gold by the Milanese goldsmith Tobia, and a casket with carved panels of crystal by Valerio Belli depicting scenes from the life of Christ. Among less important contributors to the king's collection were Renzo da Ceri, his lieutenant-general in Naples, who sent him a newly discovered ancient statue of Venus. This was installed at Amboise in 1530 and may have been be the *Venus genitrix*, ascribed to Callimachus, now in the Louvre. Another donor was the humanist Paolo Giovio, who sent a copy in grisaille by Aristotile Sangallo of Michelangelo's lost *Battle of Cascina*.[61]

Francis did not wait for gifts to enlarge his collection of works of art. He employed agents to find him paintings, statues, books and other valuable items. Some were French diplomats, such as Guillaume du Bellay, who was paid 2,050 *l.* in 1526 for sending certain *articules* from Rome; others were Italians, such as Battista della Palla and Pietro Aretino. Della Palla was a Florentine who had lived in France between 1522 and 1527, and had been in close touch with the court and, more especially, the king's sister, to whom he gave a portrait of Savonarola along with the friar's complete works. In 1528 he was commissioned by Francis to collect works of art in Florence. He was to provide 'large numbers of antiquities of every sort, that is marbles and bronzes and paintings by masters worthy of His Majesty, in which things he had greatly delighted all his life, and is now more immersed than ever'.[62] Della Palla met with resistance as he tried to plunder Florence on the king's behalf, but he did succeed in sending him some works. The only one that survives at Fontainebleau is a statue *Nature* by Niccolò Tribolo. Derived from ancient images of the multi-breasted Diana of Ephesus, it was intended to support a granite vase. Two other statues by contemporary artists sent by della Palla were Bandinelli's *Mercury Holding a Flute* and Michelangelo's *Hercules*. This was given to della Palla by its owner, Filippo Strozzi. At Fontainebleau it became part of a fountain. Originally in the Cour de la Fontaine, it was moved to the Jardin de l'Étang, where it remained until 1714 when it vanished along with the garden. There is some doubt whether it was received by Francis or by Henry II, for in a letter of February 1546 to Michelangelo Francis implied that he possessed none of his statues. The king twice invited the artist to come to France, but in vain. Michelangelo promised, if he lived long enough, to execute two works for him, one in bronze, the other in marble, but it was Francis who died first. According to Vasari, he was the intended recipient of two famous statues by Michelangelo, the *Rebellious Slave* and the *Dying Slave*, but they did not reach France until 1550. Like other collectors of his day, the king was keen to acquire ancient sculpture. In this respect della Palla was only mildly successful: he obtained some minor pieces, but nothing spectacular. Writing to Filippo Strozzi, he expressed concern about forty crates of paintings, sculptures and antiquities that had been shipped to Marseille. He was afraid that they might be unpacked carelessly, exposed to the elements or damaged in other ways. In fact, very few of the works he sent to France have survived. Even after della Palla's death in 1530, Francis continued to add Florentine works to his collection, including Michelangelo's *Leda and the Swan* (now lost) and possibly Bronzino's *Venus and Cupid* (now in the National Gallery, London).[63]

Though most of the artists represented in Francis I's collection were Florentines, Venetians were not completely overlooked. In 1538 Pietro Aretino sent two pictures to Francis, 'one magnifying the honour of man, the other magnifying the glory of God'. The first was Titian's portrait of the king, now in the Louvre, which was painted from a medal, not from life; the other was evidently a religious work, perhaps also by Titian. It may have been the *Penitent Magdalen,* now in Bordeaux. It was presumably on the evidence of these works that Francis invited Titian to France, but the artist declined, saying that he 'never wanted to abandon Venice'.[64]

Aretino began to serve as the king's artistic agent in 1529 after he had joined the circle of scholars and artists formed by the French ambassador Lazare de Baïf. In 1530 he was promised a gold chain by the king, but received it only three years later. It consisted of overlapping tongues of gold, weighed eight pounds and was worth 500 crowns. Aretino, however, failed to receive an annuity promised by Francis and warned him that 'the furnace of Murano' burning in his honour would cool unless he kept his word. About 1539 Aretino sent two portraits – one of Plato, the other of Aristotle – to the cardinal of Lorraine, who gave them to the king. As he admired them, Francis said that he recognised Aristotle as he already had his bust, but did not recall ever seeing Plato before. He ordered both pictures to be taken to the room where he kept his favourite works. In 1539 Aretino had his own portrait painted by Francesco Salviati and sent it to the king.

In addition to paintings and statues, Francis I owned no fewer than 213 tapestries. Tapestries were not only decorative; they also served to give

39. *Pietro Aretino.* Painting by Titian (Pitti Palace, Florence). The Italian man of letters (1492–1556), was employed by Francis I as one of his artistic agents in Italy. He was rewarded for his services with a gold necklace which he is seen wearing here.

warmth to a room and, following the court, they were carried from château to château. Francis seems to have commissioned them even before his accession. He also inherited some from Anne of Brittany and his mother. They depicted subjects mainly taken from the Bible or medieval romances. A few may have been woven in Paris, but the majority came from Brussels or Antwerp. In

1532 the Italian agent Marchio Baldi gave the king three tapestries after designs by Giulio Romano depicting the story of Scipio Africanus and proposed that Marc Crétif of Brussels should make a complete set illustrating the hero's deeds and triumph. Francis responded by commissioning a tapestry of twenty-two pieces. It was woven simultaneously by several workshops over three years and cost the enormous sum of 50,000 *l*. As we have seen, Primaticcio's earliest commission in France was to supervise the execution of this tapestry in Brussels. It was unfortunately destroyed in 1797 for its gold and silver thread, but several preliminary drawings and two cartoons survive. In 1532 Pierre de Pannemaker, the famous Brussels weaver, made a set of six hangings for Francis. Woven with silk, silver and gold thread, they were designed by Matteo del Nassaro, best known as an engraver of medals and gems. In 1534 another Brussels merchant supplied the king with three more sets: a *Story of Romulus and Remus*, *Espaliers* and a *Creation of the World*. The *Stories of Actaeon* and *Orpheus* 'in gold and silk with verdure and little figures' followed in 1538. Once again the purchaser was Matteo del Nassaro.

About 1540 Francis I, perhaps with an eye to economizing, set up a tapestry workshop at Fontainebleau. Apparently it was not intended to be permanent and its only known product is a set of six hangings that reproduce the decorations on the south wall of the Galerie François Ier. The king, it seems, wanted to have a movable version of his gallery and employed a minor artist, Claude Badouin, to copy Rosso's work. The tapestries are now in Vienna. They may have been given by Charles IX along with Cellini's salt-cellar at the time of his wedding to Elizabeth of Austria. Another intriguing survival – this time at the Vatican – is a copy of Leonardo's *Last Supper* woven in Flanders before 1515. Francis may have given it to Pope Clement VII at their meeting in Marseille in 1533.[65]

CHAPTER 11

'Father of Letters'

The Collège de France in Paris owns a painting by the nineteenth-century artist Guillaume Guillon, alias Lethière. It depicts Francis I signing letters patent for the creation of a royal college (see plate 11). The king is being offered a register by Guillaume Budé, the mayor of Paris, and a quill pen by a secretary. Other persons witnessing the scene are the young dauphin, Marguerite de Navarre, Janus Lascaris, Clément Marot, Primaticcio, Leonardo da Vinci and Rosso. Thus did the painter confirm with his brush the legend of Francis I as 'Father of Letters' which still commands popular, even scholarly, respect. At a conference held in Cognac to celebrate the five-hundredth anniversary of the king's birth, a distinguished professor of French literature praised the monarch's patronage of letters, describing it as operating on three levels: economically in the form of subsidies, institutionally by the creation of a royal college modelled on humanistic foundations, and linguistically by promoting the use of the French language.[1] No one would deny that his reign witnessed a remarkable flowering of humanistic studies and that the king assisted this development, but the strength of that encouragement ought not to be overstated. The king gave less than he promised; no royal college was founded in his reign; and the advancement of the French language owed little to his legislation.

Francis I enjoyed the company of intelligent and well-educated men. Among several humanists in his entourage were his secretary, Guillaume Budé, his doctor, Guillaume Cop, his old tutor, François Demoulins, and his confessor, Guillaume Petit. The most important of these men was Budé, a Parisian whose bourgeois forebears had served the French crown in various capacities. At the age of twenty-three, after studying Roman law at Orléans, he spent three years indulging his love of hunting before deciding that it was a waste of time. From then on he devoted himself to scholarship. He learnt Greek, largely on his own, and in time became sufficiently proficient to correspond in that language with eminent humanists. His mastery of Latin and

40. Francis I as a composite deity. Miniature by Nicolas Belin (*c.* 1490–1569) (Bibliothèque nationale de France). The inscription on this picture reads to the effect that Francis combined the attributes of Minerva, Mars, Diana, Venus and Mercury. Belin, a native of Modena, worked at Fontainebleau in 1533–4. Charged with fraud, he moved to England and worked for Henry VIII at Nonsuch.

Greek enabled him to become familiar with an entire field of ancient wisdom. Charles VIII received Budé at his court and appointed him as one of his secretaries, but Louis XII did not appreciate him and Budé left the court in disgust, comparing it to 'Circe's cave', a den of vice and intrigue.[2] He used his exile from court to prepare his *Annotationes ad Pandectas* and *De Asse*. Unlike

1 Anne of Brittany writing a letter to her husband, Louis XII, who has gone to war (National Library of Russia, St Petersburg, ms. fr. F. V. XIV, 8, fo. 1 verso).

2 *Banquet for the Coronation of Anne of Brittany.* Painting by André Delavigne (Waddesdon Manor).

3 Francis I in his kingdom. Colour drawing of a tapestry. The king flanked by clergy and nobility sits enthroned on an island beyond which various rural and maritime occupations are being pursued.

4 *King Francis I, c.* 1535. Painting attributed to Jean and François Clouet (Musée du Louvre, Paris). The king wears the collar of the Order of St Michael of which he was Grand Master. The knots embroidered on his doublet recall his mother's emblem of a girdle.

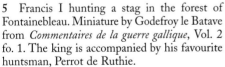

5 Francis I hunting a stag in the forest of Fontainebleau. Miniature by Godefroy le Batave from *Commentaires de la guerre gallique*, Vol. 2 fo. 1. The king is accompanied by his favourite huntsman, Perrot de Ruthie.

6 St Thomas, patron saint of architects, with the features of King Francis I. Painted enamel by Léonard Limousin (Musée du Louvre, Paris). The king is known to have sketched châteaux he wished to see built.

7 The Galerie François Ier at the château of Fontainebleau. Though much altered over the centuries, this is the most impressive vestige of Francis I's rebuilding after 1528. He was so proud of it that he kept the key on his person.

8 Elephant with the fleur-de-lis. Fresco and stucco by Rosso in the Galerie François Ier at Fontainebleau. The elephant (note the fleur-de-lis, the royal 'F' and the salamander on its trappings) symbolizes power and eternity. It dominates the elements embodied by the gods: fire by Zeus, water by Neptune and earth by Pluto.

9 King Francis I and the Emperor Charles V. Fresco by Tadeo Zuccaro for the Villa Farnese at Caprarola, commemorating the meeting in 1538 and short-lived entente of the two great rivals.

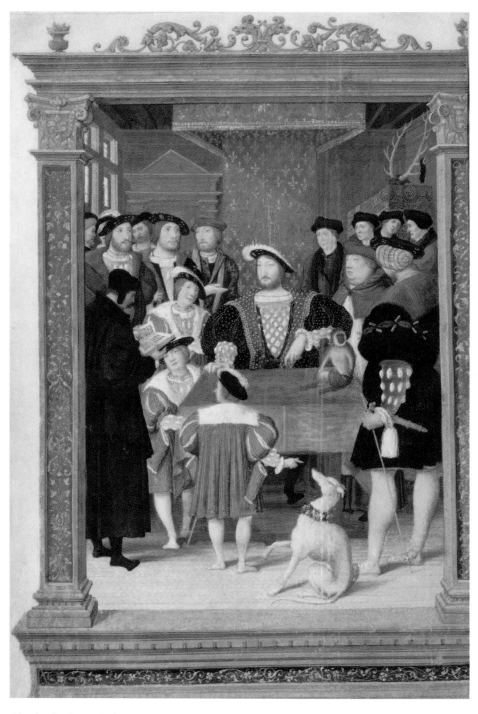

10 *Antoine Macault Offers Francis I his Translation of Diodorus Siculus.* Anonymous miniature of *c.* 1530 (Musée Condé, Chantilly). The king is surrounded by his three sons, lay courtiers on his right and churchmen (including Cardinal Duprat) on his left.

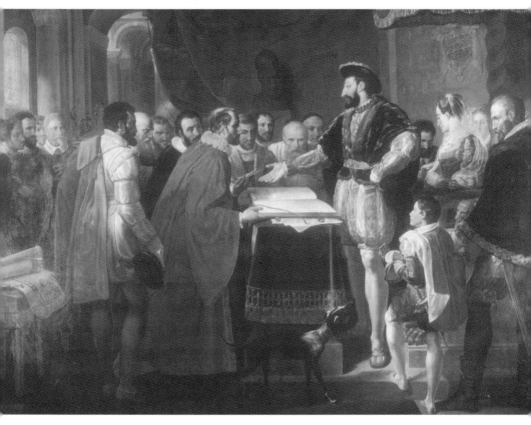

11 *The Founding of the Collège de France by King Francis I*. Painting by Guillaume Guillon, alias Lethière (Collège de France, Paris). The scene is mythical. The king never did sign a charter in the presence of the leading scholars and artists of his day.

12 *Anne de Montmorency* (1493-1567), Grand Master and Constable of France. Enamel, dated 1556, by Léonard Limousin in its original frame (Musée du Louvre, Paris).

13 Tomb of Philippe Chabot de Brion, Admiral of France (*c.* 1492-1543). This fine alabaster effigy, traditionally attributed to the sculptor Pierre Bontemps, was originally part of a larger monument erected in the monastery of the Célestins in Paris and dismantled in the French Revolution. The effigy and other fragments are now in the Musée du Louvre, Paris.

14 Henry II in his coronation robes touching victims of scrofula. Miniature from his Book of Hours (Bibliothèque nationale de France, ms. latin, 1429, fo. 107 verso).

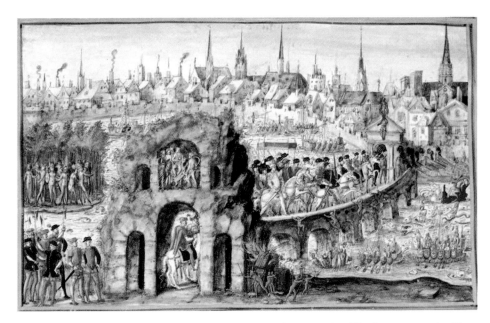

15 The royal entry festival of Henri II into Rouen, 1 October 1550. The king crosses the River Seine after passing through a grotto in which Orpheus sits on a throne playing his harp (Bibliothèque municipale de Rouen: ms.Y 28).

16 The ballroom of the château of Fontainebleau. Begun under Francis I, this hall was originally vaulted. De l'Orme replaced the vault with a flat coffered ceiling in 1550. The frescoes are after designs by Primaticcio.

17 *King Charles IX (1560-74).* Painting by François Clouet (Kunsthistorisches Museum, Vienna). The painting is dated 1569 when the king would have been twenty years old. He married Elizabeth of Austria, the daughter of the Emperor Maximilian II in 1571.

la roine mere du roi

18 *Catherine de' Medici, c.* 1560. Drawing by François Clouet (Bibliothèque nationale de France). This portrait of the queen mother in her widow's weeds was her own favourite. She appears 'almost unwrinkled', as described by the Venetian envoy, Lippomano.

19 Ball given in honour of the Polish ambassadors, 1573. Tapestry (Pitti Palace, Florence). One of a set of eight recording festivals at the court of Charles IX. The tapestries were probably commissioned by Catherine de' Medici, seen dressed in black at the centre. Two Polish envoys stand on the left.

20 *Ball at the Court of Henry III on 24 September 1581 for the Marriage of the duc de Joyeuse.* Anonymous painting (Musée du Louvre, Paris). The 'Joyeuse Magnificences', which coincided with hard times for Parisians damaged the court's reputation.

21 Henry III on his deathbed appointing Henri of Navarre as his successor (Musée national de la Renaissance, Écouen). This illustrates another myth propagated by the Huguenots in order to strengthen Henry IV's claim to be the lawful king of France.

most of his fellow humanists, Budé was a layman. At the age of thirty-eight he married a girl of fifteen who gave him eleven children; yet somehow he managed to find time to study.

Budé learnt with relief of the death of Louis XII and accession of Francis I. A new era seemed to be opening and in the final pages of *De Asse* Budé looked forward to returning to court. In 1519 he gave the new king a collection of apophthegms, subsequently published under the title of *L'Institution du Prince*, and in 1522 was appointed as royal librarian, a post that he retained for the rest of his life.[3] Two more appointments followed. In 1523 Budé became *maître des requêtes de l'hôtel* and *prévôt des marchands*, or mayor of Paris.[4] Combining the two must have been difficult since the first required

41. *Guillaume Budé*. Painting by Jean Clouet (Metropolitan Museum of Art, New York). Budé (1468–1540), the leading humanist at the court of Francis I, disliked the atmosphere there, but endured it if only to urge the king to found a college in Paris dedicated to the study of classical languages.

attendance at court and the second was based in the capital.[5] Budé and the
other *maîtres* were each paid 250 *l.* per annum for their travel expenses.

In his youth Francis was an unlikely candidate for the role of 'Father of
Letters'. As Louis XII's cousin, he only had a remote chance of succeeding
to the throne and was not therefore groomed for kingship: his education was
that normally prescribed for a young nobleman, consisting mainly of
outdoor sports and physical exercise. Pierre Du Chastel, in a funeral oration
for the king, praised his athleticism and physical powers.[6] Although taught
by François Demoulins, a churchman and humanist, Francis never
succeeded in mastering Latin. This was why Budé wrote his *L'Institution du
Prince* in French, for he knew that the king would not read it if it were in
Latin. Writing to Erasmus in February 1517, Budé wrote: 'This prince is
not lettered (which I fear is too often the case with our kings) but he is
endowed with a natural eloquence; he has intelligence, tact, suppleness and
an easy and agreeable manner.' The king, Budé continued, 'admired and
praised princes of old, particularly those who had distinguished themselves
by their high-mindedness and deeds. He disposed of resources matching his
generosity.'

Francis I had a lively and enquiring mind. He believed that the occult
sciences held the key to the hidden forces animating the universe and was
fascinated by Giulio Camillo's 'theatre of memory', a system of universal
mnemotechnics. He was also intrigued by the Cabala, the esoteric tradition
of Jewish mysticism. One of its exponents was Agrippa of Nettesheim, who
spent some time in the circle of Louise of Savoy before entering the service
of Emperor Charles V. Francis asked Jean Thenaud for a treatise on the
Cabala, but the scholar had misgivings about the king's interest. 'It is far
better', he wrote in his *Cabale métrifiée* (1519), 'to be ignorant than to ask or
to look for what cannot be known without sinning.' Undeterred, Francis
asked Thenaud for another book on the same subject, this time in prose.
Again Thenaud obliged, but repeated his warning.

Writing to Richard Pace in April 1518, Budé compared the French court
unfavourably to the English one. Henry VIII, he said, never appeared in
public or at council meetings without the presence of learned men, such as
Linacre, Pace himself, Tunstall, More and Latimer.[7] Such men, Budé
explained, had not been banished from the French court; they had simply left
of their own accord and no one was trying to bring them back. Francis had
the right qualities of body and mind, 'yet by some evil destiny study and virtue
have fled elsewhere. As far as I am concerned for the past eighteen years I
have ceased to live among courtiers.' Around 1520 Budé's relations with
Francis I changed following the presentation of *L'Institution du Prince*. This
provided the royal table with entertaining and instructive readings and Budé

was soon invited to join the king's entourage. He attended the Field of Cloth of Gold and thereafter followed the court on its travels. Though Budé disliked its way of life, he put up with it as the price of retaining the king's patronage.

Budé believed that a knowledge of history was essential to political success. 'Prudence,' he wrote, 'comes mostly from experience and from the observation of past examples as registered by history.' If in the past, he argued, kings of France had appreciated men of learning, their kingdom would have rivalled ancient Rome in greatness. Now that there was a 'lack of writing' (*faulte de la plume*), 'many nobles and valiant kings, princes and knights of this kingdom are forgotten'.[8] Francis needed to follow the example of past princes who had commissioned 'men of learning and eloquence' to immortalise their greatness and rewarded their efforts, but he needed to exercise his patronage with care, 'for a precious pearl or other jewel should only be mounted or polished by an excellent craftsman'. The king, Budé stressed, should only listen to men who had acquired their learning the hard way. He made no secret of what he expected from him in return for his own services: in *De Asse* he established a concordance between the currencies of ancient Greece and sixteenth-century France: 100 talents paid to Isocrates for a speech was worth 200 French *écus*; 100 sesterces paid to Virgil was worth 60,000 *écus*.[9]

At the start of Francis's reign the greatest need felt by humanists was for a college devoted to the teaching of Greek and Hebrew, languages excluded from the traditional university curriculum. The king responded by appointing Agostino Giustiniani, a Genoese, to teach Hebrew in Paris, but he left after only five years. In 1517 Francis announced his intention of founding a college for the study of classical languages. He may have been inspired by the college of young Greeks that Pope Leo X had set up in Rome in 1515. Francis invited Erasmus to take charge of his college: he alone among scholars had an international reputation commensurate with the prestige the king hoped to gain from his foundation. Budé was told by Guillaume Petit of a conversation between himself, François Demoulins and possibly Guillaume Cop and Étienne Poncher in the king's presence. The name of Erasmus had cropped up more than once, and Francis, 'as if inspired by Minerva's breath', had said that he wanted to attract talented men to his kingdom by offering them substantial favours. He expressed the wish to set up in France a seminary of learned men. The king's invitation was conveyed to Erasmus by Poncher during an embassy to Brussels. In a letter urging the Dutchman to accept, Budé described his master. 'This monarch', he wrote,

> is not only a Frank (which is by itself a glorious title), he is also Francis, a name borne by a king for the first time and, one can prophesy, predestined for great things. He is educated in letters, which is usual with our kings,

and also possesses a natural eloquence, wit, tact and an easy, pleasant manner; nature, in short, has endowed him with the rarest gifts of body and mind. He likes to admire and praise princes of old who have distinguished themselves by their lofty intellects and brilliant deeds, and he is fortunate in having as much wealth as any king in the world, which he gives more liberally than anyone.[10]

Erasmus, however, did not wish to tie himself to any prince, however enlightened, other than Charles of Habsburg from whom he received a pension. He therefore declined the invitation while praising the king's initiative as the dawn of a new age.[11] In April, Budé and the poet Germain de Brie tried to persuade him to change his mind, but he stood firm. 'France', Erasmus replied, 'has always smiled on me, but so far I have been detained by any number of obstacles.'

Having failed to enlist the services of Erasmus, Francis turned to Janus Lascaris, the principal of Leo X's college in Rome. A Greek from Constantinople, Lascaris had already served Charles VIII. At the end of the fifteenth century he had translated Greek texts into Latin in order to facilitate their translation into French. Francis had by now decided to set up a college in Milan, probably as a first step towards a more ambitious one in France. He allocated 10,000 *l.* to it in addition to an annual payment of 2,000 *l.* for the upkeep of twelve young Greek students and two teachers. Returning to Italy in 1520, Lascaris found suitable premises in Milan and sent agents to Greece to recruit students. In the meantime, he stayed in Venice working in the library of San Marco and collecting manuscripts for the king of France.

Budé was determined to hold Francis I to his promise to found a college. In a letter to the humanist, Christophe de Longueil, on 6 January 1521 he wrote: 'I will not go a thumb's length away from the court, as the saying is . . .. As soon as I cease to be visible to the king, his zeal and enthusiasm become lukewarm or cool completely.' One day, as Budé followed the king into his chamber, he produced a letter from Lascaris. Francis asked to see it, but Budé failed to respond, whereupon the king snatched the letter only to find that it was written in Greek. This gave Budé the chance he had been waiting for to show off his learning. 'Like a monkey among a crowd of asses', he translated the letter aloud and Francis was so impressed that he allowed Budé to say 'all that seemed opportune and useful'. Soon afterwards the king renewed his promise to found a college for the study of Greek. It was to be at the Hôtel de Nesle in Paris and to have a chapel funded out of the revenues of chapels of disused royal palaces. Yet Budé was disappointed. 'I won't say that the king's zeal is completely extinguished,' he wrote to a friend,

I even think that it won't be difficult to revive, but he is no longer doing anything. I do what I can to rekindle the fire which at present produces little but smoke, but I lack the skill to win over as I would wish the minds of the courtiers who sometimes deride my projects and seek to discredit me unfairly.

Lascaris, too, was disappointed. No money reached him from France after he had spent 2,000 *l.* recruiting young Greeks. He had paid for a building in Milan out of his own pocket, but in August 1523 he informed Montmorency that he would not be able to continue beyond the end of the month. He received no reply, so the college had to close.

Francis I had much on his mind at the time. In 1521 he declared war on the Emperor Charles V and in 1525 was defeated and taken prisoner at Pavia. In such circumstances he could be forgiven for not remembering his promise to found a college, but Budé was still there to remind him. In 1529 he dedicated the preface of his *Commentarii linguae graecae* to the king. In it, Budé compared philology to a poor girl in need of a dowry and urged Francis to provide it. The dowry he had in mind was a college capable of turning Paris into 'the sojourn of the Muses for the whole of Gaul'. It would be 'a lodging, sumptuous and magnificent from the foundations to the roof, which would be like a field for the jousters of one tongue and the other . . .'.[12]

In March 1530 Francis created four readerships: the *lecteurs royaux*. Pierre Danès and Jacques Toussaint were appointed as professors of Greek, and François Vatable and Agathias Guidacerius as professors of Hebrew. Humanists everywhere praised the move. 'The river which the king is about to let flow', wrote a Flemish scholar, 'will water many lands and make them fertile.' Erasmus declared France more fortunate than if she had conquered the whole of Italy. Rabelais in *Pantagruel* (1532) acclaimed the event as the dawn of a new age:

> Now every method of teaching has been restored, and the study of languages has been revived: of Greek, without which it is disgraceful for a man to call himself a scholar, and of Hebrew, Chaldean, and Latin. The elegant and accurate art of printing, which is now in use, was invented in my time, by divine inspiration.[13]

Yet Francis I's act fell short of Budé's vision: it was an informal measure for which no royal charter exists. The *lecteurs* often had to wait four or five years before being paid. Danès lacked patience, and in 1535 left for Italy. In fact, the lecturers only survived thanks to the generosity of some bishops, who conferred benefices on them. They were not even given a building in Paris, but had to teach in existing colleges or in the open air, where they were assailed by street noises and smells.[14]

The word 'college' was never applied to the *lecteurs royaux*. It was used, however, in connexion with another project Francis I had in mind but never implemented. Pierre Galland, the lecturer in Latin, in a funeral oration for the king pointed to three components of his literary patronage: the creation of the royal library at Fontainebleau, the setting up of a printing press in the same château dedicated to the publication of scholarly works, and the establishment of a college within the university of Paris. The sum of 200,000 gold *écus* was earmarked for its fabric and an annual revenue of 30,000 *écus* for the salaries and upkeep of its principal, teachers, priests and more than one hundred poor scholars.[15] Of these projects, however, only the library at Fontainebleau was implemented in Francis's lifetime – and even that is controversial.

The Royal Library

Louis XII founded the royal library. He collected books inherited from his family and from Charles VIII as well as others acquired in his own reign. They were kept at the château of Blois, which already housed the manuscripts of his father, the poet Charles d'Orléans. The library contained books taken by Charles VIII from the library of the kings of Naples in 1495 and those of the dukes of Milan taken by Louis himself from Pavia in 1499. There were also the books of Louis de Bruges, acquired early in the sixteenth century, and those received by Louis as gifts or as translations commissioned from copyists. Antonio de Beatis, who visited the library in 1517, described it as

> a sizeable room not only furnished with shelves from end to end but also lined with book-cases from floor to ceiling, and literally packed with books – to say nothing of those put away in chests in an inner room. These books are all of parchment, handwritten in beautiful lettering and bound in silk of various colours, with elaborate locks and clasps of silver gilt.[16]

Francis I showed little interest in the library at Blois. He added to it only occasionally, as in 1538 when he deposited a few books of scientific interest there. Almost all the books he acquired or received as gifts formed part of the library at Cognac inherited in 1496 from his grandfather Jean d'Angoulême and father, Charles. Francis added manuscripts and printed books to the library, but kept some of these in chests which he carried with him on his travels. Not content simply to own books, Francis liked to read them or have

them read to him at mealtimes. A famous miniature shows the humanist
Antoine Macault reading his translation of Diodorus Siculus to Francis, who
sits at a table surrounded by his sons, courtiers and a pet monkey (see plate
10). Reading aloud to the king was the role of the *lecteur du roi*, a post held in
1529 by Jacques Colin, the translator of Castiglione's *Il Cortegiano*, who was
succeeded in 1537 by Pierre Du Chastel. In 1536 the king's mobile library
consisted of two chests whose contents point to his favourite reading. They
contained works by Justinus, Thucydides, Appian and Diodorus Siculus as
well as the *Destruction de Troie la Grant*, the *Roman de la Rose* and other
romances. Since Francis knew no Greek, Hugues Salet and other scholars
translated the *Iliad*, some of Plutarch's *Lives* and a romance by Heliodorus
into French. The king knew the layout of his library. He once asked Germain
de Brie if he had read Vida's *Eclogues*. When de Brie admitted that he had
not, the king indicated where he might find the work on his shelves.

The king's library had relatively few printed books, and it was doubtless to
remedy this defect that the Ordinance of Montpellier was issued on 28
December 1537.[17] All printers and booksellers were required to deliver one
copy of every new book to the king's librarian at Blois. Foreign imports were
to be deposited for examination and possible purchase. In this way, the ordinance explained, contemporary works would bear witness to the literary glory
of the reign, the king's successors would acquire a taste for study and be
encouraged to continue his patronage of letters; posterity would also find texts
in their original and pure state. The ordinance, however, seems to have been
a dead letter.

Budé, who was appointed Master of the King's Library in 1521, may have
been the inspiration behind the king's search for manuscripts in Italy and the
Near East. Over five hundred were acquired in five years by agents in Venice
and Rome or by purchases or gifts of complete collections. The library of the
duc de Bourbon was added to the royal library following his treason. The
Greek manuscripts acquired by Francis I were intended for 'a fine and sumptuous library' that he wanted to found alongside the trilingual college he
planned to set up in Paris. This never materialised, but books were obtained
just the same.

Francis I's library received books from various quarters. In January 1538
Mellin de Saint-Gelais, keeper of the library at Blois, was paid 30 gold *écus*
for a trip to Toulouse to collect state papers left by the late Jean de Pins,
bishop of Rieux. During his embasssies in Venice and Rome, the bishop had
acquired Greek manuscripts, of which nineteen were now brought back by
Saint-Gelais. More manuscripts, including a translation of eight of Plutarch's
Lives, came to the king's library from the collection of Georges de Selve,
ambassador to Venice in 1533–7. A number of manuscripts also came as gifts.

Early in the 1540s Gian-Francesco Torresani, a notable Italian Hellenist, gave Francis nearly eighty Greek manuscripts; another Italian donor was Cardinal Niccolò Gaddi. In September 1538 Girolamo Fondulo, a Milanese scholar, was paid 450 *l.* for a book-buying mission to Milan on the king's behalf. He had come to France in 1537 and had become the king's secretary and tutor to the future Henry II. In 1538 he met Antonios Eparchos, a teacher of Greek and dealer in Greek manuscripts in Venice. When the latter was forced to sell his library, Fondulo tried to buy it for the king of France, but was unable to complete the purchase. He did, however, return to France in 1539 with sixty volumes, including ancient manuscripts and specially commissioned copies of ancient texts. Another important contributor to the royal library was Guillaume Pellicier, the French ambassador in Venice. In November 1540 he purchased forty volumes from Demetrio Zeno, whom he also employed as a copyist, and in August 1541 Francis I received four cases of Greek books, including many scientific and medical treatises, which one of Pellicier's servants had brought back from Venice. In addition to employing a team of copyists in the libraries of San Antonio del Castello and San Marco, Pellicier searched for books in Florence, Rome and Urbino before returning to France in 1542. Under Henry II, Cardinal Armagnac recalled that Francis I had sent a servant to Constantinople and parts of Greece to find ancient books for his library. He had gathered a large number and would have sent them if only he had received money as promised. Francis was doubtless sincere in wishing to satisfy scholars who promised him eternal glory, but all too often he failed to follow up his good intentions. A new war in 1542 caused him to relegate scholarship in his list of priorities.[18]

There is no evidence of a library at Fontainebleau before 1539 at the earliest. On 22 May 1544 Francis I ordered an inventory of the library at Blois in preparation for its transfer to Fontainebleau.[19] This lists 1,896 books as well as a terrestrial globe and a crocodile's head in a leather case. The books and objects were received at Fontainebleau on 12 June by Mathieu Lavisse, the king's private librarian, but it was only in 1546 that Nicander of Corcyra, a Greek copyist and publisher, reported the establishment of a library close to the king's lodging. This may have occupied the floor above the Galerie François Ier. Wherever it was, the library was shown in August 1546 to English ambassadors, including Cuthbert Tunstall, bishop of Durham, who was a fine Greek and Latin scholar. Francis talked to the ambassadors about French translations of Greek books he had commissioned. In 1567 Pierre Ramus, one of the *lecteurs royaux*, petitioned Catherine de' Medici for the library to be brought to Paris so as to make it more accessible to scholars. Two years later the library – now comprising 3,650 titles – was moved to an unidentified building in the capital; it was to become the nucleus of the Bibliothèque Nationale.[20]

About 1540 Francis I ordered many of his books to be rebound. Gold-tooling, the most conspicuous feature of humanistic binding, had been imported into France from Italy in the early 1500s. By 1540 French binding had embarked on a period of great stylistic innovation. Some Greek manuscripts acquired by Francis were rebound in a style called *alla greca* that was new to France. Some of the new bindings, tooled in gold and silver, are striking, but the series as a whole is unimpressive. The goatskin employed, mostly red and green, is of indifferent quality and the decorative designs are stiff and awkward. While the king provided the funds for binding, the choice of books to be bound was left to Du Chastel as Master of the Library, assisted by Angelos Vergikios in respect of the Greek books. Étienne Roffet, the King's binder (*relieur du roi*) in 1539, was succeeded in November 1547 by Gomar Estienne, a native of Brabant. Under Henry II the rebinding programme was continued. The quality of the leather used improved as well as the tooling technique and decoration of the flat surfaces. Whereas under Francis the heraldry had been simple, consisting mainly of the crowned 'F', the salamander and fleurs-de-lys, under Henry II the crescent moon, single or triple, made its appearance along with the monogram 'HC' and some elaborate interlacing. Between 1547 and 1552 no fewer than 635 books were given luxurious bindings.[21]

Francis I wanted his books to be available to scholars: hence his interest in printing. Robert Estienne, who was appointed in 1539 as the King's printer in Hebrew and Latin, and in 1542 as his printer in Greek, explained Francis's intentions as follows: 'Far from grudging to anyone the records of ancient writers that he at great and truly royal cost has procured from Italy and Greece, he intends to put them at the disposal and service of all men.' Three special founts of Greek type, the *grecs du roi*, cut by Claude Garamond and modelled on the writing of Vergikios, were funded by the king. The first work published using the new type was Eusebius's *Ecclesiastical History* (1544), and the most influential a New Testament (1550) based on nine manuscripts in the royal library. Francis himself is said to have chosen the Roman history of Dionysius of Halicarnassus for publication in 1546–7 and suggested the small Greek type used for a pocket-size New Testament in 1546.

Despite the shortcomings of his own education, Francis I deserves credit at a time when the French nobility was notoriously uncultivated for at least appreciating the value of scholarship, if only as an adornment of his own regality. The pressure of events may have caused him at times to forget well-meaning promises made to the humanists in his entourage, but overall his intellectual patronage was not negligible. Even if legend has credited him with more than he actually accomplished, he did give a significant boost to scholarship by setting up royal lectureships in subjects hitherto neglected by the French universities and he did form one of the richest collections of ancient manuscripts north of the Alps.

CHAPTER 12

A New Parnassus

Authors, however talented, could seldom lead an independent existence in early sixteenth-century France. Their rights were unprotected and royalties nonexistent. Unless an author had a private income, he needed support which could best be found by securing the notice of a well-to-do nobleman. Securing such patronage usually meant flattering the would-be patron. The biggest prize of all for an author was to attract the notice of the king or a member of his family. This could be done by presenting a book, but the degree of support an author could expect varied from reign to reign.

Charles VIII and Louis XII were not especially distinguished as literary patrons. Their main contribution was the addition to the royal library at Blois of more than a thousand books seized as war booty from the libraries of the king of Naples and duke of Milan. They also commissioned works, several of them translations of classical works, and received others as gifts. In addition, they liked histories capable of enhancing their own image. Charles VIII employed two Italians, Giovanni de Candida and Paolo-Emilio. The former was asked to revise the *Grandes Chroniques*, but failed to complete the task; Paolo-Emilio wrote *De Rebus gestis Gallorum*, but did not take it beyond 1488. Two other historians commissioned by the king, Robert Gaguin and Michele Riccio, were more successful. Guillaume Tardif translated Poggio Bracciolini's salacious *Facetiae* for Charles as well as a treatise in French on falconry. The king, it seems, was an avid reader. He read works by Christine de Pisan, Alain Chartier and Philippe de Mézières, as well as the *Roman de la Rose* and the *Cent nouvelles nouvelles*. Romances of chivalry, however, accounted for only two works in his chamber.[1] Jean d'Auton, a Benedictine monk, undertook a chronicle of the reign of Louis XII, but received no wage as historiographer royal. He was also denied access to state papers and forced to rely on hearsay for information about events.[2]

Anne of Brittany was a more significant literary patron than either of her husbands. A prolific letter writer, she also had an enquiring mind: she ordered her herald, Pierre Choque, to write accounts of his travels to Hungary and elsewhere. Her library contained works on many subjects, though they were predominantly religious. Among the many political allegories, tales of adventure and fables dedicated to the queen, the *Roman de Jehan de Paris* by André de La Vigne deserves special mention. The author began his career by composing an anti-Breton poem, but after becoming Anne's secretary, he showered her with flattery. In a poem celebrating her entry into Paris in 1504, he turned the reality of a cool reception by the Parisians into a resounding triumph. Publishers competed with each other in offering Anne luxury editions of their works. One contained a miniature of the queen, dressed in black with a large book in front of her and her ladies sitting on the ground at her feet (plate 1). The fact that the number of works dedicated to her grew substantially after her marriage to Louis XII may indicate an increase in her influence at court.[3]

Anne received innumerable tributes from poets, collectively known as the *grands rhétoriqueurs*, who have been largely dismissed by literary historians as puffed-up mediocrities. Sainte-Beuve described France as a literary wasteland from about 1460 to 1520.[4] Writing in 1894, Gustave Lanson called the work of the *rhétoriqueurs* 'a laborious and pretentious mishmash in which hollow subtleties and inept wordplay took the place of inspiration and thought'.[5] Twentieth-century scholars have been kinder, acknowledging that the *rhétoriqueurs* played a crucial role in a transitional period of French literature.[6] The most famous was Jean Lemaire de Belges, who spent most of his life looking for a patron. Margaret of Austria, duchess of Savoy, employed him for a time as administrator of her chapel at Brou, but he lost her favour after accepting a commission from Anne of Brittany. His most famous work, the *Illustrations de Gaule et Singularités de Troie*, set out to show that the Gauls were the ancestors of the Trojans and, therefore, of the Franks. Lemaire believed that Germany was the progenitrix of European nobility and that the future of Christendom would best be served by its union with France. Rejecting the notion that French was a barbaric language, he elevated Paris above Athens and Rome as 'the mother and mistress of all the world's studies'.[7]

Under Francis I a growing awareness of the classical world, a more sophisticated court and various pedagogical experiments combined to change the poetic climate. The *grands rhétoriqueurs* did not vanish overnight. Jean Bouchet (1476–1557), for example, who had presented verses to Charles VIII at Lyon in 1496, lived long enough to dedicate poems to Marguerite de Navarre and Queen Eleanor. He also organised public festivals, such as Francis I's entry into Poitiers in 1520.[8] However, if the *rhétoriqueurs* remained influential for a time, classical authors who had been neglected in the past now came into their own. Virgil and Ovid were joined by Horace, Martial and Ausonius. A Latinisation of genres got under way: the elegy came to stay, the epistle was renovated, the eclogue enjoyed some success, and the epigram and epitaph replaced older genres. The *chanson* helped to make poetry more flexible and lively. The court's influence in promoting these developments was decisive. Poetry fuelled royal propaganda by celebrating the king's victories and reviling his enemies. Royal births, marriages and deaths released floods of encomiastic verse.[9]

Among the poets who frequented Francis I's court, the most gifted was Clément Marot. His father, Jean, was among the last *rhétoriqueurs*. Having been one of Louis XII's *valets de garde-robe*, he continued to serve Francis until his death in 1526.[10] Clément, in the meantime, served as page in the household of Nicolas de Neufville, seigneur de Villeroy. In 1518 he offered a poem, the *Temple de Cupido,* to the king, who may have recommended him to his sister, Marguerite. Marot became her secretary, and in 1521 accompanied her husband, the duc d'Alençon, on a military campaign, which he described in his *Epistre du Camp d'Atigny*. Marot then disappears from the records. Scholars no longer believe that he was at the Battle of Pavia. What is certain is that he got into trouble with the religious authorities for breaking the Lenten fast. In 1526 he became a royal *valet de chambre*. As court poet, he celebrated the marriage of Princess Renée in 1528, the Peace of Cambrai in 1529 and the return of the king's sons from captivity and the arrival of Queen Eleanor in 1530. In 1531 he caught the plague but was cured by the king's physicians. He was also robbed and given 100 gold *écus* by Francis.[11]

It was only after 1526 that Marot's poetry began to show signs of originality. Rejecting the genres of the *rhétoriqueurs*, he showed a new sensitivity towards classical sources of inspiration. His gift for satire, which appeared in his poem *L'Enfer*, is also present in his epigrams. Though not an entirely accomplished Latin scholar, Marot promoted the classical influence on French poetry. Some of his earliest works involved translations from Virgil; later he turned to Ovid and above all to the Psalms. However, it was in the *épître* that he really found his form. This genre, by eliminating allegorical elements and reducing the number of metrical fireworks, helped to bring poetry closer to everyday life. Most of Marot's epistles are concerned with his personal circumstances and needs; his success ultimately depended on a more natural use of language, free from the monotonous tone and static rhythms of the *rhétoriqueurs*. His poetry, it has been said, 'gives an impression of intelligence and alertness, but rarely of depth', yet it can betray strong feelings, particularly in religious matters.

In October 1534 Marot's life was changed as a result of the Affair of the Placards.[12] Although he had taken no part in it, his evangelical views made

42. *Clément Marot.* Painting by Corneille de Lyon (Musée du Louvre, Paris). As Francis I's court poet, Marot (1496–1544) celebrated some of the court's main events in verse, but his evangelical sympathies aroused the Sorbonne's anger. Twice imprisoned, he was released at the instance of Marguerite, the king's sister, whom he had once served. Eventually forced into exile, he died in Turin. His translation of the psalms into French became immensely popular.

him suspect to the authorities. Fearing arrest, he fled to the court of Marguerite de Navarre at Nérac, then to Ferrara and finally to Venice, where he composed verses for the king and dauphin in the hope of being recalled to France. By December 1536 he was back in France and soon resumed his duties at court, but he only regained his place on the roll of household servants after bombarding Francis with epigrams. Meanwhile, he continued to serve as Marguerite's secretary. In 1538 Marot composed a *cantique* celebrating the meeting of Francis I and Charles V at Aigues-Mortes, and in the following year he was asked by the king to present a copy of his *Trente*

Psaumes de David to the emperor. In 1542 he fled to Geneva after this work had been banned by the Paris Faculty of Theology. He never returned to France and died in Turin, probably in September 1544.[13]

A court poet did not need genius to be accepted. What really mattered was his capacity to flatter the monarch and titillate the ears of his entourage. Mellin de Saint-Gelais fulfilled both requirements. He was also well connected. His family had long been associated with the House of Angoulême. After studying at Poitiers, Bologna and Padua, Saint-Gelais joined Francis I's court, where his wit and good manners soon won him admirers. He lost no opportunity to praise the king and his mistresses in verse, and entertained the courtiers with erotic ditties. Incongruous as it may seem, he was also a cleric. He was almoner to the Dauphin François, then to his younger brother, Henri. In 1536 he was appointed keeper of the royal library at Blois. In addition to the income from his office and benefices, Saint-Gelais received occasional gifts of money from the king. Much of his poetry is lost, which may be for the best. In the words of one modern commentator: 'One is tempted to think that to-day he would be lucky to obtain employment as a writer of mottoes for Christmas crackers.'[14]

Francis I himself was a poet, though his verse is a subject of great complexity.[15] Many poems attributed to him in the past are now known to have been written by others. Altogether 205 poems, including *rondeaux*, *ballades*, *épîtres*, *épitaphes* and many shorter poems, are probably by him. None survives in his own hand or is dated, but most seem to belong to the period before 1535. No collection of Francis's poems was published in his lifetime or for three hundred years thereafter. A number were set to music in his day, mainly by court composers such as Sermisy, Janequin and Sandrin.

Under Henry II Mellin de Saint-Gelais organised court entertainments. His poems, which were mostly in French, were short, pithy and easily set to music. Apart from love, they celebrated prominent persons or events. Late in life, Saint-Gelais specialised in composing challenges for tournaments or poems for use in masques. Courtiers in disguise would target onlookers with his verses. Saint-Gelais was noted for his ingenuity. The dancers in his most famous ballet, the *Mattacins*, wore helmets and carried swords and shields. They sent birds to ladies of their choice, each with a quatrain attached to one of its legs. Saint-Gelais also translated for the court's benefit Trissino's *Sophonisbe*, which was performed at Blois in 1556. It was the second tragedy given at court after Jodelle's *Cléopatre captive*. Very few of Saint-Gelais's poems were published in his lifetime, but they circulated widely as manuscript collections, earning for their author Sébillet's accolade of 'Autheur tant dous que divin' ('author as sweet as he is divine').[16]

43. *Mellin de Saint-Gelais.* Drawing by François Clouet (Musée Condé, Chantilly). A linguist and accomplished musician, Saint-Gelais (*c.* 1490–1558) was primarily a court poet. He also served Francis I and Henry II as librarian and chaplain, but specialised in reading aloud or singing his own compositions which were for the most part frivolous, witty, satirical or amorous.

Though not published till 1574, Jodelle's *Cléopatre captive* was performed in 1553 in the presence of Henry II at the Hôtel de Reims, the Parisian residence of Charles de Guise, cardinal of Lorraine. The performance was held to celebrate the successful defence of Metz against Emperor Charles V by the cardinal's brother, François duc de Guise; but the hero of the hour was the king, who was portrayed in the play as Octavian. The prologue placed him in a mythological setting and acclaimed him as the mightiest of monarchs, the ruler of earth, sea and sky, and the man who had returned the Muses to France. More god than king, his place in the heavens was already assured.[17]

Delighted by the play, Henry gave Jodelle 500 *écus*. In 1556 Jodelle published an *épître* dedicated to the king's sister, Marguerite de France, but his future was far from assured. In 1558 he was commissioned by the Parisian authorities to prepare a reception for the king and duc de Guise to celebrate the reconquest of Calais, but the result was an unmitigated disaster: it ended with the town hall being sacked by inebriated revellers.[18]

The literary significance of the reign of Henry II resides mainly in the emergence of a group of seven poets led by Pierre de Ronsard, known collectively as the Pléiade. Their connection with the court was at first tenuous. The group originated in a series of encounters stretching back to 1543 when Ronsard met his fellow poet Jacques Peletier at the funeral of Guillaume du Bellay. The poets had no formal connexion with the court: they met in Paris at the Hôtel de Baïf, a house built by Lazare de Baïf, Francis I's ambassador in Venice. All the same, the group may be seen as the precursor of the academies officially constituted under Charles IX and Henry III. The Pléiade looked to the ancient world, both Greek and Roman, and also to new models for inspiration. They aimed to equal or surpass the Italian poets; they wrote love poems, epic poems and pastoral poems in imitation of Petrarch, Ariosto and Sannazaro. At the same time, they sought to promote and improve the use of the French language, their programme being enunciated in Joachim du Bellay's *Défense et illustration de la langue française* (1549–50).

The leader of the Pléiade was Pierre de Ronsard, who was widely acclaimed, even in his own day, as France's answer to Homer and Virgil. He liked to boast of his aristocratic origins and could claim that his father and grandfather had held offices at court. As a child, he had dreamt of a military career but, as a younger son, this was denied to him. He became a page in the household of the Dauphin François, only to lose his master in 1536. He switched to Francis I's third son, Charles, but was sent away from court: once to Scotland in 1537 with Madeleine de France, and in 1540 to Germany with Lazare de Baïf. After taking minor orders in 1543, he attended the Collège de Coqueret in Paris, where he studied under Jean Dorat along with other budding poets. Knowing that advancement depended on securing royal patronage, Ronsard added his voice to the eulogies of Henry II addressed by artists and poets. He revealed his vision of the ideal king and ideal court in his *Hymne à Henri II de ce nom* (1555), the climax of which is a comparison between the court of France and Olympus. Ronsard as Apollo sings the praises of Henry's triumphant majesty. He extols the qualities expected of a prince, which Henry has in abundance. A wonderfully vivid picture of physical strength emerges as Ronsard relates the king's athletic powers: his superiority as a swordsman and rider. His majesty is made to correspond with the abundant energies of his people and the riches of his dominions. The *Hymne* is only part of a considerable poetic output that began in 1550 with the publication of four books of odes. Even so, Ronsard found it hard to live on the income from a few minor benefices. In 1559 he was appointed as councillor and king's almoner, probably at the suggestion of Charles, cardinal of Lorraine. Soon afterwards he acquired an archdeaconry and canonry, but he still felt ill-rewarded for his labours. In his elegy to Jérôme l'Huillier (1560) he wrote:

> *Et si, de mes labeurs qui honorent la France*
> *Je ne remporte rien qu'un rien pour récompense.*

> *(And yet from my works that honour France*
> *I gain only nothing as my reward.)*

Musicians

Music was omnipresent at the French Renaissance court. No coronation or royal funeral, no princely baptism or wedding, no *Te Deum* or religious procession, royal entry or interview was complete without the accompaniment of voices or instruments or a combination of both.[19] Music also accompanied the king's meals, a trumpeter announcing the arrival of each dish, as well as the dances that became so popular at court. Composers wrote works to celebrate a person or event. Music accompanied religious services, festivities, banquets and solemn processions, and served to entertain courtiers in their more private moments. There were three sets of court musicians: the Chapel, made up of choristers; the *Écurie* (stables), made up of instrumentalists; and the Chamber, comprising musicians of both kinds.

Charles VIII and Louis XII took their chapels with them when they invaded Italy, while Anne of Brittany had her own chapel whose musicians were soon to become famous: Antonius Divitis, Jean Mouton, the organist Pierre Mouton and Claudin de Sermisy. Anne's domestic servants in 1493 included a drummer, three Breton minstrels, two choristers, a lutenist and a rebec player; but her favourite musician was the organist Jacques de Loriguière, whom she elevated to the rank of *valet de chambre*. Louis XII was no singer, it seems. Glareanus's *Dodecachordon* contains a song with a part labelled 'vox regis'; it consists of only one note repeated throughout. Yet Louis liked music. In 1507 he wrote from Asti to Guillaume de Montmorency asking him to send a song by Antoine de Févin that he wanted to show to Italian ladies. Writing from Savona, he asked the Florentine authorities to release from prison a clergyman noted for his musical knowledge. Choristers from northern France and the Low Countries were much in demand; they moved from court to court and are not easily traced in the records. No document links the great Josquin des Prés with Louis XII, but he probably met the king and may have stayed at his court.

Francis I's interest in music may not have matched his love of the visual arts. The dedication of a musical work of 1555 pays tribute to his generous support of the liberal arts, including music. Legend has it that Francis, after signing a treaty with Suleyman the Magnificent, sent him a gift of musicians. After listening to them, the Ottoman sultan decided that such entertainment undermined his warlike spirit. He thanked the musicians and paid them, but destroyed their instruments and sent them away, forbidding them to remain in his empire on pain of death. This story, however, cannot be traced back further than 1645.[20] According to one nineteenth-century historian, Francis composed the words and music of a song during his Spanish captivity, but the text is not now considered to be among his authentic poems.[21] A tapestry of 1537, which shows him playing an organ under the sign of Mercury, may be just an allegory. The claim that Francis could play the lute is also unfounded, but he did sing. The English ambassador Thomas Cheyney reported on 3 July 1546 that he had seen the king, dauphin and ladies of the court pass under his window in a boat singing 'as sweetly as ever I heard'.[22]

Francis I's accounts rarely mention the buying of musical instruments. Apart from two spinets bought in 1529 and 1538, his purchases seem to have served mainly as decorative objects. In 1533 the king paid a large sum for an ivory hunting horn with silver ornaments.[23] In October 1515 a chorister in the chapel of the duke of Ferrara wrote from Vigevano: 'He [Francis] . . . does not like music as much as the late king.'[24] Yet his domestic staff in 1514 included eight musicians: an organist, four choristers, a fife player, a drummer and a rebec player. Following his accession, musical life at the court continued as before. According to Florange, the royal and papal chapels jointly produced a beautiful sound when they met in Bologna in December 1515.[25] At the Field of Cloth of Gold, the English and French royal chapels sang alternate sections of the mass. Each choir was accompanied by its own organist, the French by Pierre Mouton, a canon of Notre-Dame. In the *Credo* the French enhanced the overall effect by using sackbuts and fifes.[26] Francis occasionally exported some of his musicians as a friendly gesture. In March 1519 six choristers and wind players, dressed all in white, sang and played in the basilica of San Marco in Venice.[27]

Several members of Francis I's court liked music. Queen Claude counted two musicians among her servants, while Queen Eleanor had been taught as a child by Henri Bredemers, an organist at the court of her father, Philip the Fair. Laurent Vital wrote in 1506: 'It is a pleasure to see and hear her either playing several instruments such as the lute or manichordium, singing with others or dancing.' As queen of France, she had her own chapel, including at

least four choristers. The king's sister, Marguerite, liked musical settings of
the psalms. Charles d'Orléans, his youngest son, employed choristers and
instrumentalists. Francis's two mistresses had music dedicated to them. Little
is known about Henry II's musical tastes. He is said to have liked singing the
psalms in Marot's translation and even to have composed music for one of
them. As for Diane de Poitiers, she allegedly built two pavilions at Anet in

44. *The Concert.* Painting by the Master of the Half figures. This bears witness to the
musical accomplishments among young ladies at European courts, *c.* 1530 (State
Hermitage Museum, St Petersburg).

which to house musicians for the entertainment of the king and his courtiers. She is said to have played the lute and never to have travelled without her spinet.[28]

The royal chapel became known as the Chapelle de musique during the reign of Francis I. It consisted of choristers under the direction of a master and submaster. The mastership, an honorific post commanding a large salary, was held for many years by Cardinal François de Tournon. The effective head of the chapel was the submaster, a post occupied under Charles VIII by Johannes Ockeghem, under Louis XII by Johannes Prioris, and under Francis I first by Antoine de Longueval, then, after 1525, by Claude de Sermisy known as Claudin. In 1547 there were two submasters and, under Henry II, three. The submaster directed the chapel's music-making, and was responsible for the general welfare of the choristers, and also probably for training the choirboys.

In 1515 Francis I added the chapel of the late queen, Anne of Brittany, to his own, bringing its complement to twenty-nine choristers, an organist and a *noteur* or music copyist. This was larger than the chapels of Henry VIII of England and the Emperor Charles V. By 1533, however, Francis's chapel consisted of only twenty-five choristers, including the submaster. The choristers were all churchmen, many holding benefices that provided them with an income to supplement their normal wages of around 300 *l.* per annum. These were meant to pay for clothing, food and the upkeep of a horse. A few choristers with a long service record were paid more. Conrad Remiger, for example, who served Louis XII, Francis I and Henry II, received 400 *l.* He was a Bavarian, but the majority of choristers hailed from the north of France, which was renowned internationally for its fine singers. Despite the rise in wages, the annual cost of Francis I's chapel increased only from 8,320 *l.* in 1518 to 9,580 *l.* in the 1530s.

Within a few years of joining the chapel, choristers were given offices in the king's household, becoming almoners or chaplains, honorary titles that carried no duties. Under Louis XII, some went of their own volition to Rome to serve in the papal chapel, but under Francis they preferred to stay put. The king successfully retained the services of the best musicians left by his predecessors, such as Jean Mouton, Antonius Divitis and Claudin. Choirboys were much in demand for they alone could hit the high notes. While some were taken from the Sainte-Chapelle in Paris, others were kidnapped from cathedrals elsewhere in France. Two, for example, were snatched at night from Beauvais. The fate of such choirboys was considered enviable, since their upkeep was paid for by the king. They were dressed like pages with black breeches, a doublet and a felt hat trimmed with black velvet. When a choirboy's voice broke, the king paid for his education before re-employing him later as a mature chorister. It was a far better life than serving in one of the choirschools (*maîtrises*) attached to cathedrals and collegiate churches.[29]

A distinguished composer who served Francis I before 1522 was Jean Mouton, a disciple of Josquin. After serving in churches at Nesle, Amiens and Grenoble, he entered the service of Anne of Brittany. By 1518 he had joined Francis I's court, where he was already held in high esteem. Glareanus, who met him there, said that his music was 'in the hands of everyone'. Among several motets composed by him were *Domine salvum fac Regem* for Francis's coronation and *Exalta Regina Galliae! Jubila mater Ambasie!*, a celebration of the king's victory at Marignano and also of the birth of his first child. Mouton's style is distinguished by a 'serene, smoothly flowing polyphony, with great technical finish and superb contrapuntal command'.[30] In addition to about one hundred motets, he wrote approximately fifteen masses and twenty *chansons*. The masses span the transition from *cantus firmus* to paraphrase and parody. Like the motets, the *chansons* are in various styles: some are canonic, others are three part popular arrangements, and others still are witty, imitative pieces, influenced by popular tunes. Mouton died in 1522.

In about 1530 Francis created a new chapel, called the Chapelle de plain-chant. More modest than the Chapelle de musique, it consisted of only twelve choristers in 1533–5. These ranked as 'chaplains' and were paid less than other choristers. They were also more closely tied to the court. Whereas the choristers of the Chapelle de musique often absented themselves for several weeks at a time, those of the Chapelle de plain-chant were expected to follow the king everywhere and to celebrate mass each day wherever he happened to be.[31] Little is known about liturgy at the court of Francis I. If the poet Chappuys is to be believed, polyphonic music was performed daily, but this seems more likely to have been limited to feast days or other important occasions when members of the Chapelle de musique would have been called upon to attend. An organ would have provided additional embellishment. Musicians of the royal chapel have left us many compositions destined to replace Gregorian chants. The thirteen books of motets published by Pierre Attaingnant in 1534–5 contain some fifty pieces destined to replace in part the monody of the traditional liturgy. Following the death of Jean Mouton in 1522, the most prolific composer at Francis's court was Claude de Sermisy, to whom we owe more than seventy motets and some fifteen masses.

The musicians attached to the *écurie*, or royal stables, were all instrumentalists whose role was essentially to perform on state occasions, such as solemn entries, banquets, balls, religious processions and funerals. They wore a livery in the king's colours and were never more than humble servants. Less well paid and esteemed than the choristers of the chapel, they were expected to follow the court on foot, though the king did sometimes give them money to buy and keep a horse. A writer commented in 1533: 'If some of them now travel on foot, a time will come when they shall be raised above the clouds and placed with the consort of angels, in whose glory they participate.'[32] At the start of the sixteenth century the musicians of the *écurie* fell into three groups: trumpets; fifes and drums; sackbuts and hautbois. Between ten and twelve trumpeters formed a fanfare, but sometimes played singly or in pairs, as, for example, when an edict was proclaimed *à son de trompe*. The fifes and drums invariably played together. Sackbuts and hautbois, which were introduced under Charles VIII, commonly accompanied banquets and balls. In 1529 Francis sent them to Cambrai to liven up a banquet offered by his mother on the occasion of the Peace of the Ladies.[33] Violins, which were added to the *écurie* around 1529, were used primarily to accompany dances. Various nationalities were represented among the musicians: trumpeters were usually Italian, fifers Swiss and the rest French. Foreigners who settled in France formed musical families, a son often stepping into his father's shoes as court musician. The only promotion open to musicians of the *écurie* was to join the Chamber, but few achieved this distinction.[34]

Under Francis I a third group of court musicians developed in association with the Chamber. They represented a desire on the king's part to make his court a seat of pleasure and to attach to his person some of the leading virtuosi of his day. While relegating fifes and drums to the *écurie,* he developed within his Chamber a group of players of so-called 'noble' instruments, later to be joined by choristers. The new instruments included cornets, viols and violins. The number of cornets was fixed at two, and the six who served Francis in succession were all Italians, mostly from Verona; but the instrument that became most popular at court was the lute. The relatively small number of lutenists were acclaimed much as pop stars are today. Yet there was no post of king's lutenist. Players of the instrument were appointed to non-musical offices in order to provide them with an income commensurate with their talent and the royal favour they enjoyed. In 1524 and 1525 a lutenist called François de Bugats was listed among the *gens de mestier*, alongside the painter Jean Clouet and servants as diverse as shoemakers, tailors and barbers. From 1526, however, lutenists were elevated to the rank of *valet de chambre*, entitling them to mix with the king and his courtiers. This change coincided with the king's decision to draw a distinction between *valets de chambre ordinaires*, who served as such, and *valets de chambre extraordinaires*, who simply had the title and wages.

The first of Francis's lutenists to be appointed *valet de chambre* in 1520 was Jean Paulle (presumably a gallicisation of Giovanni Paolo); but he was eclipsed by Albert de Rippe (Alberto da Ripa), a Mantuan who arrived in 1529. Already mentioned by Aretino in a comedy of about 1526 as one of the most brilliant musicians then performing in Italy, Albert may have been recommended to Francis by Lazare de Baïf, the French ambassador in Venice, who was a friend of Aretino. His wages were roughly twice those that other lutenists had so far been paid. Among many royal gifts Albert received were the captaincy of Montils-sous-Blois and an estate in Dombes.[35] His death in 1555 brought tributes from Ronsard and other poets. Francis I evidently liked lute music. In 1538 he was captivated by the playing of Francesco Canova da Milano, called *Il divino*, whom Pope Paul III had brought to Nice.[36] About 1535 Francis created a small vocal ensemble to sing *chansons* to which he added some instruments such as flutes, hautbois and organs.

The first half of the sixteenth century witnessed important developments in French music. While some composers developed techniques first explored by Josquin and his contemporaries, others transformed the sound of music by means of new techniques and genres. Old compositions were parodied and musicians looked for ways of expressing the meaning as well as the form of words they set. An autonomous instrumental music developed independently of literary associations or the dance. At the same time, the distribution of music was transformed by printing. About 1537 Pierre Attaingnant was appointed 'king's music printer'. He sponsored, if he did not invent, a new method of printing music in which a note and its stave were cut in a single punch instead of two punches, as was the practice in Venice.

The reign of Francis also corresponded closely with the appearance of the *chanson* or polyphonic French song. *Chansons* draw on Italian and Netherlandish elements, spicing them up with grace and wit. Their charm and often broad humour were calculated to delight Francis and his courtiers. The two earliest collections of *chansons* were published by Attaingnant in 1528. Another, published a year later, contained compositions by Claude de Sermisy and Clément Janequin. Sermisy published about 160 *chansons* in addition to his motets and masses, some arranged for lute and keyboard. In his secular works his style is predominantly chordal. Without sacrificing melodic grace, he tends to use rapidly repeated notes that produce a light, declamatory effect, the whole being characterised by a dance-like quality and a simplicity that made it suitable for performance by amateurs.

Clément Janequin did not become a member of the royal chapel until 1555, but as early as 1530 he provided a song of welcome, *Chantons, sonnons trompetes*, for the return of Francis I's sons from captivity. It called on all young girls, bourgeoises and bourgeois to rejoice by singing and dancing, and became, in a sense, the official version of the songs of joy that accompanied Eleanor and the king's sons wherever they passed. Janequin may have been invited by the king to compose a song for his visit to Bordeaux in 1526. This would explain why he called himself 'king's chorister' as early as 1531 although he did not actually join the royal chapel until much later.[37] His most famous chanson, *La guerre*, imitates vividly the confused sounds of battle: the drumbeats, fanfares, rallying cries and patter of horses' hooves. First published in 1528, the work was an immediate success. According to Noël Du Fail, when it was sung before Francis, there was not a man present who did not look to see that there was a sword in his scabbard or who did not stand up on his toes to look taller. The song travelled across Europe, undergoing numerous instrumental adaptations.[38] Janequin's large *chanson* production – 286 survive – was not limited to programme music. He has left many graceful works in a more conventional style, including *Qu'est ce d'amour*, one of several settings of poems ascribed to Francis I.[39]

Music continued to flourish at the court of Henry II. Major composers attached themselves to the royal chapel, including Claude Goudimel, who was brought over from Rome, where he had directed a music school. The Fleming Jacques Arcadelt, a former member of the papal chapel, enjoyed the patronage of the cardinal of Lorraine for whom he wrote madrigals and motets. Clément Janequin, in addition to an edition of psalms (1559), published a collection of *chansons* called *Verger de musique* that were performed for Catherine de' Medici in her chamber. Other pieces by him, such as the *Siège de Metz* or *La Guerre de Renty*, were official pieces with four, five or even seven parts. The households of the king, queen and princes had on their staff a number of musical virtuosi performing on the flute, rebec, lute or spinet, to mention only a few of the many instruments now in use. Violins were increasingly popular. Marshal Brissac, governor of Piedmont, sent to the court a string orchestra which he had formed in Italy.[40]

CHAPTER 13

The Canker of Heresy

France around 1500 was a religiously united kingdom: all of its people were Catholics owing allegiance to the pope in Rome. They accepted the notion of the church as an intercessor between God and man, read the Bible in Latin, if they could read it at all, and attended mass, believing that it was a re-enactment of Christ's sacrifice on the cross. Unlike other countries, France was almost entirely free of organised heresy. England had Lollardy and Bohemia Hussitism; France had only a few Waldensians in the south.[1] Otherwise, as the great Dutch scholar Erasmus declared, it was 'the purest and most prosperous part of Christendom', the only country not infected by heresy.[2] The court of Francis I at the start of the reign reflected that religious unity. The church, closely allied to the state, was all-powerful but, like all human institutions, it sometimes fell short of its sacred mission: prominent among its abuses were pluralism, absenteeism and clerical ignorance. Not all bishops resided in their dioceses, not all parish priests cared for their flocks, not all monks followed the rules of their order. However, an awareness of the need to remedy such ills existed among the higher clergy.[3] The outstanding example of a reforming bishop was Guillaume Briçonnet, bishop of Meaux, a member of a distinguished family of royal servants.[4] He attached a great deal of importance to preaching and invited a number of like-minded men, who came to be known as the Cercle de Meaux, to assist him in his task of bringing the Gospel to the people.[5] They included Jacques Lefèvre d'Étaples, one of the founders of French humanism. A prolific editor of classical and biblical texts, Lefèvre deliberately avoided taking a doctorate in theology in order to protect his intellectual freedom which such a degree would have constrained. He graduated in arts instead and taught at the Collège du Cardinal-Lemoisne in Paris before accepting an invitation from Briçonnet, then abbot of Saint-Germain-des-Prés, to retire there in order to better pursue his studies.[6] The Cercle de Meaux was made up of Briçonnet's disciples and associates including Gérard Roussel, an arts graduate, Pierre Caroli, a brilliant Paris-trained theologian, Martial Mazurier, another theologian, François Vatable, a parish priest with a knowledge of Greek and Hebrew, Michel d'Arande, a former Augustinian hermit, and Guillaume Farel, a native of Dauphiné noted for his fiery temperament.[7] All had at some stage become closely associated with Lefèvre d'Étaples. In addition to helping Briçonnet to reform his diocese, some found time to preach at court, where they seem to have appealed strongly to the ladies, many of whom yearned to reach out to God more directly than through the traditional channels: reading the Bible in French held a strong appeal for them.

The teaching of the church rested on the theological training dispensed by the universities, notably by the Faculty of Theology of the University of Paris, commonly known as the Sorbonne, which saw itself as the guardian of orthodoxy.[8] The crown, however, was under no obligation to follow the faculty's judgment. Theology was seen at the time as the 'queen of the sciences' and controversy regarding its content aroused fierce passions. In early sixteenth-century France the dominant brand of theology was scholasticism, which followed the teaching of the thirteeth-century doctor St Thomas Aquinas and, beyond him, the metaphysical writings of Aristotle. In its more extreme form, known as Nominalism, it seemed to focus attention mainly on obscure, not to say trivial, questions of exegesis, so much so that theology itself, as taught in Paris, began to acquire a bad name.[9] Erasmus's brief experience of it put him off for life.

In the fifteenth century scholasticism had to face the challenge of humanism – basically a revival of classical languages, mainly Greek and Hebrew, coupled with a return to the original texts of Scripture, liberated from the glosses of medieval theologians, and the works of Plato and other Greek philosophers. In northern Europe humanism assumed a strongly theological dimension as it claimed a superior ability to achieve a true understanding of Scripture. At the same time it sought to communicate its findings to Christians in general by translating Scripture into the vernacular, thereby outflanking the church's traditional teaching. Such humanists became known as Christian or evangelical humanists. Many were powerfully influenced by the writings of St Paul. Their principal exponent was Erasmus; another was Lefèvre, who combined his humanism with a strong dose of late medieval mysticism. In 1519 the ideological situation became even more confused when the German monk Martin Luther publicised his famous Ninety-Five Theses at Wittemberg. His writings very soon reached Paris and aroused considerable interest and not a little sympathy among evangelical humanists. Lefèvre, for one, had anticipated some of Luther's ideas, notably that of salvation by faith alone rather than, as the church taught, by faith and good works. Luther's ideas were all the more acceptable in that he was not too radical: he still believed, for example, in the Real Presence of Christ in the eucharist, although he rejected the mass as a sacrifice. For him the mass was rather a memorial service, a view more materially expressed by John Calvin later in the Protestant Reformation; Calvin rejected even the Real Presence.

The Sorbonne viewed these developments with deep concern. It was often called upon to adjudicate in matters of belief and was intensely suspicious of any departure from the Latin Vulgate. Translations of Scripture into the vernacular were highly dangerous in its eyes, as they enabled laymen to interpret the Bible for themselves. It denounced Luther's doctrine as heretical in 1521 and, in alliance with the Parlement of Paris, tried to get all of his writings burned. The faculty's syndic, Noël Béda, could see no difference between Lutheranism and Christian humanism. As far as he was concerned, Luther, Erasmus and Lefèvre were equally detestable and needed to be silenced.

Where, we might ask, did the French court fit into this period, so aptly described by the historian Lucien Febvre as one of 'glorious religious anarchy'?[10] The court could not dissociate itself from the prevailing religious climate, for Francis I, as the 'Most Christian King', a role that he valued greatly, had the duty of protecting the church from its enemies and extirpating heresy from his kingdom. He had sworn to do these things at his coronation. His task, however, was not facilitated by the presence in his immediate entourage of churchmen holding divergent theological views: some were strict Catholics and others evangelical humanists. Guillaume Petit, the king's confessor, was a mixture: well disposed towards Erasmus, he detested Luther. Jean du Bellay, bishop of Paris, was widely seen as a Catholic liberal. The king himself, unlike his English 'cousin' Henry VIII, never showed the slightest interest in theology. He was, however, as far as we can judge, a devout Catholic who believed that the mass was a sacrifice. He also accepted the intercession of saints. Each day, whatever the circumstances, he attended mass; he also went on numerous pilgrimages; but without a solid grounding in theology he could not hope to define heresy without expert assistance, particularly in its early stages when it seemed little more than an evangelical approach to worship. He was under no obligation to accept the Sorbonne's extreme view of the matter. Francis's problem was exacerbated by the deep religious faith of his sister, Marguerite, whom he loved dearly. She was a personal friend of some of the main actors in the evangelical movement. On 10 June 1521 she wrote to Bishop Briçonnet to ask for his spiritual guidance. He agreed to help her, and Marguerite, for her part, promised to use her influence at court to advance his cause. Thus began an exchange of 123 letters – fifty-nine from Marguerite, sixty-four from the bishop – spanning the years 1521–3.[11] The relationship was not purely epistolary. In the autumn of 1521 Marguerite and her mother, Louise of Savoy, spent a fortnight with the

45. *Marguerite d'Angoulême, duchesse d'Alençon, then queen of Navarre.* Painting by Jean Clouet (Musée Condé, Chantilly). The sister of King Francis I, Marguerite (1492–1549) wrote fiction and religious poems. She sympathized with the evangelical cause without ever breaking with Rome. Much loved by her brother, she was an influential figure at his court.

bishop at Meaux. Marguerite subsequently referred to the spiritual food she had consumed at his table. She assured him that the king and her mother were strongly committed to his cause of church reform.

One lesson to be learnt from Marguerite's correspondence is the attention given by ladies of the court to preachers who visited their apartments. The ladies were often better educated than their menfolk and doubtless spent more time listening to sermons while the men were out hunting or serving in the king's army. They also came under the influence of their children's tutors, who might harbour unorthodox opinions. One of the preachers who became popular at court was Michel d'Arande, an ex-friar and a member of the Cercle de Meaux. 'I am sending you Maître Michel,' Marguerite wrote to Briçonnet in 1521, 'who, I assure you, has not wasted his time at court.' The friar, it seems, was in the habit of preaching at court, where he doubtless felt freer to speak his mind out of the Sorbonne's earshot. His activities, however, came to the notice of Guillaume Petit, the king's confessor, who lost no time in complaining to the faculty. The friar, he said, had infiltrated the ladies' apartments disguised as a secular priest; he was making fun of the Sorbonne's doctors and praising Luther. He had called him a 'holy man' while admitting that the German reformer had made errors, but no more so than Saint Augustine or Saint Bernard.[12] Alerted to the matter, Francis demanded an explanation from his mother and sister. We do not know how they replied, but apparently they succeeded in persuading the king of d'Arande's blamelessness, for Petit was reprimanded by Francis, not the preacher.[13]

In May 1521 the Sorbonne called on the Parlement to attend to the faith 'of which the Most Christian King ought to be and is the guardian and protector'.[14] Soon afterwards the faculty and Parlement imposed restrictions on the book trade in Paris; it became an offence to print or sell any religious book without the Sorbonne's imprimatur.[15] On 3 August all Parisians owning Lutheran works were ordered to hand them over or else face a fine or imprisonment.[16] Fearing an adverse impact from this legislation on his work at Meaux, Briçonnet wrote to Marguerite in November asking for her support. 'When you see an opportunity,' he wrote, 'advance God's cause so that He may be better served and honoured than He is in this kingdom wherein the king is His lieutenant-general.'[17] Marguerite reassured him. 'The best course,' she wrote, 'seems to me to silence the ignoramuses, assuring you that the king and Madame [Louise of Savoy] are determined to let it be known that the truth of God is not heresy.'[18] But Marguerite failed to comfort the bishop. In March 1522 he grew despondent: the court seemed not to care about church reform. Francis I had more pressing concerns: England had just allied with the emperor against him. In April and May Briçonnet's correspondence with Marguerite became sporadic and, after 18 May, it ceased for some months.[19] Meanwhile, the Sorbonne and Parlement took stronger measures against heresy: instead of merely censoring books, they began to target people. Among the first to feel their wrath was Louis de Berquin, a young nobleman with evangelical, even Lutheran, leanings. His home was searched and a number of suspicious books found. The Sorbonne ordered their examination and simultaneously launched an attack on Lefèvre d'Étaples. It began to examine his latest publication, a commentary on the Gospels. The chancellor, however, intervened: any errors imputed to Lefèvre, he ordered, should be referred to an episcopal commission under his own chairmanship. The Sorbonne, however, refused to give up its right to judge doctrine, and on 13 July the sale of Lefèvre's book was banned by the Parlement pending the faculty's verdict. At this critical juncture Francis raised the matter with the *Grand Conseil*. On 11 August he tested the Sorbonne by asking if it would allow the Bible to be translated into French for the benefit of a wider readership. The faculty said 'no' and sent a delegation to Francis in order to point out the error of his ways. When Louise of Savoy, acting in his absence, asked the Sorbonne how best to check the progress of Lutheranism, it replied that the crown should stop interfering and order all Lutheran books to be burned. It blamed the court for the growth of heresy, accusing its members of praising Luther and speaking ill of those who were fighting heresy. The faculty complained that the king's authority was being used to obstruct Berquin's prosecution.

Letters exchanged by Briçonnet and Marguerite between January and April 1524 show the bishop still to be on good terms with the court. Marguerite asked him to visit the royal children and also Queen Claude, who was ill. She and her mother, Marguerite added, were looking forward to meeting the bishop at Blois. She asked him for spiritual solace following the death of her aunt, the duchesse de Nemours. Briçonnet, for his part, praised the royal family's unity and Christian faith. He rejoiced over the king's participation in a religious procession on 11 March, and offered him an illuminated edition of Lefèvre's French translation of the Pauline epistles. Francis was repeatedly urged by the bishop to promote church reform by appointing worthy bishops.[20]

Following the king's defeat and captivity in 1525, the government passed into the hands of his mother, Louise of Savoy, who has been described as 'the most consistently traditional member of the royal family, the most uneasy about the spread of Lutheranism in France'.[21] She set up her court in Lyon, leaving the Sorbonne and Parlement freer to combat heresy.[22] A more repressive régime was popular with the Parisians, who were alarmed by reports of Lutheran activities along France's eastern border. Their fears focused on the court, which was seen by many as a safe haven for heretics. The king's sister was singled out for opprobrium. During a masquerade in the cloister of Notre-Dame a woman, instantly identifiable as Marguerite, appeared on a horse drawn by devils wearing placards bearing Luther's name.[23]

The Parlement was intent on silencing the Cercle de Meaux. Its members, including Briçonnet, were summoned to Paris for questioning, and Louise was asked to hand over Michel d'Arande.[24] On 12 November Francis I wrote to the Parlement from his Spanish prison, ordering all legal proceedings against Lefèvre, Pierre Caroli and Gérard Roussel to be dropped pending his return. He had obviously been informed of the situation in Paris by his sister when she visited him in Madrid. The Parlement, however, ignored his request.[25] The Cercle de Meaux was accordingly forced to break up. Lefèvre and Roussel fled to Strassburg, soon to be joined by d'Arande. Caroli sought Marguerite's protection at Alençon. As for Berquin, he was tried as a relapsed heretic, but he was still to be sentenced when the king returned to France. On 1 April 1526 Francis demanded that Berquin be either released or allowed greater freedom within his prison. Soon afterwards Berquin fell ill and Francis demanded that he should be moved to the Louvre. The Parlement refused on grounds of security, but Jean de La Barre, *bailli* of Paris, was allowed to visit him. La Barre then removed Berquin by force and took him to the Louvre.[26] In the meantime, members of the Cercle de Meaux who had fled abroad came home. Lefèvre was given charge of the royal library at Blois and appointed tutor to the king's youngest son; Roussel became Marguerite's almoner; Caroli resumed preaching in Paris.

The Sorbonne, however, was not beaten yet. On 16 May it condemned Erasmus's *Colloquies*, and soon afterwards Noël Béda published a book accusing Erasmus and Lefèvre of heresy. Erasmus complained to Francis; he described the university's theologians as 'thieves more interested in power than in defending the faith'. They would stop at nothing, he said, and might even depose the king after charging him with heresy. Francis responded by banning Béda's book, whereupon the syndic retorted that the king had been poorly advised and would act differently if only he understood the situation better.

Francis was torn between his role as defender of the Catholic faith and his willingness to listen to the evangelicals at his court. In December 1527 he promised to act as the 'Most Christian King' after an assembly of the French clergy had called on him to extirpate 'the damned and insufferable Lutheran sect'. An opportunity presented itself in June 1528, when a statue of the Virgin and Child was mutilated in Paris. It stood in a niche on a street corner in what is now the Marais district. The sacrilege revealed the existence of a more radical and iconoclastic element among French reformers. Whereas Luther opposed the destruction of religious images, iconoclasm was advocated by members of the so-called Radical Reformation, mainly to be found in Switzerland. A reward of 100 gold *écus* was offered by the king for any information leading to the arrest of those responsible for the sacrilege. House-to-house searches were carried out and expiatory processions held in Paris involving the court, clergy, students and urban magistrates. On 11 June, the feast of Corpus Christi, Francis went on foot from the Tournelles to the site of the crime. Walking bareheaded, he carried a lighted candle. With him

res scilicet maxima laude
digna : quæ paucis annis
transactis Parisij a te Christianissimo
rege Francisco celebrata est / nam cum
in vrbem hanc Lutherani quidam

46. Francis I making reparation for the mutilation of a statue of the Virgin and Child in Paris, 1528. Miniature (Musée Condé, Chantilly). In 1528 persons unknown vandalised the statue which stood in a niche at a street corner in the capital. The event signified a shift towards a more radical form of Protestant dissent. Francis expressed his revulsion by commissioning a new statue in silver and replacing it in the niche himself with his court in attendance.

were the cardinal of Lorraine, courtiers, each with a lighted candle, archers and musicians. Next day more processions converged on Notre-Dame from parish churches throughout the city. The congregation, led by the king, then went in procession to the site of the sacrilege. The bishop of Lisieux carried a new statue of the Virgin and Child in silver which the king had commissioned. This Francis placed reverently in the niche, while the damaged statue was taken to the church of Saint-Gervais.[27]

In spite of this public demonstration, doubts remained concerning Francis I's orthodoxy. Cardinal Duprat urged him in 1528 to reassure sceptics who had criticised the monarch at the recent synod of Sens. The king must have satisfied them, for soon afterwards the synod issued a declaration to the effect that 'felicity and glory have only belonged to princes who, while attaching themselves unshakeably to the Catholic faith, have hunted down and exterminated heretics as the principal enemies of their crown'.[28] Protestants were worried. On 10 May 1529 Guillaume Farel, a former member of the Cercle de Meaux, now in exile abroad, expressed disappointment with Francis in a letter to a friend: 'I cannot see what progress can be made among the French under so insane a sovereign who has allowed the New Testament to be forbidden to the people, so that there remains no way of making known the truth.'[29] Writing to Zwingli on 4 May 1530, another reformer, Oecolampadius, was equally scathing. 'It is getting too late,' he said,

> for France to turn to Christ, for persons who arrived here at Easter brought news that the bishops and theologians are extremely hostile to those who profess Christ and that the king is not merely silent about this, but actually threatens the most learned Gérard Roussel and Jacques Lefèvre and others with burning unless they dissuade his sister from the beliefs that they have induced her to embrace.[30]

Oecolampadius, however, had been misinformed: Lefèvre, at least, was safe. In May 1529 Marguerite asked Montmorency to allow him to leave Blois because the climate did not suit him. Permission was readily granted and Lefèvre moved to Nérac where he spent his last years under Marguerite's protection.[31]

During Lent in 1531 Roussel was accused by the Sorbonne of preaching heresy at the Louvre in Marguerite's presence. The charge was taken seriously by the king, who asked the preacher to give advance notice in future of what he intended to say. This placated the faculty for a time, but in 1533 Roussel was again accused of preaching heresy at court. The Sorbonne drew up a list of his errors, but foolishly also accused the king's brother-in-law, Henri d'Albret, of heresy. Furious, Francis ordered Béda's banishment from Paris.[32]

This provoked riots among students of the university. In October those of the Collège de Navarre put on a play in which Marguerite de Navarre was shown preaching heresy at the prompting of a fury called *Mégère* and tormenting anyone who would not listen. The college was raided by the *prévôt de Paris*, and two of its senior members were detained. Later that month Marguerite came under fire again. This time, her anonymously published poem *Le Miroir de l'âme pécheresse* ('Mirror of a Sinful Soul') was blacklisted by the university. The king demanded an explanation, whereupon the rector, Nicolas Cop, called a meeting of all the faculties. A theologian admitted blacklisting the poem, but denied that he had intended any offence to the king's sister. Her poem, he explained, had been banned only because it had not carried the university's imprimatur. Cop moved that it should be removed from the list of banned works and an apology sent to the king.[33]

By the 1530s French Protestants were no longer content simply with spreading the Word; they openly attacked the mass, denouncing it as blasphemy. On Sunday, 18 October 1534 Parisians were dismayed to find that printed posters or placards violently denouncing the mass and Catholic clergy had been put up overnight in a number of public places. The author of the posters, all of which carried the same 'sacramentarian' message in Gothic type, was Antoine Marcourt, a Frenchman exiled in Switzerland. Copies of the placard had been smuggled into France by Guillaume Feret, a servant of the king's apothecary. Their discovery caused panic in Paris where the rumour spread that 'Lutherans' were planning to sack the Louvre and massacre Catholic worshippers. Fears were heightened by reports of identical posters having turned up in other towns. One, it was said, had even been found on the door of the king's bedchamber.[34]

Contemporary accounts of the king's reaction to the Affair of the Placards vary widely. The Protestant martyrologist Jean Crespin states that a placard was found at the Louvre, Théodore de Bèze gives the location as Blois; both mention the bedchamber door, but Simon Fontaine states that the placard was found in the *tasse* in which the king kept his handkerchief. Florimond De Raemond says that Feret threw Protestant articles of faith into the king's closet (*cabinet*) and planted 'small bills in the salt [*nef*] from which he is served at table'. Nearly everyone mentions the king's anger. According to Crespin, he 'vomited rage through his eyes and mouth', and de Bèze states that the king decided there and then 'to exterminate everyone'. Fontaine states that he 'entered into an incredible zeal' after the placard had been read to him. The only established fact is that among the people burnt in 1535 for their part in the affair there was a chorister of the royal chapel who had allegedly introduced placards into the château of Amboise while the king was in residence there.[35]

The affair prompted a savage persecution campaign in Paris. The initiative may not have come from the king, who seems to have taken the whole thing very calmly. He did not return immediately to Paris from Amboise and no orders from him ordering the persecution have been found. It is likely to have come from the authorities on the spot, particularly the Parlement or the chancellor. Within twenty-four hours a general procession was ordered as well as a search for culprits. The prisons began to fill up and, on 13 November, a shoemaker's son was burnt at the stake, the first of a series of martyrs. Francis, meanwhile, left Amboise. On 9 December he wrote to Chancellor Duprat from Bonneval, giving his approval of the police measures so far taken. On the 16th he received a list of suspects from Duprat and five days later appointed a commission to try them.

On 13 January, soon after the court's return to the capital, there was a second affair: copies of Marcourt's *Petit Traité*, an elaboration of the doctrine of the placards, were found in the streets. Francis banned all printing until further notice and ordered a procession for 21 January 1535. This turned out to be a demonstration of Catholic solidarity on a gigantic scale, bringing together court, Parlement, university, parish clergy, religious orders, municipal authorities and guilds. Countless relics were brought out of the church treasuries, including the Crown of Thorns normally kept at the Sainte-Chapelle. At the heart of the procession was the Blessed Sacrament, the principal target of the placards: it was carried by the bishop of Paris under a canopy borne by the king's three sons and by the duc de Vendôme. Immediately behind walked Francis, bareheaded, dressed entirely in black and holding a lighted candle. Church bells, hymn-singing and instrumental music accompanied the huge cortège as it wound its way through crowded streets from Saint-Germain l'Auxerrois to Notre-Dame. Now and then it stopped and the host was placed on a temporary altar erected alongside the route. An anthem was sung and the king prayed, a sight that, according to an observer, drew tears from the crowd. Occasionally someone shouted, 'Justice, Sire!' (*Sire! Faites bonne justice!*), and Francis responded with a sign indicating that he could be trusted to do so. Mass at the cathedral was followed by a banquet at the bishop's palace, after which the king made a speech in which he called on all his subjects to denounce heretics, even if they were relatives or friends. Public burnings rounded off the day, but Francis did not stay to watch them, preferring to leave after the victims had done public penance.

The Affair of the Placards marked a watershed in the history of the French Reformation. The insult to the mass and the clergy was more than Francis or his sister could take. Even so, Marguerite's presence at court had become an embarrassment to her brother. She soon left Paris and spent several months with her husband in south-west France, but she did not abandon her evangelical friends. She offered temporary asylum at Nérac to the poet Clément Marot and even corresponded with Calvin. She reappeared from time to time at court, and attended the summit meetings at Nice in 1538 and at Aigues-Mortes later that year. On 14 June 1541 she was present at her daughter's wedding to the duke of Cleves. After 1542, however, Marguerite was most often in the Midi. Though still hoping that the church would reform itself, she never broke with Rome and even received letters of encouragement from Pope Paul III.

The persecution that followed the Affair of the Placards seriously harmed Francis I's reputation among the German Protestant princes whom he wanted as allies against Charles V. It was doubtless to repair the damage that he issued the Edict of Coucy on 16 July 1535. This ordered the release of all religious prisoners and permitted religious exiles, except sacramentarians, to return home provided they abjured within six months. Only a few people took advantage of the edict. On 30 August 1542 Francis admitted that heresy was spreading. A series of royal edicts tried to check it. More people than ever were imprisoned and burnt in Paris. The court, meanwhile, remained as divided as ever over religion. Madame d'Étampes and Charles duc d'Angoulême were described by foreign observers as 'Lutherans'. In September 1543 the duke wrote to the landgrave of Hesse expressing the wish to see the Gospel preached in France. He added that only respect for his father and brother had deterred him from introducing it into his duchy; he planned, however, to bring it into Luxemburg and asked to be admitted to the Schmalkaldic League of Protestant princes. Alongside this evangelical, not to say heretical, element at court, a strongly Catholic faction was led by the Constable of Montmorency, the Dauphin Henri, and his mistress, Diane de Poitiers.

Under Henry II the religious ambiguities of his father's court vanished. This was partly due to a clarification of the religious situation: as evangelicalism became more radical, so heresy was more easily identified. The crown found it easier to fall into line with what the Sorbonne and Parlement felt to be necessary for the defence of the faith. At the same time, the palace revolution which followed Henry's accession marked the triumph of the Catholic party. Madame d'Étampes was banished from court along with her protégés. She retired to Limours and became openly Protestant. Marguerite de Navarre returned for her daughter's wedding to Antoine de Bourbon in October 1548, but soon returned to the south where she died on 21 December 1549. These events coincided with the return to power of Montmorency and the ascendancy of the House of Guise; both, like the king, were firmly committed to the Catholic cause.

In October 1548 Henry II set up a special lawcourt in the Parlement that became known as the 'burning chamber' (*Chambre ardente*) on account of the severity of its sentences, and on 4 July he took part in an impressive procession through Paris, reminiscent of that staged by his father in 1535. A large number of relics were again brought out of the churches, and the Blessed Sacrament was again given the place of honour. This time it was carried by the cardinal de Guise, who was accompanied by the dukes of Aumale and Guise. The king walked bareheaded with candle in hand. Swiss troops, archers and officials of the household carried torches. After high mass at Notre-Dame, Henry dined at the bishop's palace. A Parisian spokesman, probably the *prévôt des marchands*, made a speech proclaiming the capital's continued adherence to its ancient motto of 'One God, one King, one faith, one law'. He admitted the presence of troublemakers hellbent on destroying church unity, but described them as foreigners. Henry, in reply, urged the clergy to pray for the destruction of all 'Lutherans', and vowed to spare no one, not even his own kith and kin, in his pursuit of that end. He urged the university to instruct the people in the Catholic verities and the secular magistrates to mete out swift justice. Afterwards he visited a number of public places in Paris and, unlike his father, stayed to watch seven heretics burn.[36]

The Edict of Châteaubriant of 27 June 1549 tightened up the heresy laws, with the result that many French dissenters were driven into the arms of Calvin, himself an exile, who was trying to turn Geneva into a godly city. It became a training ground for missionaries, who eventually returned secretly to France with the aim of evangelising it. As the Protestant Reformation, now in the form of Calvinism, spread across France, its social complexion changed. Whereas in the past it had appealed mainly to members of the lower clergy and urban bourgeoisie, it now began to make converts among the nobility. Most were young men who had been influenced by their mothers and their evangelical tutors. Their fathers and uncles continued to adhere to the old faith. Thus the Constable of Montmorency remained a die-hard Catholic while his Châtillon nephews became leading Protestants or Huguenots. As noblemen turned Protestant, they often carried their clients with them. The mass conversion in the Midi has been compared to the spread of an oil stain.[37] The court inevitably came to reflect this social transformation; it could no longer qualify as an exclusively Catholic court. On 24 July 1557 Henry II issued the Edict of Compiègne, which has been described as 'a declaration of war by the king against his Protestant subjects'.[38] They tried as far as possible to hold their conventicles in secret, but on 4 September an angry mob broke up a meeting in the rue Saint-Jacques in Paris. Some 132 Calvinists were arrested, including a number of noblewomen. Appeals on their behalf fell on deaf ears; most of the victims were kept in prison for a considerable time while charges were being prepared. They were eventually released, but only after they had endured harsh questioning and other forms of legal intimidation. The affair

47. *King Henry II.* Drawing by François Clouet (Musée Condé, Chantilly). After spending nearly five years as a hostage in Spain, Henry became king in 1547. He continued fighting the emperor and persecuted Protestants, but financial difficulties forced him to sign the Peace of Cateau-Cambrésis in 1559.

spurred Parisian Calvinists to political action: they persuaded François de Coligny, sire d'Andelot, a nephew of Montmorency, to assist in propagating the Gospel. He did so in Brittany, offering armed protection to a Calvinist preacher. On his return to court, d'Andelot was scolded by the king and dismissed as colonel-general of the infantry.[39]

On 13 May 1558 some four or five thousand Calvinists gathered in the Pré-aux-Clercs, a meadow on the left bank of the Seine within sight of the Louvre, and sang psalms. The rally, which lasted several days and was attended by the king of Navarre, convinced Henry II that his authority was under threat. He vowed to make blood flow and heads roll once peace with the emperor had been restored. Even the Parlement was now tainted with heresy: the king attended one of its sessions and was appalled by the views expressed by some councillors. Anne du Bourg suggested that heresy trials should cease pending a General Council of the church, and denounced the burning of people whose only crime had been to invoke Christ's name while adulterers and murderers went unpunished. Taking the charge of adultery personally, Henry flew into a rage and ordered the arrest of du Bourg and five councillors.[40]

The queen, Catherine de' Medici, may not have shared her husband's militancy. Under Francis I, she had belonged to the circle of Marguerite de Navarre. She apparently owned a French Bible and her close companion Marguerite, the future duchess of Savoy, was only a lukewarm Catholic. Her other friends Madeleine de Mailly, comtesse de Roye, Catherine de Longwy, duchesse de Montpensier, and Madame de Crussol, duchesse d'Uzès, all became Calvinists. Catherine was apparently upset by the cruel treatment of reformers at the end of Henry's reign and may have helped to secure the release from prison of Françoise de la Bretonnière, one of the victims of the rue Saint-Jacques affair. By the end of Henry II's reign, the court of France was deeply implicated in the religious crisis dividing the kingdom.[41]

CHAPTER 14

The Kingdom in Crisis, 1559–74

In 1559 a tournament took place in the rue Saint-Antoine in Paris as part of the celebrations following the Peace of Cateau-Cambrésis. Henry II announced on 22 May that he, the dauphin and four others would challenge *en champ clos* anyone – prince, nobleman, knight or esquire – 'so as to incite the young to virtue'. The rue Saint-Antoine, unpaved for the occasion, was provided with lists, triumphal arches and tribunes for spectators. Rich hangings bearing the arms of France, Savoy and Spain covered the timbers, and statues symbolising the benefits of peace stood between the columns. The first two days of jousting passed off well. On 30 June, however, Henry decided to joust regardless of the queen who in a nightmare had seen his face covered in blood. At 2.30 p.m. on a very warm afternoon the four *tenants* entered the lists. Henry, wearing black and white – the colours of Diane de Poitiers – proudly rode a horse called 'Malheureux', given to him by the duke of Savoy. After a brilliant performance, he shouted to the duke, who sat in one of the tribunes, that he owed his success to his mount. At this juncture, however, the queen and her ladies urged Henry to stop jousting on account of the heat, but he insisted on submitting himself to three challenges as laid down in the rule book. He successfully engaged the dukes of Nemours and Guise, but had to face a more serious challenger in the person of a young count, Gabriel de Montgomery. A first collision proved indecisive and the joust should have ended there. It was 5 p.m. and the spectators were about to leave the tribunes, but Henry refused to lay down his lance. 'I want my revenge,' he exclaimed, 'for he has shaken me and almost unhorsed me!' Once again the queen pleaded with him, but Henry would not listen. He returned to the lists and, without waiting for the traditional trumpet call, charged Montgomery. The ensuing collision was so violent that both lances shattered and the horses fell on their haunches. Recovering from the impact, Montgomery remounted with agility; but Henry, clinging to his horse's collar, stumbled to the counter-list and collapsed. Anguished cries arose from the tribunes as courtiers rushed

48. The tournament of 30 June 1559 in the rue Saint-Antoine, Paris. Engraving by Tortorel and Perrissin (Bibliothèque nationale de France). Part of the celebrations for the marriages of Henry II's sister to the duke of Savoy, and his daughter to the king of Spain. Henry II is seen here being struck by the lance of his opponent, Gabriel de Montgomery.

forward to assist the king, who was unconscious and bleeding profusely from the head. Sharp splinters of wood, one ten centimetres long, protruded from his half-open visor. As Henry regained consciousness, Montgomery begged to be punished for his crime, but the king forgave him, saying that the count had behaved as any good knight would have done: he had obeyed his sovereign. Montmorency, Marshal Tavannes and other courtiers then carried Henry to the Tournelles, where he tried with a great effort to climb a staircase unaided. His chief physician cleaned and bandaged his wounds while leading surgeons, including Vesalius and Ambroise Paré, were sent for. Five splinters were removed without anaesthetic from the king's forehead and left eye. At night Queen Catherine and leading courtiers kept a vigil by his bedside, while Parisians gathered outside the palace to pray for his recovery. For a few days Henry seemed to rally. He vowed to walk to Notre-Dame de Cléry if he recovered and dictated two letters, but on 10 July he suffered a relapse and died.[1] Devastated by her husband's death, Catherine mourned him for the rest of her life. She refused ever again to work on a Friday. 'It was my unlucky day,' she explained to her son, 'for it was the day your father was wounded, which brought us – me principally and the whole kingdom –

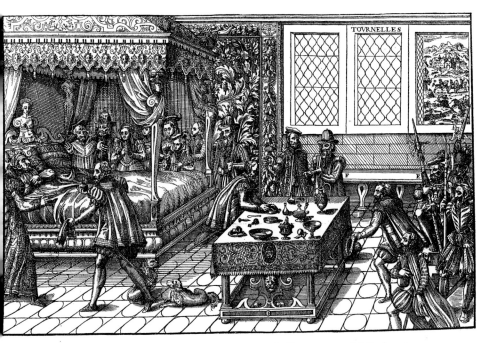

A. La Roine pleurant.
B. Le Cardinal de Lorraine.
C. M. le Conneftable,
D. Poftes courans & des medecins & Cirur-

giens bien experts, en uoyés de Flandres par
le roy d'Efpaigne.
E. Gardes de la chambre du Roy,
F. Medecins & Cirurgiens.

49. The death of Henry II on 10 July 1559. Engraving by Tortorel and Perrissin (Bibliothèque nationale de France). The absence of any religious element is indicative of the Protestant view that the king's death was a divine punishment.

so much harm that I cannot see myself ever doing anything worthwhile on that day.' Catherine never put aside her widow's weeds, except for the weddings of her children, and much of her artistic patronage was also aimed at immortalising her grief.

The death of Henry II plunged the kingdom into one of the worst crises in its history. Whereas he and his father had been strong men capable of commanding the loyalty of the nobility, Francis II, who succeeded to the throne, was only fifteen: old enough under the rules to be king, but lacking political experience or judgment. While Catherine mourned, the court fell into the hands of François duc de Guise and his brother, Charles cardinal of Lorraine. One of their first moves was to get rid of the Constable of Montmorency, who was told by the new king on 11 July that he was free to leave the court. His apartment at the Louvre was taken by the cardinal.[2] Montmorency remained constable, but had to hand over the office of *Grand maître* to Guise, who thereby gained control of the royal household. Guise

50. *Charles, cardinal of Lorraine.* Drawing by François Clouet (Musée Condé, Chantilly). A younger son of Claude, first duc de Guise, Charles (1525–74), became one of the foremost churchmen of his time. Intelligent and well educated, he became a skilful politician serving the king on many diplomatic missions. An unashamed pluralist, he was also a notable patron of the arts, building a famous grotto at his château of Meudon.

and his brother moved Francis II to the Louvre, where they themselves resided. Although Montmorency lost political influence, he was still the richest nobleman in France, with an extensive clientele. As governor of Languedoc, he continued to hold sway in the Midi. His eldest son, François, was governor of Paris and the Île-de-France, and two of his nephews held important offices: Gaspard de Coligny was Admiral of France and François d'Andelot was colonel-general of the infantry. As for Diane de Poitiers, she suffered the usual fate of a royal mistress who had lost her lover: having left

51. *François, second duc de Guise.* Drawing by François Clouet (Musée Condé, Chantilly). The elder son of Claude, first duc de Guise, François (1519–63) entered the royal family in 1548 by marrying Anne d'Este, the granddaughter of King Louis XII. An outstanding soldier, he became a national hero by wresting Calais from the English in 1558.

the court before Henry's death, she never returned. Her daughter, the duchesse de Bouillon, was also banished, but not her other daughter, the duchesse d'Aumale, who was the duc de Guise's sister-in-law. Diane was also made to surrender the crown jewels and to exchange the château of Chenonceau with Catherine de' Medici for the less attractive one of Chaumont.

The *coup d'état* mounted by the Guises was remarkably swift. Within a few days the English ambassador reported 'the house of Guise ruleth and doth all about the French king'. Within two months the cardinal was being described by a Florentine envoy as both pope and king in France. The registers of royal secretaries for April and June 1560 reveal the dominance of the brothers. The accounts of the *Épargne* are filled with gifts of money, payments of arrears and reimbursements of loans to their relatives, clients and servants. For many noblemen the obvious response was to become Guise clients themselves, but this option was not open to Protestants. The Guises were related to the royal family in several ways. The duke was married to Anne d'Este, Louis XII's granddaughter, and was the uncle of Francis II's queen, Mary Stuart, but he and his brother belonged to a family whose origins lay outside France, in the duchy of Lorraine, which still formed part of the Holy Roman Empire. For this reason they were seen by many Frenchmen as foreigners who had usurped the role rightfully belonging to the first prince of the blood, Antoine de Bourbon, king of Navarre. He was in Guyenne when Henry II died, however, and took so long coming to court that the Guises were easily able to tighten their hold upon it. When Navarre did eventually appear, he was admitted to the king's council but debarred from the inner circle of ministers.

Henry II had been forced to sign the Peace of Cateau-Cambrésis for two reasons: lack of money and the mounting threat of heresy. Both problems were now tackled head-on by the Guises. Rather than increase taxes, they decided to cut expenditure: royal troops were disbanded, the settlement of their wages deferred, pensions suppressed, alienations of royal land revoked and interest on royal debts curtailed. At the same time, the anti-heresy laws were strengthened: in September 1559 an edict ordered the destruction of houses used for Protestant worship. Two months later the death penalty was prescribed for anyone holding or attending illegal meetings. An early victim of the repression was the *parlementaire* Anne du Bourg, who was publicly burned in Paris. All this made the Guises exceedingly unpopular, especially among Protestants or Huguenots, some of whom began to plot their over-throw. They planned to arrest the Guises and make them account for their actions before a meeting of the Estates-General. They also wished to present a confession of faith to Francis II, hoping to convince him of their loyalty to the crown. Jean Du Barry, seigneur de La Renaudie, a petty nobleman from Périgord, spent five months recruiting supporters and mercenaries. In February 1560, at a meeting in Nantes, the plotters fixed 16 March as the date for their coup. News of the plot, however, reached the ears of the Guises, who ordered the court to be moved from the château of Blois to Amboise, which was easier to defend. As the conspirators gathered in woods around Amboise, they were set upon by royal troops. Some were killed; others were captured and drowned in the River Loire or hanged from the château's balconies in full view of the court. Years later the poet Agrippa d'Aubigné recalled seeing the dangling bodies as a child. His father made him swear to avenge the crime, describing it as the 'decapitation of France'.[3]

In June 1560 Michel de l'Hôpital, a distinguished lawyer and humanist, was appointed Chancellor of France. He is remembered mainly for his moderation. 'Force and violence', he maintained, 'pertain to beasts, not to man. Justice stems from reason, that most divine part of our being.' L'Hôpital put state before church, and political unity before religious conformity. He believed that France's domestic problems could best be solved by reforming the judiciary and church.[4] Before this could be done, however, the Bourbons and other great nobles needed to be given a share in government. With this end in mind, an Assembly of Notables met at Fontainebleau in August 1560. However, Antoine de Navarre and his brother, Louis prince de Condé, chose not to attend. They drew up a remonstrance in which the Guises were condemned as tyrants.[5] One result of the Fontainebleau meeting was the decision to call the Estates-General in December. Meanwhile, in various parts of France the Huguenots took up arms. As the prospect of civil war loomed, Francis II ordered Navarre to bring his brother, Condé, to court. He was said to be raising troops and the king wished to know why. The prince was arrested at Orléans, tried and sentenced to death, but, before he could be executed, Francis II fell seriously ill. He died on 5 December 1560 and Condé's life was accordingly spared.

The Regency of Catherine de' Medici

Francis's brother now became King Charles IX. At ten he was too young to rule personally, so a regent had to be appointed. On 21 December his mother, Catherine de' Medici, was appointed by the *conseil privé* as 'governor of the kingdom' (*gouvernante du royaume*) with sweeping powers. She was forty-one years old and committed neither to the Guises nor the Bourbons. 'My principal aim', she wrote to her daughter, the queen of Spain, 'is to have the honour of God before my eyes in all things and to preserve my authority, not for myself, but for the conservation of this kingdom and for the good of all your brothers.'[6] She presided over the king's council, initiated and controlled state business, directed domestic and foreign policy, and appointed to offices and benefices. She was the first to receive and open dispatches and had letters patent read out to her before the king signed them. Each of his letters was accompanied by another from Catherine. She also gave herself a great seal in which she is shown standing and holding a sceptre. The young king on his seal is shown crowned sitting on his throne.

On 28 January 1561 Catherine ordered the release of all religious prisoners and a suspension of heresy trials. Her policy, however, was misunderstood by the Huguenots: they assumed that she was coming over to their side, and at a national synod in March they decided to set up a pressure group at court, while in the kingdom at large they organised public meetings. On 8 March Condé was admitted to the council and later that month Navarre was confirmed as lieutenant-general of the kingdom. This so-called 'Huguenot Lent' provoked a Catholic backlash. The Parlement ordered the destruction of all houses used for Huguenot worship. The Guises left the court and retired to their estates. Montmorency, too, was unhappy about the turn of events. On 7 April he formed an alliance aimed at defending the Catholic faith with the duc de Guise and Marshal Saint-André which became known as 'the Triumvirate'. Their aim was to detach Navarre from the Huguenots. Catherine, for her part, still hoped to defuse the crisis. On 30 July an edict abolished the death sentence for religious offences and offered an amnesty for all crimes, religious or seditious, committed since the death of Henry II as long as the culprits swore to lead peaceful and Catholic lives in future. The Huguenots, however, encouraged by the presence at court of Calvinist preachers, wanted freedom to worship in public.

Catherine was no theologian.[7] Believing that a religious peace might be achieved through discourse, she sponsored a debate between Catholic and Protestant divines at Poissy in September 1561. The Protestant case was presented by Théodore de Bèze, Calvin's lieutenant, who was warmly received at court. He was even allowed to preach in the apartments of Condé and Coligny. Calvinism also won converts among the court's ladies, including Renée, dowager-duchess of Ferrara, and the comtesse de Roye and her daughter, the princesse de Condé. Catherine's children were said to pray in French, not Latin, and Charles IX disclosed that he only attended mass in order to please his mother. In October 1561 the Guises, who had returned to court, again left in disgust. Undeterred, Catherine continued her efforts at conciliation, but the Colloquy of Poissy merely demonstrated that the gulf between the two religious camps was unbridgeable.[8] After further talks, the government issued the Edict of January 1562 which allowed Huguenots to worship in the countryside but not inside walled towns or at night, pending a decision by the Council of Trent. Catholics could draw some comfort from Navarre's decision to join them. Catherine ordered her ladies to lead Catholic lives under threat of expulsion from court, while she herself attended mass and participated in religious processions. Her children were made to attend church.[9]

In March 1562 the duc de Guise stumbled across a group of Huguenots worshipping in a barn at Wassy in Champagne. A scuffle turned into a massacre, many worshippers being killed. The event was hailed in Paris as a great victory for orthodoxy. The *prévôt des marchands* offered to raise troops to help Guise pacify the kingdom, but the duke declined, saying that he wished only to obey the queen mother and Navarre. Hoping to defuse the situation, Catherine appointed the cardinal de Bourbon as governor of Paris. He ordered Guise and Condé to leave the capital, but the former refused. Condé obeyed, but failed to answer a call for protection from Catherine, who was at Fontainebleau. This left the way clear for Guise and Navarre to descend on the château with a thousand horse and to force Catherine and the king to return to Paris. Condé and Coligny, meanwhile, marched south, seized Orléans and issued a manifesto which marked the start of the religious wars, which were to continue intermittently until April 1598.

The Wars of Religion tore France apart. Frenchmen fought each other in a series of bloody battles.[10] Catherine herself joined her captains outside Rouen as the city was bombarded. A major victim of the siege was Antoine de Navarre, who died of his wounds on 17 November 1562. At Dreux, in December, both sides suffered heavy losses. Marshal Saint-André was killed, while Montmorency and Condé were taken prisoner. Overnight the political situation changed. The only Triumvir to survive was François de Guise, but,

52. The assassination of François duc de Guise outside Orléans, 18 February 1563. Engraving (Bibliothèque nationale de France). François de Guise was fatally wounded by a shot fired by Poltrot de Méré, a minor Protestant nobleman. The duchess, Anne d'Este, accused Admiral Coligny of complicity in the crime and the vendetta that she launched ended only in August 1572 with Coligny's murder at the hands of her son, Henri, third duc de Guise.

on 18 February 1563 he was shot in the back outside Orléans by Jean Poltrot de Méré, a Protestant nobleman; and he died soon afterwards. Following his arrest, Poltrot made a statement incriminating Admiral Coligny. The latter denied complicity in the crime, but unwisely told Catherine of the satisfaction he had felt on hearing of Guise's death. It was, he said, 'the greatest good that could befall the kingdom, God's church and my house'. Guise's widow, Anne d'Este, and her family never forgave him despite attempts by the crown to clear his name. For the time being, however, the Guises lost influence at court: the new duke, Henri, was only a child, and his uncle the cardinal of Lorraine was away in Italy attending the Council of Trent. Catherine was thus able to secure peace. The Edict of Amboise of March 1563 offered substantial concessions to the Huguenots without satisfying anyone.

In August 1563 Charles IX's majority was proclaimed in Rouen (plate 17), and soon afterwards Catherine took him on an extended progress through France.[11] In the meantime Philip II of Spain ordered the duke of Alba to crush a serious revolt in the Low Countries. The duke set off from the Milanese with an army and marched along the so-called 'Spanish road', skirting France's eastern border. No one in France, not even the government, knew the object of the march. The possibility that Alba might suddenly invade France in support of a *putsch* by the Guises could not be ruled out, and Charles IX was sufficiently alarmed to hire six thousand Swiss mercenaries. The Huguenots, too, were fearful. The threat, however, was lifted in August when Alba's army reached the Low Countries, yet Charles IX did not disband the Swiss troops. The Huguenot leaders, Condé and Coligny, decided on a pre-emptive strike. In late September, as they were relaxing at Montceaux, Catherine de' Medici and Charles IX were warned about a Huguenot army in the vicinity. They moved to the walled town of Meaux for greater security. The king's council then decided that they should return to Paris. Early on 28 September Charles and his mother left for the capital with an escort of Swiss pikemen. The Huguenots set off in pursuit. Using fast carriages, the royal party managed to reach Paris unharmed, but Catherine was furious. She described the Huguenot action, known as the 'Surprise de Meaux', as 'the greatest wickedness in the world'. It had undone all her good work since the Peace of Amboise; conciliation now seemed more remote than ever. The Huguenots further compounded their wickedness by blockading Paris; they set fire to windmills on the outskirts of the capital and cut off its food supplies.

On 10 October the king's army, led by the elderly Constable of Montmorency, marched out of Paris and advanced towards the Protestant HQ at Saint-Denis. The ensuing battle was indecisive, but Montmorency was fatally wounded. He died a few days later and was given a magnificent funeral. His removal from court facilitated a revival of Guise influence. On 11 November the rebels lifted the blockade of Paris and moved eastwards hoping to link up with a force of German *reiters* (cavalry armed with pistols). In January 1568 Catherine visited the headquarters of the royal army at Châlons-sur-Marne, determined to prevent the rebels from fleeing abroad. In February the king's army, commanded by his brother, Henri duc d'Anjou, fell back to Nogent-sur-Seine, as the Huguenots, now reinforced by the *reiters,* marched on Paris. On 21 February Condé laid siege to Chartres, but a shortage of money forced him to sign the Peace of Longjumeau.[12]

Was Catherine still committed to peace? We shall never know. On 11 June 1568 she told the Venetian envoy:

> There are circumstances which oblige one to turn upon oneself and to submit to what one did not want in order to avoid greater ills . . .. See what a miserable situation we have fallen into again. Whereas we had got used to going about the kingdom in safety, now we cannot take a step out of doors without being surrounded by guards.[13]

On learning that a force of Huguenots had been routed near the Flemish border, Catherine ordered the prisoners to be executed or sent to the galleys.[14] Speaking to Alava, the Spanish envoy, she described the execution in Brussels of counts Egmont and Hornes as 'a holy decision', which she hoped soon to see repeated in France.[15]

During the summer of 1568 Condé and Coligny, who had retired to their homes in Burgundy, began to fear a counteroffensive by the crown. On 23 August they and their families made for the Atlantic stronghold of La Rochelle, gathering so many supporters on the way that their exodus assumed biblical proportions. On 28 September the Huguenot leaders were joined by Jeanne d'Albret and her son, Henri de Navarre, who now became the official leader of the Huguenot movement, giving it legitimacy as a prince of the blood. The effective leader, however, was Louis prince de Condé. Charles IX's council, meanwhile, revoked the Peace of Longjumeau, banned any religion other than Catholicism and banished all pastors. Michel de L'Hôpital left the court after handing over the state seals to a keeper. Catherine returned to Paris on 28 September; soon afterwards her favourite son, Henri d'Anjou, took command of the king's army. On 13 March 1569 he defeated the Huguenots at Jarnac. Condé was murdered by one of Anjou's men soon after he had surrendered. His command passed to Admiral Coligny. On 7 May the latter's brother, d'Andelot, died, almost certainly poisoned. Catherine may have been implicated in the crime. Writing to the French ambassador in Spain on 19 May, she admitted: 'We greatly rejoiced over the news of d'Andelot's death ... I hope that God will mete out to the others the treatment they deserve.'[16]

Catherine doubtless hoped that Coligny, too, would soon die. No amount of excuses could expunge his guilt in her eyes.[17] On 13 September he was stripped of his offices and titles by the Parlement and sentenced to death. His property was also seized and a large reward placed on his head. His armorial bearings, tied to a horse's tail, were dragged through the streets of Paris, and a straw effigy of him hung from a gibbet. A decree of 28 September offered a reward to anyone who handed Coligny over to the crown, dead or alive.[18] The civil war, meanwhile, raged on. On 3 October another major battle was fought, this time at Moncontour. The Huguenots, under Coligny, were again routed. Marshal Tavannes wanted to pursue them, but Charles IX, who had come to Anjou's camp in the hope of sharing the fruits of victory, preferred to lay siege to Saint-Jean-d'Angély. Coligny was thus given time to regroup his forces and prepare a new spring offensive. In 1570 he crossed Languedoc, leaving behind a trail of destruction. Meanwhile, the royalists ran out of money. They urgently required peace and Catherine helped secure it. The Treaty of Saint-Germain of 5 October 1570 marked a significant advance on earlier settlements for the Huguenots.[19] Although their faith was still banned at court and in Paris, they were given four security towns (*places de sûreté*) for two years, allowed limited rights of worship, and granted access to universities, schools and hospitals. These concessions, however, enraged Catholics, who felt that they had won the war.[20]

The peace enabled Catherine to do what she liked doing best: arranging prestigious marriages for her children. In November 1570 at Mézières, Charles IX married Emperor Maximilian II's daughter, Elizabeth of Austria, whom Brantôme described as 'one of the best, sweetest, wisest and most virtuous queens ever to reign'. She spoke little and then only in Spanish, which may explain why she has left hardly any mark on French history. The union of two great dynasties, both claiming descent from Charlemagne, was seen as an event of supreme importance, heralding a universal peace.[21] Two other marriages envisaged by Catherine for her children proved more difficult to arrange. She had hoped to marry her daughter, Marguerite, to the Portuguese king, but he showed no interest in the match, so she turned to the Huguenot leader, Henri de Navarre. Was she hoping to draw him into the Catholic fold? We cannot be sure. Henri was then at La Rochelle with his mother, Jeanne d'Albret, who was deeply suspicious of Catherine's motives. She was afraid that her son, once lured to the French court, would be forced to abjure his faith and be morally corrupted. Jeanne was intensely puritanical. Catherine wanted her favourite son, Henri d'Anjou, to marry the English queen, but the Catholic world saw Elizabeth I as a bastard and a heretic. She was also twenty years older than Anjou who was only seventeen. Moreover, in 1570 she had been excommunicated by the pope. So Henri was not keen to marry her; he was also afraid of becoming a laughing stock at the French court where Elizabeth's flirtation with the earl of Leicester was common knowledge. He told Catherine that he would never marry a common whore (*putain publique*). Seeing that he was immovable, Catherine offered the hand of her youngest son, François d'Alençon, to Elizabeth.

Coligny believed that the best way to bring domestic peace to France was to unite the nobility, both Protestant and Catholic, in a war against Spain aimed at helping the Dutch rebels. He hoped to win Charles IX over to the idea, knowing that he was keen to outshine his brother, Anjou, as a military leader. Their mother, however, was vehemently opposed to a war which, she believed would bring disaster to France. Before he could persuade the king, Coligny had to return to court. Much as she disliked him, Catherine needed his support for her daughter's marriage to Navarre, so she did not oppose his presence. He was at Blois on 12 September, and stayed there for five weeks. He was given compensation for losses he had incurred during the civil war, allowed an escort of fifty noblemen and readmitted to the king's council.

Catherine had so far achieved only one of her objectives. Coligny had come to court, but Jeanne d'Albret, whose consent was required to her son's marriage, remained obdurate. In January 1572 the two ladies met at Chenonceau. Suspicious as she still was, Jeanne was afraid that if she continued to oppose her son's marriage to Marguerite, the pope might excommunicate him and deny him his right to the French throne. So eventually she agreed to come to court. Charles IX welcomed her at Blois on 2 March but, if the letters she wrote at the time are genuine, the following weeks turned into an ordeal for her.[22] Alba was informed that Jeanne would rather see her son burn than marry a Catholic. Charles IX, however, conceded all her demands on condition that Navarre would come to Paris for the wedding. On 4 April Jeanne at last agreed to the marriage. On 15 April the bishop of Mâcon informed the nuncio Salviati: 'Your Reverence can be assured that we will soon see the Prince return to the bosom of Holy Church.'[23] Later that month Jeanne moved to Vendôme hoping to meet her son, but he was ill, so she travelled to Paris alone. On 4 June, however, she fell seriously ill herself and five days later she died. A postmortem revealed that she had been suffering from tuberculosis and breast cancer, but her death was so opportune for the crown that Huguenots suspected that she had been poisoned. Be that as it may, Catholics rejoiced over Jeanne's death and the papal nuncio thought the path was now clear for Navarre's conversion. On 5 July a royal ordinance laid down strict rules of public conduct during the forthcoming marriage celebrations: no one, on pain of death, was to stir up past quarrels, start new ones, carry firearms or fight in Paris or its suburbs. Three days later Navarre arrived in the capital; he was greeted by Charles IX's two brothers and given an apartment at the Louvre.[24] On 18 August he and Marguerite were married at the cathedral of Notre-Dame.

Early on 22 August Admiral Coligny attended a council meeting at the Louvre. He then watched Charles IX play tennis before walking to his residence in the rue de Béthisy with a small group of friends. Suddenly, in the rue des Poulies, a shot was fired from the upper window of a house. A bullet struck the admiral just as he was bending down. This movement saved his life, but he was wounded in the right hand and left arm. His friends helped him to his lodging and the surgeon, Ambroise Paré, removed the bullet. Meanwhile, Coligny's companions entered the house whence the shot had been fired and found a smoking arquebus at an open window. The assailant, however, had fled.[25] He has since been identified as Charles de Louviers, seigneur de Maurevert, who in 1569 had murdered Coligny's friend the seigneur de Mouy. The house that he used for his assault on Coligny belonged to a former tutor of Henri de Guise.[26] So responsibility for the attempted assassination seems to have rested squarely with the Guises, who had long wanted to avenge the murder in 1563 of the second duke. News of the attack on Coligny caused panic at court. The rumour spread that the Huguenots were preparing to invade the Louvre, bent on slaughtering the Guises and possibly the royal family as well. Huguenots warned the king of dire consequences should he fail to act. 'Sire,' they said, 'if you do not give us justice, we will do so ourselves and the bloodshed will be such that our enemies will never be tempted to commit another outrage.'[27] According to Bellièvre, they had more than eight hundred noblemen and eight thousand followers within Paris and a force of three thousand outside. It seems that royal councillors conferred with the queen mother at the Tuileries on the afternoon of 23 August. They decided to wipe out the Huguenot leadership, but needed Charles IX's consent. This was doubtless why another council meeting took place at the Louvre around 11 p.m. this time in his presence. Others present were Catherine, the chancellor, René de Birague, the dukes of Nevers, Anjou, Montpensier and probably Guise, Albert de Gondi, comte de Retz, and Marshal Tavannes. All were hardliners. They thought it 'better to win a battle in Paris, where all the leaders were, than to risk it in the field and fall into a dangerous and uncertain war'. Later that night Jean Le Charron, the *prévôt des marchands*, was summoned to the Louvre. He was told that the Huguenots were planning a coup against the king, the state and Paris, and ordered to ensure the safety of the royal family and of all Parisians.[28] A threefold military operation was planned by the council: first, the execution of Coligny and other Huguenot nobles living in Paris; secondly, the elimination of the

Huguenot captains and noblemen in the Louvre, except for Navarre and Condé; and thirdly, the encirclement of a force of armed Huguenots in the faubourg Saint-Germain.

Early on 24 August 1572 members of the king's guard, led by the duc de Guise, burst into the Hôtel de Béthisy, murdered Coligny and threw his body out of a window. It fell in a courtyard close to where Guise was standing. As he looked at the corpse, one of his men said: 'Here then, Monseigneur, is the traitor who caused your father's death'. Coligny, however, was only the first of many more Huguenots who were to die that day; about seventy-two were killed by the king's men and their bodies dumped around a fountain in the place Saint-Honoré. The court did not escape the bloodshed. Early on 24 August Huguenots within the Louvre were rounded up, disarmed, led to a courtyard and hacked to pieces by royal troops. Charles IX is said to have watched the slaughter. Navarre and Condé were spared on account of their royal blood, but threatened with death unless they agreed to become Catholics. Henry IV's minister, the duc de Sully, recalled in his memoirs Charles IX's 'ferocious' expression and his 'eyes filled with anger' as he spoke to the two princes.

Another witness of the terrible events in the Louvre that night was the king's sister, Marguerite. In her memoirs she describes the atmosphere on the evening of 23 August. 'I saw the whole world in action: the Huguenots in despair over this wounding [of Coligny], the Guises fearing retribution and whispering in each other's ears.' As Marguerite prepared to retire for the night, her sister, Claude, begged her not to, but her mother said that she had nothing to fear. The princess accordingly retired to her bedchamber. Her husband, Navarre, who was already in bed, asked her, as she prayed, to join him. She found sleep impossible, however, as there were thirty or forty Huguenots in the room. They talked all night about the assault on Coligny and swore to call on the king in the morning to demand justice. At dawn they and Navarre left the room and Marguerite fell asleep, but not for long. A loud knocking at the door and shouts of 'Navarre! Navarre!' woke her up. Monsieur de Leyran, a Huguenot nobleman, burst into the room, closely pursued by archers; his arm was bleeding. He threw himself on Marguerite's bed. 'I did not know this man,' she wrote, 'nor did I know whether he had come to harm me or whether the archers were after him or me.' Nançai, captain of the guard, now entered the room. He angrily dismissed his archers and spared de Leyran's life. He was also able to reassure Marguerite regarding her husband's fate: he was safe and with the king in his chamber.[29]

The Massacre of St Bartholomew's Day was partly the result of a panic decision taken at court following the botched attempt to kill Coligny. The slaughter spread like wildfire to the homes of leading Huguenots, then to other parts of the capital and other towns. The death toll over several days may have reached ten thousand. On 26 August Charles IX held a *lit de justice* in the Parlement. In a speech he assumed full responsibility for the slaughter of the Huguenot leaders. An official declaration published four days later excused the massacre on the ground that it had foiled a plot by Coligny against the king, his family, Navarre and other princes and lords. The Parlement ordered the destruction of all images of the admiral. His château at Châtillon-sur-Loing was to be razed to the ground, its trees cut down and the ground sown with salt, like Carthage. A column was to be erected on the site. Huguenot survivors of the massacre were to be rounded up and hanged. Many saved themselves by abjuring; others fled to towns where Huguenots were in a majority or went abroad, principally to England and Geneva. In the past such exiles had been mainly artisans; now they included noblemen, jurists, scholars and pastors.[30]

Although many Huguenots had been wiped out in the massacre, enough survived in the south and west of France to continue the struggle. They controlled La Rochelle and refused to admit Marshal Biron as their governor. He laid siege to the town in February 1573 and was soon joined by an army led by the king's brother Henri d'Anjou. He was accompanied by his brother Alençon, Navarre, Condé, the dukes of Guise and Aumale and other lords. From the start of the siege, however, they squabbled among themselves. A number of younger nobles gathered around Alençon, who resented the fact that he had not been given a command. As a prince of the blood, he gave the so-called 'malcontents' a certain legitimacy, but as yet they lacked the cohesion needed to form a party.

The siege of La Rochelle dragged on through the spring as refugees from the recent massacres joined the defenders. On 10 May 1573, however, Anjou was elected king of Poland. He received the news on the 29th and used it as an honourable pretext for ending the siege. On 19 August a Polish delegation arrived in Paris to offer him their country's crown, and on 9 September he signed documents endorsing religious toleration in his new kingdom. Next day, at Notre-Dame, he swore to honour his promises and, three days later, received the election decree, a beautiful document adorned with the arms of France and Poland. On 14 September Anjou made his entry into Paris as king of Poland. Catherine, meanwhile, persuaded Charles IX to appoint him as his heir.

Anjou was not keen to go to Poland; he tried to delay his departure for as long as possible but eventually had to leave. The court escorted him as far as the French frontier. At Nancy, Charles III, duke of Lorraine, welcomed him and his mother. Catherine was delighted to see her daughter, the duchess Claude, who had just given birth to a boy. It was also at the court of Lorraine that Anjou first set eyes on Charles III's beautiful niece Louise de Vaudémont, who was to become his wife. From Nancy, he and his mother travelled to Blamont where they took leave of each other.[31]

The least attractive of Catherine de' Medici's children was François duc d'Alençon, who was seventeen in 1572. He had contracted smallpox in 1569 and, according to the vicomte de Turenne, had become 'unrecognizable with a completely hollowed-out face, a large and deformed nose, and eyes so red that it made him about the ugliest man one could ever hope to see'. Despite his repellent appearance, Alençon was a notorious womanizer. His mind was no better than his body: he read little except military history and knew no language other than French. His chief ambition was to be a soldier, yet he showed little aptitude for the role. It was his character, however, that prompted the loudest criticism. Navarre allegedly said of Alençon: 'He will deceive me just as he has deceived everyone who has ever trusted him . . . He is so sly and two-faced, his courage is so lacking, and he is so unfamiliar with every kind of virtue that I do not think he is capable of performing a generous act.'[32] In spite of his faults, Alençon cut a powerful figure at court; immensely rich, he had a large clientele. The historian Étienne Pasquier described him as 'a second king who had his own court'. In 1572 his household numbered some 262 persons (176 of them nobles) whose combined wages and pensions totalled 78,000 *l*. By the early 1580s it had more than a thousand staff.[33]

Alençon wanted to be lieutenant-general of the kingdom following his brother's election to the Polish throne. The sieur de Ventabren, one of his friends, was accused of having been hired by Marshal François de Montmorency to murder Henri duc de Guise. The parties concerned rejected the charge, but were punished all the same. Montmorency was banished from court and the king appointed the duke of Lorraine as lieutenant-general of the kingdom, thereby breaking a promise he had given to Alençon. The court, however, was not appeased by these measures. On 23 February 1574 a large force of Huguenots assembled near Saint-Germain-en-Laye with the aim of setting free Alençon and Navarre so that they might to go to the assistance of the Dutch rebels. Fearing a repeat of the 'Surprise de Meaux', Charles IX ordered the court to decamp from Saint-Germain. Questioned about the plot, Alençon said that it had been aimed at the Guises, who had blocked his appointment to a position of responsibility in the government. Chancellor Birague, whose severity was notorious, wanted him and Navarre executed, but the king was not prepared to go that far; instead the two princes were put under house arrest and made to take an oath of loyalty to him.

In 1574 Catherine heard that Alençon and Navarre were planning to escape to Sedan and to meet up with a force of cavalry led by the vicomte de

Turenne. The king placed the two princes under closer guard than before and ordered the arrest of fifty of their friends, including the seigneur de La Mole and the comte de Coconas. La Mole denied all knowledge of a plot, but Coconas revealed that Alençon had planned to meet Condé and the seigneur de Thoré at La Ferté before joining the Dutch rebel leader Louis of Nassau and his ally Christopher of the Palatinate at Sedan. He accused Montmorency and his brother Damville of instigating the plot. On being questioned, Alençon admitted planning to go to the Low Countries, but Navarre explained that he and Alençon had only acted out of fear of another massacre. Birague once more demanded their execution, but Charles IX again preferred to spare them. La Mole and Coconas, however, were tried, found guilty of treason and executed. As an additional safety measure, marshals Montmorency and Cossé were imprisoned. Henri de Montmorency-Damville, the governor of Languedoc, remained free, but his commission was revoked. He was not easily removed, however. On 29 May he signed a truce with the Huguenots in the Midi and subsequently formed a Union of moderate Catholics and Huguenots; in other words, an alliance of 'malcontents' of both faiths against the government. Condé, meanwhile, fled to Germany and abjured the Catholic faith that had been forced on him after the St Bartholomew's Day Massacre.[34]

On 30 May 1574 Charles IX died at Vincennes, aged twenty-three. He had been ill for some time. Before dying, he appointed his mother as regent pending the return of his brother Henri from Poland. Catherine immediately sent an envoy to inform him of his accession, and next day sent him a touching account of Charles IX's death. 'I am grief-stricken', she wrote,

> to have witnessed such a scene and the love which he showed me at the end. He could not leave me and begged me to send for you in great haste and pending your return to take charge of the government and to punish the prisoners who, he knew, were the cause of all the kingdom's ills. His last words were '*Eh, ma mère.*'

'My only consolation', added Catherine, 'is to see you here soon, as your kingdom requires, and in good health, for if France were to lose you, I would have myself buried alive with you.'[35]

CHAPTER 15

Queen Mother

In August 1563 Charles IX's majority was proclaimed in Rouen, and soon afterwards his mother, Catherine de' Medici, took him on an extended progress through France.[1] Its main purpose was to impose his authority and ensure that the recent Edict of Amboise was being applied. Writing to Coligny on 17 April 1564, she said: 'One of the main reasons for which the king, my lord and son, has undertaken his travels is to show his intention regarding that matter so clearly wherever he passes that no one will have any pretext or occasion to contravene it.'[2] Catherine also hoped to meet her son-in-law, Philip II of Spain, and his queen, Elizabeth de Valois. She also planned to use the occasion to arrange further marriages for her children.

The 'Grand Tour of France' began in Paris on 24 January 1564 and lasted until 1 May 1566. Abel Jouan, a member of the court's kitchen staff, kept a record of the places visited, the dates of arrival and departure, the distances covered and meal stops on the way. His book, entitled *Recueil et discours du voyage du roy Charles IX*, was published soon afterwards. The progress lasted 829 days during which the court moved on 201 days and stayed put on 628. In other words, it travelled on average one day in every four. Twenty-one stops lasted a week or more, accounting for a total of 486 days; 57 lasted between one and six days; 118 lasted less than a day (these were mostly overnight stops). Altogether the court covered 2,721 miles. The average distance between stops was 12 miles, with a minimum of 3 and a maximum of 36. The pace of travel quickened on the return leg.[3]

The court left Paris on 24 January 1564. It consisted of several thousand people, a multitude of horses and other beasts of burden, as well as troops. The itinerary had been settled in advance, but some stops may have been decided on the spur of the moment. Social status determined the mode of transport. Charles IX and his mother travelled by coach or litter; they also rode horses, as did most noblemen. Boats were used where rivers were navigable, but the rank and file travelled on foot. The pace of travel was leisurely, the court's van often reaching its destination before the rear had left the last halt. Nor did the court travel as a single body: its members would part company, take short cuts, cross fields and meet up on the way. Halts varied in duration from a night to a week or more. The court spent 90 days at Moulins, 46 at Toulouse, 39 at Bayonne and Saint-Jean-de-Luz, 31 at Bordeaux and 29 at Lyon.[4] The length of visits was determined by such factors as the king's health (he fell ill twice), the weather, road conditions and feast days. Overall charge of the progress was entrusted to the Constable of Montmorency. He maintained discipline, issued orders to town governors and rode ahead of the main company to ensure that all was ready for the king's reception.

The first stop on the Grand Tour was Fontainebleau, where the court remained for forty-three days celebrating carnival. The festivities took place against a background of feverish diplomatic activity and continued religious tension in the kingdom at large despite the recent settlement. They included a series of banquets offered by Montmorency and other lords in their respective lodgings. The queen mother gave hers at La Vacherie, a farm in the grounds of the château, after which she put on a play in its ballroom. Catherine was fond of the theatre. She and Henry II had attended a performance at Blois of *Sophonisbe*, a tragedy by Trissino translated into French by Mellin de Saint-Gelais. After Henry's death, however, Catherine no longer wanted to see tragedies, believing that they had brought her husband bad luck. The play staged at Fontainebleau on 13 January 1564 was *Ginevra*, an episode from Ariosto's *Orlando Furioso*: it was the first tragicomedy to be performed at the French court.

The so-called 'magnificences' at Fontainebleau included a tournament and breaking of lances, combats at the barriers and all kinds of war games. Several were jousts in fancy dress and allegorical settings. Twelve knights dressed as Greeks and Romans fought over ladies imprisoned in an enchanted tower on an island. In another entertainment, sirens swam in the canals and greeted the king in song. Neptune in a chariot pulled by sea horses floated by. Catherine, it has been suggested, laid on such entertainments to heal the differences between Catholic and Huguenot courtiers by making them share in chivalric pastimes. She may also have been seeking to enhance the king's authority by invoking the support of the 'gentle deities of nature'.

From Fontainebleau the court moved first to Sens, the scene of a recent massacre of Huguenots, then to Troyes, where a treaty was signed with England. The local judges were accused by the king of not pulling their weight and threatened with replacement unless they mended their ways. At Bar-le-Duc Catherine attended the baptism of her first grandchild, the son of the duke and duchess of Lorraine. He was christened Henri. Charles IX and his mother acted as godparents for four other noble children during the

53. *A Water Festival at Fontainebleau.* Drawing by Antoine Caron (National Gallery of Scotland, Edinburgh). Among the entertainments laid on at Fontainebleau in 1564 was a show in which sirens swimming in the canals greeted the king in song, and Neptune floated by in a chariot drawn by sea horses.

progress. The girls were all called Charlotte-Catherine.[5] On 22 March the king entered Dijon, where triumphal arches had been erected in his honour and small children, wearing his livery and playing fifes and drums, escorted him into the city. The governor, Gaspard de Saulx-Tavannes, put on a military pageant of such verisimilitude that the queen mother trembled with fear. There were 108 urban entries during the progress, some more lavish than others. Their programmes often compared Charles IX to St Louis, whose mother, Blanche de Castille, had guided him wisely in his early years. At other times Catherine was likened to Ariadne, who helped Theseus find his way through the labyrinth, to Pallas, who helped to support the pillars of Hercules, and to Juno, who suckled the young hero.[6]

One aim of the progress was to curb any show of independence by local authorities. At Dijon on 23 May, Henri duc d'Orléans, acting in the king's name, sent for the parlement's registers, and next day L'Hôpital checked that the Edict of Amboise had been duly published. He also inspected trial proceedings to see if the judges had been fair. The king meddled in the affairs of almost every town he visited, trying as far as possible to strike a proper balance between the religious parties. From Chalon-sur-Saône the royal

family sailed down the Saône to Mâcon, where Jeanne d'Albret, queen of
Navarre, met them. A proud and dignified woman, she was also a fanatical
Calvinist. Accompanying her were eight pastors and three hundred cavalry.[7]
A major reason for her coming was to be reunited with her son, Henri de
Navarre, who had been kept at the French court for some years.

During the progress foreign dignitaries attached themselves to the court,
but only two – the papal nuncio and the Spanish ambassador – stayed the
course. Nobles tagged along and dropped off as they pleased, their movements being largely determined by their religion: Huguenots, for instance,
made themselves scarce in Lorraine and other territories dominated by the
Guises. As a result, members of the king's council tended to be Catholics,
leaving the chancellor to uphold the cause of moderation.

The next major halt on the Grand Tour was Lyon, a city with a large
Huguenot population. Montmorency, riding ahead of the royal party, took
charge of the city's fortifications, artillery and keys before introducing a royal
garrison. Such steps were needed to ensure the court's safety. As a further
safeguard Protestant services were banned for the duration of the royal visit.
A similar ban was imposed in other cities soon to be visited by the court.
During their stay in Lyon, Charles IX and his mother were treated to more
pageants and celebrations in which the city's Italian and German merchants
figured prominently. Here, too, the court was joined by Emmanuel-Philibert,
duke of Savoy, and his wife, Marguerite, often likened to Minerva on account
of her learning.[8] An epidemic of plague forced the court to move to Crémieu
on 8 June where an important edict was issued designed to curb municipal
independence across the kingdom. It was here, too, that Jeanne d'Albret was
ordered to go to Vendôme and her son to remain at court.

The court's next port of call was Roussillon, where on 4 August Charles IX
ruled on the application of the Edict of Amboise. Resuming its progress on
the 15th, the court followed the Rhône Valley to Romans. After a short break
to allow the king to recover from a chill, it moved on to Montélimar, Orange
and Avignon, where it was hosted by the papal vice-legate. On 16 October
Charles and his mother called on Nostradamus at Salon de Crau. He prophesied that the king would live as long as the constable; in fact, Charles was to
outlive Montmorency by seven years. On 23 October the royal caravan
arrived at Aix-en-Provence, where the parlement was suspended for refusing
to register the Edict of Amboise and replaced by a commission of Parisian
parlementaires. The next stage of the progress was less stressful. At Brignoles
the king was greeted by young girls dancing the volta and martingale. In
Provence he admired the local flora and visited Roman remains. On 3
November at Toulon, he took a trip out to sea on a galley, and at Marseille he
and some courtiers took part in a mock sea battle dressed as Turks. In the

Camargue the royal party saw flamingos, and at Arles, where it was held up for three weeks by floods, Charles IX visited Les Alycamps – the famous avenue of Roman sarcophagi – and watched bullfights in the arena. After crossing the Rhône at Tarascon, the court visited the great Roman aqueduct, the Pont du Gard. At Nîmes, a staunchly Protestant town, Charles was given an entry notable for its mechanical devices. Then, after spending Christmas at Montpellier, the court set off on 1 January 1565 for Toulouse, but was held up at Carcassonne for ten days by snow.[9] In Guyenne Henri de Navarre, as the provincial governor, rode ahead of the main party in order to welcome the king to each town.

On 11 March after forty-six days in Toulouse, the royal caravan resumed its journey. Passing through Montauban and Agen, it reached Bordeaux, where, on 12 April, Charles IX held a *lit de justice*. The chancellor accused the *parlementaires* of treating the king's ordinances with contempt. He reaffirmed Charles's determination to enforce the Edict of Amboise. The same treatment was meted out to all the parlements, except at Grenoble and Rennes, which the king was unable to reach for various reasons.[10] On 3 May the court left Bordeaux for Bayonne, where Catherine went in disguise on 31 May to supervise preparations for the reception of her daughter, Elizabeth, the Spanish queen. Charles IX followed on 3 June, and six days later his brother Henri set off to meet his sister in Spain and escort her back to France.

The Franco-Spanish meeting at Bayonne was the diplomatic climax of the progress.[11] Catherine was keen to forge closer links with her son-in-law, Philip II, but he refused to attend, and sent in his place the duke of Alba, a noted Catholic hardliner. He had been instructed to persuade Catherine to abandon conciliation with the Huguenots in favour of persecution. She, for her part, hoped to use the occasion to arrange marriages for her children, but Alba would not discuss such matters. The Huguenots were deeply suspicious of the talks in Bayonne from which they had been excluded; they imagined that Catherine and Alba were planning their destruction. The talks were accompanied by a round of entertainments that Catherine hoped would show that France, despite her troubles, could still put on a fine show. According to Brantôme, the 'magnificence was such in everything that the Spaniards who are very contemptuous of all others, save their own, swore that they had never seen anything finer'.[12] Alba, however, was irritated by the fun and games which he viewed as an unnecessary distraction from the serious business in hand.[13]

Several printed accounts exist of the Bayonne entertainments. A banquet held on an island, the Île d'Aigueneau, on 23 June was particularly colourful. Guests were taken there in splendidly decorated boats. As they were ferried across the water, they were able to watch fishermen harpooning an artificial whale that spewed red wine from its wound. They also encountered six tritons sitting on a large turtle and blowing on conch shells, Neptune in a chariot pulled by sea horses, Arion riding two dolphins, and sirens singing their praise. On the island the guests were treated to regional dances performed by girls disguised as shepherdesses; sirens also invited them to celebrate the Franco-Spanish entente. A ballet of nymphs and satyrs followed the banquet. Next day there was a tournament between British and Irish knights, the former led by Charles IX and the latter by his brother Henri. The cartels were recited to music, and the theme of the tournament – Virtue and Love – was represented by two chariots: one drawn by four white horses, carried ladies symbolising the five Virtues; the other carried Venus and Cupid accompanied by many small cherubs. The ladies distributed devices similar to those displayed on the knights' shields. The climax of the tournament was an equestrian display in which the knights cut across each other without colliding, while little balls of fire were thrown among their horses' hooves. The event, staged in an enclosure, was accompanied by music and recitations. The royal grandstand was adorned with the magnificent *Triumphs of Scipio* tapestries that Francis I had commissioned.

The wedding of Henri de Navarre and Marguerite de Valois in August 1572 offered Catherine another chance of staging colourful entertainments. No *livret* or festival book was published describing them. Nearly everything that is known about them comes from Protestant writers who, in the light of the massacre that followed, came to view them with grave suspicion. They read all kinds of sinister meanings into the scenes that were enacted and into the roles given to the participants, yet the festivities seem to have followed a pattern already set in 1564 and 1565 at Fontainebleau and Bayonne. One of the entertainments planned was a siege in which Coligny and his fellow Huguenots were to attack a fort defended by the king and a Catholic garrison. It was dropped, however, because Coligny did not feel well enough to take part. One entertainment that did take place was a procession of chariots shaped like rocks on which marine gods and other sea creatures were perched. Another was called 'The Paradise of Love': in this the king and his brothers defended twelve nymphs who were being attacked by Navarre and other Huguenots. They ended up in Hell but were rescued by Mercury and Cupid. The nymphs celebrated their rescue by dancing a lengthy and elaborate ballet. A combat between knights ensued during which explosions of gunpowder filled the hall with fire and smoke. On the last day, before the attempted assassination of Admiral Coligny brought the festivities to an abrupt end, there was a running at the ring in the courtyard of the Louvre. Several groups of contestants turned up, including Charles IX and his brother attired as Amazons, Navarre and his companions as Turks wearing turbans and long golden robes, Condé and others as Albanian stradiots, and Guise and his friends also dressed as Amazons.

In August 1573, one year after the St Bartholomew's Day Massacre, Paris was again *en fête*, this time for the Polish ambassadors who had come to offer their country's crown to the duc d'Anjou (see plate 19). They were treated to tournaments, mock battles, barriers and running at the ring or at the quintain. Catherine also treated them to a splendid *festin* at the Tuileries, described by Jean Dorat in his *Magnificentissimi spectaculi*. This work, in Latin verse, and including French verses by Ronsard and Amadis Jamyn as well as illustrations, describes a ballet. Sixteen nymphs, each representing a French province, appeared on a moving rock from which they descended to dance a long and intricate ballet designed by Beaujoyeux. They distributed devices to the spectators. Brantôme calls this 'the finest ballet that was ever given in this world'. He justifies expenditure on such shows by arguing that they bring much prestige to France. According to d'Aubigné, the Polish ambassadors were bowled over by the entertainment; they declared that 'the ballet of France was something that no king on earth could imitate'. All these inventions, according to Brantôme, were due to Catherine alone. She often said that she wished to imitate the Roman emperors who aimed to keep their subjects out of mischief by giving them games and amusements. 'The question of Italian influence on the French *ballet de cour* seems solved', writes Frances Yates.

> It was invented, in the context of the chivalrous pastimes of the court, by an Italian, and a Medici, the Queen Mother. Many poets, artists, musicians, choreographers, contributed to the result, but it was she who was the inventor, one might perhaps say, the producer; she who had the ladies of her court trained to perform these ballets in settings of her devising.[14]

Catherine de' Medici and Court Theatre

It was during the second half of the sixteenth century that a new kind of theatrical experience reached the French court in the form of Italian comedy. Previously the theatre in France had consisted mainly of farces, moralities, mysteries and histories reaching back to the Middle Ages. Francis I had not been keen on the satirical plays staged by the Basoche, and had even legislated against them.[15] By the sixteenth century learned tragedies claiming descent from antiquity were being written by university teachers and performed by their students. Some tragedies were performed at court in the 1550s. Thus, in 1556 at the château of Blois, Mary Stuart and other royal princesses were among the actors in *Sophonisbe*, a play adapted from Trissino by Mellin de Saint-Gelais. Between 1560 and 1580 Cosimo della Gamba, alias Chasteauvieux, one of the king's *valets de chambre*, wrote and acted in comedies and tragedies, one of them being *Roméo et Juliette* after Bandello. Theatre at court was intimately associated with the idea of festival, be it a princely wedding, a ceremony or carnival. About 1570 tragedy virtually disappeared from court. According to Brantôme, Catherine de' Medici blamed it for 'bringing misfortune to the kingdom's affairs'. Courtiers now preferred ballets and new genres: the pastoral or tragicomedy. Tragedies were now performed away from Paris and outside the court in châteaux, convents, provincial towns and especially colleges.[16] Catherine cared only for comedy. In 1555 a comedy called *Flora*, written by the poet Luigi Alamanni, was performed at Fontainebleau. Some ten years later the queen mother watched a play written by Cornelio Fiesco, a gentleman of Charles IX's chamber. It prompted a lively debate among the courtiers as to whether a gentleman who had failed to take advantage of a night spent hiding in a lady's bedchamber should be praised or condemned. An Italian-style comedy was part of the entertainments laid on by Catherine at Bayonne in 1565, and two years later J.A. de Baïf offered the court *Le Brave*, a comedy inspired by Plautus. Between the acts, verses were read out in praise of the audience; such *intermedi* were a common element of Italian theatre at the time. Plays written by Italians, as distinct from plays in the Italian style written by Frenchmen, were greatly prized at the French court. Courtiers were among the large crowd that attended a performance of *Galathea* given in 1572 at the Collège de Navarre, and Italian players performed as part of the celebrations for the wedding of Marguerite de Valois and Henri de Navarre. Among high-ranking courtiers keen on the theatre were Anne d'Este, duchesse de Nemours, and Louis de Gonzague, duc de Nevers. In 1571 the latter put on an Italian comedy at his Parisian *hôtel* for an English ambassador.[17]

One of the first companies of Italian players to visit the French court was led by Alberto Naselli, also known as Ganassa. It put on a play in 1571 at Nogent-le-Roi as part of the celebrations for the baptism of a nephew of one of Catherine de' Medici's ladies. The troop remained in France for at least a year and was paid 500 *l.* as a reward for the pleasure they had given the king and also 'in order to help them live and to follow the king's suite'. Naselli, who came from Bergamo, created the character of 'zanni Ganassa' which eventually became the French 'Arlequin'. From France, Naselli's troop moved on to Spain, where it remained for several years. It was soon replaced in France by other companies, including the famous Gelosi.

The New Artemisia

In *L'Institution du Prince* Guillaume Budé advised Francis I on how to run his kingdom. Among the qualities he urged the king to cultivate was liberality; he was to use it frequently in order to enhance his prestige among foreign princes and also to promote the ascendancy of men of learning. The prince, Budé thought, needed to be the supreme Maecenas.[18] Francis, it seems, followed his advice: the extent and quality of his art patronage are indisputable. Henry II built less than his father, but was nonetheless a major patron of the arts. By contrast the patronage of the later Valois seems paltry. Francis II was too short-lived to achieve much. Charles IX did leave one ambitious project on the drawing board. He acquired an extensive domain on the banks of the River Andelle and called on the architect Jacques Androuet du Cerceau to build him a palace. It was to be called Charleval, and the plan, known from engravings, was to be vast. Had it been built, it would have been possible to fit Chambord into its *basse-cour*. Henry III was more interested in philosophy and science than art.

The most important art patron among the later Valois was Catherine de' Medici, who was keen to immortalise her husband (see plate 18). According to Vasari, she wanted Michelangelo to carve Henry II's equestrian statue, but the sculptor excused himself on the ground of age. The commission was given instead to Daniele Ricciarelli, alias Daniele da Volterra, who cast the horse in bronze before dying in 1566.[19] Giambologna (Jean Boulogne), a Flemish sculptor employed by the Medici in Florence, was then invited to make the king's statue, but he failed to deliver. Only the horse reached France, where it was eventually used for Louis XIII's equestrian statue in the Place Royale in Paris.[20] Catherine also commissioned a marble monument intended to contain Henry II's heart. Designed and carved by Germain Pilon and Domenico del Barbiere, it consists of an urn resting on the heads of the Three Graces, who, standing back to back, represent the theological virtues. Their long necks and small heads recall Primaticcio's nymphs at Fontainebleau, while the folds of their drapery fall with exquisite grace. The monument, originally erected in the convent of the Célestins in Paris, is now in the Louvre.

By far the most important memorial raised by Catherine to her husband was the Chapel of the Valois, a circular building that was to be added to the north transept at the abbey of Saint-Denis. The tomb of the king and queen was to fill the centre. The chapel was begun in 1563 on a design by Primaticcio, but little had been erected before his death in 1570. Two years later the work was entrusted to Jean Bullant: when he died in 1578, it was taken up by Jean-Baptiste du Cerceau. By 1585 the chapel had risen to the top of the second Order, only to be abandoned, perhaps because of the political situation. It fell into decay and was eventually demolished. In general design the chapel harked back to Italian models by Bramante and Michelangelo, but, unlike them, it contained six chapels – one for each of Henry II's sons and two for the altar and entrance – instead of four or eight. The external division into two storeys, each with its own Order, from which rises a drum supporting a dome, recalls Sangallo's design for St Peter's in Rome, which Primaticcio may have seen in 1540–1.[21]

Although the Chapel of the Valois was never completed, several monuments which were to be housed there survive. The tomb of Henry II and Catherine, designed by Primaticcio and executed by Germain Pilon, stands among other royal tombs in the basilica of Saint-Denis. Like those of Louis XII and Francis I, it carries two sets of effigies: on top, the *priants* – the king and queen, as living images in bronze, kneeling in prayer – and, below, the *gisants* or cadavers in white marble. Unlike its predecessors, however, the monument has no narrative bas-reliefs, and the mortuary chamber has been opened up to allow the *gisants* to be seen. By limiting the ornamentation, the sculpture has been enhanced. The *priants* are unconventional: Henry II, instead of holding his hands clasped as if in prayer, holds the right to his chest and stretches out the left. His gesture implies the presence of a missal resting on a prie-dieu, but these were removed and melted down during the French Revolution. It is often assumed that the *priants* represent the king and queen in their earthly existence, but Zerner has suggested that they may be already beyond death, presenting themselves to God in anticipation of His judgment. If so, the king's gesture may refer to his defence of the Catholic faith.[22]

The treatment of the *gisants* is also new: the king's pose recalls the body of Christ in a Renaissance *pietà*, while the queen seems to be asleep. Tall statues in bronze representing the cardinal Virtues stand at each corner of the monument. The base is adorned with marble reliefs of the theological Virtues, the fourth side being devoted to the first of the works of charity: giving drink to the thirsty. There is a notable contrast between these *gisants* and another pair, also of Henry II and Catherine, executed by Pilon from 1583. These are as rigid as thirteenth-century effigies, whereas those on the tomb are almost sensual. Draped in their coronation robes and crowned, the king and queen are cruelly realistic: Catherine's face is bloated over a double chin. These *gisants* were meant to flank the high altar of the Chapel of the Valois. Fixed in motionless prayer, they would have attended the round of masses which the priests of the abbey was expected to say for them.

Catherine favoured architecture above all the other arts. Both Jacques Androuet du Cerceau the Elder and Philibert de l'Orme dedicated treatises to her in the certain knowlege that she would read them.[23] De l'Orme in his

Architecture (1567) expresses admiration 'as your good judgment shows itself more and more and shines as you yourself take the trouble to project and sketch out the buildings which it pleases you to commission'. Catherine's earliest foray into architecture was at Montceaux-en-Brie, where Henry II had given her a château in 1556. It consisted of two long wings with a pavilion at each end. They were linked by a third wing with a central pavilion containing a straight staircase. The garden was an alley designed for pall-mall, a kind of croquet. After toying with the idea of giving it a wooden roof, Catherine commissioned a 'grotto' in the form of a tall two-storey building standing on a base made to look like a natural rock. A *salle* on the same level as the alley was to serve as a vantage point for people watching a game while taking refreshments. Nothing survives of this grotto, which was completed early in 1558.[24]

On 8 January 1570 de l'Orme died, having completed only a small part of his ambitious project. This was the central portion of the wing overlooking the garden: it comprised a pavilion flanked by two buildings and the foundations of the pavilions at each end. The central pavilion was decorated with Ionic columns on the ground floor and Corinthian pilasters above. An attic supported an elliptical dome with a lantern topped by a fleur-de-lys. The use of the Ionic order was an innovation that de l'Orme justified in his treatise on architecture by explaining that in antiquity it was associated with female deities, whereas the Doric was used in temples dedicated to gods. The central pavilion contained a staircase, once described as 'the largest, easiest and most admirable in all the world'. It was unfortunately destroyed in the seventeenth century. Flanking the pavilion was a single-storey building with an open portico overlooking the garden. It had a series of dormer windows of which some pairs shared a pediment adorned with reclining figures. De l'Orme's work was continued by Jean Bullant, who built the pavilion at the end of the palace's south wing.

Following her husband's death in 1559, Catherine de' Medici decided to leave the palace of the Tournelles which had become hateful to her. She moved to the Louvre with her son, Francis II, but felt the need to have a residence of her own with a large garden. The property known as the Tuileries, which Francis I had bought for his mother from the Villeroy family in 1518, seemed ideal as it lay close to the Louvre. In the Middle Ages the site had been occupied by a tile (*tuile*) factory: hence its name. Acquiring the property took five years, from 1563 to 1568. Meanwhile, the Tournelles was sold and demolished. Catherine hoped the proceeds would cover part of the cost of her new residence. To design it she turned, surprisingly, to Philibert de l'Orme, who had been dismissed as *surintendant des bâtiments* after Henry II's death. Perhaps she had been touched by his *Instruction* in which he rebutted

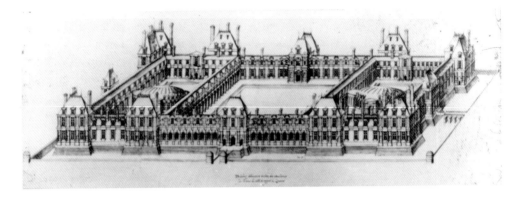

54. The Palace of the Tuileries. Engraving from Jacques Androuet du Cerceau, *Les plus excellents bastiments de France* (1576–9). This is one of two designs Philibert de l'Orme submitted. It was never completed, as Catherine abandoned the Tuileries in about 1570 although she continued to use the garden.

the charges that had been levelled against him and pleaded for fairer treatment. All that survives of the design he submitted to Catherine are two engravings by the contemporary architect Jacques Androuet du Cerceau. Those show a huge rectangular palace with five courtyards: a large one in the centre and two pairs of smaller ones at each end linked by oval halls. Serious doubt has been cast on their accuracy.[25] Blunt suggested that du Cerceau might have interpreted the engravings in a manner consistent with his own style, yet excavations carried out in 1986 revealed the foundations of a huge palace not unlike that depicted by du Cerceau. In his *Architecture* de l'Orme tells us how the queen mother with 'an admirable understanding, combined with great prudence and wisdom', had taken the trouble 'to order the organisation of her said palace as to the apartments and location of the *salles*, antechambers, chambers, *cabinets* and galleries, and to give the measurements of width and length'. She had also required de l'Orme 'to make several encrustations of different kinds of marble, gilded bronze and of minerals, like marcassite', both outside and inside.[26]

During her Grand Tour of France in 1564–5 Catherine kept in touch with her building projects, especially the Tuileries.[27] She had entrusted their supervision to a body distinct from the administration of the royal buildings, made up of some of her own ladies. The person responsible for work at the Tuileries was Marie-Catherine de Pierrevive, dame du Perron. A monumental fountain, supplied with water from Saint-Cloud, was being erected when she reported to the queen mother on work in progress. It was going reasonably well, she said, but would be going even better if money was forthcoming. She had given up hope of receiving any from the Tournelles, and warned her mistress of being cheated over supplies of wood. Madame de Pierrevive assured Catherine that a severe colic from which she was suffering had not interrupted work at the Tuileries. In May 1564 a ferry (*bac*) was laid on across the River Seine for the transportation of stone from quarries at Vaugirard and Notre-Dame-des-Champs.[28] Catherine also kept an eye on work at Fontainebleau. On 15 February she wrote to Primaticcio from Toulouse, instructing him to dig a moat around the royal apartments there and similarly at Villers-Cotterêts as a protection against a possible *coup de main*.[29] This proves that even before the 'Surprise de Meaux' Catherine feared a possible attack on the court.

De l'Orme died in January 1570 before he could complete the palace he had designed for Catherine. Two years later she halted the work. The story goes that she did so after a fortune-teller had warned her to avoid Saint-Germain if she valued her life; the Tuileries was in the parish of Saint-Germain. The tale is hard to believe, however, for Catherine continued to visit the Tuileries after she had abandoned its construction. In 1573, for example, she entertained Polish ambassadors there. It was in the garden, as we have seen, that she held an important council meeting on the eve of the Massacre of St Bartholomew's Day. It seems more likely that she gave up building the Tuileries for security reasons, as it lay outside the walls of Paris and was therefore vulnerable to attack. For whatever reason, the palace was never completed; much of it was pulled down under Louis XVI and the rest burnt down by the Communards in 1871.

According to du Cerceau, Catherine decided before 1576 to join the Tuileries to the Louvre. The first part of this link was the Petite Galerie, designed either by de l'Orme or Lescot. Only the ground floor, however, was built in part or completely in Catherine's lifetime. At some time after 1570 work also began on a pavilion at the southern end of de l'Orme's incomplete wing of the Tuileries. The architect was Jean Bullant, who evidently planned to extend the palace to the Seine whence a gallery might be run to the southern extremity of the Petite Galerie. The style of Bullant's pavilion is far less adventurous than that of de l'Orme's wing. Catherine became especially fond of the garden at the Tuileries. In 1578 this was divided along its length by six paths and across its width by eight more. The compartments in between contained clumps of trees, lawns, flowerbeds and a maze. In 1570 the famous potter Bernard Palissy was making a grotto in the garden. This has not been identified so far, but in the nineteenth century various ceramic fragments were found in the Tuileries garden, and excavations in 1986 uncovered a store for moulds as well as pottery which may have been part of the grotto or fountain.[30]

In 1572 Catherine began looking for a site for a new residence within the walls of Paris big enough to include a garden. She evidently wanted a home of her own distinct from the king's at the Louvre while remaining close enough to share in the court's life. She retained her apartment at the Louvre and divided her household accordingly, doubling its size at the same time. Between 1575 and 1583 the number of her ladies-in-waiting rose from 68 to 111, and other categories of personnel followed suit. In 1585 Catherine's household comprised nearly 800 persons, including 86 ladies-in-waiting, 25 maids of honour and 40 chambermaids and nurses.[31] Those who could not be accommodated under her roof took up lodgings close by. Catherine created a space for her new residence by sweeping away a built-up area in Paris. She began by purchasing the Hôtel Guillart near Saint-Eustache, and with papal permission moved the convent of the Filles Repenties, an order dedicated to reclaiming young girls from prostitution, to the rue Saint-Denis.[32] The convent was demolished save for the chapel. The queen mother also bought and demolished the Hôtel d'Albret and other houses nearby. On the site of these buildings Bullant built a new palace for Catherine called the Hôtel de la Reine. It has since almost entirely disappeared, but its appearance is known from engravings by Israël Sylvestre of around 1650 and a plan of about 1700. These show a central block, a courtyard and gardens. In the middle of the central block consisting of three pavilions was an arch flanked by two tall projections decorated with pilasters. A large garden attached to the Hôtel de

Prosp. de l'Hostel de Soissons.

55. *The Hôtel de la Reine.* Engraving by Israël Sylvestre, *c.* 1650 (Bibliothèque nationale de France). About 1570 Catherine de' Medici decided to build a new palace in Paris. This was built by the architect Jean Bullant on the site of several demolished buildings. Nothing survives of the palace, except a free-standing column of which the top is visible (to the right) in this engraving (and see figure 56).

la Reine included avenues of trees, flowerbeds, a lake with a jet of water, an aviary and an orangery, made of timber and 48 metres long, which could be dismantled each winter for reassembly later.[33] All that remains of the Hôtel de la Reine is a tall Doric column standing next to the Bourse du Commerce, commonly known as the Colonne de l'Horoscope. Inside the hollow fluted column is a staircase leading to a platform capable of carrying three people, topped by an iron cage. The purpose of the column has never been fully explained. According to tradition, it was used by Catherine's astrologers to scan the heavens.[34] In addition to its possible use as an observatory, the column was also a memorial to Henry II. Embedded in its fluting are various carved ornaments: fleurs-de-lys, cornucopias, shattered mirrors, torn love-knots and the letters 'C' and 'H' entwined.[35]

Outside the capital Catherine's building activities were mainly focused on two châteaux: Saint-Maur-des-Fossés and Chenonceau. She purchased the former from the heirs of Cardinal Jean du Bellay and employed de l'Orme to complete it. He submitted a design which she rejected as inadequate for the needs of her large entourage, whereupon he added two pavilions at each end of the main block. On the garden side they were joined by a terrace above a cryptoporticus. Saint-Maur was unfinished when de l'Orme died. After 1575 another architect doubled the pavilions on the garden side, raising them by two storeys and crowning them with high-pitched roofs. Two more arches were built over the cryptoporticus, which was also given a colossal pediment, but this too was never completed. The house seems not to have been habitable before the late seventeenth century.[36]

In 1560 Catherine forced Diane de Poitiers to exchange Chenonceau for Chaumont, but it was not until 1576 that she assigned large funds for building there. This consisted of two galleries on the bridge which Bullant almost certainly designed. A drawing and engraving by du Cerceau show a vast scheme that Catherine allegedly had in mind, but it may have been nothing more than a fantasy. Du Cerceau 'sometimes inserted in his book designs embodying ideas which he himself would have liked to see carried out rather than those of the actual designer of the building in question'.[37] The queen mother, however, did much to embellish the gardens at Chenonceau. She brought water from neighbouring springs, created waterfalls, laid out three parks, and set up an aviary for exotic birds and an enclosure for rare animals. She also added new stocks to the vineyard and planted mulberry trees for the rearing of silkworms. Chenonceau had its own spinning mill, and in 1582 Catherine set up a silk factory at Orléans.[38]

Catherine's building programme was expensive. In 1581 she spent 8,898 *écus* on the Hôtel de la Reine and 760 *écus* on Saint-Maur. The total cost of her buildings that year was 10,027 *écus*.[39] Such extravagance did not endear

56. The Colonne de l'Horoscope. All that remains of the Hôtel de la Reine, built by Catherine de' Medici in about 1570. Apart from standing as a memorial to the queen mother's life-long grief over her husband's death in 1559, the column may have served Catherine's interest in astrology, hence its name.

the queen mother to the Parisians, who were asked for contributions. Ronsard echoed their feelings in a poem:

Il ne faut plus que la reine batisse;
Ni que sa chaux nos trésors appetisse . . .
Peintres, maçons, engraveurs, entailleurs
Sucent l'épargne avec leurs piperies.
Mais que nous sert son lieu des Tuileries?
De rien, Moreau: ce n'est que vanité
Devant cent ans sera deshabité.[40]

(The queen must cease building;
Her lime must stop swallowing our wealth . . .
Painters, masons, engravers, stone-carvers
Drain the treasury with their deceits.
Of what use is her Tuileries to us?
Of none, Moreau: it is but vanity
It will be deserted within a hundred years.)

In 1562 Nicolas Houël, a Parisian apothecary, published a poem called *L'Histoire d'Arthemise*.[41] Artemisia II was the widow of Mausolus, prince of Caria (352–350 BC). She built the Mausoleum of Halicarnassus, one of the Seven Wonders of the Ancient World, to commemorate her grief over his death. She also vanquished his enemies and educated his children, five of whom became kings. The parallel with Catherine was obvious. Houël paid tribute to her love of architecture. 'You will find here', he writes,

the edifices, columns and pyramids that she had constructed and built both at Rhodes and Halicarnassus, which will serve as remembrances for those who reflect on our times and who will be astounded at your own buildings – the palaces at the Tuileries, Montceaux, and Saint-Maur, and the infinity of others that you have constructed, built, and embellished with sculptures and beautiful paintings.[42]

Seventy-four drawings representing events in Artemisia's life were commisioned from the painters Niccolò dell'Abbate and Antoine Caron to illustrate Houël's poem. Each of Caron's forty-four drawings has an elaborate border showing the arms of France and of the Medici with the motto: *Ardorem testantur/extincto vivere flamma.* Catherine's tears, though abundant, could not extinguish the flame of her love for Henry II. The borders also contain scythes, broken mirrors, scattered pearls and floods of tears. Among scenes represented in the drawings are the funeral procession of Mausolus, the burning of his body, the building of the temple where his ashes were deposited and the education of his son Lygdanis. Other scenes depict Artemisia's palaces and gardens. The drawings were turned into tapestries, but if any were made for Catherine, they have not survived.

Catherine was not only a builder; she was also a keen art collector. An inventory of the movables at the Hôtel de la Reine drawn up in 1589 bears witness to her collecting zeal.[43] In addition to tapestries, the contents of the ground floor included 25 hand-drawn maps of different parts of the world, more than 135 pictures and several statues. On the first floor were 341 portraits, many by Pierre and Cosme Dumoustier and Benjamin Foulon, Catherine's official painters. There were 259 pieces of Limoges ware. One room in the *hôtel* had walls covered with Venetian mirrors. Her study was lined with cupboards adorned with landscape paintings and filled with miscellaneous objects: leather fans, dolls dressed in different costumes, caskets, a stuffed chameleon, Chinese lacquer, numerous games and objects of piety. Hanging from the ceiling were seven stuffed crocodiles and countless stags' heads. Around the room were a collection of minerals, some terracotta statuettes and four miniature cannon. A cupboard between two windows was filled with books and architectural drawings. Altogether Catherine had about 4,500 books, including 776 manuscripts, but these were kept in a separate building in the rue Plâtrière. The printed books were at Saint-Maur. Finally, the inventory lists many costly fabrics, ebony furniture inlaid with ivory and 141 pieces of china, probably from Palissy's workshop.

A major item missing from the inventory is the set of eight magnificent 'Valois Tapestries', which are now in the Uffizi in Florence. They are based on six (originally eight) drawings made during Charles IX's reign by Antoine Caron and subsequently modified by another artist who added groups of full-length figures in the foreground: most are easily recognisable as Henry III and members of his family and court. In all except one, Catherine dressed in black occupies a more or less central position, albeit a modest one. Among the figures are the king's brother Alençon, the queen, Louise de Lorraine, and the Polish ambassadors who came to France in 1573. On the right of one tapestry, showing the French court leaving the château of Anet, is a group of three noblemen. All the tapestries depict festivals that took place at the court of Charles IX, notably at Fontainebleau in 1564, Bayonne in 1565 and the Tuileries in 1573, yet Charles is absent, all the identifiable portraits belonging to the next reign.

Frances Yates in her book on the tapestries argued that they were designed by Lucas de Heere, who had worked in France for Catherine during the reign of Francis II. She read into the tapestries allusions to the 'Joyeuse magnificences' of 1581 and argued that the Anet tapestry shows the court travelling to Blamont as Henri d'Anjou left France to take up his Polish crown. She identified the three noblemen in that tapestry as Louis and Henry of Nassau and Christopher of the Palatinate, who negotiated with Henry and Catherine on that occasion. Yates concluded that the tapestries were commissioned by William of Orange, made in Antwerp, and sent to Catherine as a diplomatic gift. She also suggested that Charles IX was excluded from the tapestries so as not to offend Polish sensibilities on account of his role in the St Bartholomew's Day Massacre.[44] Ingenious as it is, Yates's theory is no longer credible. Her hypothesis, as Louis de Groër has demonstrated, rests on questionable identifications, which also fail to take into account changes of fashion, notably in respect of the ruff, between 1577 and 1581. The enormous *fraises* worn by courtiers in paintings representing the Joyeuse 'magnificences' are nowhere to be seen in the tapestries. These were made in Brussels, not Antwerp, and all the evidence points to 1575 as their probable date of manufacture. They were almost certainly commissioned by Catherine herself after she had handed over power to Henry III as a lasting reminder of the magnificent festivals she had organised in the previous reign.[45]

In her will, drawn up on 5 January 1589, Catherine bequeathed her residence in Paris and half of its contents to her favourite granddaughter, Christine de Lorraine, Grand-duchess of Tuscany. About 1601 Christine received as part of her inheritance a square box containing 551 pencil portraits that Catherine had collected after her arrival in France in 1533. Some had been given to her by Francis I; the rest she had added later. For Catherine was a passionate and discriminating collector of portraits. Portraiture was a distinctively French art form in the sixteenth century, particularly drawings in black and red chalk, a technique invented in France around 1455. One of its pioneers may have been Jean Perréal, court painter to Charles VIII and Louis XII, but it was Jean Clouet and his son, François, who perfected it. Catherine preferred drawings to paintings, if only because they could be done faster. Her earliest commissions were for portraits of her children: nine were drawn in June 1548 and August 1549, and more in 1551–2. Catherine treated them as health bulletins. 'Do not fail', she wrote to Madame d'Humières on 1 June 1552, 'to require the painter who is with you to paint from life all of my said children, both my sons and daughters with the queen of Scotland as they are, without omitting anything of their faces; this can be done in crayon since it can be done faster.'[46] Albums of portraits were popular at the time, but Catherine liked to keep her drawings loose in a box so that they might be more easily rearranged or extracted to be copied. She wanted them lifelike. Thus, while admitting that a portrait of her son François by François Clouet was 'good', she did not consider it a good *likeness*. In 1569 she objected to a drawing intended to serve as model for the *teston* or silver coin of Charles IX. In addition to portraits of her children and other members of the royal family, Catherine commissioned portraits of gentlemen and ladies of the court. She wrote their names on the drawings in her big, slanting, often illegible hand before leaving this task to her secretaries. In addition to François Clouet, the queen mother employed many French artists, including Étienne, Cosme and Pierre Dumoustier. Her collection was dispersed following the extinction of the Medici dynasty in 1737. A large number of the portraits were then acquired by English visitors to Italy, notably Henry Howard, fourth earl of Carlisle, the owner of Castle Howard in Yorkshire. In 1889 they were bought by Henri d'Orléans, duc d'Aumale, who took them to his home at Chantilly, where they are now part of the glories of the Musée Condé.[47]

By comparison with architecture, painting was at a low ebb in late sixteenth-century France. Only two painters stand out as recognisable personalities: Antoine Caron and Jean Cousin the Younger.[48] Caron was not a particularly gifted artist, but his paintings are of great historical interest. They are of three kinds: allegorical subjects recalling festivities at the court of Henry III; massacre paintings; and paintings that express the astrological preoccupations of Catherine de' Medici and her circle. Caron has been described as 'the most faithful interpreter of that troubled society of the second half of the XVIth century in which the pleasures of the mind and the spectacles, festivals and games of the court stood in sharp contrast to the passions unleashed by politics and religion'.[49] He was employed by the crown in various capacities. After working at Fontainebleau, he was much concerned in the 1570s with the decoration of public ceremonies and festivals: the entry of the duc d'Anjou into Paris in 1573, the reception of the Polish ambassadors in the same year, and the 'magnificences' for the Joyeuse marriage in 1585 (see plate 19). The spirit and symbolism of such events are well conveyed in Caron's *Augustus and the Sibyl*, now in the Louvre.[50] Two large twisted columns in the centre of the painting, which are probably an allusion to the Temple in Jerusalem, are surmounted by a crown and linked by a festoon on which an eagle is perched. From the festoon hangs the motto *Pietas Augusti*. This has been identified with Charles IX's imperial device.[51] The king himself, as Augustus, is kneeling before the Tiburtine Sybil, who points to a vision of the Virgin and Child in the sky. In other words, the Most Christian King is being promised a universal empire based on the Holy Land, as in the prophecies of Guillaume Postel.

Caron is best known for his strange massacre paintings.[52] He did not invent the genre. According to the *Histoire ecclésiastique*, in 1561 three large paintings were brought to the court depicting 'the bloodiest and most inhumane executions that were once carried out in Rome under Octavius, Antoninus and Lepidus'. They were bought expensively by noblemen and shown to Huguenots by the prince de Condé. Caron's *Massacre des Triumvirs*, painted in 1566, has been called 'a veritable anthology of Roman monuments', but it does not imply a first-hand knowledge of them: Caron borrowed extensively from the engravings of Antoine Lafréry, a Franche-Comtois who had settled in Rome in 1540. The purpose behind the massacre paintings is unclear: were they condemning or glorifying violence? What is certain is that, under Henry III, Caron became closely associated with the Catholic League and that his pictures carried political messages.

CHAPTER 16

Henry III: The King and his *Mignons*

Henri duc d'Anjou was in Cracow on 15 June 1574 when news reached him of his brother's death and of his accession to the French throne: he was now king of both Poland and France. Three days later he slipped away at night with his French companions without so much as a goodbye to his Polish subjects. He rode full tilt to the Austrian border and arrived in Vienna on 24 June. The emperor entertained him splendidly, but a still grander welcome awaited him in Venice.[1] Henry III, as he now was, entered the city on board a galley escorted by the doge's gilded state barge, the *Bucintoro*, and a swarm of gondolas. During his stay in the city, he was treated to fireworks, regattas, banquets, concerts, a *Te Deum* at San Marco, balls and a visit to the Arsenal. He shopped by day, spending lavishly on jewels, glass and perfumes, and tasted the Serenissima's more dubious pleasures at night. From Venice, he travelled across northern Italy, calling at Ferrara, Mantua and Turin. In Milan he met the archbishop Carlo Borromeo, who gave him a relic of the True Cross. The future saint seems to have made a profound impression on Henry and given him a lasting taste for self-mortification.

On 6 September Henry made his entry into Lyon. One of his first acts was a public reconciliation with his brother, Alençon, and his brother-in-law, Henri de Navarre, who with the rest of the court had come down from Paris to greet him. The court remained in Lyon for several months as the political and religious situation in France deteriorated. Compounding the armed opposition of the Huguenots was a rebellion led by Henri de Montmorency-Damville, the powerful governor of Languedoc. Defying a royal command to disband his army, he issued a manifesto on 13 November in which he blamed foreigners in the king's council for the kingdom's ills. From Lyon, Henry travelled to the papal enclave of Avignon, where he took part in penitential processions, before setting off for northern France on 10 January 1575.

A matter requiring Henry's urgent attention was marriage. The future of the dynasty was at stake. In the absence of a dauphin, the crown might pass

57. *Henry III, c.* 1585. Drawing attributed to Estienne Dumoustier (Bibliothèque nationale de France). More portraits exist of Henry III than of any of his predecessors. The king kept a close watch on how he was portrayed. In this late work he seeks to project an image of sobriety and benevolence. Note the Polish-style bonnet.

either to Henry's turbulent brother, Alençon, or to Henri de Navarre, who had been forced to become a Catholic but might easily revert to his Protestant faith. As duc d'Anjou, Henry had fallen in love with Marie de Clèves, sister of the duchesse de Nevers, but in 1572 she had married the prince de Condé. So Henry turned to Louise de Vaudémont, the princess of the House of Lorraine whose beauty had dazzled him on the eve of his departure for Poland. He and Louise were married at Reims on 15 February, two days after his coronation, but no children followed. The queen soon had a miscarriage; the appalling medical treatment she received may have prevented her from ever conceiving again. Henry's political position was seriously undermined as a result.

The last Valois monarch was tall, like his father. In his youth he was also slim, but he aged prematurely, putting on weight while retaining an air of distinction. His noble and graceful bearing earned him praise, as did his refined manners. He never swore, but he could lose his temper: he once kicked a magistrate who had been accused of corruption, and in 1584 he had to be restrained from drawing his sword against one of his own councillors. The king's health was never good. A Venetian reported: 'He suffers from several serious and secret ailments, notably a continual indigestion, which is why he has been advised to drink wine.'[2] Henry was also plagued by headaches, sciatica and abscesses. In 1579 an excruciatingly painful abscess in one ear threatened his life; it burst of its own accord and left him partially deaf. The king also fell victim to scrofula, the very disease that, as king of France, he was supposed to be able to cure. He may also have contracted a venereal disease for he was treated with mercury, but physicians at the time were inclined to diagnose many ailments as syphilis: the king's trouble may have been tubercular.

It comes as no surprise that Henry III did not esteem physicians highly given the kinds of treatment they prescribed, such as inserting a foot into the jaw of a dead ox to cure an abscess. In 1574 the royal household included seventeen physicians and eighteen surgeons; ten years later the numbers had fallen to nine in each category. One treatment popular at court was bleeding. In 1574 the king and queen were bled by Léonard Botal, a barber-surgeon who wrote a treatise on the subject only to die of his own treatment. Purgation, dieting and taking the waters were also popular among courtiers. Henry consumed large amounts of Spa water, although it upset his digestion. He took it at Mézières rather than at Spa itself (which lay outside France), and had it brought by mule train.[3] The architect Baptiste du Cerceau was commissioned to build him a house at Mézières and also at Pougues, another favourite spa.[4]

Henry III was intelligent. Jacques Amyot, one of his first tutors, compared him to Francis I. Both, he thought, were bright, but Henry, unlike his grandfather, had the patience to listen, read and write.[5] At the age of sixteen his education was interrupted following his appointment as lieutenant-general of the kingdom; but he resumed his studies later. In Poland he was taught Latin and Italian by Jacopo Carbonelli. Memory interested him greatly. Giordano Bruno, whom he consulted on the subject, dedicated works to him.[6] Henry may also have attended Baïf's Academy. From February 1576 until September 1579 poets, scholars and philosophers gathered in his presence at the Louvre to discuss matters unconnected with current affairs. The Palace Academy, as these meetings were called, brought together leading writers and scholars, including Ronsard, Guy Du Faur de Pibrac, Jean-Antoine de Baïf and Philippe Desportes. Doron, the king's Latin tutor, Pontus de Tyard and Jacques Davy Du Perron were regular participants. Others who attended were Amadys Jamyn, the courtier-poet, two physicians, Miron and Cavriana, and Agrippa d'Aubigné. Ladies, too, were represented. The purpose of the meetings was to equip the king intellectually and morally for kingship. La Primaudaye, in his *Académie française*, reminded the monarch that 'republics are blessed only if kings philosophize or if philosophers govern'. Astronomy and cosmology were the main topics discussed during the first months of the Academy's existence, while later on lectures were devoted to eloquence. Although interested in astronomy, Henry did not share his mother's enthusiasm for astrology. The speeches delivered at the Academy were strongly Christian in tone, but humanism dictated the choice of topics and the ponderous classical allusions with which speakers liked to adorn their contributions.[7]

Henry combined a love of gossip with a malicious sense of humour. He spoke of Henri de Condé, a notoriously dull man, as 'the Hector of the Huguenots', and of his own disaster-prone brother, Alençon, as 'my brother, the conqueror'.[8] A born orator, he viewed speech-making as an essential tool of government, particularly when popular support was needed. His speeches were praised even by his severest critics. According to Saint-Sulpice, everyone was spellbound by Henry's opening address to the Estates-General in 1576.[9] A deputy of the clergy thought it was 'the finest and most learned speech ever heard, not only from a king but ... from any of the best orators in the world'.[10] Despite his natural eloquence, Henry always prepared his speeches with care: a member of his entourage would make a draft which the king would then edit meticulously.

A legend, largely promoted by the novels of Alexandre Dumas, has created an image of Henry III as a monarch interested only in dancing, small lapdogs and games of cup-and-ball (*bilboquet*); in reality he was serious-minded. He was not content simply to exercise authority, he also wanted to know where it came from. Travelling to Poland, he invited the humanist Pibrac to share his carriage and listened to him discourse on Aristotle's *Politics*.[11] In 1576 Louis

Le Roy offered him a collection of passages from the same work. The king also commissioned political writings, such as Pontus de Tyard's *Maximes d'Estat pour le gouvernement et la conservation des empires et royaumes*.[12] Henry's critics regarded him as a disciple of Machiavelli.[13] He was certainly familiar with the latter's ideas. According to D'Avila, each day after dinner the king would read political texts, including the *Discourses* and *The Prince*, both works were in his library. It does not follow, however, that Machiavelli shaped his policies.[14] There is evidence that in 1573, on his way to Poland, Henry called on the landgrave of Hesse, who denounced the Massacre of St Bartholomew's Day. When Henry 'defended himself with the arguments of Machiavelli', the landgrave flew into a rage, saying that no account could be taken of someone who relied on such unChristian ideas.[15] History, too, interested the king. He owned a copy of the memoirs of Philippe de Commynes, given to him by his mother, who believed that much could be learnt by comparing France's present troubles with the War of the Public Weal under Louis XI.[16]

Contemporaries were dismayed by Henry's love of desk work. His seriousness stood in sharp contrast to the childish pranks of Charles IX. Henry attended to much state business himself in spite of having many secretaries (168 in 1584). He would rise before daybreak to reply to letters, requests and dispatches. On one visit to court Duplessis-Mornay noted: 'Today the king, since three in the morning, has done nothing but write, and no one has entered his room.'[17] In 1582 he had a window inserted into a wall at the Louvre separating his *cabinet* from the *salle* where the council met, presumably to keep an eye on its discussions in readiness to intervene whenever necessary.

Secretiveness was meat and drink to Henry. In Poland he made sure that his apartment had private rooms and concealed staircases. He said that he was following his mother's example. Following his return to France, he ordered his officials to keep him informed of all that was happening in their respective provinces. They were to be very discreet in bringing him up to date. At the Louvre he would gather a few close friends at dawn to discuss matters of state with them before the *Conseil des affaires* met. He was also in the habit of consulting his mother as they walked together in the gardens of the Louvre or Tuileries out of earshot of any would-be eavesdroppers. He ordered the municipal authorities to build a high wall along the Tuileries garden to stop anyone peering into it.[18]

Unlike his predecessors, Henry travelled little. He spent most of his time in Paris, but it would be a mistake to imagine that he never left the court. As it settled more or less in Paris, close bonds were forged between it and the upper échelons of Parisian society. These were mainly members of the *noblesse de robe*: wealthy magistrates. Many acquired offices at court, and whereas in the past magistrates had been noted for their austerity, they now took to wearing fancy clothes in imitation of those worn at court, and to decorating their homes. Henry liked to call on them. He was allegedly so fond of Madame de Boulencourt, a wealthy widow, that he called her 'mother'. She kept a room for him in her house which he called his *chambre de menus-plaisirs*. Court and Parisian high society mingled on such festive occasions as the Foire Saint-Germain, where luxury goods were displayed on brightly lit stalls and gambling booths were set up. By this time France's two capitals, as I have described them, had virtually merged. This may have been to their mutual advantage, but there was another side to the coin. The court's extravagance, which in the past had been largely hidden from the lower orders of Parisian society, now became visible to all. This contributed to the court's growing unpopularity.[19]

Henry firmly believed that he knew best how to govern. His authority rested on a fount of knowledge that was an intrinsic part of his majesty. He did not think much of some of the advice given to him by courtiers. He quarrelled with the duc de Nevers as early as 1574 because the latter had criticised his handing over of fortresses in northern Italy to the duke of Savoy. He thought even less of attempts by his subjects to influence his policies. In a speech to the Estates-General in 1576 he declared plainly that mere subjects were simply not equipped to express an opinion on any aspect of government. The *vulgaire*, as he called them, lacked any perception of the 'truth of things'.[20]

Henry III was an emotional being. He was sometimes close to despair, yet never let go of his authority. In a speech to the first Estates-General of Blois, he declared: 'I know that one day I shall have to account to God for my actions, but I also want to protest before Him in this assembly that I intend to reign as a good, just and lawful king over the subjects He has entrusted to my care.'[21] His authoritarianism was tempered by kindness. Though angered by courtiers who fought duels, he treated them leniently. 'He was so kind,' wrote Brantôme, 'that he did not want to punish them harshly, for he loved his nobility.'[22] Henry raised money for the Hôtel Dieu to help it cope with a flood of patients, and arranged for poor people, driven into Paris by hunger, to be given food and money in return for cleaning out the city's moat.[23]

As duc d'Anjou, Henry had been reputed to be an excellent soldier. Following his accession, however, he appeared to lose interest in war. He was criticised for taking part in religious processions instead of fighting the Huguenots. He may have wanted to avoid exposing his kingdom to the perils that had followed Francis I's defeat and capture in 1525, but he also believed that the religious division of France would be more effectively healed by peaceful means than by war. Yet he was no coward: he could still fight if the situation so required, as he showed at the end of his reign.

Though not keen on sport, Henry did sometimes hunt and play tennis. In June 1581 Saint-Sulpice was told: '[The king] does more exercise than he has ever done and chases two or three stags in a day.'[24] In November 1583 Catherine de' Medici reported: 'The king, my lord and son, being fit and well, thank God, went hunting near Senlis five or six days ago.'[25] The duc de Joyeuse also persuaded him to hawk. 'For the past eight days,' wrote René de Lucinge, the ambassador of Savoy, on 20 May 1586, 'His Majesty has decided to become a huntsman. He has sent for greyhounds from all the lords of this court to go hunting and have fun.'[26] The king employed numerous *veneurs* and *fauconniers,* and jealously protected his hunting rights.[27] He acquired dogs and birds from time to time. An agent, sent to England to acquire dogs for him, was offered animals of all kinds. This prompted Henry to write: 'He is mad, but as long as he brings me the dogs that I have asked for, he can be as mad as he likes.'[28]

Henry had been taught by Italian masters of arms in his youth. He owned Lorino's manual on fencing and took part in mock combats.[29] From time to time he played tennis or pall-mall.[30] He also liked card games, but gave up gambling for good after losing 30,000 *écus* in 1579. Two years later he expelled the marquis d'O from court for gambling to excess. He also banned card games in his chamber.[31] In August 1585, according to Pierre de L'Estoile, 'The king began to carry a cup-and-ball in his hand, even in the street and played with it as do small children. And the dukes of Épernon and Joyeuse and several other courtiers followed suit, as did noblemen, pages, lackeys and young people of all sorts.'[32] *Canivets* – illuminations cut out of manuscripts and pasted on to coloured backgrounds – were another of Henry's pastimes.

Lapdogs became one of Henry's fads after his return from Poland. He once carried one into a council meeting, and such a dog was leaping around his feet as a Venetian ambassador took formal leave of him: Henry handed the ambassador the dog as a parting gift. In November 1575 he and the queen toured the capital in a coach, picking up small dogs as they went. They visited convents and upset the nuns by taking their pets.[33] There were kennels at the château of Madrid, and Henry also kept small dogs known as *turquets* in his apartment. In 1586 there were at least three hundred in the royal household. Many ladies at court, including Catherine de' Medici, kept them. The effigy of Valentine Balbiani, wife of Chancellor Birague, shows her reclining with a small dog at her side. Ronsard and other poets composed verses on the death of Barbiche, Madame de Villeroy's favourite pet.

Henry III's Art Patronage

Henry III was more interested in theatre, music and dancing than in architecture or painting. He was never responsible for any project comparable to those conceived or realised by his mother, which serves to explain why Jacques Androuet du Cerceau dedicated his *Plus excellents bastiments de France* (1576 and 1579) to Catherine rather than Henry. In 1578 a Venetian ambassador wrote: 'The king does not like building; first, the wars have cost him too much, then he prefers to give money to his servants so that they themselves may build.'[34] But the king did realise that his prestige depended on the proper maintenance of his official residences. Thus, he enlarged the Château-Neuf at Saint-Germain-en-Laye, carried out urgent repairs at Fontainebleau, and in Paris continued work on the south wing of the Louvre. Henry also wanted a house in the country to which he might retire for a week or so at a time. For this purpose, he purchased in September 1576 a small château at Ollainville within easy distance of Paris. It consisted of a *corps de logis* in the shape of a horseshoe surrounded by moats. Some improvements were carried out there between 1579 and 1585. Use of the property was strictly private: the king received no one there, much to the annoyance of foreign ambassadors. He eventually gave Ollainville to his queen; it was demolished in 1831.

Henry III's most important architectural achievement was the Pont-Neuf in Paris. The idea of a bridge linking the bourg Saint-Germain with the right bank of the Seine can be traced back to the reign of Charles V, but Henry was the first to take it up seriously. A commission appointed by him in November 1577 drew up a plan, the architects concerned being Baptiste Androuet du Cerceau and Pierre des Illes, and the first stone was laid in the presence of the king and queen on 31 May 1578. The funeral of the *mignons* Caylus and de Maugiron took place on the same day and it was rumoured that Henry planned to call the bridge the 'Bridge of Tears'.[35] A grand decorative scheme proposed by the commission survives in an oil painting at the Musée Carnavalet in Paris. This shows two triumphal arches recalling the Arch of Septimius Severus in Rome, a cluster of obelisks and a central pavilion at the end of the Île-de-la-Cité where the two halves of the bridge met. These may not have been purely formal features. As the historian Sauval suggested, they would have impeded a rebellious march on the Louvre. Like the bridges of ancient Rome, the Pont-Neuf was conceived as a monument of royal and civic prestige; it was not intended that part of the cost should be recouped by building houses for leasing on the bridge, but this noble resolve was soon abandoned. After an interruption due to political unrest, the bridge was completed as originally intended, without houses, in 1606 by Henry IV.[36] All that survives of the original structure are turrets decorated with bearded

58. *Project for the Pont-Neuf in Paris* (Musée Carnavalet, Paris). The first stone for the Pont-Neuf was laid in Henry III's presence in 1578. The bridge took thirty years to complete with an interruption between 1588 and 1599 caused by the religious wars. It was inaugurated in 1607.

masks, possibly by Germain Pilon. The building of the Pont-Neuf completed a process begun by the transformation of the Louvre under Francis I and his successors as the principal royal residence in Paris: it set in motion the expansion of the western side of Paris by the bourgeoisie and aristocracy which was greater than in any other direction. Henry III, it has been claimed, 'decisively altered the social geography of Paris'.[37]

Other public buildings put up by Henry III were the new porte Saint-Antoine, built in 1584 in the rustic style by Thibaut de Métezeau, a monumental porch flanked by vertical gun barrels at the Arsenal, and the Horloge du Palais with its allegorical decorations by Germain Pilon on the outside of the Tour carrée of the Palais de la Cité. Outside the capital, another building, begun by Henry III and completed by Henry IV, was a lighthouse – the phare de Cordouan – at the estuary of the River Gironde.

Henry III also sponsored the building of a large number of churches and monasteries in Paris. He may have done so not only as an expression of piety, but also to answer critics who accused him of hypocrisy or worse. The buildings included the church of Saint-Roch, the doubling in size of the collegiate church of Saint-Honoré, the addition of four bays to the nave of Saint-Nicolas-des-Champs, the continuation of work at Saint-Eustache, the

59. The Tour de l'Horloge, Paris. Among the few remains of the medieval palace on the Île-de-la-Cité is this clock donated by King Charles V in 1370. It was the first public timepiece in Paris, and in 1585 under Henry III it was set into a rich ornamental frame by the sculptor Germain Pilon.

transept of Saint-Gervais, the choir of Saint-Médard, the nave and transept of Saint-Étienne-du-Mont towards which the king gave 2000 *écus,* and the first church of Saint-Jacques du Haut Pas. Two porches inspired by de l'Orme's designs were added to the churches of Saint-Germain l'Auxerrois and Saint-Nicolas-des-Champs. The reign also saw a multiplication of religious houses in Paris. Henry founded the house of the Feuillants in the rue

60. The rood screen in the church of Saint-Étienne-du-Mont, Paris. Henry III was a notable benefactor of several churches and religious houses in Paris, including this one. The rood screen with its two spiral staircases was begun in 1530 and completed in 1545 when Pierre Nicolle was paid to erect balustrades *à l'antique* linking the columns.

Saint-Honoré alongside that of the Capuchins set up by his mother. Both king and queen mother contributed to the rebuilding of the choir of the church of the Cordeliers in the faubourg Saint-Jacques. The first stone of the Jesuit monastery in the rue Saint-Jacques was laid by Henry in 1582.

Henry III's favourite architect was Baptiste Androuet du Cerceau, who became one of the Forty-five, the bodyguard that followed him everywhere. According to the duc de Nevers, Baptiste designed more monasteries, churches, oratories and altars than any architect had done in France for the past fifty years. In September 1578 he succeeded Lescot as architect of the Louvre, and on 15 October was appointed architect of all the royal buildings in France. He also worked for some of the king's favourite courtiers. In addition to work on the Louvre in 1580–1, he was commissioned to build the first storey of the Chapel of the Valois at Saint-Denis begun by Bullant in 1563. Between 1583 and 1586 he was commissioned by the king to put up several ecclesiastical buildings. These included a monastery for the Hieronymites, one for lay penitents in the Bois de Boulogne, and a third on the site of the Tournelles. He enlarged a house owned by the queen mother at Chaillot and worked for Henri and Anne de Joyeuse. He was a Protestant, however, and in 1585 was forced to leave the court. The king nevertheless continued to employ him.

The Order of the Holy Ghost

Soon after his accession Henry planned to create a new order of chivalry dedicated to the Holy Ghost.[38] He was especially devoted to it as his birthday coincided with Pentecost, which was also the anniversary of his election as king of Poland and of his accession to the French throne. In Venice he had been shown the statutes of an Order of the Holy Ghost that had been founded in 1352 by Louis of Taranto. In the letters patent of 31 December 1578 setting up his own order, Henry asked God 'to grant us the grace of soon seeing all our subjects reunited in the Catholic faith and living for the future in good fellowship and concord under the observance of our laws and in obedience to us and our successors'. While hoping that this would enlist God's help in solving the political problems that faced him, Henry also aimed to tie the French nobility more closely to his person. The Order of St Michael, created by Louis XI, could no longer fulfil that role, having been devalued by an excessive number of creations under Charles IX: it had become known as 'every animal's collar' (*le collier à toutes bestes*). To earn respect, the new order was restricted at first to a total of one hundred knights, who were required to dedicate their lives to 'the defence of our faith and religion and of our person and state'. The order was at first to be funded by the church, but this was vetoed by the papacy. It was inaugurated at the Grands Augustins in Paris in January 1579. Unlike the knights of St Michael, the knights of the Holy Ghost did not simply hold a title: they were consulted by the king and were expected to serve him. They were called to his chamber each day at 7 a.m. and again at 2 p.m. Two were to be at his side during dinner.[39]

The Mignons

The hope of humanists that Henry III would embody the platonic ideal of the philosopher king surrounded by councillors qualified to guide him along the path of virtue was soon dashed. Instead of relying on men of learning and experience, Henry began by placing his trust in a group of young men who came to be known as *mignons*. In fifteenth-century France the word *mignon* meant simply 'companion'; it only acquired its pejorative meaning about the middle of the sixteenth century. Henry's *mignons* in 1574 were Charles de Balsac, known as Entraguet, Henri de Saint-Sulpice, Jacques de Lévis-Caylus, François de Saint-Luc, François d'O and Paul de Saint-Mégrin. They

all belonged to families that had served the monarchy as provincial adminis-
trators and came from different parts of France. Broadly of the same generation as the king, they had served under him in the third religious war and had
followed him to Poland.

The *mignons* copied the king's dress and manners. Henry III was a fop. He
wore clothes covered with gold embroidery, precious stones and pearls; his
linen was of the finest quality and his hair elaborately styled. He was also
obsessively fastidious. No one looking slovenly was admitted to his chamber.
Letters written by Henry to his *mignons* are full of expressions of love.
Describing himself as their 'master', he urges them to love him as dearly as he
loves them. A letter to Saint-Sulpice bears the sign (:S:+), used by lovers to
express the strength of their attachment.[40] Henry also gave the *mignons* affec-
tionate nicknames: Caylus, for example, was 'Petit Jacques', 'Petit' or 'Jacquet'.
Writing to Souvré in September 1577, the king tells of his burning desire to
see him soon. Such language may strike us as odd, but such hyperbole was
fashionable in sixteenth-century France. The *mignons*, for their part, assured
the king of their willingness to sacrifice their lives for him.[41]

Henry III's court was too large to accommodate all of its members under
one roof. As it settled more or less permanently in Paris during the late 1560s,
many courtiers acquired residences there. Previously only the wealthiest families, such as the Guises or Montmorencys, had Parisian *hôtels*. These stood
near the old palace of the Tournelles. When the court moved to the Louvre
in 1559, however, other courtiers began to look for accommodation nearby.
By the early 1570s a quarter of them lived near the Louvre, another quarter
in the Marais and the rest on the left bank of the Seine in the faubourg Saint-
Germain. Occasional visitors to the court rented apartments on the left bank
of the Seine or on the bridges. High-ranking courtiers who owned *hôtels* in
Paris sometimes also put up at the Louvre.[42]

In 1577 the first generation of *mignons* were joined by Anne de Joyeuse and
Jean-Louis de La Valette. Joyeuse was seventeen at the time. He became a
gentleman of the chamber in 1577, *chambellan* in 1579, and, finally, *Premier
gentilhomme de la chambre*. La Valette belonged to a noble family from
Guyenne. He had been introduced to the future Henry III at the siege of La
Rochelle in 1573. From 1579 three *mignons* – Joyeuse, La Valette and d'O –
formed an inner group enjoying the king's special favour. They served him at
table, accompanied him to parties at various private houses in Paris, and formed
a protective shield around his person. The rise of Joyeuse and La Valette,
known as the *archimignons*, was partly aimed at marginalising Henri duc de
Guise.[43] As an English envoy noted, Guise received no military command
after March 1581; nor was he received by the king in private or given any
benefice to help him pay off his debts. In 1581 Joyeuse and La Valette were

61. *Courtiers on their Way to the Louvre* (Bibliothèque nationale de France). This drawing suggests that courtiers occasionally gave each other lifts. The one in front with his Polish bonnet bears a striking resemblance to the king.

suddenly created dukes and given precedence over the other nobles at court, save princes of the blood and representatives of foreign sovereign houses. La Valette became duc d'Épernon. The two men were also appointed in January 1582 to the office of *Premier gentilhomme de la chambre*, given the right of direct access to the king's chamber, and allowed to eat at his table. In January 1585 a court regulation created a distinction between them and the other gentlemen of the chamber, known as *gentilshommes ordinaires de la chambre*. Already on 8 December 1584 the English ambassador had noted that the king had undertaken 'to reform marvellously' his household by granting access to his private apartment only to Joyeuse and Épernon while the rest of the courtiers were distributed among three antechambers leading to the *cabinet*: mere noblemen in the first, 'men of quality' in the second, and princes and knights of the Order of the Holy Ghost in the third. The *archimignons* were allowed to enter the king's *cabinet* at any time, even when he was not there; a rare privilege indeed. They could attend his *coucher* and enter his *cabinet* as he was getting dressed, all other courtiers having to wait in the antechambers until Henry was ready.[44]

Joyeuse and Épernon became extremely wealthy as a result of gifts from the king. Joyeuse received 1,200,000 *l.* on the occasion of his marriage. Épernon was given the same amount as well as a pearl necklace worth 300,000 *l.* when he married. The revenues of the two men in the 1580s have been estimated at 2,500,000 *l.* and 3,000,000 *l.* respectively. Épernon's fortune, according to his secretary, amounted to 1,300,000 *écus* in silver plate, jewels, furniture and land.[45] Henry III also brought the *archimignons* into his family by arranging marriages for them. Joyeuse married the queen's half-sister on 24 September 1581. Épernon married Marguerite de Foix-Candale, the granddaughter of the Constable of Montmorency and niece of Montmorency-Damville, on 23 August 1587.[46]

The king expected the *archimignons* to build up a clientele on whose loyalty and support he could depend. The policy seems to have paid off. In 1585 Joyeuse told the Savoyan ambassador, Lucinge, that he had made many friends who could be counted upon to turn up with four hundred noblemen each; but self-interest – the desire to clear their debts – seems to have been the main incentive for serving the *archimignons*. Henry III not only wanted to create a new court nobility devoted to the crown, but also to undermine the duc de Guise. The clienteles formed by the *archimignons* were not identical. Whereas Joyeuse recruited his clients at court or in his various *gouvernements*, Épernon drew his exclusively from Gascony, Guyenne or Béarn. Some were his cousins, others soldiers. He paid them 200 to 300 *écus* per annum. Several entered the king's household. Lucinge noted in 1585 that one reason for the Catholic League's revolt (see below p. 328) was that 'the court was being filled with Gascons'.[47] Many of Épernon's clients became gentlemen of the chamber between 1580 and 1583. Their attachment to Épernon, however, proved fickle. In March 1587 Lucinge reported that the duke had been abandoned by most of them; the rest seemed likely to desert him at the first downward turn in his fortunes.[48]

Among clients recruited by Épernon in south-west France were the famous Forty-five (*Quarante-cinq*): gentlemen of the chamber, who also constituted the king's personal bodyguard. They were under orders to watch over his person day and night, and unlike the other gentlemen of the chamber, who served by quarter, they served all the year round. The Forty-five took an oath 'to guard and recognise no one but the king' and were handsomely remunerated: they were paid 1,200 *écus* per annum and 600 *l.* for their equipment. Catherine de' Medici thought them too expensive and in 1586 she urged

Henry to disband them, but the king would not hear of it. He even promised them a New Year gift of 400 *écus*. The *Cent gentilshommes*, who had traditionally protected the king's person, resented their displacement by the Forty-five and many joined the League.[49]

In addition to controlling the court, the *archimignons* also acquired considerable authority over the armed forces. Joyeuse became Admiral of France in May 1582 and Épernon was appointed Colonel-general of the infantry in September 1581. His office, which was for life, gave him control of the infantry and the ability to form a large network of military *fidélités*. As governors of Metz and Piedmont, Épernon and his brother controlled 41 per cent of the kingdom's garrisons. Henry III's aim was to deprive the Guises not only of their government offices, but also of their provincial power bases.[50]

The Court Reformed

Henry III stamped his personality on his court. Though convivial, he hated crowds. He also disliked travel, preferring to reside mostly in Paris or Blois, except for breaks, lasting a week or so, at Ollainville, Saint-Germain, Vincennes or Madrid. When Henry was at Ollainville the court became a court without a king.[51] A more static court facilitated the introduction of a stricter etiquette similar to that of the imperial court, which Henry had been able to observe on his return from Poland.

In 1574 Henry III decided that his *lever* would henceforth be private. All but three or four people were denied access to his chamber. The king also had a barrier erected around his table and insisted on being served by gentlemen of the chamber and on their doing so hatless. No one was to talk during his meals. Many courtiers, upset by these innovations, left the court in disgust and Henry had to backtrack: the ban on their entering his chamber or observing silence during his meals was lifted and the barrier around his table removed. But the innovations returned in 1578 in the form of new regulations.[52] Two features were new: the king's timetable was fixed with clock-like precision, and admission to his chamber was given a strict order of precedence – courtiers could only approach him in carefully regulated stages. The day began in the king's *cabinet*. While valets and a barber attended to his toilette, princes, great officers of the crown and councillors entered the chamber. Once Henry had signalled his readiness, members of the *conseil des affaires* joined him in the *cabinet* while the gentlemen of the chamber entered the antechamber. After the king had been handed his cloak and sword, he walked to the chapel accompanied by all the lords. In 1582 additions were made to the regulations of 1578. A dozen courtiers were invited to share a round table with the king every Sunday, and the chief steward was instructed to lay two

23

REPRESENTATION DE l'orgueil de Henry de Valois, enuers la Noblesse de France, au commencement de son retour de Poulongne.

il auoit apprife en peu de temps, fe rendre vn demy Dieu, & fembler que les Princes & Seigneurs du Royaume ne fuffent dignes de l'approcher: dont les plus aduifez fe fcandalizerent, & les autres n'y prindrent garde de tant pres, difans que c'eftoient des petites nouueautez qu'il auoit apporté de Poulongne. D'autre cofté fes Mignons, defquels entre autres eftoiět Quelus, & Maugiron, difoient que c'eftoit bien

62. Henry III behind his barrier. Engraving from *Vie et faits notables de Henry de Valois* (Bibliothèque municipal de Lyon). Disliking crowds, Henry III tried to gain more privacy by having a barrier erected around his table at meal times. This proved so unpopular with courtiers that it had to be removed, but was restored later.

places at the end of the king's table for Joyeuse or Épernon. Such favouritism was not new, but never before had actual names been written into a court ruling. Henry also insisted on his officials committing themselves to his service alone; he did not want them to serve his brother as well. Access to the sovereign was also meticulously controlled: he was only to be approached by

63. Henry III dining 'en public' (Folger Library, Washington). Drawing in Richard Cook's account of his stay in France in 1584. The king is seated, his back to a fire, flanked by two armed halbardiers. Sharing his table are an ecclesiastic and a nobleman, possibly one of the *archimignons*, Joyeuse or Épernon. A procession of servants is bringing food to the table as choristers sing and courtiers, wearing huge ruffs, stand and talk.

persons whom he had invited and they were to be preceded by Swiss guards; no one was to accompany Henry unless invited to do so. His agenda for the day was to be communicated to courtiers after dinner by the captain of the guards, and access to his chamber was controlled 'to avoid the confusion that is seen each day in the said chamber where each person wishes to enter freely without the ushers being able to stop him'. Henceforth, only the gentlemen of the chamber on duty were to be given the key to the room; no one was to enter the *cabinet* unless invited to do so.

In January 1585 the king's apartment was reshaped and the circulation of courtiers within it controlled. The *chambre* was now reached through an enfilade of four rooms: *salle, antichambre, chambre d'état* and *chambre de l'audience*. All who attended on the king were to wear a suit and bonnet of black velvet and a gold chain. The *lever* and *coucher* still took place in the chamber, as did meetings of the council, but Henry no longer slept there, preferring to share the queen's bed. According to the historian, De Thou, the antechambers were an English idea. The 1585 regulations also restored the barrier around the king's table, which was now set up in the antechamber. Responsibility for the smooth running of the court was entrusted to Guillaume Pot for whom the office of *Grand Maître des cérémonies de France* was created on 2 January 1585. He had to see that courtiers were correctly placed in the various ceremonies, and to keep a list of them.

At a time of endemic civil unrest, security became crucially important. Henry III lived in a climate of fear: fear of disease and of assassination, in particular by poisoning. His father and elder brothers had died tragically. The Huguenots had attempted to capture Francis II at Amboise in 1560 and Charles IX at Meaux seven years later. Several foreign princes suffered violent deaths: William of Orange was assassinated by a Spanish agent in 1584; Mary Stuart was executed by command of Queen Elizabeth in 1587. Fear of poisoning was omnipresent. The king's food and drink were tasted before being presented to him and it was for reasons of security that Henry usually ate alone.[53]

The court's population in 1577 was estimated at eight thousand and the number of domestic servants at between 1,500 and two thousand. An English ambassador noted in 1575 that courtiers quarrelled each day outside the king's door.[54] One drew a dagger inside the king's chamber. So far policing the court had been left to the baron de Senecey, but he was often absent, so in February 1575 he was replaced by François du Plessis-Richelieu, the father of the future cardinal, who was given the new title of *Grand Prévôt de l'Hôtel*. He had a staff of ten lawyers and seventy-eight halberdiers. Every Saturday morning he was to report to the king after making a list of the week's misdemeanours. The captains of the guard also helped to maintain order. When the king was at mass, they had to ensure that the congregation knelt devoutly and desisted from chatter. During Henry's meals the captains were to prevent people from approaching his table: following its removal, they were to sort the people who wished to meet the king from the rest. Archers, stationed in the halls and on staircases, were to prevent mischief by pages and lackeys, and to stifle any blasphemous talk.

Troops attached to Henry III's household numbered 2,650 in 1579. They comprised a company of *archers de la Porte*, two bands of *Cent gentilshommes*, four companies of one hundred *gardes du corps*, another of *Cent Suisses* and a regiment of *gardes françaises*. The *Capitaine de la Porte*, who kept the keys to king's residence, had to guard it at all times. The captains of the *Cent gentilshommes* were to accompany Henry everywhere with twenty-five men. The *gardes françaises*, consisting of twelve companies of between fifty and two hundred men, were based in Paris. According to De Thou, Henry III strengthened his guards after 1585 as popular discontent mounted; he ceased to wander about the streets of Paris alone as he had been in the habit of doing.

Henry waited a few years before carrying out major changes to his household staff. The duc de Guise retained the largely honorific office of *Grand maître*. He had to keep an up-to-date roll of the staff and assemble them on the fourth day of the first month of each quarter. He was to be nearest the king at his meals, and was allowed his own table with some twenty guests. The office of *Grand chambellan* was likewise retained by the duc de Mayenne, who was theoretically responsible for the king's chamber. He, too, had a table to which twelve gentlemen of the chamber were invited. The office of *Premier gentilhomme de la chambre* was shared by Retz and Villequier from 1574 until 1582, when the former lost it for good. From 1578 to 1581 a third person, François d'O, called himself *Premier gentilhomme de la chambre* in addition to being *Maître de la garde-robe*. The *Premier maître d'hôtel* commanded an annual wage of 3,000 *l.* in 1580. He was responsible for the household's finances and was its effective head, as the *Grand maître* was often absent. Other important officials were the *Grand écuyer* and *Grand maréchal des logis*.

An important administrative development during Henry's reign concerned the secretaries of state. A regulation of 1585 provided for their full participation in the deliberations of the *Conseil d'état* and *Conseil privé*. Until 1588 they continued to take their oath of office before the chancellor, but in that year they began taking it before the king: this was after Henry had sacked his ministerial team. Villeroy, who served under five kings as secretary of state, states in his memoirs that he was never more than an executive officer. In fact, he and other secretaries are known to have taken decisions. A regulation of 1588 forbade new secretaries of state from opening packages containing dispatches or from writing letters under their own signature, but in fact there was no stopping their rise. Villeroy was truly a minister, so much so that the leaders of the League in 1588 did not believe that the king could do without him. The secretaries used to receive demands for favours and gifts and drew up lists of beneficiaries for the king to sign. They employed a large staff who, in addition to their normal remuneration, hoped to be found places at court. Some took employment in the households of great nobles, which could prove embarrassing at a time of civil unrest.[55]

Henry was anxious to end the monopoly of offices at court which some noble families had enjoyed during his mother's rule; he wanted to bring the monarchy into closer touch with the nobility as a whole. The number of court offices held by noblemen doubled accordingly to about 1,000, compared with some 500 under Charles IX. A total of between 650 and 700 served successively as *gentilshommes de la chambre*, as compared with 157 under Henry II and only 99 under Charles IX. In 1585 it was laid down that they should accompany the king from 6 a.m., and be at his disposal from 2 p.m. until supper time. Under Charles IX, the number of gentlemen of the chamber had been fixed at 48 (or 12 per quarter). Under Henry it rose to 128 in 1574, 274 in 1580, 300 in 1582 and 380 in 1583. The king then reduced the number, partly as an economy measure and partly because he no longer needed to compete for clients with his brother, Anjou, following his death in 1584.

Richard Cook's Account of Henry III's Court

Oddly enough, it is to an Englishman, Richard Cook, that we owe one of the most vivid accounts of the court of France in the 1580s. He had accompanied Sir Henry Cobham, the English resident ambassador in the early 1580s, and may have stayed on under Sir Edward Stafford. His account, written between November 1583 and September 1584, was presented to the Earl of Derby when he visited Paris in February 1585.

Cook begins by describing the three royal councils: the *Grand Conseil*, the *conseil privé* and the *conseil du cabinet*. The *Grand Conseil*, a purely judicial body, met three or four miles from the court, except in a town large enough to accommodate the whole court. The king never sat in it. The *conseil privé*, which had been set up to deal with affairs of state, had lost some of its prestige after Francis I created the *conseil du cabinet*. Its members were chosen by the king, who attended it almost every day. They dealt with affairs of state, financial matters and 'particular men's causes'. Certain days were reserved for certain types of business. The council was chaired by the chancellor, who was assisted by four clerks and three secretaries of state. Each secretary was expected to report any news reaching him to the king and council; he was also to keep a record of royal gifts and of petitions addressed to the king. The *conseil du cabinet*, also called the *conseil des affaires*, was created by Francis I because he did not wish to impart his 'weightiest affairs' to a body as large as the privy council. Each morning, therefore, following his *lever*, he would talk about such matters 'to some such only as pleased His Majesty to call thereunto'.

A typical day in Henry III's life is described by Cook as follows:

When the king is ready to rise, which is ordinarily between six and seven, he calleth unto one that lieth near unto him to give him his night gown and a pair of little buskins lined with soft and very fine leather, and when he retireth himself into another chamber where divers valets do attend to make him ready, and being set down before the fire, one of the valets of his chamber bringeth him his doublet, another gartereth his hose, the third, while he is thus making himself ready, kenneth and trimmeth his head and the fourth plucketh on his shoes. When these valets have all done, the king riseth out of his chair and, standing by the fire, one of the gentlemen of his chamber bringeth and presenteth unto him a certain bouillon or broth the which he receiveth in his hand and suppeth it up without any spoon. After this he showeth himself ready to speak with all men that be in his chamber. But before any other do enter, and during the time that he is making himself ready, the three secretaries ordinarily first come in and such other only as be of the Council of the cabinet, there every secretary according to his several department do read and report unto his majesty all such news as be sent to the court . . .. When the secretaries have done, the usher is commanded to open the door of the presence, and while the nobility do enter and then attend, his Majesty after he hath heard a little short mass in his cabinet and after the said mass broken his fast, as they term it there '*en bon escient*', he cometh out into the presence, and, having there devised awhile among his noblemen and with those of his council, he goeth publicly to the chapel of Bourbon accompanied with the queen and with the queen mother and with many other princes and nobility to his high mass. So soon as he is descended down into the castle yard, he is there received by his guard of Swiss to the number of three score, who march before him three and three, everyone carrying a halberd on his shoulder, and two of these Swiss sound upon the taber and the fife the stroke of marching in battle after the manner of their own country, not ceasing till the king be entered into the chapel, then as well these Swiss as all the rest of king's guard making a lane between the castle gate and the chapel where the king is entered to stand and attend his return. The king being at his high mass, the greatest prince which is there present giveth a French crown for his offering, and the greatest prelate presenteth unto him the pix.

The king's dinner normally takes place at 10 a.m. in the antechamber

where the chiefest prince presenteth him a napkin very finely and thick-plaited being first wet at one end and with the same he washeth his hands and wipeth them at the other end. But this office is always executed by the young queen his wife when she dineth with him. The king being set at his table and while he is at dinner, it is permitted and lawful for all men to enter into the antechamber to see him dine and to hear him talk and devise among his nobility. Also during the time that he dineth he giveth liberally audience to all that be desirous to move him of anything secretly in his ear unto whom he answereth *submissa voce*. The king sitteth every week thrice at supper at a round table among his queens and greatest ladies of the court.

After His Majesty hath dined, he retireth himself into the presence and sometimes into his cabinet for two or three hours where he heareth his secretaries and delivereth to every of them their commissions to make their dispatches to all parts, and, after he hath spent some time in this fashion, he cometh again into the presence and from thence goeth accompanied with his princes and noblemen to the queen mother's chamber where also the young queen meeteth him. And if it be needful by reason of any urgent affairs to hold council that afternoon, then they go both together unto the council chamber, otherwise they abide still there devising among their nobility till evensong. And this order they commonly keep on Sundays and holidays, for on other days the king is accustomed to play after dinner at a certain Italian game called commonly *Palle Maille* or tennis among his noblemen, or at *premiere* with the queen mother at the Tuileries or some other garden where oftentimes they sup together.

When the court is united altogether in any great town or in any place commodious to receive the whole train, the king is accustomed to banquet twice every week with all the great princes and ladies of the court, and that is commonly on Thursdays and Sundays at night, at what time he himself doth openly sup at a round table with the queens and other ladies in the antechamber where it is lawful for all men to enter and see them at supper. After supper, having a while devised together, His Majesty goeth to revels into the great hall, where he himself danceth among the ladies and so passeth away the time for two or three hours ... then the King leaveth and sitteth down between his queen and the queen mother giving the looking on to his young princes and ladies and after retireth himself into his cabinet having first given the goodnight to the queens and all the company.[56]

The Penitent King

In December 1583 Henry III set up a confraternity of Hieronymites in the forest of Vincennes. The seventy-two members, drawn mainly from the royal entourage, included the duc de Joyeuse and his three brothers, Épernon and Bernard de La Valette, and officers of the royal household, including Retz, Villequier, Combault and Maulévrier. They were given small, sparsely furnished cells to which they made occasional retreats, each time putting on a friar's garb and following a strict rule. The Hieronymites were closely associated with another royal foundation, created in 1584, called the *Congrégation de l'Oratoire de Notre-Dame de Vie Saine*. This, too, was located at Vincennes (hence the pun) in a priory specially acquired by the king for the purpose. Henry spent much time there in the winter of 1583–4, wearing the community's habit and following a strict régime. Not every courtier, however, shared the king's love of austerity. Maulévrier smuggled some fish into his cell at a time of fasting. The smell drew the king's attention, but Maulévrier only opened the door of his cell after he had eaten the fish. Sacred oratory became a major activity of the congregation. The king himself preached on the feast of St Jerome in 1585.[57] Other speakers included the humanist Jacques Amyot and the poet Desportes. The Palace Academy was thus 'transposed to the plane of a sacred academy'.[58]

On 9 March 1584 Henry III left Paris with forty-seven penitents each wearing a tunic, a white hood and a scourge at the waist. They reached Chartres on the 13th where they prayed to the Virgin for the king to be granted a male heir. They then moved to Notre-Dame de Cléry, near Orléans, before returning exhausted to Paris on the 22nd. Henry made a general confession to Father Mathieu, the provincial of the French Jesuits, but it was to another Jesuit, Edmond Auger, one of the best orators of his day, that he mainly turned for spiritual guidance.[59] Auger had founded an order of penitents at Toulouse, Lyon and Dole, and in March 1583 Henry sought his aid regarding a similar foundation in Paris. This was the Congregation of White Penitents of Our Lady's Annunciation, which was formally set up on 21 March. Four days later, on the feast of the Annunciation, the king and his *mignons* walked in procession through Paris from the Grands Augustins to Notre-Dame wearing tall pointed hoods of white cloth with holes for the eyes. Undeterred by heavy rain, they sang psalms and litanies before falling on their knees at Notre-Dame and intoning the *Salve regina*. On Maundy Thursday the king and his courtiers repeated their penitential procession, this time at night and by torchlight which revealed their backs bloodied by self-flagellation. This event prompted a flood of lampoons, most of them fastening on the unnatural practices ascribed to the king and his *mignons*.

Henry III's penitential mania contrasted bizarrely with the court's foppery and extravagance. It need not have been the manifestation of an unbalanced mind: it may have been intended to boost his authority by pointing to his close rapport with God.[60] Not everyone was convinced of the king's sincerity. His public demonstrations of penance prompted a flood of satirical lampoons. On 27 March 1583 Henry ordered the imprisonment of a monk named Poncet who had denounced the new confraternity as being made up of hypocrites and atheists. Two days later eighty pages and lackeys were flogged in the Louvre for staging a mock procession in which they had covered their heads with handkerchiefs pierced with holes for the eyes.[61]

In the spring of 1585 Henry III was very gloomy. The pacific policy he had pursued since the Peace of Bergerac (1577) had failed, and the kingdom stood once more on the brink of civil war. He again sought a mystical escape from his predicament, only this time he avoided publicity: the statutes of his new order of courtly penitents remained in manuscript only. In May 1585 Henry formed a group of twenty-one people at the Louvre under the name of the

Confrérie de la Mort et Passion de Notre Seigneur Jésus Christ.[62] They were mostly prominent courtiers. Wearing a black habit and a hood, they met on Fridays in an oratory at the Louvre. Here they would kneel in darkness and recite the psalms *Miserere* and *De profundis*, before beating themselves with a scourge, or *discipline*.[63] The brotherhood, however, was soon wound up, perhaps in response to the papal nuncio Ragazzoni's expression of alarm at its excesses. Miron, the king's physician, and Combault, his steward, were also concerned by its existence, but Henry retorted that he was only doing God's will.[64] His mother, too, disapproved of actions that distracted her son from his political duties, but was rebuked by him. He would be even more distracted if he were to hunt as often as his predecessors had done.[65]

In December 1585 the Louvre *Confrérie* was followed by a new foundation: the *Oratoire et Compagnie de benoît Saint François*. This may have been inspired by Henri du Bouchage. Following his wife's death in 1587, the comte entered a Franciscan monastery under the name of Frère Ange, and a close spiritual bond was formed between him and the king who sought his advice on how to become a lay Franciscan.[66] Henry's letters to Bauchage and the provincial of the Capuchins in Paris bear witness to the sincerity of his faith. In 1585 he spent eight days over Christmas at the Capuchin monastery, dividing his time mainly between attending church and private prayer. The rest of the time he took part in processions or listened to Auger preaching; afterwards all lights were extinguished and the king and his companions flogged themselves strenuously for half an hour. At dinner Henry ate only one cooked pear while listening to a reading from Scripture. Before sitting at table, he kissed the ground, as did the friars. Throughout his stay he insisted on sleeping on a straw mattress. He aimed to bring the lifestyle of his White Penitents into line with that of the Capuchins. Comparing the scapular that he wore against his skin with that of the Capuchins, he found his own too soft and changed it for a harsher one.[67]

CHAPTER 17

The Court 'en fête'

Henry III visited few provincial towns in the course of his reign and was given only four entries as compared with the 108 of Charles IX's 'Grand Tour of France'. He was not even given a formal entry into Paris as king of France. For almost half his reign, of course, he was at war with some of his subjects, and the crown's acute financial problems after 1576 restricted the court's freedom to perambulate the kingdom. In 1577 Henry informed the pope that he could not afford to move his court, and in April the secretary of state, Pinart, told the duc de Nevers that the king lacked the means to move the court from Chenonceau. No entry could avoid crowds, which presented a security risk and could also be destructive. A garden with grottoes, statues and jasper vases which had formed the centrepiece of the duc d'Anjou's entry into Tours in 1576 was vandalised by a crowd soon after the duke's departure.[1]

Henry III's four entries were at Lyon on 6 September 1574, Reims on 11 February 1575, Orléans on 15 November 1576 and Rouen on 13 June 1588. At Lyon the municipal authorities built a *Bucintoro* in which to convey the king across the Saône, though this may have been no more than a refurbishment of a Venetian gondola that the archbishop Ippolito d'Este had imported at his own expense for Henry II's entry in 1548. While the Lyon entry made use of the traditional heroic imagery, including figures of Mars and Pallas, that of Reims, which preceded the coronation, invoked the King of Peace and his mission to restore harmony to the kingdom. The young woman who handed over the city's keys was surrounded by small girls symbolising Peace and Concord; they wore antique costumes and played lutes and citterns. On a scaffold along the processional route were figures representing the four cardinal virtues: Temperance, Justice, Fortitude and Prudence. These framed the royal motto: *Manet ultimo caelo* ('His last crown awaits him in Heaven'). Entries often made reference to the political context. Thus the Orléans entry, which took place only seven months after the Peace of Monsieur of 6 May 1576, was an attempt by Henry III to reassert his authority at a time when it was being challenged by his brother, the duc d'Anjou, who held several entries of his own in the towns of his *apanage*. The entry was notable for three speeches delivered respectively by the university's rector, the lieutenant-general and a magistrate, who vied with each other in expounding similes and metaphors in praise of the king. Henry was compared to the sun, Augustus, a phoenix and Alexander the Great. The solar symbolism was again used in speeches delivered at Rouen in 1588, only this time it was applied to the disturbed state of the kingdom. The entry occurred at the lowest point in Henry III's fortunes. He had been driven out of Paris by the duc de Guise and the League, and was desperately looking to France's richest province for funds with which to continue the war. The entry was not especially sumptuous: a procession staged by the various corporations was followed by a number of warlike pageants. There were sea battles that lasted several days and attacks on artificial sea monsters.

Henry III seems to have attached little importance to establishing close ties with the urban authorities in his kingdom: 1576 was the last year in which he showed any interest in civic festivals. He treated them with an indifference bordering on contempt. The citizens of Rouen were twice rebuffed by him. In 1578 he refused an entry that they had offered him, instead ordering them to hand over the sum of 20,000 *écus* that had been earmarked to pay for it; in 1584 he ordered the municipality to address him only through the mouth of the provincial governor, the sieur de Carrouges. Henry left the task of visiting the provincial cities to the *archimignons*, Joyeuse and Épernon, who held a number of provincial governorships. Their entries were comparable in magnificence to royal ones. When Joyeuse entered Rouen on 25 March 1583, he was greeted by a banner acknowledging his role as the eye of the king. At Caen on 5 April he was treated to theatrical displays designed to enhance his authority. Henry III preferred to take part in ceremonies of a different sort. He attended five *Te Deums* in Paris, either at Notre-Dame or the Sainte-Chapelle, between 1576 and 1587. The purpose of such ceremonies was to give thanks to God for a military victory or peace treaty; they also served to underscore the sacred nature of the king's authority. *Te Deums*, unlike entries, tended to widen the gulf between the monarch and his subjects.

Neglecting traditional ceremonial, Henry aimed to turn his court into a place dedicated to the daily exaltation of his majesty. The organisation of its protocol was left to a master of ceremonies, who had to reach the chapel first every morning and to oversee the placing of courtiers at high mass and later at vespers. He did likewise at marriages, baptisms, banquets and diplomatic receptions. He controlled the order of precedence by keeping a list of all the nobles present at court as well as a register of ceremonies past and present to ensure that tradition was being correctly followed. As we have seen Henry had created the office of master of the ceremonies of France for Guillaume Pot, sieur de Rhodes. Pot first performed his duties in February 1585 when an English embassy came to confer the Order of the Garter on the French king.

Henry III ran to excess: one minute he would be walking barefoot and hooded in a penitential procession; the next he would be leaping about the court like a gilded butterfly. No wonder his subjects were baffled and read hypocrisy into his antics. Yet they may have misjudged him. Henry may not have been insincere: he always had to show off, whether it was his religious conscience or his sense of fun. These qualities may not have appeared contradictory to him: he may have regarded both as permissible in the appropriate context. The court, in spite of the political turmoil that surrounded it, was anything but austere. Alongside the plots and counterplots, duels and poisonings, even massacres, it continued to enjoy itself by staging banquets, balls and masquerades that offered the king and his courtiers opportunities of sartorial and choreographic display.

In 1580 Sir Henry Cobham noted that Henry gave more time to ballet than to war.[2] The king was certainly crazy about dancing. He had loved it since childhoood when he had been taught the art by Italian dancing masters. During his visit to Italy in 1574 he had witnessed entertainments in the great halls of palaces in Venice, Mantua and Turin. At his own court he ordered ballets to be held on Mondays and Thursdays. The expense was to be borne by courtiers, each in turn, and the lords and ladies were expected to turn up with the right dancing equipment. Even in the privacy of Ollainville, Henry liked to dance. He invited local ladies to join him regardless of rank and was praised for his agile footwork and high leaps. He tried never to miss an opportunity to dance; he did so at the wedding celebrations of courtiers and in their Parisian *hôtels*. During carnival Henry danced all night three times a week with Parisian ladies. 'In truth,' wrote an English observer in 1584, 'there has been nothing but dancing, banqueting, from one house and company to another, bravery in apparel glittering like the Sun.' A most spectacular ballet was laid on at the Louvre by Henry for an English embassy that visited Paris in February 1585 to confer on him the Order of the Garter. One hundred and twenty dancers and musicians took part. After entering the *grande salle*, they danced across it twice, ensuring that their steps exactly matched the rhythm of the music. The climax was a ballet in which twenty-four richly attired couples traced on the floor the letters of the names of the king and queen. Ballet was seen by Henry as more than an entertainment; it was the means by which the glory of his court could be relayed to other courts in the dispatches of ambassadors.[3]

64. The *Balet comique de la royne* in the Salle Bourbon on 15 October 1581. Engraving from R. de Beaujoyeux, *Balet comique de la royne* (Paris, 1582). In the foreground sits Henry III flanked by his mother and a nobleman. On the right is a wood in which sits the god Pan and, opposite, concealed by clouds, the 'golden vault' containing singers and players. At the far end, in an artificial garden framed by trelliswork, sits Circe the enchantress. A gentleman standing before the king has just escaped from her garden and calls on him to free the world from her baneful rule.

Costume

Unlike today when everyone in Western countries dresses more or less alike, costume in western Europe in the sixteenth century was richly varied. It was characterised by geographical provenance, whether national or provincial; every nation had its own style of dress. One remembers how appalled Henry VIII was on first seeing the German clothes worn by Anne of Cleves and her ladies: they doubtless wore multiple gold chains like those adorning the bosoms of ladies painted by Lucas Cranach. Francis I, as we have seen, sought dolls from Isabella d'Este so that her ladies' dresses might be copied and worn by those of his court. One remembers, too, Portia's judgment on Falconbridge, the young baron of England who came to Belmont seeking her hand. 'I think he bought his doublet in Italy, his round hose in France, his bonnet in Germany, and his behaviour everywhere.'[4] Within France, each province also had its distinctive dress. When the court visited Bayonne in 1565, young ladies wearing dresses representing different provinces danced for the king.

65. Frenchwomen's costumes. Engraving from A. de Bruyn, *Omnium pene Europae, Asiae, Aphricae atque Americae gentium habitus* (Antwerp, 1581).

Clothes also varied according to occupation and social status. In France flashy clothes made out of costly fabrics, such as silk or velvet, were officially restricted to the nobility. Not even wealthy merchants were supposed to wear them. Scholars and lawyers invariably wore black or grey, colours deemed compatible with the seriousness of their occupations. In December 1543 Francis I forbade anyone other than his own children to wear clothes made of cloth of gold or silver on pain of a heavy fine and confiscation of the clothes concerned. Silks were exempted as long as they were not embroidered with more costly materials. The edict was justified on economic grounds, but under Henry II a new motive came into play as members of the old nobility viewed with alarm rich bourgeois who were trying to pass themselves off as nobles by wearing rich clothes. In July 1549 Henry II regulated clothing according to social rank. Only princes and princesses were allowed to wear red silk. Noblemen and their ladies could only use such material for doublets, breeches, tunics and sleeves. The ladies who served the king's sister and daughters were allowed to wear brightly coloured velvet, but those who served princesses or other ladies could wear only black velvet or tan. Pages were forbidden to wear anything but cloth, though they might be allowed a single

66. Frenchmen's costumes. Engraving from A. de Bruyn, *Omnium pene Europae, Asiae, Aphricae atque Americae gentium habitus* (Antwerp, 1581).

silk band. Artisans, peasants, valets and the like were strictly forbidden to wear silk, and any bourgeoise who sought to be taken for a noblewoman by wearing rich clothes was told to wait until her husband had become a nobleman. Yet it seems clear that the sumptuary laws were commonly flouted even in the king's presence. Participants in royal entries often wore clothes above their station. Henry III tried to reinforce the sumptuary legislation of his predecessors. 'God', he explained, 'was much offended and modesty was extinguished' by the sartorial excesses of his subjects. He even tried to restrict the amount of jewellery worn by women and forbade pages to wear anything but cloth, albeit with borders of velvet or silk.[5] This edict was followed by an attempt at enforcement. On 13 November 1583, according to L'Estoile, fifty or sixty women were arrested by the *Prévôt de l'Hôtel* and fined for wearing clothes above their station.[6] Montaigne thought the sumptuary laws were misconceived. If rich fabrics were restricted to the nobility, they were made more desirable; the only way to ensure that they were not usurped, he suggested, was to restrict them to prostitutes. 'The rest of the country', he wrote,

> adopts as canon the canons of the Court. Let the Court stop liking those vulgar codpieces which make a parade of our hidden parts . . . and our armour so hard to put on; those long effeminate tresses . . . and so on for similar recent and depraved innovations: then they would soon all vanish in disapproval. [7]

Letters exchanged by members of the nobility in late sixteenth-century France bear witness to the importance attached to costume. The court set the fashion and those who absented themselves from it for a time wanted to keep abreast of any changes in order not to be found wanting. For fashion at the court of Henry III changed with bewildering rapidity: anyone seen wearing last year's fashion would be dismissed as 'an overripe fruit' (*un fruit suranné*). Fashion was a mark of social status and of being 'in the swim'. Madame de Saint-Sulpice, who went to court only occasionally, was kept abreast of current fashions by her husband. In May 1570 he wrote: 'Dresses with hanging sleeves are no longer worn; they are now much pleated and several have high collars.' In September 1578 the same lady was told by a friend that *bergugales* which made dresses seem short on the sides were now the rage.[8] Such rapid changes of fashion aroused Montaigne's disdain: 'The most monstrous clothes imaginable include, to my taste, our doctoral bonnets, that long tail of pleated velvet hanging down from the heads of our womenfolk with its motley fringes.'[9] Blaise de Vigenère, a member of the duc de Nevers's household, was equally scathing: in less than twenty years, he said, there had been more than two hundred kinds of hat and sword belt. He described some of these confections: one was an Albanian hat shaped like an obelisk, another hat was large and flat like a plate.[10] Doublets also varied widely: some had sleeves and were tight-fitting while others were huge and slashed. Some, known as *penserons à la poulaine*, protruded at the front. Breeches, too, varied in style. Some covered only the upper thigh, while others reached down the leg, giving the wearer the appearance of a male ostrich or 'Lombardy chicken'. Such fashions were all the rage at court in the late sixteenth century. A courtier who was taken prisoner in a fight in 1590 wore a cassock with four sleeves, two of them serviceable and the others hanging like wings.

The probate inventories of courtiers under the last Valois kings list quantities of precious buttons and rich silk fabrics in many colours. They betokened social eminence and power. Even as a prisoner, the vicomte de Turenne asked one of his servants to supply him with two outfits for the summer, but he wanted them pretty and well-made as evidence of his social eminence.[11] A satirist, Nöel du Fail, poked fun at ladies whose dresses were so voluminous that they could not pass through doors. Queen Louise, who had simple tastes, nevertheless left a sizeable wardrobe at her death containing some extremely luxurious dresses. One of them took so much time to put on that she arrived late at a reception offered by the queen mother in 1580. She explained to the wife of the English ambassador that, being a sovereign only by marriage, she had to be sure to dress like one.[12] Henry III, for his part, liked to dress up. In 1574 Zuñiga described him as a thespian figure. An equestrian portrait at Chantilly shows him wearing a doublet with green and gold stripes, a maroon overgarment crisscrossed in silver, a black cape, crimson breeches embroidered with gold, green hose and white shoes. An early miniature in the Uffizi shows Henry wearing an enormous ruff and his hair curled and brushed up from behind. In January 1577 at the Estates-General of Blois, Henry wore a doublet and hose adorned with 4,720 metres of gold and silver thread and a short coat of gold cloth lined with silver cloth.

Moralists, who criticized the court under the late Valois, focused their attention on the ladies' dresses. For much of the sixteenth century these were long and covered the whole body, falling away from a ruff at the neckline. In the last third of the century, however, they became more or less low-cut. A high collar replaced the ruff enclosing the sides and back of the head. Alternatively a large circular lace collar might be worn across the shoulders. Henry III's sister, the future Reine Margot, who was anything but prudish, wore dresses that were lower-cut than most. Male attire also underwent a radical transformation. The padded codpiece, which had figured so prominently in portraits in the reign of Charles IX, disappeared to be replaced by short and close-fitting breeches that covered the thigh and stopped at the knee. These were similar to the undergarments of silk or velvet that ladies wore for riding to protect their modesty in the event of a fall. The confusion of male and female attire was interpreted by the court's critics as evidence of an androgynous tendency seen equally in the costumes worn in masquerades. In February 1586 a Lyonnais deplored the 'androgynous masquerades' that he had witnessed at court during carnival. In one of his satires Noël du Fail compared the men of his day with their predecessors under Francis I, who had fed on good meat. Now they were but half-men: they fed on appearance, smoke, talk, hand-kissing and salutations.[13] Pierre de L'Estoile was equally contemptuous of current male fashion. He made fun of the young men who accompanied Henry III on his return from Poitiers in October 1577 'with their ruffs, curls, raised crests, wigs . . . combed, diapered and powdered with scent of violet which aromatised the streets, squares and houses they frequented'.[14]

In time, however, the king tried to match his image to the lofty sentiments he expressed in a speech to the Estates-General of Blois in 1576. Contradiction once again governed his behaviour. He appeared before the deputies dressed soberly in black with a single jewel pinned to his cloak. In January he wore earrings which he had not done for months; retaining thereafter only a single pearl, sometimes accompanied by an λ (for the queen). In his later portraits his collar is turned down and the hairstyle is simple. Henry is invariably shown wearing a black toque adorned with a feathered aigrette. He was the first king of France to have his portrait widely circulated in the form of engravings.[15]

The Theatre

Theatre at the court of Henry III was essentially comedy. The king shared his mother's dislike of tragedy. He never showed the slightest interest in the works of Robert Garnier, the most prolific of the humanist playwrights in the ambit of the Pléiade. Likewise the comedies *à l'antique* written in the 1580s by Pierre de Larivey, Odet de Turnèbe, François d'Amboise and Jean Godard appear to have been performed only in erudite circles outside Paris. Henry III and his court reserved their enthusiasm for the *commedia dell'arte*; this Italian import became all the rage. During his stay in Venice in 1574, the king asked to see a performance by the famous company of Italian actors called I Gelosi. The Venetian authorities were told that 'the king is very keen to see them, particularly the woman who performed last winter'. This may have been Vittoria, a famous actress. Although the Gelosi were due to leave for Mantua, they delayed their departure and called on the king. He remembered them two years later when he wrote to his ambassador in Venice: 'now that the kingdom is at peace, I wish to invite the Magnifico who came to me in Venice

67. A commedia dell'arte troupe, *c.* 1580 (Musée Carnavalet, Paris), probably that of the Gelosi with their leading lady, Isabella Andreini, as the *innamorata* confronting an angry Pantalone. Such itinerant Italian actors were invited to France by the king and various noblemen from 1570 onwards.

on my return from Poland with all his troop of players, the Gelosi.'[16] The ambassador replied that they were at the imperial court, but that he would convey the king's invitation on their return. Next winter the Gelosi were kidnapped by Huguenots as they were travelling to Blois. Henry secured their release by paying a ransom. Their arrival at court was greeted with joy; they immediately performed a comedy before the king in the hall where the Estates-General met. The Magnifico, who led the company, played Pantalone, and Isabella Andreini was his lover. When she died at Lyon in 1604 the parish register described her as 'one of the rarest women in the world on account of her learning and command of languages'. After entertaining the court, the Gelosi settled at the Hôtel de Bourbon, an enormous hall opposite the Louvre. They rented it from the *Confrères de la Passion*, who had a monopoly of Parisian spectacles. Other Italian players, who performed for the queen mother and leading courtiers in 1584–5 were the Confidenti. There was also a troop led by Battista Lazaro at the Hôtel de Bourgogne and the Raccolti, who performed in the faubourg Saint-Germain. Such companies did not entertain only the court and Parisians: they went all over the kingdom. One troupe entertained the king of Navarre at Nérac in 1575 and 1587. But players were not always welcome. Certain local authorities were distinctly hostile and tried to ban their activities. In 1588 the Parlement of

Paris took advantage of the king's absence from the capital to silence the Italian players, describing them as 'one of the century's great evils'. Cardinal de Bourbon complained to Catherine de' Medici about plays being performed during Lent, but neither she nor her son would be swayed. Henry III defended the Gelosi, saying that they gave him pleasure. But for the court's support, theatre in France might not have survived its modern form.

The Italian actors had a considerable impact on the manners and even on the language of the court, whose members were not in the least put out by the rather scabrous content of the plays: they were used to their own lax morals and could take them in good part. The actors, being accomplished flatterers, gained the friendship of courtiers and sent them poems. Battista Amorcvoli, one of the Gelosi, sent a verse to the king after a *mignon* had been killed in a duel. Isabella Andreini was on close terms with the duchesse de Nemours and other court ladies. Several princely masquerades drew inspiration from the *commedia dell'arte*. On the eve of one Shrove Tuesday Henry III and his courtiers rode through the streets of Paris wearing parti-coloured trousers like those worn by Zanni, Harlequin and the rest. Even letter-writing was influenced by the *commedia*. Thus, in June 1574 Henry III wrote from Vienna to the duc de Nevers: 'There is no better or more perfect Pantalone than yourself.'[17] Such names occur frequently in letters written by courtiers. Brantôme, who had inside knowledge of the court, often alluded to characters from the *commedia* in his writings.[18]

The Joyeuse 'Magnificences'

Anne de Joyeuse's apotheosis was his marriage to Marguerite de Lorraine, the queen's half-sister, on 24 September 1581. The ceremony took place at the church of Saint-Germain l'Auxerrois. The king, who gave away the bride, wore the same attire as the groom: covered with embroidery, pearls and precious stones, it was valued at 10,000 *écus*. The wedding was followed by festivities that Henry had planned since July.[19] The intention may have been not only to gather the nobility around him, but also to detach the Guises from the Catholic extremists who were threatening the crown. The festivities, described by L'Estoile as 'mummeries, finery, dances, music, masques, tournaments and similar follies and superfluities', cost an estimated 3,600,000 *l*. and had not been paid for in full fifteen years later.

The entertainments laid on during the fortnight after the wedding included tournaments in chivalric settings, an aquatic fête, an equestrian ballet and a stupendous firework display. Temporary buildings designed by the best artists were erected in the streets and squares of the capital, and the various shows were accompanied by music acclaimed as 'the most harmonious that had ever been heard'. The first entertainment took place in the *salle* of the hôtel de Bourbon, behind the Louvre, on the evening of 19 September. It took the form of a combat in which the dukes of Guise, Mercoeur and Montmorency defended Cupid, chained to a rock, against another team led by the king. On the 24th a ball took place in the upper hall of the Louvre after a dinner and a supper; and the day after the wedding Joyeuse offered a banquet and a ball at the Hôtel de Guise. A small painting on copper, now in the Louvre, shows Henry III and his entourage in the upper hall of the Louvre on the evening after the wedding. Joyeuse and his wife are in the centre, about to dance (plate 20). She wears a long white dress; he a small black hat, a green doublet, breeches of the same colour, a short grey cape and stockings that cling to his thighs. In short, he is portrayed as the new ideal courtier, slim and graceful.[20]

The most famous of the 'magnificences' was the *Balet comique de la royne* on 15 October which lasted five hours. It was prepared by Balthasar de Beaujoyeux, one of the queen mother's *valets de chambre*, and written by the king's almoner, Nicolas Filleul de La Chesnaye. Both were strongly influenced by the pastoral: hence their choice of symbolic places (grotto, grove) and of mythological beings (Pan, nymphs, naiads, tritons and Circe). The spectacle expressed the conflict between the forces of Harmony and Reason, on the one hand, and of the passions, on the other. The solar metaphor was used to characterise the king's superiority over his subjects. Charles IX had already appeared in the carnival of 1571 dressed as the Sun; ten years later Henry III adopted the same imagery, only more grandly. He rode into the courtyard of the Louvre in a chariot dressed as the Sun god surrounded by planets and stars.

The music composed for the *Balet comique de la royne* was aimed at producing 'effects', while the plot constituted an invocation of cosmic forces in aid of the French monarchy. The theme was the transference of power from the hands of the enchantress Circe into those of the royal family. At one end of the hall was the garden of Circe before whom passed men she had turned into beasts; at the other was the 'golden vault', representing the celestial world, in which singers and instrumentalists were divided into ten *concerts de musique*. The action began with the escape of a nobleman from Circe's garden. He crossed the hall, fell at the king's feet and implored him to rid the world of the sorceress. In the mythological drama that followed, Circe with her entourage of sirens and satyrs was not immediately defeated. This was only achieved by an alliance of the four cardinal Virtues and Minerva. When the Virtues appeared in star-spangled robes, they called on the gods to descend from heaven. The musicians in the 'golden vault' replied to their music, and it was at this point that the celestial forces began to gain the upper hand. Circe's defeat was signalled by a loud clap of thunder and the appearance of Jupiter seated on an eagle. His descent was accompanied by the 'most learned and excellent music that had ever been seen or heard'. Once Circe had surrendered, she was taken before the king as a prisoner. The performers then knelt before him in acknowledgment of the power of his wisdom as guided by his mother's advice. The festivities continued with a ballet celebrating the establishment of harmony in which dancers passed fifteen times in front of Henry and formed a great chain with four interlacings. Finally, medals bearing engraved images of animals were distributed to the principal spectators. The queen offered one with a dolphin to Henry as a presage of the hoped-for birth of a son.[21]

CHAPTER 18

The Court under Fire

A Divided Court

From the start of his reign Henry III had to contend with the intrigues of his younger brother, François duc d'Alençon.[1] Ill-favoured physically, Alençon was devoured by jealousy and ambition. He built up a large clientele with which the king felt obliged to compete. Many noblemen were attracted to Alençon's service by the expectation of his eventual succession to the throne. In the meantime, the duke seized every opportunity of embarrassing the king politically. Disappointed at not having been made lieutenant-general of the kingdom during Henry's absence in Poland, Alençon left Paris in September 1575 and went to Dreux, where he issued a manifesto calling for three things: the removal of foreigners from the court, a religious settlement and a meeting of the Estates-General. As prince of the blood, he could give the political opposition legitimacy by placing himself at its head. Henry III used his mother to negotiate a truce with his brother in November 1575, but Alençon soon repudiated it and joined the opposition, which now included Henri de Navarre who, after escaping from court, had reverted to his Calvinist faith. The rebels presented a long list of demands to the king, who, lacking financial resources, had to accept the Treaty of Beaulieu of May 1576, better known as the Peace of Monsieur (the title traditionally given to the king's younger brother). Alençon was made duc d'Anjou and, when civil war broke out again, he fought on the king's side against the Huguenots. He captured La Charité in May 1576, earning for himself a hero's welcome at court; later he sacked the town of Issoire.

In 1576 Anjou's household was larger than the king's and still growing. At its head was Louis de Clermont, baron de Bussy, who seized every opportunity of taunting the king's men. On 1 November 1575 the *mignon*, the sieur Du Guast, was murdered by masked men in Paris. Though deeply upset, Henry III chose not to pursue the murderers; he did, however, give Du Guast a splendid funeral. Peace between his household and that of Anjou followed, but in the autumn of 1576 the brothers attended the Estates-General at Blois. Monsieur felt stronger now that he was duc d'Anjou and his entourage grew accordingly. On 20 December another *mignon*, Henri de Saint-Sulpice, was murdered by one of Anjou's clients. By 1578 fights between servants of the king and Anjou became daily events. In January the English ambassador reported witnessing nine or ten clashes between them. Three days after quarrelling with Philibert de Gramont during a ball at the Louvre, Bussy d'Amboise went to the porte Saint-Antoine with three hundred armed nobles in the hope of challenging him. A pitched battle was narrowly averted by the king, but Gramont tried to attack Bussy in his lodging. Both men were imprisoned in the Louvre, but the violence continued. On 1 February some *mignons* fell upon Bussy at the porte Saint-Honoré, but he managed to get away and demanded justice from the king. An ordinance was issued banning quarrels at court, and on 6 February an attempt was made by the *prévôt des marchands* to broker a reconciliation between the parties at the Hôtel de Ville.[2]

On 14 February 1578 Anjou left the court at night after climbing through a window of his sister's bedchamber; he fled to Angers, soon to be followed by his mother. Catherine hoped to persuade him to return to Paris, but he refused even to see her.[3] The removal of his household from court, however, did not end the violence, for the *mignons* began quarrelling among themselves. At 5 a.m. on 27 April Caylus, Maugiron and Livarot met Entraguet, Ribérac and the young Schomberg near the porte Saint-Antoine. A pitched battle, known as the *duel des mignons*, ensued; Maugiron and Schomberg were killed, while Ribérac was fatally injured and Livarot seriously wounded. The funerals ordered by the king for Caylus and Maugiron seemed designed to immortalise their intimacy with him. Caylus lay in state with his face uncovered, an honour normally reserved for persons of the highest rank. On 21 July another *mignon*, Saint-Mégrin, was hacked to pieces by a group of men as he left the Louvre.[4] Henry III commissioned Desportes and Ronsard to compose verses in praise of the three *mignons*, while a Latin encomium by Jean Dorat was engraved in letters of gold on the black marble at the base of their tombs. The king's preacher, Arnauld Sorbin, who had spoken at Charles IX's funeral, did so again for the three *mignons*, thereby linking them by association with the royal family. The church of Saint-Paul where they were buried became the centre of a veritable cult and in 1580 was a regular halt along the route followed by processions of penitents. The tombs of the *mignons* were commissioned by Henry III from Germain Pilon. Each consisted of a sarcophagus of black marble standing on a pedestal. An entablature above the sarcophagus served as a platform for the effigy of the deceased, who was portrayed kneeling at a prie-dieu on which rested an open Book of Hours. His coat of arms was engraved on the prie-dieu and a trophy adorned the sarcophagus.[5]

Anjou's departure from the court in 1578 prompted a major reshuffle of court personnel. Henry no longer needed to compete with his brother; he could afford to cut staff without fear of losing prestige. The reorganisation affected the first generation of *mignons*. Those who were not murdered or killed in duels fell out with the king for a variety of reasons. The first was Roger de Bellegarde, who led a revolt in July 1579 but died soon afterwards.[6] The fall of Souvré, Beauvais-Nangis and François d'O was less spectacular and only temporary.[7] Meanwhile, Anjou pursued his ambitions abroad. Following the peace of Bergerac in September 1577, he intervened militarily in the Low Countries on the side of the Dutch rebels against Spain, but let them down badly. In August 1581 he captured Cambrai, only to be driven back to the Channel coast by the Spaniards. In October he visited the English court in the vain hope of marrying Elizabeth I. Returning to the Low Countries, he assumed the title of Duke of Brabant, and in January 1583 tried unsuccessfully to seize Antwerp. In October he returned to France for good. As the king's health seemed precarious, Catholics looked to the duke as his successor, but in June 1584 he died of consumption, clearing the path to the throne for Navarre.

An Unpopular Court

The rivalry between the households of Henry III and Anjou, and the violent quarrels among the *mignons* that so often disrupted the life of the court, were not calculated to impress the king's subjects. Rather, they served to fuel an ever-growing corpus of hostile literature. Anti-courtier satire had a history reaching back to the Middle Ages and beyond. Much of it had disparaged court life by comparing it to a more peaceful rural existence, but in the 1570s it rounded more specifically on the king's entourage. The old analogy between parts of the human body and the social estates was brought into play and the rise of favourites was seen as a reversal of the natural order over which virtue had presided. The ancient French nobility, it was argued, was being displaced by social upstarts who had captured the king's attention by flattery and by pandering to his baser instincts. The *Reveille-Matin des Français et de leurs voisins* (1574), attributed to the Protestant, Nicolas Barnaud, portrayed the court as a Sodom ruled by avarice and atheism. Its vicious ways were proof enough, it argued, that France had become a tyranny.

The relationship between king and nobility came under critical scrutiny from many writers who deplored the advancement of courtiers without regard for virtue, that essential quality of nobility which earlier kings had respected in dispensing their favours. Virtue was deemed to be inborn; its outward manifestation was virility, a quality in short supply at the court of Henry III. Writers argued that, in dispensing his favour, the king should not allow personal feelings to influence him. Friendship itself was called into question, as it stemmed from the passions, not reason. Catherine de' Medici was accused of filling the court with her degenerate compatriots, a much-hated figure being the *Premier gentilhomme de la chambre*, Albert de Gondi-Retz, who was described as the son of a bankrupt banker and a Lyon courtesan. For the author of *La France Turquie* the religious division of France was used by the crown to destroy the old nobility and replace it by a new one modelled on the Ottoman janissaries.[8] Dignities and honours were no longer a reward for virtue and loyalty but a bait held up by the king without moral justification. Dissimulation and hypocrisy, allied to sodomy and usury, were contrasted by writers with the simplicity and naïve virtue they ascribed to the French.

Contemporary French critics of Henry III's court blamed Italians for the changes. Italians were prominent among the court's personnel. They had come to France even before the start of the Italian Wars, but the process had gathered momentum since. Italian merchant-bankers, who had long been settled in Lyon and other French towns, set up branches in Paris in response to Henry III's prolonged residence there. They wanted to be close to the court; and Paris was also the principal market for luxury goods in France. Italian artists came there as their superiority was recognised, not only in architecture, sculpture and painting, but also in music, dancing, gardening and fountain-making.

The Italian presence among royal servants under Henry III was significant.[9] Many of the gentlemen of the chamber between 1574 and 1584 were Italians, including Albert de Gondi, marshal de Retz, and his brother Charles, baron de la Tour. Another Italian, René de Birague, became Chancellor of France in 1571. A Milanese, he had been president of the Parlement of Turin during the French occupation of Piedmont. He and two other Italians – Louis de Gonzague, duc de Nevers, and Retz – attended the fateful council meetings that had preceded the Massacre of St Bartholomew. In 1584 Retz and another brother, Pierre de Gondi, bishop of Paris, were part of a group of ten whom the king consulted on matters of importance. The number of Italians receiving pensions from the crown rose dramatically from seventy-seven under Henry II to 243 in 1577.

The Italian presence in the arts remained significant under Henry III. They were also important as producers of court entertainments. Baldassare Belgiojoso, alias Balthasar de Beaujoyeux, had come to France under Henry II in the suite of Marshal Brissac, governor of Piedmont. His *Balet comique de la Royne* was a precursor of opera, a new genre that was taking root in Italy. Court entertainments called on the services of a large number of musicians and dancers, many of them Italians. Under Henry III nearly 25 per cent of the choristers in the royal chapel were Italian and 47 per cent of instrumentalists, including 76 per cent of violinists. Many Italian dancers also came to France.

Italian immigrants showed a willingness to integrate into French society through marriage and the acquisition of property. The court offered them opportunities of abandoning trade and entering the nobility by marriage. Thus, Guillaume de Gadagne, a member of an Italian family of merchant bankers of Lyon, married a Frenchwoman and purchased several *seigneuries*. He became a gentleman of the king's chamber and his four daughters married into the French aristocracy. Among the more successful Italian social climbers in France was the Florentine merchant Ludovico Dadiaceto, who had come to France in 1553. After lucrative business deals in Lyon and Marseille, he joined the court of Henry III and purchased a Parisian *hôtel* which he filled with statues and paintings by Italian masters. He entertained members of the court, including Ronsard. Dadiaceto became a royal secretary in 1578 and a steward in the king's household. In 1580, two years after acquiring the *comté* of Châteauvillain, he married Anne d'Aquaviva, an exiled Neapolitan duchess who was one of Marguerite de Navarre's ladies. The marriage was celebrated at court in the presence of the royal family. Another prominent Italian at Henry III's court was Sébastien Zamet, a wealthy financier who frequently received the king at his house in Paris and also lent him money.[10] Not all Italians, however, were keen to settle permanently in France. Orazio Ruccellaï, for example, having made a fortune in France, returned to Florence after Henry III's death and joined the Grand Duke's court. Such behaviour offended Frenchmen, who felt that they were being exploited.

Many French courtiers went to Italy to complete their education. Some attended universities; more frequented schools of fencing, dancing and riding. No one at Henry III's court was considered properly educated unless he had been touched by Italian culture. For this reason courtiers took to speaking Italian, much to the irritation of Frenchmen. Henry III, for his part, spoke Tuscan fluently and used it when conversing with Italian ambassadors; 16 per cent of his books were Italian.[11] It was in his reign, as we have seen, that Italian actors became prominent at court.

The French did not like to think of the court's vices as homegrown, so they blamed the Italians who had invaded it.[12] One had only to read Machiavelli or Castiglione, they claimed, to see where French courtiers had picked up their bad habits. The principal opponent of Machiavellians at court was Innocent Gentillet, author of the *Anti-Machiavel*. Appalled by the Massacre of St Bartholomew and, even more, by the exultation that greeted it at court, he traced their source to Machiavelli's works. As Gentillet knew them only in translation, he sometimes misrepresented them, but this did not lessen his impact. The notion that Machiavelli was the chief repository of evil political aphorisms spread like wildfire. Jean Bodin, in the preface to his *République*, lamented the vogue enjoyed by Machiavelli among courtiers. The *Vindiciae contra tyrannos* (1579) blamed Machiavelli for the civil dissension dividing the state. Though allegedly conceived as a riposte to Machiavelli, it justified rebellion and even legitimised a tyrant's assassination by a single individual acting on his own initiative.[13]

The work that above all others denounced Italian-inspired manners at court was that of printer–publisher Henri Estienne, *Deux dialogues du nouveau langage françois Italianizé* (1578). This accused courtiers of speaking a jargon, half-French and half-Italian, and of debasing both languages in the process. Estienne criticized their affected use of adverbs, such as *infiniment, extrêmement* and, especially, *divinement*; also the absurd salutations they exchanged. Without citing Castiglione by name, Estienne condemned as against all reason the cult of 'accommodation' prescribed by him as a recipe for successful advancement at court.[14]

Criticism of the Court

Under Henry III criticism of the court became more barbed. The target for invective also narrowed: at first it was the king's *mignons*; then the *archimignons*; then Épernon alone; finally the king. Henry was portrayed as an effeminate, hypocritical and profligate debauchee presiding over a court riddled with vice and corruption.[15] Clément Marchant in his *Remonstrance aux Francoys* (1576) denounced the reversal of values whereby the most highly esteemed person at court was the most perfumed. He blamed Satan for the fact that the body and stomach were now rated above the soul. He it was who, with the assistance of heretics, had bamboozled France; but no follower of Satan had ever escaped punishment: witness the great fire that consumed the Sodomites. The *Vindiciae contra tyrannos* (1579) by Du Plessis-Mornay and Hubert Languet condemned 'today's courtiers'. Only bad princes and unworthy favourites, it claimed, could argue that the court's dissolute life was not subject to any law.

A major critic of the court was Pierre de L'Estoile, a lawyer attached to the Parlement of Paris, who kept a day-by-day record of events in the capital. In addition to expressing his own views, he avidly collected and reproduced lampoons that were sold in the streets of the capital. L'Estoile was especially shocked by Henry III's extravagance. In February 1577 he wrote:

L'HERMITAGE PREPARE
POVR HENRY DE VALOIS.

Les Hermites i   Ne porte gayement vne belle figure,

68. Henry III's Covenant with the Devil. Engraving from *Recueil de l'Estoile*, fo. XIXa. The unpopularity of Henry III and his court was expressed in countless pamphlets, often illustrated with engravings, which poured off the Parisian presses. Here, two religious figures with clawed feet are trying to get the king to enter the mouth of Hell. The print forms part of a series that parodied his religious activities.

the king ordered jousts, tournaments, ballets and countless masquerades in which he normally appeared dressed as a woman with his doublet open, baring his neck on which he wore a necklace of pearls and a ruff in three layers, two *à fraise* and one 'reversed', as was then worn by ladies of his court. It was said that, but for the recent death of *Messire* Nicolas de Lorraine, comte de Vaudémont, his father-in-law, he would have spent 100,000 or 200,000 francs in games and masquerades at the carnival. Such was the luxury rooted in the heart of this prince![16]

L'Estoile was also shocked by the festivities at Plessis-lès-Tours on 15 May 1577. A banquet in honour of the king's brother, Anjou, was served by ladies in male attire. Their assistants wore green silk that had cost 60,000 francs. The queen mother was reported to have spent close on 100,000 *l.* on a banquet at Chenonceau, money that had been borrowed from the king's wealthiest servants and Italians who had charged interest of one hundred per cent. 'At this fine banquet,' wrote L'Estoile, 'the service was done by the most beautiful and honest ladies of the court, who were topless and had their hair loose and flowing.'[17] The 'magnificences' for the duc de Joyeuse were said to have cost 12,000 *écus* (see plate 20). In September 1581 L'Estoile wrote: 'Everyone was stunned by so much luxury and such an enormous and superfluous expense . . . at a time, which was . . . wretched and hard for the people who, in the country, were being gnawed to the bone by the soldiery and in the towns by new offices, taxes and subsidies.'[18]

Henry III's court was also condemned as licentious.[19] His relations with his *mignons* came in for special censure. In July 1576 L'Estoile reported:

> The name of *mignons* began at this time to fall from the lips of the people to whom they were odious as much because of their flippant and haughty ways as of their make-up and effeminate and indecent attire, but especially because of the outrageous gifts and liberalities they received from the king.

The *mignons* were portrayed as pimps pandering to Henry's lust. An anonymous poem, *Les Vertus et Propriétés des Mignons* (1576), likened them to caterpillars and locusts whose voracious appetites spread waste and desolation over a wide area and whose prodigality, subsidised by crippling taxes, was dissipating the hard-won rewards of honest workers. The poem ends with a wake-up call: 'Frenchmen, open your eyes!'

The penitential processions in which the king and his courtiers took part in the 1580s were seen by many as exercises in hypocrisy designed to camouflage their own disreputable conduct. A preacher at Notre-Dame exclaimed: 'Ah! you miserable hypocrites; thus do you mock God beneath your masks and the scourge you carry at your belt is just for show.'[20] The public was also shocked by the courtiers' lawlessness. In September 1577 Madame de Villequier was murdered by her husband. 'This murder', writes L'Estoile,

> was considered cruel in that the victim was a woman pregnant with twins and also strange, as it was committed in the king's lodging while he was there, and also at the court where debauchery is publicly and notoriously practised among the ladies (*entre les Dames*) who take it as virtue. But the outcome and ease with which Villequier obtained his pardon and remission caused people to think that there had been a secret command or tacit consent from the king who hated that lady (although he had abused her for a long time with her husband acting as go-between).[21]

In February 1586 a Dutchman named Van Buchen was shocked to see the *mignons* riding through Paris, knocking people over, beating them up or pelting them with eggs, sand or flour.[22] In 1588 a work entitled *Histoire tragique et memorable de Pierre de Gaverston,* attributed to Jean Boucher, drew a parallel between disorders provoked by Épernon, who was a Gascon, and those committed in England under Edward II by his Gascon favourite, Piers Gaveston.

In his *Discours politiques et militaires* (1587), François de La Noue, a Huguenot captain, is highly critical of the extravagance of courtiers, particularly in the matter of clothing. No one, he writes, now dares to appear in high society without being 'gilded like a chalice'. The worst offenders are courtiers who are prepared to give up their homes for several months at a time in order to see themselves 'covered in silk and silver' for a few days. La Noue deplores the frequent changes of fashion at court. This, he explains, had begun under Francis I and had developed under Henry II, but now it had become a craze; even pages and lackeys were dressed in cloth of silver. 'At present,' La Noue writes, 'if one sees someone at court wearing last year's costume, one says of him: "We know him well; he won't bite us; he is an overripe fruit." Such mockery causes him to leave the court.' Sartorial waywardness was seen by La Noue as a sign of foolishness ('une grande légèreté d'esprit'), as were the fashions that earned courtiers the derision of foreigners: their huge ruffs, their long hair and their habit of letting their swords dangle behind their backs.[23]

The poem *Les Vertus et Propriétés des Mignons,* which Nicolas Barnaud included in his virulent *Le Cabinet du Roy de France* (1582), suggests that the effeminacy of the king and his entourage points to the prevalence of homosexuality, a theme taken up by Agrippa d'Aubigné in his famous poem *Les Tragiques.* He describes Henry III at a ball as follows:

> *De cordons emperlez sa chevelure pleine,*
> *Sous un bonnet sans bord fait à l'Italienne,*
> *Faisoit deux arcs voutez; son menton pinceté,*
> *Son visage de blanc & de rouge emâsté,*
> *Son chef tout empoudré nous monstrerent ridée,*
> *En la place d'un Roy, une putaine fardée . . .*
> *Pour nouveau parement il porta tout ce jour*
> *Cet habit monstrueux, pareil à son amour:*
> *Si qu'au premier abord chascun estoit en peine*
> *S'il voyait un Roy femme ou bien un homme Reyne.*[24]

> *(His hair covered with strings of pearls*
> *Beneath a rimless bonnet in the Italian style*
> *Made two round arches; his pinched chin,*
> *His face caked with white and red paste,*
> *His head all powdered revealed to us,*

Instead of a king, a wrinkled and made-up whore . . .
The whole of today he wore a new outfit,
A costume as monstrous as was his love,
So that at first no one was sure if he was
Seeing a female king or a male queen.)

Critics of the court viewed its alleged homosexuality not only as contrary to Christian morality, but also as a sure sign of national decadence. A clever satire, *L'Isle des Hermaphrodites*, though not published until 1605, is an allegory on the court of Henry III. A group of people, shipwrecked on an island, discover a beautiful palace where, in a heavily perfumed room, a masked and gloved Hermaphrodite is waited upon by an army of minions. The observer is both amused and shocked by the comic, grotesque and macabre elements of a society instantly recognisable as Henry's court. The Hermaphrodites reject all cults and divinities save those concerned with the fulfilment of human desires.[25] Atheism was a charge repeatedly levelled at Henry's court. Its use of magic and blasphemy were held responsible by La Noue for France's ruin.

CHAPTER 19

Nemesis

On the night of 20 January 1583 Henry III had a nightmare: he saw himself being devoured by the wild animals in his menagerie.[1] The vision was prophetic, only instead of animals, the devourers were to be the king's own subjects. Following Anjou's death in 1584, the Huguenot leader Henri de Navarre became heir presumptive to the throne, a situation unacceptable to France's Catholic majority. In September Henri duc de Guise, his brothers, Charles duc de Mayenne and Louis cardinal de Guise, and two other noblemen formed an association at Nancy aimed at excluding Navarre from the throne. In December they signed the Treaty at Joinville with Philip II of Spain aimed at defending the Catholic faith and extirpating Protestantism from France. Cardinal de Bourbon was recognised as heir to the throne, and Philip agreed to subsidise an armed rising by the Catholic League. This was a grouping of armed associations, closely associated with the House of Guise and dedicated to preserving France as a Catholic kingdom. The movement soon gained control of a number of important towns.[2] In April 1585 Catherine de' Medici tried unsuccessfully to negotiate with Guise and the other leaders of the League. In July she had to sign the Treaty of Nemours which committed Henry III to pay the Leaguers' troops and conceded to them a number of surety towns, the lion's share being given to Guise himself whose clients received favours, pensions and governorships. An edict arising from the treaty banned all Protestant worship and ordered pastors to quit the kingdom instantly. Huguenots were debarred from public office and required to surrender their own surety towns. Setting aside the Salic law, the treaty deprived Navarre of his right to the throne.[3] As for Henry III, he had never been in so much danger. Guise had the support of several towns, including Paris which had its own league, founded in 1584 by Catholic zealots who became known as 'the Sixteen'.

Throughout his reign Henry III was bedevilled by a shortage of money. The military campaign of 1576 had been particularly costly. He had to promise John Casimir of the Palatinate the colossal sum of 3,388,549 florins, to be paid in instalments over four years. Henry had been forced to pawn the crown jewels in order to secure loans from Italian princes. He had also seized money intended to repay annuities, known as the *rentes sur l'Hôtel de Ville*, a move that had alienated the Parisian bourgeoisie. In spite of his efforts the crown's debts rose to 101 million *l.* whereas they had been only 43.7 million on the eve of the civil wars. In 1588 they exceeded 133 million. Yet Henry never ceased to be generous to his favourites. Writing to the abbé de l'Isle in September 1575, he said that 'liberality and magnificence were the badge (*le propre*) of a great prince'.[4]

In June 1586 Lucinge noted that Henry III's 'extraordinary devotions' had won him much credit among his subjects, but the Leaguers interpreted them as signs of royal duplicity. Early in 1586 a courtier wrote: 'The king is still at his devotions where he has been for the past fortnight. He will be here tomorrow . . . . He is more addicted to solitude than ever; nevertheless he enjoys himself in private.'[5] In January 1587 Henry III ordered Jean de La Barrière, who had introduced a regime of the strictest austerity into the Cistercian abbey of Notre-Dame-de-Feuillant in the diocese of Rieux, to bring sixty of his monks to Paris. They travelled on foot, preaching as they went. Henry gave them a building close to the Tuileries and reserved a place for himself, but in April 1588, before it could receive him, he was driven out of Paris by the League. When eventually he returned, he did so as a soldier rather than as a penitent. In the meantime, the Leaguers invaded and pillaged the oratory at Vincennes. Inside the king's cell they found a crucifix flanked by two candlesticks of crude workmanship with feet recalling those of satyrs. They accused Henry of witchcraft, a charge which he rejected with contempt in a letter of March 1589 to the curé of Saint-Eustache thanking him and his parishioners for their prayers.[6]

The Peace of Nemours was no peace at all as Navarre refused to be bound by it; so the civil war continued. On 15 February 1586 Guise entered Paris with an escort of six hundred horse. Acclaimed as their saviour by the inhabitants, his presence spread panic at court. Joyeuse and Épernon strengthened security in their apartments while the king shut himself up in the Louvre and ceased to go on retreats. Joyeuse, who competed with Guise for the leadership of the Catholic party, left the court soon afterwards on a number of military campaigns against the Huguenots. He conducted these with ferocity and a fair measure of success, which earned him plaudits from Parisian pulpits and presses. His popularity, indeed, threatened to eclipse that of Guise, but his prolonged absences from court enabled Épernon to monopolize the king's favour.[7] Meanwhile, the queen mother once again placed her diplomatic skills at her son's service.[8] She left the court early in 1587 in an attempt to persuade

Navarre to revert to the Catholic faith, a conversion which would not only have decapitated the Huguenot party but also made him more acceptable to Catholics as prospective king. She met him at Saint-Brice, near Cognac, in March, but he merely strung her along while waiting for military support to reach him from Germany.

In August 1587 reports reached the court of an impending invasion of France by German *reiters*. At a special council meeting Henry III proposed to lead his army against them but was dissuaded by all the councillors except Nevers, who thought such a move might enhance his popularity. In the end Henry set up three armies: one led by Joyeuse, another by Guise, and the third by himself. The plan was for Joyeuse to march south against Navarre and for Guise to impede the *reiters'* advance. As for Henry himself, he was to stop them crossing the Loire with the bulk of the army. He probably hoped that Guise and Navarre would both be defeated, leaving him to gather the laurels; but the turn of events did not match his intentions. Joyeuse complained of being starved of troops and funds. He returned to court on 27 August and, after spending a few days at the Louvre, set off once more to fight the Huguenots. His campaign was seen as a final attempt to win back royal favour: it may also have been a final bid to wrest the leadership of the Catholic cause from Guise. Joyeuse's army, according to Sully, contained 'the most agile and splendid noblemen of the court'. Battle with Navarre was joined at Coutras on 20 October. It lasted less than three hours and resulted in the annihilation of the royal army. Royal losses were put at four thousand dead, including 250 leading nobles. Joyeuse surrendered, only to be murdered by a Huguenot soldier.

News of the disaster caused dismay among Catholics. Funeral services were held in all the major towns. Pamphlets put out by the League suggested that Joyeuse's demise had been contrived by Épernon, who emerged as the event's main beneficiary: on 7 November, Henry III appointed him in place of Joyeuse as Admiral of France and governor of Normandy, a concentration of favours that infuriated the League. A few weeks later Guise routed the *reiters* at Auneau, thereby ensuring his role as undisputed leader of the Catholic party. One of the consequences of Joyeuse's death was the destruction of the 'system of favour', the balancing act between the two *archimignons* that the king had performed for some years.[9] Henceforth, he would have to rely on Épernon alone in facing up to Guise and the League. Shortly before Christmas Henry returned to Paris in triumph. The people acclaimed him and a solemn *Te Deum* was sung at Notre-Dame, but few were deceived: the real victors were the king's enemies, Guise and Navarre.

The bodies of Joyeuse and his brother, Saint-Sauveur, were brought to Paris on 4 March 1588. Their effigies were exposed at Saint-Jacques-du-

Haut-Pas in a *salle de parade*. Such a custom was not reserved for royalty alone; the effigy of the Constable of Montmorency had been similarly exposed in 1567. However, instead of being shown in courtly attire, Joyeuse was in a penitent's habit. For three days the effigy attracted large crowds. On the 6th it was made to sit at a table for a funeral repast. Next day, the king and Épernon, accompanied by many courtiers, paid their last respects to the deceased. On 8 March a huge procession of penitents, religious orders, officers of the king's household, knights of the Holy Ghost and corporations of Paris escorted the bodies of Joyeuse and his brother to the church of the Grands Augustins for the funeral. The effigies were placed in a *chapelle ardente* in the choir, and on 9 March a eulogy was delivered by the bishop of Senlis after a requiem mass. On the 12th the bodies were taken to their final resting place at the Capuchin monastery in the faubourg Saint-Honoré. A number of poetic eulogies were composed for the occasion. The king's grief was compared to that of Phoebus over the fall of Phaëthon; others identified Joyeuse with Christ or gave him the title of 'prince of martyrs'.[10]

The favours showered on Épernon by Henry III following the death of Joyeuse did not enhance the king's popularity or bolster his flagging authority. Many noblemen who felt that they had been unfairly overlooked in the promotion stakes left the court and joined Guise and the League. As Pasquier noted, without a blow being struck, the king had lost more nobles than at the Battle of Coutras. He was also denounced for not lifting a finger to prevent the execution of Mary Stuart, an event seen by French Catholics as a warning of things to come if a Protestant were ever to become king of France. Henry had also allowed the *reiters* to return home with Épernon as escort after their defeat at the hands of Guise. Preachers in Paris poured scorn on the king while scurrilous pamphlets attacking him and his entourage poured from the presses; they accused Henry of the basest duplicity. The hate campaign was orchestrated by the duchesse de Montpensier, Guise's sister, from her Parisian *hôtel*.

Early in 1588 the League submitted various demands to the king: Épernon's dismissal, acceptance of Guise's tutelage in dealing with heresy, and publication of the decrees of the Council of Trent. In May Guise accepted an invitation from the Sixteen to come to Paris in defiance of a royal ban. Instead of having him arrested, however, Henry planted troops around the Louvre and elsewhere in Paris, thereby breaching the inhabitants' traditional privilege of self-defence. They poured into the streets, set up barricades and attacked the royal troops, injuring some of them. Rather than face the music, Henry decided to leave Paris. On 13 May, the so-called 'Day of the Barricades', he fled to Chartres, leaving Guise free to tighten his hold on the capital.[11] The leader of the Sixteen became mayor and took an oath of loyalty to the duke as the representative of cardinal de Bourbon, the League's chosen candidate for the throne.

The king was accompanied to Chartres by the dukes of Montpensier and Longueville, and by a few great officers of the crown. Épernon, who had been in Normandy on the 'Day of the Barricades', arrived on 20 May with a suite of five hundred noblemen. His presence, however, did not alter the king's resolution regarding the League's demands. He accepted them on the 28th and called a meeting of the Estates-General. Épernon agreed to surrender all his offices provided they were not given to Guise. The king also recognised the cardinal de Bourbon as his heir and appointed the duke as lieutenant-general of the kingdom. Henry's humiliation seemed complete, but appearances were deceptive: he was playing for time. In September he surprised everyone by sacking all his ministers, including the chancellor, Cheverny, and replacing them with younger men, many of them clients of Épernon, who evidently still exercised an indirect influence on the court.[12] Pasquier was not far wrong in suggesting that Henry wished to turn over a new leaf and rid himself of the ministers appointed by Catherine who were suspected of sympathising with Guise. The queen mother was still in Paris and on amicable terms with the duke. The king even dismissed his physician, Marc Miron, who had served him for twenty years.[13] Henry's new team included his last *mignon*: Roger II de Saint-Lary, baron de Bellegarde. Having entered the court at the age of thirteen, he became a gentleman of the chamber thanks largely to Épernon's support. Eventually he was promoted *Maître de la garde-robe*, then *Grand écuyer* and finally *Premier gentilhomme de la chambre*.[14]

Henry hoped that the Estates-General would provide him with the means needed to fight the Huguenots. He tried to influence the elections, but most of the deputies supported the League: they feared that any money granted to the king would be squandered on his pleasures. Henry concluded that the deputies were being manipulated by Guise and decided to get rid of him. He announced his decision to a few close friends. Some advised caution: they thought the duke should be imprisoned and tried. Others backed Henry's decision, believing that in crimes of *lèse-majesté* the punishment should precede the judgment.

Various contemporary accounts exist of the tragic events that followed at the château of Blois. None can be regarded as wholly reliable; an approximation of the truth must suffice. On 23 December the king asked to be roused at 4 a.m. but he was already awake when his valet called. A council meeting had been fixed for 6 a.m. In the meantime Henry assembled his Gascon bodyguard, the Forty-five, and told them of his decision to murder the duc de Guise. After they had assured him of their loyalty, they were distributed around the king's apartment. Some were posted in the antechamber between the chamber where the council met and the king's cabinet. The council was already in session when the duke arrived. He had come regardless of warnings he had received of a plot against his life. On entering the council chamber, the duke complained of feeling cold; he asked for a fire to be lit and for some fruit or sweetmeats to be brought to him. As the council resumed its business, the secretary of state, Revol, entered and whispered in the duke's ear that the king wished to see him in his *cabinet*. Guise accordingly left the room. Outside he encountered the Forty-five who saluted him and formed up around him as an escort. Suddenly one stabbed him in the chest, another in the throat and a third transfixed him with his sword. Guise shouted for help. Though badly wounded, he summoned enough strength to drag his assailants across the floor of the antechamber. He then collapsed, but was still breathing as Henry stepped out of the *cabinet* to survey the scene. He ordered the duke to be finished off. As he looked upon the corpse lying at his feet, he allegedly said: 'My God, isn't he tall! He seems even taller dead than alive.'[15] The duke's body was then searched and a document found inside a pocket. This laid out a plan to take over the government. The king listened carefully as it was read out to him. The document also urged Guise to draw closer to the queen mother and to flatter the king's current favourites, Bellegarde and Laugnac. The plan, if genuine, was not to depose the king, but for Guise to set himself up as a kind of prime minister acting as intermediary between sovereign and nobility. Meanwhile, the cardinal de Guise, who had risen from the council table to investigate the commotion outside, was pinned down by his fellow councillors. He was interrogated at length by Retz about the League's intentions. The cardinal is said to have confessed that the Catholic princes planned to seize the king; he was then murdered by Henry's order. Both bodies were burnt to deprive the League of its martyrs. The skill with which Henry had carried out his coup amazed contemporary observers. The Florentine Filippo Cavriana was particularly impressed by the secrecy that Henry had succeeded in maintaining.[16]

Far from ridding the king of his difficulties, the double murder triggered an armed rising by the Parisians. The preacher Guincestre asked the congregation at the church of Saint-Barthélemy to raise a hand and swear to spare neither the smallest coin in their purses nor the last drop of their blood in avenging the deaths of the two princes of Lorraine.[17] On 2 January 1589 a mob destroyed the tombs of the *mignons* in the church of Saint-Paul. On 10 January more than ten thousand small children dressed in white went in procession from the cemetery of the Innocents to the church of Sainte-Geneviève. On the following day they were joined by adults wearing only shirts in spite of the cold weather, walking barefoot and holding burning candles. On 25 February a large picture behind the high altar of the church

of the Grands Augustins depicting the foundation of the Order of the Holy
Ghost was burnt and replaced by another showing Christ among the pilgrims
of Emmaus.[18] Meanwhile requiem masses were held in all the capital's
churches. The christening of Guise's posthumous son on 7 February 1589 was
almost turned into a canonisation.[19] And the outpouring of grief by the
Parisians was coupled with rage. Henry III had become Satan in their eyes.
The Sorbonne freed them from their allegiance and deleted Henry's name
from their prayers.

'Oh wretched man! What has he done? . . . Pray for him, for he needs [your
prayers] more than ever. I see him rushing to his ruin. I fear that he may lose
his body, soul and kingdom.'[20] Such were the words allegedly spoken by
Catherine de' Medici following the murder of Guise. On 31 December her
physician, Filippo Cavriana, reported that she was in deep shock; she could
see no cure, now or in the future, for the kingdom's ills. On the following day
she visited the cardinal de Bourbon, who was now a prisoner. She tried to tell
him that he would soon be pardoned and set free, but he rounded on her.
'Madame! Madame!' he said. 'We are all dying because of your actions and
your tricks, Madame!' Silently and in tears, Catherine returned to her apartment. Three days later she ran a high fever. On 5 January she asked to make
her will and to see a confessor. Later that morning her speech grew faint and
the king had to dictate her last wishes. Catherine died at 1.30 p.m. An
autopsy revealed that her lungs were rotten, her brain blood-soaked, and that
she had an abscess on her left side. The modern verdict is that she died of
pleurisy. After her body had been embalmed and placed in a wooden coffin
lined with lead, her effigy, decked out in robes that had been used for the
funeral of Anne of Brittany, was put on public display at the château of Blois,
where it remained for nearly four weeks.

Catherine's funeral took place on 4 February 1589 in the church of Saint-
Sauveur at Blois. Renault de Beaune, archbishop of Bourges, gave the eulogy
describing her as the best of French queens. In Paris, however, news of her
death aroused mixed feelings. Some Leaguers swore to cast her body in the
Seine if anyone dared to bring it to Paris for burial. Others were more charitable. A preacher described Catherine as having done both good and evil,
though probably less of the former than of the latter. He allowed his congregation to offer up one *Our Father* and one *Hail Mary* for her soul.[21] A pamphlet
expressed the mixed feelings of Parisians:

> *La reine qui ci-gît fut un diable et un ange*
> *Toute pleine de blâme et pleine de louange*
> *Elle soutint l'État, et l'État mit à bas;*
> *Elle fit maints accords et pas moins de débats;*

Elle enfanta trois rois et cinq guerres civiles,
Fit bâtir des châteaux et ruiner des villes,
Fit bien des bonnes lois et de mauvais édits.
Souhaite lui, passant, Enfer et Paradis.[22]

(Here lies the queen who was both devil and angel,
Full of blame and full of praise:
She upheld the state and brought down the state;
She made many treaties and as many disputes;
She gave birth to three kings and to five civil wars;
Had châteaux built and towns ruined;
Made many good laws and bad edicts;
Passer-by, wish her Hell and Paradise.)

The mood of Paris deterred the king from transferring his mother's remains to Saint-Denis. They consequently remained at Blois for the time being. According to Pasquier, the body had not been correctly embalmed and began to smell; it had, therefore, to be buried in an unmarked grave where it remained for the next twenty-one years until Diane de France, Henry II's natural daughter, had it exhumed and taken to the Chapel of the Valois at Saint-Denis. When this was demolished in 1719, Catherine's remains were moved to another resting place within the abbey. In 1793, however, a revolutionary mob tossed them into a mass grave along with the bones of other kings and queens.

In her will Catherine remembered all those people who had served her. She distributed 400,000 *écus* among some five hundred members of her household. Among them were 112 ladies-in-waiting and *demoiselles d'honneur*, 76 *gentilshommes servants*, 6 dwarfs, 58 councillors, 108 secretaries, 51 clerks of her chapel. 23 doctors and 50 chambermaids, not to mention kitchen staff and other humble domestics. The bequests must have been welcome, for many of the servants had not been paid for years: the arrears for the past year alone totalled 50,000 *écus*.[23] The queen mother's principal legatees were her granddaughter, Christine de Lorraine, who became Grand Duchess of Tuscany, her daughter-in-law, Queen Louise, and Charles d'Angoulême, Grand Prior of France, the bastard son of Henry II. Christine received all the queen's property in Italy, including her claim to the duchy of Urbino; also the Hôtel de la Reine in Paris along with half of its furniture, as well as rings and jewels. Louise got Chenonceau, and Charles the counties of Clermont, Auvergne and Lauraguais. A notable absentee from the will was Catherine's daughter, Marguerite, whom she had disinherited. As executor, Henry III was required to fund a chapter that Catherine had founded in the church of the

Annonciade that was attached to her Paris residence. He was also required to provide dowries for poor girls, and to give money to the poor in return for their prayers. Moreover, he was given responsibility for the settlement of Catherine's debts, said to have amounted to 800,000 *écus*. This necessitated the sale of the contents of the Hôtel de la Reine, but the duc de Mayenne and duchesse de Montpensier, who now occupied the building, refused to admit Catherine's creditors. They had to wait until 1593 for any settlement. It was then decided that they should be paid out of the proceeds of the sale of three of Catherine's estates: Chenonceau, Montceaux and Saint-Maur-des-Fossés.[24]

The Assassination of Henry III, 1 August 1589

Virtually alone, having lost Joyeuse, several of his *mignons* and now his mother, and with the majority of Parisians howling for his blood, Henry III had only to await the final blow. But he was nothing if not courageous. Only by coming to terms with one of his enemies could he hope to survive. In April 1589 he signed a truce with Navarre that soon turned into an alliance. This earned him a monitory from Pope Sixtus V threatening excommunication unless Henry did penance for the murder of the cardinal de Guise and set free the cardinal de Bourbon and the archbishop of Lyon whom he had imprisoned. Combining forces, Henry and Navarre laid siege to Paris, setting up their headquarters at Saint-Cloud and Meudon respectively. Meanwhile an anti-Valois frenzy in the capital boiled over. Identifying Henry with Satan, preachers called for his extermination.

Henry III had taken up residence at Saint-Cloud in the home of Jérôme de Gondi. On the evening of 31 July 1589 Jacques de La Guesle, *procureur général* of the Parlement of Paris, and his brother were travelling from Vanves to Saint-Cloud when they overtook a Jacobin friar. His name was Jacques Clément and he claimed that he had been sent to the king from Paris by de Harlay, the president of the Parlement, with important news.[25] La Guesle agreed to give him a lift on his horse. On arrival at Gondi's house, Clément produced a letter of introduction from de Harlay and a passport signed by the comte de Brienne who was a prisoner of the League. It was arranged that he should see the king at his next *lever*. Henry was sitting, half-undressed, on his close-stool when the friar was ushered into his presence. The king looked at the documents he had brought and, turning to the friar, asked him to disclose the important message he claimed to be carrying. Clément said that de Harlay was well. He then asked if he might draw closer to Henry to impart a confidence. The king ordered La Guesle and Bellegarde to stand aside, and the friar drew closer to him as if to whisper in his ear. As he did so, he pulled a knife from his sleeve and plunged it into Henry's abdomen. 'Oh my God!' cried the king as he rose from the stool. He managed to pull the knife out of his body and with it struck the friar in the face and chest. La Guesle and Bellegarde hurled themselves on the friar, who fell next to the king's bed. Members of the Forty-five burst into the room and hacked the friar to death with their swords. Then, in time-honoured fashion, Clément's body was thrown out of a window into a courtyard below. Meanwhile, frantic efforts were made to save the king's life. Blood poured from his wound, which was wide enough for the intestines to be visible. Even so, he was still conscious. He dictated a note to the queen, who was at Chenonceau, telling her not to worry and to stay put; but the doctors, who examined Henry did not rate highly his chances of survival. That night he ran a high fever and suffered great pain. With him were Épernon, the *Grand prieur*, Bellegarde, François d'O and two captains of the guard, Larchant and Clermont d'Entragues. They all wept, none more so than the king's nephew, the *Grand prieur*, who had come to regard Henry as his father. Navarre then arrived, having travelled

69. The assassination of Henry III at Saint-Cloud, on 1 August 1589.

posthaste from his camp outside Paris. He was at the king's bedside about 10 a.m. and returned to Meudon later that day. Legend has it that Henry III acknowledged him as his successor and ordered his entourage to do likewise (see plate 21), but a letter written by Navarre following his return to Meudon indicates clearly that at the time of their meeting Henry believed he would survive.[26] The legend may be ascribed to *post-facto* Bourbon propaganda aimed at reinforcing Navarre's claim to the throne.[27] Early next morning, however, around 2 a.m., Henry III died. Navarre was told that evening that the king's state had got worse. He promptly left his camp for Saint-Cloud but arrived to find that the last Valois was no more. If Sully is to be believed, Navarre was saluted as their new sovereign by the dignitaries present and the Scottish guards.[28]

Henry III's death was acclaimed by the League as an act of God. 'A new David has killed Goliath,' exclaimed Jean Boucher, curé of Saint-Benoît in Paris, 'a new Judith has killed Holofernes.'[29] Catherine de Lorraine, duchesse de Montpensier, Guise's sister, was ecstatic. 'What joy you bring me!' she said to the messenger who brought her the news; 'my only regret is that he did not know before his death that I had ordered it!' The duchess and her mother, Anne d'Este, duchesse de Nemours, toured Paris in a coach, calling out to Parisians: 'Good news, my friends! The tyrant is dead! There is no more Henri de Valois in France!' Parisians expressed their jubilation by lighting bonfires in the squares of the capital. The Spanish ambassador, Mendoza, writing to Philip II, acclaimed the news as good for the Catholic cause everywhere.[30]

Henry III's body was laid to rest in the church of Saint Corneille in Compiègne where it remained; for Henri IV did not order its transfer to Saint-Denis.[31] Henry III was the first king of France to be murdered by one of his own subjects, yet his court survived. Some members of his entourage joined Henry IV without demur; others made his conversion a condition of their serving him. Épernon and Bellegarde thought of retiring. The former only rallied to Henry IV once the military situation had turned in his favour. Only a few of Henry III's former companions went over to the League. As for the king's household, it remained largely intact, for Henry IV confirmed all the staff, if only to demonstrate that he was now king and no longer just a party leader.[32] When he eventually decided to become a Catholic, he opened up the court to many more people. That is not to say that there was no change in its character under the new monarch, for his personality was markedly different from that of his predecessor. A countryman at heart, he was also gregarious and anything but fastidious in his personal habits.[33]

The court's survival was only to be expected, since no one questioned its right to exist. The fatal blow by the Jacobin friar was aimed only at the person of Henry III, not at his office. Monarchy as a form of government was never called into question in sixteenth-century France, not even by the people who had been howling for Henry's blood. It was because they believed that he had betrayed the trust placed in him by God that they clamoured for his removal. Monarchy was the only form of government they knew; it was also an integral part of their religious faith. The king of France was, in their eyes, the 'Most Christian King' and they expected him to behave as such. Henry had forsaken their allegiance by conduct they construed as tyrannical. The last straw was the alliance he had concluded with the heretical leader Henri de Navarre. The only constitutional issue over which they sometimes argued was the source of royal authority: had the king been directly appointed by God or had he been elected under some divine dispensation?

The fact that monarchy was the only form of government known to Frenchmen in the sixteenth century explains why the existence of the court, however unpopular, was never disputed. Everyone accepted it as being at the heart of government. That is why it survived the traumas that beset it in the late sixteenth century. Yet something had obviously gone wrong. Why had Henry III brought his court into such disrepute? Had it played any part in his unhappy demise? As we have seen, the court closely reflected the monarch's personality: he dictated its shape, size, character and mobility. Charles VIII, Louis XII, Francis I and Henry II may be said to have used the court in a way both intelligible and acceptable to their subjects. It is true that even in their day it came in for criticism. Courtiers were denounced as flatterers and hypocrites; at times of economic hardship court entertainments were regarded as indecently expensive. Humanists believed that the king should pick his councillors from among themselves rather than from semi-educated noblemen. No one, however, dared to question his right to surround himself with friends, ministers and servants of his own choosing.

The court underwent significant changes during the first half of the sixteenth century: it became much larger as it recruited more staff and as people flocked to it in search of employment and patronage. Its manners became more polished as a consequence of the greater role given to women in its activities. Such changes, however, did not affect the court's essential function of serving the monarch, not merely for his own enjoyment, but also as a means of bonding him with his subjects. The kings of France traditionally took pride in their accessibility; they seized every opportunity of familiarising themselves with the various parts of the kingdom by visiting them. As they did so, they were given entries which provided them with opportunities of projecting their authority and publicising their aims and aspirations. Thus they proclaimed themselves to be champions of peace and providers of fruitfulness and plenty. The imagery and symbolism of public ceremonial achieved a new sophistication in the early sixteenth century, which, particularly under

Henry II, evoked memories of the glories of ancient Rome. At the same time the court became a focus of artistic excellence that enhanced its prestige internationally. The many fine châteaux erected mainly by Francis I and his courtiers, the leading painters and sculptors who came from Italy to work at the French court and the collections of paintings, statues and books built up painstakingly by the king served to make his court an object of admiration among foreigners. Ambassadors sent home enthusiastic accounts of its splendid banquets and balls. All of this, however, underwent a great shock around the middle of the century, mainly for two reasons. The first was the rise of a new religion – Protestantism – which offered the king's subjects an alternative to the faith officially endorsed by the king and the court. The nation was more profoundly divided than it had ever been before. The second reason was the accidental death of Henry II, which plunged the kingdom into one of the gravest political crises of its history. The fact that his son was only a boy offered competing aristocratic houses a chance to seize power. The Guises were the first to do so, thereby provoking the enmity of the house of Bourbon, which had a far better claim to run the government. Others, like the Montmorencys, tried to hold the balance, while differences of religion helped to embitter the rivalries further. These were inevitably played out at court as well as in the kingdom at large. The court was torn apart as noble factions struggled to control it. As the kingdom drifted into civil war, the queen mother, Catherine de' Medici, tried unsuccessfully to reconcile the parties. She also tried, as best she could, to maintain a normal court life, with its usual round of ceremonies and entertainments. She served her second son, Charles IX, as regent until his majority was declared, and remained a powerful voice in the government thereafter. Historians are divided as to whether she was a force for good or evil. Wherever the truth may lie, as a woman and an Italian she could never hope to command the same authority as a Frenchman, and her dominance at court helped to fuel its growing unpopularity. Rightly or wrongly she was held responsible for the Massacre of St Bartholomew which destroyed any hope of an early solution of the kingdom's problems. It was certainly due to her initiative that her third son, Henry, was elected king of Poland, and, in retrospect, this may be seen as a mistake, for his sojourn in that country fuelled the political ambitions of his younger brother, the duc d'Alençon. Following Henry's return to France, the court witnessed a fierce rivalry for clients between the brothers. It became a sort of battleground on which their households tried to outdo each other in size and splendour. The contest only ended in 1584 when Alençon, now duc d'Anjou, died; but this event, far from simplifying the situation, made it worse, for Henry had no son and under the Salic law the next in line to the throne was the Protestant leader Henri de Navarre. He was unacceptable to the majority of the king's

Catholic subjects. The Catholic League was formed in order to exclude him from the throne and a rival candidate was chosen in the person of the cardinal de Bourbon. Looking ahead, courtiers weighed up the pros and cons of supporting Navarre or the League even while Henry III was still king.

There is no doubt that Henry III, highly intelligent as he was, misused the court. Instead of following tradition and using it to gain the affection of his subjects, to foster and retain their loyalty, he used it rather as a plaything of his own; he sought to adapt it to the needs of his own autocratic, reserved and morbid personality. He tried to enhance his authority by distancing himself from the mass of his subjects while surrounding himself with a small group of intimate friends. Erecting a barrier around his dining table was only one example of his exclusiveness; others were the sequence of antechambers that he introduced into the royal apartment in order to make himself less accessible to courtiers and the strict etiquette governing their movement from room to room. Henry also travelled much less than his predecessors: he spent far more time in and near Paris, and consequently took part in only four urban entries as compared with more than a hundred under Charles IX. On the other hand, he liked attending *Te Deums* which helped to underscore his special relationship with the Almighty. Paradoxically, the almost continual presence of the court in Paris brought it more into the public eye. Its activities prompted all those satirical pamphlets which the Parisian chronicler L'Estoile collected with such glee. Henry's addiction to favourites alienated all those noblemen who felt excluded from that circle, and his participation in processions of hooded penitents brought him into ridicule among some of his more cynical and outspoken critics. Whether the king was as morally depraved as they affirmed is difficult to tell; a precise answer would require a foolproof filtering of all the scurrilous rumours that circulated around the court, an exercise beyond the powers of any historian. Henry's conduct certainly played into the hands of the rumour-mongers.

Yet, in spite of all the disasters that befell the court in the half-century that followed Henry II's death, it survived, and in the next century took on a new lease of life, culminating in the static grandeur of Louis XIV's palace at Versailles, which for many people is the very epitome of court life. It should not, however, be allowed to eclipse the splendours of the French Renaissance court which this book has tried to evoke. Nor should the tribulations it suffered in the second half of the sixteenth century obliterate all memory of the 'golden years'.

Notes

Introduction

1. *The Life of Benvenuto Cellini Written by Himself*, tr. J.A. Symonds, ed. J. Pope-Hennessy (London, 1949), p. 264.
2. C. Terrasse, *François Ier: le roi et le règne*, 3 vols (Paris, 1945–70), vol. 3, p. 23.

Chapter 1: The Golden Years, 1483–1559

1. Yvonne Labande-Mailfert, *Charles VIII et son milieu (1470–1498): La jeunesse au pouvoir* (Paris, 1975), pp. 55–80.
2. *Ibid.*, pp. 13–115.
3. E. Albèri (ed.), *Relazioni degli ambasciatori veneti al Senato*, 14 vols (Florence, 1839–63), vol. 4, pp. 15–16. Cited by Labande-Mailfert, *Charles VIII et son milieu*, p. 155.
4. Labande-Mailfert, *Charles VIII et son milieu*, pp. 265–414, 475–88.
5. Bernard Quilliet, *Louis XII* (Paris, 1986), pp. 194–217.
6. *Ibid.*, p. 328.
7. *Ibid.*, pp. 334–55. For a penetrating analysis of Louis XII's reputation across the centuries, see N. Hochner, *Louis XII: les dérèglements de l'image royale (1498–1515)* (Seyssel, 2006), pp. 28–30.
8. R.J. Knecht, 'Marignan: François Ier "vainqueur des Suisses"', in Catherine Arminjon, Denis Lavalle, Monique Chatenet and Claude d'Anthenaise (eds), *De l'Italie à Chambord: François Ier et la chevauchée des princes français* (Paris, 2004), pp. 23–39.
9. R. de Maulde La Clavière, *Louise de Savoie et François Ier: Trente ans de jeunesse, 1485–1515* (Paris, 1895), pp. 122–54.
10. A. Renaudet, *Préréforme et humanisme à Paris pendant les premières guerres d'Italie (1494–1517)* (Paris, 1953), pp. 171–2.
11. Maulde La Clavière, *Louise de Savoie*, p. 184.
12. An Assembly of Notables was an enlarged royal council. It met three times in the sixteenth century: at Tours in 1506, and in Paris in 1527 and 1558. In 1506 it included representatives of some twenty towns which each sent one bourgeois and one nobleman.
13. Maulde La Clavière, *Louise de Savoie*, pp. 218–22. The author assumes wrongly that the Assembly of Notables was a meeting of the Estates-General.
14. Louise de Savoie, *Journal*, in J.-F. Michaud and J.-J.F. Poujoulat, *Nouvelle collection de mémoires pour servir à l'histoire de France*, 1st ser., vol. 5 (1836), p. 88.
15. Charles Giry-Deloison, '"Une haquenée . . . pour le porter bientost et plus doucement en enfer ou en paradis": The French and Mary Tudor's marriage to Louis XII in 1514', in D. Grummitt (ed.), *The English Experience of France, c. 1450–1558* (Aldershot, 2002), pp. 132–59.

16. *CSP Ven.*, vol. 2, p. 196; *LP*, vol. 1 (pt 2), pp. 1343, 1351.

17. Florange, *Mémoires du maréchal de Florange dit le jeune adventureux*, ed. R. Goubaux and P.A. Lemoisne, 2 vols (Paris, 1913–24), vol. 1, p. 163. 'Basoche' was a name given to the Palais de Justice in Paris. Its clerks were ill-disciplined young men whose farces and morality plays provided the only comic element in the French theatre during the Renaissance. See H.G. Harvey, *The Theatre of the Basoche: The Contribution of the Law Societies to French Mediaeval Comedy* (Cambridge, MA, 1941), pp. 228–31.

18. For the reign of Francis I generally see Jean Jacquart, *François Ier* (2nd edn, Paris, 1994), and R.J. Knecht, *Renaissance Warrior and Patron: The Reign of Francis I* (Cambridge, 1994).

19. Florange, *Mémoires*, vol. 1, p. 152; *CAF*, vol. 5, nos 15674–5. Cf. C.A. Mayer and D. Bentley-Cranch, *Florimond Robertet (?–1527), homme d'état français* (Geneva, 1994).

20. P. Morgan, 'Un chroniqueur gallois à Calais', *Revue du nord*, 47 (1965), p. 199.

21. Antonio de Beatis, *The Travel Journal of Antonio de Beatis: Germany, Switzerland, the Low Countries and Italy, 1517–1518*, ed. J.R. Hale (London, 1979), pp. 107–8.

22. *LP*, vol. 6, p. 308, no. 692.

23. See below, pp. 228–35.

24. De Beatis, *The Travel Journal*, p. 107.

25. Knecht, *Renaissance Warrior and Patron*, p. 116.

26. *LP*, vol. 3, no. 2879.

27. Knecht, *Renaissance Warrior and Patron*, pp. 200–15. See also A. Lebey, *Le connétable de Bourbon, 1490–1527* (Paris, 1904), pp. 112–99; D. Crouzet, *Charles de Bourbon, Connétable de France* (Paris, 2003).

28. A. Champollion-Figeac (ed.), *Captivité du roi François Ier* (Paris, 1847).

29. G. Jacqueton, *La politique extérieure de Louise de Savoie* (Paris, 1892).

30. Ghislaine de Boom, *Archiduchess Éléonore, reine de France, soeur de Charles Quint* (Brussels, 2003). This biography was originally published under a different title in 1943.

31. Mark Greengrass, 'Property and Politics in Sixteenth-Century France: The Landed Fortune of Constable Anne de Montmorency', *French History*, 2 (1988), pp. 371–98.

32. F. Decrue, *Anne de Montmorency à la cour, aux armées et au conseil du roi François Ier* (Paris, 1885), p. 164.

33. P. Paris, *Études sur François Ier*, 2 vols (Paris, 1895), vol. 2, pp. 204–323; E. Desgardins, *Anne de Pisseleu duchesse d'Étampes et François Ier* (Paris, 1904); *CAF*, vol. 2, pp. 7189, 7256; vol. 9, p. 8768.

34. *SP*, vol. 7, p. 891. I have modernized the spelling.

35. *LP*, vol. 6, p. 308, no. 692.

36. There is a list of Eleanor's household staff at the Bibliothèque Sainte-Geneviève in Paris: MS. 848. This yields twelve Spanish names among some fifty ladies and *demoiselles d'honneur*. There was also an unusually large number of musicians.

37. Monique Chatenet, *La cour de France au XVIe siècle: vie sociale et architecture* (Paris, 2000), pp. 27–8.

38. Pierre de Brantôme, *Oeuvres complètes*, ed. L. Lalanne, 11 vols (Paris, 1864–82), vol. 7, p. 341.

39. N. Tommaseo, *Relations des ambassadeurs vénitiens sur les affaires de France au XVIe siècle*, 2 vols (Paris, 1838), vol. 1, p. 287.

40. Françoise Bardon, *Diane de Poitiers et le mythe de Diane* (Paris, 1963), p. 50.

41. Decrue, *Anne de Montmorency*, p. 360.

42. R.J. Knecht, 'Charles V's Journey through France, 1539–40', in J.R. Mulryne and Elizabeth Goldring (eds), *Court Festivals of the European Renaissance: Art, Politics and Performance* (Aldershot, 2002), pp. 152–70.

43. L. Romier, *Les origines politiques des guerres de religion*, 2 vols (Paris, 1913), vol. 1, p. 22.

44. Ivan Cloulas, *Henri II* (Paris, 1985), pp. 337–47; Romier, *Les origines politiques*, vol. 1, pp. 1–33.

45. A. Castan, 'La mort de François Ier et les premiers temps du règne de Henri II d'après les dépêches secrètes de l'ambassadeur impérial, Jean de Saint-Mauris', *Mémoires de la Société d'Émulation du Doubs*, 5th ser., vol. 3 (1878), p. 449; *CSP Span.*, vol. 9, pp. 73–7; Cloulas, *Henri II*, pp. 142–3.

46. A. Jouanna et al. (eds), *La France de la Renaissance* (Paris, 2001), p. 785; K. Brandi, *The Emperor Charles V*, tr. C.V. Wedgwood (London, 1939), p. 641.
47. F. Decrue, *Anne duc de Montmorency, Connétable et pair de France sous les rois Henri II, François II et Charles IX* (Paris, 1889), pp. 1–20.
48. Jean-Marie Constant, *Les Guise* (Paris, 1984), pp. 20–36.
49. Cloulas, *Henri II*, pp. 185–8; John Guy, *'My Heart Is My Own': The Life of Mary Queen of Scots* (London, 2004), pp. 38–42.
50. Romier, *Les origines politiques*, vol. 1, pp. 65–77.
51. *Lettres de Catherine de Médicis*, ed. Hector de la Ferrière and Baguenault de Puchesse, 10 vols (Paris, 1880–1909), vol. 8, p. 181.
52. J.-H. Mariéjol, *Catherine de Médicis* (Paris, 1920), p. 43.
53. *Ibid.*, p. 44.
54. Thierry Wanegffelen, *Catherine de Médicis: le pouvoir au féminin* (Paris, 2005), pp. 11–19.
55. N.M. Sutherland, *The Huguenot Struggle for Recognition* (New Haven, CT, 1980), pp. 342–3; D. Crouzet, *La genèse de la réforme française, 1520–1562* (Paris, 1996), pp. 419–21.
56. Robert M. Kingdon, *Geneva and the Coming of the Wars of Religion in France, 1555–1563* (Geneva, 1956), pp. 54–67.
57. Cloulas, *Henri II*, pp. 315–33.
58. Decrue, *Anne de Montmorency*, pp. 203–9.
59. Cloulas, *Henri II*, pp. 582–3.
60. *Ibid.*, pp. 589–94.

Chapter 2: One Kingdom, Two Capitals

1. G. Zeller, *Les institutions de la France au XVIe siècle* (Paris, 1948), pp. 1–9; H. Stein and L. Legrand, *La frontière d'Argonne* (Paris, 1905).
2. F. Braudel, *The Mediterranean and the Mediterranean World in the Age of Philip II*, tr. S. Reynolds, 2 vols (London, 1972–3), i. 360; F. Braudel, *The Identity of France*, tr. S. Reynolds, 2 vols (London, 1989–1), vol. 1, p. 112; C. Estienne, *Le guide des chemins de France de 1553*, ed. J. Bonnerot, 2 vols (Paris, 1936); R. Mousnier, *Études sur la France de 1494 à 1559* (Cours de Sorbonne, 1964), pp. 9–13.
3. Jouanna et al., *La France du XVIe siècle*, p. 11.
4. J. Dupâquier (ed.), *Histoire de la population française*, vol. 2: *De la Renaissance à 1789* (2nd edn, Paris, 1991); Jouanna et al., *La France du XVIe siècle*, pp. 23–37.
5. B. Chevalier, *Les bonnes villes de France du XIVe au XVIe siècle* (Paris, 1982), pp. 13, 40, 46–7, 54; P. Benedict (ed.), *Cities and Social Change in Early Modern France* (London, 1989), pp. 24–5.
6. P. Chaunu and R. Gascon (eds), *Histoire économique et sociale de la France*, vol. 1 (1450–1660), pt 1: *L'état et la ville* (1977), pp. 256–60; Jouanna et al., *La France du XVIe siècle*, pp. 109–13.
7. L. Febvre and H.-J. Martin, *The Coming of the Book: The Impact of Printing* (London, 1986), pp. 170–7, 181–6.
8. P. Goubert, *L'ancien régime*, 2 vols (Paris, 1969), vol. 1, pp. 81–5; G. Duby and A. Wallon (eds), *Histoire de la France rurale*, vol. 2 (Paris, 1975), pp. 108–20, 134–47.
9. Chevalier, *Les bonnes villes*, pp. 35–6.
10. Arlette Jouanna, *Ordre social: mythes et hiérarchies dans la France du XVIe siècle* (Paris, 1977), pp. 54–85.
11. Donna Bonahan, *Crown and Nobility in Early Modern France* (Basingstoke, 2001), pp. 7–33.
12. Jean-Marie Constant, *La vie quotidienne de la noblesse française aux XVIe–XVIIe siècles* (Paris, 1985), p. 194; Arlette Jouanna, *Le devoir de révolte: la noblesse française et la gestation de l'état moderne, 1559–1661* (Paris, 1989), p. 98.
13. Claude de Seyssel, *The Monarchy of France*, ed. D.R. Kelley (New Haven, CT, 1981), pp. 61–2.

14. Fanny Cosandey and Robert Descimon, *L'absolutisme en France: histoire et historiographie* (Paris, 2002); R. Bonney, 'Absolutism: What's in a Name?', *French History*, 1 (1987), 93–117; R. Bonney, *L'absolutisme* (Paris, 1989).

15. B. Barbiche, *Les institutions de la monarchie française à l'époque moderne* (Paris, 1999), pp. 28–33.

16. P. Hamon, *L'argent du roi: les finances sous François Ier* (Paris, 1994), pp. 65–133.

17. *Ibid.*, pp. 251–4.

18. E. Maugis, *Histoire du Parlement de Paris*, 3 vols (1913–16); J.H. Shennan, *The Parlement of Paris* (2nd edn, Stroud, 1998).

19. See below, pp. 64–5.

20. Jouanna, *La France*, pp. 142–4; M. Harsgor, *Recherches sur le personnel du conseil du roi sous Charles VIII et Louis XII*, 4 vols (Lille, 1980); F. Decrue, *De consilio regis Francisci I* (1885); R. Mousnier, *Le conseil du roi de Louis XII à la révolution* (Paris, 1970); J.A. Guy, 'The French King's Council, 1483–1526', in R.A. Griffiths and J. Sherborne (eds), *Kings and Nobles in the Later Middle Ages* (New York, 1986), pp. 274–94;

21. Jouanna, *La France*, p. 142.

22. Barbiche, *Les institutions*, pp. 121–3; M. Etchechoury, *Les maîtres des requêtes de l'hôtel du roi sous les derniers Valois (1553–1589)* (Paris, 1991), pp. 19–36.

23. Barbiche, *Les institutions*, pp. 153–72; Helène Michaud, *La Grande Chancellerie et les écritures royales au XVIe siècle* (Paris, 1967).

24. Chatenet, *La cour de France*, p. 20; Jean-Pierre Babelon, *Nouvelle histoire de Paris: Paris au XVIe siècle* (Paris, 1986), pp. 45, 53.

25. Labande-Mailfert, *Charles VIII et son milieu*, p. 457.

26. Chatenet, *La cour de France*, p. 20.

27. *CAF*, vol. 8, pp. 411–567.

28. Chatenet, *La cour de France*, p. 20

29. Babelon, *Nouvelle histoire*, pp. 148–9, 151.

30. Lawrence M. Bryant, *The King and the City in the Parisian Royal Entry Ceremony: Politics, Ritual, and Art in the Renaissance* (Geneva, 1986), *passim*; Babelon, *Nouvelle histoire*, pp. 55–60.

31. Anne-Marie Lecoq, 'Une fête italienne à la Bastille en 1518', in *'Il se rendit en Italie': études offertes à André Chastel* (Paris, 1987), pp. 149–68. See also below, pp. 72–4.

32. V.-L. Bourrilly (ed.), *Journal d'un Bourgeois de Paris sous le règne de François Ier* (Paris, 1910), p. 49; C. Whibley (ed.), *Henry VIII* (London, 1904), vol. 1, p. 175.

33. *Registres des délibérations du Bureau de la Ville de Paris*, vol. 1 (1499–1526), ed. F. Bonnardot (Paris, 1883), pp. 102–3.

34. R.J. Knecht, 'Francis I and the "Lit de Justice": A "Legend" Defended', *French History*, 7 (1993), pp. 53–83.

35. *Registres des délibérations du Bureau de la Ville de Paris*, vol. 2 (1527–39), ed. Alexandre Tuetey (Paris, 1886), p. 17.

36. See below, p. 284.

Chapter 3: The Court

1. *Ordonnances des rois de France, règne de François Ier*, 9 vols (Paris, 1902–75), vol. 6, no. 547.

2. J.-F. Solnon, *La cour de France* (Paris, 1987), p. 15.

3. F. Lot and R. Fawtier, *Histoire des institutions françaises au Moyen Âge*, vol. 2: *Institutions royales* (Paris, 1958), pp. 66–8.

4. BNF, MS. Clairambault 832, pp. 128–9. Cited in *ibid.*, p. 70.

5. D. Potter (ed.), *France in the Later Middle Ages, 1200–1500* (Oxford, 2002), pp. 160–3.

6. Labande-Mailfert, *Charles VIII et son milieu*, pp. 139–41.

7. Chatenet, *La cour de France*, p. 24.

8. See below, pp. 80–6.

9. *CAF*, vol. 2, p. 506, no. 6238.

10. *LP*, vol. 4, nos 2087, 2092.

11. Christelle Cazaux, *La musique à la cour de François Ier* (Paris, 2002), pp. 69–106.
12. AN, KK94, f. 60r; BNF, Ms. fr. 2953, f. 20r.
13. *Ordonnances*, vol. 7, pp. 136–7.
14. Cazaux, *La musique*, p. 96.
15. '*Il buttar' grande che fa il Re ogni giorno*': *Correspondance des nonces en France, 1541-46*, ed. J. Lestocqouy (Rome/Paris, 1965), p. 113.
16. P. Hamon, *L'argent du roi. Les finances sous François Ier* (Paris, 1994), pp. 4–5.
17. *LP*, vol. 24 (pt 2), no. 492.
18. Chatenet, *La cour de France*, p. 25.
19. Decrue, *Anne de Montmorency à la cour*, p. 77; Brigitte Bedos-Rezak, *Anne de Montmorency* (Paris, 1990), p. 115.
20. Chatenet, *La cour de France*, p. 34.
21. AS Mantua, A.G. 634.
22. *Ibid.*, 638.
23. Chatenet, *La cour de France*, p. 33.
24. Raffaele Tamalio, *Federico Gonzaga alla corte di Francesco I di Francia nel carteggio privato con Mantova (1515–1517)* (Paris, 1994), p. 239.
25. 'Mémoires de la vie de François de Scépeaux, sire de Vieilleville', in *Collection complète des mémoires relatifs à l'histoire de France*, ed. M. Petitot, vol. 26 (Paris, 1822), pp. 78–9.
26. Chatenet, *La cour de France*, p. 20.
27. Annie Cosperec, *Blois: la forme d'une ville* (Paris, 1994), p. 106.
28. *Ibid.*, p. 20.
29. See below, pp. 80–6.
30. N. Tommaseo (ed.), *Relations des ambassadeurs vénitiens sur les affaires de France au XVIe siècle* (Paris, 1838), vol. 1, pp. 106–10.
31. *CAF*, vol. 8, pp. 419–25.
32. C. Estienne, *Le guide des chemins de France de 1553*, ed. J. Bonnerot, 2 vols (1936).
33. *CAF*, vol. 2, p. 676, no. 7047.
34. J. Boutier, A. Dewerpe and D. Nordman, *Un tour de France royal: le voyage de Charles IX (1564–1566)* (Paris, 1984), pp. 44–7.
35. Chatenet, *La cour de France*, p. 40.
36. BNF, Ms. fr. 10390, ff. 1–33; F. Bournon, 'Inventaire des tapisseries emportées du château de Blois en 1533', *Nouvelles archives de l'art français*, 2nd ser., vol. 1 (1979), pp. 334–2; Chatenet, *La cour de France*, pp. 31–2. See S. Schneebalg-Perelman, 'Richesses du garde-meuble parisien de François Ier: inventaires inédits de 1542 et 1551', *GBA*, 6th ser., 78 (1971), pp. 253–304.
37. M. de Montaigne, *The Complete Essays*, tr. M.A. Screech (London, 1993), p. 1019.
38. Chatenet, *La cour de France*, pp. 126–7.
39. Machiavel, *Portrait de la France*, in *Oeuvres*, ed. Vollard (Paris, 1793), vol. 6, p. 185. Cited by Boutier, Dewerpe and Nordman, *Un tour de France*, p. 135.
40. C. Terrasse, *François Ier*, vol. 3 (Paris, 1970), p. 23.
41. AS Modena, Ambasciatori in Francia 23 (Scipio Piovene, Brie-Comte-Robert, 10 June 1546). Cited by Chatenet, *La cour de France*, p. 41.
42. AS Mantua, A.G. 638.
43. BNF Ms. ital. 2182. Cited by Boutier, Dewerpe and Nordman, *Un tour de France*, p. 135.
44. Tommaseo, *Relations des ambassadeurs*, vol. 2, p. 529.
45. AS Mantua, A.G. 639. Cited by Chatenet, *La cour de France*, p. 45.
46. *CSP Ven.*, vol. 4, no. 902.
47. AS Mantua, A.G. 638. Cited by Chatenet, *La cour de France*, p. 35.
48. *CSP Span.*, vol. 6 (i), no. 120.
49. A. Jouanna, P. Hamon, D. Biloghi and G. Le Thiec, *La France de la Renaissance* (Paris, 2001), pp. 1004–6. See also J.-N. Biraben, *Les hommes et la peste en France et dans les pays européens et méditerranéens* (Paris/The Hague, 1975–6).
50. G. Guiffrey (ed.), *Cronique du roy Françoys premier de ce nom* (Paris, 1860), p. 93.

Chapter 4: The Courtier

1. E. Haddad, 'Noble Clientèles in France in the Sixteenth and Seventeenth Centuries: A Historiographical Approach', *French History*, 20 (2006), pp. 75–109.
2. R. Mousnier, *La Vénalité des offices sous Henri IV et Louis XIII* (Paris, 1971), pp. 35–92.
3. Knecht, *Renaissance Warrior and Patron*, pp. 90–103.
4. J. Le Goff and R. Rémond, *Histoire de la France religieuse*, vol. 2, p. 188. The figures are those of M. Perronet. See also Marilyn M. Edelstein, 'The Social Origins of Episcopacy in the Reign of Francis I', *French Historical Studies*, 8 (1974), pp. 377–92. Her figures are slightly different: 123 bishops out of 129 Frenchmen whose origins are known were nobles; six were commoners. The nobles comprised 9 princes of the blood, 93 nobles of the sword and 21 nobles of the robe. At least 23 foreigners were noble.
5. M. Foisil, *Le sire de Gouberville* (Paris, 1981).
6. R.J. Knecht, 'Military Autobiographies in Sixteenth-Century France', in J.R. Mulryne and Margaret Shewring (eds), *War, Literature and the Arts in Sixteenth-Century Europe* (London, 1989), pp. 3–21.
7. Ambroise Paré, *Apologie et Traité contenant les voyages faits en divers lieux; 1585*, in *Oeuvres complètes*, ed. J.-F. Malgaigne (Paris, 1840–1), vol. 3, pp. 703–4.
8. Jouanna, *Le devoir de révolte*, p. 23.
9. Chatenet, *La cour de France*, pp. 258–60.
10. *Ibid.*, pp. 279, 282–3.
11. R.R. Harding, *Anatomy of a Power Elite: The Provincial Governors of Early Modern France* (New Haven, CT, 1978), *passim*; D. Potter, *War and Government in the French Provinces: Picardy 1470–1560* (Cambridge, 1993), pp. 65–112.
12. Harding, *Anatomy of a Power Elite*, pp. 21–31; Kristen B. Neuschel, *Word of Honor: Interpreting Noble Culture in Sixteenth-Century France* (Ithaca, NY, 1989), pp. 1–37.
13. Bernard Chevalier, *Guillaume Briçonnet (v. 1445–1514): Un cardinal-ministre au début de la Renaissance* (Rennes, 2005).
14. C. Michon, 'Les richesses de la faveur à la Renaissance: Jean de Lorraine (1498–1550) et François Ier', *RHMC*, 50 (2003), pp. 34–61.
15. L. Byatt, *Dizionario biografico degli Italiani*, 43 (Rome, 1993), pp. 367–74; J. Tricou, 'Un archevêque de Lyon au XVIe siècle: Hyppolyte d'Este', *Revue des études italiennes* (1958), pp. 147–66; Chatenet, *La cour de France*, pp. 262, 284–5.
16. A. Buisson, *Le Chancelier Antoine Duprat* (Paris, 1935).
17. C.-A. Mayer and D. Bentley-Cranch, *Florimond Robertet (?–1527), homme d'état français* (Paris, 1994).
18. A. Spont, *Semblançay (?–1527): La bourgeoisie financière au début du XVIe siècle* (Paris, 1895); Hamon, *L'Argent du roi*, pp. 293–304.
19. M. Greengrass, 'Noble Affinities in Early Modern France: The Case of Henri I de Montmorency, Constable of France', *EHQ*, 16 (1986), pp. 275–311.
20. Decrue, *Anne de Montmorency*.
21. *St P*, vol. 11, 277.
22. *LP*, vol. 17, 935; *St P*, vol. 9, 192.
23. *LP*, vol. 19 (pt 1), 573; A. Desjardins, *Négociations diplomatiques de la France avec la Toscane* (Paris, 1859–86), vol. 3, p. 140.
24. Jouanna et al., *La France de la Renaissance*, pp. 812–13.
25. Raffaele Tamalio (ed.), *Ferrante Gonzaga alla corte spagnola di Carlo V nel carteggio privato con Mantova (1523–1526). La formazione da "cortegiano" di un generale dell'Impero* (Paris, 1994), p. 203.
26. *Ibid.*, p. 277.
27. Brantôme, *Œuvres complètes*, vol. 7, p. 314.
28. *Ibid.*
29. *Ibid.*, vol. 3, p. 127.
30. Chatenet, *La cour de France*, pp. 27–8.

31. Sydney Anglo, 'The Courtier: The Renaissance and Changing Ideals', in A.G. Dickens (ed.), *The Courts of Europe: Politics, Patronage and Royalty, 1400–1800*, (London, 1977), pp. 33–53, and Anglo, *Machiavelli: The First Century* (Oxford, 2006), pp. 578–88.
32. Pauline M. Smith, *The Anti-Courtier Trend in Sixteenth Century French Literature* (Geneva, 1966), p. 29.
33. *Ibid.*, pp. 32–4.
34. *Ibid.*, p. 144; Anglo, *Machiavelli*, pp. 590–9. See also D. Javitch, 'The Philosopher of the Court: A French Satire Misunderstood', *Comparative Literature*, 23 (1971).
35. Anglo, 'The Courtier', p. 50.
36. Anglo, *Machiavelli*, pp. 590–9.

Chapter 5: The Daily Round

1. The letter is often said to have been written to Charles IX, but this is clearly wrong. The internal evidence points to 1576 as the likeliest date. J.-H. Mariéjol, *Catherine de Médicis* (Paris, 1920), pp. 269–70; N. Le Roux, *La faveur du roi: Mignons et courtisans au temps des derniers Valois (vers 1547, vers 1589)* (Seyssel, 2000), p. 164.
2. R. Scheurer (ed.), *Correspondance du cardinal Jean du Bellay*, 2 vols (Paris, 1969), vol. 1, pp. 153–4.
3. Tommaseo, *Relations des ambassadeurs vénitiens*, vol. 1, pp. 512–13.
4. Tamalio, *Federico Gonzaga*, p. 408.
5. *LP*, vol. 8 (pt 2), no. 993, p. 426. A buskin was a boot reaching to the calf or knee.
6. Chatenet, *La cour de France*, p. 120.
7. Cellini, *The Life of Benvenuto Cellini*, p. 264.
8. Cazaux, *La musique*, p. 112.
9. Chatenet, *La cour de France*, pp. 112–33.
10. Tommaseo, *Relations des ambassadeurs vénitiens*, vol. 1, pp. 371–3.
11. G. Zeller, *Les institutions de la France au XVIe siècle* (Paris, 1948), p. 97.
12. M. Smith, 'Familiarité française et politesse italienne au XVIe siècle', *Revue d'histoire diplomatique*, vol. 102 (1988), p. 206.
13. *Ibid.*, p. 215.
14. B. Castiglione, *The Book of the Courtier*, tr. George Bull (Harmondsworth, 1967), p. 129.
15. M. Smith, 'Familiarité française', p. 196.
16. *Ibid.*, p. 200.
17. *Ibid.*, p. 201.
18. *Ibid.*, p. 202.
19. *Ibid.*, p. 208.
20. AS Mantua, A.G. 639 (5 Jan. 1540. G.B. Gambara to duke of Mantua). Cited by Chatenet, *La cour de France*, p. 122.
21. AS Mantua, A.G. 636 (5 Oct. 1520. Paris; Stazio Gadio). Cited by Chatenet, *La cour de France*, p. 122.
22. Fanny Cosandey, *La reine de France: symbole et pouvoir* (Paris, 2000), pp. 139–42.
23. Anne-Marie Cocula-Vaillières, *Brantôme: amour et gloire au temps des Valois* (Paris, 1986), and M. Lazard, *Pierre de Bourdeille, seigneur de Brantôme* (Paris, 1995).
24. M. Smith, 'Familiarité française', pp. 206–7, 229. Chatenet, *La cour de France*, p. 187.
25. Brantôme, *Oeuvres complètes*, vol. 7, pp. 376–7.
26. Chatenet, *La cour de France*, p. 189.
27. Tamalio, *Federico Gonzaga*, p. 387.
28. Chatenet, *La cour de France*, pp. 189–90.
29. My account of this event is indebted to Lecoq, 'Une fête italienne à la Bastille en 1518', and to Stephen Bamforth and Jean Dupèbe, 'The Silva of Bernardino Rincio (1518)', *Renaissance Studies*, 8 (Sept. 1994), pp. 256–315. The English ambassadors were the Lord Chamberlain, Charles Somerset, earl of Worcester, Nicholas West, bishop of Ely, Thomas Docwra, Grand Prior of St John's, and Nicholas Vaux, captain of Guînes.

30. The two editions (BNF, Réserve Lb 31A and Lb 31) are reproduced in full in the original Latin and translated in *Renaissance Studies*, 8 (Sept. 1994), pp. 292–311.

31. Galeazzo was granted a pardon in March 1516 (*CAF*, vol. 1, p. 106 [no. 616]; vol. 5, p. 320 [no. 16331]. In November he recovered all his goods, *CAF*, vol. 5, p. 307 [no. 16261]. On 24 November 1516 Federico Gonzaga mentioned Galeazzo's presence at the French court in a letter to his father (Tamalio, *Federico Gonzaga*, p. 349).

32. While Lecoq ('Une fête italienne', p. 153) places the two sideboards with gold plate in the corners of the *tribunal*, Bamforth and Dupèbe place all four in the corners of the *orchestra* ('The *Silva*', pp. 267–8).

33. Lecoq, 'Une fête italienne', p. 155.

34. Only two of Galeazzo's three daughters accompanied him to France. Both were married in 1509: Chiara to Pietro da Pusterla and Veronica to Federico Borromeo, count of Arona. One of them – possibly Veronica, who became one of Queen Claude's ladies – was rumoured to have been seduced by Francis I ('una di qual, se dice, è graveda dil Re': Sanuto, *I diarii di Marino Sanuto* [Venice, 1889], vol. 26, p. 55). According to F. Calvi, *Famiglie notabili milanesi*, 4 vols (Milan, 1875–85), vol. 2, she was delivered of a boy soon after coming to France. He was baptised François at the request of the king, his godfather, who paid for his education. Bamforth and Dupèbe, 'The *Silva*', p. 280, n. 89.

35. On masques at the court of Henry VIII, see Sydney Anglo, *Spectacle, Pageantry and Early Tudor Policy* (Oxford, 1969), p. 117. He dismisses the 1512 masque as of 'little artistic significance, and . . . more noteworthy as an illustration of Henry's desire to increase the brilliance of his court by introducing fashionable continental revels into England'.

36. Chatenet, *La cour de France*, p. 231.

37. *Ibid.*, pp. 217–20. For the letter from Marcantonio Bendidio to the marchioness of Mantua (dated Paris, 12 January 1539) see AS Mantua, A.G. 638.

38. For Soranzo's report (1550), see MS. Venice, Bibl. Correr, Cod. Cigogna 1134, ff. 20b–21a. Cited by Chatenet, *La cour de France*, pp. 218–20.

39. *Ibid.*, pp. 142–56.

40. *Ibid.*, pp. 144–7.

41. *Ibid.*, pp. 147–50.

42. De l'Orme, *Premier Tome de l'Architecture* (Paris, 1567), book 4, chap. 1.

43. Chatenet, *La cour de France*, pp. 159–71.

44. See below, pp. 162, 176–8.

45. David Potter and P.R. Roberts, 'An Englishman's View of the Court of Henri III, 1584–1585: Richard Cook's "Description of the Court of France"', *French History*, 2 (1988), p. 340.

46. Chatenet, *La cour de France*, pp. 179–86.

Chapter 6: Outdoor Pursuits

1. De Beatis, *The Travel Journal*, ed. J.R. Hale (London, 1979), p. 134.

2. *St P*, vol. 6, 58. I have modernised the spelling.

3. J. Cummins, *The Hound and the Hawk. The Art of Medieval Hunting* (London, 1988), pp. 1–11.

4. Chatenet, *La cour de France*, pp. 128–9.

5. BNF, Ms. fr. 13429. 'Perot' is identifiable with Perrot de Ruthie to whom Francis gave 20,000 *l.* towards his marriage in April 1533. See *CAF*, vol. 2, 5676, p. 382.

6. Claude d'Anthenaise, 'La chasse, le plaisir et la gloire', in *De l'Italie à Chambord: François Ier et la chevauchée des princes français* (Paris, 2004), p. 106.

7. In 1539 Francis I paid 46 *l.* to Pierre de Sos, *valet des lymiers*, to go to St Hubert after he had been bitten by a rabid dog. Louis Cimber and Charles Danjou (eds), *Archives curieuses de l'histoire de France*, ser. 1, vol. 3, p. 99.

8. D'Anthenaise, 'La chasse', p. 103.

9. *LP*, vol. 3, nos 1160, 1176.

10. See below, p. 159.

11. D'Anthenaise, 'La chasse', pp. 96–7.
12. The finest manuscript of this text is BNF, Ms. fr. 616 at the Bibliothèque Nationale de France.
13. De Beatis, *The Travel Journal*, p. 108.
14. H. Chevreul, *Traité de la Venerie par Feu Monsieur Budé, conseiller du roy François Ier et maistre des requestes ordinaire de son hostel, traduit du latin en français par Louis Le Roy* (Paris, 1861). Cited by d'Anthenaise, 'La chasse', p. 98.
15. *St P*, vol. 6, no. 27, pp. 57–8. I have modernised the spelling.
16. D'Anthenaise, 'La chasse', p. 99.
17. *St P*, vol. 6, no. 27, pp. 57–8. I have modernised the spelling.
18. Desjardins, *Négociations diplomatiques*, vol. 3, p. 16.
19. Guillaume Budé, *De Venatione*, in *De Philologia libri II* (Paris, 1532), tr. Chevreul, *Traité de la vénerie* (Paris, 1861). Cited by d'Anthenaise, 'La chasse', p. 102.
20. D'Anthenaise, 'La chasse', pp. 100–2.
21. *Ibid.*, p. 102.
22. *CAF*, vol. 2, no. 7047.
23. Vincent Carloix, 'Mémoires de la vie de François de Scépeaux, sire de Vieilleville', in M. Petitot (ed.), *Collection complète des mémoires relatifs à l'histoire de France*, vols 16–18 (Paris, 1822), vol. 1, pp. 398–9. Cited by Chatenet, *La cour de France*, pp. 127–8.
24. Abel Lefranc, *La vie quotidienne au temps de la Renaissance* (Paris, 1938), p. 23.
25. Chatenet, *La cour de France*, p. 129.
26. R.J. Knecht (ed.), *The Voyage of Sir Nicholas Carewe to the emperor Charles V in the Year 1529* (Roxburghe Club, 1959), pp. 48–9.
27. Cloulas, *Henri II*, pp. 345–6.
28. Florange, *Mémoires*, vol. 1, p. 226.
29. E. Baux, V.-L. Bourrilly and P. Mabilly, 'Le voyage des reines et de François Ier en Provence et dans la vallée du Rhône (décembre 1515–février 1516), *Annales du Midi*, 16 (1904), p. 51.
30. *Journal de Jean Barrillon*, ed. P. de Vaissière (Paris, 1899), vol. 2, p. 179; *Mémoires de Martin et Guillaume du Bellay*, ed. V.-L. Bourrilly and F. Vindry (Paris, 1908), vol. 1, p. 103; Bourrilly, *Journal d'un Bourgeois de Paris*, p. 76; *Livre de raison de Me Nicolas Versoris*, ed. G. Fagniez (Paris, 1885), p. 16.
31. Chatenet, *La cour de France*, p. 109.
32. See above, pp. 128–9, 140.
33. J. de Saint-Gelais, *Histoire de Louis XII, Roy de France, Père du peuple et de plusieurs choses mémorables advenues en France et en Italie jusques en l'an 1510* (Paris, 1622), p. 179.
34. The event was described by Pierre Sala, a former servant of Charles VIII and Louis XII who was also a man of letters and an 'antiquarian', well versed in old romances of chivalry. (See P. Fabia, *Pierre Sala, sa vie et son oeuvre, avec la légende et l'histoire de l'Antiquaille* [Lyon, 1934].) Two versions exist of a book which he wrote in Lyon. The first, *Hardiesses des grands rois et empereurs* (BNF, Ms. fr. 584), was probably written before the imperial election of 1519; the second, called *Les prouesses de plusieurs roys* (BNF, MS. FR. 10420), may have been written after Francis I's visit to Lyon in April–July 1522. It is modelled on the *Decameron*: Sala imagines a visit by four ladies to l'Antiquaille, his home at Lyon. After one has expressed her love of tales of heroism by ancient kings, the ladies all praise Francis's bravery at Marignano. They then tell a story of past bravery, starting with David and the bear. Sala's offering is Francis I and the boar of Amboise. See Anne-Marie Lecoq, *François Ier imaginaire. Symbolique et politique à l'aube de la Renaissance française* (Paris, 1987), pp. 207–11.
35. Vieilleville, *Mémoires de la vie de François de Scépeaux, sire de Vieilleville*, ed. V. Carloix (Paris, 1822), vol. 1, p. 162.
36. V. Dufour, *La ménagerie royale du château de Vincennes* (Paris, 1890), pp. 53–63.
37. Montaigne, *The Complete Essays*, p. 756.
38. François Billacois, *Le duel dans la société française des XVIe–XVIIe siècles* (Paris, 1986), pp. 21–40.

39. *Mémoires de Martin et Guillaume du Bellay*, vol. 3, pp. 442–4; *Cronique du Roy Françoys premier de ce nom*, ed. G. Guiffrey (Paris, 1860), pp. 232–6; *CAF*, vol. 8, no. 29692.
40. A. Franklin, *Le duel de Jarnac et de La Châtaigneraie* (Paris, 1909); Cloulas, *Henri II*, pp. 147–51.
41. *Commentaires de Blaise de Monluc*, ed. P. Courteault (Paris, 1925), vol. 3, p. 60.
42. Michelet, *Histoire de France*, vol. 9, p. 32.
43. Billacois, *Le duel*, pp. 89–91.

Chapter 7: Ceremonies

1. Helen Watanabe-O'Kelly, 'The Early Modern Festival Book: Function and Form', in J.R. Mulryne, Helen Watanabe-O'Kelly and Margaret Shewring (eds), *Europa Triumphans: Court and Civic Festivals in Early Modern Europe*, 2 vols (Aldershot, 2004), vol. 1, pp. 5–6.
2. For the coronation of Louis XII, see N. Hochner, *Louis XII: les dérèglements de l'image royale (1498–1515)* (Seyssel, 2006), pp. 43–51.
3. Richard A. Jackson, *Vive le Roi! A History of the French Coronation from Charles V to Charles X* (Chapel Hill, NC, 1984), pp. 48–9, 51–2, 57, 59; Cloulas, *Henri II*, pp. 154–7.
4. Fanny Cosandey, *La reine de France. Symbole et pouvoir* (Paris, 2000), pp. 127–62.
5. George Cavendish, *The Life and Death of Cardinal Wolsey*, ed. Richard S. Sylvester (London, 1959), p. 54.
6. Marc Bloch, *Les rois thaumaturges* (Paris, 1961), pp. 309–15.
7. Cosandey, *La reine de France*, p. 202.
8. For details of music played in Francis I's entries, see Cazaux, *La musique*, pp. 184–96.
9. P. Gringore, *Les entrées royales à Paris de Marie d'Angleterre (1514) et Claude de France (1517)*, ed. Cynthia J. Brown (Geneva, 2005), pp. 127–55.
10. Watanabe-O'Kelly, 'The Early Modern Festival Book', vol. 1, pp. 3–17.
11. R. Cooper's introduction to M. Scève, *Entry of Henry II into Lyon, Sep. 1548* (Tempe, AZ, 1997), pp. 128–9.
12. Iain Fenlon, 'Music and Festival', in Mulryne et al. (eds), *Europa Triumphans*, vol. 1, pp. 47–55.
13. For a detailed account of Louis XII's entry into Paris in 1498 and its symbolic significance, see Hochner, *Louis XII*, pp. 52–69.
14. Josèphe Chartrou, *Les entrées solennelles et triomphales à la Renaissance (1484–1551)* (Paris, 1928), pp. 22–3.
15. *Ibid.*, pp. 24–5.
16. *Ibid.*, pp. 26–7.
17. *Ibid.*, pp. 27–8.
18. *Ibid.*, pp. 29–42; N. Hochner, 'Louis XII and the Porcupine: Transformation of a Royal Emblem', *Renaissance Studies*, 15 (2001), pp. 17–36. Although Louis XII's overall military record was undistinguished, his pursuit of bravery and knightly virtue earned him high praise from contemporary writers and artists. His emblem – a porcupine – symbolised invincibility and strength. See Hochner, *Louis XII*, pp. 70–100.
19. Hochner, *Louis XII*, pp. 59–60.
20. Chartrou, *Les entrées solennelles*, pp. 45–7.
21. *Ibid.*, pp. 48–9.
22. The frescos are now at Hampton Court Palace.
23. Wolfenbütfel, Herzog August Bibliothek Cod. 86.4 Extravagantium.
24. Lecoq, *François Ier imaginaire*, pp. 187–94.
25. *Ibid.*, pp. 194–9.
26. *Ibid.*, pp. 144–8; Chartrou, *Les entrées solennelles*, p. 32.
27. Lecoq, *Francois Ier Imaginaire*, pp. 199–201.
28. Hochner, *Louis XII*, pp. 52–68.
29. Lecoq, *Francois Ier Imaginaire*, pp. 171–6.
30. I.D. McFarlane (ed.), *The Entry of Henri II into Paris, 16 June 1549* (Binghamton, NY, 1982).
31. Margaret McGowan, *Ideal Forms in the Age of Ronsard* (Berkeley, CA, 1985), pp. 23–4.

32. McFarlane, *The Entry*, pp. 28–35.
33. The Fontaine des Innocents that stands in Paris today is a reconstruction on a square plan with a fourth side added by the sculptor Augustin Pajou. It has been moved from the original site on the rue Saint-Denis to a square near the Halles. See J.-M. Pérouse de Montclos (ed.), *Le guide du patrimoine de Paris* (Paris, 1994), p. 240.
34. R. Descimon, 'Le corps de ville et le système cérémoniel parisien au début de l'âge moderne', in M. Boone and M. Prak (eds), *Statuts individuels, statuts corporatifs et statuts judiciaires dans les villes européennes (Moyen Âge et Temps modernes)* (Louvain, 1996).
35. Cosandey, *La reine de France*, p. 183.
36. McGowan, *Ideal Forms*, pp. 144–7, 152–5; Margaret M. McGowan, *The Vision of Rome in Late Renaissance France* (New Haven, CT, and London, 2000), pp. 330–4.
37. Richard Cooper, 'Court Festival and Triumphal Entries under Henri II', in J.R. Mulryne and Elizabeth Goldring (eds), *Court Festivals of the European Renaissance: Art, Politics and Performance* (Aldershot, 2002), pp. 51–75.
38. *Ibid.*, p. 55.
39. *La magnificence de la superbe et triomphante entrée de la noble et antique cité de Lyon faicte au Treschrestien Roy de France Henry, deuxiesme de ce nom, et à la Royne Catherine son Espouse, le xxiii de Septembre M.D.XLVIII* (Lyon, 1549), ed. R.A. Cooper (Tempe, AZ, 1997).
40. Cooper, 'Court Festival', p. 59.
41. The many different arches are described in *ibid.*, pp. 59–61.
42. Labande-Mailfert, *Charles VIII et son milieu*, pp. 101–15.
43. Bernard Quilliet, *Louis XII, Père du peuple* (Paris, 1986), p. 229.
44. Jamie Cameron, *James V. The Personal Rule, 1528–1542* (East Linton, 1998), pp. 131–3.
45. Chatenet, *La cour de France*, pp. 220–1.
46. *CSP Ven.*, vol. 6 (pt 3), pp. 1486–7.
47. Antonia Fraser, *Mary Queen of Scots* (London, 1969), pp. 70–3; J. Guy, *'My Heart Is My Own': The Life of Mary Queen of Scots* (London, 2004), pp. 85–90.
48. Fraser, *Mary Queen of Scots*, p. 71.
49. *CSP Ven.*, vol. 6, pt 3, p. 1486.
50. T. and D. Godefroy, *Ceremonial François* (Paris, 1649), vol. 2, p. 139.
51. Chatenet, *La cour de France*, p. 229 n.
52. Cazaux, *La musique*, p. 165.
53. Godefroy, *Ceremonial François*, vol. 2, pp. 139–43.
54. Chatenet, *La cour de France*, pp. 225–30.
55. Godefroy, *Ceremonial François*, vol. 2, pp. 146–8. The author wrongly dates the baptism 1545 instead of 1546: Cloulas, *Henri II*, p. 128.
56. Ralph Giesey, *The Royal Funeral Ceremony in Renaissance France* (Geneva, 1960), p. 166.
57. A. Tuetey (ed.), *Registres des délibérations du Bureau de la Ville de Paris* (Paris, 1886), vol. 2, pp. 127–8.
58. Bourrilly, *Journal d'un Bourgeois de Paris* (Paris, 1910), pp. 352–3.
59. Y. Labande-Mailfert, *Charles VIII* (Paris, 1986), pp. 462–4.
60. Quilliet, *Louis XII*, p. 446.
61. Giesey, *The Royal Funeral Ceremony*, p. 169.
62. *Ibid.*, pp. 79–104.
63. *Ibid.*, p. 183.
64. Pierre Du Chastel, *Deux sermons funèbres prononcez es obseques de François premier de ce nom*, ed. Pascale Chiron (Geneva, 1999).

Chapter 8: Summit Meetings

1. *Opus Epistolarum Des. Erasmi Rotorodami*, ed. P.S. Allen et al. (Oxford, 1906–58), vol. 2, no. 541. Letter to Wolfgang Fabricius Capito.
2. For the diplomacy leading to this treaty, see P. Gwyn, *The King's Cardinal: The Rise and Fall of Thomas Wolsey* (London, 1992), pp. 58–103.
3. Lecoq, *François Ier imaginaire*, p. 159.

4. *LP,* vol. 3 (pt 1), no. 626.
5. Hamon, *L'argent du roi,* p. 50. The crown borrowed 200,000 *l.* from the Lyon bankers. A debt of 124,099 *l.* for the purchase of cloth of gold and silk remained unsettled in 1543. The master of the *chambre aux deniers* spent 30,290 *l.* mainly on the banquets. Normandy alone contributed 99,100 *l.* to funding the meeting.
6. Du Bellay, *Mémoires,* vol. 1, pp. 101–2.
7. It has been argued that the Field of Cloth of Gold owed its name to the Val Doré, but according to du Bellay it was called after the magnificent clothes worn by the lords and their servants. *LP,* vol. 3 (pt 1), no. 643; Du Bellay, *Mémoires,* vol. 1, p. 100.
8. Edward Hall, *Henry VIII,* ed. C. Whibley, 2 vols (1904), vol. 1, p. 196.
9. *LP,* vol. 3, pt 1, no. 702; Joycelyne G. Russell, *The Field of Cloth of Gold* (London, 1969), pp. 48–9.
10. *LP,* vol. 3 (pt 1), nos 698, 806.
11. *LP,* vol. 3 (pt 1), no. 841.
12. Hall, *Henry VIII,* vol. 1, pp. 186–7.
13. *Ibid.,* pp. 189–93; Sydney Anglo, 'Le Camp du Drap d'Or et les entrevues d'Henri VIII et de Charles Quint', in Jean Jacquot (ed.), *Fêtes et cérémonies au temps de Charles-Quint* (Paris, 1960), pp. 116–18; Anglo, *Spectacle,* pp. 141–3; Russell, *The Field of Cloth of Gold,* pp. 31–42.
14. BNF, Ms. fr. 10383; Russell, *The Field of Cloth of Gold,* pp. 29–30.
15. *CSP Ven.,* vol. 3, nos 60, 80.
16. Hall, *Henry VIII,* vol. 1, pp. 193–4; the design of the rotunda has been ascribed to Domenico da Cortona. See J. Guillaume, 'Léonard de Vinci, Dominique de Cortone et l'escalier du modèle de bois de Chambord', *GBA,* 1 (1968), p. 108 n. 22.
17. Florange, *Mémoires,* vol. 1, p. 263.
18. Russell, *The Field of Cloth of Gold,* p. 31.
19. *LP,* vol. 3 (pt 1), no. 747.
20. *LP,* vol. 3 (pt 1), nos 861, 874; *CAF,* vol. 1, no. 1193.
21. *CSP Ven.,* vol. 3, nos 68, 73; Sanuto, *I Diarii di Marino Sanuto,* vol. 29, col. 28.
22. *CSP Ven.,* vol. 3, nos 50, 60, 67, 68, 71, 72, 73; Hall, *Henry VIII,* vol. 1, pp. 196–200; *LP,* vol. 3, (pt 1), nos 869, 870; Sanuto, *I Diarii,* vol. 19, col. 19; Russell, *The Field of Cloth of Gold,* pp. 95–104; Anglo, *Spectacle,* pp. 145–9.
23. Hall, *Henry VIII,* vol. 1, pp. 200–1; Anglo, *Spectacle,* pp. 150–1; Russell, *The Field of Cloth of Gold,* pp. 112–14.
24. Russell, *The Field of Cloth of Gold,* p. 119.
25. Anglo, *Spectacle,* pp. 153–4.
26. *Ibid.,* p. 156.
27. *CSP Ven.,* vol. 3, no. 50.
28. Florange, *Mémoires,* vol. 1, p. 272; J. Michelet, *La Réforme,* vol. 10 of *L'Histoire de France* (Paris, n.d.), pp. 77–8, 90.
29. Hall, *Henry VIII,* vol. 1, p. 208; Florange, *Mémoires,* vol. 1, pp. 268–70; *CSP Ven.,* vol. 3, nos 50, 77, 78, 90.
30. Hall, *Henry VIII,* vol. 1, pp. 208–9; *CSP Ven.,* vol. 3, nos 50, 90, 91; *LP,* vol. 3, (pt 1), p. 1554.
31. *The Anglica Historia of Polydore Vergil, A.D. 1485–1537,* ed. D. Hay (London, 1950), p. 269.
32. Paul Kast, 'Remarques sur la musique et les musiciens de la chapelle de François Ier au Camp du Drap d'Or', and Hugh Baillie, 'Les musiciens de la chapelle d'Henri VIII au Camp du Drap d'Or', in Jean Jacquot (ed.), *Fêtes et cérémonies au temps de Charles Quint* (Paris, 1975), pp. 135–59; Cazaux, *La musique,* pp. 204–7.
33. *CSP Ven.,* vol. 3, no. 50; Jacobus Sylvius, *Francisci Francorum Regis et Henrici Anglorum Colloquium,* ed. and tr. Stephen Bamforth and Jean Dupèbe, *Renaissance Studies,* 5 (1991), pp. 28–32, 94–7; Anglo, *Spectacle,* p. 157; Russell, *The Field of Cloth of Gold,* p. 176. Anglo indicates that 23 June is the Eve of the Nativity of St John the Baptist, a festival long associated with the summer solstice and customarily celebrated with bonfires and fireworks. The English expense accounts for Guînes contain a payment for canvas to be used as

covering for a dragon. But the dragon at the Field of Cloth of Gold came from Ardres rather than Guînes. This suggests that it was a mischievous salamander launched by the French rather than a dragon.

34. *CSP Ven.*, vol. 3, nos 50, 93, 95.
35. *LP*, vol. 5, nos 1373, 1484–5, 1492, 1523; *CSP Ven.*, vol. 5, nos 820, 823–4, 827, 829, 831–2. For music at the meeting, see Cazaux, *La musique*, pp. 216–17.
36. For a discussion of what may have passed between them, see A. Hamy, *Entrevue de François Ier avec Henri VIII à Boulogne-sur-Mer en 1532* (Paris, 1898), pp. 77–9.
37. They were elected at the order's chapter on 27 October: *LP*, vol. 5, p. 620 (no. 1474).
38. See above, p. 43–4.
39. A. Hamy, *Entrevue de François Ier avec Clément VII à Marseille, 1533. D'après le journal d'Honoré de Valbelle* (Paris, 1900), p. 4. Before leaving Marseille, the Grand Master dismissed a large number of artisans (*compagnons*) who had come to play the drums. At first he would not pay them, but was persuaded to do so as they had come at the invitation of the baron d'Ollières, the local proctor.
40. 'Outre le sang royal, je crois qu'il n'était pas demeuré seigneur en France et que tous ne fussent venus accompagner le roi.' Hamy, *Entrevue de François Ier avec Clément VII à Marseille*, p. 6.
41. Francis gave his musicians new clothes for the occasion. See Cazaux, *La musique*, pp. 217–20.
42. Martin and Guillaume Du Bellay, *Mémoires de Martin et Guillaume du Bellay*, ed. V.-L. Bourrilly and F. Vindry (Paris, 1908–19), vol. 2, pp. 225–31; Hamy, *Entrevue de François Ier avec Clément VII*; Cloulas, *Catherine de Médicis*, pp. 53–8.
43. Valbelle states (Hamy, *Entrevue de François Ier avec Clément VII*, pp. 16–17) that she had come from Nice where she had been left by Albany while he returned to Italy to fetch the pope, but she and her suite are unlikely to have travelled overland from Nice to Marseille along a rough and tortuous road. Almost certainly Catherine had come to Marseille with Clement but had effaced herself since, perhaps by staying just outside Marseille at Aubagne, until protocol dictated that it was time for her to appear.
44. L. von Pastor, *The History of the Popes*, tr. F.J. Antrobus and R.F. Kerr (London, 1891–1933), vol. 11, pp. 274–5; M. François, *Le Cardinal François de Tournon* (Paris, 1951), p. 163.
45. *CSP Span.*, p. 456 and no. 184.
46. AN, X1a 1541, ff. 484 a–b, 485a.
47. Xavier Le Person, 'A moment of "resverie". Charles V and Francis I's encounter at Aigues-Mortes (July 1538)', *French History*, 19 (2005), pp. 1–27.
48. On music at this meeting, see Cazaux, *La musique*, pp. 222–3.
49. L.-P. Gachard, *Relation des troubles de Gand sous Charles-Quint par un anonyme* (Brussels, 1846), pp. 40–3.
50. *Papiers d'état du cardinal de Granvelle*, ed. C. Weiss (Paris, 1841–52), vol. 2, pp. 540–2; Decrue, *Anne de Montmorency*, p. 372. See also *CSP Span.*, vol. 6 (pt 1), p. 92; Musée Condé, MS. 899, ff. 64–66b: *Mémoire de ce qui fault commandez et ordonnez aux consuls, manans et habitants des villes et villages par ou passera lempereur par ce Royaume.*
51. J. Jacquot, 'Panorama des fêtes et cérémonies du règne', in Jacquot (ed.) *Les fêtes de la Renaissance*, vol. 2 (Paris, 1975), pp. 434–45.
52. *LP*, vol. 14 (pt 2), no. 686 (pp. 251–5).
53. J.-P. Babelon, *Châteaux de France au siècle de la Renaissance* (Paris, 1989), pp. 119–23.
54. L. Dimier, *Le Primatice* (Paris, 1928), pp. 8–9.
55. M.H. Smith, 'La première description de Fontainebleau', *Revue de l'art*, 91 (1991), pp. 44–6.
56. *Ibid.*, p. 7.
57. For the music performed, see Cazaux, *La musique*, pp. 223–5.
58. J. Pope-Hennessy, *Cellini* (London, 1985), pp. 103–4.
59. *Cronique du roy Françoys premier*, ed. G. Guiffrey (Paris, 1860), p. 315.
60. Monique Chatenet, *Le château de Madrid au bois de Boulogne* (Paris, 1987), p. 27.
61. Babelon, *Châteaux de France*, pp. 213–18.
62. *CSP Span.*, vol. 6 (pt 1), no. 117.

Chapter 9: Royal Builders

1. Babelon, *Châteaux de France*, pp. 124–7, 138–42.
2. Guy Coquille, *Oeuvres*, 2 vols (Paris, 1665).
3. Babelon, *Châteaux de France*, pp. 300–4.
4. *Ibid.*, pp. 119–23.
5. Pierre Lesueur, 'Les jardins du château de Blois', *Mémoires de la Société des Sciences et Lettres de Loir-et-Cher*, 29 (1936), p. 239.
6. Babelon, *Châteaux de France*, pp. 23–8; Labande-Mailfert, *Charles VIII et son milieu*, pp. 500–1; Ivan Cloulas, *La vie quotidienne dans les châteaux de la Loire au temps de la Renaissance* (Paris, 1983), pp. 47–50.
7. Cosperec, *Blois*, pp. 107–8.
8. *Ibid.*, pp. 108–22; Babelon, *Châteaux de France*, pp. 41–7.
9. De Beatis, *The Travel Journal*, pp. 134–5. This seems to be the earliest reference to an orangery in France. Pacello de Mercogliano was made a canon of Saint-Sauveur in 1501 and given the seigneurie of Château-Gaillard in 1505. He was paid 300 *l.* per annum for looking after the main garden at Blois.
10. AS Mantua 638. Cited by Chatenet, *La cour de France*, pp. 45, 48.
11. M.H. Smith, 'François Ier, l'Italie et le château de Blois', *Bulletin monumental*, 147 (1989), pp. 315–19.
12. F. Gebelin, *Les châteaux de la Renaissance* (Paris, 1927), pp. 55–62; A. Blunt, *Art and Architecture in France, 1500–1700* (Harmondsworth, 1957), pp. 9–10; Babelon, *Châteaux de France*, pp. 110–18; P. Lesueur, *Le château de Blois* (Paris, 1914–21), pp. 76–105.
13. BNF, Ms. fr. 25720 (142). Printed in L. Jarry, 'Documents inédits servant à rectifier la date de la construction et les noms des premiers architectes du château de Chambord', *Mémoires de la Société archéologique et historique de l'Orléanais*, 22 (1889), pp. 579–80; Monique Chatenet, *Chambord* (Paris, 2001), p. 37.
14. Chatenet, *Chambord*, p. 35.
15. AS Mantua 635. Cited by Chatenet, *Chambord*, p. 35.
16. *Ibid.*, pp. 52–3.
17. J. Guillaume, 'Léonard et l'architecture', in *Léonard de Vinci ingénieur et architecte* (Montreal, 1987), pp. 282–4.
18. Jean Guillaume, 'Léonard de Vinci et l'architecture française, I: Le problème de Chambord', *Revue de l'art*, 25 (1974), pp. 71–84.
19. Chatenet, *Chambord*, pp. 93, 96.
20. Henri Zerner, *Renaissance Art in France: The Invention of Classicism* (Paris, 2003), p. 66.
21. *Registres des délibérations du Bureau de la Ville de Paris*, vol. 2, p. 17.
22. Bourrilly, *Le Journal d'un Bourgeois de Paris*, p. 274.
23. M. Chatenet, 'Le logis de François Ier au Louvre', *Revue de l'art*, 97 (1992), pp. 72–5.
24. Mary Whiteley, 'Le Louvre de Charles V: dispositions et fonctions d'une résidence royale', *Revue de l'art*, 97 (1992), pp. 60–75.
25. M. Fleury and W. Kruta, *Le château du Louvre* (Paris, 1990), pp. 71, 74.
26. Sabine Frommel, *Sebastiano Serlio* (Milan, 1998), pp. 267–84.
27. Chatenet, *Le château de Madrid*, pp. 49–63.
28. L. de Laborde, *Les comptes des bâtiments du roi (1528–71)*, 2 vols (Paris, 1878–80), vol. 1, p. 7.
29. Chatenet, *Le château de Madrid*, pp. 43–8.
30. Monique Chatenet, 'Une nouvelle "Cheminée de Castille" à Madrid en France', *Revue de l'art*, 91 (1991), pp. 36–8.
31. Chatenet, *Le château de Madrid*, pp. 65–71.
32. *Ibid.*, pp. 76–86.
33. See above, pp. 139–40.
34. Chatenet, *Le château de Madrid*, pp. 21–4, 129–30.
35. *Diary of John Evelyn*, ed. E.S. De Beer (London, 1959), p. 64.
36. H. Sauval, *Histoire et recherches des antiquités de la ville de Paris* (Paris, 1724), vol. 2, p. 309.

37. F. Marias, 'De Madrid à Paris: François Ier et la Casa de Campo', *Revue de l'art*, 91 (1991), pp. 26–35; Chatenet, 'Une nouvelle "cheminée de Castille"'.
38. Monique Chatenet, 'Une demeure royale au milieu du XVIè siècle: La distribution des espaces au château de Saint-Germain-en-Laye', *Revue de l'art*, 81 (1988), p. 22.
39. AS Modena, Ambasciatori in Francia 22 (Paris, 17 Jan. 1546). Giulio Alvarotti. Cited by Chatenet, *La cour de France*, p. 51.
40. Babelon, *Châteaux de France*, pp. 325–7.
41. *Ibid.*, pp. 323–5.
42. AS Modena, Ambasciatori in Francia 22. Cited by Chatenet, *La cour de France*, p. 52.
43. AS Mantua, A.G. 638. Cited by Chatenet, *La cour de France*, p. 52.
44. A. Chastel, 'L'Escalier de la Cour Ovale à Fontainebleau', in D. Fraser, H. Hibbard and M.J. Lewine (eds), *Essays in the History of Architecture Presented to Rudolf Wittkower* (London, 1967), pp. 74–80.
45. G. Vasari, *The Lives of the Painters, Sculptors and Architects*, ed. W. Gaunt (London, 1963), vol. 2, pp. 355, 362.
46. *St P*, vol. 8 (pt 5), pp. 482–4.
47. Henry VIII also had sunken baths and hot water. Excavations at Whitehall palace in the 1930s revealed a large square sunken bath together with fragments of a green-glazed stove. S. Thurley, *The Royal Palaces of Tudor England* (London, 1993), p. 170.
48. Tommaseo, *Relations des ambassadeurs vénitiens*, vol. 1, p. 101.
49. Chatenet, *Le château de Madrid*, pp. 16–17; and her 'Le coût des travaux dans les résidences royales d'Île-de-France entre 1528 et 1550', in A. Chastel and J. Guillaume (eds), *Les chantiers de la Renaissance* (Paris, 1991), pp. 115–29.
50. David Thomson, *Renaissance Paris* (London, 1984), p. 90.
51. *Ibid.*, pp. 77–9.
52. Anthony Blunt, *Art and Architecture in France 1500–1700* (Harmondsworth, 1957), p. 48.

Chapter 10: Art Patronage

1. M.H. Smith, 'François Ier, l'Italie et le château de Blois', *Bulletin monumental*, 147 (1989), pp. 307–8, 320.
2. *Ibid.*, pp. 309, 322.
3. Cécile Scailliérez, *François Ier et ses artistes dans les collections du Louvre* (Paris, 1992), pp. 76–7.
4. Vasari, *Lives of the Painters*, vol. 2, p. 167.
5. Carlo Vecce, 'Léonard de Vinci et la France', in *Léonard de Vinci: dessins et manuscrits*, exh. cat. the Louvre, Paris, May–July 2003 (Paris, 2003), pp. 21–6.
6. A. Chastel, *L'Art français: temps modernes, 1430–1620* (Paris, 1994), pp. 114–15; see also Zerner, *Renaissance Art*, p. 197.
7. Vasari, *Lives*, vol. 2, p. 162.
8. Carlo Vecce, *Léonard de Vinci* (Paris, 1998), p. 283.
9. K. Clark, *Leonardo da Vinci* (Harmondsworth, 1958), p. 147.
10. De Beatis, *The Travel Journal*, pp. 132–3.
11. B. Cellini, 'Discorso dell'architettura', in *Opere*, ed. B. Maier (Milan, 1968), pp. 858–60.
12. C. Pedretti, *Leonardo da Vinci: The Royal Palace at Romorantin* (Cambridge, MA, 1972); Jean Guillaume, 'Léonard et l'architecture', in *Léonard de Vinci, ingénieur et architecte* (Montreal, 1987), pp. 278–82.
13. Vecce, *Léonard de Vinci*, pp. 291–3.
14. Vasari, *Lives*, vol. 2, pp. 312–13; J. Shearman, *Andrea del Sarto* (Oxford, 1965), pp. 1, 3–4, 77, 314; S.J. Freedberg, *Andrea del Sarto* (Cambridge, MA, 1963), vol. 1, p. 47; Scailliérez, *François Ier*, pp. 23, 116; Janet Cox-Rearick, *The Collection of Francis I: Royal Treasures* (Antwerp, 1995), pp. 181–9.
15. Caroline Elam, 'Art in the Service of Liberty: Battista della Palla, Art Agent for Francis I', *I Tatti Studies: Essays in the Renaissance*, 5 (1993), pp. 63–4, 78–9. The painting is now in the Uffizi in Florence.

16. Vasari, *Lives*, vol. 4, p. 192.

17. AN, Minutier Central vol. CCXII, 1045.

18. G.-M. Leproux, *La peinture à Paris sous le règne de François Ie. Corpus vitrearum, France, Étude IV* (Paris, 2001).

19. Zerner, *Renaissance Art*, p. 107.

20. Sylvie Béguin, 'Aspects sur la Chambre du Roi', in Chastel (ed.), *L'Art de Fontainebleau* (Paris, 1975), pp. 199–230.

21. Louis Golson, 'Rosso et Primatice au Pavillon de Pomone', in Chastel (ed.), *L'Art de Fontainebleau*, pp. 231–40.

22. Sylvie Béguin, 'New Evidence for Rosso in France', *Burlington Magazine*, 131 (1989), pp. 828–38.

23. See above, p. 162–3.

24. Pierre et Françoise Joukovsky, *À travers la galerie François Ier* (Paris, 1992), pp. 17–18.

25. A.-M. Lecoq, 'La fondation du Collège royal et *L'Ignorance chassée* de Fontainebleau', in M. Fumaroli (ed.), *Les origines du Collège de France (1500–1560)* (Paris, 1998), pp. 185–206.

26. S. Pressouyre, 'L'Emblème du Naufrage à la Galerie François Ier', in *Actes du colloque international sur l'art de Fontainebleau (Fontainebleau et Paris, 1972)* (Paris, 1975), pp. 127–39.

27. D. and E. Panofsky, 'The iconography of the Galerie François Ier at Fontainebleau', *GBA*, 6th ser., 52 (1958), pp. 113–90.

28. Joukovsky, *À travers la galerie François Ier*, p. 5.

29. 'Regarder vos bastiments sans ouïr sur cela votre intencion, c'est lire en esbreu.' *Lettres de Marguerite d'Angoulême, soeur de François Ier, reine de Navarre*, ed. F. Génin (Paris, 1841), p. 382.

30. Cited by E.A. Carroll in 'Rosso in France', in A. Chastel (ed.), *Actes du Colloque international sur l'art de Fontainebleau* (Paris, 1975), p. 17.

31. Zerner, *Renaissance Art*, p. 116.

32. Letter from Calcagnino, published by L. Dimier in *Archivio Storico dell'Arte*, vol. 2 (1889), p. 377.

33. Dana Bentley-Cranch, *The Renaissance Portrait in France and England* (Paris, 2004), pp. 87–139.

34. Zerner, *Renaissance Art*, pp. 200–1.

35. Cécile Scailliérez, *François Ier par Clouet* (Paris, 1996), p. 84.

36. Zerner, *Renaissance Art*, p. 199.

37. Bertrand Jestaz, 'Benvenuto Cellini et la cour de France', in B. Jestaz (ed.), *Art et artistes en France de la Renaissance à la Révolution* (Paris, 2003), p. 72.

38. Cellini, *The Life of Benvenuto Cellini*, p. 264.

39. *Ibid.*

40. Jestaz, 'Benvenuto Cellini', pp. 78–9.

41. *Ibid.*, pp. 79–80.

42. Cellini, *The Life of Benvenuto Cellini*, pp. 272–3.

43. Pope-Hennessy, *Cellini*, p. 105.

44. Cellini, *The Life of Benvenuto Cellini*, p. 273.

45. *Ibid.*, p. 274.

46. *Ibid.*, p. 306.

47. Jestaz, 'Benvenuto Cellini', pp. 99–105.

48. Cellini, *The Life of Benvenuto Cellini*, pp. 284–5.

49. Jestaz, 'Benevenuto Cellini', pp. 120–1.

50. Cellini, *The Life of Benvenuto Cellini*, p. 318.

51. *Ibid.*, pp. 312–14.

52. C. Occhipinti, *Carteggio d'arte degli ambasciatori estensi in Francia (1536–1553)* (Pisa, 2001), p. 99.

53. Cellini, *The Life of Benvenuto Cellini*, p. 321.

54. *Ibid.*, p. 335.

55. Pope-Hennessy, *Cellini*, pp. 144–6.

56. Scaillérez, *François Ier et ses artistes*, pp. 21, 106; Lecoq, *François Ier imaginaire*, pp. 441–6.

57. Scailliérez, *François Ier et ses artistes*, pp. 21, 108–9, 111; Cox-Rearick, *The Collection of Francis I*, pp. 75–81, 191–9, 201–17.
58. Francesco II Gonzaga sent the picture to Francis on 30 November 1518. See C.M. Brown, 'Lorenzo Costa in Mantua – Five Autograph Letters', *L'arte*, 11–12 (1970), 120ff. The painting has been identified with Costa's *Venus*, now in Budapest. See Scailliérez, *François Ier et ses artistes*, p. 21.
59. Scailliérez, *François Ier et ses artistes*, pp. 21, 112–13; Lecoq, *Français Ier imaginaire*, pp. 44–8; Cox-Rearick, *The Collection of Francis I*, p. 388. The engraving is by Marcantonio Raimondi.
60. Scailliérez, *François Ier et ses artistes*, p. 21. According to Père Dan (1642), it was embalmed in Venice and valued at 6,000 ducats.
61. Scaillérez, *François Ier et ses artistes*, pp. 27–8. The painting is now at Holkham Hall, Norfolk.
62. Caroline Elam, 'Art and Diplomacy in Renaissance Florence', *Royal Society of Arts Journal*, 136 (1988), p. 821.
63. Vasari writes of Bronzino: 'He made a picture of singular beauty, which was sent into France to King Francis. In it was a nude Venus and Cupid who kissed her.' See E. Panofsky, *Studies in Iconology* (New York, 1962), pp. 86–91; M. Levey, 'Sacred and Profane Significance in Two Paintings by Bronzino', *Studies in Renaissance and Baroque Art presented to Anthony Blunt on his 60th birthday* (London, 1967), pp. 30–3; Cox-Rearick, *The Collection of Francis I*, pp. 227–34, 237–41.
64. Cox-Rearick, *The Collection of Francis I*, pp. 248–54.
65. Sophie Schneebalg-Perelman, 'Richesses du garde-meuble parisien de François Ier: Inventaires inédits de 1542 et 1551', *GBA*, 6th period, 78 (1971), pp. 253–304; Scaillérez, *François Ier et ses artistes*, pp. 120–1; Cox-Rearick, *The Collection of Francis I*, pp. 363–8.

Chapter 11: 'Father of Letters'

1. C.-G. Dubois, 'François Ier et François Rabelais: Aspects de la vie culturelle au temps de François Ier', in *François Ier du château de Cognac au trône de France* (Colloque de Cognac, septembre et novembre 1994. Annales du G.R.E.H.), p. 253.
2. Marie-Madeleine de La Garanderie, *Christianisme et lettres profanes. Essai sur l'Humanisme français (1515–1535) et sur la pensée de Guillaume Budé* (Paris, 1995), p. 207.
3. La Garanderie (*ibid.*, p. 207) states that Budé was put in charge of the library at Fontainebleau, but as yet there was no library at that château. .
4. For the text of *L'Institution du Prince*, see C. Bontems, L.-P. Raybaud and J.-P. Brancourt, *Le Prince dans la France des XVIe et XVIIe siècles* (Paris, 1965), pp. 1–143.
5. La Garanderie, *Christianisme*, p. 208.
6. Pierre Du Chastel, *Deux sermons funèbres prononcez es obseques de François Premier de ce nom*, ed. Pascale Chiron (Geneva, 1999), p. 15.
7. La Garanderie, *Christianisme*, p. 222.
8. Bontems et al., *Le Prince*, p. 90.
9. *Ibid.*, p. 86; G. Gadoffre, *La révolution culturelle dans la France des humanistes* (Geneva, 1997), p. 254.
10. A. Lefranc, *Histoire du Collège de France* (Paris, 1893), pp. 48–9.
11. Erasmus, *Opus epistolarum*, ed. P.S. Allen and H.M. Allen (Oxford, 1906–34), vol. 2, pp. 454–8.
12. La Garanderie, *Christianisme*, p. 233.
13. F. Rabelais, *The Histories of Gargantua and Pantagruel*, tr. J.M. Cohen (Harmondsworth, 1955), p. 194. For the original French text, see F. Rabelais, *Pantagruel*, ed. V.-L. Saulnier (Geneva, 1965), pp. 43–5.
14. A. Lefranc et al., *Le Collège de France (1530–1930)* (Paris, 1932), pp. 31, 35–8; André Chastel, 'François Ier et le Collège de France', in *Culture et demeures en France au XVIe siècle* (Paris, 1989), pp. 37–9; J.K. Farge, *Le parti conservateur au XVIe siècle. L'Université de Paris à l'époque de la Renaissance et de la Réforme* (Paris, 1992), p. 37.

15. Farge, *Le parti conservateur*, pp. 20–1. The oration is in BNF Rés. Lb. 108.
16. De Beatis, *The Travel Journal*, p. 133.
17. *Ordonnances*, vol. 8, no. 828, pp. 494–500.
18. Marie-Pierre Laffitte and Fabienne Le Bars, *Reliures royales de la Renaissance. La librairie de Fontainebleau, 1544–1570* (Paris, 1999), pp. 14–19.
19. *Ibid.*
20. A. Coron, 'Collège royal et *Bibliotheca regia*; la bibliothèque savante de François Ier', in M. Fumaroli (ed.), *Les origines du Collège de France (1500–1560)* (Paris, 1998), pp. 143–83; A. Hobson, *Humanism and Bookbinders: the Origins and Diffusion of the Humanistic Bookbinding, 1459–1559* (Cambridge, 1989), pp. 172–213.
21. Laffitte and Le Bars, *Reliures royales*, pp. 36–63.

Chapter 12: A New Parnassus

1. Labande-Mailfert, *Charles VIII et son milieu*, pp. 160–3.
2. Jouanna et al., *La France de la Renaissance*, pp. 614–15.
3. G. Minois, *Anne de Bretagne* (Paris, 1999), pp. 446–61.
4. D. Hollier (ed.), *A New History of French Literature* (Cambridge, MA, 1994), p. 127.
5. 'Un laborieux et prétentieux fatras où les subtilités creuses et les ineptes jeux de mots tenaient lieu d'inspiration et d'idées.' G. Lanson, *Histoire de la littérature française* (Paris, 1951), p. 186.
6. Paul Zumthor, *Le masque et la lumière. La poétique des grands rhétoriqueurs* (Paris, 1978).
7. Yves Giraud and Marc-René Jung, *La Renaissance I, 1480–1548* (Paris, 1972), pp. 187–202.
8. Jouanna et al., *La France de la Renaissance*, pp. 647–48; A. Hamon, *Jean Bouchet (1476–1557?)* (Paris, 1901).
9. I.A. McFarlane, *A Literary History of France: Renaissance France, 1470–1589* (London, 1974), pp. 31–50, 91–2.
10. *Ibid.*, pp. 94–6.
11. P.M. Smith, *Clément Marot* (London, 1979), pp. 2–16; C. Marot, *Les Épitres*, ed. C.A. Mayer (London, 1954), pp. 5–11.
12. See below, pp. 235–6.
13. P.M. Smith, *Clément Marot*, pp. 16–36, 53–6.
14. H.-J. Molinet, *Mellin de Saint-Gelays (1490?-1558): Étude sur sa vie et sur ses oeuvres* (1910); McFarlane, *A Literary History*, pp. 130–1.
15. François Ier, *Oeuvres poétiques*, ed. J.E. Kane (Geneva, 1984), *passim*.
16. Giraud and Jung, *La Renaissance I*, pp. 321–2.
17. Hollier (ed.), *A New History of French Literature*, p. 205.
18. Cloulas, *Henri II*, p. 486.
19. For a full account of such musical participation, see Cazaux, *La Musique*, pp. 163–96.
20. G. Du Peyrat, *L'Histoire ecclésiastique de la cour ou les antiquitez et recherches de la chapelle et oratoire du roi de France depuis Clovis I jusques à nostre temps* (Paris, 1645), pp. 479–80; Cazaux, *La Musique*, pp. 50–1.
21. A. Champollion-Figeac, *Captivité du roi François Ier* (Paris, 1847), p. 561; François Ier, *Oeuvres poétiques*, pp. 46–7.
22. Cazaux, *La musique*, p. 54.
23. *Ibid.*, p. 55.
24. 'Non gusta la musica come el re passato' (Jean-Michel to Sigismondo d'Este, Vigevano, 29 Oct. 1515). Cited by L. Lockwood, 'Jean Mouton and Jean Michel: new evidence on French music and musicians in Italy, 1505–1520', *Journal of the American Musicological Society*, 32 (1979), p. 204.
25. Cazaux, *La musique*, pp. 199–201.
26. P. Kast, 'Remarques sur la musique et les musiciens de la chapelle de François Ier au Camp du Drap d'Or', in J. Jacquot (ed.), *Fêtes et cérémonies au temps de Charles-Quint* (Paris, 1960), pp. 135–7; Cazaux, *La musique*, pp. 204–7.

27. Sanudo, *I diarii*, vol. 27, cols 230, 238; Cazaux, *La musique*, pp. 203–4.
28. Cazaux, *La musique*, pp. 58–63.
29. *Ibid.*, pp. 69–95.
30. H.M. Brown, *Music in the Renaissance* (Englewood Cliffs, NJ, 1976), p. 176. On Mouton, see also G. Reese, *Music in the Renaissance* (New York, 1959), pp. 280–5.
31. Cazaux, *La musique*, pp. 95–100.
32. Isabelle Cazeaux, *French Music in the Fifteenth and Sixteenth Centuries* (Oxford, 1975), p. 19.
33. Cazaux, *La musique*, p. 213.
34. *Ibid.*, pp. 107–26.
35. *CAF*, vol. 2, no. 5611; vol. 3, nos 8594, 10393; vol. 7, nos 28327, 26876, 27334.
36. Reese, *Music*, pp. 527, 553.
37. Cazaux, *La musique*, p. 191.
38. *Ibid.*, p. 198.
39. Reese, *Music*, pp. 295–9; Brown, *Music*, pp. 214–16.
40. Cloulas, *Henri II*, p. 355.

Chapter 13: The Canker of Heresy

1. Gabriel Audisio, *The Waldensian Dissent: persecution and survival, c. 1170–c. 1570* (Cambridge, 1999).
2. Margaret Mann, *Érasme et les débuts de la réforme française, 1517–36* (Paris, 1934), p. 23.
3. See Nicole Lemaître, *Le Rouergue flamboyant* (Paris, 1988), pp. 217–45 on another reforming bishop, François d'Estaing.
4. He was the son of Guillaume Briçonnet (1445–1514), who became a cardinal following the death of his wife, Raoulette de Beaune.
5. M. Veissière, *L'évêque Guillaume Briçonnet (1470–1534)* (Provins, 1986), p. 198.
6. A. Renaudet, *Préréforme et humanisme à Paris pendant les premières guerres d'Italie (1494–1517)* (Paris, 1953), *passim*; H. Heller, 'Lefèvre d'Étaples', in *Contemporaries of Erasmus*, ed. P.G. Bietenholz and T.B. Deutscher (Toronto, 2003), vol. 2, pp. 315–18; Jean-François Pernot (ed.), *Jacques Lefèvre d'Étaples (1450?–1536)* (Paris, 1995).
7. D. Crouzet, *La génèse de la réforme française* (Paris, 1996), pp. 138–40.
8. J.K. Farge, *Orthodoxy and Reform in Early Reformation France: The Faculty of Theology of the University of Paris, 1500–1543* (Leiden, 1985), pp. 160–213. Sorbonne was the name of a college of the university distinct from the Faculty of Theology. The name is used simply for convenience.
9. Knecht, *Renaissance Warrior and Patron*, pp. 144–6.
10. Lucien Febvre, *Au coeur religieux du XVIe siècle* (Paris, 1957), p. 66.
11. Veissière, *L'évêque Guillaume Briçonnet*, pp. 187–96.
12. *Ibid.*, pp. 225–6.
13. *Ibid.*, pp. 525–7.
14. Farge, *Orthodoxy*, p. 254.
15. *Ibid.*, p. 168.
16. Bourrilly, *Journal d'un Bourgeois de Paris*, p. 101.
17. G. Briçonnet and Marguerite d'Angoulême, *Correspondance*, ed. C. Martineau and M. Veissière, 2 vols (Geneva, 1975–9), vol. 1, p. 61 and n. 117.
18. *Ibid.*, vol. 1, p. 71 and n. 1; Veissière, *L'évêque Guillaume Briçonnet*, p. 221.
19. Veissière, *L'évêque Guillaume Briçonnet*, p. 222.
20. *Ibid.*, pp. 272–4.
21. Farge, *Orthodoxy*, p. 132.
22. *Ibid.*, p. 258; J. Fraikin (ed.), *Nonciatures de France: nonciatures de Clément VII* (Paris, 1906), p. 428; R. Doucet, *Étude sur le gouvernement de François Ier dans ses rapports avec le Parlement de Paris*, 2 vols (Paris and Algiers, 1921–6), vol. 2, pp. 160–4, 168–9; *Ordonnances*, vol. 4, no. 387.
23. AN, X1a 1530, ff. 33b–34a.
24. Veissière, *L'évêque Guillaume Briçonnet*, pp. 348–9.

25. *Ibid.*, pp. 351–5.
26. Doucet, *Étude sur le gouvernement*, vol. 1, pp. 336–40; W.G. Moore, *La réforme allemande et la littérature française* (Strasbourg, 1930), pp. 102–4; P. Imbart de la Tour, *Les origines de la réforme* (Melun, 1944), vol. 2, p. 228; Bourrilly, *Journal d'un Bourgeois de Paris*, p. 142; Farge, *Orthodoxy*, pp. 173–4, 255–6. Berquin's luck ran out. At a later stage he was again tried and sentenced to life imprisonment. He foolishly appealed and the sentence was changed to death. He was burned in Paris during the king's absence. See Knecht, *Warrior and Patron*, p. 284.
27. Imbart de la Tour, *Les origines*, vol. 3, p. 262; Bourrilly, *Journal d'un bourgeois de Paris*, pp. 290–3; *Registres des délibérations du Bureau de la Ville de Paris*, vol. 2, pp. 24–6.
28. Imbart de la Tour, *Les origines*, vol. 3, pp. 262–7; Buisson, *Le chancelier Antoine Duprat*, pp. 293–8; Veissière, *L'évêque Guillaume Briçonnet*, pp. 402–3.
29. A. Herminjard (ed.), *Correspondance des réformateurs dans les pays de langue française* (Geneva, 1886–7), vol. 2, p. 179.
30. *Ibid.*, vol. 2, p. 249.
31. *Ibid.*, vol. 2, pp. 250–1; P.E. Hughes, *Lefèvre, Pioneer of Ecclesiastical Renewal in France* (Grand Rapids, MI, 1984), pp. 178–9.
32. Farge, *Orthodoxy*, pp. 201–3.
33. *Ibid.*, pp. 203–4.
34. R. Hari, 'Les placards de 1534', in G. Berthoud et al. (eds), *Aspects de la propagande religieuse* (Geneva, 1957), pp. 114, 119–20; G. Berthoud, *Antoine Marcourt* (Geneva, 1973), pp. 174–6, 181–7.
35. Knecht, *Warrior and Patron*, pp. 313–21.
36. D. Crouzet, *La génèse de la réforme française, 1520–1562* (Paris, 1996), p. 417.
37. Janine Garrisson, *Protestants du Midi, 1559–1598* (Toulouse, 1980), p. 26.
38. N.M. Sutherland, *The Huguenot Struggle for Recognition* (New Haven, CT, 1980), p. 345; Crouzet, *La genèse*, pp. 419–21.
39. R.M. Kingdon, *Geneva and the Coming of the Wars of Religion in France, 1555–1563* (Geneva, 1956), pp. 62–3; Crouzet, *La genèse*, pp. 461–2.
40. M. Lelièvre, 'Les derniers jours d'Anne du Bourg', *Bulletin de la Société de l'Histoire du Protestantisme Français*, 37, pp. 517ff.; Cloulas, *Henri II*, pp. 585–7.
41. R.J. Knecht, *Catherine de' Medici* (London, 1998), pp. 53–4.

Chapter 14: The Kingdom in Crisis, 1559–74

1. Cloulas, *Henri II*, pp. 589–93.
2. Wanegffelen, *Catherine de Médicis*, p. 165.
3. Lucien Romier, *La conjuration d'Amboise* (Paris, 1923), pp. 80–125.
4. Seong-Hak Kim, *Michel de L'Hôpital: The Vision of a Reformist Chancellor during the French Religious Wars* (Kirksville, MI, 1997); D. Crouzet, *La Sagesse et le malheur: Michel de l'Hospital, Chancelier de France* (Seyssel, 1998); Michel de l'Hospital, *Discours pour la majorité de Charles IX*, ed. R. Descimon (Paris, 1993).
5. J. Shimizu, *Conflict of Loyalties: Politics and religion in the career of Gaspard de Coligny, Admiral of France, 1519–72* (Geneva, 1970), pp. 39–47.
6. *Lettres de Catherine de Médicis*, vol. 1, p. 158.
7. *Ibid.*, vol. 1, p. 181.
8. D. Nugent, *Ecumenism in the Age of the Reformation: The Colloquy of Poissy* (Cambridge, MA, 1974); Knecht, *Catherine de' Medici*, pp. 77–82.
9. Mariéjol, *Catherine de Médicis*, p. 115.
10. Mack P. Holt, *The French Wars of Religion, 1562–1629* (Cambridge, 1995); R.J. Knecht, *The French Civil Wars* (London, 2000), pp. 99–104, 150–2, 229–31; James B. Wood, *The King's Army: Warfare, soldiers and society during the Wars of Religion in France, 1562–1576* (Cambridge, 1996), pp. 184–204.
11. Boutier, Dewerpe and Nordman, *Un tour de France*; Pierre Champion, *Catherine de Médicis présente à Charles IX son royaume, 1564–1566* (Paris, 1937).

12. *Lettres de Catherine de Médicis*, vol. 3, p. xxvi.
13. *Ibid.*, vol. 3, pp. xxvii–xxviii.
14. *Ibid.*, vol. 3, pp. 166–7.
15. Cloulas, *Catherine de Médicis*, p. 235.
16. *Lettres de Catherine de Médicis*, vol. 3, p. 241.
17. Mariéjol, *Catherine de Médicis*, p. 175.
18. D. Crouzet, *Le haut coeur de Catherine de Médicis* (Paris, 2005), pp. 371–2.
19. Shimizu, *Conflict of Loyalties*, pp. 135–40.
20. Sutherland, *The Huguenot Struggle*, pp. 175–7, 358–60.
21. *Bref et sommaire recueil de ce qui a esté faict & de l'ordre tenûe à la joyeuse & triumphante Entrée du tres-puissant, tres magnanime & tres chrestien Prince Charles IX, de ce nom Roy de France, en sa bonne ville de Paris, capitale de son Royaume, le Mardy seiziesme iour de Mars* (Paris, 1570); Frances Yates, *Astraea: The Imperial Theme in the Sixteenth Century* (London, 1975), pp. 127–48.
22. The letters of Jeanne d'Albret are problematic. Roelker (*Queen of Navarre*) cites them as authentic; other historians (e.g., Ritter, Cazaux) dismiss them as fakes. Many survive only in seventeenth-century copies. David Bryson (in *Jeanne d'Albret et sa cour*, ed. Evelyne Berriot-Salvadore, Philippe Chareyre and Claude Martin-Ulrich [Paris, 2004], p. 502) writes: 'Mais ces textes importants et émouvants ne sont pas nécessairement des faux, et il ne faut pas les écarter entièrement. [But these important and moving texts are not necessarily fakes, and ought not to be set aside completely].' Denis Crouzet's view is that the letters, even if genuine, may reflect Jeanne's fanatical puritanism and persecution mania.
23. Desjardins, *Négociations diplomatiques*, vol. 3, p. 765; Roelker, *Queen of Navarre*, p. 383.
24. D. Crouzet, *La nuit de la Saint-Barthélemy: Un rêve perdu de la Renaissance* (Paris, 1994), pp. 337–8.
25. *Ibid.*, pp. 378–81.
26. *Ibid.*, pp. 378–94.
27. *Ibid.*, p. 388.
28. *Ibid.*, pp. 396–7.
29. Élianne Viennot, *Marguerite de Valois* (Paris, 1995), p. 55.
30. Janine Garrisson, *Les protestants au XVIe siècle* (Paris, 1988), pp. 285–90.
31. For Henri's experiences in Poland, see P. Chevallier, *Henri III* (Paris, 1985), pp. 209–31; Robert Sauzet (ed.), *Henri III et son temps* (Paris, 1992), pp. 67–117; and J.R. Mulryne, Helen Watanabe-O'Kelly and Margaret Shewring (eds), *Europa Triumphans*, 2 vols (Aldershot, 2004), vol. 1, pp. 130–9.
32. Mack P. Holt, *The Duke of Anjou and the Politique Struggle during the Wars of Religion* (Cambridge, 1986), pp. 13–16.
33. *Ibid.*, p. 17.
34. *Ibid.*, pp. 34–44.
35. *Lettres de Catherine de Médicis*, vol. 4, pp. 310–12.

Chapter 15: Queen Mother

1. Boutier, Dewerpe and Nordman, *Un tour de France*; Champion, *Catherine de Médicis présente*.
2. Boutier, Dewerpe and Nordman, *Un tour de France*, p. 177.
3. *Ibid.*, pp. 13–23.
4. *Ibid.*, pp. 19–21.
5. *Commentaires de Blaise de Monluc*, ed. P. Courteault (Paris, 1925), vol. 1, p. 18, vol. 3, p. 341.
6. V.E. Graham and W. McAllister Johnson, *The Royal Tour of France by Charles IX and Catherine de Medici* (Toronto, 1979), pp. 8–9, 11–13.
7. Roelker, *Queen of Navarre*, pp. 229–30; J.-P. Babelon, *Henri IV* (Paris, 1982), p. 127.
8. Champion, *Catherine de Medicis présente*, pp. 99–111.
9. Mariéjol, *Catherine de Médicis*, pp. 146–47.

10. Boutier, Dewerpe and Nordman, *Un tour de France*, pp. 245–6; Champion, *Catherine de Médicis présente*, pp. 248–52.
11. Boutier, Dewerpe and Nordman, *Un tour de France*, pp. 87–104; Champion, *Catherine de Médicis présente*, pp. 262–3; Mariéjol, *Catherine de Médicis*, pp. 149–54; Graham and Johnson, *The Royal Tour*, pp. 29–57.
12. See below, pp. 264–5.
13. Champion, *Catherine de Médicis présente*, p. 292.
14. Frances A. Yates, *The Valois Tapestries* (2nd edn, London, 1975), p. 68.
15. R.J. Knecht, 'Popular theatre and the court in sixteenth-century France', *Renaissance Studies*, 9 (1995), pp. 364–73.
16. Madeleine Lazard, 'Le Théâtre', in R. Aulotte (ed.), *Précis de littérature française du XVIe siècle: la Renaissance* (Paris, 1991), pp. 70–1.
17. Jacqueline Boucher, *Société et mentalités autour de Henri III* (Lille, 1981), vol. 3, pp. 1009–12.
18. Bontemps et al., *Le Prince*, p. 53.
19. Vasari, *Lives of the Painters*, vol. 4, pp. 79–80; C. Avery, *Giambologna* (London, 1993), pp. 159–61.
20. C. Avery, 'An Equestrian Statuette of Louis XIII Attributed to Simon Guillain (1581–1658)', *The Burlington Magazine*, 126 (Sept. 1984), pp. 553–6.
21. Blunt, *Art and Architecture in France*, pp. 54–5; Zerner, *L'art de la Renaissance*, pp. 351–4.
22. Zerner, *Renaissance Art*, pp. 379–80.
23. Historians of French Renaissance architecture are heavily indebted to the fifteen books of engravings which Jacques Androuet du Cerceau the elder published between 1549 and 1584. His first known work – a collection of triumphal arches – was published at Orléans in 1549, and in 1566 he entered the service of Renée de France, for whom he supervised the construction of the château of Montargis. He was also employed at Verneuil-sur-Oise by her brother-in-law, the duc de Nemours. His books of engravings had three purposes: to spread knowledge of antiquity, to provide pattern books for various kinds of grotesque decoration, and to provide designs for houses great and small. Du Cerceau's *Livre d'Architecture* (1559) was the first practical architectural handbook to appear in France; but his fame rests mainly on his *Les Plus Excellents Bastiments de France*, published between 1576 and 1579. The engravings are a major source of information about buildings that have since been altered or have vanished altogether. Du Cerceau was also an architect in his own right; he favoured a style of mannerist decoration that Blunt described as 'barbarous'. It did, nonetheless, exert a powerful influence in France for more than half a century. Jacques Androuet du Cerceau founded a dynasty of architects. His son, Baptiste, became Henry III's favourite architect.
24. Babelon, *Châteaux de France*, pp. 691–2.
25. A. Blunt, *Philibert de l'Orme* (London, 1958), pp. 92–3.
26. M.N. Baudoin-Matuszek (ed.), *Paris et Catherine de Médicis* (Paris, n.d.), p. 89.
27. Boutier et al., *Un tour de France*, pp. 217, 223–4, 261–4.
28. Baudoin-Matuszek, *Paris*, pp. 89–90.
29. See above, p. 163, figure 28.
30. Baudoin-Matuszek, *Paris*, p. 97.
31. Cloulas, *Catherine de Médicis*, pp. 330–1.
32. J.-P. Babelon, *Paris au XVIe siècle* (Paris, 1986), pp. 229, 232.
33. Baudoin-Matuszek, *Paris*, pp. 108–20.
34. D. Thomson, *Renaissance Paris: architecture and growth, 1475–1600* (London, 1984), pp. 175–6; Babelon, *Paris au XVIe siècle*, pp. 141–2; Mariéjol, *Catherine de Médicis*, p. 215.
35. Baudoin-Matuszek, *Paris*, pp. 121–4.
36. Blunt, *Philibert de l'Orme*, pp. 89–91.
37. *Ibid.*, p. 64.
38. *Ibid.*, pp. 61–4; Babelon, *Châteaux de France*, pp. 598–602.
39. Cloulas, *Catherine de Médicis*, pp. 328–30, 339.
40. *Ibid.*, p. 322.
41. Babelon, *Paris au XVIe siècle*, pp. 83, 254.

42. McGowan, *Ideal Forms*, p. 126.
43. E. Bonnaffé, *Inventaire des meubles de Catherine de Médicis en 1589* (Paris, 1874). See also Chantal Turbide, 'Les collections de Catherine de Médicis (1519–89): quelques vestiges d'un patrimoine', in J.-Y. Ribault (ed.), *Mécènes et collectionneurs: les variantes d'une passion*, vol. 1 (Paris, 1999), pp. 51–63.
44. Yates, *The Valois Tapestries*.
45. Louis de Groër, 'Les tapisseries des Valois du Musée des Offices à Florence', in *Art, Objets d'art, collections: hommage à Hubert Landais* (Brussels, 1987).
46. BNF. Ms. fr. 3133, f. 8.
47. Alexandra Zvereva, *Les Clouet de Catherine de Médicis: chefs-d'oeuvre graphiques du Musée Condé* (Paris, 2002), pp. 6–18.
48. On the problem of distinguishing between Jean Cousin the Elder and his son, see Zerner, *Renaissance Art*, pp. 227–65. Neither seems to have had much contact with the court.
49. G. Lebel, 'Notes sur Antoine Caron et son oeuvre', *Bulletin de la Société de l'Histoire de Paris et de l'Île-de-France* (1940), pp. 7–34.
50. J. Ehrmann, *Antoine Caron: peintre des fêtes et des massacres* (Paris, 1986), pp. 129–34.
51. Yates, *Astraea*, p. 145.
52. J. Ehrmann, 'Massacre and Persecution Pictures in Sixteenth-Century France', *JWCI*, 8 (1945), pp. 195–9.

Chapter 16: Henry III: The King and his *Mignons*

1. For an account of the entertainments offered to Henry III in Venice and elsewhere in northern Italy in 1574, see Margaret McGowan, 'Festivals and the Arts in Henri III's Journey from Poland to France (1574)', in J.R. Mulryne, Helen Watanabe-O'Kelly and Margaret Shewring (eds), *Europa Triumphans: Court and Civic Festivals in Early Modern Europe*, 2 vols (Aldershot, 2004), vol. 1, pp. 122–8.
2. Tommaseo, *Relations des ambassadeurs vénitiens*, vol. 2, pp. 235–7.
3. 'Sa Majesté se porte très bien et boit mieux de son eau que le plus grand ivrogne d'Allemagne ne boit de vin du Rhein.' E. Charrière, *Négociations de la France dans le Levant* (Paris, 1855–60), vol. 4, p. 196.
4. J. Boucher, *Société et mentalités autour de Henri III*, 3 vols (Lille, 1981), vol. 1, pp. 18–22.
5. M. Quentin, in *Bulletin de la Société des sciences historiques et naturelles de l'Yonne* (1888), pp. 397–422. Cited by Boucher, *Société*, pp. 32–3.
6. Boucher, *Société*, pp. 32–6.
7. Robert J. Sealy, *The Palace Academy of Henry III* (Geneva, 1981); Frances A. Yates, *The French Academies of the Sixteenth Century* (London, 1988), pp. 105–30.
8. *Lettres de Catherine de Médicis*, vol. 5, pp. 147–9.
9. 'Le roi fit une harangue, la mieux dite, la plus éloquente et prononcée de la meilleure grâce qui se peut désirer, tellement que tout le monde en est ébahi.' E. Cabié, *Les guerres de religion dans le sud-ouest de la France et principalement en Quercy d'après les papiers des seigneurs de Saint Sulpice* (Albi, 1906), p. 316.
10. Guillaume de Taix, *Mémoires des affaires du clergé de France* (Paris, 1625), pp. 20–2. Cited by Boucher, *Société*, p. 50; N. Le Roux, *Un régicide au nom de Dieu: l'assassinat d'Henri III* (Paris, 2006), p. 66.
11. 'Le roi prend bien la peine quelquefois de réciter lui même ce qu'il a ouï et comme il a la mémoire excellente, peu de choses lui échappent, de sorte, Madame, que j'en vois le fruit tout présent.' A. Cabos, 'Gui du Faur de Pibrac, un magistrat poète au XVIe siècle, 1529–1584' (Thesis of University of Toulouse, 1922), pp. 151–2. Cited by Boucher, *Société*, p. 54.
12. Boucher, *Société*, pp. 54–7.
13. Innocent Gentillet, *Discours sur les moyens de bien gouverner et maintenir en bonne paix un royaume: Contre Nicolas Machiavel, Florentin* (1576), p. 11. Cited by Boucher, *Société*, p. 60.
14. Boucher, *Société*, pp. 57–60. Anglo cautions against accepting d'Avila's statement in '*Le plus gentil esprit qui soit apparu au monde depuis les demiers siècles*'. The Popularity of Machiavelli

in Sixteenth-Century France', in Pauline Smith and Trevor Peach (eds), *Renaissance Reflections: Essays in memory of C.A. Mayer* (Paris, 2002), p. 198.

15. Sydney Anglo, *Machiavelli: The First Century* (Oxford, 2005), p. 347 n. 58.
16. La Popelinière, *Histoire de France . . . depuis 1550*, 2 vols (Paris, 1581), vol. 1.
17. Boucher, *Société*, p. 68.
18. Le Roux, *Un régicide*, pp. 58–61.
19. See below p. 320.
20. Le Roux, *Un régicide*, p. 61.
21. Boucher, *Société*, p. 72.
22. Brantôme, *Oeuvres complètes*, vol. 6, pp. 384–6.
23. Boucher, *Société*, p. 74.
24. Cabié, *Les guerres de religion dans le sud-ouest*, pp. 681–2.
25. *Lettres de Catherine de Medicis*, vol. 8, p. 71.
26. René de Lucinge, *Lettres de la cour d'Henri III en 1586*, ed. Alain Dufour (Geneva, 1966), p. 190.
27. Boucher, *Société*, p. 85.
28. *Lettres de Henri III*, ed. P. Champion and M. François (Paris, 2000), vol. 5, p. 310.
29. S. Anglo, *The Martial Arts of Renaissance Europe* (London, 2000), pp. 109–10.
30. Boucher, *Société*, p. 87.
31. *CSP*, vol. 14, pp. 504–8; vol. 15, pp. 333–5.
32. Pierre de L'Estoile, *Registre-Journal du règne de Henri III*, ed. M. Lazard and G. Schrenck, 6 vols (Geneva, 1992–2003), vol. 5, p. 39.
33. *Ibid.*, vol. 1, p. 207.
34. Tommaseo, *Relations des ambassadeurs vénitiens*, pp. 381–3.
35. H. Sauval, *Histoire et recherches des Antiquités de la Ville de Paris* (Paris, 1724), Book III, p. 231.
36. Babelon, *Paris au XVIe siècle*, pp. 137–9; Thomson, *Renaissance Paris*, p. 178; Jean-Marie Pérouse de Montclos (ed.), *Le guide du patrimoine: Paris* (1994), p. 401.
37. Thomson, *Renaissance Paris*, p. 180.
38. Daniel Alcouffe, 'A propos de l'orfèvrerie commandée par Henri III pour l'ordre du Saint-Esprit', in *Art, objets d'art, collections*, pp. 135–42.
39. L'Estoile, *Registre-Journal*, vol. 3, pp. 11–13, 20–2; P. Chevallier, *Henri III* (Paris, 1985), pp. 495–501; J. Boucher, *La cour de Henri III* (Rennes, 1986), p. 194.
40. 'Aymez le bien toujours et croyez qu'yl vous ayme fort . . . et, s'il se peust plus.'
41. N. Le Roux, *La Faveur du roi: Mignons et courtisans au temps des derniers Valois (vers 1547–vers 1589)* (Seyssel, 2000), pp. 280–8.
42. *Ibid.*, pp. 288–96.
43. *Ibid.*, pp. 461–71.
44. Historical Manuscripts Commission, *Calendar of Hatfield Manuscripts*, vol. 3, pp. 74–5.
45. Le Roux, *La Faveur*, pp. 471–9.
46. *Ibid.*, pp. 479–86.
47. René de Lucinge, *Lettres sur les débuts de la Ligue, 1585*, ed. A. Dufour (Geneva, 1964), p. 22.
48. René de Lucinge, *Lettres de 1587*, ed. James J. Supple (Geneva, 1994), p. 100.
49. Le Roux, *La Faveur*, pp. 519–27.
50. *Ibid.*, pp. 528–33.
51. Le Roux, *Un régicide*, p. 47.
52. Le Roux, *La Faveur*, p. 182.
53. Le Roux, *Un régicide*, p. 53.
54. *CSP, Foreign of the Reign of Elizabeth*, vol. 11, pp. 78, 133.
55. Arlette Jouanna et al. (eds), *Histoire et dictionnaire des guerres de religion* (Paris, 1998), pp. 1293–5.
56. D. Potter and P.E. Roberts, 'An Englishman's View of the Court of Henry III', *French History*, vol. 2 (Sept. 1988), pp. 312–44. I have modernised the spelling and inserted some punctuation.
57. L'Estoile, *Registre-Journal*, vol. 5, p. 46.

58. Yates, *The French Academies*, p. 163.
59. *Ibid.*, pp. 165–7
60. Le Roux, *La Faveur*, p. 596.
61. *Ibid.*, pp. 77–8.
62. Boucher, *La cour de Henri III*, p. 197.
63. Le Roux, *Un régicide*, pp. 73–4.
64. Chevallier, *Henri III*, p. 548.
65. Boucher, *La cour*, p. 194.
66. Le Roux, *La Faveur*, pp. 599–602.
67. Chevallier, *Henri III*, pp. 553–4.

Chapter 17: The Court '*en fete*'

1. M. Greengrass, 'Henry III, festival culture and the rhetoric of royalty', in J.R. Mulryne, Helen Watanabe-O'Kelly and Margaret Shewring (eds), *Europa Triumphans: Court and Civic Festivals in Early Modern Europe*, 2 vols (Aldershot, 2004), vol. 1, p. 110.
2. *CSP Elizabeth, 1579–80*, p. 69, no. 62.
3. Margaret McGowan, 'L'essor du ballet à la cour de Henri III', in Isabelle de Conihout, Jean-François Maillard and Guy Poirier (eds), *Henri III, mécène des arts, des sciences et des lettres* (Paris, 2006), pp. 82–9.
4. W. Shakespeare, *The Merchant of Venice*, act 1, sc. ii.
5. Jacqueline Boucher, 'Le costume autour des derniers Valois: signe de pouvoir et objet de polémique', in Marie Viallon (ed.), *Paraitre et se vêtir au XVIe siècle* (Saint-Etienne, 2006), pp. 213–16.
6. L'Estoile, *Registre-Journal*, vol. 4, p. 104.
7. Montaigne, *The Complete Essays*, p. 301.
8. Boucher, 'Le costume', pp. 216–17.
9. Montaigne, *The Complete Essays*, p. 133.
10. Boucher, 'Le costume', p. 217.
11. *Ibid.*
12. *CSP Elizabeth* (London, 1914), vol. 14, pp. 161–4.
13. Boucher, p. 220.
14. L'Estoile, *Registre-Journal*, vol. 2, p. 145.
15. Alexandra Zvereva, 'La génèse du portrait de Henri III', in de Conihout et al. (eds), *Henri III, mécène*, pp. 56–65, and Isabelle Oger, 'Le rôle de Henri III dans l'invention et la diffusion de son portrait gravé', in *ibid.*, pp. 68–80.
16. *Lettres de Henri III*, ed. M. François, vol. 2 (Paris, 1965), p. 433, no. 1854.
17. *Lettres de Henri III, roi de France*, ed. M. François, vol. 1 (Paris, 1959), p. 359, no. 969.
18. Boucher, *Société*, vol. 3, pp. 1009–33.
19. Yates, *Astraea*, pp. 149–72.
20. *Ibid.*, p. 488.
21. Le Roux, *La Faveur*, pp. 486–92; Yates, *The French Academies*, pp. 236–74; Yates, *Astraea*, pp. 165–7.

Chapter 18: The Court under Fire

1. Holt, *The Duke of Anjou, passim.*
2. Le Roux, *La Faveur*, pp. 364–82.
3. *Ibid.*, pp. 384–7.
4. *Ibid.*, pp. 389–95.
5. *Ibid.*, pp. 412–16.
6. *Ibid.*, pp. 421–7.
7. *Ibid.*, pp. 428–56.

8. Le Roux, *Un régicide*, p. 51.
9. The proportion of Italians in the household of Catherine de' Medici between 1570 and 1589 was as follows (Boucher, *La cour de Henri III*, p. 99):

> ladies-in-waiting: 15–16 per cent
> chambermaids (*filles de chambre*): 10–18 per cent
> stewards (*maîtres d'hôtel*): 10–33 per cent
> *gentilshommes servans*: 14–18 per cent
> secretaries: 3–7 per cent
> almoners: 18–41 per cent

The percentage of Italians in Henry III's household between 1574 and 1589 was as follows:

> almoners: 6–11 per cent
> stewards: 11 per cent
> gentlemen of the chamber: 9–12 per cent
> *gentilshommes servans*: 11 per cent
> *valets de chambre*: 20–25 per cent
> *secrétaires de la chambre*: 2–3 per cent
> *fourriers*: 7–11 per cent
> physicians: 15–17 per cent

The percentage of Italians in the queen's household between 1575 and 1590 was as follows:

> ladies: 11 per cent
> *gentilshommes servans* and doctors: 28 per cent
> *valets de chambre*: 23 per cent
> almoners: 10 per cent

10. Boucher, *La cour de Henri III*, pp. 102–4.
11. *Ibid.*, pp. 104–6.
12. Henry Heller, *Anti-Italianism in Sixteenth-Century France* (Toronto, 2003), pp. 114–36.
13. Anglo, *Machiavelli*, pp. 271–324.
14. P.M. Smith, *The Anti-Courtier Trend*, pp. 206–16.
15. Le Roux, *La Faveur*, pp. 621–70.
16. L'Estoile, *Registre-Journal*, vol. 2, p. 104.
17. *Ibid.*, pp. 112–13. Jacqueline Boucher suggests that L'Estoile may have been thinking of the new style of low-cut dresses: *Paraître et se vêtir au XVIe siècle* (Saint-Etienne, 2006), p. 219.
18. L'Estoile, *Registre-Journal*, vol. 3 , pp. 155–6.
19. *Ibid.*, vol. 5 , p. 212.
20. J.-H. Mariéjol, *La Réforme, la Ligue, l'Édit de Nantes, 1559–1598* (Paris, 1983), p. 240.
21. L'Estoile, *Registre-Journal*, vol. 2, pp. 128.
22. See above, p. 31.
23. François de La Noue, *Discours politiques et militaires*, ed. F.E. Sutcliffe (Geneva, 1967), p. 194.
24. P.M. Smith, *The Anti-Courtier Trend*, p. 191.
25. *Ibid.*, pp. 193–6.

Chapter 19: Nemesis

1. Le Roux, *Un régicide*, p. 73
2. Jean-Marie Constant, *La Ligue* (Paris, 1996), pp. 112–16.
3. Sutherland, *The Huguenot Struggle*, p. 364; Chevallier, *Henri III*, pp. 574–7.
4. *Lettres de Henri III roi de France*, vol. 2, p. 133. See also Le Roux, *Un régicide*.
5. Le Roux, *La Faveur*, p. 599.
6. Chevallier, *Henri III*, pp. 554–5.
7. Le Roux, *La Faveur*, pp. 592–3.
8. Le Roux, *Un régicide,* p. 69.
9. Le Roux, *La Faveur*, pp. 616–20.

10. Le Roux, *La Faveur*, pp. 640–4.
11. Chevallier, *Henri III*, pp. 62–8; Le Roux, *Un régicide*, pp. 127–33.
12. Le Roux, *La Faveur*, p. 685.
13. *Ibid.*, pp. 685–6.
14. *Ibid.*, pp. 687–8.
15. L'Estoile, *Registre-Journal*, vol. 6, p. 87.
16. Constant, *La Ligue*, pp. 201–12; Le Roux, *La Faveur*, p. 699.
17. L'Estoile, *Registre-Journal*, vol. 6, p. 129
18. Le Roux, *Un régicide*, p. 162
19. L'Estoile, *Registre-Journal*, vol. 6, p. 144.
20. Chevallier, *Henri III*, p. 672.
21. L'Estoile, *Registre-Journal*, vol. 6, p. 132.
22. Cloulas, *Catherine de Médicis*, p. 604.
23. *Ibid.*, p. 605.
24. *Ibid.*, pp. 605–7.
25. On Jacques Clément, see Le Roux, *Un régicide*, pp. 279–84.
26. *Ibid.*, p. 22.
27. *Ibid.*, pp. 26–31.
28. *Ibid.*, pp. 30–1.
29. Mark Greengrass, *France in the Age of Henry IV* (2nd edn, London, 1995), p. 60.
30. Le Roux, *Un régicide*, pp. 32–3.
31. Chevallier, *Henri III*, pp. 696–704.
32. Le Roux, *La Faveur*, pp. 704–6.
33. Jean-François Solnon, *La cour de France* (Paris, 1987), pp. 164–5.

Bibliography

Primary Sources

Albèri, E. (ed.), *Relazioni degli ambasciatori veneti al Senato*, 14 vols (Florence, 1839–63)

Aubigné, Agrippa d', *Histoire universelle*, ed. André Thierry, 9 vols (Geneva, 1981–95)

Auton, Jean d', *Chronique de Louis XII*, ed. R. de Maulde La Clavière, 4 vols (Paris, 1889–95)

Barrillon, Jean, *Journal de Jean Barrillon*, ed. P. de Vaissière, 2 vols (Paris, 1899)

Bonnaffé, E. (ed.), *Inventaire des meubles de Catherine de Médicis en 1589* (Paris, 1874)

Bontems, C., L.-P. Raybaud and J.-P. Brancourt, *Le Prince dans la France des XVIe et XVIIe siècles* (Paris, 1965)

Bourrilly, V.-L. (ed.), *Journal d'un bourgeois de Paris sous le règne de François Ier* (Paris, 1910)

Brantôme, Pierre de Bourdeille, seigneur de, *Œuvres complètes*, ed. Ludovic Lalanne, 11 vols (Paris, 1864–82)

Bref et sommaire recueil de ce qui a esté faict & de l'ordre tenüe à la joyeuse & triumphante Entrée du tres-puissant, tres magnanime & tres chrestien Prince Charles IX, de ce nom Roy de France, en sa bonne ville de Paris, capitale de son Royaume, le Mardy seiziesme iour de Mars (Paris, 1570)

Briçonnet, G., and Marguerite d'Angoulême, *Correspondance*, ed. C. Martineau and M. Veissière, 2 vols (Geneva, 1975–9)

Calendar of State Papers, Foreign: Edward VI, Mary, Elizabeth I, ed. W.B. Turnbull et al., 25 vols. (London, 1861–1950)

Calendar of State Papers, Spanish, ed. C. Bergenroth, P. de Gayangos and M.A.S. Hume, 12 vols (London, 1862– 95)

Calendar of State Papers, Venetian, ed. R. Brown, C. Bentinck and H. Brown, 9 vols (London, 1864–98)

Captivité du roi François Ier, ed. A. Champollion-Figeac (Paris, 1847)

Castiglione, Baldesar, *The Book of the Courtier*, tr. George Bull (Harmondsworth, 1967)

Catalogue des actes de François Ier, 10 vols (Paris, 1887–1910)

Cellini, Benvenuto, *The Life of Benvenuto Cellini Written by Himself*, tr. John Addington Symonds, revised by John Pope-Hennessy (London, 1949)

Cimber, L., and C. Danjou, *Archives curieuses de l'histoire de France depuis Louis XI jusqu'à Louis XVIII*, 30 vols (Paris, 1834–49)

Comptes de l'hôtel des rois de France aux XIVe et XVe siècles, ed. M.K. Douët-d'Arcq (Paris, 1865)

Comptes de Louise de Savoie et de Marguerite d'Angoulême, ed. Abel Lefranc and Jacques Boulenger (Paris, 1905)

Coquille, Guy, *Œuvres*, 2 vols (Paris, 1665)

Correspondance des nonces en France: Capodiffero, Dandino et Guidiccione (1541–1546), ed. Jean Lestocquoy (Rome/Paris, 1963)

De Beatis, Antonio, *The Travel Journal of Antonio De Beatis: Germany, Switzerland, the Low Countries and Italy, 1517–1518*, ed. J.R. Hale (London, 1979)

De l'Orme, Philibert, *Premier Tome de l'Architecture* (Paris, 1567)

Desjardins, A. (ed.), *Négociations diplomatiques de la France avec la Toscane*, 6 vols (Paris, 1859–86)

Discours merveilleux de la vie, actions et deportements de Catherine de Médicis, Royne-mère, ed. Nicole Cazauran (Geneva, 1995)

Du Bellay, Martin and Guillaume, *Mémoires de Martin et Guillaume du Bellay*, ed. V.-L. Bourrilly and F. Vindry, 4 vols (Paris, 1908–19)

Dubois, Claude-Gilbert (ed.), *L'Isle des hermaphrodites* (Geneva, 1996)

Du Cerceau, J.-A., *Le premier livre des plus excellents bastiments de France* (Paris, 1976)

Du Chastel, Pierre, *Deux sermons funebres prononcez es obseques de Françoys premier de ce nom*, ed. Pascale Chiron (Geneva, 1999)

Erasmus, *Opus epistolarum*, ed. P.S. Allen and H.M. Allen, 8 vols (Oxford 1906–34)

Estienne, C., *Le guide des chemins de France de 1553*, ed. J. Bonnerot, 2 vols (Paris, 1936)

Europa Triumphans: Court and Civic Festivals in Early Modern Europe, ed. J.R. Mulryne, Helen Watanabe-O'Kelly and Margaret Shewring, 2 vols (Aldershot, 2004)

Florange, *Mémoires du maréchal de Florange, dit Le jeune Adventureux*, ed. R. Goubaux and P.A. Lemoisne, 2 vols (Paris, 1913–24)

Fraikin, J. (ed.), *Nonciatures de France: nonciatures de Clément VII*, 2 vols (Paris, 1906)

François Ier, *Œuvres poétiques*, ed. J.E. Kane (Geneva, 1984)

Gachard, L.-P., *Relation des troubles à Gand sous Charles-Quint par un anonyme* (Brussels, 1846)

Godefroy, T., *Le céremonial françois*, 2 vols (Paris, 1649)

[Granvelle] *Papiers d'état du cardinal de Granvelle*, ed. C. Weiss, 9 vols (Paris, 1841–52)

Gringore, Pierre, *Les entrées royales à Paris de Marie d'Angleterre (1514) et Claude de France (1517)*, ed. Cynthia J. Brown (Geneva, 2005)

Guiffrey, G. (ed.), *Cronique du Roy Françoys premier de ce nom* (Paris, 1860)

Hall, Edward, *Henry VIII*, ed. C. Whibley, 2 vols (London, 1904)

Haton, Claude, *Mémoires de Claude Haton*, ed. Laurent Bourquin, 4 vols (Paris, 2001–7)

Herminjard, A. (ed.) *Correspondance des réformateurs dans les pays de langue française*, 9 vols (Geneva, 1886–7)

Hurtubise, P. (ed.), *Correspondance du nonce en France Antonio-Maria Salviati* (Rome, 1975)

Knecht, R.J. (ed.), *The Voyage of Sir Nicholas Carewe to the emperor Charles V in the year 1529* (Roxburghe Club, 1959)

L'Entrée de Henri II à Rouen 1550, with an introduction by Margaret McGowan (Amsterdam, 1974)

La magnificence de la superbe et triomphante entrée de la noble et antique cité de Lyon faicte au Treschrestien Roy de France Henry, deuxiesme de ce nom, et à la Royne Catherine son Espouse, le xxiii de Septembre M.D.XLVIII (Lyon, 1549), ed. R.A. Cooper (Tempe, 1997)

La Noue, François de, *Discours politiques et militaires*, ed. F.E. Sutcliffe (Geneva, 1967)

Laborde, L. de, *Les comptes des bâtiments du roi (1528–71)*, 2 vols (Paris, 1878–80)

L'Estoile, Pierre de, *Registre-Journal du règne de Henri III*, ed. Madeleine Lazard and Gilbert Schrenck, 6 vols (Geneva, 1992–2003)

Letters and Papers, Foreign and Domestic of the Reign of Henry VIII, ed. J.S. Brewer, J. Gairdner and R.H. Brodie, 21 vols (London, 1862–1910)

Lettres de Catherine de Médicis, ed. Hector de la Ferrière and Baguenault de Puchesse, 10 vols (Paris, 1880–1909)

Lettres de Henri III, roi de France, ed. Pierre Champion, Michel François and Jacqueline Boucher, 6 vols to date (Paris, 1959–2006)

Lettres de Marguerite d'Angoulême, ed. F. Génin (Paris, 1841)

L'Hôpital, Michel de, *Discours pour la majorité de Charles IX*, ed. R. Descimon (Paris, 1993)

Livre de raison de Me Nicolas Versoris , ed. G. Fagniez (Paris, 1885)

Louise de Savoie, *Journal*, in S. Guichenon, *Histoire généalogique de la royale maison de Savoie* (Lyon, 1660), vol. 2, p. 457. Also in Michaud and Poujoulat, *Nouvelle collection* (1836)

Lucinge, René de, *Dialogue du françois et du savoysien (1593)*, ed. Alain Dufour (Geneva, 1961)

Lucinge, René de, *Lettres sur les débuts de la Ligue, 1585*, ed. A. Dufour (Geneva, 1964)

Lucinge, René de, *Lettres sur la cour d'Henri III en 1586*, ed. Alain Dufour (Geneva, 1966)

Lucinge, René, *Lettres de 1587. L'année des reîtres*, ed. James J. Supple (Geneva, 1994)

McFarlane, I.D. (ed.), *The Entry of Henri II into Paris, 16 June 1549* (Binghamton, NY, 1982)

McGowan, Margaret, *L'Entrée de Henri II, Rouen 1550* (Amsterdam, 1974)

Marguerite d'Angoulême, *Heptaméron*, ed. M. François (Paris, 1942)

Marguerite d'Angoulême, *Lettres de Marguerite d'Angoulême, sœur de François Ier, reine de Navarre*, ed. F. Génin (Paris, 1841)

[Marguerite d'Angoulême,] *Nouvelles lettres de Marguerite d'Angoulême*, ed. F. Génin (Paris, 1842)

Marguerite de Navarre, *Heptaméron*, ed. Rena Salminen (Geneva, 1999)

[Marguerite de Valois,] *Mémoires de Marguerite de Valois*, ed. Yves Cazaux (Paris, 1971)

Marot, Clément, *Les épîtres*, ed. C.A. Mayer (London, 1958)

Marot, Clément, *Les épigrammes*, ed. C.A. Mayer (London, 1970)

Michaud, J.-F., and J.-J.F. Poujoulat (eds), *Nouvelle collection de mémoires pour servir à l'histoire de France*, 1st ser., vol. 5 (1836)

[Monluc, Blaise de,] *Commentaires de Blaise de Monluc*, ed. P. Courteault, 4 vols (Paris, 1925)

Montaigne, M. de, *The Complete Essays*, tr. M. Screech (London, 1993)

Ordonnances des rois de France: règne de François Ier, 9 vols (Paris, 1902–75)

Pasquier, Estienne, *Lettres historiques pour les années 1556–1594*, ed. D. Thickett (Geneva, 1966)

Petitot, M. (ed.), *Collection complète des mémoires relatifs à l'histoire de France*, 52 vols (Paris, 1819–26)

Procédures politiques du règne de Louis XII, ed. R. de Maulde La Clavière (Paris, 1885)

Rabelais, François, *The Histories of Gargantua and Pantagruel*, tr. J.M. Cohen (Harmondsworth, 1955)

Rabelais, François, *Pantagruel*, ed. V.-L. Saulnier (Geneva, 1965)

Registres des délibérations du Bureau de la Ville de Paris, vol. 1 (1499–1526), ed. F. Bonnardot (Paris, 1883); vol. 2 (1527–39), ed. A. Tuetey (Paris, 1886); vol. 3 (1539–52), ed. P. Guérin (Paris, 1886)

Saint-Gelais, Jean de, *Histoire de Louis XII, Roy de France, Père du peuple et de plusieurs choses mémorables advenues en France et en Italie jusques en l'an 1510* (Paris, 1622)

Sanuto, M., *I diarii di Marino Sanuto*, 58 vols (Venice, 1879–1903)

Scheurer, R. (ed.), *Correspondance du cardinal Jean du Bellay*, 2 vols (Paris, 1969)

Seyssel, Claude de, *La monarchie de France*, ed. J. Poujol (Paris, 1961); English edition: *The Monarchy of France*, tr. J.H. Hexter and D.R. Kelley (New Haven, CT, 1981)

State Papers of Henry VIII, 11 vols (London, 1830–52)

Sylvius, Jacobus, *Francisci Francorum Regis et Henrici Anglorum Colloquium*, ed. and tr. Stephen Bamforth and Jean Dupèbe, *Renaissance Studies*, 5 (1991)

Tamalio, Raffaele (ed.), *Federico Gonzaga alla corte di Francesco I di Francia nel carteggio privato con Mantova (1515–1517)* (Paris, 1994)

Tommaseo, Niccolò, *Relations des ambassadeurs vénitiens sur les affaires de France au XVIe siècle*, 2 vols (Paris, 1838)

[Tournon,] *Correspondance du cardinal François de Tournon*, ed. M. François (Paris, 1946)

[Valbelle, Honoré de,] *Entrevue de François Ier avec Clément VII à Marseille, 1533. D'après le journal d'Honoré de Valbelle*, ed. A. Hamy (Paris, 1900)

Vasari, G., *Le vite de' piu eccelenti pittori, scultori ed architettori*, ed. G. Milanesi, 9 vols (Florence, 1878–85); English edition: *Lives of the Painters, Sculptors and Architects*, ed. William Gaunt, 4 vols (London, 1963)

[Vieilleville,] *Mémoires de la vie de François de Scépeaux, sire de Vieilleville*, ed. V. Carloix, in *Collections complètes des mémoires relatifs à l'histoire de France*, ed. M. Petitot, vols 26–28 (Paris, 1822)

Books

Adamson, John (ed.), *The Princely Courts of Europe* (London, 1999)

Anglo, Sydney, *Spectacle, Pageantry and Early Tudor Policy* (Oxford, 1969)

Anglo, Sydney, *The Martial Arts of Renaissance Europe* (New Haven and London, 2000)

Anglo, Sydney, *Machiavelli: The First Century* (Oxford, 2005)

Arlette, Jouanna, *La Saint-Barthélemy: le mystère d'un crime d'Etat* (Paris 2007)

Arminjon, Catherine, Denis Lavalle, Monique Chatenet and Claude d'Anthenaise (eds), *De l'Italie à Chambord: François Ier et la chevauchée des princes français* (Paris, 2004)

Armstrong, E., *Robert Estienne, Royal Printer* (Cambridge, 1954; revised edn, 1986)
Aulotte, Robert (ed.), *Précis de Littérature française du XVIe siècle* (Paris, 1991)
Babelon, J.-P., *Henri IV* (Paris, 1982)
Babelon, J.-P., *Nouvelle histoire de Paris: Paris au XVIe siècle* (Paris, 1986)
Babelon, J.-P., *Châteaux de France au siècle de la Renaissance* (Paris, 1989)
Balsamo, Jean (ed.), *Passer les monts: Français en Italie - l'Italie en France (1494–1525* (Paris, 1998)
Barber, Richard W., and Juliet Barker, *Tournaments, Jousts, Chivalry and Pageants in the Middle Ages* (Woodbridge, 1989)
Barbiche, B., *Les institutions de la monarchie française à l'époque moderne* (Paris, 1999)
Bardon, Françoise, *Diane de Poitiers et le mythe de Diane* (Paris, 1963)
Baudouin-Matuszek, M.N. (ed.), *Paris et Catherine de Médicis* (Paris, n.d.)
Baurmeister, U., and M.-P. Lafitte (eds), *Des livres et des rois* (Paris, 1992)
Beaune, Colette, *Naissance de la nation française* (Paris, 1985); English edition: *The Birth of an Ideology: Myths and Symbols of Nation in Late Medieval France* (Berkeley, CA, 1991)
Bedos-Rezak, Brigitte, *Anne de Montmorency, seigneur de la Renaissance* (Paris, 1990)
Béguin, Sylvie, *L'École de Fontainebleau: le maniérisme à la cour de France* (Paris, 1960)
Béguin, Sylvie, Jean Guillaume and A. Roy, *La galerie d'Ulysse à Fontainebleau* (Paris, 1985)
Bellenger, Yvonne (ed.), *Le Mécénat et l'influence des Guises* (Paris, 1887)
Bély, Lucien, *La société des princes, XVIe–XVIIIe siècle* (Paris, 1999)
Benedict, Philip (ed.), *Cities and Social Change in Early Modern France* (London, 1989)
Berriot-Salvadore, Evelyne, *Les femmes dans la société française de la Renaissance* (Geneva, 1990)
Berriot-Salvadore, Evelyne, Philippe Chareyre and Claude-Martin Ulrich (eds), *Jeanne d'Albret et sa cour* (Paris, 2004)
Berthoud, G., *Antoine Marcourt* (Geneva, 1973)
Berthoud, G., et al., *Aspects de la propagande religieuse* (Geneva, 1957)
Billacois, François, *Le duel dans la société française des XVIe–XVII siècles: essai de psychosociologie historique* (Paris, 1986)
Biraben, J.-N., *Les hommes et la peste en France et dans les pays européens et méditerranéens* (Paris-The Hague, 1975–6)
Bloch, Marc, *Les rois thaumaturges* (Paris, 1961); English edition: *The Royal Touch: Sacred Monarchy and Scrofula in England and France* (London, 1973)
Blunt, Anthony, *Art and Architecture in France, 1500–1700* (Harmondsworth, 1953)
Blunt, Anthony, *Philibert de l'Orme* (London, 1958)
Bohanan, Donna, *Crown and Nobility in Early Modern France* (Basingstoke, 1981)
Boucher, Jacqueline, *Société et mentalités autour de Henri III* (Thesis of University of Lyon, 1977), 3 vols (Lille, 1981)
Boucher, Jacqueline, *La cour de Henri III* (Rennes, 1986)
Boucher, Jacqueline, *Deux épouses et reines à la fin du XVIe siècle: Louise de Lorraine et Marguerite de France* (Saint-Etienne, 1995)
Boudon, Françoise and Jean Blécon, *Le château de Fontainebleau de François Ier à Henri IV: le bâtiment et ses fonctions* (Paris, 1998)
Bourgeon, Jean-Louis, *L'Assassinat de Coligny* (Geneva, 1992)
Bourgeon, Jean-Louis, *Charles IX devant la Saint-Barthélemy* (Geneva, 1995)
Bourquin, Laurent, *Noblesse seconde et pouvoir en Champagne aux XVIe et XVIIe siècles* (Paris, 1994)
Bourrilly, V.-L., *Jacques Colin, abbé de Saint Ambroise* (Paris, 1905)
Bourrilly, V.-L., *Guillaume du Bellay, seigneur de Langey* (Paris, 1905)
Boutier, Jean, Alain Dewerpe and Daniel Nordman, *Un tour de France royal: Le voyage de Charles IX (1564–1566)* (Paris, 1984)
Brandi, Karl, *The Emperor Charles V*, tr. C.V. Wedgwood (London, 1939)
Braudel, F., *The Mediterranean and the Mediterranean World in the Age of Philip II*, tr. S. Reynolds (London, 1972–3)
Braudel, F., *The Identity of France*, tr. S. Reynolds, 2 vols (London, 1989–91)
Brown, H.M., *Music in the Renaissance* (Englewood Cliffs, NJ, 1976)
Bryant, Lawrence M., *The King and the City in the Parisian Royal Entry Ceremony: Politics, Ritual and Art in the Renaissance* (Geneva, 1986)

Buisson, A., *Le Chancelier Antoine Duprat* (Paris, 1935)

Cameron, Keith (ed.), *From Valois to Bourbon: Dynasty, State and Society in Early Modern France* (Exeter, 1989)

Cameron, Keith, *Henri III: A Maligned or Malignant King: Aspects of the Satirical Iconography of Henri de Valois* (Exeter, 1978)

Carroll, E.A., *Rosso Fiorentino: Drawings, Prints and Decorative Arts* (Washington, DC, 1987)

Cazaux, Christelle, *La musique à la cour de François Ier* (Paris, 2002)

Cazeaux, Isabelle, *French Music in the Fifteenth and Sixteenth Centuries* (Oxford, 1975)

Champion, Pierre, *Catherine de Médicis présente à Charles IX son royaume (1564–1566)* (Paris, 1937)

Chantérac, B. de, *Odet de Foix, vicomte de Lautrec* (Paris, 1930)

Chartrou, Josèphe, *Les entrées solennelles et triomphales à la Renaissance (1484–1551)* (Paris, 1928)

Chastel, André (ed.), *Actes du colloque international sur l'Art de Fontainebleau: Fontainebleau et Paris, 18–20 octobre 1972* (Paris, 1975)

Chastel, André, *Le cardinal Louis d'Aragon: un voyageur princier de la Renaissance* (Paris, 1986)

Chastel, André, *Culture et demeures en France au XVIe siècle* (Paris, 1989)

Chastel, André, *L'Art français: temps modernes, 1430–1620* (Paris, 1994)

Chatenet, Monique, *Le château de Madrid au bois de Boulogne* (Paris, 1987)

Chatenet, Monique, *La cour de France au XVIe siècle: vie sociale et architecture* (Paris, 2000)

Chatenet, Monique, *Chambord* (Paris, 2001)

Chatenet, Monique (ed.), *Maisons des champs dans l'Europe de la Renaissance* (Paris, 2006)

Chaunu, P., and R. Gascon (eds), *Histoire économique et sociale de la France*, vol. 1 (1450–1660): pt 1: *L'état et la ville* (Paris, 1977)

Chevalier, Bernard, *Les bonnes villes de France du XIVe au XVIe siècle* (Paris, 1982)

Chevalier, Bernard, *Guillaume Briçonnet (v. 1445–1514): Un cardinal ministre au début de la Renaissance* (Rennes, 2005)

Chevallier, Pierre, *Henri III, roi shakespearien* (Paris, 1985)

Clark, Kenneth, *Leonardo da Vinci* (Harmondsworth, 1958)

Cloulas, Ivan, *Catherine de Médicis* (Paris, 1979)

Cloulas, Ivan, *La vie quotidienne dans les châteaux de la Loire au temps de la Renaissance* (Paris, 1983)

Cloulas, Ivan, *Henri II* (Paris, 1985)

Cloulas, Ivan, *Diane de Poitiers* (Paris, 1997)

Cocula-Vaillières, Anne-Marie, *Brantôme: amour et gloire au temps des Valois* (Paris, 1986)

Conihout, Isabelle de, Jean-François Maillard and Guy Poirier (eds), *Henri III, mécène des arts, des sciences et des lettres* (Paris, 2006)

Constant, Jean-Marie, *Les Guise* (Paris, 1984)

Constant, Jean-Marie, *La vie quotidienne de la noblesse française au XVIe et XVIIe siècles* (Paris, 1995)

Constant, Jean-Marie, *La Ligue* (Paris, 1996)

Constant, Jean-Marie, *La noblesse en liberté* (Rennes, 2004)

Cosandey, Fanny, *La reine de France: symbole et pouvoir, XVe–XVIIIe siècle* (Paris, 2000)

Cosperec, Annie, *Blois: la forme d'une ville* (Paris, 1994)

Courteault, P., *Blaise de Monluc, historien* (Paris, 1908)

Cox-Rearick, Janet, *The Collection of Francis I: Royal Treasures* (Antwerp, 1995)

Crouzet, Denis, *Les guerriers de Dieu: la violence au temps des troubles de religion (vers 1525–vers 1610)*, 2 vols (Paris, 1990)

Crouzet, Denis, *La Nuit de la Saint-Barthélemy: un rêve perdu de la Renaissance* (Paris, 1994)

Crouzet, Denis, *La genèse de la réforme française, 1529–62* (Paris, 1996)

Crouzet, Denis, *La sagesse et le malheur: Michel de l'Hospital, Chancelier de France* (Seyssel, 1998)

Crouzet, Denis, *Charles de Bourbon, Connétable de France* (Paris, 2003)

Crouzet, Denis, *Le haut cœur de Catherine de Médicis* (Paris, 2005)

Cummins, John, *The Hound and the Hawk. The Art of Medieval Hunting* (London, 1988)

d'Anthenaise, Claude and Monique Chatenet (eds), *Chasses princières dans l'Europe de la Renaissance* (Arles, 2007)

De Boom, Ghislaine, *Archiduchesse Éléonore, reine de France, sœur de Charles Quint* (Brussels, 2003)

Decrue, Francis, *Anne de Montmorency à la cour, aux armées et au conseil du roi François Ier* (Paris, 1885)

Decrue, Francis, *Anne duc de Montmorency, Connétable et Pair de France sous les rois Henri II, François II et Charles IX* (Paris, 1889)

Delaruelle, L., *Guillaume Budé* (Paris, 1907)

Desgardins, E., *Anne de Pisseleu duchesse d'Étampes et François Ier* (Paris, 1904)

Desplat, Christian and Paul Mironneau (eds), *Les Entrées: gloire et déclin d'un cérémonial* (Biarritz, 1997)

Devèze, M., *La vie de la forêt française au XVIe siècle*, 2 vols (Paris, 1961)

Dickens, A.G. (ed.), *The Courts of Europe: Politics, Patronage and Royalty, 1400–1800* (London, 1977)

Diefendorf, Barbara B., *Beneath the Cross: Catholics and Huguenots in Sixteenth-Century Paris* (Oxford, 1991)

Dimier, Louis, *Le Primatice* (Paris, 1928)

Dimier, Louis, *Le Château de Fontainebleau et la cour de François Ier* (Paris, 1930)

Doucet, Roger, *Étude sur le gouvernement de François Ier dans ses rapports avec le Parlement de Paris*, 2 vols (Paris and Algiers, 1921–6)

Doucet, Roger, *Les institutions de la France au XVIe siècle*, 2 vols (Paris, 1948)

Dubois de Groër, Anne, *Corneille de La Haye, dit Corneille de Lyon (1500/1510–1575)* (Paris, 1996)

Dubost, Jean-François, *La France italienne, XVIe–XVIIe siècle* (Paris, 1997)

Duby, G., and A. Wallon (eds), *Histoire de la France rurale*, vol. 2: *L'âge classique* (Paris, 1975)

Dumaître, Paule, *Amboise Paré, chirurgien de quatre rois de France* (Paris, 1986)

Dupâquier, J. (ed.), *Histoire de la population française: 2. De la Renaissance à 1789* (2nd edn, Paris, 1991)

Ehrmann, J., *Antoine Caron, peintre à la cour des Valois* (Paris, 1955)

Etchechoury, *Les maîtres des requêtes de l'hôtel du roi sous les derniers Valois* (Paris, 1991)

Farge, James K., *Orthodoxy and Reform in Early Reformation France: The Faculty of Theology of Paris, 1500–1543* (Leiden, 1985)

Farge, James K., *Le parti conservateur au XVIe siècle. L'Université de Paris à l'époque de la Renaissance et de la Réforme* (Paris, 1992)

Febvre, Lucien, *Amour sacré, amour profane: autour de l'Heptaméron* (Paris, 1944)

Febvre, Lucien, *Au Cœur religieux du XVIe siècle* (Paris, 1957)

Febvre, L., and H.-J. Martin, *The Coming of the Book: The Impact of Printing* (London, 1986)

Fenlon, Iain, *The Ceremonial City: History, Memory and Myth in Renaissance Venice* (New Haven and London, 2007)

Foisil, M., *Le Sire de Gouberville* (Paris, 1981)

Ford, Philip, and Gillian Jondorf (eds), *Humanism and Letters in the Age of François Ier* (Cambridge, 1996)

François, Michel, *Le Cardinal François de Tournon* (Paris, 1951)

Franklin, Alfred, *Précis de l'histoire de la Bibliothèque du Roi* (2nd edn, Paris, 1875)

Franklin, Alfred, *Le Duel de Jarnac et de La Chataigneraie* (Paris, 1909)

Freedberg, S.J., *Andrea del Sarto*, 2 vols (Cambridge, MA, 1963)

Frommel, Sabine, *Sebastiano Serlio, architect* (Milan, 1998)

Frommel, Sabine (ed.), *Primaticcio, architetto* (Milan, 2005)

Fumaroli, M. (ed.), *Les origines du Collège de France (1500–1560)* (Paris, 1998)

Gadoffre, Gilbert, *La Révolution culturelle dans la France des humanistes* (Geneva, 1997)

Gaehtgens, Thomas W., and Nicole Hochner (eds), *L'Image du roi de François Ier à Louis XIV* (Paris, 2008)

Garrisson, Janine, *Tocsin pour un massacre: la saison des Saint-Barthélemy* (Paris, 1968)

Garrisson, Janine, *Protestants du Midi, 1559–1598* (Toulouse, 1980)

Garrisson, Janine, *Les Protestants au XVIe siècle* (Paris, 1988)

Gebelin, F., *Les châteaux de la Renaissance* (Paris, 1927)

Giesey, R., *The Royal Funeral Ceremony in Renaissance France* (Geneva, 1960)

Giesey, R., *Cérémonial et puissance souveraine: France, XVe–XVIIe siècle* (Paris, 1987)

Giraud, Yves, and Marc-René Jung, *La Renaissance 1: 1480–1548* (Paris, 1972)

Goubert, P., *L'Ancien régime*, 2 vols (Paris, 1969)

Graham, V.E., and W. McAllister Johnson, *The Paris entries of Charles IX and Elizabeth of Austria, 1571* (Toronto, 1974)

Graham, V.E., and W. McAllister Johnson, *The Royal Tour of France by Charles IX and Catherine de Medici* (Toronto, 1979)

Greengrass, Mark, *France in the Age of Henry IV* (2nd edn, London, 1995)

Greengrass, Mark, *Governing Passions: Peace and Reform in the French Kingdom, 1576–1585* (Oxford, 2007)

Grummitt, David (ed.), *The English Experience in France c. 1450–1558* (Aldershot, 2002)

Guénée. B., and F. Lehoux, *Les entrées royales françaises de 1328 à 1515* (Paris, 1968)

Gwyn, P. *The King's Cardinal: The Rise and Fall of Thomas Wolsey* (London, 1992)

Hamon, Philippe, *L'argent du roi: les finances sous François Ier* (Paris, 1994)

Hamon, Philippe, *'Messieurs des finances'. Les grands officiers de finance dans la France de la Renaissance* (Paris, 1999)

Hamy, Alfred, *Entrevue de François premier avec Henry VIII à Boulogne-sur-Mer en 1532* (Paris, 1898)

Harding, Robert R., *Anatomy of a Power Élite: The Provincial Governors of Early Modern France* (New Haven, CT, 1978)

Harsgor, M., *Recherches sur le conseil du roi sous Charles VIII et Louis XII*, 4 vols (Lille, 1980)

Harvey, H.G., *The Theatre of the Basoche: The Contribution of the Law Societies to French Mediaeval Comedy* (Cambridge, MA, 1941)

Heller, Henry, *Anti-Italianism in Sixteenth-Century France* (Toronto, 2003)

Herbet, F., *Le château de Fontainebleau* (Paris, 1937)

Hobson, Anthony, *Great Libraries* (London, 1970)

Hobson, Anthony, *Humanists and Bookbinders: The Origins and Diffusion of the Humanistic book-binding, 1459–1559* (Cambridge, 1989)

Hochner, Nicole, *Louis XII: les dérèglements de l'image royale (1498–1515)* (Seyssel, 2006)

Holt, Mack P., *The Duke of Anjou and the Politique Struggle during the Wars of Religion* (Cambridge, 1986)

Holt, Mack P., *The French Wars of Religion, 1562–1629* (Cambridge, 1995)

Hughes, P.E., *Lefèvre, Pioneer of Ecclesiastical Renewal in France* (Grand Rapids, MI, 1984)

Imbart de la Tour, P., *Les origines de la réforme*, 4 vols (Paris, 1905–35)

Jackson, Richard A., *Vive le Roi! A History of the French Coronation from Charles V to Charles X* (Chapel Hill, NC, 1984)

Jacquart, Jean, *François Ier* (2nd edn, Paris, 1994)

Jacqueton, G., *La politique extérieure de Louise de Savoie* (Paris, 1892)

Jacquot, J. (ed.), *Fêtes et cérémonies au temps de Charles Quint* (Paris, 1975)

Jestaz, Bertrand, *Art et artistes en France de la Renaissance à la Révolution* (Paris, 2003)

Jouanna, Arlette, *Ordre social: mythes et hiérarchies dans la France du XVIe siècle* (Paris, 1977)

Jouanna, Arlette, *Le devoir de révolte: la noblesse française et la gestation de l'état moderne, 1559–1661* (Paris, 1989)

Jouanna, Arlette, *La France du XVIe siècle, 1483–1598* (Paris, 1996)

Jouanna, Arlette, Jacqueline Boucher, Dominique Biloghi and Guy Le Thiec (eds), *Histoire et dictionnaire des guerres de religion* (Paris, 1998)

Jouanna, Arlette, Philippe Hamon, Dominique Biloghi and Guy Le Thiec, *La France de la Renaissance: Histoire et dictionnaire* (Paris, 2001)

Joukovsky, Pierre and Françoise, *À travers la Galerie François Ier* (Paris, 1992)

Jourda, Pierre, *Marguerite d'Angoulême, Duchesse d'Alençon, Reine de Navarre (1492–1549)*, 2 vols (Paris, 1930)

Kettering, Sharon, *French Society, 1589–1715* (Harlow, 2001)

Kingdon, Robert M., *Geneva and the Coming of the Wars of Religion in France, 1555–1563* (Geneva, 1956)

Knecht, Robert J., *Renaissance Warrior and Patron: The Reign of Francis I* (Cambridge, 1994)

Knecht, R.J., *Catherine de' Medici* (London, 1998)

Knecht, R.J., *The French Civil Wars* (London, 2000)

Knecht, R.J. *The Rise and Fall of Renaissance France, 1483–1610* (2nd edn, Oxford, 2001)

Krynen, Jacques, *L'Empire du roi. Idées et croyances politiques en France, XIIIe–XVe siècle* (Paris, 1993)

Kusenberg, K., *Le Rosso* (Paris, 1931)

Labande-Mailfert, Yvonne, *Charles VIII et son milieu (1470–1498): la jeunesse au pouvoir* (Paris, 1975)

Labande-Mailfert, Yvonne, *Charles VIII* (Paris, 1986)

Laffitte, Marie-Pierre, and Fabienne Le Bars, *Reliures royales de la Renaissance. La librairie de Fontainebleau, 1544–1570* (Paris, 1999)

La Garanderie, Marie-Madeleine de, *Christianisme et lettres profanes: Essai sur l'Humanisme français (1515–1535) et sur la pensée de Guillaume Budé* (Paris, 1995)

Lazard, Madeleine, *Le théâtre en France au XVIe siècle* (Paris, 1980)

Lazard, Madeleine, *Pierre de Bourdeille, seigneur de Brantôme* (Paris, 1995)

Lazard, Madeleine, *Les avenues de Fémynie: les femmes et la Renaissance* (Paris, 2001)

Lebey, A., *Le connétable de Bourbon, 1490–1527* (Paris, 1904)

Le Clech-Charton, S., *Chancellerie et culture au XVIe siècle. Les notaires et secrétaires du roi de 1515 à 1547* (Toulouse, 1993)

Lecoq, Anne-Marie, *François Ier imaginaire: symbolique et politique à l'aube de la Renaissance française* (Paris, 1987)

Lefranc, Abel, *Histoire du Collège de France* (Paris, 1893)

Lefranc, Abel, *La vie quotidienne au temps de la Renaissance* (Paris, 1938)

Lefranc, Abel, et al. (eds), *Le Collège de France (1530–1930)* (Paris, 1932)

Le Goff, J., and R. Rémond, *Histoire de la France religieuse*, vol. 2: *Du christianisme flamboyant à l'aube des Lumières, XIVe–XVIIIe siècle* (Paris, 1988)

Le Person, Xavier, *'Practiques' et 'Practiqueurs': la vie politique à la fin du règne de Henri III (1584–1589)* (Geneva, 2002)

Leproux, G.-M., *La peinture à Paris sous le règne de François Ier. Corpus vitrearum; France. Étude IV* (Paris, 2001)

Le Roux, Nicolas, *La faveur du roi: mignons et courtisans au temps des derniers Valois (vers 1547–vers 1589)* (Seyssel, 2000)

Le Roux, Nicolas, *Un régicide au nom de Dieu: l'assassinat d'Henri III* (Paris, 2006)

Lesueur, F., and P. Lesueur, *Le château de Blois* (Paris, 1914–21)

Lesueur, Pierre, *Les jardins du château de Blois et leurs dépendances* (Blois, 1906)

Lesueur, Pierre, *Dominique de Cortone, dit Le Boccador* (Paris, 1928)

Loades, David, *The Tudor Court* (London, 1986)

Lot, Ferdinand, and R. Fawtier, *Histoire et institutions françaises au Moyen Âge*, vol. 2: *Institutions royales* (Paris 1958)

McFarlane, I.A., *A Literary History of France: Renaissance France, 1470–1589* (London, 1974)

McGowan, Margaret, *L'Art du ballet de cour en France* (Paris, 1963)

McGowan, Margaret, *Ideal Forms in the Age of Ronsard* (Berkeley, CA, 1985)

McGowan, Margaret, *The Vision of Rome in Late Renaissance France* (New Haven and London, 2000)

Mann, Margaret, *Érasme et les débuts de la réforme française, 1517–36* (Paris, 1934)

Mariéjol, J.-H., *Catherine de Médicis* (Paris, 1920)

Mariéjol, J.-H., *La Réforme, la Ligue, l'Édit de Nantes, 1559–1598* (Paris, 1983)

Maulde La Clavière, R. de, *Louise de Savoie et François Ier: trente ans de jeunesse, 1485–1515* (Paris, 1895)

Mayer, C.A., and D. Bentley-Cranch, *Florimond Robertet (?–1527), homme d'état français* (Paris, 1994)

Mehl, Jean-Michel, *Les jeux au royaume de France du XIIIe au début du XVIe siècle* (Paris, 1990)

Mellen, Peter, *Jean Clouet* (London, 1971)

Michaud, Helène, *La Grande Chancellerie et les écritures royales au XVIe siècle* (Paris, 1967)

Michelet, Jules, *Histoire de France*, vol. 9: *La Renaissance*; vol. 10: *La Réforme* (Paris, n.d.)

Minois, G., *Anne de Bretagne* (Paris, 1999)

Molinier, H.-J., *Mellin de Saint-Gelays (1490?–1558): étude sur sa vie et sur ses œuvres* (Paris, 1910)

Mousnier, R., *Le conseil du roi de Louis XII à la révolution* (Paris, 1970)

Mousnier, R., *La Vénalité des offices sous Henri IV et Louis XIII* (Paris, 1971)

Mulryne, J.R., and Elizabeth Goldring (eds) *Court Festivals of the European Renaissance: Art, politics and performance* (Aldershot, 2002)

Neuschel, Kristen B., *Word of Honor: Interpreting Noble Culture in Sixteenth-Century France* (Ithaca, NY, 1989)

Nouaillac, Jules, *Villeroy, secrétaire d'État et ministre de Charles IX, Henri III et Henri IV* (Paris, 1909)

Nugent, D., *Ecumenism in the Age of the Reformation: The Colloquy of Poissy* (Cambridge, MA, 1974)

Oursel, H., and Julia Fritsch (eds), *Henri II et les arts* (Paris, 2003)

Paris, P., *Études sur François Ier*, 2 vols (Paris, 1885)

Pastor, Ludwig von, *The History of the Popes*, tr. F.J. Antrobus and R.F. Kerr, 23 vols (London, 1891–1933)

Pedretti, Carlo, *Leonardo da Vinci: The Royal Palace at Romorantin* (Cambridge, MA, 1972)

Pernot, Jean-François (ed.), *Jacques Lefèvre d'Étaples (?1450–1536)* (Paris, 1995)

Pinvert, L., *Lazare de Baïf (1496?–1547)* (Paris, 1900)

Poncet, Olivier, *Pomponne de Bellièvre (1529–1607). Un homme d'état au temps des guerres de religion* (Paris, 1998)

Pope-Hennessy, John, *Cellini* (London, 1985)

Potter, David, *A History of France, 1460–1560: The Emergence of a Nation State* (London, 1995)

Potter, David, *France in the Later Middle Ages, 1200–1500* (Oxford, 2002)

Poutrin, Isabelle and Marie-Karine Schaub, *Femmes et pouvoir politique: les princesses d'Europe, XVe–XVIIIe siècle* (Rosny-sous-Bois, 2007)

Primatice, maître de Fontainebleau (exh. cat., the Louvre, Paris, Sept. 2004–Jan. 2005)

Quentin-Bauchart, E., *La bibliothèque de Fontainebleau 1515–89* (Paris, 1891)

Quilliet, Bernard, *Louis XII* (Paris, 1986)

Reese, G., *Music in the Renaissance* (New York, 1959)

Renaudet, Augustin, *Préréforme à Paris pendant les premières guerres d'Italie (1494–1517)* (Paris, 1953)

Richet, Denis, *De la Réforme à la Révolution. Études sur la France moderne* (Paris, 1991)

Roelker, Nancy Lyman, *Queen of Navarre, Jeanne d'Albret, 1528–1572* (Cambridge, MA, 1968)

Romagnoli, Daniela, *La Ville et la Cour: des bonnes et des mauvaises manières* (Paris, 1995)

Romier, Lucien, *Les origines politiques des guerres de religion*, 2 vols (Paris, 1913)

Romier, Lucien, *Le royaume de Catherine de Médicis*, 2 vols (Paris, 1913)

Romier, Lucien, *La conjuration d'Amboise* (Paris, 1923)

Roy, Maurice, *Artistes et monuments de la Renaissance en France*, 2 vols (Paris, 1929–34)

Russell, Joycelyne Gledhill, *The Field of Cloth of Gold: Men and manners in 1520* (London, 1969)

Russell, Nicolas, and Hélène Visentin (eds), *French Ceremonial Entries in the Sixteenth Century: Event, Image, Text* (Toronto, 2007)

Sabatier, Gérard and Sylvène Édouard, *Les monarchies de France et d'Espagne (1556–1715)* (Paris, 2001)

Salvadori, Philippe, *La chasse sous l'Ancien Régime* (Paris, 1996)

Sauval, H., *Histoire et recherches des antiquités de la ville de Paris*, 2 vols (Paris, 1724)

Sauzet, Robert (ed.), *Henri III et son temps* (Paris, 1992)

Scailliérez, Cécile, *François Ier et ses artistes dans les collections du Louvre* (Paris, 1992)

Scailliérez, Cécile, *François Ier par Clouet* (Paris, 1996)

Schmidt, C., *Gérard Roussel, prédicateur de la reine Marguerite de Navarre* (Strasbourg, 1845)

Screech, M., *Rabelais* (London, 1979)

Sealy, Robert J., *The Palace Academy of Henry III* (Geneva, 1981)

Seong-Hak Kim, *Michel de l'Hôpital: The Vision of a Reformist Chancellor during the French Religious Wars* (Kirksville, MO, 1997)

Shearman, John, *Andrea del Sarto* (Oxford, 1965)

Shennan, J.H., *The Parlement of Paris* (2nd edn, Stroud, 1998)

Shimizu, J., *Conflict of Loyalties: Politics and religion in the career of Gaspard de Coligny, Admiral of France, 1519–72* (Geneva, 1970)

Simonin, Michel, *Charles IX* (Paris, 1995)

Smith, Pauline M., *The Anti-Courtier Trend in Sixteenth-Century French Literature* (Geneva, 1966)

Smith, Pauline M., *Clément Marot, Poet of the French Renaissance* (London, 1970)
Smith, Pauline M., and Trevor Peach (eds) *Renaissance Reflections: Essays in Memory of C.A. Mayer* (Paris, 2002)
Solnon, Jean-François, *La Cour de France* (Paris, 1987)
Spont, A., *Semblançay (?–1527). La bourgeoisie financière au début du XVIe siècle* (Paris, 1895)
Sutherland, Nicola M., *The French Secretaries of State in the Age of Catherine de Medici* (London, 1962)
Sutherland, Nicola M., *The Massacre of St. Bartholomew and the European Conflict, 1559–1572* (London, 1973)
Sutherland, Nicola M., *The Huguenot Struggle for Recognition* (New Haven, CT, 1980)
Sutherland, Nicola M., *Princes, Politics and Religion, 1547–1580* (London, 1984)
Terrasse, Charles, *François Ier: le roi et le règne*, 3 vols (Paris, 1945–70)
Thomson, David, *Renaissance Paris: architecture and growth, 1475–1600* (London, 1984)
Thurley, Simon, *The Royal Palaces of Tudor England* (London, 1993)
Vaissière, Pierre de, *Charles de Marillac, ambassadeur et homme politique sous les règnes de François Ier, Henri II et François II (1510–1560)* (Paris, 1896)
Vaissière, Pierre de, *De quelques assassins* (Paris, 1912)
Vale, Malcolm, *War and Chivalry: Warfare and Aristocratic Culture in England, France and Burgundy at the end of the Middle Ages* (London, 1981)
Vale, Malcolm, *The Princely Court: Medieval Courts and Culture in North-West Europe 1270–1380* (Oxford, 2001)
Vecce, Carlo, *Léonard de Vinci* (Paris, 2001)
Veissière, Michel, *L'évêque Guillaume Briçonnet (1470–1534)* (Provins, 1986)
Viennot, Éliane, *Marguerite de Valois* (Paris, 1993)
Viennot, Éliane, *La France, les femmes et le pouvoir: l'invention de la loi salique (Ve–XVIe siècle)* (Paris, 2006)
Wanegffelen, Thierry, *Catherine de Médicis: Le pouvoir au féminin* (Paris, 2005)
Wilson-Chevalier, Kathleen (ed.), *Patronnes et mécènes en France à la Renaissance* (Saint-Etienne, 2007)
Wilson-Chevalier, Kathleen, and Éliane Viennot (eds), *Royaume de fémynie: Pouvoirs, contraintes, espaces de liberté des femmes de la Renaissance à la Fronde* (Paris, 1999)
Wood, James B., *The King's Army: Warfare, Soldiers and Society during the Wars of Religion in France, 1562–1576* (Cambridge, 1996)
Woodbridge, Kenneth, *Princely Gardens: The origins and development of the French formal style* (London, 1986)
Yates, Frances A., *Astraea. The Imperial Theme in the Sixteenth Century* (London, 1975)
Yates, Frances A., *The Valois Tapestries* (2nd edn, London, 1975)
Yates, Frances A., *The French Academies of the Sixteenth Century* (London, 1988)
Zeller, G., *Les institutions de la France au XVIe siècle* (Paris, 1948)
Zerner, Henri, *The School of Fontainebleau* (London, 1969)
Zerner, Henri, *L'Art de la Renaissance en France: L'invention du classicisme* (Paris, 1996). English edition: *Renaissance Art in France: The Invention of Classicism* (Paris, 2003)
Zumthor, Paul, *Le masque et la lumière. La poétique des grands rhétoriqueurs* (Paris, 1978)
Zvereva, Alexandra, *Les Clouet de Catherine de Médicis: chefs-d'œuvre graphiques du Musée Condé* (Paris, 2002)

Articles

Adhémar, J., 'The Collection of Francis the First', *GBA*, 6th ser., 30 (1946), pp. 5–16
Adhémar, J., 'Aretino, Artistic adviser to Francis I', *JWCI*, 17 (1954), pp. 311–18
Alcouffe, Daniel, 'À propos de l'orfèvrerie commandée par Henri III pour l'ordre du Saint-Esprit', in *Art, objets d'art, collections (Hommage à Hubert Landais)* (Paris, 1987), pp. 135–42
Anglo, Sydney, 'Le Camp du Drap d'or et les entrevues d'Henri VIII et de Charles Quint', in J. Jacquot (ed.), *Fêtes et cérémonies au temps de Charles Quint*, (Paris, 1975), pp. 113–34

Anglo, Sydney, 'The Courtier: The Renaissance and changing ideals', in A.G. Dickens (ed.), *The Courts of Europe: Politics, Patronage and Royalty, 1400–1800* (London, 1977), pp. 33–53

Anglo, Sydney, '*Le plus gentil esprit qui soit apparu au monde depuis les derniers siècles.* The Popularity of Machiavelli in Sixteenth-Century France', in Pauline M. Smith and Trevor Peach (eds), *Renaissance Reflections: Essays in Memory of C.A. Mayer* (Paris, 2002), pp. 195–212

Bamforth, Stephen, and Jean Dupèbe, 'The *Silva* of Bernardino Rincio (1518)', *Renaissance Studies*, 8 (Sept. 1994), pp. 256–315

Baux, E., V.-L. Bourrilly and P. Mabilly, 'Le voyage des reines et de François Ier en Provence et dans la vallée du Rhône (décembre 1515–février 1516)', *Annales du Midi*, 16 (1904), pp. 31–64

Béguin, Sylvie, 'Remarques sur la Chambre du Roi', in A. Chastel (ed.), *L'Art de Fontainebleau* (Paris, 1975), pp. 199–230

Béguin, Sylvie, 'New Evidence for Rosso in France', *Burlington Magazine*, 131 (1989), pp. 828–38

Béguin, Sylvie et al., 'La Galerie François Ier au château de Fontainebleau', *Revue de l'art*, 16–17 (1972)

Boucher, Jacqueline, 'Le costume autour des derniers Valois: signe de pouvoir et objet de polémique', in Marie Viallon (ed.), *Paraître et se vêtir au XVIe siècle* (Saint-Etienne, 2006), pp. 213–22

Boudon, Françoise, and Monique Chatenet, 'Les logis du roi de France au XVIe siècle', in Jean Guillaume (ed.), *Architecture et vie sociale: l'organisation intérieure des grandes demeures à la fin du Moyen Âge et à la Renaissance* (Paris, 1994), pp. 65–81

Bournon, F., 'Inventaire des tapisseries emportées du château de Blois en 1533', *Nouvelles archives de l'art français*, 2nd ser., vol. 1 (1979), pp. 334–42

Brown, Horatio, 'The Assassination of the Guises as described by the Venetian ambassador', *EHR*, 10 (1895), pp. 304–32

Carroll, E.A., 'Rosso in France', in A. Chastel (ed.), *Actes du colloque international sur l'art de Fontainebleau* (Paris, 1975)

Castan, A., 'La mort de François Ier et l'avènement de Henri II d'après des dépêches secrètes de l'ambassadeur impérial, Jean de Saint Mauris', *Mémoires de la Société d'Émulation du Doubs*, 5th series, vol. 3 (1878), pp. 420–54

Chastel, André, 'L'escalier de la Cour Ovale à Fontainebleau', in D. Fraser, H. Hibbard and M.J. Lewine (eds), *Essays in the History of Architecture presented to Rudolf Wittkower* (London, 1967), pp. 74–80

Chastel, André, 'La demeure royale au XVIe siècle et le nouveau Louvre', in *Studies in Renaissance and Baroque Art presented to Antony Blunt* (London, 1967), pp. 78–82

Chatenet, Monique, 'Une demeure royale au milieu du XVIe siècle: la distribution des espaces au château de Saint-Germain-en-Laye', *Revue de l'art*, 81 (1988), pp. 20–30

Chatenet, Monique, 'Une nouvelle "Cheminée de Castille" à Madrid en France', *Revue de l'art*, 91 (1991), pp. 36–8

Chatenet, Monique, 'Le coût des travaux dans les résidences royales d'Ile-de-France entre 1528 et 1550', in A. Chastel and J. Guillaume (eds), *Les chantiers de la Renaissance* (Paris, 1991), pp. 115–29

Chatenet, Monique, 'Etiquette and Architecture at the Court of the Last Valois', in J.R. Mulryne and Elizabeth Goldring (eds), *Court Festivals of the European Renaissance* (Aldershot, 2002), pp. 76–100

Chatenet, Monique, 'Henri III et "L'Ordre de la court". Évolution de l'étiquette à travers les règlements généraux de 1578 et 1585', in R. Sauzet (ed.), *Henri III et son temps* (Paris, 1992), pp. 133–9

Chatenet, Monique, 'Le logis de François Ier au Louvre', *Revue de l'art*, 97 (1992), pp. 72–4

Chatenet, Monique, '*Cherchez le lit*: the Place of the Bed in Sixteenth-Century French Residences', *Transactions of the Ancient Monuments Society*, 43 (1999), pp. 7–24

Chatenet, Monique, 'Les logis des femmes à la cour des derniers Valois', in Jan Hirschbiegel and Werner Paravicini (eds), *Das Frauenzimmer: Die Frau bei Hofe in Spätmittelalter und früher Neuzeit* (Stuttgart, 2000), pp. 175–92

Chatenet, Monique, 'Quelques aspects des funérailles nobiliaires au XVIe siècle', in Jean Balsamo (ed.), *Les funérailles à la Renaissance* (Geneva, 2002), pp. 37–54

Chatenet, Monique, 'Henri III et le cérémonial du diner', in *Tables royales et festins de cour en Europe, 1661–1789* (Paris, 2005), pp. 17–27

Chatenet, Monique, 'Piteux triomphes et lamentables pompes: les obsèques des Orléans-Longueville aux XVe et XVIe siècles', in Jean Guillaume (ed.), *Demeures d'éternité: Églises et chapelles funéraires aux XVe et XVIe siècles* (Paris, 2005) pp. 225–46

Chatenet, Monique, and Christian Cussonneau, 'Le devis du château de Jarzé: la place du lit', *Bulletin monumental*, 155–II (1997), pp. 103–26

Clément-Simon, G., 'Un conseiller du roi François Ier, Jean de Selve', *RQH*, 73 (1903), pp. 45–120

Colliard, L., 'Tableaux représentant des bals à la cour des Valois', *GBA*, 6th series, vol. 61 (1963), 147–56

Cooper, Richard, 'The Aftermath of the Blois Assassinations of 1588: Documents in the Vatican', *French History*, 3 (1989), pp. 404–26

Cooper, Richard, 'The Blois Assassinations: Sources in the Vatican', in K. Cameron (ed.), *From Valois to Bourbon* (Exeter, 1989), pp. 51–72

Cooper, Richard, 'Court Festival and Triumphal Entries under Henri II', in J.R. Mulryne and Elizabeth Goldring (eds), *Court Festivals of the European Renaissance: Art, Politics and Performance* (Aldershot, 2002), pp. 51–75

Coron, A., 'Collège royal et *Bibliotheca regia*: la bibliothèque savante de François Ier', in M. Fumaroli (ed.), *Les origines du Collège de France (1500–1560)* (Paris, 1998), pp. 143–83

D'Anthenaise, Claude, 'La chasse, le plaisir et la gloire', in Catherine Arminjon et al. (eds), *De l'Italie à Chambord: François Ier et la chevauchée des princes français* (Paris, 2004)

De Groër, Léon, 'Les tapisseries des Valois du Musée des Offices à Florence', in *Art, objets d'art, collections (Hommage à Hubert Landais)* (Paris, 1987), pp. 125–34

Dermenghem, E., 'Un ministre de François Ier: la grandeur et la disgrace de l'amiral Claude d'Annebault', *Revue du XVIe siècle*, 9 (1922), pp. 34–50

Dodu, G., 'Les amours et la mort de François Ier', *RH*, 161 (1929), pp. 237–77

Doucet, R., 'La mort de François Ier', *RH*, 113 (1913), pp. 309–16

Doucet, R. 'Pierre du Chastel, grand aumônier de France', *RH*, 133 (1920), pp. 212–57; 234 (1920), pp. 1–57

Dubois, C.-G., 'François Ier et François Rabelais. Aspects de la vie culturelle au temps de François Ier', in *François Ier du château de Cognac au trône de France* (Colloque de Cognac, septembre et novembre 1994. Annales du G.R.E.H.), pp. 251–60

Ehrmann, J., 'Massacre and Persecution Pictures in Sixteenth-Century France', *JWCI*, 8 (1945), pp. 195–9

Elam, Caroline, 'Art and Diplomacy in Renaissance Florence', *Royal Society of Arts Journal*, 136 (1988), pp. 1–14

Elam, Caroline, 'Art in the Service of Liberty: Battista della Palla, Art Agent for Francis I', *I Tatti Studies: Essays in the Renaissance*, 5 (1993)

Freedman, R., 'Paris and the French court under Francis I', in Ian Fenlon (ed.), *The Renaissance* (London, 1989)

Giry-Deloison, Charles, '"Une haquenée . . . pour le porter bientost et plus doucement en enfer ou en paradis": The French and Mary Tudor's marriage to Louis XII in 1514', in D. Grummitt (ed.), *The English Experience in France, c. 1450–1558* (Aldershot, 2002), pp. 132–59

Golson, Louis, 'Serlio, Primaticcio and the Architectural Grotto', *GBA*, 77 (1971), pp. 95–108

Golson, Louis, 'Rosso et Primatice au Pavillon de Pomone', in A. Chastel (ed.), *L'art de Fontainebleau* (Paris, 1975), pp. 231–40

Greengrass, Mark, 'Noble Affinities in Early-Modern France: The Case of Henri I de Montmorency, Constable of France', *EHQ*, 16 (1986), pp. 275–311

Greengrass, Mark, 'Property and Politics in Sixteenth-Century France: The Landed Fortune of Constable Anne de Montmorency', *French History*, 2 (1988), pp. 371–98

Guillaume, Jean, 'Léonard de Vinci, Dominique de Cortone et l'escalier de bois de Chambord', *GBA*, 1 (1968), pp. 93–108

Guillaume, Jean, 'Léonard de Vinci et l'architecture française, 1: Le problème de Chambord', 2: La villa de Charles d'Amboise et le château de Romorantin: reflexion sur un livre de Carlo Pedretti', *Revue de l'art*, 25 (1974), pp. 71–91

Guillaume, Jean, 'Fontainebleau 1530: le pavillon des Armes et sa porte égyptienne', *Bulletin monumental*, 137 (1979), pp. 225–40

Guillaume, Jean, 'Léonard de Vinci et l'architecture', in *Léonard de Vinci ingénieur et architecte* (Montreal, 1987), pp. 207–86

Guillaume, Jean, and C. Grodecki, 'Le jardin des Pins à Fontainebleau', *Bulletin de la société de l'histoire de l'art français* (1978), pp. 43–51

Guy, John, 'The French King's Council, 1483–1526)', in R.A. Griffiths and J. Sherborne (eds), *Kings and Nobles in the Later Middle Ages* (New York, 1986), pp. 274–94

Haddad, E., 'Noble Clientèles in France in the Sixteenth and Seventeenth Centuries: A Historiographical Approach', *French History*, 20 (2006), pp. 75–109

Hari, R., 'Les placards de 1534', in G. Berthoud et al., *Aspects de la propagande religieuse* (Geneva, 1957), pp. 79–142

Heller, H., 'Marguerite of Navarre and the Reformers of Meaux', *Bibliothèque d'humanisme et Renaissance*, 33 (1971), pp. 271–310

Heydenreich, L.H., 'Leonardo da Vinci, Architect of Francis I', *Burlington Magazine*, 94 (1952), pp. 277–85

Hochner, Nicole, 'Louis XII and the porcupine: transformation of a royal emblem', *Renaissance Studies*, 15 (2001), pp. 17–36

Jestaz, Bertrand, 'Benvenuto Cellini et la cour de France', in B. Jestaz (ed.), *Art et artistes en France de la Renaissance à la Révolution* (Paris, 2003)

Joannides, P., 'Michelangelo's Lost Hercules', *Burlington Magazine*, 119 (1977), pp. 550–5

Joannides, P., 'A supplement to Michelangelo's Lost Hercules', *Burlington Magazine*, 123 (1981), pp. 20–3

Kast, Paul, 'Remarques sur la musique et les musiciens de la chapelle de François Ier au Camp du Drap d'or', in J. Jacquot (ed.), *Fêtes et cérémonies au temps de Charles Quint* (Paris, 1975), pp. 135–46

Knecht, R.J., 'Francis I. Prince and Patron of the Northern Renaissance', in A.G. Dickens (ed.), *The Courts of Europe* (London, 1977), pp. 98–119

Knecht, R.J., 'The Court of Francis I', *European Studies Review*, 8 (1978), pp. 1–22

Knecht, R.J. 'Royal Patronage of the Arts in France, 1574–1610', in Keith Cameron (ed.), *From Valois to Bourbon* (Exeter, 1989), pp. 145–59

Knecht, R.J., 'Francis I and Fontainebleau', *The Court Historian*, 4 (1999), pp. 93–118

Knecht, R.J., 'Charles V's Journey through France, 1539–40', in J.R. Mulryne and Elizabeth Goldring (eds), *Court Festivals of the European Renaissance: Art, Politics and Performance* (Aldershot, 2002), pp. 153–70

Knecht, R.J., '*Haulse (Paris) haulse bien hault ta porté*'. The Entry of the Emperor Charles V into Paris, 1540', in Pauline M. Smith and Trevor Peach (eds), *Renaissance Reflections: Essays in memory of C.A. Mayer* (Paris, 2002), pp. 85–105

Knecht, R. J., 'Sir Nicholas Carew's Journey through France in 1529', in D. Grummitt (ed.), *The English Experience in France, c.1450–1558* (Aldershot, 2002), pp. 160–81

Knecht, R.J., '"Our Trinity": Francis I, Louise of Savoy and Marguerite d'Angoulême', in Jessica Munns and Penny Richards (eds), *Gender, Power, and Privilege* (London, 2003)

Knecht, R.J., 'Court Festivals as Political Spectacle: the Example of Sixteenth-Century France', in J.R. Mulryne, Helen Watanabe-O'Kelly, Margaret Shewring (eds), *Europa Triumphans* (Aldershot, 2004), vol. 1, pp. 19–31

Knecht, R.J., 'I mecenati', in *Francesco Primaticcio architetto*, ed. S. Frommel (Milan, 2005), pp. 44–55

Lebel, G., 'Notes sur Antoine Caron et son œuvre', *Bulletin de la Société de l'Histoire de Paris et de l'Ile-de-France* (1940), pp. 7–34

Lecoq, Anne-Marie, 'La salamandre royale dans les entrées de François Ier', in J. Jacquot and E. Konigson (eds), *Les fêtes de la Renaissance*, vol. 3 (1975), pp. 93–104

Lecoq, Anne-Marie, 'Un portrait "kabbalistique" du roi de France vers 1520', *Bulletin de la Société de l'art français* (1981), pp. 15–20

Lecoq, Anne-Marie, 'La symbolique de l'État: les images de la monarchie des premiers Valois à Louis XIV', in *Les lieux de mémoire*, vol. 2: *La nation*, ed. P. Nora (Paris, 1986), pp. 145–92

Lecoq, Anne-Marie, 'Une fête italienne à la Bastille en 1518', in *'Il se rendit en Italie': études offertes à André Chastel* (Rome/Paris, 1988), pp. 149–68

Lecoq, Anne-Marie, 'La fondation du Collège royal et *L'ignorance chassée* de Fontainebleau', in M. Fumaroli (ed.), *Les origines du Collège de France (1500–1560)* (Paris, 1998), pp. 185–206

Le Person, Xavier, 'A moment of "resverie". Charles V and Francis I's Encounter at Aigues-Mortes (July 1538)', *French History*, 19 (2005), pp. 1–27

Le Roux, Nicolas, 'The Politics of Festivals at the Court of the Last Valois', in J.R. Mulryne and Elizabeth Goldring (eds), *Court Festivals of the European Renaissance* (Aldershot, 2002), pp. 101–17

Le Roux, Nicolas, 'La cour dans l'espace du palais. L'exemple de Henri III', in Marie-Françoise Auzepy and Joel Cornette (eds), *Palais et pouvoir. De Constantinople à Versailles* (Saint-Denis, 2003), pp. 229–67

Le Roux, Nicolas, 'Henri III and the Rites of Monarchy', in J.R. Mulryne, Helen Watanabe, J. O'Kelly and Margaret Shewring (eds), *Europa Triumphans: Court and Civic Festivals in Early Modern Europe* (Aldershot, 2004), vol. 1, pp. 116–21

Lesueur, Pierre, 'Pacello de Mercogliano, et les jardins d'Amboise, de Blois et de Gaillon', in *Bulletin de la Société de l'Histoire de l'Art Français* (1935), pp. 90–117

Levey, M., 'Sacred and Profane Significance in Two Paintings by Bronzino', in *Studies in Renaissance and Baroque Art presented to Anthony Blunt on his 60th birthday* (London, 1967), pp. 30–3

MacMahon, Luke, 'Courtesy and Conflict: The Experience of English Diplomatic Personnel at the Court of Francis I', in D. Grummitt (ed.), *The English Experience in France, c. 1450–1558* (Aldershot, 2002), pp. 182–99

McAllister Johnson, W., 'Once More the Galerie François Ier at Fontainebleau', *GBA*, 6th ser., 103 (1984), pp. 127–44

McGowan, Margaret, 'Les images du pouvoir royal au temps de Henri III', *Théorie et pratique politiques à la Renaissance* (Paris, 1977), pp. 301–20

McGowan, Margaret, 'Impaired Vision: the experience of Rome in Renaissance France', *Renaissance Studies*, 8 (Sept. 1994), pp. 244–55

McGowan, Margaret, 'L'essor du ballet de cour à la cour de Henri III', in Isabelle de Conihout, Jean-François Maillard and Guy Poirier (eds), *Henri III mécène des arts, des sciences et des lettres* (Paris, 2006), pp. 82–9

Marias, Fernando, 'De Madrid à Paris: François Ier et la Casa de Campo', *Revue de l'Art*, 91 (1991), pp. 26–35

Michon, Cédric, 'Les richesses de la faveur à la Renaissance: Jean de Lorraine (1498–1550) et François Ier', *RHMC*, (2003), pp. 34–61

Michon, Cédric, 'Quand l'église fait l'État', *Annuaire-Bulletin de la Société de l'Histoire de France* Année 2005 (2007), pp. 127–47

Morgan, P., 'Un chroniqueur gallois à Calais', *Revue du Nord*, 42 (1965), pp. 195–202

Oger, Isabelle, 'Le rôle de Henri III dans l'invention et la diffusion de son portrait gravé', in Isabelle de Conihout, Jean-François Maillard and Guy Poirier (eds), *Henri III, mécène des arts, des sciences et des lettres* (Paris, 2006), pp. 68–80

Paillard, C., 'La mort de François Ier et les premiers temps du règne de Henri II d'après les dépêches de Jean de Saint-Mauris (avril–juin 1547)', *RH*, 5 (1877), pp. 84–120

Paillard, C., 'Le voyage de Charles-Quint en France en 1539–1540', *RQH*, 25 (1879), pp. 506–50

Panofsky, Dora, and Erwin Panofsky, 'The Iconography of the Galerie François Ier at Fontainebleau', *GBA*, 2 (1958), pp. 113–90

Pedretti, C., 'Leonardo da Vinci: Manuscripts and Drawings of the French Period, 1517–18', *GBA*, 6th ser. 76 (1970), pp. 285–318

Picot, E., 'Les italiens en France au XVIe siècle', *Bulletin italien*, 1 (Bordeaux, 1901), pp. 92–137; 2 (Bordeaux, 1902), pp. 19–20; 3 (Bordeaux 1903), pp. 21–2

Potter, David, 'Kingship in the Wars of Religion: the Reputation of Henri III of France', *European History Quarterly*, 25 (1995), pp. 485–528

Potter, David, 'Politics and faction at the court of Francis I: the Duchesse D'Etampes, Montmorency and the Dauphin Henri', *French History*, vol. 21 (June 2007), pp. 127–46

Potter, David, and Roberts, Peter, 'An Englishman's view of the court of Henri III, 1584–1585: Richard Cook's "Description of the Court of France"', *French History*, 2 (1988), pp. 312–44

Pressouyre, Sylvia, 'Les fontes de Primatice à Fontainebleau', *Bulletin monumental* (1969), pp. 223–39

Pressouyre, Sylvia, 'L'emblème du Naufrage à la Galerie François Ier', in *Actes du Colloque international sur l'art de Fontainebleau (Fontainebleau et Paris, 1972)* (Paris, 1975), pp. 127–39

Reymond, M., and M.-R. Reymond, 'Léonard de Vinci, architecte du château de Chambord', *GBA*, 1 (1913)

Rice, E.F., 'Humanist Aristotelianism in France', in A.H.T. Levi (ed.), *Humanism in France at the End of the Middle Ages and in the Early Renaissance* (Manchester, 1970), pp. 132–49

Richardson, Glenn, '"Most Highly to be Regarded": The Privy Chamber of Henry VIII and Anglo-French Relations, 1515–1520', *The Court Historian*, vol. 4 (Aug. 1999), pp. 119–40

Ruble, A. de, 'La cour des enfants de France sous François Ier', *Notices et documents publiés pour la Société de l'Histoire de France* (1884), pp. 323–30

Saulnier, V.-L., 'Charles Quint traversant la France: ce qu'en disent les poètes français', in J. Jacquot (ed.), *Fêtes et cérémonies au temps de Charles Quint* (Paris, 1975), pp. 207–33

Schneebalg-Perelman, Sophie, 'Richesses du garde-meuble parisien de François Ier. Inventaires inédits de 1542 et 1551', *GBA*, 6th ser., vol. 78 (1971), pp. 253–304

Shell, L., and G. Sironi, 'Salaì and Leonardo's legacy', *Burlington Magazine* (1991), pp. 95–108

Smith, Marc Hamilton, 'Familiarité française et politesse italienne au XVIe siècle', *Revue d'histoire diplomatique* 102ᵉ année, nos 3–4 (1988), pp. 193–232

Smith, Marc Hamilton, 'François Ier, l'Italie et le château de Blois', *Bulletin monumental*, 147 (1989), pp. 307–23

Smith, Marc Hamilton, 'La première description de Fontainebleau', *Revue de l'art*, 91 (1991), pp. 44–6

Solmi, Edmondo, 'Documenti inediti sulla dimora di Leonardo da Vinci in Francia nel 1517 e 1518', *Archivio Storico Lombardo*, 4th ser., vol. 2 (1904), pp. 389–410

Tolley, Thomas, 'States of independence: women Regents as patrons of the Visual Arts in Renaissance France', *Renaissance Studies*, 10 (June 1996), pp. 237–58

Tricou, J., 'Un archevêque de Lyon au XVIe siècle: Hippolyte d'Este', *Revue des études italiennes* (1958), pp. 147–66

Turbide, Chantal, 'Les collections de Catherine de Médicis (1519–1589): quelques vestiges d'un patrimoine', in J.-Y. Ribault (ed.), *Mécènes et collectionneurs: les variantes d'une passion*, vol. 1 (Paris, 1999), pp. 51–63

Venard, M., 'Arretez le massacre!', *RHMC*, 39 (1992), pp. 645–61

Wardropper, Ian, 'Le mécénat des Guise. Art, religion et politique au milieu du XVIe siècle', *Revue de l'Art*, 94 (1991), pp. 27–44

Weary, William, 'La maison de La Trémoille pendant la Renaissance: une seigneurie agrandie', in B. Chevalier (ed.), *La France de la fin du XVe siècle. Renouveau et apogée* (Paris, 1985)

Wormald, Francis, 'The Solemn Entry of Mary Tudor in Montreuil-sur-Mer in 1514', in J. Conway Davies (ed.), *Studies Presented to Sir Hilary Jenkinson* (Oxford, 1957), pp. 475–9

Zvereva, Alexandra, 'La génèse du portrait de Henri III', in Isabelle de Conihout, Jean-François Maillard and Guy Poirier (eds), *Henri III, mécène des arts, des sciences et des lettres* (Paris, 2006), pp. 56–65

Glossary

Academy	A gathering of persons meeting to discuss literature, science or the fine arts and to promote their diffusion. Academies were set up by royal letters patent. A famous Parisian academy in the sixteenth century was the *Académie de Poésie et de Musique,* founded by the poet Jean-Antoine de Baïf (1532-89) from 1567 to 1573. Such gatherings held at court by King Henry III became known as the Palace Academy.
Aisés	The well-to-do.
Apanage	Part of the royal domain assigned by the king to a younger son to ensure his livelihood. The beneficiary or *apanagiste* did not own the land which could not be alienated; he was only tenant for life.
Apparati	Roadside spectacles of a symbolic nature, both classical or biblical, specially devised for a royal entry into a town.
Assembly of notables	A consultative assembly called by the king, usually to avoid summoning the Estates-General. Its members, drawn from the nobility, clergy and third estate, were not elected but chosen by the king without his following any set rules as to membership or consultation.
Bailliage	The basic unit of royal administration at the local level, administered by the *bailli.* An alternative name, mainly used in the south of France was *sénéchaussée.* There were 86 such units at the start of the sixteenth century and 97 at the end.
Ballet de cour	A type of ballet danced at the French court as from the sixteenth century in which dance, poetry and music were combined in a single scenario.
Basse-cour	The outer courtyard of a castle or *château.*
Bureau de la ville	Municipal government. In Paris it comprised the *prévôt des marchands* or mayor and the *échevins* or aldermen.
Cabinet	Closet.
Cantus firmus	In sixteenth-century polyphony, a plainchant melody, often in long and equal note values.
Cartel	A written challenge in a tournament.
Chambre des comptes	The Paris *Chambre des comptes* was an offshoot of the king's council with a special jurisdiction over fiscal matters. There were also provincial *chambres des comptes.*
Chapeau de triomphe	A floral wreath in celebration of a person or event.
Chapelle ardente	A chapel draped in black and lit with candles for a lying-in-state.

Château	Originally a castle, but from the sixteenth century usually a country house. A medieval castle is now described as a *château-fort*.
Châtelet	The tribunal of the *prévôté* and *vicomté* of Paris.
Chemin de ronde	A walkway, often enclosed, around the top of a fortified building.
Compagnies d'ordonnance	The armoured cavalry of *gens d'armes* (hence their other name, *gendarmerie*) forming the core of the king's standing army.
Conseiller	A member of a parlement under the rank of *président*.
Corps-de-logis	Main building as distinct from the wings or pavilions.
Cuisine de bouche	The kitchen that provided food and wine for the king and his circle.
Cuisine du commun	The kitchen that provided food and wine to the court's officials, servants and visitors.
Curia regis	The royal court in the early Middle Ages. Departments which became detached from it were said to have 'gone out of court'.
Device	A motto.
Domestiques et commensaux du roi	Visitors to the court who were allowed to eat and drink there at the king's expense.
Échanson	A cup-bearer.
Échevin	An alderman in a municipal government.
Écu	A gold crown. In 1515 it was worth 36 *sous* 3 *deniers*, or about 4 English shillings.
Écuyer	The lowest rank of the nobility of the sword.
Edict	A royal act on a single matter as distinct from an *ordonnance*, which ranged more widely.
Enfant d'honneur	A page in the king's household.
Enfants de France	The king's children.
Enfants de la ville	The sons of rich bourgeois.
Épargne	The central treasury set up by Francis I. Its full name was *Trésor de l'Épargne*.
Estates-General	The national representative body comprising elected representatives of the three orders of clergy, nobility and third estate. They met at irregular intervals as ordered by the king.
Evangelical	A Christian, not necessarily a Protestant, who stressed the importance of the Bible in worship.
Évocation	The transference by royal writ of a case from a lawcourt to the *Grand conseil*.
Fauconnier	A falconer.
Fraise	A type of ruff.
Fripier	A dealer in second-hand clothes.
Gabelle	The tax on salt.
Gallican	A member of the French church who stood for the defence of its liberties against the claims of the papacy.
Généralité	One of 17 fiscal regions outside the *pays d'états*, each with a *recette générale*.
Gens de finance	Collective name for officials of the crown's fiscal administration.
Gens de métiers	Artisans.
Gouvernement	A provincial governorship.
Gouverneur	A provincial representative of the king at the head of a *gouvernement*.
Grand' Chambre	The principal lawcourt in the Parlement of Paris.
Grand Conseil	A judicial offshoot of the king's council. Though an independent 'sovereign court' as from 1497, it continued to follow the king on his travels.

Grand maître de l'Hôtel	One of the highest offices of state. He supervised the running of king's household in addition to discharging military and ceremonial functions.
Grands Officiers de la Couronne	The most important officers of state, including the Chancellor of France, the Constable of France, the Admiral of France and the Marshals of France.
Hôtel	An important town house.
Hôtel-Dieu	The oldest hospital in Paris, situated on the Île-de-la-Cité, allegedly founded by St Landry, bishop of Paris, in 651 AD. Although it grew in size over time, it was never able to accommodate the thousands of poor people who flocked there.
Hôtel du roi	The king's household.
Innocents, Cimetière des	The oldest and most important cemetery in Paris. Destroyed in 1786, it now lies under a square.
Lieutenant-général du royaume	A title conferring general command of the kingdom. It was given in 1557 to François, duc de Guise, in 1561 to Antoine de Bourbon and in 1588 to Henri duc de Guise.
Lists	Barriers enclosing a space set apart for tilting.
Lit de justice	A session of the Parlement held in the king's presence usually to enforce the registration of an edict.
Livret	A printed festival book, sometimes illustrated, describing a royal entry or other festival.
Machicolation	In military architecture, a series of openings in a stone parapet through which missiles or boiling liquid could be dropped on assailants beneath.
Maître des requêtes	A senior office-holder in a sovereign court, above the *conseillers* but below the *présidents*. The masters of requests deputized for the chancellor, served the king's council and were sent on missions to the provinces.
Marshal of France	The highest military dignitary with his own jurisdiction exercised in a court called *table de marbre*.
Menu peuple	The lowest rank in society: the proletariat.
Menus plaisirs	The king's privy purse.
Mignon	A royal favourite. Often used pejoratively.
Nef	A saltcellar in the shape of a ship, usually made of gold or silver.
Noblesse d'épée	(Nobility of the sword) The nobility owing its status to military prowess.
Noblesse de robe	(Nobility of robe) Nobility acquired through the holding of an *office*.
Notables	Important persons drawn from the magistracy or municipal government.
Office	A permanent government post (as distinct from a *commission*, which was temporary). It was often sold and could confer nobility.
Order	One of the architectural Orders, such as Doric, Ionic, Corinthian or Composite, the capitals in each case being of different design. Philibert de l'Orme invented a French Order in the form of a banded column.
Ordo	A manuscript in which the rules to be followed in a coronation ceremony are laid down. In France the most famous *ordo* was that of Charles V, compiled in the 1360s. It made a number of liturgical additions, including prayers, to an existing Capetian *ordo* and provided a firm foundation for the ceremony's future development.

Ordonnance	(Ordinance) A law of wider coverage than an edict.
Palais	Former royal palace on the Île-de-la-Cité in Paris which had become the seat of the Parlement of Paris.
Panetier	An official of the royal bakehouse or pantry.
Parlement	The highest court of law under the king, also responsible for registering royal edicts and possessing administrative duties. In addition to the Parlement of Paris, there were seven provincial parlements (Aix-en-Provence Bordeaux, Dijon, Grenoble, Rennes, Rouen and Toulouse).
Parlementaire	Magistrate serving in a parlement.
Parties casuelles	A treasury set up by Francis I to receive revenues from the sale of offices.
Pays d'états	Provinces that retained their representative estates as distinct from the *pays d'élections* which had lost theirs.
Place de sûreté	A fortified town which Protestants were allowed to garrison. Under the Peace of Saint-Germain (1570) they obtained four (La Rochelle, Cognac, La Charité and Montauban) for two years. The number was raised to eight in the Peace of Monsieur (1576).
Politique	A moderate during the civil wars, who opposed Catholic and Protestant extremism equally.
Premier président	The leading magistrate in a parlement.
Prévôt des marchands	The mayor of Paris.
Procureur	A solicitor. In every royal court there was a *procureur du roi*, known in the Parlement as the *procureur-général*.
Quintain	A stout post or some object mounted upon it set up as a target to be tilted at with a lance in a tournament.
Reiters	German mercenary cavalry, usually armed with pistols.
Remontrance	(Remonstrance) A petition to the king listing grievances.
Rente	A government bond issued on the security of municipal revenues: e.g. *rentes sur l'Hôtel de Ville de Paris*. A *rentier* was a person living off such an investment.
Rhétoriqueurs or *Grands rhétoriqueurs*	A group of poets active from *c.* 1450 to 1530 who shared an intense interest in rhetoric, the art of persuasion and speaking well.
Sacramentarian	A Protestant who rejected the doctrine of the Real Presence of Christ in the Eucharist.
Sacre	The French coronation ceremony.
Salle	A hall or vestibule. Often qualified according to size as *grande* or as a *sallette*. In England it was often called Presence chamber.
Secrétaire d'état	(Secretary of state) One of the king's chief ministers whose importance grew during the sixteenth century.
Seigneurie	The basic economic unit in rural France. A *seigneur* exercised varying degrees of jurisdiction, called 'high', 'middle' and 'low', over his tenants.
Sénéchaussée	Another name for a *bailliage*, mainly used in the south of France.
Sorbonne	Strictly, one of the colleges of the university of Paris, but commonly used to describe the university's Faculty of Theology.
Sovereign courts	Courts that had once formed part of the royal court (*curia regis*) and had since detached themselves or 'gone out of court' and become fixed in Paris. They included the Parlement of Paris and the *Chambre des comptes*.
Stradiots	Light cavalry recruited in the Balkans.

Surintendant des finances	Minister responsible for the general management of the royal finances. The title only came into regular use in 1564.
Table de marbre	A table of black marble in the Palais de la Cité in Paris. It was normally used by the marshals of France when exercising their jurisdiction over the military so that their tribunal took the name of *Table de marbre*, but the table itself was used occasionally by the king for banquets.
Taille	The principal direct tax. It was levied on the person in the north of France (*taille personnelle*) and on non-noble land in the south (*taille réelle*).
Teston	A small silver coin bearing the engraved portrait of the reigning monarch.
Veneur	A huntsman specialising in the use of dogs.

The Later Valois

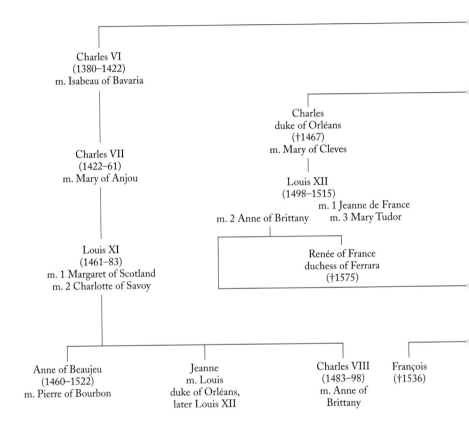

Charles VI
(1380–1422)
m. Isabeau of Bavaria

Charles VII
(1422–61)
m. Mary of Anjou

Louis XI
(1461–83)
m. 1 Margaret of Scotland
m. 2 Charlotte of Savoy

Charles
duke of Orléans
(†1467)
m. Mary of Cleves

Louis XII
(1498–1515)
m. 1 Jeanne de France
m. 2 Anne of Brittany   m. 3 Mary Tudor

Renée of France
duchess of Ferrara
(†1575)

Anne of Beaujeu
(1460–1522)
m. Pierre of Bourbon

Jeanne
m. Louis
duke of Orléans,
later Louis XII

Charles VIII
(1483–98)
m. Anne of
Brittany

François
(†1536)

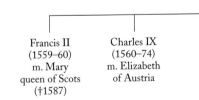

Francis II
(1559–60)
m. Mary
queen of Scots
(†1587)

Charles IX
(1560–74)
m. Elizabeth
of Austria

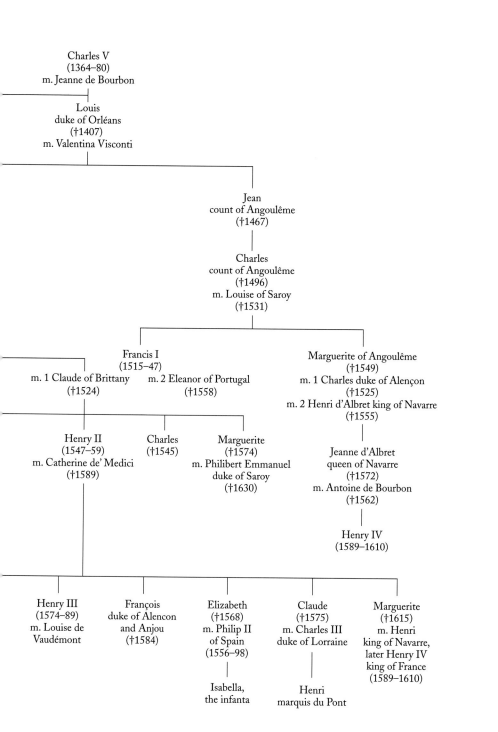

Charles V
(1364–80)
m. Jeanne de Bourbon

Louis
duke of Orléans
(†1407)
m. Valentina Visconti

Jean
count of Angoulême
(†1467)

Charles
count of Angoulême
(†1496)
m. Louise of Saroy
(†1531)

Francis I
(1515–47)

m. 1 Claude of Brittany
(†1524)

m. 2 Eleanor of Portugal
(†1558)

Marguerite of Angoulême
(†1549)
m. 1 Charles duke of Alençon
(†1525)
m. 2 Henri d'Albret king of Navarre
(†1555)

Henry II
(1547–59)
m. Catherine de' Medici
(†1589)

Charles
(†1545)

Marguerite
(†1574)
m. Philibert Emmanuel
duke of Saroy
(†1630)

Jeanne d'Albret
queen of Navarre
(†1572)
m. Antoine de Bourbon
(†1562)

Henry IV
(1589–1610)

Henry III
(1574–89)
m. Louise de
Vaudémont

François
duke of Alencon
and Anjou
(†1584)

Elizabeth
(†1568)
m. Philip II
of Spain
(1556–98)

Claude
(†1575)
m. Charles III
duke of Lorraine

Marguerite
(†1615)
m. Henri
king of Navarre,
later Henry IV
king of France
(1589–1610)

Isabella,
the infanta

Henri
marquis du Pont

INDEX